The Social Movements Reader

BLACKWELL READERS IN SOCIOLOGY

Each volume in this authoritative series aims to provide students and scholars with comprehensive collections of classic and contemporary readings for all the major subfields of sociology. They are designed to complement single-authored works, or to be used as stand-alone textbooks for courses. The selected readings sample the most important works that students should read and are framed by informed editorial introductions. The series aims to reflect the state of the discipline by providing collections not only on standard topics but also on cutting-edge subjects in sociology to provide future directions in teaching and research.

1. *From Modernization to Globalization: Perspectives on Development and Social Change* edited by J. Timmons Roberts and Amy Hite
2. *Aging and Everyday Life* edited by Jaber F. Gubrium and James A. Holstein
3. *Popular Culture: Production and Consumption* edited by C. Lee Harrington and Denise D. Bielby
4. *Self and Society* edited by Ann Branaman
5. *Qualitative Research Methods* edited by Darin Weinberg
6. *Cultural Sociology* edited by Lyn Spillman
7. *Sexuality and Gender* edited by Christine L. Williams and Arlene Stein
8. *Readings in Economic Sociology* edited by Nicole Woolsey Biggart
9. *Classical Sociological Theory* edited by Craig Calhoun, Joseph Gerteis, James Moody, Steven Pfaff, Kathryn Schmidt, and Indermohan Virk
10. *Contemporary Sociological Theory* edited by Craig Calhoun, Joseph Gerteis, James Moody, Steven Pfaff, and Indermohan Virk
11. *Race and Ethnicity: Comparative and Theoretical Approaches* edited by John Stone and Rutledge Dennis
12. *Social Movements*, second edition, edited by Jeff Goodwin and James M. Jasper
13. *Cities and Society* edited by Nancy Kleniewski

The Social Movements Reader

Cases and Concepts

Second Edition

Edited by

Jeff Goodwin and James M. Jasper

A John Wiley & Sons, Ltd., Publication

This second edition first published 2009
Editorial material and organization © 2009 Blackwell Publishing
Edition history: Blackwell Publishing Ltd (1e, 2003)

Blackwell Publishing was acquired by John Wiley & Sons in February 2007. Blackwell's publishing program has been merged with Wiley's global Scientific, Technical, and Medical business to form Wiley-Blackwell.

Registered Office
John Wiley & Sons Ltd, The Atrium, Southern Gate, Chichester, West Sussex, PO19 8SQ, United Kingdom

Editorial Offices
350 Main Street, Malden, MA 02148-5020, USA
9600 Garsington Road, Oxford, OX4 2DQ, UK
The Atrium, Southern Gate, Chichester, West Sussex, PO19 8SQ, UK

For details of our global editorial offices, for customer services, and for information about how to apply for permission to reuse the copyright material in this book please see our website at www.wiley.com/wiley-blackwell.

Library of Congress Cataloging-in-Publication Data

The social movements reader : cases and concepts / edited by Jeff Goodwin and James M. Jasper.—2nd ed.
p. cm.—(Blackwell readers in sociology)
Includes bibliographical references and index.
ISBN 978-1-4051-8764-0 (pbk. : alk. paper) 1. Social movements. 2. Social movements—Case studies. I. Goodwin, Jeff. II. Jasper, James M., 1957– III. Title. IV. Series.

HM881.S64 2009
303.48′4—dc22

2008052032

A catalogue record for this book is available from the British Library.

Set in 10/12pt Sabon
by SPi Publisher Services, Pondicherry, India
Printed in Singapore by C.O.S.Printers Pte Ltd

7 2012

Contents

List of Key Concepts and Chronologies

List of Activist Biographies

Acknowledgments

All part introductions, key concepts, chronologies, and biographies are by Jeff Goodwin and James M. Jasper. The editors and publisher gratefully acknowledge the permission granted to reproduce the copyright material in this book:

Alinsky, Saul D. 1971. Extract from *Rules for Radicals: A Pragmatic Primer for Realistic Radicals*. Copyright © 1971 by Saul D. Alinsky. Reproduced by permission of Random House Inc.

Auyero, Javier. 2004. Extract from "When Everyday Life, Routine, Politics and Protest Meet," *Theory and Society*, Vol. 33, 2004. Reproduced with kind permission from Springer Science and Business Media.

Bernstein, M. 1997. Extract from "Celebration and Suppression: The Strategic Uses of Identity by the Lesbian and Gay Movement," *American Journal of Sociology*, Vol. 103, The University of Chicago. Reproduced by permission of the University of Chicago Press.

Blumberg, R. L. 1984. Extract from *Civil Rights: The 1960s Freedom Struggle*, pp. 17–36. Reproduced by permission of Twayne Publishers.

Bob, Clifford. 2002. "The Quest for International Allies," originally published as "Merchants of Morality," from *Foreign Policy* Mar./Apr. (129):36–45. Reproduced by permission of *Foreign Policy*.

Brockett, Charles. 1993. "The Repression/Protest Paradox in Central America," originally published as "A Protest Cycle Resolution of the Repression/Popular Protest Paradox," from *Social Science History* 17(3):457–84. Copyright © The Social Science History Association. Used by the permission of the publisher.

Brym, Robert. J. 2007. "Suicide Bombing," originally published as "Six Lessons of Suicide Bombing," from *Contexts* 6(4):40–45. Copyright © The American Sociological Association. Reproduced by permission of the University of California Press.

"Classic Protest Songs" (chapter 18). 2006. From *Contexts* 5(1):10. Copyright © The American Sociological Association. Reproduced by permission of the University of California Press.

Clemens, E. S. 1993. From "Organizational Repertoires and Institutional Change : Women's Groups and the Transformation of U.S. Politics, 1890–1920," by Elisabeth S Clemens, *American Journal of Sociology*, Vol. 98, The University of Chicago. Reproduced by permission of the University of Chicago Press.

Cotgrove, S., and A. Duff. 1980. "Environmentalism, Middle-Class Radicalism and Politics," from *Sociological Review* 28(2):333–49. Reproduced by permission of Blackwell Publishing.

D'Emilio, John. 1983. "The Gay Liberation Movement," from *Sexual Politics, Sexual Communities*. Reproduced by permission of the University of Chicago Press.

Epstein, Barbara. 2001. "What Happened to the Women's Movement?" from *Monthly Review* 53(1) (May). Reproduced by permission of the Monthly Review Foundation.

Freeman, Jo. 1973. "The Origins of the Women's Liberation Movement," from *American Journal of Sociology* 78(4):792–811. Reproduced by permission of the author.

Gamson, J. 1995. "Must Identity Movements Self-Destruct? A Queer Dilemma," from *Social Problems* 42(3):390–407. Reproduced by permission of the University of California Press.

Gamson, W. A. 1990. Extract from *The Strategy of Social Protest*. Reproduced by permission of Cengage Learning.

Gitlin, T. 1980. Extract from *The Whole World is Watching*. Copyright © 1980 The Regents of the University of California. Reproduced by permission of the University of California Press.

Hirsch, E. L. 1990. "Sacrifice for the Cause: Group Processes, Recruitment, and Commitment in a Student Social Movement," from *American Sociological Review* 55 (Apr.):243–54. Reproduced by permission of the American Sociological Association.

Jasper, James M. 1998. "The Emotions of Protest," from *Sociological Forum* 13(3). Reproduced by permission of Kluwer Academic/Plenum Press.

Jenkins, J. C., and C. Perrow. 1977. "Insurgency of the Powerless," from *American Sociological Review* 42(Apr.):248–68. Reproduced by permission of the American Sociological Association.

Klandermans, B. 1997. Extracts from *The Social Psychology of Protest*. Reproduced by permission of Blackwell Publishing.

Kurzman, Charles. 1996. "Structural and Perceived Opportunity: The Iranian Revolution of 1979," from *American Sociological Review* 61(Feb.):153–70. Reproduced by permission of the American Sociological Association.

Kurzman, Charles. 2002. "Who Are the Radical Islamists?" originally published as "Bin Laden and Other Thoroughly Modern Muslims," from *Contexts* 1(2):13–20. Copyright © The American Sociological Association. Reproduced by permission of the University of California Press.

Lalich, Janja. 2004. Extracts from *Bounded Choice: True Believers and Charismatic Cults*. Copyright © 2004 The Regents of the University of California. Reproduced by permission of the University of California Press.

Lerner, Stephen. 2007. "Global Corporations, Global Unions," from *Contexts* 6(3):16–22. Copyright © The American Sociological Association. Reproduced by permission of the University of California Press.

Luker, K. 1984. Extract from *Abortion and the Politics of Motherhood*. Copyright © 1984 The Regents of the University of California. Reproduced by permission of the University of California Press.

Mansbridge, J. J. 1986. "Ideological Purity in the Women's Movement," from *Why We Lost the ERA*. Reproduced by permission of the University of Chicago Press.

McAdam, D. 1988. Extracts from *Freedom Summer.* Reproduced by permission of Oxford University Press, New York.

McCarthy John D., and Mayer N. Zald. 1977. From "Resource Mobilization and Social Movements: A Partial Theory," *American Journal of Sociology*, Vol. 82, The University of Chicago. Reproduced by permission of the University of Chicago Press.

Meyer, David S. 2003. "How Social Movements Matter," from *Contexts* 2(4):30–35. Copyright © The American Sociological Association. Reproduced by permission of the University of California Press.

Morris, A. D. 1984. Extract from *The Origins of the Civil Rights Movement.* Reprinted and edited with the permission of The Free Press, a Division of Simon & Schuster Adult Publishing Group.

Olson, Mancur. 1965. Extract from *The Logic of Collective Action: Public Goods and the Theory of Groups*, pp. 1–2, 10–16, 104–107, 132–133, 140, 165–167, Cambridge, Mass.: Harvard University Press, Copyright © 1965, 1971 by the President and Fellows of Harvard College. Reprinted by permission of the publisher.

Pellow, David Naguib, and Robert J. Brulle. 2007. "Environmental Justice," originally published as "Poisoning the Planet: The Struggle for Environmental Justice," from *Contexts* 6(1):37–41. Copyright © The American Sociological Association. Reproduced by permission of the University of California Press.

Ron, James, Howard Ramos, and Kathleen Rodgers. 2006. "What Shapes the West's Human Rights Focus?" from *Contexts* 5(3):23–28. Reproduced by permission of the American Sociological Association.

Ryan, Charlotte, and William A. Gamson. 2006. "Are Frames Enough?" originally published as "The Art of Reframing Political Debate," from *Contexts* 5(1):13–18. Copyright © The American Sociological Association. Reproduced by permission of the University of California Press.

Roxborough, Ian. 2007. "Counterinsurgency," from *Contexts* 6(2):15–21. Copyright © The American Sociological Association. Reproduced by permission of the University of California Press.

Seidman, Gay. 2001. "Armed Struggle in the South African Anti-Apartheid Movement," originally published as "Guerrillas in Their Midst: Armed Struggle in the South African Anti-Apartheid Movement," from *Mobilization* 6(2):111–27. Reproduced by permission of San Diego State University.

Sherkat, Darren E., and T. Jean Blocker. 1997. "The Personal Consequences of Protest," originally published as "Explaining the Political and Personal Consequences of Protest," from *Social Forces* 75(3):1049–76. Copyright © The University of North Carolina Press. Used by permission of the publisher.

Smith, Jackie. 2008. Extract from *Social Movements for Global Democracy.* Reprinted by permission of the Johns Hopkins University Press.

Wapner, Paul. 1995. "Politics Beyond the State: Environmental Activism and World Civic Politics," from *World Politics* 47(3): 311–40. Copyright © The Johns Hopkins University Press. Reprinted by permission of the Johns Hopkins University Press.

Whittier, N. 1995. Extract from *Feminist Generations*. Reproduced by permission of Temple University Press.

Every effort has been made to trace copyright holders and to obtain their permission for the use of copyright material. The publisher apologizes for any errors or omissions in the above list and would be grateful if notified of any corrections that should be incorporated in future reprints or editions of this book.

Part I

Introduction

Part I

Introduction

1 Editors' Introduction

Jeff Goodwin and James M. Jasper

Throughout history, humans have complained about the things they disliked. Sometimes they do more than complain; they band together with others to change things. In modern societies, more than ever before, people have organized themselves to pursue a dizzying array of goals. There are the strikes, pickets, and rallies of the labor movement, aimed at unionization but also at political goals. In the early nineteenth century the Luddites broke into early British factories and smashed new machines. There have been dozens of revolutions like those in France, Russia, China, Cuba, and Iran. The women's movement has tried to change family life and gender relations. We have seen Earth Day and organizations like the Union of Concerned Scientists and the Natural Resources Defense Council. Animal rights activists have broken into labs and "liberated" experimental animals. There have been plenty of conservative and right-wing movements as well, from Americans opposed to immigrants in the 1840s to those who fought federally mandated busing in the 1970s to those who have bombed abortion clinics in more recent years.

Some of these movements have looked for opportunities to claim new rights while others have responded to threats or violence. Some have sought political and economic emancipation and gains, while others have fought lifestyle choices they disliked or feared. Some have created formal organizations, others have relied upon informal networks, and still others have used more spontaneous actions such as riots. Movements have regularly had to choose between violent and nonviolent activities, illegal and legal ones, disruption and persuasion, extremism and moderation.

> **Political or Social Protest** Protest refers to the act of challenging, resisting, or making demands upon authorities, powerholders, and/or cultural beliefs and practices by some individual or group.

Social movements are conscious, concerted, and sustained efforts by ordinary people to change some aspect of their society by using extra-institutional means. They are more conscious and organized than fads and fashions. They last longer than a single protest or riot. There is more to them than formal organizations, although such organizations usually play a part. They are composed mainly of ordinary people as opposed to army officers, politicians, or economic elites. They need not be explicitly political, but many are. They are protesting against something, either explicitly as in antiwar movements or implicitly as in the back-to-the-land movement that is disgusted with modern urban and suburban life.

* * *

Why study social movements? First, you might be interested in them for their own sake, as a common and dramatic part of the world around you. You might simply wish to understand protestors and their points of view, especially when they seem to want things that to you seem undesirable. Why do some people think animals have rights? Others that the United Nations is part of a sinister conspiracy? Understanding social movements is a good way to comprehend human diversity.

But there are other reasons for studying social movements, which are windows onto a number of aspects of social life. You might study social movements if you are interested in politics, as movements are a main source of political conflict and change. They are often the first to articulate *new* political issues and ideas. As people become attuned to some social problem they want solved, they typically form some kind of movement to push for a solution. Political parties and their leaders are rarely asking the most interesting questions, or raising new issues; bureaucracy sets in, and politicians spend their time in routines. It is typically movements outside the political system that force insiders to recognize new fears and desires.

Social Movement A social movement is a collective, organized, sustained, and noninstitutional challenge to authorities, powerholders, or cultural beliefs and practices. A **revolutionary movement** is a social movement that seeks, at minimum, to overthrow the government or state.

You might also study social movements because you are interested in human action more generally, or in social theory. Scholars of social movements ask why and how people do the things they do, especially why they do things together: this is also the question that drives sociology in general, especially social theory. Social movements raise the famous Hobbesian problem of social order: why do people cooperate with each other when they might get as many or more benefits by acting selfishly or alone? The study of social movements makes the question more manageable: if we can see why people will voluntarily cooperate in social movements, we can understand why they cooperate in general. Political action is a paradigm of social action that sheds light on action in other spheres of life. It gets at the heart of human motivation. For example, do people act to maximize their material interests? Do they act out rituals that express their beliefs about the world, or simply reaffirm their place in that world? What is the balance between symbolic and "instrumental" action? Between selfish and altruistic action?

You will also benefit from the study of social movements if you are interested in social change. This might be a theoretical interest in why change occurs, or it might be a practical interest in encouraging or preventing change. Social movements are one central source of social change. Other sources include those formal organizations, especially corporations, that are out to make a profit: they invent new technologies that change our ways of working and interacting. Corporations are always inventing new ways of extracting profits from workers, and inventing new products to market. These changes typically disrupt people's ways of life: a new machine makes people work harder, or toxic wastes have to be disposed of near a school. People react to these changes, and resist them, by forming social movements.

But while formal organizations are the main source of technical change, they are rarely a source of change in values, in social arrangements. Why? In modern societies with tightly knit political and economic systems, the big bureaucracies demand economic and political control, stability. So they try to routinize everything in order to prevent the unexpected. They resist changes in property relations, for example, which are one of the key components of capitalism.

So innovation in values and political beliefs often arises from the discussions and efforts of social movements. Why don't societies just endlessly reproduce themselves intact? It is often social movements that develop new ways of seeing society and new ways of directing it. They are a central part of what has been called "civil society" or the "public sphere," in which groups and individuals debate their own futures.

If you have a *practical* interest in spreading democracy or changing society, there are tricks to learn, techniques of organizing, mobilizing, influencing the media. There have been a lot of social movements around for the last 40 years, and people in those movements have accumulated a lot of know-how about how to run movements. This is not the main focus of this reader, but we hope there are a few practical lessons to be learned from it.

Finally, you might want to study social movements if you have an interest in the moral basis of society. Social movements are a bit like art: they are efforts to express sensibilities that have not yet been well articulated, that journalists haven't yet written about, that lawmakers have not yet addressed. We all have moral sensibilities—including unspoken intuitions as well as articulated principles and rules—that guide our action, or at least make us uneasy when they are violated. Social movements are good ways to understand these moral sensibilities.

Social movements play a crucial role in contemporary societies. We learn about the world around us through them. They encourage us to figure out how we feel about government policies and social trends and new technologies. In some cases they even inspire the invention of new technologies or new ways of using old technologies. Most of all, they are one means by which we work out our moral visions, transforming vague intuitions into principles and political demands.

* * *

Research on social movements has changed enormously over time. Until the 1960s, most scholars who studied social movements were frightened of them. They saw them as dangerous mobs who acted irrationally, blindly following demagogues who sprang up in their midst. In the nineteenth century, the crowds that attracted the most attention were those that periodically appeared in the cities of Europe demanding better conditions for workers, the right to vote, and other conditions we now take for granted. Most elites, including university professors, had little sympathy for them. Crowds were thought to whip up emotions that made people do things they otherwise would not do, would not want to do, and should not do. They transformed people into unthinking automatons, according to scholars of the time. The last hurrah of this line of thinking was in the 1950s, as scholars analyzed the Nazis in the same way they had crowds: as people who were fooled by their leaders, whom they followed blindly and stupidly. For more than one hundred years, most scholars feared political action outside of normal, institutionalized channels.

These attitudes changed in the 1960s, when for one of the first times in history large numbers of privileged people (those in college and with college educations) had considerable sympathy for the efforts of those at the bottom of society to demand freedoms and material improvements. The civil rights movement was the main reason views changed, as Americans outside the South learned what conditions of repression Southern blacks faced. It was hard to dismiss civil rights demonstrators as misguided, immature, or irrational. As a result, scholars began to see aspects of social movements they had overlooked when they had used the lens of an angry mob. There were several conceptual changes or "turns" made in social movement theories.

First was an economic turn. In 1965 an economist named Mancur Olson wrote a book, *The Logic of Collective Action*, in which he asked when and why individuals would protest if they were purely rational, in the sense of carefully weighing the costs and benefits of their choices. Although Olson portrayed people as overly individualistic (caring only about the costs and benefits to them individually, not to broader groups), he at least recognized that rational people could engage in protest. Within a few years, John McCarthy and Mayer Zald worked out another economic vision of protest, taking formal organizations as the core of social movements and showing that these social movement organizations (SMOs, for short) act a lot like firms: they try to accumulate resources, hire staff whose interests might diverge from constituents', and "sell" their point of view to potential contributors. SMOs even compete against one another for contributions; together they add up to a "social movement industry." Because of their emphasis on SMOs' mobilization of time and money, they came to be known as "resource mobilization" theorists. Just as Olson saw individuals as rational, so McCarthy and Zald saw their organizations as rational. Protestors were no longer dismissed as silly or dangerous.

Around the same time, scholars also discovered the explicitly political dimension of social movements. Most older social movements, like the labor or the civil rights movements, were making demands directly of the state. Foremost were claims for new rights, especially voting rights. Thus the state was involved as not only the target but also the adjudicator of grievances. In this view, which came to be known as "political process" theory, social movements were also seen as eminently rational; indeed, they were little more than normal politics that used extra-institutional means. As in the economic models of mobilization theories, protestors were seen as normal people pursuing their interests as best they could. By highlighting social movements' interactions with the state, these process theories have focused on conflict and the external environments of social movements, to the extent that they even explain the emergence of social movements as resulting from "opportunities" provided by the state (such as a lessening of repression or a division among economic and political elites).

In the late 1980s, yet another dimension of social movements came to be appreciated: their cultural side. Whereas the economic and political "turns" had both featured protestors as straightforwardly rational and instrumental, scholars now saw the work that goes into creating symbols, convincing people that they have grievances, and establishing a feeling of solidarity among participants. Two cultural components have been studied more than others. The processes by which organizers "frame" their issues in a way that resonates with or makes sense to potential recruits and the broader public is one such component. The other is the "collective identity" that organizers can either use or create in arousing interest in and loyalty to their cause. Most fortunate are those activists who can politicize an existing identity, as when black college students in the South around 1960 began to feel as though it was up to them to lead the civil rights movement into a more militant phase. Other activists may try to create an identity based on membership of the movement itself, as communists did for much of the twentieth century.

Recently scholars have begun to recognize and study even more aspects of social movements. For example, many movements have a global reach, tying together protest groups across many countries or having international organizations. The environmental movement, or the protest against the World Trade Organization and the unregulated globalization of trade, are examples. Yet most of our models still assume a national movement interacting with a single national state.

The emotions of protest are also being rediscovered. A variety of complex emotions accompany all social life, but they are especially clear in social movements. Organizers must arouse anger and outrage and compassion, often by playing on fears and anxieties. Sometimes these fears and anxieties need to be mitigated before people will protest. Typically, organizers must also offer certain joys and excitements to participants in order to get them to remain in the movement. These represent some of the future directions that research on social movements seems likely to take in coming years.

Our understanding of social movements has grown as these movements themselves have changed. Like everyone else, scholars of social movements are influenced by what they see happening around them. Much protest of the nineteenth century took the form of urban riots, so it was natural to focus on the nature of the crowd. In the 1950s, it was important to understand how the Nazis could have taken hold of an otherwise civilized nation, so "mass society" theories were developed to explain this. Scholars who have examined the labor movement and the American civil rights movement recognized that claims of new rights necessarily involve the state, so it was natural for them to focus on the political dimensions of protest. Social scientists who came of age in the 1960s and after were often favorably disposed toward the social movements around them, and so portrayed protestors as reasonable people. Many of the movements of the 1960s and after were not about rights for oppressed groups, but about lifestyles and cultural meanings, so it was inevitable that scholars sooner or later would turn to this dimension of protest. Likewise in recent years, several important social movements have become more global in scope. Many movements are also interested in changing our emotional cultures, especially movements influenced by the women's movement, which argued that women were disadvantaged by the ways in which different emotions were thought appropriate for men and for women.

Research on social movements will undoubtedly continue to evolve as social movements themselves evolve.

* * *

Scholars and activists themselves have asked a number of questions about social movements. We have grouped the readings in this volume around nine main questions. Foremost, of course, why do social movements form, and why do they form when they do? Who joins and supports them? What determines how long a person stays in a social movement: who stays and who drops out? What kinds of things do participants think, want, and feel? How are movements organized? What do they do? In other words, how do they decide what tactics to deploy? How are they affected by the media? By the state and elites? What happens to them over time? Why and how do they decline or end? What changes do they bring about? The pages that follow give a variety of answers to each of these questions.

So that students can learn something about specific movements as well as theoretical questions and hypotheses, we have chosen a disproportionate number of readings about several movements in the United States, especially civil rights, the women's movement, environmentalism, and the gay and lesbian movement. Although we apologize to non-American readers for this emphasis, we felt these cases would interest a large number of curious students. Movements with these concerns, of course, have also arisen outside the United States.

Part II

When and Why Do Social Movements Occur?

Introduction

The most frequently asked question about social movements is why they emerge when they do. Not only does this process come first in time for a movement, but it is also basic in a logical sense as well. Until a movement takes shape, there is not much else we can ask about it. Where we think a movement comes from will color the way we view its other aspects too: its goals, personnel, tactics, and outcomes. In general, theories of movement origins have focused either on the characteristics of participants or on conditions in the broader environment which the movement faces. Only in recent years have cultural approaches tried to link these two questions.

Theorists before the 1960s addressed the question of origins to the exclusion of almost all others, for they frequently saw movements as mistakes that were best avoided! For them, the urgent political issue was how to prevent them, and to do this you needed to know why they appeared. "Mass society" theorists, for instance, argued that social movements occurred when a society had lost other, "intermediary" organizations that discontented individuals could join (Kornhauser 1959). These might be trade unions, community groups, churches—or any other organization that could mediate between the individual and government, aggregating individual preferences and providing outlets for letting off steam. These "regular" organizations were thought to be stable and normal and healthy, unlike social movements. Other theorists emphasized the kind of people they thought likely to join movements, which would form when enough people were "alienated" from the world around them, or had infantile psychological needs that absorption in a movement might satisfy (Hoffer 1951). In general, early theorists saw movements as a function of discontent in a society, and they saw discontent as something unusual. Today, scholars see social movements as a normal part of politics, and so these early theories are no longer taken very seriously.

In the 1960s and 1970s, a group of researchers known as the "resource mobilization" school noticed that social movements usually consisted of formal organizations (McCarthy and Zald 1977, excerpted in part VI). And one prerequisite for any organization was a certain level of resources, especially money, to sustain it. They argued that there were always enough discontented people in society to fill a protest movement, but what varied over time—and so explained the emergence of movements—was the resources available to nourish it. They accordingly focused on how movement leaders raise funds, sometimes by appealing to elites, sometimes through direct-mail fundraising from thousands of regular citizens. As a society grows wealthier, moreover, citizens have more discretionary money to contribute to social movement organizations, and so there are more movements than ever before. With this point of view, the focus shifted decisively away from the kinds of individuals who might join a movement and toward the infrastructure necessary to sustain a movement. Today, scholars still consider resources an important part of any explanation of movement emergence.

The paradigm that has concentrated most on movement emergence is the "political process" approach (Jenkins and Perrow 1977; McAdam 1982; Tarrow 1998). In this view, economic and political shifts occur, usually independently of protestors' own efforts, that open up a space for the movement. Because they perceive movements as primarily political, making demands of the state and asking for changes in laws and policies, they see changes in the state as the most important opportunity a movement needs. Most often, this consists of a slackening in the repression that organizers are otherwise assumed to face, perhaps because political elites are divided (the movement may have found some allies within the government), or because political and economic elites have divergent interests. There may be a general crisis in the government, perhaps as a result of losing a foreign war, that distracts leaders (Skocpol 1979). In many versions, the same factors are seen as explaining the rise of the movement and its relative success (e.g., Kitschelt 1986).

Rhoda Blumberg's description of the preconditions of the American civil rights movement (taken from her book, *Civil Rights*) reflects the process perspective, although it adds a few other factors as well. The migration of African-Americans out of the rural South provided more resources and denser social ties, a church and organizational infrastructure through which money could be channeled to civil rights work, as well as an entirely new cultural outlook. These in turn allowed a greater degree of mobilization, especially through the NAACP, which in turn won inspiring legal victories (especially *Brown v. Board of Education* in 1954). Resources, organization, the emotions of raised expectations, and a sense of new opportunities all encouraged the civil rights movement that grew rapidly beginning in 1955.

Alongside mobilization and process approaches, a number of scholars have emphasized the social networks through which people are mobilized into social movements. Although networks have been used primarily to explain *who* is recruited (as we will see in part III), the very existence of social ties among potential recruits is seen as a prerequisite for the emergence of a social movement. If most process theorists emphasize conditions in the external world (especially the state) that allow a movement to emerge, network theorists look at the structural conditions within the community or population of those who might be recruited. Those with "dense" ties, or pre-existing formal organizations, will find it easier to mobilize supporters, and build a movement.

Jo Freeman's article, "The Origins of the Women's Liberation Movement," was one of the first accounts of a movement to place networks front and center. She was arguing against early theorists who saw discontented and unorganized masses as spontaneously appearing in the streets. (Freeman herself was one of the founders of the younger branch of the movement in Chicago.) Freeman asserts that, if spontaneous uprisings exist at all, they remain small and local unless they have pre-existing organizations and social ties. Those networks are important for communication, vital to the spread of a movement. Like most network theorists, however, she does not discuss the emotions that are the real life blood of networks: people respond to the information they receive through networks because of affective ties to those in the network. She also admits that organizers can set about building a new network suited to their own purposes, an activity that takes longer than mobilizing or coopting an existing network.

John D'Emilio's account of the 1969 Stonewall rebellion in New York City and subsequent development of a militant gay and lesbian movement also emphasizes the critical importance of social networks. This apparently spontaneous eruption of gay militancy in fact marked the public emergence of a long-repressed, covert urban subculture. D'Emilio points out that the movement was also able to draw upon preexisting networks of activists in the radical movements then current among American youth. The "gay liberation" movement recruited from the ranks of both the New Left and the women's movement. It also borrowed its confrontational tactics from these movements. Many lesbians and gay men, D'Emilio notes, had already been radicalized and educated in the arts of protest by the feminist and antiwar movements.

These structural approaches redefined somewhat the central question of movement emergence. Scholars began to see movements as closely linked to one another, because leaders and participants shifted from one to the other, or shared social networks, or because the same political conditions encouraged many movements to form at the same time. So researchers began to ask what caused entire waves of social movements to emerge, rather than asking about the origins of single movements (Tarrow 1998:ch. 9). In this structural view, all movements are equivalent.

In the cultural approach that has arisen in recent years, not all movements are seen as structurally similar. In one version, movements are linked to broad historical developments, especially the shift from an industrial or manufacturing society to a postindustrial or knowledge society, in which fewer people process physical goods and more deal with symbols and other forms of knowledge (Touraine 1977). Social movements are seen as efforts to control the direction of social change largely by controlling a society's symbols and self-understandings. This often involves shaping or creating their own collective identities as social movements (Melucci 1996).

In cultural approaches, the goals and intentions of protestors are taken seriously. For instance, the origin of the animal protection movement has been linked to broad changes in sensibilities of the last 200 years that have allowed citizens of the industrial world to recognize the suffering of nonhuman species—and to worry about it (Jasper and Nelkin 1992). Such concerns would simply not have been possible in a society where most people worked on farms and used animals both as living tools (horses, dogs, dairy cows) and as raw materials (food, leather, etc.). The point is to observe or ask protestors themselves about their perceptions and desires and fantasies, without having a theory of history that predicts in advance what protestors will think and feel. Perceptions are crucial in this view.

From this perspective, Charles Kurzman's article, excerpted below, helped change the way scholars think about political opportunities. Process theorists had insisted that these were objective changes, independent of protestors' perceptions, but for the case of the Iranian Revolution, Kurzman shows that the perceptions matter more than some underlying "reality." A movement can sometimes succeed merely because it thinks it can. In other words, cultural perceptions can play as important a role as changes in state structure. Process theorists had apparently not tested their model in cases where perceptions and objective realities diverged. We are tempted to go even further than Kurzman does: the objective shifts in repression, elite alliances, and so on (the "opportunities" of process theorists) may only have an effect if they are perceived as such. In other words, perceptions, rhetoric, symbols, and emotions matter as much or more than structural shifts in the state.

Structural and cultural approaches disagree in part because they have examined different kinds of social movements (on the conflict between these two views, see Goodwin and Jasper 2003). Most process theorists have focused on movements of groups who have been systematically excluded from political power and legal rights—in other words groups who are demanding the full rights of citizenship. Cultural approaches have been more likely to examine movements of those who already have the formal rights of citizens—who can vote, pressure legislators, run for office—but who nonetheless feel they must step outside normal political channels to have a greater impact (such as the so-called new social movements). In a related difference, structural theorists usually assume that groups of people know what they want already, and merely need an opportunity to go after it; culturalists recognize that in many cases people need to figure out what they want, often because organizers persuade them of it (e.g., that animals can suffer as much as humans, that marijuana is a danger to respectable society, that the U.S. government is the tool of Satan).

There are a number of factors to look for in explaining why a movement emerges when and where it does, drawn from all these perspectives: political factors such as divisions among elites, lessened repression from the police and army; economic conditions such as increased discretionary income, especially among those sympathetic to a movement's cause; organizational conditions such as social-network ties or formal organizations among aggrieved populations; demographic conditions such as the increased population density that comes with industrialization (if you live a mile from your nearest neighbor, it is hard to organize collectively); cultural factors such as moral intuitions or sensibilities that support the movement's cause. And in many cases, potential protestors must frame and understand many of these factors as opportunities before they can take advantage of them.

Culturalists have reasserted the importance of perceptions, ideas, emotions, and grievances, all of which mobilization and process theorists once thought did not matter or could simply be taken for granted. But these are examined today in the context of broader social and political changes, not in isolation from them. It is not as though people develop goals, then decide to go out and form movements to pursue them; there is an interaction between ideas, mobilization, and the broader environment. But some people hold ideas that others do not, so that the question of the origins of a social movement begins to overlap with that of who is recruited to it.

Discussion Questions

1. In what ways might the *Brown v. Board of Education* decision of 1954 have encouraged the civil rights movement? (Think about emotional dynamics as well as cognitive ones.)
2. What were the two branches of the women's movement of the late 1960s and how do they differ?
3. In what ways did the New Left and women's movement spur the development of the gay liberation movement?
4. Did the Iranian Revolution occur because people perceived opportunities for collective action that didn't actually exist?
5. What is the relationship between "objective" political opportunities and people's perceptions of them? What effect does each have?
6. What are the competing sets of factors that might explain popular participation in the Iranian Revolution of 1979? Which does Kurzman favor?

2 The Civil Rights Movement

Rhoda Lois Blumberg

Trends and events in the first half of the twentieth century significantly affected black people and provided the necessary conditions for the successful take-off of the civil rights movement. Militant free and ex-slave black leaders had come forward prior to the Civil War; whites as well as blacks had struggled in the abolitionist movement. Yet by the end of the nineteenth century, the main spokesperson for the race was the accommodationist leader, Booker T. Washington, who espoused gradual change rather than political action.

Poverty, segregation, and violence were rampant when Washington came to prominence. Most former slaves had been deprived of their newly won right to vote and were still members of a rural peasantry in the South. Washington advised adjustment to the biracial situation and to disenfranchisement. He stressed self-help, racial solidarity, economic accumulation, and industrial education. His polite, conciliatory stance toward whites was coupled with the premise that black folk should take responsibility for their own advancement – to prove themselves worthy of the rights many thought they had already won.

Washington's 1895 speech at the Cotton States and International Exposition in Atlanta was hailed by whites. He gained the financial backing of foundations and controlled, through the "Tuskegee machine," important governmental appointments of black individuals during the Theodore Roosevelt and Taft administrations.

Protest had not entirely died out, however. The Afro-American Council, in existence from 1890 to 1908, had a militant outlook. Antilynching crusader Ida Wells-Barnet and William Monroe Trotter, editor of the outspoken *Boston Guardian*, lashed out against Washington. W. E. B. Du Bois gradually made public his growing disagreements with Washington, and through his role as editor of *Crisis* magazine, Du Bois renewed the move toward integration and equal rights. But until his death in 1915, and despite some erosion of his power, Booker T. Washington probably remained the most influential political figure of the race.

What happened to move a people from accommodation to protest? The most important interacting events that made the transition possible included:

1. A mass migration of black peasantry out of the South, eventuating in their transformation to a predominantly urban group
2. White violence against the black urban newcomers which demanded response
3. Two world wars and an economic depression
4. Years of litigation culminating in important legal victories
5. The development of community institutions and organizations in the cities
6. The rise of leaders who utilized opportunities for protest and were able to mobilize potential participants
7. A changed international climate confronting American racism

[...]

World War II stimulated another major migration to the North, so that by 1950 almost one-third of all black people lived outside the South. Over 20 million people, more than 4 million of them black, were forced to leave the land after 1940.

.. Chronology of the U.S. Civil Rights Movement

1896: Supreme Court upholds "separate but equal" doctrine in *Plessy v. Ferguson*

1905: W. E. B. Du Bois and others form the Niagara Movement, demanding abolition of racially discriminatory laws

1909: The National Association for the Advancement of Colored People (NAACP) is formed

1941: Labor leader A. Philip Randolph threatens massive march on Washington; President Roosevelt orders the end of racial discrimination in war industries and government

1948: President Truman ends segregation in the armed forces

1954: Supreme Court, in *Brown v. Board of Education of Topeka*, rules that segregated public schools are unconstitutional

1955: Emmett Till is lynched in Mississippi; Rosa Parks is arrested for violating the bus segregation ordinance in Montgomery, Alabama; the Montgomery bus boycott begins

1956: Supreme Court rules that segregation on public buses is unconstitutional

1957: Southern Christian Leadership Conference (SCLC) is formed with Martin Luther King, Jr., as president; President Eisenhower sends paratroopers to Little Rock, Arkansas, to enforce school integration

1960: Sit-ins at segregated lunch counters begin in Greensboro, North Carolina, Nashville, Tennessee, and elsewhere; student activists form the Student Nonviolent Coordinating Committee (SNCC, pronounced "Snick")

1961: "Freedom Riders" expose illegal segregation in bus terminals

1963: Major demonstrations are begun by the SCLC in Birmingham, Alabama, to protest segregation; Medgar Evers, head of the Mississippi NAACP, is assassinated; the March on Washington attracts hundreds of thousands of demonstrators to Washington, DC; four black girls are killed by a bomb at Birmingham's Sixteenth Street Baptist Church

1964: Hundreds of white college students participate in Freedom Summer, a Mississippi voter registration project; three civil rights workers are murdered near Philadelphia, Mississippi; the Civil Rights Act of 1964, banning discrimination in voting and public accommodations, is passed; the Mississippi Freedom Democratic Party challenges the state's all-white delegation to the Democratic national convention in Atlantic City, NJ; Martin Luther King, Jr., receives the Nobel Peace Prize

1965: Malcolm X is assassinated in New York City; police brutally attack a planned march in Selma, Alabama; a massive march takes place from Selma to Montgomery after a U.S. District Court rules that protestors have the right to march; President Johnson signs the Voting Rights Bill into law; riot in the Watts section of Los Angeles is the largest race riot in U.S. history up to that time

1966: SNCC leader Stokely Carmichael popularizes the slogan, "Black power"; the Black Panther Party is formed in Oakland, CA; riots occur in major cities, continuing through 1967; SNCC votes to exclude white members

1968: Martin Luther King, Jr., is assassinated in Memphis; riots occur in more than 100 cities; Richard Nixon is elected president

Although the federal government subsidized farmers to take land out of production in order to reduce agricultural surpluses at the end of the war, few sharecroppers received their share of the subsidies. Vastly increased mechanization made much human labor power obsolete. The result was the loss of 1 million farms between 1950 and 1969, with only the larger ones remaining. By 1960, 73 percent of black people were urban and by 1965, the figure had risen to 80 percent. Another important fact was that, by 1960, about half of the black population lived outside of the most repressive areas – the old slave states.

The movement to the cities resulted in conditions favorable to protest: the amassing of large numbers of people with similar grievances, a slight economic improvement over rural poverty so that folks could be less concerned about their daily bread, a nucleus of organizations through which communication and mobilization could occur, and a cultural support system for black pride and militancy. The segregated black world contained contradictions, from which both problems and strengths derived. Among the latter was the possibility of high population concentrations creating a rich, varied, all-black group life. On the other hand, urban conditions were crowded, dangerous, and unhealthy, and the black population was subject to exploitation. There also came to be vested interests in preserving segregation.

Even during slavery, free African Americans had gravitated to cities, finding relatively more freedom there to seek their rights. They acquired property, created schools and churches, met in conventions, petitioned state legislatures, and protested segregation. As abolitionists, they were largely responsible for the escape route to the North and Canada – the underground railroad. Denmark Vesey, the leader of a major slave revolt in Charleston, South Carolina, in 1822 was a freeman and a successful carpenter. These urban-dwelling free Negroes and former slaves became the nucleus of a more educated class. Within the black communities, a vast network of organizations grew – churches, fraternal orders, and lodges. Many local and state organizations – some temporary and some long-lived – provided forums for the working out of survival and protest strategies.

Mass migration to northern cities in the twentieth century provided an even stronger base for dealing with racism. Unlike the white immigrants who preceded them, ghetto blacks found no escape route to "better," more healthful neighborhoods. Housing segregation became increasingly rigid; neighborhood businesses continued to be controlled by whites. The separate black world came to share a sense of oppression and a sense of community. The black press grew and became a vital source of communication, supplementing white newspapers with race news – full coverage of black problems, issues, personalities, and cultural life. Through their own publications, leaders publicly and heatedly debated the correct course of action for their people. Fiery critics, such as Marcus Garvey and Malcolm X after him, seemed best able to capture the imaginations of urban blacks and to verbalize their smoldering resentment.

These large concentrations of people had ready access to one another and to the mass communication media. They were voters or potential voters; by the early 1940s, New York's Harlemites were able to elect one of their own, the young minister and race leader Adam Clayton Powell, Jr., to the city council. In 1945, black urbanites of the new 18th Congressional District started sending him to Congress. A vocal advocate for equal rights, Powell had followed his father as pastor of the Abyssinian Baptist Church. Although most African Americans were concentrated in unskilled or semiskilled jobs, some found additional avenues of employment and status. The city became the center of intellectual thought and cultural development. It placed black protest leaders in contact with white liberals and radicals and created the possibility of a northern support system for the southern-based civil rights movement of the 1960s.

Harlem, the mecca of African American culture, began to take shape and character as a Negro community around 1910. The Harlem Renaissance, a creative outburst of talent and nationalism, was led by black poets like Langston Hughes, Countee Cullen, and Claude McKay. Black theater and black music became popular.

Many of the writings of the 1930s projected themes of protest. Richard Wright's works, such as *Native Son*, gained him recognition as a major American writer. This literary movement accelerated, with such giants as Ralph Ellison and James Baldwin incisively examining the effects of white racism on black life. Another cultural renaissance would mark the transition from the civil rights movement to the black power movement in the 1960s. The growth of a literature of protest provided ideological and emotional impetus for the movement and gave sympathetic whites a greater understanding of black life.

White liberals had supported the Harlem Renaissance. Without an adequate economic base, black artists were often dependent on white sponsors and white patronage. Critics, such as Harold Cruse (1967), say that white patrons influenced the directions of black artistic expression, preventing it from fully achieving its promise. Others view this cultural era as significantly fostering black pride and black consciousness. Always there would be this debate about the influence of white liberals. They brought black interests to the attention of the public, but, it was argued, they did so in a patronizing fashion that would have to lead, eventually, to rejection. A somewhat different criticism would be made intermittently of white Communists, who also focused public attention on black issues. They were frequently accused of using racial issues for their own purposes. The question of whether or not to work with white leftists would plague black organizations; paradoxically some of the most anti-communist black organizations would be accused of being reds by their white enemies....

Relative Deprivation The poor are not always the most rebellious people in a society, nor do people always protest during the worst of times. Rather, people typically become angry and feel that their situation is unjust when there is a significant difference between the conditions of their lives and their expectations. In other words, people judge the fairness of their social situation and of the society in which they live not against some absolute standard, but relative to the expectations that they've come to hold about themselves or their society. Such relative deprivation may be found among quite comfortably-off and even privileged people. Relative deprivation may also become widespread when a long period of prosperity is followed by an abrupt economic downturn (the J-curve theory). When this happens, people cannot quickly or easily adjust their expectations to fit their new situation; instead, they may feel that something is badly wrong with the society in which they live. See Gurr (1970) and Gurney and Tierney (1982).

As World War II approached, black leaders remembered the bitter experiences of World War I – the segregated units, the struggle to be allowed into combat, the difficulty in gaining access to any but the lowest of assignments, and the Red Summer of 1919. Two issues loomed large – continued segregation in the armed forces and the inability of blacks to work in defense industries. As whites began to profit from these burgeoning industries, African Americans were once more being discriminated against. They were blocked from entering training for some of the newly available jobs. The 1940 statistics on the employment of blacks in war industries showed that only a tiny proportion had been hired. The armed forces were strongly racist: the Selective Service System operated under discriminatory quotas; the navy restricted blacks to messmen and other menial positions; the army segregated them. As national rhetoric proclaimed the contrast between the free and totalitarian worlds, black leadership initiated a "double V" campaign – victory abroad and victory over racism at home.

Black anger was growing. Leaders attempted to negotiate with the national government. In September 1940, the executive secretary of the NAACP, Walter White, along with Randolph and other prominent blacks, met with President Roosevelt to protest segregation in the armed forces. This effort proved futile, despite the fact that the black vote had helped FDR gain a second term. Not only did the president reaffirm the policy of segregation in the armed forces, but his press statement seemed to imply that the black leaders had gone along with it. This they immediately denied. The NAACP held a national protest day, January 26, 1941, calling it "National Defense Day." African American newspapers, firmly supported by the black public (as shown in polls), unanimously called for an end to racial discrimination during the national emergency. In contrast, the white press ignored the grievances of blacks, confining itself to the usual reporting of black crimes.

It was in this context that Randolph, who had tried so hard to move organized labor from within, took bolder action. He created the March on Washington Movement (MOWM), threatening a mass protest demonstration of 100,000 black people in Washington on the first of July 1941. The black press fully supported the proposed march, the aims of which were to secure the admission of blacks into defense industries on a nondiscriminatory basis and to end segregation in the armed forces. After first resisting the demands, FDR became convinced that he could not deter the leaders. At the last moment, on June 25, 1941, he created the first national Fair Employment Practices Commission through Executive Order 8802. Thus only the threat of a major demonstration, combined with a situation perceived as a national emergency, could move the federal government into the area of employment discrimination.

A student of the first March on Washington action ranks it as a high point in black protest and sees it as the best example of pressure unanimously and militantly applied against a president up to that point. A short-lived but extremely significant event, the MOWM incorporated several elements that would reappear in the civil rights movement of the 1960s. Randolph tried to build mass participation and recognized the importance of black consciousness in the development of a racial protest movement. Besides his belief in the need to mobilize the black masses, Randolph had become distrustful of white allies. The CP opposed the planned march until close to its deadline, when an event abroad led it to reverse its position – the Nazi attack on the Soviet Union in June 1941. Randolph planned an all-black march. Integrationist in orientation, the NAACP was lukewarm about it, providing little coverage in its official publications. But much grass-roots recruiting took place, with the formation of neighborhood committees, speaking tours by leaders, and huge outdoor meetings.

The NAACP and the Urban League had become the main bastions of black leadership following the demise of Garvey. Yet for a year and a half, from the inception of the MOWM until its decline, A. Philip Randolph was the major black leader in America. A member of the board of directors of the NAACP, Randolph was never averse to starting a new organization when he thought one was needed. This strong leader met tremendous opposition from white unionists and received little of the acknowledgment from other white Americans that King later would.

Shortly after the first FEPC hearing, the Japanese bombed Pearl Harbor and the United States became formally involved in the shooting war. Black leaders persisted in seeking equality during the war but were unable to achieve desegregation in the armed forces. That would not occur until President Truman signed an executive order in 1948. Nevertheless, the mood of black people during the war is probably accurately reflected in this statement by Ottley in a book published in 1943:

> Tradition must be overturned, and democracy extended to the Negro.... The color problem has become a world-wide issue to be settled here and now. Should tomorrow the Axis surrender unconditionally, Negroes say, the capitulation would provide only a brief interlude of peace.... There is nothing mystical about the Negro's aggressive attitude. The noisy espousal of democracy in the last war gave stimulus to the Negro's cause, and set the race implacably in motion. By advancing it in this war, democracy has become an immediate goal to the Negro. His rumblings for equality in every phase of American life will reverberate into a mighty roar in the days to come. (344)

Ottley's dramatic projection into the future was based not only on internal developments within the United States but also on a changing international environment. During the war, black soldiers went abroad again in the name of democracy, experienced segregation in the armed forces and their recreational facilities, and met Europeans who were far less prejudiced than white Americans. Racial clashes between white and black servicemen occurred. But the aftermath of World War II would differ from that of the first war. White supremacy in Africa and Asia was in decline: between 1945 and 1960, forty new independent nation-states were formed. The impact on the United States was considerable. Says Isaacs, "The downfall of the white-supremacy system in the rest of the world made its survival in the United States suddenly and painfully conspicuous. It became our most exposed feature and in the swift unfolding of the world's affairs, our most vulnerable weakness" (1963, 6–7).

The United States competed for the friendship of the newly independent nations, but reports of American segregation and discrimination interfered. The Soviet Union, engaged in a cold war with the United States, could point to this country's hypocrisy. The CP-USA publicized cases of racial injustice and championed the victims. The foreign press gave full coverage to America's racial disgraces, such as the 1955 murder of the teenager Emmett Till in Mississippi. Battles over school desegregation following the 1954 Supreme Court decision also made headlines. In particular, a famous incident at Little Rock, Arkansas, gained national attention. A reluctant President Eisenhower was forced to send in airborne troops to enforce a federal desegregation order and escort nine black students into high school. Vivid pictures showing angry adults screaming at black students were flashed around the world. The incident so embarrassed the president that he went on television and radio to criticize the actions of the governor of the state and justify his own.

Other incidents, involving ambassadors or citizens of new African or Asian states, were causing the country acute chagrin. A number of them were refused service or segregated in restaurants and motels along U.S. Route 40, which leads into Washington, D.C. Sometimes official apologies were necessary. Of course, Washington itself, the nation's capital, discriminated against dark-skinned peoples. Route 40 would become the target of demonstrations by CORE, intended to test desegregation laws. But meanwhile, the NAACP was continuing its pursuit of desegregation through the courts.

Another area of discrimination was the world of sports, from which blacks had been almost totally excluded. In the fight ring, where they could compete, Joe Louis reigned as world heavyweight champion. The color barrier in baseball was finally breached when Jackie Robinson was hired by the Brooklyn Dodgers in 1945, which some saw as a hopeful sign.

The end of World War II did not see a resurgence of race riots for several reasons. Labor shortages provided some employment gains for blacks, and the country did not experience a severe recession. Larger numbers of black people now lived in the North, where they could vote and did. The 1948 Democratic party convention adopted a strong civil rights plank, but was challenged by a separate Dixiecrat candidate drawing off party voters. Against this rival and Progressive and Republican party candidates, Harry S. Truman pulled off his surprising victory. In the same year, black citizens received their reward for support – Truman's executive order ending segregation in the armed forces. Black voters were beginning to play a pivotal role in national elections....

A final but major precondition to the modern civil rights movement was the continuing battle in the nation's courts. The NAACP had taken as a mission the investigation of cases where justice had been mishandled in the courts as well as in the streets. It fought and finally won a number of cases against segregation in graduate and professional education, successfully demonstrating the inferiority of schools for blacks.

As early as the 1930s, the Supreme Court had begun to reverse its post-Civil War negativity to the black cause. A 1938 Missouri case was decided favorably, with the Court insisting that equal educational opportunities had to be made available to black students. Two important cases followed. In *Sweatt v. Painter*, the Court ruled that the state law school set up in Texas for blacks was not comparable to the white school. The following year the Court went even further in *McLaurin v. Oklahoma*. By maintaining segregation in the classroom, cafeteria, and library, the University of Oklahoma was judged to have deprived a black student of the equality guaranteed by the Fourth Amendment. By the fall of 1953, blacks had been integrated, in a token manner, into twenty-three publicly supported colleges in southern or border states at the graduate level. There was even a small amount of integration at the undergraduate level. But in the five states of the lower South, the public schools were totally segregated, and data showed that black schools were vastly unequal in resources and in the education they offered. Many of the southern states made a last ditch effort to try to improve black schools. Cautious at first, the NAACP decided to attack the principle of segregation itself. Five cases challenging the constitutionality of school segregation were moving up to the Supreme Court from South Carolina, Virginia, Kansas, Delaware, and the District of Columbia. In December 1952, the Supreme Court ordered the litigants to submit briefs on a list of questions for a new hearing in the case of *Oliver Brown et al. v. Board of Education of Topeka, Kansas*.

The unanimous ruling of the Court under Chief Justice Earl Warren favored the black plaintiffs. In often-quoted words, the Court declared that segregation has a detrimental effect upon colored children because it "generates a feeling of inferiority as to their status in the community that may affect their hearts and minds in a way unlikely ever to be undone" (Woodward 1974, 147). These victories of the litigation phase were crucial developments.

The Supreme Court decision was greeted with hope by black Americans, who did not realize at the time how long and hard a struggle lay ahead. Soon they would turn to nonviolent action to protest the much-hated, humiliating segregation in public transportation. Courts and law were not abandoned as an avenue of redress, but more and more it was felt that mass action was necessary to supplement the legal process. Beginning in 1955, nonviolent protest spread significantly, backed by a clearly enunciated ideology. The proliferation of leaders and escalation of involvement lasted over most of the 1960s and was popularly called – at the time – the civil rights movement.

References

Cruse, Harold 1967 *The Crisis of the Negro Intellectual*. London: W. H. Allen.

Isaacs, Harold R. 1963 *The New World of Negro Americans*. London: Phoenix House.

Ottley, Roi 1943 *'New World A-Coming': Inside Black America*. Boston: Houghton Mifflin.

Woodward, C. Vann 1974 *The Strange Career of Jim Crow*. 3rd edn. New York: Oxford University Press.

Biography – Martin Luther King, Jr.: Prophet of Nonviolence

In the days following Rosa Parks' arrest for refusing to yield her bus seat to a white man, leaders of the African-American community in Montgomery, Alabama, scrambled to organize a city-wide bus boycott. It was a challenge to reach the 45,000 African-Americans in this city of 120,000, and the social networks of the black churches were the only way to do it. Unfortunately, there were longstanding tensions among them, and several different preachers probably felt they should be chosen to lead the new Montgomery Improvement Association. Perhaps for this very reason, a young, 26-year-old preacher, who had been in Montgomery only two years and had not yet become embroiled in the infighting, was selected. Few outside his own Dexter Avenue Baptist Church knew who he was.

That night, Martin Luther King, Jr., delivered his first big speech to an audience of thousands. He spoke for only a few minutes. He began awkwardly, fumbling for images that would stir the crowd, most of whom could not fit in the church and were listening to loudspeakers outside. Then King said, "And you know, my friends, there comes a time when people get tired of being trampled over by the iron feet of oppression." The line was a winner, and occasional "yeses" and "Amens" combined into a great sustained cheer. King had the audience now, surprising himself and the members of his own congregation who were present. His rhetoric would only improve during his remaining twelve, remarkable years.

King was born to the African-American elite, son of an Atlanta preacher and educated at Morehouse College, Crozer Theological Seminary, and Boston University, where he earned his Ph.D. in 1955. He was ordained at age 19. But stardom was thrust upon him, through his rather accidental choice to lead the Montgomery bus boycott. His charisma was, some have argued, created by his structural position. At the same time, he more than lived up to expectations. King had a resonant voice, a good store of Biblical allusions, a keen sense of what would rouse his audience, and a mastery of the theory and art of civil disobedience. Not everyone would have played the role so well.

The Montgomery boycott, which succeeded after a grueling year, helped bring national attention to the Southern civil rights movement, even landing King on the cover of *Time* magazine. He helped form, and was selected leader of, a new organization that would apply Montgomery's lessons elsewhere in the South, the Southern Christian Leadership Conference (SCLC). Black preachers, familiar figures in their dark blue suits, were respected leaders of the African-American community. They brought to the civil rights movement important resources such as places to meet and organize, a flow of funds from African-American churches in northern cities, and social networks that helped spread the word about successful tactics.

King's SCLC simply was the civil rights movement in the late 1950s. It eclipsed the older National Association for the Advancement of Colored People (NAACP), which pursued legal solutions to the problems of segregation, discrimination, and disenfranchisement. In 1960 the SCLC was joined by a more radical organization, composed of students, which grew out of lunch-counter sit-ins, the Student Nonviolent Coordinating Committee (SNCC). Later, the Nation of Islam, the Black Panther Party, and other radicals and black "nationalists" would create a more separatist movement and pugnacious brand of protest. Inspired by Gandhi's philosophy of nonviolence, however, King continued to favor large rallies, marches, and arrests for civil disobedience. His style of civil rights protest reached its apogee with the 1963 March on Washington, attended by a quarter million people. With "I Have a Dream," King delivered one of the most famous speeches in history. He was awarded the Nobel Prize for Peace the following year. But King continued to evolve.

After the passage of the Civil Rights Act of 1964 and the Voting Rights Act of 1965, King increasingly turned his attention to states outside the South. He came to see poverty as the key problem of black Americans, and of America generally, and he hoped to forge a broad antipoverty coalition. King's rhetoric became increasingly radical in his last years, calling for a "radical revolution of values." "You can't talk about solving the economic problem of the Negro without talking about billions of dollars," King proclaimed in 1966. "Now this means that we are treading in difficult waters, because it really means that we are saying that something is wrong . . . with capitalism . . . . There must be a better distribution of wealth and maybe America must move toward a Democratic Socialism." In 1967 King initiated a "Poor People's Campaign" which focused on providing jobs for the poor of all races. He began planning a new March on Washington, which he did not live to see, which would demand an Economic Bill of Rights guaranteeing employment for able-bodied individuals, incomes for those unable to work, and an end to housing discrimination.

King was also an early and vocal opponent of the Vietnam War, at a time when most liberals as well as conservatives supported the war. He encouraged young men to become conscientious objectors. King viewed the war as a grotesque waste of life and resources. He suggested that "A nation that continues year after year to spend more money on military defense than on programs of social uplift is approaching spiritual death."

King was assassinated on April 4, 1968, while supporting a strike of black sanitation workers in Memphis, Tennessee. In 1986 the third Monday of January was designated a federal holiday in his honor.

3 The Women's Movement

Jo Freeman

The emergence in the last few years of a feminist movement caught most thoughtful observers by surprise. Women had "come a long way," had they not? What could they want to be liberated from? The new movement generated much speculation about the sources of female discontent and why it was articulated at this particular time. But these speculators usually asked the wrong questions. Most attempts to analyze the sources of social strain have had to conclude with Ferriss (1971, p. 1) that, "from the close perspective of 1970, events of the past decade provide evidence of no compelling cause of the rise of the new feminist movement." His examination of time-series data over the previous 20 years did not reveal any significant changes in socioeconomic variables which could account for the emergence of a women's movement at the time it was created. From such strain indicators, one could surmise that any time in the last two decades was as conducive as any other to movement formation.

[...]

An investigation into a movement's origins must be concerned with the microstructural preconditions for the emergence of such a movement center. From where do the people come who make up the initial, organizing cadre of a movement? How do they come together, and how do they come to share a similar view of the world in circumstances which compel them to political action? In what ways does the nature of the original center affect the future development of the movement?

Most movements have very inconspicuous beginnings. The significant elements of their origins are usually forgotten or distorted by the time a trained observer seeks to trace them out, making retroactive analyses difficult. Thus, a detailed investigation of a single movement at the time it is forming can add much to what little is known about movement origins. Such an examination cannot uncover all of the conditions and ingredients of movement formation, but it can aptly illustrate both weaknesses in the theoretical literature and new directions for research. During the formative period of the women's liberation movement, I had many opportunities to observe, log, and interview most of the principals involved in the early movement. The descriptive material below is based on that data. This analysis, supplemented by five other origin studies made by me, would support the following three propositions:

Proposition 1: The need for a preexisting communications network or infrastructure within the social base of a movement is a primary prerequisite for "spontaneous" activity. Masses alone don't form movements, however discontented they may be. Groups of previously unorganized individuals may spontaneously form into small local associations – usually along the lines of informal social networks – in response to a specific strain or crisis, but, if they are not linked in some manner, the protest does not become generalized: it remains a local irritant or dissolves completely. If a movement is to spread rapidly, the communications network must already exist. If only the rudiments of one exist, movement formation requires a high input of "organizing" activity.

Proposition 2: Not just any communications network will do. It must be a network that is *co-optable* to the new ideas of the incipient movement. To be co-optable, it

A Chronology of the U.S. Women's Movement

1961: President Kennedy forms President's Commission on the Status of Women, chaired by Esther Peterson and Eleanor Roosevelt; only 3.6 percent of law students are women

1963: Betty Friedan's book, *The Feminine Mystique*, becomes a best-seller; the Equal Pay Act is signed into law

1964: The Civil Rights Act of 1964 is signed into law; Title VII of the Act bars sex discrimination in employment; Mary King and Casey Hayden write a paper decrying the treatment of women in the Student Nonviolent Coordination Committee (SNCC)

1965: The U.S. Supreme Court, in *Griswold v. Connecticut*, bans laws that prohibit the use of, or the dissemination of information about, birth control; King and Hayden's paper on "Sex and Caste" is circulated widely (and published in the journal *Liberation* in 1966).

1966: National Organization of Women (NOW) founded with Betty Friedan as president

1967: Women's consciousness-raising (CR) groups formed in Berkeley and elsewhere; CR groups proliferate, especially during 1968 and 1969

1968: Protests are staged against the Miss America Pageant in Atlantic City; Shirley Chisholm becomes the first African-American woman elected to Congress; women are hissed and thrown out of a convention of Students for a Democratic Society (SDS) for demanding a women's liberation plank in the group's platform

1969: Feminist activists disrupt Senate hearings on the birth control pill for excluding testimony about its dangerous side-effects

1970: Tens of thousands participate in the Women's Equality March in New York City; much feminist work is published, including Kate Millett's *Sexual Politics*, Shulamith Firestone's *The Dialectic of Sex*, *The Black Woman*, edited by Toni Cade Bambara, and *Sisterhood is Powerful*, edited by Robin Morgan; the Feminist Press is founded; Rita Mae Brown spurs the "Lavender Menace" protest in favor of including lesbian rights as part of the women's movement; lesbian feminist CR groups proliferate during 1970 and 1971; the U.S. House passes the Equal Rights Amendment (ERA); four states, including New York, pass liberal abortion laws

1971: The first courses in women's history and literature are offered at many colleges; the National Women's Political Caucus is founded by Bella Abzug, Shirley Chisholm, Betty Friedan, and Gloria Steinem, among others

1972: Title IX of the 1972 education bill prohibits sex discrimination in educational programs (including sports programs) that receive federal assistance; 12 percent of law students are now women; Shirley Chisholm runs for the Democratic nomination for president; the first rape crisis and battered women's shelters open; *Ms.* magazine begins publishing

1973: Supreme Court, in *Roe v. Wade*, eliminates restrictions on first-trimester abortions; the National Black Feminist Organization is formed

1974: The Equal Opportunity Act forbids discrimination on the basis of sex or marital status; the Coalition of Labor Union Women is founded; the Combahee River Collective of Black Women begins meeting in Boston; eleven women are ordained as Episcopal priests in violation of church law

1978: The first "Take Back the Night March" is held in Boston

1979: The Moral Majority is founded by Rev. Jerry Falwell, opposing the ERA, abortion, and gay rights

Early 1980s: The women's movement is divided over the issue of pornography

1982: The ERA is defeated, falling three states short of the thirty-eight needed for ratification

must be composed of like-minded people whose background, experiences, or location in the social structure make them receptive to the ideas of a specific new movement.

Proposition 3: Given the existence of a co-optable communications network, or at least the rudimentary development of a potential one, and a situation of strain, one or more precipitants are required. Here, two distinct patterns emerge that often overlap. In one, a crisis galvanizes the network into spontaneous action in a new direction. In the other, one or more persons begin organizing a new organization or disseminating a new idea. For spontaneous action to occur, the communications network must be well formed or the initial protest will not survive the incipient stage. If it is not well formed, organizing efforts must occur; that is, one or more persons must specifically attempt to construct a movement. To be successful, organizers must be skilled and must have a fertile field in which to work. If no communications network already exists, there must at least be emerging spontaneous groups which are acutely atuned to the issue, albeit uncoordinated. To sum up, if a co-optable communications network is already established, a crisis is all that is necessary to galvanize it. If it is rudimentary, an organizing cadre of one or more persons is necessary. Such a cadre is superfluous if the former conditions fully exist, but it is essential if they do not.

Before examining these propositions in detail, let us look at the structure and origins of the women's liberation movement.

The women's liberation movement manifests itself in an almost infinite variety of groups, styles, and organizations. Yet, this diversity has sprung from only two distinct origins whose numerous offspring remain clustered largely around these two sources. The two branches are often called "reform" and "radical," or, as the sole authoritative book on the movement describes them, "women's rights" and "women's liberation" (Hole and Levine 1971). Unfortunately, these terms actually tell us very little, since feminists do not fit into the traditional Left/ Right spectrum. In fact, if an ideological typography were possible, it would show minimal consistency with any other characteristic. Structure and style rather than ideology more accurately differentiate the two branches, and, even here, there has been much borrowing on both sides.

I prefer simpler designations: the first of the branches will be referred to as the older branch of the movement, partly because it began first and partly because the median age of its activists is higher. It contains numerous organizations, including the lobbyist group (Women's Equity Action League), a legal foundation (Human Rights for Women), over 20 caucuses in professional organizations, and separate organizations of women in the professions and other occupations. Its most prominent "core group" is the National Organization for Women (NOW), which was also the first to be formed.

While the written programs and aims of the older branch span a wide spectrum, their activities tend to be concentrated on legal and economic problems. These groups are primarily made up of women – and men – who work, and they are substantially concerned with the problems of working women. The style of organization of the older branch tends to be traditionally formal, with elected officers, boards of directors, bylaws, and the other trappings of democratic procedure. All started as top-down national organizations, lacking in a mass base. Some have subsequently developed a mass base, some have not yet done so, and others do not want to.

Conversely, the younger branch consists of innumerable small groups – engaged in a variety of activities – whose contact with each other is, at best, tenuous. Contrary to popular myth, it did not begin on the campus nor was it started by the Students for a Democratic Society (SDS). However, its activators were, to be trite, on the other side of the generation gap. While few were students, all were "under 30" and had received their political education as participants or

Social Networks The web of social ties that connects individuals (and organizations) to others is often referred to as a social network. An individual's network typically includes friends, relatives, neighbors, and co-workers. One's ideas and attitudes are typically strongly influenced and reinforced by one's social network, and scholars have emphasized how recruitment to movements often occurs through network ties. (Finding a job typically depends on one's network ties, too. Friends of friends turn out to be especially important for job-seekers.) Movements, then, are often built upon pre-existing networks, although they also bring together previously unconnected networks and organizations. The individuals who bring together such networks are sometimes called **brokers**.

concerned observers of the social action projects of the last decade. Many came direct from New Left and civil rights organizations. Others had attended various courses on women in the multitude of free universities springing up around the country during those years.

The expansion of these groups has appeared more amoebic than organized, because the younger branch of the movement prides itself on its lack of organization. From its radical roots, it inherited the idea that structures were always conservative and confining, and leaders, isolated and elitist. Thus, eschewing structure and damning the idea of leadership, it has carried the concept of "everyone doing her own thing" to the point where communication is haphazard and coordination is almost nonexistent. The thousands of sister chapters around the country are virtually independent of each other, linked only by numerous underground papers, journals, newsletters, and cross-country travelers. A national conference was held over Thanksgiving in 1968 but, although considered successful, has not yet been repeated. Before the 1968 conference, the movement did not have the sense of national unity which emerged after the conference. Since then, young feminists have made no attempt to call another national conference. There have been a few regional conferences, but no permanent consequences resulted. At most, some cities have a coordinating committee which attempts to maintain communication among local groups and to channel newcomers into appropriate ones, but these committees have no power over any group's activities, let alone its ideas. Even local activists do not know how big the movement is in their own city. While it cannot be said to have no organization at all, this branch of the movement has informally adopted a general policy of "structurelessness."

Despite a lack of a formal policy encouraging it, there is a great deal of homogeneity within the younger branch of the movement. Like the older branch, it tends to be predominantly white, middle class, and college educated. But it is much more homogenous and, unlike the older branch, has been unable to diversify. This is largely because most small groups tend to form among friendship networks. Most groups have no requirements for membership (other than female sex), no dues, no written and agreed-upon structure, and no elected leaders. Because of this lack of structure, it is often easier for an individual to form a new group than to find and join an older one. This encourages group formation but discourages individual diversification. Even contacts among groups tend to be along friendship lines.

In general, the different style and organization of the two branches was largely derived from the different kind of political education and experiences of each group of women. Women of the older branch were trained in and had used the traditional forms of political action, while the younger branch has inherited the loose, flexible, person-oriented attitude of the youth and student movements. The different structures that have evolved from these two distinctly different kinds of experience have, in turn, largely determined the strategy of the two branches, irrespective of any conscious intentions of their participants. These different structures and strategies have each posed different problems and possibilities. Intramovement differences are often perceived by the participants as conflicting, but it is their essential complementarity which has been one of the strengths of the movement.

Despite the multitude of differences, there are very strong similarities in the way the two branches came into being. These similarities serve to illuminate some of the microsociological factors involved in movement formation. The forces which led to NOW's formation were first set in motion in 1961 when President Kennedy established the President's Commission on the Status of Women at the behest of Esther Peterson, to be chaired by Eleanor Roosevelt. Operating under a broad mandate, its 1963 report (*American Women*) and subsequent committee publications documented just how thoroughly women are still denied many rights and opportunities. The most concrete response to the activity of the president's commission was the eventual establishment of 50 state commissions to do similar research on a state level. These commissions were often urged by politically active women and were composed primarily of women. Nonetheless, many believe the main stimulus behind their formation was the alleged view of the governors that the commissions were excellent opportunities to pay political debts without giving women more influential positions.

The activity of the federal and state commissions laid the groundwork for the future movement in three significant ways: (1) it brought together many knowledgeable, politically active women who otherwise would not have worked together around matters of direct concern to women; (2) the investigations unearthed ample evidence of women's unequal status, especially their legal and economic difficulties, in the process convincing many previously uninterested women that something should be done; (3) the reports created a climate of expectations that something would be done. The women of the federal and state commissions who were exposed to these influences exchanged visits, correspondence, and staff and met with each other at an annual commission convention. Thus, they were in a position to share and mutually reinforce their growing awareness and concern over women's issues. These commissions thus created an embryonic communications network among people with similar concerns.

During this time, two other events of significance occurred. The first was the publication of Betty Friedan's (1963) book, *The Feminine Mystique*. An immediate best seller, it stimulated many women to question the status quo and some to suggest to Friedan that a new organization be formed to attack their problems. The second event was the addition of "sex" to Title VII of the 1964 Civil Rights Act. Many men thought the "sex" provision was a joke. The Equal Employment Opportunity Commission (EEOC) certainly treated it as one and refused to adequately enforce it. The first EEOC executive director even stated publicly that the provision was a "fluke" that was "conceived out of wedlock." But, within the EEOC, there was a "pro-woman" coterie which argued that "sex" would be taken more seriously if there were "some sort of NAACP for women" to put pressure on the government. As government employees, they couldn't organize such a group, but they spoke privately with those whom they thought might be able to do so. One who shared their views was Rep. Martha Griffiths of Michigan. She blasted the EEOC's attitude in a June 20, 1966 speech on the House floor declaring that the agency had "started out by casting disrespect and ridicule on the law" but that their "wholly negative attitude had changed – for the worse."

On June 30, 1966, these three strands of incipient feminism were knotted together to form NOW. The occasion was the last day of the Third National Conference of Commissions on the Status of Women, ironically titled "Targets for Action." The participants had all received copies of Rep. Griffiths's remarks. The opportunity came with a refusal by conference officials to bring to the floor a proposed resolution that urged the EEOC to give equal enforcement to the sex provision of Title VII as was given to the race provision. Despite the fact that these state commissions were not federal agencies, officials replied that one government agency could not be allowed to pressure another. The small group of women who had desired the resolution had met the night before in Friedan's hotel room to discuss the possibility of a civil rights organization for women. Not convinced of its need, they chose instead to propose the resolution. When the resolution was vetoed, the women held a whispered conversation over lunch and agreed to form an action organization "to bring women into full participation in the mainstream of American society now, assuming all the privileges and responsibilities thereof in truly equal partnership with men." The name NOW was coined by Friedan, who was at the conference researching her second book. Before the day was over, 28 women paid $5.00 each to join.

By the time the organizing conference was held the following October 29–30, over 300 men and women had become charter members. It is impossible to do a breakdown on the composition of the charter membership, but one of the first officers and board is possible. Such a breakdown accurately reflected NOW's origins. Friedan was president, two former EEOC commissioners were vice-presidents, a representative of the United Auto Workers Women's Committee was secretary-treasurer, and there were seven past and present members of the State Commissions on the Status of Women on the 20-member board. Of the charter members, 126 were Wisconsin residents – and Wisconsin had the most active state commission. Occupationally, the board and officers were primarily from the professions, labor, government, and the communications industry. Of these, only those from labor had any experience in organizing, and they resigned a year later in a dispute over support of the Equal Rights Amendment. Instead of organizational expertise, what the early NOW members had was media experience, and it was here that their early efforts were aimed.

As a result, NOW often gave the impression of being larger than it was. It was highly successful in getting publicity, much less so in bringing about concrete changes or organizing itself. Thus, it was not until 1969, when several national news media simultaneously decided to do major stories on the women's liberation movement, that NOW's membership increased significantly. Even today, there are only 8,000 members, and the chapters are still in an incipient stage of development.

In the meantime, unaware of and unknown to NOW, the EEOC, or to the state commissions, younger women began forming their own movement. Here, too, the groundwork had been laid some years before. Social action projects of recent years had attracted many women, who were quickly shunted into traditional roles and faced with the self-evident contradiction of working in a "freedom movement" without being very free. No single "youth movement" activity or organization is responsible for the younger branch of the women's liberation movement; together they created a "radical community" in which like-minded people continually interacted with each other. This community consisted largely of those who had participated in one or more of the many protest activities of the sixties and had established its own ethos and its own institutions. Thus, the women in it thought of themselves as "movement people" and had incorporated the adjective "radical" into their personal identities. The values of their radical identity and the style to which they had been trained by their movement participation directed them to approach most problems as political ones which could be solved by organizing. What remained was to translate their individual feelings of "unfreedom" into a collective consciousness. Thus, the radical community provided not only the necessary network of communication; its radical ideas formed the framework of analysis which "explained" the dismal situation in which radical women found themselves.

Papers had been circulated on women, and temporary women's caucuses had been held as early as 1964, when Stokely Carmichael made his infamous remark that "the only position for women in SNCC is prone." But it was not until late 1967 and 1968 that the groups developed a determined, if cautious, continuity and began to consciously expand themselves. At least five groups in five different cities (Chicago, Toronto, Detroit, Seattle, and Gainesville, Florida) formed spontaneously, independent of each other. They came at a very auspicious moment. The year 1967 was the one in which the blacks kicked the whites out of the civil rights movement, student power had been discredited by SDS, and the organized New Left was on the wane. Only draft-resistance activities were on the increase, and this movement more than any other exemplified the social inequities of the sexes. Men could resist the draft; women could only counsel resistance.

What was significant about this point in time was that there was a lack of available opportunities for political work. Some women fit well into the "secondary role" of draft counseling. Many did not. For years, their complaints of unfair treatment had been ignored by movement men with the dictum that those things could wait until after the revolution. Now these movement women found time on their hands, but the men would still not listen.

A typical example was the event which precipitated the formation of the Chicago group, the first independent group in this country. At the August 1967 National Conference for New Politics convention, a women's caucus met for days but was told its resolution wasn't significant enough to merit a floor discussion. By threatening to tie up the convention with procedural motions, the women succeeded in having their statement tacked to the end of the agenda. It was never discussed. The chair refused to recognize any of the many women standing by the microphone, their hands straining upward. When he instead called on someone to speak on "the forgotten American, the American Indian," five women rushed the podium to demand an explanation. But the chairman just patted one of them on the head (literally) and told her, "Cool down little girl. We have more important things to talk about than women's problems."

The "little girl" was Shulamith Firestone, future author of *The Dialectic of Sex* (1971), and she didn't cool down. Instead, she joined with another Chicago woman, who had been trying to organize a women's group that summer, to call a meeting of those women who had half-heartedly attended the summer meetings. Telling their stories to those women, they stimulated sufficient rage to carry the group for three months, and by that time it was a permanent institution.

Another somewhat similar event occurred in Seattle the following winter. At the University of Washington, an SDS organizer was explaining to a large meeting how white college youth established rapport with the poor whites with whom they were working. "He noted that sometimes after analyzing societal ills, the men shared leisure time by 'balling a chick together.' He pointed out that such activities did much to enhance the political consciousness of the poor white youth. A woman in the audience asked, 'And what did it do for the consciousness of the chick?'" (Hole and Levine 1971, p. 120). After the meeting, a handful of enraged women formed Seattle's first group.

Groups subsequent to the initial five were largely organized rather than emerging spontaneously out of recent events. In particular, the Chicago group was responsible for the creation of many new groups in that city and elsewhere and started the first national newsletter. The 1968 conference was organized by the Washington D.C. group from resources provided by the Center for Policy Studies (CPS), a radical research organization. Using CPS facilities, this group subsequently became a main literature-distribution center. Although New York groups organized early and were featured in the 1969–70 media blitz, New York was not a source of early organizers.

Unlike NOW, the women in the first groups had had years of experience as local-level organizers. They did not have the resources, or the desire, to form a national organization, but they knew how to utilize the infrastructure of the radical community, the underground press, and the free universities to disseminate ideas on women's liberation. Chicago, as a center of New Left activity, had the largest number of politically conscious organizers. Many traveled widely to Left conferences and demonstrations, and most used the opportunity to talk with other women about the new movement. In spite of public derision by radical men, or perhaps because of it, young women steadily formed new groups around the country.

Initially, the new movement found it hard to organize on the campus, but, as a major congregating area of women and, in particular, of women with political awareness, campus women's liberation groups eventually became ubiquitous. While the younger branch of the movement never formed any organization larger or more extensive than a city-wide co-ordinating committee, it would be fair to say that it has a larger "participationship" than NOW and the other older branch organizations. While the members of the older branch knew how to use the media and how to form national structures, the women of the younger branch were skilled in local community organizing.

From this description, there appear to be four essential elements contributing to the emergence of the women's liberation movement in the mid-sixties: (1) the growth of a preexisting communications network which was (2) co-optable to the ideas of the new movement; (3) a series of crises that galvanized into action people involved in this network, and/or (4) subsequent organizing effort to weld the spontaneous groups together into a movement. To further understand these factors, let us examine them in detail with reference to other relevant studies.

1. Both the Commissions on the Status of Women and the "radical community" created a communications network through which those women initially interested in creating an organization could easily reach others. Such a network had not previously existed among women. Historically tied to the family and isolated from their own kind, women are perhaps the most organizationally underdeveloped social category in Western civilization. By 1950, the 19th-century organizations which had been the basis of the suffrage movement – the Women's Trade Union League, the General Federation of Women's Clubs, the Women's Christian Temperance Union, the National American Women's Suffrage Association – were all either dead or a pale shadow of their former selves. The closest exception was the National Women's Party (NWP), which has remained dedicated to feminist concerns since its inception in 1916. However, since 1923, it has been essentially a lobbying group for the Equal Rights Amendment. The NWP, having always believed that a small group of women concentrating their efforts in the right places was more effective than a mass appeal, was not appalled that, as late as 1969, even the majority of avowed feminists in this country had never heard of the NWP or the ERA.

[...]

Other evidence also attests to the role of previously organized networks in the rise and spread of a social movement. According to Buck (1920, pp. 43–44), the Grange established a degree of organization among American farmers in the 19th century which greatly facilitated the spread of future farmers' protests. In Saskatchewan, Lipset (1959) has asserted, "The rapid acceptance of new ideas and movements . . . can be attributed mainly to the high degree of organization. . . . The role of the social structure of the western wheat belt in facilitating the rise of new movements has never been sufficiently appreciated by historians and sociologists. Repeated challenges and crises forced the western farmers to create many more community institutions . . . than are necessary in a more stable area. These groups in turn provided a structural basis for immediate action in critical situations. [Therefore] though it was a new radical party, the C.C.F. did not have to build up an organization from scratch." More recently, the civil rights movement was built upon the infrastructure of the Southern black church (King 1958), and early SDS organizers made ready use of the National Student Association (Kissinger and Ross 1968, p. 16).

[...]

The development of the women's liberation movement highlights the salience of such a network precisely because the conditions for a movement existed *before* a network came into being, but the movement didn't exist until afterward. Socioeconomic strain did not change for women significantly during a 20-year period. It was as great in 1955 as in 1965. What changed was the organizational situation. It was not until a communications network developed among like-minded people beyond local boundaries that the movement could emerge and develop past the point of occasional, spontaneous uprising.

2. However, not just any network would do; it had to be one which was co-optable by the incipient movement because it linked like-minded people likely to be predisposed to the new ideas of the movement. The 180,000-member Federation of Business and Professional Women's (BPW) Clubs would appear to be a likely base for a new feminist movement but in fact was unable to assume this role. It had steadily lobbied for legislation of importance to women, yet as late as "1966 BPW rejected a number of suggestions that it redefine... goals and tactics and become a kind of 'NAACP for women' ...out of fear of being labeled 'feminist' " (Hole and Levine 1971, p. 81). While its membership has become a recruiting ground for feminism, it could not initially overcome the ideological barrier to a new type of political action.

On the other hand, the women of the President's and State Commissions on the Status of Women and the feminist coterie of the EEOC were co-optable, largely because their immersion into the facts of female status and the details of sex-discrimination cases made them very conscious of the need for change. Likewise, the young women of the "radical community" lived in an atmosphere of questioning, confrontation, and change. They absorbed an ideology of "freedom" and "liberation" far more potent than any latent "antifeminism" might have been. The repeated contradictions between these ideas and the actions of their male colleagues created a compulsion for action which only required an opportunity to erupt. This was provided by the "vacuum of political activity" of 1967–68.

[...]

A co-optable network, therefore, is one whose members have had common experiences which predispose them to be receptive to the particular new ideas of the incipient movement and who are not faced with structural or ideological barriers to action. If the new movement as an "innovation" can interpret these experiences and perceptions in ways that point out channels for social action, then participation in social movement becomes the logical thing to do.

3. As our examples have illustrated, these similar perceptions must be translated into action. This is the role of the "crisis." For women of the older branch of the movement, the impetus to organize was the refusal of the EEOC to enforce the sex provision of Title VII, precipitated by the concomitant refusal of federal officials at the conference to allow a supportive resolution. For younger women, there were a series of minor crises. Such precipitating events are common to most movements. They serve to crystallize and focus discontent. From their own experiences, directly and concretely, people feel the need for change in a situation that allows for an exchange of feelings with others, mutual validation, and a subsequent reinforcement of innovative interpretation. Perception of an immediate need for change is a major factor in predisposing people to accept new ideas. Nothing makes desire for change more acute than a crisis. If the strain is great enough, such a crisis need not be a major one; it need only embody symbolically collective discontent.

4. However, a crisis will only catalyze a well-formed communications network. If such networks are only embryonically developed or only partially co-optable, the potentially active individuals in them must be linked together by someone. As Jackson et al. (1960, p. 37) stated, "Some protest may persist where the source of trouble is constantly present. But interest ordinarily cannot be maintained unless there is a welding of spontaneous groups into some stable organization." In other words, people must be organized. Social movements do not simply occur.

The role of the organizer in movement formation is another neglected aspect of the theoretical literature. There has been great concern with leadership, but the two roles are distinct and not always performed by the same individual. In the early stages of a movement, it is the organizer much more than any "leader" who is important, and such an individual or cadre must often operate behind the scenes. Certainly, the "organizing cadre" that young women in the radical community came to be was key to the growth of that branch of the women's liberation movement, despite the fact that no "leaders" were produced (and were actively discouraged). The existence of many leaders but no organizers in the older branch of the women's liberation movement and its subsequent slow development would tend to substantiate this hypothesis.

The crucial function of the organizer has been explored indirectly in other areas of sociology. Rogers (1962) devotes many pages to the "change agent" who, while he does not necessarily weld a group together or "construct" a movement, does do many of the same things for agricultural innovation that an organizer does for political change. Mass-society theory makes reference to the "agitator" but fails to do so in any kind of truly informative way. A study of farmers' movements indicates that many core organizations were organized by a single individual before the spontaneous aspects of the movement predominated. Further, many other core groups were subsidized by older organizations, federal and state governments, and even by local businessmen. These organizations often served as training centers for organizers and sources of material support to aid in the formation of new interest groups and movements.

Similarly, the civil rights movement provided the training for many another movement's organizers, including the young women of the women's liberation movement. It would appear that the art of "constructing" a social movement is something that requires considerable skill and experience. Even in the supposedly spontaneous social movement, the professional is more valuable than the amateur.

[...]

References

Buck, Solon J. *The Agrarian Crusade*. 1920. New Haven, Conn.: Yale University Press.

Ferriss, Abbott L. 1971. *Indicators of Trends in the Status of American Women*. New York: Russell Sage.

Firestone, Shulamith. 1971. *The Dialectic of Sex*. New York: Morrow.

Friedan, Betty, 1963. *The Feminine Mystique*. New York: Dell.

Hole, Judith, and Ellen Levine. 1971. *Rebirth of Feminism*. New York: Quadrangle.

Jackson, Maurice, Eleanora Petersen, James Bull, Sverre Monsen, and Patricia Richmond. 1960. "The Failure of an Incipient Social Movement." *Pacific Sociological Review* 3, no. 1 (Spring): 40.

King, Martin Luther, Jr. 1958. *Stride toward Freedom*. New York: Harper.

Kissinger, C. Clark, and Bob Ross. 1968. "Starting in '60: Or From SLID to Resistance." *New Left Notes*, June 10.

Lipset, Seymour M. *Agrarian Socialism*. Berkeley: University of California Press, 1959.

Rogers, Everett M. 1962. *Diffusion of Innovations*. New York: Free Press.

Biography – Betty Friedan and *The Feminine Mystique*

Ideas are crucial to social movements, and in the literate modern world those ideas are often expressed in books. The volume that did the most to revive the women's movement in the 1960s was packaged as a critique of housewives written by one: *The Feminine Mystique*. Its author, Betty Friedan, was born in Peoria, Illinois, in 1921, only one year after the Nineteenth Amendment had given women the right to vote. Her father was an ambitious immigrant who had put himself through medical school. Her mother was a housewife who, when young, had wanted to go to Smith College, something her parents did not allow.

From childhood, Friedan was known to have a brilliant mind and a quick temper, two things girls were not supposed to have in Peoria. Having skipped a grade, she felt like an outsider, a status probably exacerbated by local anti-Semitism and her lack of traditional good looks. At Smith College she developed, despite her own affluent background, radical sympathies as well as a rabble-rousing reputation as editor of the school newspaper. She supported, for instance, a strike by the maids who cleaned students' rooms and served them in the dining halls. Between her junior and senior years she spent several weeks at the Highlander Folk School in Tennessee, a training ground for leftist labor organizers.

After graduating in 1942, Friedan went to Berkeley to study psychology. She shone there as well, and was soon offered a lucrative fellowship that would have supported her through finishing her Ph.D. She panicked when a boyfriend implied that his envy would ruin their relationship if she took the scholarship, and – feeling torn between love and career – she left the university. For the next nine years she would work for a left-wing news service, then the newspaper of a leftist union, the United Electrical, Radio and Machine Workers of America.

At the age of 26, Friedan met a veteran named Carl Friedman and fell in love. He was a college drop-out, and no intellectual, but he loved the theater and seemed to love Betty. Despite misgivings on each side, they soon married. Their first child was born in late 1948, and Betty was given a maternity leave by the union (which was later cut short, however). She became pregnant again in 1952, during a crisis for the union, which had lost two thirds of its members in the face of redbaiting by the government and the Congress of Industrial Organizations (CIO). The four-person newspaper staff, two men and two women, had to be cut in half, and both the women left (how voluntarily is not altogether clear). Brilliant, radical Betty became a housewife in Queens.

Sort of. She continued to write articles, now for women's magazines, in which any political and economic analysis, or anything that implied that women might be more satisfied working than raising children, was assiduously edited out. A serious debate was raging over whether women should go to college at all, or instead be schooled in the skills of managing a home, since that is what they were going to do. Many otherwise sensible scholars argued that college was wasted on women. Friedan wrote an article arguing the opposite, only to see it rejected by *McCall's* and published by the *Ladies' Home Journal* only after it was edited to make the opposite point. At the same time, she also helped organize community groups for various causes, from a rent strike to sex education in the schools. Friedan was not your typical housewife.

In 1957, Friedan and two of her Smith classmates wrote a lengthy questionnaire to distribute at their fifteenth reunion that spring. Inspired by their own experiences in therapy, and a sense from the tenth reunion that most of the women were overwhelmed with child-rearing, they asked a number of proto-feminist questions, like "What problems have you had working out your role as a woman?" Friedan did other research on women's issues, and realized that she might be able to publish her ideas as a book, since they were too controversial for most magazines. W. W. Norton gave her an advance, and in 1963 she published *The Feminine Mystique*.

Her book became a bestseller, in part due to her own ferocious self-promotion (she replaced her agent, forced Norton to hire an outside publicist for the book, and went on her own publicity tour). Even more, it touched a nerve among millions of women, and by 1970 it had sold 1.5 million copies. It described and analyzed the dissatisfaction felt by so many American housewives and mothers, each locked up in her own "comfortable concentration camp": "Each suburban wife struggled with it alone. As she made the beds, shopped for groceries, matched slipcover material, ate peanut butter sandwiches with her children, chauffeured Cub Scouts and Brownies, lay beside her husband at night – she was afraid to ask even of herself the silent question – 'Is this all?'" Friedan had packaged the ideas of Simone de Beauvoir and

Margaret Mead for middle-class housewives. She had also carefully avoided linking her analysis to Marxism, and suppressed any mention of her own years in the Left, now discredited by years of McCarthyism. The plight of women, it seemed, was distinct. To help sell her book, Friedan shrewdly but inaccurately presented herself as a simple suburban housewife who just couldn't take it any more.

The Feminine Mystique helped the women's movement coalesce in the mid-1960s, providing an ideology for the networks that had formed around the National Commission on the Status of Women (and state-level equivalents). Many of these women (and some men) were active in forming the National Organization for Women (NOW) in 1966. Its goal was to integrate women into the mainstream of American society and institutions, and it would remain the central organization of the liberal, reformist wing of the women's movement. Friedan, now a celebrity, was elected its first president. She would remain active in the cause the rest of her life. But her foremost contribution was her writing, her ability to articulate discontent, to provide a rationale for what would become one of the most successful social movements of the twentieth century.

4 The Gay Liberation Movement

John D'Emilio

On Friday, June 27, 1969, shortly before midnight, two detectives from Manhattan's Sixth Precinct set off with a few other officers to raid the Stonewall Inn, a gay bar on Christopher Street in the heart of Greenwich Village. They must have expected it to be a routine raid. New York was in the midst of a mayoral campaign – always a bad time for the city's homosexuals – and John Lindsay, the incumbent who had recently lost his party's primary, had reason to agree to a police cleanup. Moreover, a few weeks earlier the Sixth Precinct had received a new commanding officer who marked his entry into the position by initiating a series of raids on gay bars. The Stonewall Inn was an especially inviting target. Operating without a liquor license, reputed to have ties with organized crime, and offering scantily clad go-go boys as entertainment, it brought an "unruly" element to Sheridan Square, a busy Village intersection. Patrons of the Stonewall tended to be young and nonwhite. Many were drag queens, and many came from the burgeoning ghetto of runaways living across town in the East Village.

However, the customers at the Stonewall that night responded in any but the usual fashion. As the police released them one by one from inside the bar, a crowd accumulated on the street. Jeers and catcalls arose from the onlookers when a paddy wagon departed with the bartender, the Stonewall's bouncer, and three drag queens. A few minutes later, an officer attempted to steer the last of the patrons, a lesbian, through the bystanders to a nearby patrol car. "She put up a struggle," the *Village Voice* (July 3, 1969, p. 18) reported, "from car to door to car again." At that moment,

> the scene became explosive. Limp wrists were forgotten. Beer cans and bottles were heaved at the windows and a rain of coins descended on the cops.... Almost by signal the crowd erupted into cobblestone and bottle heaving.... From nowhere came an uprooted parking meter – used as a battering ram on the Stonewall door. I heard several cries of "let's get some gas," but the blaze of flame which soon appeared in the window of the Stonewall was still a shock.

Reinforcements rescued the shaken officers from the torched bar, but their work had barely started. Rioting continued far into the night, with Puerto Rican transvestites and young street people leading charges against rows of uniformed police officers and then withdrawing to regroup in Village alleys and side streets.

By the following night, graffiti calling for "Gay Power" had appeared along Christopher Street. Knots of young gays – effeminate, according to most reports – gathered on corners, angry and restless. Someone heaved a sack of wet garbage through the window of a patrol car. On nearby Waverly Place, a concrete block landed on the hood of another police car that was quickly surrounded by dozens of men, pounding on its doors and dancing on its hood. Helmeted officers from the tactical patrol force arrived on the scene and dispersed with swinging clubs an impromptu chorus line of gay men in the middle of a full kick. At the intersection of Greenwich Avenue and Christopher Street, several dozen queens screaming "Save Our Sister!" rushed a group of officers who were clubbing a young man and dragged him to safety. For the next few hours, trash fires blazed, bottles and stones flew through the air, and cries of "Gay Power!" rang in the streets as the police, numbering over 400, did battle with a crowd estimated at more than 2,000.

After the second night of disturbances, the anger that had erupted into street fighting was channeled into intense discussion of what many had begun to memorialize as the first gay riot in history. Allen Ginsberg's stature in the 1960s had risen almost to that of guru for many counterculture youth. When he arrived at the Stonewall on Sunday evening, he commented on the change that had already taken place. "You know, the guys there were so beautiful," he told a reporter. "They've lost that wounded look that fags all had ten years ago." The New York Mattachine Society hastily assembled a special riot edition of its newsletter that characterized the events, with camp humor, as "The Hairpin Drop Heard Round the World." It scarcely exaggerated. Before the end of July, women and men in New York had formed the Gay Liberation Front, a self-proclaimed revolutionary organization in the style of the New Left. Word of the Stonewall riot and GLF spread rapidly among the networks of young radicals scattered across the country, and within a year gay liberation groups had sprung into existence on college campuses and in cities around the nation.

The Stonewall riot was able to spark a nationwide grassroots "liberation" effort among gay men and women in large part because of the radical movements that had so inflamed much of American youth during the 1960s. Gay liberation used the demonstrations of the New Left as recruiting grounds and appropriated the tactics of confrontational politics for its own ends. The ideas that suffused youth protest found their way into gay liberation, where they were modified and adapted to describe the oppression of homosexuals and lesbians. The apocalyptic rhetoric and the sense of impending revolution that surrounded the Movement by the end of the decade gave to its newest participants an audacious daring that made the dangers of a public avowal of their sexuality seem insignificant.

In order to make their existence known, gay liberationists took advantage of the almost daily political events that young radicals were staging across the country. New York's Gay Liberation Front had a contingent at the antiwar march held in the city on October 15, 1969, and was present in even larger numbers at the November moratorium weekend in Washington, where almost half a million activists rallied against American involvement in Southeast Asia. Gay radicals in Berkeley performed guerrilla theater on the campus during orientation that fall and carried banners at the November antiwar rally in San Francisco. In November 1969 and again the following May, lesbians from GLF converged on the Congress to Unite Women, which brought to New York women's liberationists from around the East. Gay activists ran workshops at the 1969 annual convention of the National Student Association. In May 1970 a GLF member addressed the rally in New Haven in support of Bobby Seale and Ericka Huggins, the imprisoned Black Panther leaders. A large contingent of lesbians and gay men attended the national gathering called by the Panthers in the fall of 1970, and the next year a gay "tribe" took part in the May Day protests in Washington against the war. In raising the banner of gay liberation at these and other local demonstrations, radical gays reached closeted homosexuals and lesbians in the Movement who already had a commitment to militant confrontational politics. Their message traveled quickly through the networks of activists created by the New Left, thus allowing gay liberation to spread with amazing rapidity.

The first gay liberationists attracted so many other young radicals not only because of a common sexual identity but because they shared a similar political perspective. Gay liberationists spoke in the hyperbolic phrases of the New Left. They talked of liberation from oppression, resisting genocide, and making a revolution against "imperialist Amerika." GLF's statement of purpose, printed in the New Left newspaper *RAT* (August 12, 1969), sounded like many of the documents produced by radicals in the late 1960s, except that it was written by and about homosexuals:

> We are a revolutionary group of men and women formed with the realization that complete sexual liberation for all people cannot come about unless existing social institutions are abolished. We reject society's attempt to impose sexual roles and definitions of our nature. We are stepping outside these roles and simplistic myths. We are going to be who we are. At the same time, we are creating new social forms and relations, that is, relations based upon brotherhood, cooperation, human love, and uninhibited sexuality. Babylon has forced us to commit ourselves to one thing – revolution!

Gay liberation groups saw themselves as one component of the decade's radicalism and regularly addressed the other issues that were mobilizing American youth. The Berkeley GLF, for instance, passed a resolution on the Vietnam War and the draft demanding that "all troops be brought home at once" and that homosexuals in the armed forces "be given Honorable discharges immediately." Its Los Angeles counterpart declared its "unity with and support for all oppressed minorities who fight for their freedom" and expressed its intention "to build a new, free and loving Gay counter-culture." Positions such as these made it relatively easy for previously closeted but already radicalized homosexuals and lesbians to join or form gay liberation organizations, and the new movement quickly won their allegiance.

Gay liberationists targeted the same institutions as homophile militants, but their disaffection from American society impelled them to use tactics that their predecessors would never have adopted. Bar raids and street arrests of gay men in New York City during August 1970 provoked a march by several thousand men and women from Times Square to Greenwich Village, where rioting broke out. Articles hostile to gays in the *Village Voice* and in *Harper's* led to the occupation of publishers' offices. In San Francisco a demonstration against the *Examiner* erupted into a bloody confrontation with the police. Chicago Gay Liberation invaded the 1970 convention of the American Medical Association, while its counterpart in San Francisco disrupted the annual meeting of the American Psychiatric Association. At a session there on homosexuality a young bearded gay man danced around the auditorium in a red dress, while other homosexuals and lesbians scattered in the audience shouted "Genocide!" and "Torture!" during the reading of a paper on aversion therapy. Politicians campaigning for office found themselves hounded by scruffy gay militants who at any moment might race across the stage where they were speaking or jump in front of a television camera to demand that they speak out against the oppression of homosexuals. The confrontational tactics and flamboyant behavior thrust gay liberationists into the public spotlight. Although their actions may have alienated some homosexuals and lesbians, they inspired many others to join the movement's ranks.

As a political force, the New Left went into eclipse soon after gay liberation appeared on the scene, but the movement of lesbians and gay men continued to thrive throughout the 1970s. Two features of gay liberation accounted for its ability to avoid the decline that most of the other mass movements of the 1960s experienced. One was the new definition that post-Stonewall activists gave to "coming out," which doubled both as ends and means for young gay radicals. The second was the emergence of a strong lesbian liberation movement.

From its beginning, gay liberation transformed the meaning of "coming out." Previously coming out had signified the private decision to accept one's homosexual desires and to acknowledge one's sexual identity to other gay men and women. Throughout the 1950s and 1960s, leaders of the homophile cause had in effect extended their coming out to the public sphere through their work in the movement. But only rarely did they counsel lesbians and homosexuals at large to follow their example, and when they did, homophile activists presented it as a selfless step taken for the benefit of others. Gay liberationists, on the other hand, recast coming out as a profoundly political act that could offer enormous personal benefits to an individual. The open avowal of one's sexual identity, whether at work, at school, at home, or before television cameras, symbolized the shedding of the self-hatred that gay men and women internalized, and consequently it promised an immediate improvement in one's life. To come out of the "closet" quintessentially expressed the fusion of the personal and the political that the radicalism of the late 1960s exalted.

Coming out also posed as the key strategy for building a movement. Its impact on an individual was often cathartic. The exhilaration and anger that surfaced when men and women stepped through the fear of discovery propelled them into political activity. Moreover, when lesbians and homosexuals came out, they crossed a critical dividing line. They relinquished their invisibility, made themselves vulnerable to attack, and acquired an investment in the success of the movement in a way that mere adherence to a political line could never accomplish. Visible lesbians and gay men also served as magnets that drew others to them. Furthermore, once out of the closet, they could not easily fade back in. Coming out provided gay liberation with an army of permanent enlistees.

A second critical feature of the post-Stonewall era was the appearance of a strong lesbian liberation movement. Lesbians had always been a tiny fraction of the homophile movement. But the almost simultaneous birth of women's liberation and gay liberation propelled large numbers of them into radical sexual politics. Lesbians were active in both early gay liberation groups and feminist organizations. Frustrated and angered by the chauvinism they experienced in gay groups and the hostility they found in the women's movement, many lesbians opted to create their own separatist organizations. Groups such as Radicalesbians in New York, the Furies Collective in Washington, D.C., and Gay Women's Liberation in San Francisco carved out a distinctive lesbian-feminist politics. They too spoke in the radical phrases of the New Left, but with an accent on the special revolutionary role that lesbians filled because of their dual oppression as women and as homosexuals. Moreover, as other lesbians made their way into gay and women's groups, their encounters with the chauvinism of gay men and the hostility of heterosexual feminists provided lesbian liberation with ever more recruits.

Although gay liberation and women's liberation both contributed to the growth of a lesbian-feminist movement, the latter exerted a greater influence. The feminist movement offered the psychic space for many women to come to a self-definition as lesbian. Women's liberation was in its origins a separatist movement, with an ideology that defined men as the problem and with organizational forms from consciousness-raising groups to action-oriented collectives that placed a premium on female solidarity. As women explored their oppression together, it became easier to acknowledge their love for other women. The seeming contradiction between an ideology that focused criticism on men per se and the ties of heterosexual feminists to males often provoked a crisis of identity. Lesbian-feminists played upon this contradiction. "A lesbian is the rage of all women condensed to the point of explosion," wrote New York Radicalesbians in "The Woman-Identified Woman," one of the most influential essays of the sexual liberation movements:

> Lesbian is the word, the label, the condition that holds women in line. . . . Lesbian is a label invented by the man to throw at any woman who dares to be his equal, who dares to challenge his prerogatives, who dares to assert the primacy of her own needs. . . . As long as women's liberation tries to free women without facing the basic heterosexual structure that binds us in one-to-one relationships with our own oppressors, tremendous energies will continue to flow into trying to straighten

> up each particular relationship with a man.... It is the primacy of women relating to women, of women creating a new consciousness of and with each other which is at the heart of women's liberation, and the basis for the cultural revolution.

Under these circumstances many heterosexual women reevaluated their sexuality and resolved the contradiction between politics and personal life by coming out as lesbians. Lesbian-feminist organizations were filled with women who came not from the urban subculture of lesbian bars but from the heterosexual world, with the women's liberation movement as a way station. As opponents of feminism were quick to charge, the women's movement was something of a "breeding ground" for lesbianism.

Besides the encouragement it provided for women to come out, women's liberation served lesbians – and gay men – in another way. The feminist movement continued to thrive during the 1970s. Its ideas permeated the country, its agenda worked itself into the political process, and it effected deep-seated changes in the lives of tens of millions of women and men. Feminism's attack upon traditional sex roles and the affirmation of a nonreproductive sexuality that was implicit in such demands as unrestricted access to abortion paved a smoother road for lesbians and homosexuals who were also challenging rigid male and female stereotypes and championing an eroticism that by its nature did not lead to procreation. Moreover, lesbians served as a bridge between the women's movement and gay liberation, at the very least guaranteeing that sectors of each remained amenable to the goals and perspectives of the other. Feminism helped to remove gay life and gay politics from the margins of American society.

By any standard of measurement, post-Stonewall gay liberation dwarfed its homophile predecessor. In June 1970 between 5,000 and 10,000 men and women commemorated the first anniversary of the riot with a march from Greenwich Village to Central Park. By the second half of the decade, Gay Freedom Day events were occurring in dozens of cities, and total participation exceeded half a million individuals. The fifty homophile organizations that had existed in 1969 mushroomed into more than 800 only four years later; as the 1970s ended, the number reached into the thousands. In a relatively short time, gay liberation achieved the goal that had eluded homophile leaders for two decades – the active involvement of large numbers of homosexuals and lesbians in their own emancipation effort.

Numerical strength allowed the new breed of liberationists to compile a list of achievements that could only have elicited awe from homophile activists. In 1973 the American Psychiatric Association altered a position it had held for almost a century by removing homosexuality from its list of mental disorders. During the 1970s more than half the states repealed their sodomy laws, the Civil Service Commission eliminated its ban on the employment of lesbians and homosexuals, and several dozen municipalities passed antidiscrimination statutes. Politicians of national stature came out in favor of gay rights. Activists were invited to the White House to discuss their grievances, and in 1980 the Democratic party platform included a gay rights plank.

The stress gay liberation placed upon coming out also gave the movement leverage of another kind. Not only did men and women join groups that campaigned for equality from outside American institutions; they also came out within their professions, their communities, and other institutions to which they belonged. Gay Catholics, for instance, formed Dignity, and gay Episcopalians, Integrity. In some denominations gay men and women sought not only acceptance but also ordination as ministers. Military personnel announced their homosexuality and fought for the right to remain in the service. Lesbian and gay male academicians, school teachers, social workers, doctors, nurses, psychologists, and others created caucuses in their professions to sensitize their peers to the needs of the gay community and to combat discrimination. Openly gay journalists and television reporters brought an insider's perspective to their coverage of gay-related news. The visibility of lesbians and gay men in so many varied settings helped make homosexuality seem less of a strange, threatening phenomenon and more like an integral part of the social fabric.

Finally, the post-Stonewall era witnessed a significant shift in the self-definition of gay men and women. As pressure from gay liberationists made police harassment the exception rather than the rule in many American cities, the gay subculture flourished as never before. The relative freedom from danger, along with the emphasis the movement placed on gay pride, led not only to an expansion of the bar world but also to the creation of a range of "community" institutions. Gay men and lesbians formed their own churches, health clinics, counseling services, social centers, professional associations, and amateur sports leagues. Male and female entrepreneurs built record companies, publishing houses, travel agencies, and vacation resorts. Newspapers, magazines, literary journals, theater companies, and film collectives gave expression to a distinctive cultural experience. The subculture of homosexual men and women became less exclusively erotic. Gayness and lesbianism began to encompass an identity that for many included a wide array of private and public activities.

Stonewall thus marked a critical divide in the politics and consciousness of homosexuals and lesbians. A small, thinly spread reform effort suddenly grew into a large, grassroots movement for liberation. The quality of gay life in America was permanently altered as a furtive subculture moved aggressively into the open.

Reference

Radicalesbians, 1992 "The Woman-Identified Woman," in Karla Jay and Allen Young *Out of the Closets,* New York: Douglas Book Corp, pp. 172–7.

5 The Iranian Revolution

Charles Kurzman

> "When a people which has put up with an oppressive rule over a long period without protest suddenly finds the government relaxing its pressure, it takes up arms against it."
>
> —*Tocqueville 1955: 176*

Alexis de Tocqueville's famous dictum is based on two observations about the French Revolution. On one hand, the government undercut and alienated its bases of support through ill-conceived efforts at reform. On the other hand, the populace perceived a lessening of "pressure" and rose up to take advantage. The strength of Tocqueville's analysis lies in its combination of objective and subjective factors. It is not only the structural weakness of the state that precipitates revolution in Tocqueville's model, or the subjective sentiments of collective efficacy, but the combination of the two.

Social-movement theory has recently revived this combined approach after years of veering between structuralist and subjectivist extremes. McAdam's (1982) oft-cited book, *Political Process and the Development of Black Insurgency*, may be the model for contemporary social-movement theorizing on structure and consciousness. McAdam argues that the "structure of political opportunities" is one of two major determinants of political protest, the other being organizational strength: "The opportunities for a challenger to engage in successful collective action... vary greatly over time. And it is these variations that are held to be related to the ebb and flow of movement activity" (pp. 40–41). The "crucial point," he states, is that the political system can be more open or less open to challenge at different times (p. 41). But structural conditions, McAdam argues, do not automatically translate into protest: They are mediated by "cognitive liberation," an oppressed people's ability to break out of pessimistic and quiescent patterns of thought and begin to do something about their situation (pp. 48–51).

McAdam's (1982) analysis shows the tight fit between subjective perceptions and the structure of opportunities. The optimism of African Americans in the 1930s (pp. 108–10) and early 1960s (pp. 161–63) reflected structural shifts in Federal policies (pp. 83–86, 156–60). Conversely, in the late 1960s, perceptions of diminishing opportunities reflected the actual diminishing of opportunities (p. 202). State structure and subjective perceptions are treated as closely correlated.

Structural opportunities generally coincide with perceived opportunities in other recent studies in the Tocquevillean tradition. Tarrow (1994), for instance, recognizes the interplay between the macro- and micro-levels of analysis. He notes that "early risers" – protest groups at the beginning stages of a cycle of widespread protest activity – may make opportunities visible that had not been evident, and their actions may change the structure of opportunities (pp. 96–97). However, over most of the protest cycle, perceptions closely follow the opening and closing of objective opportunities (pp. 85–96, 99). "The main argument of this study," Tarrow emphasizes, "is that people join in social movements in response to political opportunities" (p. 17).

[. . .]

These Tocquevillean analyses recognize that structural opportunities and perceived opportunities may not always match. Cognitive liberation is a distinct variable that is not reducible to political opportunity structure, according to McAdam; "early risers" may protest despite unfavorable structural conditions in Tarrow's model; not all state crises lead to revolution, Goldstone (1991a) notes. The Tocquevillean tradition, however, has focused on cases in which the opportunity structure and perceptions agree, and has not examined mismatches.

[. . .]

I explore this latter possibility through an examination of the Iranian Revolution of 1979. Protestors *were* concerned with prospects for success – they did not participate in large numbers until they felt success was at hand. However, most Iranians did not feel that the state had weakened or that structural opportunities had opened up. Indeed, I argue that the state was *not*, by several objective measures, particularly vulnerable in 1978 when widespread protest emerged. Instead, Iranians seem to have based their assessment of the opportunities for protest on the perceived strength of the opposition. In other words, Iranians believed the balance of forces shifted, not because of a changing state structure, but because of a changing opposition movement.

Unlike the Tocquevillean cases, then, structural opportunities and perceived opportunities may have been at odds. Thus, the Iranian Revolution may constitute a "deviant" case for social-movement theory, one that allows a comparison between the relative effects of structural versus subjective factors. This is a historic issue in sociological theory, and far too weighty for the imperfectly documented Iranian case. However, the case at least raises the historic issue in a new guise for social-movement theory. In addition to researching the links between the structural and subjective levels of analysis, as social-movement theory has attempted to do in recent years, the case suggests that conflicts and disjunctures between these levels are also worth examining.

[. . .]

Because I do not proceed chronologically, a brief summary of the events leading to the fall of the Iranian monarchy in February 1979 is in order. The revolutionary movement is generally dated from mid-1977, when liberal oppositionists began to speak out publicly for reforms in the Iranian monarchy. Late in 1977, some of Iran's Islamic leaders called for the removal of Shâh Muhammad Rizâ Pahlavî, and their followers embarked on a series of small demonstrations that the regime suppressed with force. Casualties at each incident generated a cycle of mourning demonstrations throughout the first half of 1978. The bulk of Iran's population, however, did not participate in these events. The revolutionary movement attracted a large following only in September 1978, following a suspicious theater fire and a massacre of peaceful demonstrators; both events persuaded many Iranians that the Pahlavî regime must fall. Beginning in September 1978, strikes began to shake the country and built up to a virtual general strike that lasted until the revolution's success in February 1979. By the end of 1978, the shah was actively seeking a reformist prime minister. When he finally found an oppositionist willing to take the

Charisma Some political or religious leaders are popular not simply because of their ideas, but also because they are viewed as possessing some extraordinary personal quality, a "gift" of superhuman power, which requires loyalty and obedience even in the face of great risks. Indeed, people are willing and even eager to sacrifice their lives for charismatic leaders. (If they are not, then the leader is not charismatic.) People seem to attribute or "project" magical or prophetic powers upon certain exemplary leaders during times of political chaos or uncertainty, when people have become frustrated with politics-as-usual and are looking for someone or something to lead them to a more glorious future. (Note: Many people now incorrectly use the word "charismatic" as a synonym for "popular.") Notable charismatic leaders include Adolf Hitler and the Ayatollah Khomeini.

position and left for a "vacation" in mid-January, the country had become ungovernable. Exiled religious leader Imâm Rûhullah Khumeinî returned to Iran to great acclaim at the end of January and named his own prime minister. Two weeks later, a mutiny in one of the air force barracks in Tehran sparked an unplanned citywide uprising. Within 40 hours, the military declared its "neutrality" and allowed the revolutionaries to take power.

The Structure of Political Opportunity

Scholars of the Iranian Revolution have generally characterized the Pahlavî regime as highly susceptible to collapse. Four structural weaknesses are often cited as constituting a structure of political opportunities conducive to revolution.

Monarchy's Social Support Undermined by Reforms

One alleged weakness of the state is the undermining of the state's social support, particularly by the elite, as a result of the monarchy's vigorous efforts at reform. This argument takes different forms depending on the affected group. For instance, the shah's land reforms of the 1960s threw the landed oligarchy into the opposition. The shah's industrialization policies and punitive price-control measures threw the traditional *bazaari* sector into the opposition. Harsh labor repression threw workers into the opposition. The overheated oil-boom economy led to the inflation of urban housing prices, throwing poor migrants into the opposition. Political repression threw intellectuals and the middle classes into the opposition. Secularizing reforms threw religious leaders into the opposition. In sum, the state "destroyed its traditional class base while failing to generate a new class base of support" (Moshiri 1991:121).

There are three problems with this argument. First, the affected groups were not entirely oppositional. Second, even as reforms created enemies for the state, they also created new allies. Third, the shah needed relatively little internal support because of the state's oil revenues and international support, and this internal autonomy may have strengthened rather than weakened the state.

The most affected elite group was the Islamic clerics. State reforms took away their longstanding judicial roles, limited their educational roles, and challenged their role in welfare distribution. Clerics had the clearest reason to resent the Pahlavî state. Yet prior to the revolution, relatively few clerics favored Khumeinî's revolutionary proposals. During the revolutionary movement, senior clerics tried to dissuade protestors from confronting the state, and one cleric even met secretly with government representatives to seek a compromise.

Similarly, leading oppositionist *bazaaris* and intellectuals opposed the revolutionary tide; they favored reforming the monarchy, not ousting it. Workers' demands centered on workplace gains and only switched to revolutionary demands in the fall of 1978, months after the revolutionary movement began. Urban migrants who suffered the most from the state's policies did not participate in large numbers in the revolutionary movement. Indeed, strikers at one factory blamed recent urban migrants for being too apolitical. In sum, the extent to which the shah's reform policies undermined his popular support should not be exaggerated.

Meanwhile, the state created new classes dependent on state patronage and therefore inclined to support the shah. The most important of these was the military, which expanded greatly during the shah's decades in power. The loyalty of the military remained largely unshaken to the end (see below). Another class created by state fiat was the industrial bourgeoisie, which emerged through credit subsidies and royal patronage. This class allegedly abandoned the shah by transferring its assets overseas and then emigrating at the first hint of trouble. Certainly rumors to this effect were circulating during the fall of 1978.

But evidence suggests that some of the bourgeoisie stayed and actively supported the shah to the end. Groups of industrialists met in November 1978 and January 1979 to determine common solutions to strikes and money shortages; representatives worked with the prime minister on these matters. Thus, the shah was not totally abandoned by his allies.

In any case, the shah's access to oil revenues and foreign support made internal support less important than it was for most regimes. On theoretical grounds, it is difficult to say whether this is a sign of state weakness or strength. While reliance on foreign powers may create an image of a puppet regime, state autonomy is often identified as a strength, as the state can impose collective solutions on recalcitrant social groups. If the basis for autonomy breaks down, of course, the state is left without a reed to lean on. However, the shah retained international support during the revolutionary movement.

International Pressure on the Monarchy

The second alleged weakness of the state is the widespread impression that international constraints stayed the monarchy's hand and prevented the crackdown that would have crushed the protest movement. Many academic analyses have applied Skocpol's (1979) structural model to the Iranian Revolution, arguing that international pressures weakened the state and made it vulnerable to revolution (Ashraf and Banuazizi 1985:19–20; Liu 1988:202–203; Milani 1988:30–31). However, none of these analysts presents evidence of such pressure.

Jimmy Carter campaigned for President in 1976 on a platform that included the consideration of human rights in U.S. foreign policy, and he threatened to weaken U.S. support for the shah. But this threat never materialized. When the shah visited Washington in November 1977, Carter's meetings with him barely touched the subject of human rights. A month later, Carter made his famous New Year's toast to the shah in Tehran: "Iran, because of the great leadership of the Shah, is an island of stability in one of the more troubled areas of the world. This is a great tribute to you, Your Majesty, and to your leadership and to the respect and the admiration and love which your people give to you" (*Weekly Compilation of Presidential Documents*, January 2, 1978, p. 1975).

As the revolutionary movement grew during 1978, the shah received no international complaints about his handling of Iranian protests, even when his troops shot hundreds, perhaps thousands, of unarmed demonstrators in Tehran on September 8. In fact, Carter telephoned the shah from Camp David two days later to express his continuing support. When the shah installed a military government on November 6, U.S. officials voiced their full approval (*New York Times*, November 7, 1978, p. 14). National Security Advisor Zbigniew Brzezinski had telephoned the shah several days earlier to encourage him to be firm. Riot-control equipment, blocked for months on human-rights grounds, was then shipped to Iran (*Newsweek*, November 20, 1978, p. 43). As late as December 28, 1978, the U.S. Secretary of State cabled to his ambassador in Tehran the firm statement "that U.S. support is steady and that it is essential, repeat essential, to terminate the continuing uncertainty."

Throughout the fall of 1978, the shah met regularly with the U.S. ambassador, William Sullivan. The shah's final autobiography notes that "the only word I ever received from Mr. Sullivan was reiteration of Washington's complete support for my rule" (Pahlavi 1980:161). In fact, according to Sullivan (1981), "the Shah himself in due course told me he was somewhat embarrassed by the constant reiteration of our public support, saying it made him look like a puppet" (p. 204).

The shah was apparently unaware of divisions within the U.S. administration. Carter's cabinet was split into hostile camps over the extent of force the shah should use, the advisability of a coup d'état, and the desirability of a nonmonarchical government in

Iran – in short, how to respond to the Iranian revolutionary movement. This debate was never resolved. As a result, Washington never sent detailed recommendations to Iran. Ambassador Sullivan in Tehran repeatedly told the shah that he had "no instructions" from his superiors.

This lack of instructions may have deepened the shah's suspicions about the United States' true intentions. The head of the French secret service insisted to the shah that the United States was secretly planning his ouster, and the shah asked visitors on several occasions whether the United States had abandoned him. Offhand public remarks by U.S. officials suggesting that the United States was considering various contingencies in Iran reached the shah and worried him, despite official denials and reassurances.

In sum, the United States continued to pledge its support, although the shah did not entirely believe it. But there is no evidence of international pressure constraining the monarchy's response to protest.

Overcentralization and Paralysis of the State

A third alleged weakness focuses on the structure of the Iranian state. According to this argument, a concerted crackdown would have worked, but the state lacked the will to carry it out. At its basest, this explanation accuses individual officeholders of treason. At its most theoretical, this analysis argues that the Iranian state was structurally susceptible to paralysis because of its overcentralization around the person of the shah. Fatemi's (1982) analysis is perhaps the most succinct: "Since the *raison d'être* of this organizational structure was mostly to protect the shah and his throne from potential threats, such as military *coups d'état* and strong political rivals" (p. 49), the state demanded loyalty to the monarch, arranged overlapping responsibilities and rivalries, and forbade lateral communication. "To operate this system the shah had effectively made himself the sole decision-making authority in every significant phase of Iran's political affairs" (p. 49). Therefore, the system depended for its operation on a fully functioning shah. In 1978, however, the shah was ill with cancer. According to this thesis, the state was thereby paralyzed in its response to the protest movement.

There is abundant evidence of the centralization of the state around the person of the shah. There is also evidence of the shah's illness. He was under medication and appeared at times to be depressed or listless and not his usual decisive self. But evidence of paralysis is much less convincing. To be sure, the shah repeatedly stated his unwillingness to massacre his subjects in order to save his throne. "The instructions I gave were always the same: 'Do the impossible to avoid bloodshed'" (Pahlavi 1980:168). One general allegedly offered to kill a hundred thousand protestors to quell the disturbances. Another supposedly proposed to bomb the holy city of Qum. The head of a neighboring country suggested the execution of 700 mullahs. The shah vetoed all these plans.

However, the refusal to authorize slaughter does not necessarily indicate lack of will or structural paralysis. Less extreme measures were vigorously pursued. Throughout the fall of 1978, security forces routinely broke up protests at gunpoint. They arrested virtually every prominent oppositionist in the country at least once. At one time or another they occupied virtually all key economic and governmental institutions and forced striking personnel back to work in the oil fields, power stations, airlines, customs offices, and telecommunications centers. Plans began to be drawn up for a possible pro-shah military coup.

Moreover, the Pahlavî regime – despite its pretensions – was a Third World state and not overly efficient in the best of times: Iran's intelligence service was hardly more than a glorified police force, according to the head of the French secret service; Tehran had no sewage system; and industry suffered frequent power shortages. The flurry of state actions in response to the revolutionary movement hardly represents paralysis.

State Vacillation

A fourth possible weakness concerns the state's "vacillating" (Abrahamian 1982: 518); or "inconsistent" (Arjomand 1988: 115) responses to the protest movement. The combination of concession and repression is said to have encouraged protestors while providing them with new reasons to protest. Because of this vacillation, according to these analyses, the Iranian revolution grew from a small and sporadic movement into a massive and continuous upheaval. The implication is that a more one-sided policy – either reform *or* crackdown – would have been more effective in stifling protest.

Such a conclusion goes against the advice of numerous royal advisors. In ancient India, Kautilîya (1972:414) instructed kings on how to deal with revolts: "Make use of conciliation, gifts, dissension and force." In eleventh-century Persia, Nizam al-Mulk (1960, chaps. 40, 44) urged caliphs to imitate the mercy and liberality of Harun ar-Rashid, but also the deviousness and repression of Nushirwan. In sixteenth-century Italy, Machiavelli advised princes to gain both the fear of the people and the love of the people, combining punishment and reward, cruelty and clemency. [. . .] On theoretical grounds, then, it is not clear whether a combined state response constitutes vacillation and vulnerability, or carrot-and-stick and co-optation.

In any case, the shah had used a similar strategy for years. The two major prerevolutionary studies of the Iranian political system make this point repeatedly. Zonis (1971) notes that co-operation of the opposition had become routine, to the extent that the shah told one foreign visitor not to worry about youthful subversives. "We know just who those young men are and will be offering them high-level jobs as appropriate" (pp. 331–32). Bill (1972:100) describes the state's "three-pronged strategy of intimidation, bribery, and selected concessions" toward student oppositionists. Both authors view the shah's repression and his co-optive concessions as complementary parts of a single coherent system of political opportunities.

This combined approach continued through 1978. At several crucial junctures, the shah cracked down on protestors, but at the same time offered minor concessions and promised future reforms. In mid-May, soldiers opened fire on a demonstration in Tehran, but troops were removed from the seminary city of Qum and a ban was announced on pornographic films, clearly gestures toward religious oppositionists. In early August, the shah announced that free elections were going to be held, but soon placed the city of Isfahan under martial law. In late August, the shah placed 11 cities under martial law, but also granted various concessions, including freedom of the press, and appointed a new prime minister thought to be more acceptable to the religious opposition. In November, the shah installed a military government that flooded Tehran with armored vehicles and cracked down on the oilfield strikes. At the same time, the shah made an apologetic televised speech and promulgated limits on the royal family's business activities.

There was a definite logic to these state responses. The government sent protestors a mixed but consistent message: Continue protesting and you'll be killed; stop protesting and you'll get reforms. The combination of crackdowns with promises of future reforms was intended to defuse the short-term situation while reaffirming the long-term commitment to liberalization. The shah stuck to the structure of political opportunities he had maintained for decades, one that was conducive to co-optive political participation and inimical to revolutionary street protests.

The Perception of Political Opportunity

Perceptions of the State's Coercive Power

Casualties increased as the protest movement progressed. Moreover, the Iranian people recognized that street protests were dangerous, including the large demonstrations that were legal, well-organized, and rarely repressed. For instance, marches on the religious holidays of Tâsû'â and 'Âshûrâ in December 1978 were certain to attract millions of participants, but they still inspired fear. The leading cleric in Shiraz warned on the eve of the demonstrations: "Maybe we'll be killed tomorrow. We're facing guns, rifles and tanks. Whoever is afraid shouldn't come" (Hegland 1986:683).

[. . .]

But recognition of the state's coercive power did not translate into obedience. Frequently, repression led to increased militancy. In late August, after the immolation of several hundred moviegoers in Abadan – a tragedy many Iranians blamed on the state – protests increased from several thousand participants to hundreds of thousands. In early September, the day after hundreds and perhaps thousands of peaceful demonstrators were gunned down in Tehran's Zhâlih Square, wildcat strikes spread across the country. In early November, within weeks of the installation of a military government, the opposition denounced the government as illegal and began planning for huge confrontations during the Shi'i holy month of Muharram.

On an individual level, acts of repression that hit close to home were a major source of revolutionary zeal. An anthropologist who spent much of the revolutionary period in a village near Shiraz reports that this response was called "*az khud guzashtih*" or "*az jân guzashtih*" (literally, "abandoning oneself" or "abandoning life"):

> People felt this emotion and gained this attitude through hearing about or participating in events in which government forces treated people with violence and injustice.... Villagers reported to me their horror, fury, and frustration upon hearing about such events, as well as their resolve that they would never rest until the shah and the government that did such inhuman things to their fellow Iranians no longer existed. (Hegland 1983:233–34)

Repression was such a mobilizing force that the opposition circulated a hoax audio cassette, along with other opposition cassettes, on which an indistinct voice resembling the shah's was heard giving his generals formal orders to shoot demonstrators in the streets. If scare tactics of this sort were revolutionary propaganda, and not counterrevolutionary propaganda, then something was clearly amiss with the shah's carrot-and-stick strategy.

Perceptions of the Opposition's Power

What was amiss, I propose, was the Iranian people's perception of political opportunities. Iranians continued to recognize and fear the state's coercive powers. However, they felt that these powers were insignificant compared with the strength of the revolutionary movement. [. . .] Popular perceptions are difficult to identify, particularly during a period of repression and unrest. But this is no excuse for leaving popular perceptions unexamined. The bits of evidence that exist show consistently that Iranians considered the strength of the protest movement to be a decisive factor in their decisions to participate.

At the first mass demonstration of the protest movement, on September 4 in Tehran, journalists reported a sense of euphoria among the protestors: "'The shah is finished,' they cry above all" (Brière and Blanchet 1979:46). This judgment was premature, but the sentiment seems genuine. Protestors felt that revolution was not only possible, but practically inevitable.

[. . .]

On a smaller scale, it appears that Iranians preferred to participate in a particular protest only if they had assurances that others would protest as well. U.S. diplomats in Tehran noted during the strike day of October 16, 1978:

> Most shops have closed during [the] morning, however, as shopkeepers evaluated [the] local situation: no one wants to have the only open shop on the block.... Everyone knew of Khomeini's appeal [to strike], yet [the] vast majority came to work, they decided to stay or return based on what

> neighbors were doing. (National Security Archive 1989: Document 1594)

At its margins, this desire to go with the flow shaded into fear of persecution for non-participation. "I could not go to [the] office against the will of my employees," said the managing director of a state agency that was on strike. "Besides, anything could happen to me" (Farazmand 1989:172). The owner of a tiny shop in central Tehran expressed a similar opinion:

> He explained candidly that he had put a photograph of the Ayatollah, whom he said he respected, in his store window because he feared it would be smashed otherwise. "Most of the people want an Islamic Republic," he said wearily. "And I want anything that most of the people want." (*New York Times*, February 2, 1979, p. A9)

The fear of violence should not be overestimated, however, despite the dark suspicions of several foreign observers – notably British Ambassador Anthony Parsons, U.S. military envoy Robert Huyser and U.S. diplomats. The Iranian Revolution exhibited remarkably little retribution against backsliders, especially when compared with the revolutionary violence reported in South Africa, Palestine, and the Sikh independence movement in India.

Rather, the fear of violence should probably be considered part of the overall "bandwagon effect" (Hirsch 1986:382), whereby individuals' willingness to participate in a protest is correlated with their expectations of the size and success of the protest. [. . .]

Perhaps the best evidence of the bandwagon effect comes from the reformist oppositionists who opposed outright revolution. These liberals are more fully represented than are other social groups in the government, journalistic, and oral-history sources available for this research. Liberals were highly sensitive to the structure of opportunities – they had begun to speak out publicly for reform in 1977 when the shah allowed such opposition to be voiced. In late 1977, when the shah clamped down again after his cordial meetings with Carter, liberals muted their protests. In the summer of 1978, when the shah made a few concessions and promised to hold free elections, liberals were elated and rushed to take advantage of the new freedoms. During the fall of 1978, liberals began to sense that the opposition movement was larger than they had imagined, and "out of our hands." This sense crystallized for some on September 4, when liberal *bazaar* oppositionists chased in vain after a massive revolutionary demonstration, trying to disperse the crowd and reminding people that they were not supposed to be demonstrating.

In the following months, liberals joined the revolutionary movement, not because they now favored revolution, but because they felt the revolutionary movement was too strong to oppose. [. . .] In a memorandum dated December 8, 1978, a U.S. diplomat reported asking a moderate Iranian religious leader if he and other clerics would approve a constitutional settlement to the crisis and go against Khumeinî. The cleric, "perhaps not wanting his followers to understand, replied in broken English, 'That would be dangerous and very difficult'" (*Asnâd-i Lânih-yi Jâsûsi* 1980–1991, vol. 26, p. 61). By the end of 1978, when the shah was casting about for a prime minister, a series of liberal oppositionists turned down the position. Several months earlier they would have considered the appointment a dream come true – now they considered it futile.

Perception Versus Structure

Confident of the revolution's ultimate victory, millions of Iranians participated in mass protests against the shah in the final months of 1978. Yet, at the end of the year, the shah's military remained largely intact. The two sides faced a potentially cataclysmic confrontation. But as protestors' perception of political opportunities clashed with the state's structural position, the structure of the state gave way.

As late as early December 1978, top generals still thought they could subdue the protest movement. Thus, the collapse of the military followed, rather than preceded, mass mobilization of the protest movement. Like the broad state-breakdown argument, this suggests that military breakdown may be an outcome of mobilization rather than a necessary precondition.

During demonstrations, protestors handed flowers to soldiers and chanted slogans such as: "Brother soldier, why do you kill your brothers?" and "The army is part of the nation" (Kamalî 1979). On several occasions, large throngs of protestors persuaded soldiers to give up their arms, throw off their uniforms, and join the demonstration. On other occasions, protestors attacked security personnel and even military bases.

Nonetheless, the effectiveness of popular pressure on the military is unclear. Even in mid-January 1979, as the shah was about to leave Iran, desertions remained relatively low, only about a thousand a day out of several hundred thousand troops, according to the Iranian chief of staff. However, authorized leaves may have been increasing dramatically as soldiers requested furloughs to check on their families and property after riots and other disturbances. (In a Crisis Meeting on January 23, the chief of staff estimated that the armed forces were only at 55 percent of their strength, although the tone of his comments suggests that this figure was picked more for effect than for accuracy.) Small mutinies increased. [. . .]

Whether or not popular pressure was effective, however, military leaders were clearly worried about it. This concern prevented the military from being used to its full capacity because each military operation exposed the troops to fraternization and further appeals from protestors. On January 15, 1979, the head of the ground forces proposed keeping the soldiers away from this nefarious influence:

> We should round up the units and send them someplace where [the demonstrators] won't have any contact with the soldiers. Because yesterday they came and put a flower in the end of a rifle barrel, and another on the [military] vehicle. . . . The soldiers' morale just disappears. (*Misl-i Barf* 1987:50)

During the largest demonstrations, military commanders kept their troops well away from the march routes, guarding "key" sites and neighborhoods. On a few occasions they ordered the military back to barracks, twice as a direct result of defections.

[. . .]

But several hundred thousand troops could not be held in their barracks for long. A number of soldiers, even officers, slipped out and joined protests – out of uniform, of course, because a uniform would attract dangerous attention from protestors and security forces that remained loyal. In early February of 1979 when whole units of troops began to demonstrate in uniform against the shah, the military's disintegration was imminent. After only a day and a half of street fighting, the chiefs of staff declared the military's "neutrality" and allowed the revolutionaries to take power.

Implications for Social-Movement Theory

I have argued that the Iranian state was not particularly vulnerable to revolution in 1978, according to several indicators. The Pahlavî regime's domestic support had not withered away, nor had its international support. State centralization and the shah's illness did not prevent the state from responding actively to the revolutionary movement, combining carrot and stick, cracking down on opposition activities while promising future reforms, as it had done for decades.

In terms of popular perceptions, the Iranian people considered the coercive power of the state to be intact right up to the end. At the same time, however, evidence suggests that the Iranian people considered political opportunities to have increased as a result of the growth of the opposition. The strength of the revolutionary movement induced even non-revolutionary liberals to join in. Acting on this perception of opposition strength, Iranians altered the structure of opportunities by fraternizing with the military and making it partially unusable as a coercive force.

In more theoretical terms, there was a mismatch between the structure of political opportunities and popular perceptions of political opportunities. Rather than calculate opportunities solely on the basis of changes in the state, as Tocquevillean theory suggests, Iranians appear to have calculated opportunities on the basis of changes in the opposition. Ultimately, their perceptions proved self-fulfilling: The balance of forces had indeed tilted toward the opposition, and perceptions proved stronger than the state structure.

This finding suggests that social-movement theory should reconsider the relation between "objective" and "subjective" definitions of political opportunity. If opportunity is like a door, then social-movement theory generally examines cases in which people realize the door is open and walk on through. The Iranian Revolution may be a case in which people saw that the door was closed, but felt that the opposition was powerful enough to open it. These people were not millenarians, masochists, fanatics, or martyrs – the case is not dismissed so easily. It turns out that Iranians were able to open the door on their own.

[. . .]

References

Abrahamian, Ervand. 1982. *Iran Between Two Revolutions*. Princeton, NJ: Princeton University Press.

Arjomand, Said Amir. 1988. *The Turban for the Crown: The Islamic Revolution in Iran*. New York: Oxford University Press.

Ashraf, Ahmad and Ali Banuazizi. 1985. "The State, Classes, and Modes of Mobilization in the Iranian Revolution." *State, Culture, and Society* 1:3–40.

Bill, James A. 1972. *The Politics of Iran*. Columbus, OH: Charles E. Merrill.

Brière, Claire and Pierre Blanchet. 1979. *L'Iran: La Révolution au Nom de Dieu* (The Revolution in the Name of God). Paris, France.

Farazmand, Ali. 1989. *The State, Bureaucracy, and Revolution in Modern Iran: Agrarian Reforms and Regime Politics*. New York: Praeger.

Fatemi, Khosrow. 1982. "Leadership by Distrust: The Shah's *Modus Operandi*." *Middle East Journal* 36:48–61.

Goldstone, Jack A. 1991a. "Ideology, Cultural Frameworks, and the Process of Revolution." *Theory and Society* 20:405–53.

Hegland, Mary Elaine. 1983. "Two Images of Husain." Pp. 218–35 in *Religion and Politics in Iran*, edited by Nikki R. Keddie. New Haven, CT: Yale University Press.

—— 1986. "Imam Khomaini's Village: Recruitment to Revolution." Ph.D. dissertation. Department of Anthropology, State University of New York, Binghamton, NY.

Hirsch, Eric L. 1986. "The Creation of Political Solidarity in Social Movement Organizations." *The Sociological Quarterly* 27:373–87.

Kamalî, Alî. 1979. *Inqilâb* (Revolution). Tehran, Iran: Massoud Publishing House.

Kautilîya. 1972. *The Kautilîya Arthaśâstra*. Pt. 2, 2nd ed. Edited by R. P. Kangle. Bombay, India: University of Bombay.

Liu, Michael Tien-Lung. 1988. "States and Urban Revolutions: Explaining the Revolutionary Outcomes in Iran and Poland." *Theory and Society* 17:179–209.

McAdam, Doug. 1982. *Political Process and the Development of Black Insurgency, 1930–1970*. Chicago, IL: University of Chicago Press.

Milani, Mohsen. 1988. *The Making of Iran's Islamic Revolution: From Monarchy to Islamic Republic*. Boulder, CO: Westview Press.

Misl-i Barf Âb Khwâhîm Shud: Muzâkirât-i "Shûrâ-yi Farmândihân-i Artish" (Dey-Bahman'1357) (We Will Melt Like Snow: Conversations of the "Council of the Army Commanders" [January 1979]). 1987. 3rd printing. Tehran, Iran: Nashr-i Ney.

Moshiri, Farrokh. 1991. "Iran: Islamic Revolution Against Westernization." Pp. 116–35 in *Revolutions of the Late Twentieth Century*, edited by Jack A. Goldstone, Ted Robert Gurr, and Farrokh Moshiri. Boulder, CO: Westview Press.

National Security Archive. 1989. *Iran: The Making of U.S. Policy, 1977–1980*. Microfiche Collection, Index, and Guide. Alexandria, VA: Chadwyck-Healey.

Nizam al-Mulk. 1960. *The Book of Government*. London, England: Routledge and Kegan Paul.

Pahlavi, Mohammad Reza. 1980. *Answer to History*. New York: Stein and Day.

Skocpol, Theda. 1979. *States and Social Revolutions*. Cambridge, England: Cambridge University Press.

Sullivan, William. 1981. *Mission to Iran*. New York: W.W. Norton.

Tarrow, Sidney. 1994. *Power in Movement: Social Movements, Collective Action and Politics*. Cambridge, England: Cambridge University Press.

Tocqueville, Alexis de. 1955. *The Old Regime and the French Revolution*. Translated by S. Gilbert. Garden City, NY: Doubleday Anchor.

Zonis, Marvin. 1971. *The Political Elite of Iran*. Princeton, NJ: Princeton University Press.

Part III

Who Joins or Supports Movements?

Introduction

Once initial activists in a social movement form groups and begin to think of themselves as a movement, their next step is usually to try to expand their movement by recruiting others to their cause. Like theories of movement origins, theories of recruitment have evolved through several stages, from an emphasis on individual traits to one on structural availability, and finally toward a synthesis of these dimensions.

Before the 1960s, researchers tended to see protestors as swept up in crowds, acting in abnormal and sometimes irrational ways because of frustration with their individual circumstances. In some theories marginal and alienated members of society were seen as most likely to join social movements (Kornhauser 1959); in others it was those who were insecure or dogmatic (Adorno et al. 1950; Hoffer 1951). Such claims were usually demeaning to protestors, who were thought to be compensating for some sort of personal inadequacy, and subsequent empirical research did not generally support the image of protestors as more angry or alienated than others.

In 1965 an economist, Mancur Olson (1965), took the opposite view of potential protestors, arguing that they are so rational (and self-interested) that they will not join groups if they think they can gain the benefits that the groups pursue without taking the time to participate. In other words, they will be "free riders" on the efforts of others. You don't have to join the environmental movement to enjoy the clean air that it wins for all of us. One reason to free ride is that your own participation won't make a difference, something especially true in very large groups. To attract participants, Olson said, movements must provide "selective incentives" that go only to those who participate, such as an interesting newsletter or insurance for trade union members. Olson challenged scholars to show how organizers manage to overcome the free rider problem.

Framing and Frame Alignment In order to attract people to join and remain committed to a movement, its issues must be presented or "framed" so that they fit or resonate with the beliefs, feelings, and desires of potential recruits. Like a picture-frame that highlights what is in the frame but excludes everything outside it, frames are simplifying devices that help us understand and organize the complexities of the world; they are the filtering lenses, so to speak, through which we make sense of this world. Frames may take the form of appealing stories, powerful clusters of symbols, slogans and catch words, or attributions of blame for social problems. Social-movement leaders and recruiters work hard to find the right frames, ones "aligned" with the understandings of potential recruits. Framing is thus one of the principal activities in which movement activists participate, and activists are often involved in framing contests or "framing wars" with their opponents in an attempt to win the "hearts and minds" of the public. See Snow et al. (1986) and Snow and Benford (1988).

Problems in the crowd paradigm, combined with Olson's challenge, helped inspire the resource mobilization paradigm, which shifted attention from what kinds of *people* protested to what kinds of *structural conditions* facilitated protest. Attitudes were summarily dismissed as unimportant or at least insufficient, for many people had the right attitudes but did not participate. As part of this new agenda, "biographical availability" was seen as necessary for participation: those with few family or work obligations—especially young people—were available to devote time to movement activities (McCarthy and Zald 1973; McAdam 1986).

More importantly, researchers found that the best predictor of who will join is whether a person knows someone else already in the movement (Snow, Zurcher and Ekland-Olson 1980). In many movements, a majority of participants are recruited this way. Social networks were seen as a precondition for the emergence of a movement as well as the explanation for who was recruited. In the extreme case of "bloc recruitment" organizers bring a social network almost intact into a movement (Oberschall 1973). Social structures like these suggest that—contrary to Olson—people do not make choices as isolated, selfish individuals.

Different kinds of social networks can be used for recruitment. They may not be political in origin or intent. Black churches were crucial to the Southern civil rights movement in the 1950s (Morris 1984); fundamentalist churches helped defeat the Equal Rights Amendment in the 1980s (Mansbridge 1986); and mosques facilitated the Iranian Revolution (Snow and Marshall 1984). Networks developed for earlier political activities can also aid recruitment into a new movement—one reason that a history of previous activism makes someone more likely to be recruited (McAdam 1988). The clustering of movements in waves makes this mutual support especially important, as one movement feeds into the next (Tarrow 1998). Because of these networks, prior activism and organizational memberships help predict who will be recruited (and who will not be).

This view of recruitment is summed up in our excerpt from Doug McAdam's book on "Freedom Summer" of 1964, when hundreds of mostly white college students went South to help in voter registration drives. McAdam's methodological strategy is to look first at the students who applied to the project (compared implicitly to college students generally), then at those who actually participated (as opposed to those who were accepted but did not show up). He finds three factors important in explaining who applied: biographical availability, ideological compatibility, and social-network ties. In explaining those who showed up and those who did not, the first two factors drop out and the third factor becomes crucial. Those who knew others who were going were the most likely to follow through on their plans.

Recent work on recruitment has criticized the mechanical image of networks in much of the earlier research. Without denying the importance of personal contacts, this work has examined the cultural messages transmitted across these networks. Edward Walsh (1981), for example, described "suddenly imposed grievances": dramatic and unexpected events that highlight some social problem. In his case the Three Mile Island accident in 1979 alerted people to the risks of nuclear energy, giving a big boost to the antinuclear movement. Recruitment involves a cognitive shift for participants. McAdam (1982) called this "cognitive liberation," when potential participants begin to think they may have a chance of success.

In this view, direct personal contacts are seen as important because they allow organizers and potential participants to "align" their "frames," to achieve a common definition of a social problem and a common prescription for solving it (see Snow et al. 1986). In successful recruitment, organizers offer ways of seeing a social problem that resonate with the views and experiences of potential recruits. Networks are important *because* of the cultural meanings they transmit. Networks and meanings are not rival explanations; they work together.

Snow and Benford (1988) distinguish three successive types of framing necessary for successful recruitment: *diagnostic*, in which a movement convinces potential converts that a problem needs to be addressed; *prognostic*, in which it convinces them of appropriate strategies, tactics and targets; and *motivational*, in which it exhorts them to get involved in these activities (this last seems primarily about arousing the right emotions). They argue that frames are more likely to be accepted if they fit well with the existing beliefs of potential recruits, if they involve empirically credible claims, if they are compatible with the life experiences of the audiences, and if they fit with the stories or narratives the audiences tell about their lives. Frames, in other words, must resonate with the salient beliefs of potential recruits. (We'll read a chapter on frames in part V.)

Collective identity is another concept used to get at the mental worlds of participants that might help explain participation: in order to devote time and effort to protest, people must usually feel part of a larger group they think they can help (Melucci 1996). (On collective identity, read also the selection by Mary Bernstein in part VII, where she shows how different kinds of identity claims can be important strategic moves.) Pieces of culture such as frames and identities have audiences outside the movement as well as inside it.

This emphasis on culture challenges the arguments of many structuralists who promoted the idea that individual characteristics do not help explain who will be recruited to a social movement, an idea that is a kind of half-truth. The structuralists concentrated on arguing against personality traits as a predictor—without ever gathering serious evidence about personality traits (Klandermans 1983, 1989). But they also rejected attitudes and grievances as part of an explanation, in favor of structural traits (Gurney and Tierney 1982; Klandermans and Oegema 1987; Useem 1980). But this kind of argument went to ridiculous extremes: bigots don't join civil rights campaigns just because they are in the right network; leftists don't join right-wing movements because a "bloc" of their fellow parishioners do. The fact that not *everyone* with a set of beliefs or personality traits gets recruited does not mean that supportive ideas or other traits are not a necessary condition. They are just not sufficient.

Another cultural approach, broader than frame alignment, shows how attitudes and worldviews matter. Political scientist Ronald Inglehart (1977) has argued that new "postmaterial" values and beliefs have emerged in the advanced industrial nations since the 1960s. Through most of human history, in his view, people have been forced to worry about basic material needs such as food, shelter, and security, but since World War II the advanced industrial world has been largely spared traditional privations. Those born after World War II (especially the college-educated and

"Moral Shocks" and Self-Recruitment

Sometimes in the course of daily life something happens to us that distresses, surprises, and outrages us. A loved one may be killed by a drunk driver. Our boss may ask us for sexual favors. Construction on a nuclear power plant may begin down the street. Sometimes we are shocked by information we receive (perhaps from a newspaper or political pamphlet) rather than by personal experience. We learn that cosmetics are tested by being put into the eyes of rabbits, or that NATO is deploying a new type of nuclear missile throughout Europe. These "moral shocks" are often strong enough to propel us into trying to do something. We may seek out a social movement organization if we know one exists. We may even try to found our own. Although people who join a social movement typically know someone involved in it, a moral shock may still be the trigger that gets them to join. In some cases it can even push us into participation when we do not know anyone at all in the movement. In such cases, we see a process of "self-recruitment" to a movement: people actively seek out a movement or movement organization in which they can participate, as opposed to being recruited by the movement itself.

Free-Rider Problem People who would benefit from a social movement may not in fact protest but rather "free ride" on the efforts of others. Such people calculate that their own contribution to the movement (assuming that its constituency is large) is likely to be minimal and that they will enjoy the achievements of the movement anyway. So why should they bother to protest? Of course, this problem assumes that (and only arises when) people are rather narrowly self-interested. But many people protest because they feel morally obligated to do so, or because they derive pleasures or benefits from protesting (e.g., new friends) whether or not they think it will succeed. See Olson (1965).

affluent middle class) were "freed" to pursue "higher" goals such as control over their lives, environmental protection, and satisfying work, rather than worrying primarily about their paychecks. The spread of mass communications and higher education contributed to the same trends. Together, the result has been less emphasis on economic redistribution, class-based political organizations, or the pursuit of political power. Instead we have seen movements critical of large bureaucracies, complex technologies, and many different forms of oppression.

Stephen Cotgrove and Andrew Duff try to explain who is likely to support the environmental movement, depending on their relationship to industrial production, by using the concept of postmaterial politics articulated by Inglehart. They show how a movement can have a middle-class social base, even though it is not pursuing the economic interests of this class. So the growth of a post-industrial sector of the economy can help explain not only changes over time (Inglehart's interest) but different sympathies across parts of the population at any given time.

In the final excerpt, Charles Kurzman shows that Osama bin Laden's followers tend to be well educated, middle-class, and "modern." He is implicitly addressing a remnant of crowd theory, in which Westerners assume that the Islamic world is mired in religious superstition in a rejection of modern rationality. While they do question some aspects of the modern world, looking nostalgically backward to a golden age of Islam, they also use the latest technologies and media. We may not accept a particular religious orientation, but that does not mean we can dismiss it as irrational or primitive.

Recruitment involves more than cognitive beliefs about how the world works. Its moral and emotional dimensions are equally important. All the key concepts used to explain recruitment depend heavily on their emotional dynamics. The term "moral shock" is meant to incorporate some of these other dimensions, as events or information raise such a sense of outrage in people that they become inclined toward political action, with or without a network of contacts (Jasper 1997; Jasper and Poulsen 1995). Social networks are also grounded in the emotional bonds among their members: we pay attention to people in our networks because we are fond of them or trust them.

The new synthesis pays more attention to what goes on inside people's heads (and hearts). Protest is no longer seen as a compensation for some lack, but part of an effort to impose cognitive meaning on the world, to forge a personal and collective identity, to define and pursue collective interests, and to create or reinforce affective bonds with others. These are things that all humans desire and pursue. There is today considerable consensus that structural positions in networks and cultural (including cognitive, moral, and emotional) orientations and transformations are equally important in recruitment. But there are also cases in which cultural messages can be used to recruit people in the absence of social networks, relying on moral shocks instead of personal contacts. For virtually all social movements, only a small fraction of potential recruits actually join, and it takes all the factors we have considered to understand who does and who does not sign up.

Discussion Questions

1. What is the role of daily life in affecting one's likelihood of joining a social movement, even a movement one is sympathetic to?
2. Why must social-movement organizers take care how they "frame" their arguments and choose their symbols in trying to recruit members?
3. What are postmaterial values? Who is most likely to have them and why?
4. What kinds of people are more likely to sympathize with the environmental movement? Does this mean they will join it?
5. What are some of the ways that Osama bin Laden is "modern"? Have these helped him to be more effective in recruiting followers? In attaining his goals?
6. How do individual traits and structural conditions interact in recruitment to social movements?
7. What do scholars mean by the "free-rider problem"? What would be an example of free riding? How might movements address this problem?

6 The Free-Rider Problem

Mancur Olson

It is often taken for granted, at least where economic objectives are involved, that groups of individuals with common interests usually attempt to further those common interests. Groups of individuals with common interests are expected to act on behalf of their common interests much as single individuals are often expected to act on behalf of their personal interests. This opinion about group behavior is frequently found not only in popular discussions but also in scholarly writings. Many economists of diverse methodological and ideological traditions have implicitly or explicitly accepted it. This view has, for example, been important in many theories of labor unions, in Marxian theories of class action, in concepts of "countervailing power," and in various discussions of economic institutions. It has, in addition, occupied a prominent place in political science, at least in the United States, where the study of pressure groups has been dominated by a celebrated "group theory" based on the idea that groups will act when necessary to further their common or group goals. Finally, it has played a significant role in many well-known sociological studies.

The view that groups act to serve their interests presumably is based upon the assumption that the individuals in groups act out of self-interest. If the individuals in a group altruistically disregarded their personal welfare, it would not be very likely that collectively they would seek some selfish common or group objective. Such altruism, is, however, considered exceptional, and self-interested behavior is usually thought to be the rule, at least when economic issues are at stake; no one is surprised when individual businessmen seek higher profits, when individual workers seek higher wages, or when individual consumers seek lower prices. The idea that groups tend to act in support of their group interests is supposed to follow logically from this widely accepted premise of rational, self-interested behavior. In other words, if the members of some group have a common interest or objective, and if they would all be better off if that objective were achieved, it has been thought to follow logically that the individuals in that group would, if they were rational and self-interested, act to achieve that objective.

But it is *not* in fact true that the idea that groups will act in their self-interest follows logically from the premise of rational and self-interested behavior. It does *not* follow, because all of the individuals in a group would gain if they achieved their group objective, that they would act to achieve that objective, even if they were all rational and self-interested. Indeed, unless the number of individuals in a group is quite small, or unless there is coercion or some other special device to make individuals act in their common interest, *rational, self-interested individuals will not act to achieve their common or group interests*. In other words, even if all of the individuals in a large group are rational and self-interested, and would gain if, as a group, they acted to achieve their common interest or objective, they will still not voluntarily act to achieve that common or group interest. The notion that groups of individuals will act to achieve their common or group interests, far from being a logical implication of the assumption that the individuals in a group will rationally further their individual interests, is in fact inconsistent with that assumption.

If the members of a large group rationally seek to maximize their personal welfare, they will *not* act to advance their common or group objectives unless there is coercion to force them to do so, or unless some separate incentive, distinct from the achievement of the common or group interest, is offered to the members of the group individually on the condition that they help bear the costs or burdens involved in the achievement of the group objectives. Nor will such large groups form organizations to further their common goals in the absence of the coercion or the separate incentives just mentioned. These points hold true even when there is unanimous agreement in a group about the common good and the methods of achieving it.

The widespread view, common throughout the social sciences, that groups tend to further their interests, is accordingly unjustified, at least when it is based, as it usually is, on the (sometimes implicit) assumption that groups act in their self-interest because individuals do. There is paradoxically the logical possibility that groups composed of either altruistic individuals or irrational individuals may sometimes act in their common or group interests. But, as later, empirical parts of this study will attempt to show, this logical possibility is usually of no practical importance. Thus the customary view that groups of individuals with common interests tend to further those common interests appears to have little if any merit.

[...]

Consider a hypothetical, competitive industry, and suppose that most of the producers in that industry desire a tariff, a price-support program, or some other government intervention to increase the price for their product. To obtain any such assistance from the government, the producers in this industry will presumably have to organize a lobbying organization; they will have to become an active pressure group. This lobbying organization may have to conduct a considerable campaign. If significant resistance is encountered, a great amount of money will be required. Public relations experts will be needed to influence the newspapers, and some advertising may be necessary. Professional organizers will probably be needed to organize "spontaneous grass roots" meetings among the distressed producers in the industry, and to get those in the industry to write letters to their congressmen. The campaign for the government assistance will take the time of some of the producers in the industry, as well as their money.

There is a striking parallel between the problem the perfectly competitive industry faces as it strives to obtain government assistance, and the problem it faces in the marketplace when the firms increase output and bring about a fall in price. *Just as it was not rational for a particular producer to restrict his output in order that there might be a higher price for the product of his industry, so it would not be rational for him to sacrifice his time and money to support a lobbying organization to obtain government assistance for the industry. In neither case would it be in the interest of the individual producer to assume any of the costs himself. A lobbying organization, or indeed a labor union or any other organization, working in the interest of a large group of firms or workers in some industry, would get no assistance from the rational, self-interested individuals in that industry.* This would be true even if everyone in the industry were absolutely convinced that the proposed program was in their interest (though in fact some might think otherwise and make the organization's task yet more difficult).

Some critics may argue that the rational person will, indeed, support a large organization, like a lobbying organization, that works in his interest, because he knows that if he does not, others will not do so either, and then the organization will fail, and he will be without the benefit that the organization could have provided. This argument shows the need for the analogy with the perfectly competitive market. [...] When the number of firms involved is large, no one will notice the effect on price if one firm increases its output, and so no one will change his plans because of it. Similarly, in a large organization, the loss of one dues payer will not noticeably increase the burden for any other one dues payer, and so a rational person would not believe that if he were to withdraw from an organization he would drive others to do so.

[...]

However similar the purposes may be, critics may object that attitudes in organizations are not at all like those in markets. In organizations, an emotional or ideological element is often also involved. Does this make the argument offered here practically irrelevant?

A most important type of organization—the national state—will serve to test this objection. Patriotism is probably the strongest non-economic motive for organizational allegiance in modern times. This age is sometimes called the age of nationalism. Many nations draw additional strength and unity from some powerful ideology, such as democracy or communism, as well as from a common religion, language, or cultural inheritance. The state not only has many such powerful sources of support; it also is very important economically. Almost any government is economically beneficial to its citizens, in that the law and order it provides is a prerequisite of all civilized economic activity. But despite the force of patriotism, the appeal of the national ideology, the bond of a common culture, and the indispensability of the system of law and order, no major state in modern history has been able to support itself through voluntary dues or contributions. Philanthropic contributions are not even a significant source of revenue for most countries. Taxes, *compulsory* payments by definition, are needed. Indeed, as the old saying indicates, their necessity is as certain as death itself.

If the state, with all of the emotional resources at its command, cannot finance its most basic and vital activities without resort to compulsion, it would seem that large private organizations might also have difficulty in getting the individuals in the groups whose interests they attempt to advance to make the necessary contributions voluntarily.

The reason the state cannot survive on voluntary dues or payments, but must rely on taxation, is that the most fundamental services a nation-state provides are, in one important respect, like the higher price in a competitive market: they must be available to everyone if they are available to anyone. The basic and most elementary goods or services provided by government, like defense and police protection, and the system of law and order generally, are such that they go to everyone or practically everyone in the nation. It would obviously not be feasible, if indeed it were possible, to deny the protection provided by the military services, the police, and the courts to those who did not voluntarily pay their share of the costs of government, and taxation is accordingly necessary. The common or collective benefits provided by governments are usually called "public goods" by economists, and the concept of public goods is one of the oldest and most important ideas in the study of public finance. A common, collective, or public good is here defined as any good such that, if any person X_i in a group $X_1, \ldots, X_i, \ldots, X_n$ consumes it, it cannot feasibly be withheld from the others in that group. In other words, those who do not purchase or pay for any of the public or collective good cannot be excluded or kept from sharing in the consumption of the good, as they can where noncollective goods are concerned.

Students of public finance have, however, neglected the fact that *the achievement of any common goal or the satisfaction of any common interest means that a public or collective good has been provided for that group*. The very fact that a goal or purpose is *common* to a group means that no one in the group is excluded from the benefit or satisfaction brought about by its achievement. Almost all groups and organizations have the purpose of serving the common interests of their members. It is of the essence of an organization that it provides an inseparable, generalized benefit. It follows that the provision of public or collective goods is the fundamental function of organizations generally. A state is first of all an organization that provides public goods for its members, the citizens; and other types of organizations similarly provide collective goods for their members.

And just as a state cannot support itself by voluntary contributions, or by selling its basic services on the market, neither can other large organizations support themselves without providing some sanction, or some attraction distinct from the public good itself, that will lead individuals to help bear the burdens of maintaining the organization. The individual member of the typical large organization is in a position analogous to that of the firm in a perfectly competitive market, or the taxpayer in the state: his own efforts will not have a noticeable effect on the situation of his organization, and he can enjoy any improvements brought about by others whether or not he has worked in support of his organization.

[...]

Marx's emphasis on self-interest, and his assumption that classes will be conscious of their interests, has naturally led most critics to think of Marx as a utilitarian and a rationalist. Some think that this is his main failing and that he emphasizes self-interest and rationality far too much. [...] They feel that most people must not *know or care* what their class interests are, since class conflict is not the overwhelming force Marx thought it would be. [...]

It is *not* in fact true that the absence of the kind of class conflict Marx expected shows that Marx overestimated the strength of rational behavior. On the contrary, the absence of the sort of class action Marx predicted is due in part to the predominance of rational utilitarian behavior. *For class-oriented action will not occur if the individuals that make up a class act rationally.* If a person is in the bourgeois class, he may well want a government that represents his class. But it does not follow that it will be in his interest to work to see that such a government comes to power. If there is such a government he will benefit from its policies, whether or not he has supported it, for by Marx's own hypothesis it will work for his class interests. Moreover, in any event one individual bourgeois presumably will not be able to exercise a decisive influence on the choice of a government. So the *rational* thing for a member of the bourgeoisie to do is to ignore his *class* interests and to spend his energies on his *personal* interests. Similarly, a worker who thought he would benefit from a "proletarian" government would not find it rational to risk his life and resources to start a revolution against the bourgeois government. It would be just as reasonable to suppose that all of the workers in a country would voluntarily restrict their hours of work in order to raise the wages of labor in relation to the rewards for capital. For in both cases the individual would find that he would get the benefits of the class action whether he participated or not. (It is natural then that the "Marxian" revolutions that have taken place have been brought about by small conspiratorial elites that took advantage of weak governments during periods of social disorganization. It was not Marx, but Lenin and Trotsky, who provided the theory for this sort of revolution. See Lenin's *What Is to Be Done* for an account of the communist's need to rely on a committed, self-sacrificing, and disciplined minority, rather than on the common interests of the mass of the proletariat.)

Marxian class action then takes on the character of any endeavor to achieve the collective goals of a large, latent group. A class in Marxist terms consists of a large group of individuals who have a common interest arising from the fact that they do or do not own productive property or capital. As in any large, latent group, each individual in the class will find it to his advantage if all of the costs or sacrifices necessary to achieve the common goal are borne by others. "Class legislation" by definition favors the class as a whole rather than particular individuals within the class and thus offers no incentive for individuals to take "class-conscious" action. The worker has the same relation to the mass of the proletariat, and the businessman has the same relation to the mass of the bourgeois, as the taxpayer has to the state, and the competitive firm to the industry.

[...]

If the individuals in a large group have no incentive to organize a lobby to obtain a collective benefit, how can the fact that some large groups are organized be explained? Though many groups with common interests, like the consumers, the white-collar workers, and the migrant agricultural workers, are not organized, other large groups, like the union laborers, the farmers, and the doctors have at least some degree of organization. [...]

The large economic groups that are organized do have one common characteristic which distinguishes them from those large economic groups that are not, and which at the same time tends to support the theory of latent groups offered in this work.

The common characteristic which distinguishes all of the large economic groups with significant lobbying organizations is that these groups are also organized for some *other* purpose. The large and powerful economic lobbies are in fact the by-products of organizations that obtain their strength and support because they perform some function in addition to lobbying for collective goods.

The lobbies of the large economic groups are the by-products of organizations that have the capacity to "mobilize" a latent group with "selective incentives." The only organizations that have the "selective incentives" available are those that (1) have the authority and capacity to be coercive, or (2) have a source of positive inducements that they can offer the individuals in a latent group.

A purely political organization—an organization that has no function apart from its lobbying function—obviously cannot legally coerce individuals into becoming members. A political party, or any purely political organization, with a captive or compulsory membership would be quite unusual in a democratic political system. But if for some nonpolitical reason, if because of some other function it performs, an organization has a justification for having a compulsory membership, or if through this other function it has obtained the power needed to make membership in it compulsory, that organization may then be able to get the resources needed to support a lobby. The lobby is then a by-product of whatever function this organization performs that enables it to have a captive membership.

[...]

By providing a helpful defense against malpractice suits, by publishing medical journals needed by its membership, and by making its conventions educational as well as political, the American Medical Association has offered its members and potential members a number of selective or noncollective benefits. It has offered its members benefits which, in contrast with the political achievements of the organization, can be withheld from nonmembers, and which accordingly provide an incentive for joining the organization.

The American Medical Association, then, obtains its membership partly because of subtle forms of coercion, and partly because it provides noncollective benefits. It would have neither the coercive power to exercise, nor the noncollective benefits to sell, if it were solely a lobbying organization. It follows that the impressive political power of the American Medical Association and the local groups that compose it is a by-product of the nonpolitical activities of organized medicine.

[...]

Unorganized groups, the groups that have no lobbies and exert no pressure, are among the largest groups in the nation, and they have some of the most vital common interests.

The white-collar workers are a large group with common interests, but they have no organization to care for their interests. The taxpayers are a vast group with an obvious common interest, but in an important sense they have yet to obtain representation. The consumers are at least as numerous as any other group in the society, but they have no organization to countervail the power of organized or monopolistic producers. There are multitudes with an interest in peace, but they have no lobby to match those of the "special interests" that may on occasion have an interest in war. There are vast numbers who have a common interest in preventing inflation and depression, but they have no organizations to express that interest.

Nor can such groups be expected to organize or act simply because the gains from group action would exceed the costs. Why would the people of this (or any other) country organize politically to prevent inflation when they could serve their common interest in price stability just as well if they all spent less as individuals? Virtually no one would be so absurd as to expect that the individuals in an economic system would voluntarily curtail their spending to halt an inflation, however much they would, as a group, gain from doing this. Yet it is typically taken for granted that the same individuals in a political or social context will organize and act to further their collective interests. The rational individual in the economic system does not curtail his spending to prevent inflation (or increase it to prevent depression) because he knows, first, that his own efforts would not have a noticeable effect, and second, that he would get the benefits of any price stability that others achieved in any case. For the same two reasons, the rational individual in the large group in a socio-political context will not be willing to make any sacrifices to achieve the objectives he shares with others. There is accordingly no presumption that large groups will organize to act in their common interest. Only when groups are small, or when they are fortunate enough to have an independent source of selective incentives, will they organize or act to achieve their objectives.

The existence of large unorganized groups with common interests is therefore quite consistent with the basic argument of this study. But the large unorganized groups not only provide evidence for the basic argument of this study: they also suffer if it is true.

7 Recruits to Civil Rights Activism

Doug McAdam

The roots of the Summer Project are to be found in the strategic stalemate that confronted SNCC's Mississippi operation in the fall of 1963. For all the courage, hard work, and sacrifice its field workers had expended in the state since 1961, the organization had achieved few concrete victories. They had been able to persuade only a small number of prospective voters to try registering, and had succeeded in registering only a fraction of these. Three factors had combined to limit the effectiveness of SNCC's campaign in Mississippi. The first was simply the state's intransigence to any form of racial equality. The second was the absence of any aggressive federal presence in the state that might have blunted the effectiveness of state resistance. The third was SNCC's inability to generate the type of publicity that Martin Luther King, Jr. had used so effectively elsewhere in coercing supportive federal action.

[...]

At a loss as to how to counter these obstacles, the SNCC braintrust grasped at a straw of a plan offered it by Allard Lowenstein. Lowenstein, a peripatetic Democratic Party activist and sometime college administrator, had come to Mississippi in July of 1963 to investigate the racial situation. Never one to wait for a formal invitation, Lowenstein had made himself welcome in the SNCC office in Jackson, and in the course of discussion there had offered up a suggestion that spoke to the strategic impasse SNCC found itself facing. With the state's gubernatorial election scheduled for the fall, Lowenstein proposed a protest vote to demonstrate the desire of blacks to participate in the electoral process. In the context of the dilemma confronting SNCC, the plan offered much that was attractive. There was the distinct possibility that such a campaign might generate the kind of national publicity that had thus far eluded SNCC. Second, the very effort of coordinating a statewide campaign promised to strengthen SNCC's organizational presence throughout Mississippi. Finally, the symbolic nature of the project was likely to forestall the type of violent opposition that had undermined virtually all of SNCC's previous campaigns in the state.

With few workable alternatives before them, SNCC's Mississippi staff opted for the plan. The basic idea called for SNCC fieldworkers to conduct a mock gubernatorial election among Mississippi's black population. The first step in the process took place in August with the casting of protest votes in the regular state Democratic primary. In all, some 1,000 blacks cast votes in the election, principally in Greenwood and Jackson. Encouraged by the success of the primary campaign, SNCC, under the direction of Bob Moses, set about planning for the regular gubernatorial election in November. Two changes were proposed and approved for the fall campaign. First, blacks would be asked to vote, not in the regular election, but in a parallel "Freedom Vote" designed to minimize the potential for violence, and thereby insure maximum voter turnout. To give Mississippi's black population someone to vote for, a slate of "freedom" candidates was selected, headed by Aaron Henry, the president of the Mississippi NAACP, and Tougaloo College's white chaplain, Ed King. Finally, to offset the increased need for staff during the "Freedom Vote" campaign, the decision was made to import Northern college students for the duration of the project. This decision was reached partly in response to Lowenstein's assurance that he could supply as many students as the project required. Lowenstein made good on his promise. Drawing upon contacts established during earlier administrative stints at Stanford and Yale, Lowenstein was able to recruit some 100 students to come South to help with the vote.

Most arrived late in October and stayed through the November 4 conclusion of the campaign. During that time, the volunteers worked with SNCC staffers in all phases of the project, from canvassing black neighborhoods and registering black voters to staging the actual election. In all, nearly 80,000 blacks cast votes in the election, testament both to SNCC's organizing skills and the electoral willingness of Mississippi's black minority.

SNCC insiders, most important, Bob Moses, deemed the project and the use of the white volunteers a success. While the presence of so many upper-middle-class whites had exacerbated racial tensions on the project, these new volunteers had also contributed a great deal of valuable labor to the effort. Moreover, their presence had also insured a great deal of favorable publicity for SNCC as well as the campaign itself. Then too, the attention lavished on the volunteers helped popularize Southern civil rights work among Northern college students. [...]

Back in Mississippi, Bob Moses wasted little time in proposing an ambitious extension of the Freedom Vote campaign. At SNCC's November 14–16 staff meeting in Greenville, Mississippi, the idea of bringing an even larger, though unspecified, number of white students to Mississippi for the summer of 1964 was raised. Debate on the proposed plan was heated. Opponents used the occasion to raise the whole issue of white participation in the movement. Citing the Freedom Vote campaign as an example, several black staffers warned of the tendency of white students to appropriate leadership roles. This tendency, they argued, retarded the development of indigenous black leadership while also reinforcing traditional patterns of racial dominance and submission within the movement. Overall, though, sentiment at the Greenville meeting seemed to favor the plan.

[...]

Finally, there was the little matter of recruiting volunteers. How was SNCC to get word of the project to prospective applicants? How were applications to be handled? Who was to produce and distribute the forms? Who would select the volunteers? What criteria would guide the selection process? These and hundreds of other details of the recruitment process were still to be worked out. In one sense, though, the underlying rationale for the project had long since resolved the most important issue of all, that being the basic aim of the recruiting process. The fundamental goal of the project was to focus national attention on Mississippi as a means of forcing federal intervention in the state. For the project to be successful, then, it had to attract national media attention. What better way to do so than by recruiting the sons and daughters of upper-middle-class white America to join the effort? Their experiences during the Freedom Vote campaign had convinced the SNCC high command that nothing attracted the media quite like scenes of white college kids helping "the downtrodden Negroes of Mississippi." The SNCC veterans had also learned that the presence of well-heeled white students insured the conspicuous presence of federal law enforcement officials. Describing the Freedom Vote campaign, SNCC veteran, Lawrence Guyot, said:

> Wherever those white volunteers went FBI agents followed. It was really a problem to count the number of FBI agents who were there to protect the [Yale and Stanford] students. It was just that gross. So then we said, "Well, now, why don't we invite lots of whites... to come and serve as volunteers in the state of Mississippi?" (Quoted in Raines, 1983: 287).

In a 1964 interview, Bob Moses (quoted in Atwater, 1964) put the matter a bit more obliquely when he remarked that "these students bring the rest of the country with them. They're from good schools and their parents are influential. The interest of the country is awakened and when that happens, the government responds to that issue." Or as James Forman, SNCC's Executive Director at the time of the Summer Project, put it more recently, "we made a conscious attempt...to recruit from some of the Ivy League schools...you know, a lot of us knew...what we were up against. So that we were, in fact, trying to consciously recruit a counter power-elite."

The financial straits SNCC found itself in on the eve of the project served to reinforce the strategic decision to recruit at elite colleges and universities. The organization simply lacked the resources to subsidize the participation of the summer volunteers.[...]

Faced with such severe financial constraints, SNCC would have been hard pressed to pay the volunteers even had strategic considerations argued for doing so. In the end, the strategic and financial imperatives of the project combined to convince project organizers to pitch their recruiting appeals to those who could bear the costs of a summer in Mississippi. Practically, this translated into a recruitment campaign geared to the nation's elite colleges and universities. Schools, such as Stanford, Harvard, and Princeton, offered project recruiters large numbers of students who not only could pay their own way, but whose social and political connections fit the public relations aims of the project.

[...]

The Applicants: A Profile

The information from the applications provides a broad-brush portrait of the Freedom Summer applicants. There are three components to this portrait: the applicants' background characteristics, motives for applying, and what might be called their "social relationship" to the Summer Project.

Background Characteristics

No doubt the single most salient characteristic of the Freedom Summer applicants is the comfortable, if not elite backgrounds from which they were drawn. [...] That meant that some of the least privileged persons in America were to play host to the offspring of some of the most privileged. This clash of class backgrounds was to produce some of the most poignant and eye-opening moments of the summer for both volunteers and residents alike.

The privileged character of the applicants makes sense, given two features of SNCC's recruiting efforts. First, SNCC's policy requiring the volunteers to be self-supporting encouraged the class bias noted above. Secondly, SNCC's stress on recruiting at elite colleges and universities also favored the well-to-do over the average student. Again, the figures show clearly just how much emphasis SNCC placed on recruiting at high-status colleges and universities. While 233 schools contributed applicants, the majority of students who applied came from the top thirty or so schools in the country. Elite private universities, such as Harvard, Yale, Stanford, and Princeton, accounted for nearly 40 percent of the total. In fact, those four schools alone contributed 123 of the 736 students who applied to work on the project. An additional 145 applicants were drawn from among the dozen most prestigious state universities – including Berkeley, Wisconsin, Michigan – in the country. All told, then, students from the nation's highest ranking public and private colleges and universities made up 57 percent of the total applicant pool.

The class advantages that account for the elite educational backgrounds of the volunteers may also help to explain the relatively small numbers of blacks who applied to the project. Less than 10 percent of the applicants were black. [...]

A bit more surprising is the relatively large number of women who applied to the project. Forty-one percent of all applicants were female. This represents a slight overrepresentation of women among the applicants when compared to their proportion among all college students. In 1964, women comprised only 39 percent of all undergraduates. Then, too, it must be remembered that the women applicants had come of age during one of the more romanticized and traditional eras of gender socialization in this country's history. For them to have even applied required a level of rejection of traditional sex roles not demanded of the male applicants.

[...]

Taken together, these various bits and pieces of information yield a reasonably coherent portrait of the applicants. The central theme of that portrait is one of biographical availability. For all the social-psychological interpretations that have been proposed to account for the conspicuous role of students in social protest there may be a far more mundane explanation. Students, especially those drawn from privileged classes, are simply free, to a unique degree, of constraints that tend to make activism too time consuming or risky for other groups to engage in. Often freed from the demands of family, marriage, and full-time employment, students are uniquely available to express their political values through action. Certainly, this view is consistent with the information we have on the applicants. Only 22 percent of those who applied held full-time jobs, and nearly 70 percent of this group were teachers out of school for the summer. The rest of the applicants were spared the need to work during the summer by virtue of their advantaged class backgrounds. The same story applies on a personal level. Barely 10 percent of the applicants were married, more often than not to another applicant. Less than 2 percent were parents.

Attitudes and Values

[...]

The applicants were exactly who we would have expected them to be, given the era in which they were raised and the class advantages most of them enjoyed. To the extent that they were drawn from that privileged segment of the American middle and upper-middle classes who came of age in postwar America, they shared in the generalized optimism, idealism, and sense of potency that was the subjective heritage of their class and generation.

[...] The following excerpts capture the dominant tone of the applications:

> As Peter Countryman said at the Conference on Racial Equality held at Pomona in February, "The only thing necessary for the triumph of evil is for the good men to do nothing."... I have always known that discrimination was wrong and that *now* is the time to overcome these obstacles.... Until we do, all that we stand for in democracy and Christianity is negated, mocked while such oppression exists.... I can not sit by idly, knowing that there is discrimination and injustice, knowing that there is terror and fear, while I do nothing.

> I want to work in Mississippi this summer because... there is a great deal of work to be done and... just as great [a] need for workers.... But more than that, I feel that I *must* help. There is so much to do, so many barriers between men to be broken, so much hate to be overcome. I think that this is most acutely true of Mississippi, where barriers of ignorance, fear and hate are only now beginning to be effectively attacked. I want to contribute what I can to the effort so that we might at long last build a truly colorblind [*sic*] society "with liberty and justice for all."

Cognitive Liberation People will not usually rebel against the status quo, no matter how wretched they are, unless they feel that it is unjust or illegitimate (as opposed to natural or inevitable) and that they have the capacity to change it for the better. Together, these feelings of injustice and efficacy constitute what Doug McAdam (1982) has called "cognitive liberation." Of course, it is possible that people only develop or discover a sense of efficacy or empowerment *after* they have begun protesting with others. At first, and sometimes for a long time, people may be uncertain as to whether their protests will actually make a difference. In this sense, cognitive liberation is sometimes a product rather than a cause of protest.

[...]

What strikes the reader first about these statements is the depths of idealism they express. Indeed, that idealism is so passionately stated that it occasionally sounds naive and a bit romanticized. That it does may tell us as much about the lack of idealism in contemporary America as it does about any lack of sophistication on the part of the applicants. In any case, what is more important than *our* reaction to the statements is, first, the consistency with which these views were expressed, and second, what they tell us about the applicants. These were deeply idealistic individuals, dedicated to achieving equal rights and human dignity for all. What sets the applicants apart from a good many others who espouse similar values was their optimism that these values could be realized through a kind of generational mission in which they shared. Wrote one applicant:

> I no longer can escape the tension, the spirit, the anxiety that fills my heart and mind concerning the movement in the South. It is impossible for me to deny the fact that the fight against racial prejudice, intolerance, ignorance – the fight for Civil Rights – is the most significant challenge and the most crucial war my generation will ever be called to fight.

[...]

So the applicants' idealism was informed by a sense of generational potency that made them extremely optimistic about the prospects for social change. One even referred to the need "to solve the racial question, so we can move on to eliminate hunger and poverty in America." Never let it be said that the applicants lacked either imagination or confidence!

These quotes also say something about the ideological diversity of the applicants on the eve of the Summer Project. Clearly, their perceptions of the world were not being filtered through a single dominant interpretive frame. Their narrative statements predate the emergence of the mass New Left and the dissemination of its political perspective throughout mainstream youth culture. So unlike activists in the late Sixties, for whom the "correct" *political* analysis became de rigueur, the Freedom Summer applicants display a remarkably eclectic mix of world views and reasons for wanting to go to Mississippi. In fact, many of the answers on the applications make no mention of larger political issues or motivations. As Elinor Tideman Aurthur told me in the course of her interview:

> [D]uring that period [prior to Freedom Summer] I was... apolitical... I was into the humanities, and culture... and literature. I was kind of impatient with my father and his involvement with social causes. I felt that was dead... I wanted to write... I didn't have the confidence to write but I saw myself as a writer, and I did not do anything political.

[...]

Those applicants whose statements evidence the least political orientation to the project fall into one of two groups. The first are teachers or education majors whose primary motivation for applying represents a simple extension of their occupational roles or future career plans.

[...]

The second group of "nonpolitical" applicants consists of persons whose reasons for applying appear to be primarily religious. For them the project represented an extension of the social gospel in action or, reflecting the existential theology of the day, an opportunity to bear "personal witness" to the idea of Christian brotherhood. One applicant put it this way: "Christ called us to *act* in the service of brotherhood, not just talk about it. I'm tired of talking. Mississippi is my opportunity to act."

The widespread salience of religious motives among the applicants may surprise some readers unfamiliar with America's longstanding tradition of church-based activism. From religious pacifists to Quaker abolitionists to Catholic settlement workers, much of America's activist history has had deep roots in the church. With its ministerial leadership and strong ideological ties to Southern black theology, the civil rights movement merely continued this tradition. It is hardly surprising, then, to find religious sentiments being voiced by many of the volunteers.

Among the more political applicants, a kind of conventional patriotic rhetoric was more often invoked than a radical leftist analysis. Many applicants cited a desire to "honor the memory" or "carry out the legacy of John F. Kennedy" as their principal reason for applying. Another sounded particularly Kennedyesque when he said that he was attracted to the project "by a desire to enhance the image of the United States abroad, thereby undercutting Communist influence among the underdeveloped nations of the world."

[...]

The impression that one gets from reading the applications, then, is one of healthy ideological diversity. All of the groups identified here seem to have been present in roughly equal numbers in the ranks of the applicants. What is interesting is that these ideological differences mask a common source of inspiration for whatever values the applicants espouse. Regardless of ideological stripe, the vast majority of applicants credit their parents with being the models for their actions. [...]

This, then, is one case in which the popular view of the Sixties activist is *not* consistent with the evidence. Far from using Freedom Summer as a vehicle for rebellion against parents, the applicants simply seem to be acting in accord with values learned at home. This finding is consistent with most previous research on the roots of student activism.

Social Relationship to the Project

Were freedom from adult responsibilities and sympathetic attitudes enough to account for the applicant's decision to apply to the project? Or were there ways in which concrete social ties served to "pull" people into the project? The answer to this last question would appear to be "yes." The image of the activist as a lone individual driven only by the force of his or her conscience applies to very few of the applicants. Rather, their involvement in the project seems to have been mediated through some combination of personal relationships and/or organizational ties.

Organizationally the applicants were a very active group. Only 15 percent of the prospective volunteers reported no group memberships, while 62 percent list two or more. The percentage of volunteers listing various types of organizations is shown below:

Civil rights organization	48%
Student club or social group	21
Church or religious group	21
Socialist or other leftist organization	14
Democrat or Republican party affiliate	13
Academic club or organization	13
Teachers' organization	10

Not surprisingly, the highest percentage of memberships are to civil rights groups. Within this category, CORE or Friends of SNCC chapters account for better than half of all the affiliations. Given that SNCC and CORE supplied 100 percent of the field staff for the Summer Project, it seems reasonable to assume that membership in one of their chapters would have insured a certain knowledge of and loyalty to the project.

The remaining organizational categories mirror the ideological diversity touched on above. Each of the informal divisions discussed in the previous section corresponds to one of the next six largest organizational categories. [...]

The real importance of these organizations lies not so much in the ideological divisions they reflect as in the role they played in drawing the applicants into civil rights activity *before* Freedom Summer. One volunteer described her initiation into the Movement in this way:

> [The] Church was very important to me. I was studying to be a minister at the time that I went to Mississippi and actually that is how I got involved in it [Freedom Summer]

> because I went to Beaver College which was an all female institution, wanting to be a missionary eventually, got involved in the YWCA there and was sent on a voter registration drive, which Al Lowenstein headed, in Raleigh, North Carolina . . . he . . . told us about the Mississippi summer project and after having my eyes opened by the whole Raleigh experience I knew I wanted to go.

[. . .]

For the vast majority of applicants, then, Freedom Summer did *not* mark their initial foray into the civil rights movement. Instead, through a variety of sponsoring organizations, some 90 percent of the applicants had already participated in various forms of activism. Not that the nature of their involvements was in all cases terribly significant. Most of the applicants had confined their activities to such safe forms of participation as "on-campus civil rights organizing" (36 percent) or fund-raising (10 percent). But it is not the intensity of these earlier involvements as much as the fact that they took place that is significant. Extremely risky, time-consuming involvements such as Freedom Summer are almost always preceded by a series of safer, less demanding instances of activism. In effect, people commit themselves to movements in stages, each activity preparing the way for the next. The case of the volunteer, who engaged in voter registration work in Raleigh, North Carolina, prior to Freedom Summer, illustrates the process. While in Raleigh, three very important things happened to her. First, she met activists she had not known previously, thus broadening her range of movement contacts. Second, talking with these activists and confronting segregation firsthand clearly deepened the volunteer's understanding of and commitment to the movement. Finally, at the level of identity, the week in Raleigh allowed her to "play at" and grow more comfortable with the role of activist. As the research on identity transformation suggests, it is precisely such tentative forays into new roles that pave the way for more thoroughgoing identity change. Playing at being an activist is usually the first step in becoming one. As a result, the volunteer left Raleigh knowing more people in the movement and more ideologically and personally disposed toward participation in the Summer Project. As she herself said, "the trip to Raleigh really laid the foundation for Mississippi . . . I don't think I would have even applied to the project otherwise."

So most of the applicants were already linked to the civil rights movement either through the organizations to which they belonged or their own modest histories of civil rights activism. But what about their links to one another? How extensive were the ties *between* prospective volunteers on the eve of the summer? The presumption, of course, is that an individual would have found it easier to apply had they known someone else who had done so.

Fortunately, one question on the application allows for a very conservative estimate of the extent of such ties. That question asked the applicant to "list at least ten persons who . . . would be interested in receiving information about your [summer] activities." These names were gathered in an effort to mobilize a well-heeled, Northern, liberal constituency who might lobby Washington on behalf of protection for civil rights workers as well as other changes in civil rights policy. Judging from the names they listed, most of the applicants seem to have been well aware of this goal. The names most often provided by the applicants were those of parents, parents' friends, professors, ministers, or other noteworthy or influential *adults* with whom they had contact. On occasion, however, the applicant also included another applicant in their list of names. Just how often was surprising.

Exactly a fourth of the applicants listed at least one other prospective volunteer on their applications. What makes this figure impressive is the fact that the intent of the question was not to have the applicants identify other applicants. That 25 percent did so suggests that the personal ties between the applicants were extensive. Interviews with the applicants confirm this impression. Forty-nine of the eighty applicants said they knew at least one other applicant in advance of the summer. And their accounts make it clear that these ties were important in their decision to apply to the project. Several even described their decision to apply as more a group than an individual process. As one volunteer put it:

> [T]he group that went down to Raleigh... were from Cornell, Dartmouth, Amherst, BU [Boston University], Yale... and I just felt that I was with a very special group of people and I wanted to be with them for as long as I could and we would sit up at night talking about whether we would go down [to Mississippi] and [then] we communicated with each other after that Raleigh experience... [and] talked each other into going.

Together, the bits and pieces of information presented above yield a fairly coherent portrait of the Freedom Summer applicants. The central themes embodied in this portrait are those of "biographical availability," "attitudinal affinity" and "social integration." Raised by parents who espoused values consistent with the project, the applicants found themselves disposed to participate on attitudinal grounds. Then too, their freedom from family and employment responsibilities (the latter owing largely to their privileged class backgrounds) made it possible for them to act on their attitudes and values. Finally, a combination of organizational ties, personal links to other applicants, and their own histories of activism served to pull the applicants into the project even as their values were pushing them in that direction. [...]

The Survivors: Distinguishing Volunteers from No-Shows

Confronted by various hurdles, roughly a quarter of the applicants fell by the wayside prior to the start of the project. Can these no-shows be distinguished from those who did make it to Mississippi? Are there specific factors that account for the different courses of action taken by those in each group? The answer is yes. Expressed in terms of the three broad factors touched on earlier in the chapter, it appears that going or not going to Mississippi had more to do with the applicants' biographical availability and social links to the project than to any apparent differences in attitude between the volunteers and the no-shows. What is more, it would seem that the impact of these factors is closely related to the three major hurdles – staff rejection, parental opposition, and applicant fears – already noted.

[...]

Biographical Availability Many people are deterred or prevented from protesting by the responsibilities and constraints of daily life which are imposed by work, parents, spouses or partners, children, or friends. Not everyone, in other words, is "biographically available" for protest, even if they are sympathetic to the cause. Of course, some people try to work around these constraints, or try to change them, if they are especially motivated to protest. In other words, people sometimes *make* themselves biographically available for protest. See McAdam (1988).

Together, the findings reported here offer a consistent picture of the Freedom Summer volunteers. Stated simply, the volunteers enjoyed much stronger social links to the Summer Project than did the no-shows. They were more likely to be members of civil rights (or allied) groups, have friends involved in the movement, and have more extensive histories of civil rights activity prior to the summer. The practical effect of this greater "proximity" to the movement would have been to place the volunteer at considerable "risk" of being drawn into the project via the application process. Having applied, the volunteer's close ties to the civil rights community would then have served another function. Given the extended time commitment expected of Freedom Summer volunteers and the highly publicized dangers of the campaign, it seems reasonable to assume that individual applicants – even highly committed ones – would have considered withdrawing from the campaign prior to the summer. What might have discouraged applicants from acting on these fears was the presence of strong *social* constraints discouraging withdrawal. If one acted alone in applying to the project and remained isolated in the months leading up to the campaign, the social costs of withdrawing from the project would not have been great. On the other hand, the individual who applied in consort with friends or as a movement veteran undoubtedly risked considerable social disapproval for withdrawal. One can also stress a more positive interpretation of the same process. In the months leading up to the summer, well-integrated applicants were no doubt encouraged to make good on their commitment through the reinforcement and sense of strength they derived from other applicants. As one volunteer explained, his relationship with another applicant was "probably the key to me making it to Mississippi... [he] and I just sort of egged each other on... I'm pretty sure I wouldn't have made it without him and probably that was true for him too." Whichever interpretation one chooses, it is clear from the data that participants *do* differ significantly from no-shows in the extent and strength of their social links to the project.

Those applicants who finally made it to Mississippi, then, were an interesting and very special group. They were independent both by temperament and by virtue of their class advantages and relative freedom from adult responsibilities. They were not children, however, but young adults whose slightly older age granted them an immunity from parental control not enjoyed by the no-shows. Owing to the formidable obstacles the female applicants faced, the volunteers were disproportionately male. Academically, they numbered among "the best and the brightest" of their generation, both in the levels of education they had obtained and the prestige of the colleges and universities they were attending. Reflecting their privileged class backgrounds as much as the prevailing mood of the era, the volunteers held to an enormously idealistic and optimistic view of the world. More important, perhaps, they shared a sense of efficacy about their own actions. The arrogance of youth and the privileges of class combined with the mood of the era to give the volunteers an inflated sense of their own specialness and generational potency. This message was generally reinforced at home by parents who subscribed to values consistent with those of the project. Finally, the volunteers were already linked to the civil rights community. Whether these links took the form of organizational memberships, prior activism, or ties to other applicants, the volunteers benefited from greater "social proximity" to the project than did the no-shows. In fact, nothing distinguishes the two groups more clearly than this contrast. Biographical availability and attitudinal affinity may have been necessary prerequisites for applying, but it was the strength of one's links to the project that seems to have finally determined whether one got to Mississippi or not.

References

Atwater, James 1964 " 'If we can crack Mississippi . . .'." *Saturday Evening Post*, July 25, p. 16.

Raines, Howell 1983 *My Soul Is Rested.* New York: Penguin Books.

8 Middle-Class Radicalism and Environmentalism

Stephen Cotgrove and Andrew Duff

There has been increasing interest in recent years in the possibility of fundamental changes in the political system, with the emergence of new social groups, new interests and new values which cut across traditional class-based alignments and cleavages. Moreover, in recent decades, there has been a marked increase in direct action, and the growth of outsider politics, a decline in partisan support for the traditional parties, and other indications of a loss of legitimacy. Such indications of strain and stress take on a special significance with the possibility that industrial societies, which have relied so heavily on policies of sustained and rapid economic growth for maintaining a broad spectrum of consensus and support, may be facing special challenges with intransigent problems of unemployment and inflation, exacerbated by increasing shortages of materials and energy.

The environmentalist movement provides an important case study and focus for exploring such issues. In the last decade the awareness of environmental problems has not only increased dramatically, but has taken on a new political significance. Environmentalist groups have been at the centre of protest, locally and nationally, against motorways, airports and dams, and have vigorously opposed the nuclear programme in a number of countries. And in the last few years, newly formed 'ecology parties' have captured a sizeable proportion of the votes at elections. The significance of the environment has shifted from a preoccupation with the preservation of the countryside, historic buildings and local amenities, to become the focus for radical protest. Above all, environmentalists have challenged the central values and ideology of industrial society. It is with this dimension of the environmentalist movement that this analysis is concerned. Is environmental protest indicative of a fundamental change in social values, and if so, what strains and problems will this generate for the political system? What are the sources of support? Is there a potentially larger political constituency?

In order to clarify the analysis, it is necessary first to emphasize the heterogeneous character of those who come under the broad umbrella of environmentalists. On the one hand there are those who are mainly interested in protecting wildlife, preserving the countryside, and our national heritage of buildings. They wish simply to give a higher priority to the protection of the environment. But at the other extreme there are those who argue that the problem requires more than simply a shift in priorities, and that fundamental changes are essential if we are to survive growing threats to the environment and the exhaustion of materials which result from a high-growth, energy-consuming and environmentally-damaging way of life. It is environmentalists in this 'strong' sense, and who have joined associations which promote such policies, who are the object of this analysis.

Environmental Awareness and Beliefs

The most plausible explanation for environmental activism is that those who join such

A Chronology of the U.S. Environmental Movement

1845: Henry David Thoreau moves to Walden Pond, where he stays for two years, and writes one of a series of careful observations of the New England environment which he made throughout his life.

1872: U.S. Congress creates the first national park, Yellowstone, but also passes legislation (still in effect today) allowing private individuals and companies to stake mining claims in public lands for a nominal fee.

1891: Forest Reserve Act allows the President to set aside public lands with only restricted uses.

1892: The Sierra Club is founded by outdoorsmen to conserve California's wilderness, with John Muir as its first president.

1913: After long controversy, Congress passes a law to allow the damming of California's Hetch Hetchy, a dramatic and beautiful valley much like Yosemite. The conflict pitted pragmatic conservationists like Gifford Pinchot, who favored the dam for the electric power it would produce, against more radical preservationists like John Muir.

1949: Aldo Leopold publishes *The Sand Country Almanac*, which argues that all life (human and nonhuman) is connected through its presence in balanced habitats. We all benefit, he said, from the biological diversity of ecosystems.

1962: Marine biologist Rachel Carson publishes *Silent Spring* in serial form in *The New Yorker*, on the unintended effects of DDT and other chemical pesticides.

1964: President Johnson signs the Wilderness Act, which allows large tracts of land to be protected from development.

1966: Victor Yannacone and others sue to stop the spraying of DDT on Long Island; a year later they form the Environmental Defense Fund (EDF). The Ford Foundation provides startup grants to several legally oriented environmental groups, including EDF, the Natural Resources Defense Council, and the Sierra Club Legal Defense Fund.

1968: Paul Ehrlich publishes *The Population Bomb*, warning of the many risks of rapid population growth around the world.

1969: David Brower, dynamic head of the Sierra Club who has radicalized that organization, is forced out and founds the Friends of the Earth. When he is later ousted from that group, he will form the Earth Island Institute.

1970: On January 1, President Nixon signs the National Environmental Policy Act; within a decade two dozen other environmental acts will be passed, creating among other things the Environmental Protection Agency and the Occupational Safety and Health Administration.

1970: Twenty million Americans participate in the first Earth Day, April 22, aiming to spread awareness of environmental problems and solutions. This is probably the largest single show of support for any cause in U.S. history.

Mid-1970s: Within several years, a number of direct-action ecology groups are founded, including Greenpeace, the Environmental Policy Institute, and the Sea Shepherd Conservation Society.

Late 1970s: Ecology movement helps inspire antinuclear movement against civilian nuclear reactors.

1978: Love Canal makes headlines and places toxic waste at the top of environmental agenda; thousands of local environmental groups (sometimes called "NIMBYs" for "Not In My BackYard") are formed.

1980: Led by Dave Foreman, former lobbyist for the Wilderness Society, Earth First! is founded on the principle of sabotage against logging, mining, and other incursions into wilderness areas.

1981: President Reagan appoints James Watt of Wyoming as Secretary of the Interior as part of the "sagebrush rebellion" of western businesses and politicians against federal intervention to protect the environment or slow down commercial exploitation; millions join the major environmental groups in response.

1990: A conference in Michigan and a book, *Dumping in Dixie* by Robert Bullard, help create the environmental justice movement, which emphasizes that poor communities are the biggest victims of pollution and hazards.

associations are particularly aware of the problems. To test this we asked a series of questions about environmental issues. The questionnaire was distributed to three target groups: environmentalists (members of Friends of the Earth and the Conservation Society), leading industrialists (drawn from *Business Who's Who* and *Who's Who in British Engineering*), and a sample of the general public from Bath and Swindon. The results were surprising. On items testing awareness of environmental damage such as 'Rivers and waterways are seriously threatened by pollution' and 'Some animals and plants are being threatened with extinction', both environmentalists and the public generally agreed that the environment was being damaged, although the strength of agreement was greater for environmentalists. On a cluster of items testing awareness of shortages, such as 'There are likely to be serious and disruptive shortages of essential raw materials if things go on as they are', there was still substantial agreement about the threat of shortages. So it is clear that awareness of environmental dangers can only account in part for membership of the more activist environmental groups.

It is when we turn to an exploration of the significance and meaning of beliefs about the environment in the context of wider systems of belief and action that larger differences between environmentalists and others begin to emerge. Firstly, environmentalists see environmental dangers and problems to be much more serious: 93 per cent define them as extremely serious or very serious, compared with 56 per cent of the general public. Environmentalists differed too in their attitude toward science and technology. In answer to items such as 'Science and technology can solve our problems by finding new sources of energy, materials, and ways of increasing food production' and 'We attach too much importance to reason and science to the neglect of our intuition', it was the environmentalists who showed their lack of confidence in, and even hostility to science and technology by contrast with the public. And on a scale of opposition to the institutions of industrial society environmentalists were significantly more opposed than members of the general public. Substantial differences in values and ideals between the two groups also emerged. Using a modified form of Inglehart's scale for measuring 'material' and 'post-material' values, we found a marked polarization between environmentalists and the public, the former scoring higher on items indicating support for post-material values, and much lower on material items. Support for material values was indicated by high priority given to items such as 'Maintaining a high rate of economic growth' and 'Maintaining a stable economy'. By contrast, the environmentalists gave high priority to 'Progressing toward a less impersonal, more humane society', and 'Progressing toward a society where ideas are more important than money'.

The second source of empirical evidence is more complex. Our study of environmentalists' literature pointed to the probability that environmentalists held strongly negative views about many features of industrial society. In order to explore this, we devised a series of items to enable respondents to indicate their preferences for the kind of society they would like to see. [...]

At the top of the list for the general public was preference for a society with more emphasis on law and order, followed by satisfying work, economic growth, differentials, and rewards for achievement. By contrast, environmentalists want a society which above all attaches more importance to humanly satisfying work, in which production is selective rather than aiming to satisfy the demand for consumer goods, which sets limits to economic growth, and emphasizes participation, as against the influence of experts.

Environments at Risk

What differentiates the environmentalists then from the general public is not primarily their awareness of environmental dangers.

Rather, it is the use to which they have put environmental beliefs which distinguishes them. They are opposed to the dominant values and institutions of industrial society, and want to change them. Now such a challenge faces enormous odds. But the environment has provided ammunition for their case. Beliefs about environmental dangers have been harnessed and put to work to support their challenge to the dominant values and ideology. What they are saying is that the society we have got is bad: that the way we behave is against Nature, our children will suffer, and time is running out. They are adopting a practice which is widespread in human societies. In the words of Mary Douglas, 'Time, money, God and Nature are the universal trump cards plunked down to win an argument'. So, she says, the 'laws of nature are dragged in to sanction the moral code: this kind of disease is caught by adultery, that by incest; this meteorological disaster is the effect of political disloyalty, that the effect of impiety'. In advanced industrial societies too, the environment has become a doom-point: a trump card thrown down by the environmentalists to win a moral argument. Nuclear power stations in particular have come to have a deep symbolic significance: centralized, technologically complex and hazardous, and reinforcing all those trends in society which environmentalists most fear and dislike – the increasing domination of experts, threatening the freedom of the individual, and reinforcing totalitarian tendencies. Opposition to nuclear power is seen for many as a key issue on which to take a stand against the further advance of an alliance between state power and commercial interests. For the objectors, the material advantages from nuclear power cannot justify the risks involved.

As was stressed earlier, environmentalists are far from being a homogeneous group. This raises problems in testing ideas about the political significance of the environmentalists' movement. Some members of the environment associations do not share such radical views, nor wish to harness environment beliefs to challenging the dominant values. Their main concern is rather with the protection of the countryside. Indeed, a significant minority of our sample support both material values and 'economic individualism'. The most important distinguishing factor was position on the political spectrum. Those on the left had less confidence in science, higher scores on the anti-industrial society scale, higher post-material scores, and were more opposed to economic individualism. And despite the fact that their perceptions of environmental damage and shortages did not differ from those on the right, it was this group who were most likely to rate environmental dangers as extremely or very serious. Such evidence lends even stronger support to the view that it is the use to which environmental beliefs are put which is the key to the political significance of the environmentalist movement.

Competing Paradigms

The environmentalist movement then has provided a vehicle for harnessing beliefs about environmental dangers to support an attack on the central values and beliefs of industrial capitalism – the hegemony of economic goals and values, and the rational and systematic orientation of action to these ends. In industrial societies economic criteria become the bench-mark by which a wide range of individual and social action is judged and evaluated. And belief in the market and market mechanisms is quite central. Clustering round this core belief is the conviction that enterprise flourishes best in a system of risks and rewards, that differentials are necessary incentives to maximize effort and to call forth talent and achievement, and in the necessity for some form of division of labour, and a hierarchy of skills and expertise. In particular, there is a belief in the competence of experts in general and of scientists in particular. More than this, scientific knowledge and the scientific method enjoy a special epistemological status as superior ways of knowing, so that statements of the form 'it is a scientific fact that . . . ' are treated with special deference. And as a corollary, there is an emphasis on quantification. In short, it is possible to identify a dominant social paradigm – a set of beliefs about the nature of society which provides both a guide to action and a legitimation of policies.

The alternative environmental paradigm polarizes on almost every issue. The first and most obvious point of difference is the environmentalists' opposition to the dominant value attached to economic growth. This in turn rests on beliefs that the earth's resources are finite – a view encapsulated in Boulding's telling metaphor 'space ship earth'. But their disagreement with the central values and beliefs of the dominant social paradigm runs deeper than this. Not only do they challenge the importance attached to material and economic goals, they by contrast give much higher priority to the realization of non-material values – to social relationships and community, to the exercise of human skills and capacities, and to increased participation in decisions that affect our daily lives. They disagree too with the beliefs of the dominant social paradigm about the way society works. They have little confidence in science and technology to come up with a technical fix to solve the problems of material and energy shortages. And this is in part rooted in a different view of nature which stresses the delicate balance of ecological systems and possibly irreversible damage which may result from the interventions of high technology. They question whether the market is the best way to supply people with the things they want, and the importance of differentials as rewards for skill and achievement. They hold a completely different world-view, with different beliefs about the way society works, and about what should be the values and goals guiding policy and the criteria of choice. It is, in short, a counter-paradigm.

What is being argued then is that what differentiates environmentalists is a complex of beliefs about the nature of industrial society, about both the effectiveness and desirability of many of its core institutions and values. Their world-view differs markedly from the dominant view. It constitutes an alternative paradigm, with different beliefs about nature and man's relations with his environment, about how the economy can best be organized, about politics and about the nature of society (figure 8.1).

Middle-Class Radicalism

How then can we explain the existence of a group within industrial societies which rejects the dominant social paradigm? The most plausible explanation is to be found when we look at the occupations of environmentalists. What is particularly striking is the high proportion of environmentalists in our sample occupying roles in the non-productive service sector: doctors, social workers, teachers, and the creative arts (table 8.1). In short, it will be argued, environmentalists are drawn predominantly from a specific fraction of the middle class whose interests and values diverge markedly from other groups in industrial societies. Firstly, environmentalism is an expression of the interests of those whose class position in the non-productive sector locates them at the periphery of the institutions and processes of industrial capitalist societies. Hence, their concern to win greater participation and influence and thus to strengthen the political role of their members. It is a protest against alienation from the processes of decision making, and the depoliticization of issues through the usurpation of policy decisions by experts, operating within the dominant economic values. It is the political dimension of their role which goes far to account for their particular form of dissent. Their sense of being political outsiders is reflected especially in the attitudes of environmentalists towards working through the existing political parties. As many as 17 per cent rejected the left-right dimension in political beliefs, compared with 4.7 per cent of the industrial sample. And 64 per cent

	Dominant Social Paradigm	*Alternative Environmental Paradigm*
CORE VALUES	Material (economic growth) Natural environment valued as resource Domination over nature	Non-material (self-actualization) Natural environment intrinsically valued Harmony with nature
ECONOMY	Market forces Risk and reward Rewards for achievement Differentials Individual self-help	Public interest Safety Incomes related to need Egalitarian Collective/social provision
POLITY	Authoritative structures (experts influential) Hierarchical Law and order	Participative structures (citizen/worker involvement) Non-hierarchical Liberation
SOCIETY	Centralized Large-scale Associational Ordered	Decentralized Small-scale Communal Flexible
NATURE	Ample reserves Nature hostile/neutral Environment controllable	Earth's resources limited Nature benign Nature delicately balanced
KNOWLEDGE	Confidence in science and technology Rationality of means Separation of fact/value, thought/feeling	Limits to science Rationality of ends Integration of fact/value, thought/feeling

Figure 8.1 Competing social paradigms

would support direct action to influence government decisions on environmental issues, compared with 60 per cent of the industrial sample who were opposed.

But this is only part of the answer. Their attack is not simply rooted in their subordinate position. It is also a challenge to the goals and values of the dominant class, and the structures and institutions through which these are realized. Environmentalists' rejection of beliefs in the efficacy of the market, risk-taking and rewards for achievement, and of the overriding goal of economic growth and of economic criteria is a challenge to the hegemonic ideology which legitimates the institutions and politics of industrial capitalism. Central to the operation of such societies is the role of the market. It is the relation between individuals and those subsystems of society which operate either within or largely outside the market which we will argue is the clue to the clash of value systems and social paradigms.

If this explanation is correct, then we would expect support for the dominant social paradigm to be strongest in precisely those occupations which are the polar opposite of the environmentalists – among those who occupy dominant positions in the market sector. Support for the dominant social paradigm is markedly stronger amongst our industrial sample. It is here that we find overwhelming support for economic individualism; for differentials, rewards for achievement, for a society in which market forces and private interests predominate and for managerial authority.

What we are arguing then is that the clue to understanding the quite different values and beliefs of environmentalists and 'industrialists' is to be found in part in their relations to the core economic institutions of

Table 8.1 Occupations of environmentalists and public

	Environmentalists %	*Public* %
Commerce and industry		
— professional and supervisory	14.3	13.6
— clerical	5.6	12.2
Self-employed	9.6	4.8
Service, welfare, creative	38.4	12.2
Manual	5.4	28.2
Retired	9.1	7.8
Housewife	8.0	18.0
Unemployed	1.6	1.7
Student	8.0	1.4
	100.0	99.9
	(N = 427)	(N = 294)

society. It is class position and the interests and values which this generates to which we now turn.

The New Middle Class

Analyses of class in industrial societies, especially those in the Marxist tradition, have been overwhelmingly preoccupied with the way in which the capitalist relations of production generate antagonisms and conflicts of interest within societies in which the production of goods and services is the dominant activity. Such a model has faced considerable difficulty in relating a 'middle' class of managers, technicians, and service workers, to the two main antagonistic classes. What is notable is the almost complete omission of any extended discussion of the particular fraction of the middle class which has been identified in this analysis: those operating in those subsystems in industrial societies concerned with the pursuit of non-economic values, and functioning outside the market, and in this sense, non-capitalistic elements persisting within capitalist societies.

The central question raised by this analysis is the extent of any relative autonomy of such subsystems within the framework of the dominant institutions of industrial capitalism. The Marxist tradition sees the institutions of health and welfare as functionally necessary for the reproduction of labour, thus serving the interests of a capitalist class. Now while this may possibly explain state support for 'non-productive' sectors, such an explanation does not offer a satisfactory account of either the interests or values of those who work in the personal service, intellectual, and artistic sectors. Our evidence demonstrates that many such hold values and beliefs which are sharply antagonistic to the dominant ideology.

The precise connection between occupation and values is problematic, though there are strong grounds for concluding that values are a major factor influencing occupational choice. What our evidence does is to draw attention to the relationship between opposition to the dominant ideology and occupational role. Non-productive sub-systems functioning outside the market, orientated to non-economic goals and values persist in all industrial societies. Those who work in them resist in varying degrees the intrusion of market values and processes (the commercialization of art, the vocationalizing of all education and learning). To the extent that schools, hospitals and welfare agencies operate outside the market-place, and those who work in them are dedicated to maximizing non-economic values, they constitute non-industrial enclaves within industrial societies and are the carriers of alternative non-economic values. And they may well provide a more congenial environment for those for whom the values and ideology of industrial capitalism do not win unqualified enthusiasm and unquestioning support. In short, those who reject the ideology and values of industrial capitalism are likely to choose careers outside the market-place. Moreover, such occupations can offer a substantial degree of personal autonomy for those who have little taste for a subordinate role in the predominantly hierarchical structures of industrial society.

Discussion: Ideologies, Paradigms, and Political Legitimacy

It is not being suggested that the traditional antagonisms of capital and labour are no longer relevant. Conflicts of power and interest deriving from the ownership and control of production persist. But such conflicts tend to be focused primarily around economic values. What the new politics brings to the surface and feeds in to the political system are demands stemming from non-economic values. These have always constituted an element in left-wing politics, which has never lent support to unbridled economism, and whose dream of a new Jerusalem has gone beyond material goals, however important these have been for those suffering material deprivation and inequality. Any attempt to assimilate the ideology of this particular fraction of the middle class to that of either the bourgeosie or the proletariat flies in the face of the evidence. Nor can their values and beliefs be explained away as 'false consciousness', being firmly rooted in their structural position. But although the new politics cuts across the trade union economism which dominates Labour Party policies, the new dimension is much closer to the left than it is to the right with its strong commitment to the dominant social paradigm. The radicalism located in this particular fraction of the middle class is then much more than an emotional satisfaction derived from the expression of personal values in action, as Parkin argued from his study of the C.N.D. movement, and has much more radical potential than most theorists have recognized. Although position on the political spectrum accounted for much of the variance in scores on post-materialism and economic individualism, environmentalists had significantly higher post-material scores and were more strongly anti-economic individualism than the general public with the same political affiliations.

[...]

Now it is not being suggested that environmentalists are about to man the barricades. Nevertheless, environmental issues have provided a focus for direct action – ranging from the disruption of inquiries on motorways, the massive protests against nuclear power sites in Germany and France, our own Windscale inquiry, to the violent opposition to the opening of Tokyo airport and even the strong reaction against the culling of grey seals. But more important, the dominant social paradigm provides not only a set of beliefs about how society works, and taken-for-granted assumptions about goals and criteria: it functions also as an ideology, legitimating and justifying the dominant political institutions and processes. And it is at the level of legitimacy that the environmentalist movement may provide its greatest challenge to the political system. Because of its taken-for-granted character, the dominant social paradigm can systematically repress the articulation of alternative view points. Given support for economic values and growth, confidence in experts, and in the power of science and technology to come up with answers, then the conclusions of Mr. Justice Parker at Windscale can be seen to be not only reasonable but right. Given the acceptance of the dominant goals and values of society, problems are seen to be essentially questions of means, soluble by harnessing knowledge and expertise to the political process. Rationality is defined in narrowly technical or instrumental terms. What are properly political questions involving conflicts of values and interest are de-politicized and treated as technical questions. This, it is argued, is precisely what happened at

Windscale. It is under such conditions that political institutions distort communications and there is no genuine dialogue. There is little doubt that alternative social paradigms generate major problems of communication and understanding. Hence the charges and counter-charges of unreason and irrationality between environmentalists and supporters of the status quo. From the environmentalist perspective, it is modern industrial societies dominated by the value of 'technology–organization–efficiency–growth–progress ...' whose sanity is called into question: '... only such single-valued mindlessness would cut down the last redwoods, pollute the most beautiful beaches, invent machines to injure and destroy plant and human life. To have only one value, is, in human terms, to be mad. It is to be a machine'. And from the industrialists' perspective, environmentalist policies look silly, utopian, or plain mad.

Those who seek to promote alternative goals and values look with exasperation at the failure of the main parties to grasp the essential issues, and to formulate appropriate policies. The traditional left-right polarization is seen to be no longer relevant. The normal channels for feeding interests and demands into the system are clogged by incomprehension: the hegemony of the dominant taken-for-granted values and beliefs of liberal capitalism blocks off meaningful dialogue and communication. The charges and counter-charges of unreason are rooted in the failure to grasp that what is at stake is competing world-views and ideologies. The debate about environmental issues becomes a dialogue of the blind talking to the deaf. It is such experiences which, it can be argued, contribute to the decline in political legitimacy, a falling-off in support for traditional political parties and processes, and an increase in direct action.

This analysis suggests that many prescriptions for increasing the rationality of the environmentalist debate fail to penetrate to the heart of the problem. Its 'irrational' character is generally diagnosed as being due to a failure to settle crucial scientific and technical issues. Opposition to nuclear energy is seen to be irrational, because the scientific evidence demonstrates it to be safer than windmills. A more sophisticated version recognises that the evidence of those who have an interest in an issue may be partial or distorted. So, it is argued, the way to ensure a rational debate for the inquiry on fast-breeder reactors is to set up more broad-based machinery which would not be dependent on those institutionally committed to official options, but would be able to initiate, conduct or commission independent research. In short, the problem of achieving rationality is seen to be fundamentally one of getting the facts right, and of discovering the right technical and organizational solutions. Such an approach fails to recognise the problems of communication and understanding rooted in alternative paradigms. What is not appreciated is the existence of what may be described as an anthropological problem of competing cultures and meaning systems. If this is correct, then the 'new' politics will present a serious challenge to the parties of the left to come to grips with conflicts of values and beliefs which run deeper than simply a reordering of priorities. Such conflicts have always been evident in the left. But any decisive generational shift away from the overriding materialism and economism of industrial societies, reinforced by intransigent economic problems of 'stagflation' and material and energy shortages, could place new strains on any tenuous consensus.

9 Who Are the Radical Islamists?

Charles Kurzman

As the United States wages war on terrorism, media coverage has portrayed the radical Islamism exemplified by Osama bin Laden as medieval, reactionary, and eager to return the Islamic world to its seventh century roots.

In one sense this is accurate: Islamists, like almost all Muslims, regard the early years of Islam as a golden era, and they aspire to model their behavior after the Prophet Muhammad and his early followers, much as Christians idealize the example of Jesus.

Islamists seek to regain the righteousness of the early years of Islam and implement the rule of *shari'a*, either by using the state to enforce it as the law of the land or by convincing Muslims to abide by these norms of their own accord. Litmus-test issues for Islamists, as for traditional Muslims, include modest dress for women—ranging from headscarves to full veils—abstention from alcohol and other intoxicants, and public performance of prayers. However, Islamists have no wish to throw away electricity and other technological inventions. Most have graduated from modern schools, share modern values such as human equality and rule of law, and organize themselves along modern lines, using modern technologies and—some of them—the latest methods of warfare.

Indeed, radical Islamists have much in common with Islamic liberalism, another important movement in the Islamic world. Both Islamic liberals and radical Islamists seek to modernize society and politics, recasting tradition in modern molds. Both Islamist movements maintain that there are multiple ways of being modern, and that modernity is not limited to Western culture.

Islamists may ally themselves on occasion with traditionalist Islamic movements, and they may share certain symbols of piety, but they are quite distinct in sociological terms. Traditionalists such as the Taliban of Afghanistan, by contrast with Islamists such as bin Laden's Al Qaeda network, draw on less educated sectors of society, believe in mystical and personal authority, and are skeptical of modern organizational forms. For this reason, traditionalist movements are finding it increasingly difficult to survive in a competitive religious environment and occupy only isolated pockets of Muslim society. Modern movements have taken over the rest.

The Islamists' Roots in Secular Education

Start with bin Laden himself. Though he issued *fatwas* (religious judgments) as though he were a seminary-educated Islamic scholar, his training was in civil engineering. Similarly, many other Islamist leaders have university rather than seminary backgrounds: Hasan Turabi of the Sudan is a lawyer trained in Khartoum, London, and Paris; Necmettin Erbakan of Turkey studied mechanical engineering in West Germany; Hasan al-Banna of Egypt, who founded the first mass Islamist group, the Muslim Brotherhood, in the 1920s, was a teacher educated and employed in secular schools.

These leaders railed against seminary-trained scholars, the *'ulama*, for being obscurantist and politically inactive. Bin Laden lambasted the *'ulama* of Saudi Arabia as playing "the most ominous of roles.

Regardless of whether they did so intentionally or unintentionally, the harm that resulted from their efforts is no different from the role of the most ardent enemies of the nation." Even Islamist leaders with traditional seminary educations—such as Abu'l-'Ala Maudoodi of Pakistan, Ruhollah Khomeini of Iran, 'Abd al-Hamid Kishk of Egypt—frequently railed against their alma maters for similar reasons. Seminaries were considered so backward in Islamist eyes that for decades Maudoodi hid the fact that he had a seminary degree.

Not only the Islamist leaders but also the rank and file emerge disproportionately from secular universities. The classic study on this subject was performed in the late 1970s by Saad Eddin Ibrahim, the Egyptian sociologist who was recently jailed for his pro-democracy activities. Of the 34 imprisoned Islamist activists whom he interviewed, 29 had some college education. In a follow-up study in the 1990s, Ibrahim found the Islamist movement had added poorer and less educated members, but as political scientist Carrie Wickham has discovered through interviews with Islamists in Cairo, Islamist recruitment efforts are still geared toward university graduates in Egypt. Outside of Egypt, too, bin Laden's 1996 open letter identified "high school and university students" and the "hundreds of thousands of unemployed graduates" as prime targets for mobilization. The 19 alleged hijackers of September 11, 2001 included a city planner, a physical education instructor, a business student, a teacher, and two engineers; even the Saudi "muscle" among them were largely middle-class youths educated in state-run high schools.

Contrast this with the Taliban. Afghanistan's school system was virtually demolished in two decades of civil war, so the Islamists' usual constituency of educated young men was unavailable. Taliban leader Mullah Muhammad Omar had no advanced education. Other top officials had seminary backgrounds as well; according to reports, many were educated at the Haqqani seminary near Peshawar, Pakistan, and three of six members of the Taliban ruling council studied at the same seminary in Karachi. The foot soldiers were drawn largely from students at Haqqani and other refugee seminaries in Pakistan—hence the name *Taliban*, which means seminary students or seekers. (The singular is *talib*, so references to a single American Taliban are grammatically incorrect.) This force was created in large part by the Pakistani intelligence ministry, which is staffed at its higher ranks by well-educated Muslims from secular universities; it made an alliance with Al Qaeda, which also appears to draw on the highly educated. But these connections should not obscure the fact that the Taliban had an entirely different social base. According to an Egyptian Islamist, top officials of Al Qaeda considered their Afghan hosts to be "simple people" who lacked the "ability to grasp contemporary reality, politics and management."

Indeed, the rise of Islamist movements in the 20th century is closely associated with the sidelining of the seminary educational system. Beginning in Ottoman Turkey and Egypt in the early 19th century and ending in the 1950s with the Arab emirates of the Persian Gulf, states—colonial or local—have founded their own schools to operate in competition with the seminaries. At first these were small elite schools, designed to produce government officials. In the past two generations, however, state-run school systems have expanded to include significantly larger sectors of the population. In one sample of 22 Muslim-majority countries, 70 percent of adults had no formal education in 1960; by 1990, this figure had been reduced to 44 percent. In 1960, only four of these countries had more than 1 percent of the adult population with some higher education; in 1990, only four of these countries had less than 1 percent with some higher education. Seminaries have grown, too, in some countries; but even where seminarians control the state, as in the Islamic Republic of Iran, these schools remain marginal to the nation's educational system.

The growth of secular education has led expanding numbers of Muslims to approach religious questions without the skills—or blinders, depending on one's perspective—inculcated in the seminaries. College graduates have turned to the sacred texts and analyzed them in a sort of do-it-yourself theology, developing liberal interpretations in addition to radical ones. In Pakistan, for example, a study group of educated Muslim women met and produced a feminist interpretation, "For Ourselves: Women Reading the Koran" (1997). In North America, a gay convert to Islam produced a Web site called Queer Jihad that espoused tolerance for homosexuality. In Syria, a soil engineer named Muhammad Shahrour decided that traditional scholarship on the Koran was unscientific and that he had a better approach, one that happened to support liberal political positions. According to booksellers interviewed by anthropologist Dale Eickelman, Shahrour's tomes are best-sellers in the Arab world, even where they are banned.

In addition, governments have waded into the religious field throughout the Islamic world. In each country, the state has established its own official religious authorities, which may be pitted against every other state's religious authorities. Many states produce their own schoolbooks to teach Islamic values in the public schools. In Turkish textbooks, these values include secular government; in Saudi textbooks, these values include monarchy; in Palestine National Authority textbooks, according to a review by political scientist Nathan J. Brown, these values include the defense of the Palestinian homeland (though they do not, as often charged, include the destruction of Israel).

The result is a tremendous diversity of Islamic opinion and a corresponding diversity of Islamic authority. There is no universally recognized arbiter to resolve Islamic debates. For most of Islamic history, at least a symbolic arbiter existed: the caliph (*khalifa*), that is, the successor to the Prophet. Caliphs could never impose interpretive uniformity on all Muslims, although some were more inclined than others to try. But since the Turkish Republic abolished the Ottoman caliphate in 1924, even this symbol of authority is gone. Any college graduate in a cave can claim to speak for Islam.

Modern Goals, Modern Methods

Just as the social roots of Islamism are modern, so too are many of its goals. Do not be misled by the language of hostility toward the West. Islamist political platforms share significant planks with Western modernity. Islamists envision overturning tradition in politics, social relations, and religious practices. They are hostile to monarchies, such as the Saudi dynasty in Arabia; they favor egalitarian meritocracy, as opposed to inherited social hierarchies; they wish to abolish long-standing religious practices such as the honoring of relics and tombs.

Bin Laden, for example, combined traditional grievances such as injustice, corruption, oppression, and self-defense with contemporary demands such as economic development, human rights, and national self-determination. "People are fully occupied with day-to-day survival; everybody talks about the deterioration of the economy, inflation, ever-increasing debts and jails full of prisoners," bin Laden wrote in 1996. "They complain that the value of the [Saudi] *riyal* is greatly and continuously deteriorating against most of the major currencies."

These mundane concerns do not mean that Islamist states look just like Western states, but they are not entirely different, either. The Islamic Republic of Iran, for example, has tried to forge its own path since it replaced the Pahlavi monarchy in 1979. Yet within its first year it copied global norms by writing a new constitution, ratifying it through a referendum with full adult suffrage, holding parliamentary and presidential elections, establishing a cabinet system, and occupying itself with myriad other tasks that the modern world expects of a state, from infrastructure expansion to narcotics interdiction. The 1986 Iranian census conducted by the Islamic Republic was scarcely different from the 1976 census conducted by the monarchy. Similarly in Pakistan and the Sudan, where Islamic laws were introduced in the 1980s, there were changes, but there were also massive continuities. The modern state remained.

Contrast this continuity with the traditionalist Taliban. While most well-educated Islamists disdain relics as verging on idol worship, Taliban leader Mullah Muhammad Omar literally wrapped himself in the cloak of the Prophet—a cherished relic in Qandahar—one April day in 1996. While successful Islamist movements have ensconced themselves in the offices of their predecessors, Omar remained in his home province. The Taliban government reproduced a few of the usual ministries—foreign affairs, for example—but did not bother with most. The Taliban preferred informal and personal administration to the rule-bound bureaucracies favored by modern states.

Western bias tends to lump Khomeini's Iran and the Taliban's Afghanistan in the same category, and indeed both claimed to be building an Islamic state. However, one is a modern state and the other was not. Perhaps the most vivid distinction involved gender. While the Taliban barred girls from attending school, the Islamic Republic of Iran more than doubled girls' education from pre-revolutionary levels. While the Taliban barred women from working at most jobs, Iranian women entered the labor force in unprecedented numbers, as television anchors, parliamentary deputies, government typists, and sales clerks—even while dressed in headscarves and long coats. Iranian leaders were as outspoken as Western feminists in condemning Taliban policies on gender and other subjects and felt the Taliban were giving Islam a bad name.

The Taliban reintroduced tradition; Khomeini and other Islamists reinvented it. This process is entirely consistent with the "invention of tradition" identified by historians Eric Hobsbawm and Terence Ranger. The Victorians in England, for example, developed anthems, symbols, and a mythical lineage that they then projected backward in time, pretending that these were the outgrowth of an ancient tradition. Similarly, the Islamists' ideals of early Islamic society are contemporary constructions. The Islamists wish to return to God's law and the sacred practices of the first Muslims, but they downplay early Islamic practices such as slavery that are at odds with their modern values. In place of the clear social hierarchies in early Islam based on tribe, lineage, and seniority, Islamists emphasize human equality. In place of personal regimes, Islamists insist on codified law. In place of submission to authority, Islamists speak the language of individual rights. These modern values set Islamists apart from their precursors in earlier periods, such as Ibn Taymiyya in the 14th century and Muhammad Ibn 'Abd al-Wahhab and Shah Wali-Allah in the 18th century.

Not all Islamist demands are consonant with modern norms, of course. Islamists are openly hostile to certain elements of modernity in its Western forms, such as dating, decriminalized drug use, and separation of church and state. Moreover, certain high-profile Islamist goals such as corporal punishment, legalized polygyny, automatic male custody in divorce, restrictive garb for women, bans on heresy and apostasy, and judicial authority keyed to sacred texts are unpalatable to modern Western sensibilities. Yet even these demands are framed in the familiar modern idiom of rediscovering authenticity. The goal is to "Islamicize modernity," in the phrase of Moroccan Islamist leader Abdessalam Yassine: to forge an alternative modernity that combines basic elements of modernity with selected elements of Islamic heritage.

Ironically, the West, generally the underminer of tradition, now supports traditional elites in the Islamic world. The British and French installed monarchies in much of the Middle East after World War I. More recently, Western military might forced a republic to disgorge a monarchy—albeit a liberalized one—when Kuwait was liberated in 1991. Since that time, U.S. troops have been stationed in Saudi Arabia to defend an absolute monarchy. Bin Laden and other Islamists make repeated use of the irony: America, supposed proponent of democracy and rights, clings to a regime that detests these modern concepts.

Not just in ideology but also in practice, bin Laden and other radical Islamists mirror Western trends. They term their mobilization *jihad*, or sacred struggle, although many Muslims point out that the Prophet called struggle against others the "lesser jihad," with the internal struggle to lead a good life being the "greater jihad." Regardless of the ancient terminology, Al Qaeda and other Islamist groups operate globally like transnational corporations, with affiliates and subsidiaries, strategic partners, commodity chains, standardized training, off-shore financing and other features associated with contemporary global capital. Indeed, insiders often referred to Al Qaeda as the "company."

Documents discovered by *The New York Times* in Afghan training camps after Al Qaeda's departure show a bureaucratic organization with administrative lines of authority and an insistence on budgeting. Islamists use the latest high-tech skills, not just airplane piloting and transponder deactivation, as the world learned tragically on September 11, 2001, but also satellite phones, faxes, wired money orders, and the like. Mullah Muhammad Omar was so suspicious of modern technology that he refused to be photographed; bin Laden, by contrast, distributed videotapes of himself to the world's media.

Like other covert networks, such as mafiosi and narcotraffickers, Islamists organize themselves through informal personal ties. Political scientist Quintan Wiktorowicz was able to document this phenomenon among radical Islamists in Jordan, who allowed him to attend their illegal meetings. These activists are harassed by the security forces, frequently arrested, and barred from regular employment. In this repressive context their main avenue for collective action is to draw on friendship networks, people whom they trust to maintain the secrecy that their illegal activities require.

Some Islamists also benefit from "front" organizations that gain legitimacy and launder money. Indeed, some of these organizations do tremendous good works, such as supporting medical clinics in poor neighborhoods in Egypt, offering earthquake relief in Turkey, and mobilizing women into microenterprises in Yemen. Surprisingly, however, many of these welfare organizations are quite unsuccessful in mobilizing political support among the poor. Political scientist Janine Clark, who has conducted extensive fieldwork among these organizations in the Arab world, found that the beneficiaries of Islamic charity often receive such a pittance of financial aid that they are forced to seek benefits from other charities as well—state-run, missionary-run, secular, or otherwise—and have no particular loyalty to the Islamists.

Like other political movements, Islamists are divided as to how to achieve their goals. Some prefer a hearts-and-minds strategy, "calling" Muslims to increased piety. "There is no compulsion in religion," they argue, quoting the Koran, so conquering the state without preparing the populace is both morally impermissible and strategically foolhardy. Others argue that state conquest cannot be delayed. Oppression, foreign and domestic, operates through the state and can only be addressed at that level. But state-oriented Islamists are themselves divided: some seek to take power democratically, while others pursue putsches and terrorism. This division reveals one of the least-known aspects of the Islamist movement: for all their notoriety, Islamists remain unpopular among Muslims.

The Radical Minority

A minority of Muslims support Islamist organizations, and not just because they are illegal in many countries. There are only a handful of reputable surveys on the subject, but they show consistently that most Muslims oppose Islamists and their goals. Surveys in 1988 found that 46 and 20 percent of respondents in Kuwait and Egypt, respectively, favored Islamist goals in religion and politics. A 1986 survey in the West Bank and Gaza found 26 percent calling for a state based on *shari'a*, and polls in the same regions showed support for Hamas and other Islamist groups dropping from 23 percent in 1994 to 13 to 18 percent in 1996–97. A 1999 survey in Turkey found 21 percent favoring implementation of *shari'a*, consistent with other surveys in the mid-1990s. In a Gallup poll of nine Muslim societies at the end of 2001, only 15 percent of respondents said they considered the September 11 attacks to be morally justifiable.

When free or partially free elections are held, Islamists rarely fare well. Islamist candidates and parties have won less than 10 percent of the vote in Bangladesh, Egypt, Pakistan, and Tajikistan. They have won less than 25 percent of the vote in Egypt, Malaysia, Sudan, Tunisia, Turkey, and Yemen. Their best showings have been in Kuwait, where they won 40 percent of seats in 1999, and Jordan, where moderate Islamists won 43 percent of seats in 1989 before dropping to 20 percent in the next election. Virtually the only majority vote that Islamists have ever received was in Algeria in 1991, when the Islamic Salvation Front dominated the first stage of parliamentary elections, winning 81 percent of the seats; it was about to win the second stage of voting when the military annulled the elections and declared martial law.

In the few elections where Islamists fared relatively well, success followed from promises to abide by democratic norms. The Algerian Islamist leader 'Abbasi Madani, who earned a doctorate in education from the University of London, developed a Muslim Democrat position analogous to the Christian Democrat parties of Europe: culturally conservative but committed to democracy. "Pluralism is a guarantee of cultural wealth, and diversity is needed for development. We are Muslims, but we are not Islam itself," Madani said while campaigning. "We do not monopolize religion. Democracy as we understand it means pluralism, choice and freedom." These sentiments may have been insincere, but we will never know. A secular military regime barred Madani from office before he could develop a track record, just as secular military officials in Turkey removed Necmettin Erbakan as prime minister in 1997, after less than a year in office. Islamists now cite Algeria and Turkey while debating whether it is naive to think that they will ever be allowed to play by the same rules as other parties.

Still, when given a choice between liberal and radical Islamists, Muslim voters prefer the liberal. In Indonesia, Abdurrahman Wahid's liberal party received 17 percent of the vote in 1999, and Amien Rais's semi-liberal party received 7 percent, compared with 11 percent for the more radical United Development Party. In Kuwait in 1996 and 1999, more than twice as many candidates associated with the moderate Islamic Constitutional Movement were elected than candidates associated with the more hard-line Islamic Popular Movement. Most dramatically, in Iran, for years the role model for Islamists, the liberal reform movement swept a series of elections as soon as it was allowed to run against hard-liners: the presidency in 1997, city councils in 1998, parliament in 1999 and the presidency again in 2001. The reformists must still contend with other branches of government that the constitution sets aside as unelected. However, President Muhammad Khatami and his allies, all former radicals themselves, serve as high-profile defectors from the Islamist cause.

Islamists thus face a dilemma that is common to other radical movements of the past century: whether to water down their message to attract popular support or maintain a pure vision and mobilize a relatively small cadre. Like leftist splinter groups that rejected democratic socialism, bin Laden and his ilk have opted for the second path. Like radical leftists, radical Islamists fare best when the liberals are forcibly removed from the scene: by repressive regimes, as in Pahlavi-era Iran, contemporary Saudi Arabia, and elsewhere; or by the Islamists themselves, as in the Algeria, Chechnya, and Kashmir assassination campaigns, among others.

Sadly, the U.S.-led war on terrorism may inadvertently benefit the Islamists. This is the great debate among scholars of Islamic studies in the months since September 2001. Do the United States and its allies appear hypocritical in supporting autocrats in Muslim-majority countries while claiming to defend human rights and democracy? Will Muslims perceive the war on terrorism as evidence of Western hostility toward Islam? Will military action stoke Islamist radicalism or extinguish it?

In the short run, the war on terrorism has not generated the massive negative reaction among Muslims that some observers expected. Yet there is evidence to suggest that Islamism is gaining in popularity. Gallup polls of nine Muslim societies at the end of 2001 found that a majority considered the United States and the West to be hostile to Islam and Muslims. Since the beginning of 2002, Israel's military operations in Palestinian territories, with Western acquiescence, may have further radicalized Muslim attitudes.

Longer term approaches to the war on terrorism also face ambivalences. The modernization of Muslim societies, promoted by the United States and its allies as a buffer against traditionalism, may wind up fueling Islamism. Modern schools produce Islamists as well as liberals; modern businesses fund Islamist as well as other causes; modern communications can broadcast Islamist as well as other messages. Western culture, we are learning, is not the only form that modernity may assume.

Recommended Resources

Abou El Fadl, Khaled. *Rebellion and Violence in Islamic Law.* Cambridge, U.K.: Cambridge University Press, 2001. A thorough critique of Islamists' misuse of sacred sources as justification for terrorism.

Eickelman, Dale F., and James Piscatori. *Muslim Politics.* Princeton, N.J.: Princeton University Press, 1996. A valuable globe-trotting overview of variation in contemporary Muslim politics.

Ernst, Carl W. *Following Muhammad: An Introduction to Islam in the Contemporary World.* Boston: Shambala, 2002. A sensitive and insightful introduction to historical and contemporary developments in Islam.

Kurzman, Charles (ed.). *Liberal Islam: A Source-Book.* New York: Oxford University Press, 1998. An anthology of 32 influential writings, mostly late 20th century, by Muslims favoring democracy, multireligious coexistence, women's rights, and other liberal themes.

Kurzman, Charles (ed.). *Modernist Islam: A Source-Book, 1840–1940.* New York: Oxford University Press, 2002. An anthology of 52 influential writings by Muslims in the 19th and early 20th centuries favoring constitutionalism, nationalism, science, women's rights, and other modern values.

Lawrence, Bruce. *Shattering the Myth: Islam Beyond Violence.* Princeton, N.J.: Princeton University Press, 1998. A highly readable examination of key issues in contemporary Islamic debates.

Lubeck, Paul. "The Islamic Revival: Antinomies of Islamic Movements Under Globalization." In *Global Social Movements*, ed. Robin Cohen and Shirin M. Rai. New Brunswick, N.J.: Athlone Press, 2000. A provocative analysis linking economic globalization with global Islamic activism.

Wickham, Carrie. *Mobilizing Islam: Religion, Activism and Political Change in Egypt.* New York: Columbia University Press, 2002. The definitive work on Islamists in Egypt, documenting the methods through which secular university students are drawn to Islamist activism.

Wiktorowicz, Quintan. *The Management of Islamic Activism: Salafis, the Muslim Brotherhood, and State Power in Jordan.* Albany: State University of New York Press, 2001. A path-breaking study of radical Islamist groups in Jordan, based on extensive interviews with activists in illegal cells.

Part IV

Who Remains In Movements, and Who Drops Out?

Introduction

Recruiting activists and supporters is one obvious challenge that movements confront. Keeping these recruits active within the movement is quite another. Meeting this challenge is important because most movements need to work for many years or even decades to bring about desired changes. A movement that constantly needs to replace recruits who have dropped out is not likely to be very effective. And, of course, if too many people drop out and cannot be replaced, then the movement will decline or disappear altogether, an issue we take up more directly in part IX.

The reasons that people remain active in movements may be very different from the reasons they became involved in the first place. Recruits may greatly enjoy (or come to dislike!) their lives with other activists or movement supporters. The movement or movement organization may head in a direction that supporters either applaud or reject. Why people remain committed to a movement for some significant period of time, then, is a different question than asking why they joined in the first place; likewise, why some people drop out of movements is a different question than asking why some never joined in the first place.

> **Mass Society** Before the 1960s, most scholars took a dim view of protest. They preferred politics within normal institutional channels. They usually argued that people protested because they were swept up in irrational crowds, or because they had personality flaws for which they were trying to compensate. One popular theory claimed that people joined social movements when they had lost other organized contacts with the main institutions of their society, like clubs or churches. This makes them susceptible to demagogues like Lenin or Hitler. (The theory was heavily influenced by fears of communism and fascism.) In today's "mass society," people watch television as individuals, the argument goes, rather than going out and joining bowling leagues and volunteer groups. Few scholars still accept this argument, having shown that protestors are usually well integrated into their communities and social networks. See Kornhauser (1959).

Despite their importance, these questions have received less attention from scholars than the recruitment issue, but they have not been neglected altogether. The issue of commitment to a cause was taken up years ago by Rosabeth Moss Kanter (1972) in her study of nineteenth-century communes like Brook Farm and Oneida—communities that share a number of characteristics with social movements, including voluntary membership, idealism, and a rejection of certain aspects of the larger society (see also Hall 1988). Kanter emphasizes that commitment to a cause or group is simultaneously cognitive, affective, and moral—it involves people's beliefs, feelings, and moral judgments. Kanter catalogues a variety of "commitment mechanisms" that helped to keep people in the communes she studied, some of which lasted for many decades. Communes were more successful, for example, when they did not have to compete for their members' loyalties. The opportunities and temptations of the "outside world" would often pull people out of communes (just as they pull people out of movements), so they tried to insulate themselves in various ways, sometimes geographically. Radical movement groups, which generally demand a lot from their members, also typically try to limit members' relationships with outsiders. Of course, the heavy time commitment that some such groups require of their members has the same practical effect, although activists notoriously "burn out" if too much is demanded of them for too long.

Another threat to commitment which Kanter found came from within the communes themselves, namely the possibility that members would spend too much time with family, friends, or people to whom they were romantically or sexually attracted, neglecting their obligations to the larger group. To prevent this, communes often separated family members, raised children communally, and prohibited monogamous marriages. Movements also face the potential threat of "dyadic withdrawal," as when movement activists meet, fall in love, and gradually withdraw from public activities for the pleasures of a more private life (Goodwin 1997).

Leaders Research tends to focus on networks, organizations, and groups, but individuals matter to mobilization in many ways. Some social movement "organizations" are actually the work of a single person, even though she may be able to mobilize others for specific events. In more complex organizations, decisions at various levels are often made, in the end, by one or a few individuals. Some individuals become leaders because they are effective **brokers**, bringing together previously unconnected groups and organizations. In addition to these "influential" individuals, there are "symbolic" ones. A person such as Martin Luther King Jr. or Nelson Mandela may come to embody the aspirations, indignation, and other ideals of a movement in a way that can inspire members—or arouse opponents. This is one source of charisma.

Kanter also found that communes lasted longer the more they engaged in collective activities that forged a strong group identity and *esprit de corps*. Working, eating, singing, playing, praying, and making decisions together—all these activities, which movements also practice, helped to develop strong affective bonds among commune members as well as a strong moral commitment to their common enterprise. The reading by Eric Hirsch similarly emphasizes how collective "consciousness-raising" discussions and collective decisionmaking helped to build solidarity among members of a student movement opposed to university investments in South Africa. (Consciousness-raising groups were first popularized by the women's movement, especially its more radical wing, during the late 1960s and early 1970s.) Hirsch also argues that polarization and the escalation of conflict may build group solidarity as outside threats induce members to turn inward for mutual support and protection (intellectual, moral, and sometimes physical). The resulting "ideological purity" binds activists together, although it may also prevent them from understanding potential allies or making compromises (see the selection by Jane Mansbridge in part V).

The reading by Nancy Whittier explores how some women in Columbus, Ohio, continued to identify themselves as radical feminists, and remained committed to radical feminist principles, even though the women's movement as a whole had declined. They sustained their radical feminist identity through a number of mechanisms that overlap with those stressed by Hirsch: collective activities, including consciousness-raising groups and protest itself; interactions among a dense network of like-minded friends and acquaintances; the use of feminist language; and, interestingly, the ritual telling of "cautionary tales" about women who have "sold out" their feminist principles. These and other factors establish group boundaries between radical feminists and others.

Whittier suggests, however, that while group boundaries often become rigidified and exclusive when movements are in decline, the boundaries drawn by the radical feminists whom she studied generally became more permeable. Radical feminists became more accepting of and emotionally open to non-feminists and men, especially gay men.

In contrast to "nice" movements like these, Janja Lalich has written about cults that demand the full commitment—sometimes even the lives—of participants. Rescuing the idea of a "true believer" from older crowd and mass-society traditions, she shows that people become true believers, not because of their own personality flaws, but through group processes that remake people's views of the world, pressure them to obey charismatic leaders, and limit their perceived options. Although she discusses extreme types of groups, the same kinds of pressure for conformity are present in milder forms in all groups that depend on a serious time commitment by members.

Finally, Bert Klandermans explores why people disengage from movements, whether passively and unobtrusively or actively and loudly. Again, a variety of factors may push people to disengage, depending upon the movement they are in and their level of commitment to it. Unlike Hirsch, Klandermans suggests that polarization can lead people to pull out of a movement, rather than deepening their commitment to it. Sometimes people receive negative reactions from their "significant others" about their political commitments. (This is why communes and some movements try to limit contact with such people.) Disengagement often results from bad relationships—or few contacts at all—with fellow members. Activists often "burn out" from time-consuming and stressful work. People may withdraw from a movement organization when its strategy and tactics seem ill advised, although some then may jump to another group with a different strategy or tactics. Changes in the political environment may convince people that their enthusiasm for certain causes was misplaced or unrealistic.

Social scientists still have a lot to learn about why people stay in or pull out of movements, but the readings in this section make a good start.

Discussion Questions

1 What type of collective activities might help to sustain commitment to a particular movement? Might some such activities seem too demanding?
2 How might the escalation of a conflict between a movement and its opponents reinforce the solidarity of that movement? When might an escalating conflict lead people to disengage from a movement?
3 How do people sustain their commitment to a cause that has fallen upon hard times?
4 What traits and actions make a leader charismatic? Why do people follow him or her?
5 Why do activists "burn out"? What might movements do to prevent this?

10 Generating Commitment Among Students

Eric L. Hirsch

[...] This article develops an alternative perspective on recruitment and commitment to protest movements; it emphasizes the importance of the development of *political solidarity*, that is, support for a group cause and its tactics. Mobilization can then be explained by analyzing how group-based political processes, such as *consciousness-raising*, *collective empowerment*, *polarization*, and *group decision-making*, induce movement participants to sacrifice their personal welfare for the group cause. Empirical support for this perspective comes from a detailed analysis of a Columbia University student movement that demanded that the university divest itself of stock in companies doing business in South Africa.

[...]

Affective Ties Social relationships based on friendship or sexual attraction are often important in recruiting people to protest events and social movements, and these relationships also help to keep people in a group or movement once they have joined. (It is alleged, for example, that many young men became involved in the Reverend Jim Lawson's civil disobedience workshops in Nashville in order to be close to Diane Nash.) Such affective ties are thus an important component of "indigenous organization." These ties, however, may also hurt movements. Strong affective ties to people outside a movement may prevent one from joining that movement or developing a strong commitment to it; such ties, in other words, may make one biographically *un*available for protest. And people may meet in a movement, fall in love, and drop out, a phenomenon known as "dyadic withdrawal." See Goodwin (1997).

Impact of Group Processes

[...]

Consciousness-Raising

Potential recruits are not likely to join a protest movement unless they develop an ideological commitment to the group cause and believe that only non-institutional means can further that cause. Consciousness-raising involves a group discussion where such beliefs are created or reinforced. It may occur among members of an emerging movement who realize they face a problem of common concern that cannot be solved through routine political processes. Or it may happen in an ongoing movement, when movement activists try to convince potential recruits that their cause is just, that institutional means of influence have been unsuccessful, and that morally committed individuals must fight for the cause. Effective consciousness-raising is a difficult task because protest tactics usually challenge acknowledged authority relationships. Predisposing factors, such as prior political socialization, may make certain individuals susceptible to some appeals and unsympathetic to others.

Consciousness-raising is not likely to take place among socially marginal individuals because such isolation implies difficulty in communicating ideas to others. And it is not likely to happen among a group of rational calculators because the evaluation of society and of the chances for change is often influenced more by commitment to political or moral values than by self-interest calculations (Fireman and Gamson 1979; Ferree and Miller 1985). Consciousness-raising is facilitated in non-hierarchical, loosely structured, face-to-face settings that are isolated from persons in power; in such *havens* (Hirsch 1989), people can easily express concerns, become aware of common problems, and begin to question the legitimacy of institutions that deny them the means for resolving those problems.

Collective Empowerment

The recruitment and commitment of participants in a protest movement may also be affected by a group process called collective empowerment. While recruits may gain a sense of the potential power of a movement in consciousness-raising sessions, the real test for the movement comes at the actual protest site where all involved see how many are willing to take the risks associated with challenging authority. If large numbers are willing to sacrifice themselves for the movement, the chances for success seem greater; a "bandwagon effect" (Hirsch 1986) convinces people to participate in this particular protest because of its presumed ability to accomplish the movement goal. Tactics are more easily viewed as powerful if they are highly visible, dramatic, and disrupt normal institutional routines.

Polarization

A third important group process is polarization. Protest challenges authority in a way that institutional tactics do not because it automatically questions the rules of the decision-making game. The use of non-routine methods of influence also means that there is always uncertainty about the target's response. For these reasons, one common result of a protest is unpredictable escalating conflict. Each side sees the battle in black and white terms, uses increasingly coercive tactics, and develops high levels of distrust and anger toward the opponent.

Polarization is often seen as a problem since it convinces each side that their position is right and the opponent's is wrong; this makes compromise and negotiation less likely. Since it leads each side to develop the independent goal of harming the opponent, movement participants may lose sight of their original goal. Finally, escalation of coercive tactics by those in power can result in demobilization of the movement as individual participants assess the potential negative consequences of continued participation.

But if other group processes, such as consciousness-raising and collective empowerment, have created sufficient group identification, the protesters will respond to threats as a powerful, angry group rather than as isolated, frightened individuals. Under these circumstances, polarization can have a strong positive impact on participation (Coser 1956, 1967; Edelman 1971). The sense of crisis that develops in such conflicts strengthens participants' belief that their fate is tied to that of the group. They develop a willingness to continue to participate despite the personal risks because they believe the costs of protest should be collectively shared. Greater consensus on group goals develops because the importance of social factors in perception increases in an ambiguous conflict; protesters become more likely to accept the arguments of their loved fellow activists and less likely to accept those of their hated enemy. Because of the need to act quickly in a crisis, participants also become willing to submerge their differences with respect to the group's tactical choices.

Collective Decision-Making

Finally, collective decision-making often plays an important role in motivating the continuing commitment of movement participants. Movements often have group discussions about whether to initiate, continue, or end a given protest. Committed protesters may feel bound by group decisions made during such discussions, even when those decisions are contrary to their personal preferences. Participation in a protest movement is often the result of a complex group decision-making process, and not the consequence of many isolated, rational individual decisions.

The Columbia Divestment Campaign: A Case Study

The importance of these four group processes – consciousness-raising, collective empowerment, polarization, and group decision-making – in recruitment and commitment in a protest movement is illustrated by the Columbia University divestment protest. In April of 1985, several hundred Columbia University and Barnard College students sat down in front of the chained doors of the main Columbia College classroom and administrative building, Hamilton Hall, and stated that they would not leave until the university divested itself of stock in companies doing business in South Africa. Many students remained on this "blockade" for three weeks. This was a particularly good case for the analysis of movement recruitment and commitment because the majority of the participants in the protest had not been active previously in the divestment or other campus protest movements.

Protest actions of this kind can create problems for researchers because the organizers' need for secrecy often prevents the researcher from knowing of the event in advance. The best solution is to use as many diverse research methods as possible to study the movement after it has begun. I spent many hours at the protest site each day observing the activities of the protesters and their opponent, the Columbia administration. I also discussed the demonstration with participants and non-participants at the protest site, in classrooms, and other campus settings; and examined the many leaflets, position papers, and press reports on the demonstration.

During the summer of 1985, I completed 19 extended interviews, averaging one and one-half hours each, with blockaders and members of the steering committee of the Coalition for a Free South Africa (CFSA), the group that organized and led the protest. The interviews covered the protester's political background, previous experience in politics and protest movements, her/his experiences during the three weeks of the protest, and feelings about the personal consequences of participation. All quotes are taken from transcripts of these interviews.

[...]

Consciousness-Raising

The Coalition for a Free South Africa (CFSA) was founded in 1981 to promote Columbia University's divestment of stock in companies doing business in South Africa. It was a loosely structured group with a predominantly black steering committee of about a dozen individuals who made decisions by consensus, and a less active circle of about fifty students who attended meetings and the group's protests and educational events. The group was non-hierarchical, non-bureaucratic, and had few resources other than its members' labor. The CFSA tried to convince Columbia and Barnard students that blacks faced injustice under apartheid, that U.S. corporations with investments in South Africa profited from the low wages paid to blacks, that Columbia was an accomplice in apartheid because it invested in the stock of these companies, and that divestment would advance the anti-apartheid movement by putting economic and political pressure on the white regime of South Africa.

This consciousness-raising was done in a variety of small group settings, including dormitory rap sessions, forums, and teach-ins. Coverage of the CFSA's activities in the Columbia student newspaper and television reports on the violent repression of the anti-apartheid movement in South Africa increased student consciousness of apartheid and encouraged many students to support divestment.

Even in this early period, conflict between the CFSA and the Columbia administration affected the views of potential movement recruits. At first, the CFSA tried to achieve divestment by using traditional avenues of influence. In 1983, the organization was able to gain a unanimous vote for divestment by administration, faculty, and student representatives in the University Senate, but Columbia's Board of Trustees rejected the resolution. As one protester pointed out, that action was interpreted by many students as an indication that traditional means of influence could not achieve divestment:

> I remember in '83 when the Senate voted to divest. I was convinced that students had voiced their opinion and had been able to convince the minority of administrators that what they wanted was a moral thing. It hadn't been a bunch of radical youths taking buildings and burning things down, to destroy. But rather, going through the system, and it seemed to me that for the first time in a really long time the system was going to work. And then I found out that it hadn't worked, and that just reaffirmed my feelings about how the system at Columbia really did work.

The result of CFSA's extensive organizing work was that many students were aware of the oppressed state of blacks in South Africa, the call for divestment by anti-apartheid activists, and the intransigence of the university President and Trustees in the face of a unanimous vote for divestment by the representative democratic body at the university.

Collective Empowerment: The Initiation of the Blockade

In the next phase of the movement, the CFSA sponsored rallies and vigils to call attention to the intransigence of the Trustees. Few students attended these demonstrations, probably because few supporters believed they would result in divestment. Deciding that more militant tactics were necessary, the CFSA steering committee began to plan a fast by steering committee members and a takeover of a campus building. The plan called for chaining shut the doors of the building and blocking the entrance with protesters; this, it was assumed, would lead to a symbolic arrest of a few dozen steering committee members and other hard-core supporters of divestment. The intent was to draw media coverage to dramatize the continuing fight for divestment.

Because they had worked hard on publicity, the steering committee of CFSA expected a large turnout for their initial rally, but fewer than 200 students gathered at the Sundial in the center of campus on the morning of April 4. Speeches were made by a local political official, a representative of the African National Congress, several black South African students, and members of the CFSA steering committee. Many of those interviewed had been at the rally, but none felt that the speeches were any more or less inspiring than speeches they had heard at previous CFSA events.

At the conclusion of the speeches, nearly all of those present agreed to follow one of the CFSA steering committee members on a march around campus. Most expected to chant a few anti-apartheid and pro-divestment slogans and return to the Sundial for a short wrap-up speech. Instead, they were led to the steps in front of the already-chained doors at Hamilton Hall. The protesters did not understand at first why they had been led to this spot, and few noticed the chained doors.

The steering committee member then revealed the day's plan, stating that this group of protesters would not leave the steps until the university divested itself of stock in companies doing business in South Africa. At least 150 students remained where they were; no one recalls a significant number of defections. Within two hours, the group on the steps grew to over 250.

Why did so many students agree to participate in this militant protest? The CFSA steering committee did not have an answer. Student participation in their relatively safe rallies and vigils had been minimal, so they certainly did not expect hundreds to join a much riskier act of civil disobedience. According to one steering committee member:

> Needless to say, I was quite startled by the events of April 4. By noon, there must have been hundreds more people than I expected there would be. I was hoping for 50 people, including the hard core. We would all get carted off, and whatever obstacles were blockading the door would be cut, removed, or thrown up. That's what everyone was expecting. We would have a story written and the press would report that we had done this. Jesus Christ, what happened that day was absolutely mind boggling! I still haven't gotten over it.

It was hard for anyone to predict the high level of mobilization based on the prior actions and attitudes of the participants because so few had been active in the divestment movement prior to April 4. Only 9 percent of the random sample of students reported that they had been at least somewhat active in the divestment movement, yet 37 percent participated in blockade rallies and/or slept overnight on the steps of Hamilton Hall. In fact, these students did not know that they would join this militant protest until it was actually initiated.

It is unlikely that the decision to participate was due to a narrow individual cost/benefit analysis including such costs as the time involved and the definite possibilities of arrest and/or disciplinary action by the university. Regarding personal benefits, it is hard to see how any Columbia student could gain from the divestment of South Africa-related stock.

Rather, participation was due to a belief in the cause and the conviction that this protest might work where previous CFSA actions had failed. Consciousness-raising had convinced these students of the importance of divestment, but they had not participated in the movement because they did not believe its tactics would work. Once several hundred were in front of the doors, many demonstrators felt that such a large group using a dramatic tactic would have the power to call attention to the evils of apartheid and cause the university to seriously consider divestment:

> Often when I would see a rally, I'd think that here was a bunch of people huffing and puffing about an issue who are going to be ignored and things are going to go on just as they were before this rally. The fact that there were a couple of hundred people out there with the purpose of altering the way the University does business gave me the feeling that this would be noticed, that people would pay attention.

The belief in the potential power of the tactic was reinforced by the willingness of several leaders of the movement to sacrifice their individual interests to achieve divestment. Two black South African students who spoke at the rally faced the possibility of exile or arrest and imprisonment upon their return home. About half a dozen CFSA steering committee members had fasted for nearly two weeks simply to get a meeting with the university President and Trustees; two of these students were eventually hospitalized. As one blockader testified:

> The fasters were doing something that personally took a lot of willpower for them, and that gave you a little extra willpower. To have to go into the hospital because you were off food for fifteen days, and the Trustees won't even speak to you. It really made me angry at the Trustees, so I was determined that this was not something that was just going to wimper off. At least I was going to be there, and I know others felt the same way.

The leaders of the protest recruited participants by taking personal risks that demonstrated their own commitment to the cause and to this particular tactic; other students in the blockade ignored individual interests in favor of the cause as well.

> I do think it has something to do with the support of peers, just seeing that there were people who were willing to extend themselves and put their own asses on the line. I guess it's the self-sacrifice aspect of it that appealed to me, that really drew my attention. These people were willing to sacrifice their own personal interests in a big way, or a larger way than usual. That's something that hit a chord with me. It was the degree to

which people were willing to give up self-interest.

Another factor influencing participation may have been the fact that the protesters were not forced to decide to join the protest at all. Instead, they were led as a group to a position in front of the doors, unaware that this was an act of civil disobedience; the only decision to be made was whether or not to leave the protest. Although this was done because CFSA did not want to reveal its plans to campus security prematurely, the unintended consequence was to maximize participation; it was difficult for demonstrators to leave the steps because of the public example of self-sacrificing black South Africans and the fasters.

Of course, each protester had many less public opportunities to leave the protest during the three weeks after April 4th. Most stayed, partly because of growing evidence of the power of this tactic. The protest soon gained the public support of a variety of groups locally and nationally, including Harlem community groups and churches, the Columbia faculty, unions on and off the campus, the African National Congress, and the United Nations. Students on other campuses engaged in similar protests. This support made the blockaders believe that their challenge to the authority of the Columbia administration was moral, necessary, and powerful. One blockader described this as being "part of something that was much larger than myself." Another suggested:

One thing I believe now is that people in a grassroots movement can actually have an impact, that we're not all completely helpless. I guess it was that sense of power that I didn't have before.

Polarization and Increased Commitment

Because the blockade was an unconventional attempt to gain political influence, the steering committee of CFSA was unable to predict how many would participate. For the same reason, they were unable to predict their opponent's reaction to their tactic. Based on the information they had on recent South African consulate and embassy protests, they assumed they would be arrested soon after the doors of Hamilton Hall were chained. As these expectations of a mostly symbolic arrest were communicated to the less politically experienced blockaders, a consensus developed that the blockade would be short-lived.

However, the administration did not order the arrest of the protesters. Instead, Columbia's President sent a letter to everyone at the university arguing that the students were "disruptive" and "coercive," and that they were trying to impose their will on the rest of the university. He suggested that "countless avenues of free speech" in the university community were open to them and that what they were doing was illegal, that divestment would probably hurt rather than help blacks in South Africa, and that the university was doing all it could to fight apartheid.

University officials began to videotape the protesters in order to prosecute them under university regulations on obstructing university buildings and disrupting university functions. They sent letters threatening suspension or expulsion to the members of the CFSA steering committee and a few others. Guarantees were given that those who reported for individual disciplinary hearings would be treated more leniently than those who did not. They also obtained a court order calling on participants in the blockade to cease and desist.

By threatening suspensions and expulsions, the administration had raised the stakes; the protesters felt much more threatened by these academic penalties than by symbolic arrests. There were other costs associated with participating in this protest, including dealing with the cold and freezing rain; missing classes, exams, and study time; and losing close relationships with non-blockaders. Ignoring these costs, the steering committee members who received letters refused to go to the disciplinary hearings, suggested that the administration was engaging in unfair selective prosecution, and reiterated their determination to remain in front of Hamilton Hall until the university divested.

Such actions were to be expected from the strongly committed CFSA steering committee. The surprise was that the less experienced majority of protesters also refused to be intimidated and remained on the blockade. They did so in part because of an example of self-sacrifice by one of their own. One of the politically inexperienced students, a senior with three weeks to go before graduation, received a letter threatening him with expulsion. Initially, he was scared:

> I was petrified, especially since Columbia has not been fun for me but rather painful. I really wanted to get out of here, and I was horrified by the thought that I would either have to come back to Columbia or go somewhere else and lose credits by transfering. My reaction was, "Why do they have to pick me? Why do I have to be the focal point of this whole thing?"

But he decided not to report for disciplinary action. He felt that he could not give in to his fears in the face of the sacrifices being made by the fasters and South African students.

> Listening to the commitment on the part of the steering committee people who had received letters made me feel bad that I even considered leaving the blockade. One other factor was the fasters, the fact that there were South Africans involved in it, and that these people had more on the line than I did. I felt like I could not let these people down. I also felt that I was a sort of representative of a lot of people on the blockade and I felt I could not set a precedent by leaving and backing down.

His example was extremely important for the maintenance of commitment by the other inexperienced blockaders:

> They threatened (the blockader) with expulsion. It was sobering in a way. But it helped bond us together. It was stupid to do that because it just made people more furious, and it made people more resolved to stay. We just said we're not going to let him be expelled. We're all going to stick together in this.

The protesters responded as a group to administration threats, not as isolated individuals. Individual concerns about disciplinary actions were now secondary; each blockader saw her or his welfare as tied to the group fate. Paradoxically, the potential for high personal costs became a reason for participation; protesters wanted to be part of an important and powerful movement and they did not want fellow activists to face the wrath of the authorities alone. The night the threat of arrest was assumed to be greatest, Easter Sunday, was also the one night out of twenty-one with the greatest number sleeping out on the blockade. Soon after this, 500 students signed a statement accepting personal responsibility for the blockade.

Collective Decision-Making and the End of the Blockade

Another group process which influenced participation in this protest was collective decision-making. Open-ended rap sessions among the blockaders, lasting up to four or five hours, were begun after administration representatives delivered the first disciplinary letters to the protesters. In all cases, a serious attempt was made to reach consensus among all those on the steps; votes were held on only a few occasions. One of the main questions was whether to continue the protest. This discussion was initiated by members of the CFSA steering committee because of their commitment to democratic decision-making, and because they understood that the blockaders would be more likely to continue the protest if they participated in a collective decision to do so. During the first two weeks of the protest, the consensus was to continue the blockade.

By the third week, though, some of the protesters began to feel that the protest should be ended. The sense of crisis had been dulled by the lack of action by the administration to back up their threats. It was now clear that there were no plans to call in the police to make arrests. As one blockader put it, the "university's policy of waiting it out was becoming effective." Also, an event can be news for only so long, and the image of Columbia students sitting on some steps became commonplace. Diminishing television and print coverage reduced the collective belief in the power of this particular tactic. As one protester suggested:

> It was during the third week that I started spending nights at home and coming up in the morning. During the last week I probably spent three nights out [on the steps] and four nights at home. During that third week a kind of mood of lethargy hit, and it became a chorelike atmosphere. There was a lot of feeling that it was kind of futile to stay out there.

In the face of declining participation, long and heated discussions were held about ending the protest. Proponents of continuing the action argued that protesters ought to honor their commitment to stay in front of the doors until Columbia divested. Those who advocated ending the protest argued that divestment was not imminent and that the blockade was no longer effective. As one protester put it:

> The blockade ended because a very thoughtful and carefully planned decision was made. It was a question of what we could do that would be most effective for divestment. We decided that the blockade had done a lot, but at this point other things would be better, seeing how the administration was willing to sit us out.

On the 25th of April, the blockade officially ended with a march into Harlem to a rally at a Baptist Church. Five months later, the Columbia Trustees divested.

[...]

Conclusion

[...]

Years of well-organized activities by the CFSA were crucial in raising consciousness about the apartheid issue and on the need for noninstitutional means of influence to achieve divestment. The blockade itself was initiated only after two months of careful planning by the CFSA steering committee.

The blockaders were not just isolated individuals with preferences for divestment nor a set of confused, insecure people; rather, they were people who had been convinced by CFSA meetings that apartheid was evil, that divestment would help South African blacks, and that divestment could be achieved through protest. They joined the blockade on April 4th because it appeared to offer a powerful alternative to previously impotent demonstrations and because of the example of self-sacrificing CFSA leaders. The solidarity of the group increased after the administration's escalation of the conflict because group identification among the protesters was already strong enough so that they responded to the threat as a powerful group rather than as powerless individuals. Protesters remained at this long and risky protest partly because of the democratic decision-making processes used by the group.

This analysis of the 1985 Columbia University divestment protest indicates that useful theories of movement mobilization must include insights about how individual protesters are convinced by group-level processes to sacrifice themselves for the cause. This means asking new kinds of questions in movement research: What kinds of arguments in what kinds of settings convince people to support a political cause? Why do potential recruits decide that non-institutional means of influence are justified and necessary? Under what circumstances is the example of leaders sacrificing for the cause likely to induce people to join a risky protest? Why do some tactics appear to offer a greater chance of success than others? Under what conditions do threats or actual repression by authorities create greater internal solidarity in a protest group? Under what conditions do threats or repression result in the demobilization of protest? What kinds of group decision-making processes are likely to convince people to continue to participate in a protest movement?

Generalizing from case studies is always difficult. Some aspects of student movements make them unusual, especially the ability of organizers to take advantage of the physical concentration of students on campuses. But the important impact of group processes on movement recruitment and commitment is not unique to the 1985 Columbia anti-apartheid movement. The development of solidarity based on a sense of collective power and polarization was also found in a Chicago community organization (Hirsch 1986). And these same group processes were crucial in the mobilization and development of the Southern civil rights movement of the 1950s and 1960s. Consciousness-raising occurred in black churches and colleges. The collective power of protest was evident to those who participated in bus boycotts, sit-ins, freedom rides, and in Freedom Summer. The movement relied heavily on the creation of polarized conflict between the white Southern segregationist elite and black protesters to recruit participants, to gain national media attention, and ultimately to force federal intervention to redress the social and political grievances of Southern blacks (McAdam 1982; Morris 1984).

References

Coser, Lewis. 1956. *The Functions of Social Conflict*. New York: Free Press.

——. 1967. *Continuities in the Study of Social Conflict*. New York: Free Press.

Edelman, Murray. 1971. *Politics and Symbolic Action*. New York: Academic.

Ferree, Myra Marx and Frederick D. Miller. 1985. "Mobilization and Meaning: Toward an Integration of Social Psychological and Resource Perspectives on Social Movements." *Sociological Inquiry* 55: 38–61.

Fireman, Bruce and William Gamson. 1979. "Utilitarian Logic in the Resource Mobilization Perspective." Pp. 8–44 in *The Dynamics of Social Movements*, edited by Mayer N. Zald and John D. McCarthy. Cambridge: Winthrop.

Hirsch, Eric L. 1986. "The Creation of Political Solidarity in Social Movement Organizations." *Sociological Quarterly* 27: 373–87.

——. 1989. *Urban Revolt: Ethnic Politics in the Nineteenth Century Chicago Labor Movement*. Berkeley, Cal.: University of California Press.

McAdam, Douglas. 1982. *Political Process and the Development of Black Insurgency*. Chicago: University of Chicago.

Morris, Aldon. 1984. *The Origins of the Civil Rights Movement*. New York: Free Press.

11 Sustaining Commitment Among Radical Feminists

Nancy Whittier

Remaining Radical Feminists

What does it mean to say that a political generation has retained a radical feminist collective identity? In terms of practices – women's real lives – it means that participants have kept in touch with each other, believe they have things in common that they do not share with others, hold fast to central tenets of feminist ideology, and think of themselves as "radical feminist" and therefore different from the mainstream. Virtually all the women I interviewed continue to identify with the term "feminist" and most with "radical feminist," and this identification remains important to them. "If someone asks me, 'Who are you?' I'm a radical feminist," declared a woman who now works for a public interest organization. "And I see radical feminism as my life's work, even though I'm spending most of my days, most of my weeks, most of my years, doing something else." Seeing oneself this way still sets women apart from the majority of the population. As one woman succinctly put it, "Like most radical feminists, I'm really odd wherever I go." This "oddness" stems from her beliefs or consciousness and from her membership in a distinct group of women's movement veterans. Radical feminists' political consciousness about the world and their construction of group boundaries both set them apart from others and bind them together. I will first discuss consciousness and how it has changed, then turn to group boundaries and their changes.

Feminist Consciousness

Developing feminist consciousness was, and is, a central task of the radical women's movement. Most movements possess a formal body of writings and scholarship that communicate interpretive frameworks and explain the group's position in the social structure, and members also interweave political understandings into their daily life and interactions. The radical women's movement of the 1970s took the meshing of politics and everyday life to a new height. In consciousness-raising groups and other

> **Collective Identity** Before members of any group can present "their" demands to authorities or strategize about how "they" can best bring about desired changes, they need to know who "they" are. In whose name do activists speak? Feeling part of a broader group can be exhilarating, providing a major incentive for collective action. Some collective identities are widely accepted, and activists can take them for granted. Martin Luther King, Jr., for example, did not have to persuade African-Americans who lived in Birmingham in 1955 that they faced discrimination by virtue of their skin color. Under other circumstances, however, activists have to work hard to get a certain category of people to think of themselves as belonging to a group with distinctive problems and interests. Collective identities such as "Hispanic" or "gay" (or "queer") do not always come naturally to people (that is, they do not always result from ordinary, everyday interactions). These identities may have to be consciously created, and in fact they are often as much a result as a cause of protest. Some collective identities, in fact, are based solely on participation in a movement, such as "animal protectionist" or "human rights activist." Even a favored tactic can provide an identity, as with those who espouse nonviolent "direct action." And membership in an organization is also a potential basis for collective identity.

settings, women discussed their experiences and politics with the aim of rethinking their understandings of the world. From this work grew elaborate theoretical frameworks that explained women's oppression, male dominance, and patriarchy, and politicized all aspects of life with the notion of the personal as political.

In the late 1970s, WAC's (Women's Action Collective, a radical feminist group in Columbus, Ohio, founded in 1971) orientation sessions were a political education for many women that included analyzing their own experiences through a feminist framework and constructing and learning theoretical analyses. As one woman explained, "It taught me everything I know about feminism, racism, classism." Whether individuals experienced "consciousness raising" through a consciousness-raising group, in the course of protest, or through a political orientation session, these transforming experiences forever changed the way a generation of feminist activists looked at the world. As one succinctly put it, "It's like once you realize that the world is round, you can never again believe that it's flat."

Most women I interviewed were emphatic that the beliefs they formed during the women's movement had endured, although they were aware of the popular stereotype of 1960s radicals selling out. A woman who has not remained active in feminist organizations maintained that her feminist principles still exist, saying, "We continued to believe that a better world is possible, that we do need a creation of a new culture." Another woman, who became part of WAC in the mid-1970s, explained that the women's movement had a lasting and profound effect on how she looks at the world despite her belief that feminism is now in "the doldrums."

> It helped me learn how to construct principles.... And that was in a sense the beginning of a real life for me, of choosing to live a principled life.... And so, even if the doldrums continue forever and ever, I am light years ahead of them, personally.

Participating in consciousness-raising groups, activist organizations, and political actions such as boycotts or pickets gave women a new interpretation of themselves and the events around them. A former member of WAC explained how her feminist framework grew from consciousness-raising groups.

> Everything that happens in the world, I have a framework for understanding it. And that framework comes from the consciousness raising first, and understanding women's common experiences and my own experiences and the validity of that, and then seeing the rest of that through that validity.... If I didn't have a feminist framework to look at the world, I'd be, like most people, kind of adrift.

The women's movement developed highly complex interpretive frameworks. Feminist theory analyzes the sources and operation of patriarchy and male dominance, women's economic and social oppression, violence against women, the links between sexism and racism and classism, the role of homophobia in perpetuating female subordination, and a variety of other phenomena. Such analyses are widespread in written works but are not limited to the printed page. Women's movement organizations in Columbus and elsewhere discussed and refined feminist theory as part of their daily operation, and activists were sufficiently well-versed in feminist analysis to explain the reasons for a demonstration to the press, argue with each other, and interpret their own lives in light of feminist theory in consciousness-raising groups. The large number of discussion groups that emerged in the late 1970s around specific issues such as women and economics, the workplace, radical feminism, and white supremacy are a testimonial to the importance of theory to the women's movement. An antirape activist explained the centrality of theory development to WAC strategy during the 1970s.

> In the [Women's Action] Collective when we were doing theory [we used the process

> of] trying to figure out what you are doing by starting with your metaprinciples, and then going down to your principles, and then your objectives, and your goals, and then your strategies, and then your tactics. Everything relates back up to your metaprinciple, which in the case of rape prevention was respect for persons. The easiest way to get rid of rape would be to kill all the men, but that's not respectful of persons, therefore you can't do it. You have to keep going up and down this, to try to figure out. Whatever you do is going to be principled.

Theory remained important. Many respondents reported forming discussion groups in the late 1980s and early 1990s on topics including feminist theory, women and economics, feminist art criticism, and "How do we keep hanging on?" in hard times.

Despite the complexity of feminist theory, the lasting beliefs that respondents attributed to their participation in the women's movement were a general ethic of personal responsibility, egalitarianism, skepticism, freedom, and a policy of treating others well. Just over half of the women I talked to spontaneously mentioned the Golden Rule ("Do unto others as you would have them do unto you") as part of their core values. Although the Golden Rule was part of feminist ideology earlier in the century, its biblical origins make it widely known and consistent with mainstream culture. Yet longtime feminists translated it into a radical political context. The following statements by three different women illustrate the broad definitions of feminist principles.

> Just nonsexist, nonracist, nonclassist, treating people fairly, nonhomophobic, all those -isms.... Mostly, I just try to use the Golden Rule, I guess. I just try to treat people the same way I would want them to treat me.

> That ethic of the sixties is very egalitarian, political, and realizing there's politics in everything personal. And not always believing what your government says, and questioning everything. And questioning authority above all.

> I still have the same idealism. I'd still like people to be free to do what they want, and I'd still like people to have choices, and I'd like us all to be working on important issues. Bringing peace to the world, ending war.

Respondents have not forgotten or disregarded the more specific and complex elements of feminist consciousness over the years. Rather, they take for granted the application of feminist theory to specific topics. Feminist analyses of rape, for example, as an act of violence rather than sex, of sexual harassment, and of sexism in advertising, have become so intrinsic to participants' views of the world that they did not articulate them when I asked about their feminist principles.

Most respondents thought that their feminist beliefs have been a positive force in their lives, even in the 1980s and 1990s, when support for radical feminism made them increasingly politically marginal. One activist described the far-reaching effects.

> I think it's made me stronger. I think it's made me really clear about who I am. It's made me very clear about what the problems are that women face in society.... I almost feel like my life has a theme. It's not just like I'm this little ant out there living and working with all the other ants on the anthill. There are things that I care really, really deeply about, and that sort of infuses my whole life with meaning. And I've retained that, and I think I always will.

Attributing the difficulties in one's life to structural rather than personal causes (seeing the personal as political) is an important component of oppositional consciousness and helps motivate people to participate in collective action aimed at changing their circumstances. It also makes daily life easier for respondents and motivates activism, as one woman who is now a professor explained.

> If you really understand that the problems are out there, instead of blaming yourself, it makes you willing to take more risks. It makes you more motivated to fight the

> motherfuckers!... If I didn't have that base to latch onto, I would just go nuts.

A few respondents, however, felt that their feminist beliefs, although accurate, made their lives more difficult. As one woman who has not remained active in feminist organizations explained:

> From becoming active in the women's movement...I've gotten a different perspective on politics and how government is conducted, how business is conducted, almost everything that goes on in our society. And I don't like a lot of what I see. Much of what I see is extremely disturbing. Some of it frightens me or depresses me or angers me. And there are times that I wish I had never joined that first women's CR group and learned to look at the world differently.

Despite her regrets, she, too, has been changed irrevocably. Yet there have been some important changes in feminist consciousness as well as continuities over the past two decades.

Changes in Consciousness

Reflecting changes in the larger women's movement, respondents reported that they have become less concerned with "political correctness," or taking a strict political line on everything. Instead, they criticize some features of the 1960s–1970s movement, view feminism as broader and encompassing a variety of social reform issues, and are more aware of race and class differences. One woman articulated the declining significance of political correctness, commenting, "I don't look at life now in terms of feminism and what's politically correct and what's not." This remark must be placed in the larger social context of the 1990s, where a backlash against multiculturalism has taken the form of attacks on so-called mandated political correctness within universities. It has become unfashionable and perhaps politically dangerous to appear to be overly concerned with language use, subtle forms of discrimination, verbal harassment, and the like.

Nevertheless, many participants reacted against what they perceived as the excess and mistakes of the women's movement in the 1970s. Many singled out collective structure as an experiment they did not want to repeat. One former member of WAC proclaimed that she no longer believed in the collective process.

> To be honest, we got really sick of consensual decision making...Some of us feel like, I wouldn't go to a meeting if that was the way it was going to be! I don't want to be part of it, I have no patience with it.

Another WAC veteran commented in a similar vein:

> We did a lot of experimentation with the collective process, thinking that was the ideal structure, and found out that it wasn't. And now, I wouldn't be involved in a collective if you paid me a million bucks. Absolutely not!

Participants' reactions against perceived errors in the women's movement of the 1970s have led not only to disillusionment but to new and perhaps more effective organizational structures as well. "I've got to have radicals [on the board of directors] who at this point are so mellow on their own stuff that they're going to say to me, 'It's your vision, do what you want. Run with it...,' " explained a woman who founded a feminist organization in the 1980s. "I wanted some way to counter the fact that we got so bound up by the end of the seventies. We've got to give women the chance in their lifetimes to fly, and this is mine." Further, some women commented that they simply wanted their lives to be less serious than in the 1970s. "We had some fun in the seventies, but we were also quite grim a lot of the time," commented one woman about her changing approach to activism. "And I want to have some good times for the rest of my life. I want to do some fun things."

A second major change in the women's movement in the 1980s and 1990s has been an increase in attention to differences among women, particularly to issues of race and class. Sustainers and others began discussing race and class in the late 1970s. These discussions and feminist writings by women of color changed the outlook of the entire political generation. Longtime feminists reported a growing awareness that women are not an undifferentiated group and reflected critically on the race and class homogeneity of the women's movement in the 1960s and 1970s. One woman described the changes in her consciousness as follows:

> Back in the Ohio days I would have described myself as a radical feminist and since then I'd describe myself as a socialist feminist... [In the early 1980s] we started wondering why we were all white, and what was wrong... So I had a heavy infusion of thinking about race and class. It means that instead of viewing women as this undifferentiated group that are oppressed more or less equally by men, there are differences of class as well as race.

Only three of the women I interviewed reported that their identification had changed from radical to socialist feminist, but most reported an increasing concern with race and class.

A third change is a broadening of the goals and analyses of feminism. The women I interviewed increasingly define feminism as encompassing other struggles such as peace, environmental protection, animal rights, humanism, lesbian and gay freedom, socialism, and human rights. One woman who has become involved with the movement for recovery from addictions articulated the shift in her consciousness this way:

> I haven't forgotten the women's movement. But to me it's a piece of this larger issue, in which we need to think about how all people can be empowered, as who they are. It's the feminist criticism, I think, that has expanded our consciousness to the point where we can even see that there's a problem. But I guess I don't see feminism as my guiding call anymore. It's sort of part of the whole picture.

[...]

The broadening of concerns and the increasing incorporation of race and class issues do not signify a drastic or discontinuous shift in feminist consciousness for this generation. Rather, respondents are applying the basic principles of feminist consciousness to additional issues. In addition, women who came to the women's movement from the New Left are returning to some of their earlier concerns and examining them in a feminist light. When asked if her beliefs or view of the world had changed over the past twenty years, almost every interviewee first answered, "No," and then described some shifts. In other words, the core of feminist consciousness has remained consistent for this generation although there have been modifications. As one woman said, "I still retain my feminist principles absolutely, although they have evolved and changed."

Group Boundaries

Although participants construct their consciousness interactively in a movement context, individuals internalize it. Much of the foregoing evidence addresses this individual level. But collective identity is about far more than consciousness. At root it is about seeing oneself as part of a group, a collectivity. The mechanism by which this is accomplished is the construction of group boundaries, or symbolic and material distinctions between members of the collectivity and others. Participants establish group boundaries through a symbolic system and by constructing an alternative culture or network that serves as a "world apart" from the dominant society. These manifestations of collective identity are visible in interactions among group members and in the actions of individuals; they are not limited to the attitudes or beliefs of individuals.

The notion of group boundaries may imply rigid delineation of who is permitted to be a feminist. But in fact it refers to a much more ambiguous process by which people try to make sense of their lives and of their similarities to and differences from others. Group boundaries can be rigid or permeable and vary in their importance. For longtime feminist activists, boundaries between themselves and others became less important in the 1980s even as their sense of self remained inextricably linked to feminism. Boundaries have both persisted and been transformed between feminists and nonfeminists, women and men, and different political generations. A network of relationships among feminist veterans helps them to maintain their collective identity.

Distinguishing feminists from nonfeminists. Despite rhetoric of sisterhood, the "we" defined by radical feminists twenty-five years ago did not include all women. The labels "feminist" and "radical feminist" distinguished between women who adopted such labels and those who did not. For participants, a transformed individual identity as a woman meant seeing oneself as a member of the collectivity "feminists"; adopting "feminist" or "radical feminist" as a public identity signified membership in the group of women who had experienced such a transformation.

Despite the continuing importance of feminism for self-definition, the distinction between feminists and nonfeminists has become less significant in two ways. First, many women I interviewed said that they are less likely to form negative impressions of people who do not identify publicly as feminists. As one woman who now leads workshops on sexual harassment put it:

> I'm much kinder to women who aren't feminists and who are deferring to men when it's clearly against their best interests. I'm much better in discussing it with her and helping her overcome that than I would have been five years ago. Fifteen years ago I would have kind of jumped down her throat, and she would have had to avoid me. [*Laughs*]

Another woman, now a lawyer, remarked that she, too, is less critical of those who differ politically from her.

> I used to size people up in two minutes concerning their politics, and if their politics weren't right, I didn't have any use for them. I would cast them aside and be on my way...And that was stupid, and I've stopped doing that.

In other words, the boundary between feminists and nonfeminists has become more permeable, and feminists are willing to cooperate more with those outside the group.

Second, many longtime feminists reported that they are less likely to see themselves as part of a common group with someone simply because she calls herself a feminist. As one professor of women's studies declared:

> One thing I know now is that just because someone calls herself, or himself, a feminist does not mean that person's values or behavior or way of operating in the world is going to be something that I identify with...So I'm much less influenced by someone marching up to me and announcing they're a feminist. I'm much more wanting to watch how that person operates before I make a decision about whether I'm really in league with them.

[...]

Language use is an additional marker of the boundary between feminists and nonfeminists. The women's movement developed a sweeping critique of sexism in language that brought about substantial change in language use. Derogatory terms used to refer to women – chick, cunt, bitch, girl, and so forth – were a special target of feminists in the initial years of the movement and have remained so since then. Like the label "feminist," the use of language remains an important boundary marker, but, as one woman indicated, failure to conform to feminist terminology (indicating "outsider" status) carries fewer consequences than it did during the 1970s.

> I paid too much attention to language [in the 1970s] as a means to assess politics. I think language is important, and to this day I'd have real problems having a close personal friendship with somebody who referred to women as chicks. But it got to

> be so crazy, and if people didn't use your exact terminology they were an enemy.

Other feminists suggested that even their own use of language has changed to include terms that would previously have been used only by outsiders, as this lawyer commented:

> I can remember the time that my tongue would have rotted in my cheeks before I would have said the word "girl" in relation to a woman at all. And at least now I've gotten to the point where I can joke with some of my friends and at least use the word. But I can't even imagine being in a meeting and talking about a young woman as being a girl. That still would really make me nuts.

In short, what would previously have been a fairly serious boundary violation has become acceptable, but only within limits and in certain settings.

Distinguishing women from men. Another means by which radical feminists established boundaries in the 1970s was by emphasizing women's difference from men and denigrating many masculine traits. Some feminists made this argument in essentialist terms – the view that the differences between women and men reflected the sexes' innate natures. Many others, however, viewed the differences as a socially constructed product of socialization and structural position. One woman explained how being a feminist kept her from forming close relationships with men during the 1970s.

> It made it impossible to be close to men anymore, because ... I was entering a universe that [they] couldn't come into ... All men became aliens when I realized that I didn't have to live as though I approved of patriarchy. They just can't relate.

Most feminist veterans reported that their close friendships and their political alliances are still primarily with women. Like other boundary markers, however, the division between women and men has lessened. Many lesbians reported increasing political work and a feeling of commonality with gay men. Both lesbian and heterosexual participants indicated a tension between a continuing view of men as untrustworthy and different from themselves and increasing cooperative contact with men. This woman's comment illustrates the ambivalence.

> I have to deal with men on a day-by-day basis, so I do deal with them. I'm not sure that I like them or I trust them any more than I did twenty years ago. But I've also learned that there are really some very, very good men out there who do try and are very supportive. And I don't think when I was truly involved with the women's movement that I would have admitted that, at all.

Like the distinction between feminists and nonfeminists, the boundary between women and men is more permeable than it was ten years ago.

Two kinds of changes can occur in how challenging groups construct their boundaries when their social movement falls on hard times. One model is illustrated by the National Woman's Party in the 1950s, which developed an elite-sustained structure. Boundaries become rigidified, increasing the commitment of a small cadre of activists but keeping out new recruits and allies. The second possibility, which has occurred in the Columbus women's movement, is that boundaries may become more permeable and differences less salient. Although members still see radical feminists as a distinct group, they are more willing to cross the boundaries between their group and others, opening up the possibility for the coalitions that have developed in the 1980s.

Accompanying this development is a reframing of emotions, from anger to acceptance or openness. Almost everyone I interviewed said she felt an increasing "mellowness," more tolerance for people with different political views or lifestyles, less stridency, a growth in spirituality, and an increasing reluctance to be motivated by anger. One woman's comments were typical.

> In the early seventies, when I was eating and breathing and sleeping feminist activity, I was so angry! I was really fueled by fury a lot of the time. And at this point in my life, to be angry is too hard. I just can't do it. It doesn't feel good to be angry, and I also had the realization that I didn't like the way things went for me when I was angry. When you're angry, other people are intimidated and they don't want to do what you want them to do. It really sets up an opposition.

Relationships among feminists, once stormy, calmed somewhat for these women. "Now I'm much more into why can't we all get along, and getting people to deal more on a one-to-one or in small groups of people," explained one. Many women saw their changed attitudes as a function of age, as this woman did.

> When you reach your thirties and forties, you have a more overall view of life. I don't in any way think that I have become less radical or that I have mellowed, I think that's not a proper use of your greater age. It's just that I have a wider view of things and I'm more tolerant of other people because I'm more compassionate now than I was then.

It is difficult to know how much of this change is actually due to age, but "mellowing" in political attitudes is not biologically determined. Years of experience and the need for unity in a hostile environment made feminists less angry and more willing to compromise.

Generational boundaries. Unlike the differences between feminists and nonfeminists and between women and men, which have been socially reconstructed and minimized, the women I interviewed perceived a variety of differences between themselves and people who did not share their experiences in the women's movement of the 1960s and 1970s because of age or politics. One woman who was very active in lesbian feminist protest during the mid- to late 1970s described her perception of younger lesbians who had not shared her experience in the women's movement.

> When I am involved with women who have not been through the experience I've been through, I feel a little bit sad for them. I feel that they have lost a major part of what it is to be a feminist, and to be a lesbian.... And it's hard to convey to them what feminism is, let alone what lesbian feminism is, in the sense that I learned it, and how encompassing it is.

Another veteran of the earliest days of WL, who now works in a mainstream corporation, felt that her social movement participation set her apart from people of different ages.

> I talk to some of these young kids at work, and it's like they don't know anything about the politics in El Salvador, they don't know anything about anything. They've just been yuppified. And they don't see the big political picture. Or people that are ten or fifteen years older. It's like [they say], "What's wrong with you?" when I start ranting about politics, or Bush, or Reagan.

Movement veterans symbolically underscore the importance of remaining true to one's political commitments by telling "cautionary tales" about women who were formerly radical feminists and have "sold out" in the 1980s and 1990s. One woman, who is employed by a nonprofit organization and owns a modest house, told such a tale.

> I'm not a big consumer or a real high materialist. But I know some women who went the other way. I know one woman who makes a lot of money, well over a hundred thousand dollars a year. And she used to be in WAC. ... And now she's just very different.

Another told a similar story about a woman who "went from being a radical lesbian to being a Reagan Republican who wanted to get rich." A variation on this theme concerns a rumored social group for professional lesbians, including former radical feminists, that limits membership to women above a certain income. A sense of identity and commonality is reinforced by those who are different. Thus, stories of women who have sold out serve to support others' status as "dedicated feminists" and symbolically underscore the boundary between those who have retained commitment and those who have abandoned it.

Lesbian feminist identity. Throughout the 1970s lesbians became more visible in the radical women's movement; lesbian feminist ideology developed, and in practice activists often conflated the categories "lesbian" and "radical feminist." By the end of the decade, heterosexual women were a shrinking minority in radical feminist groups at the same time that a lesbian feminist subculture was growing. Large women's movement organizations embraced lesbian issues, but animosities remained between heterosexual and lesbian women. The new source of conflict was some heterosexual women's charge that lesbians dominated the movement. "I think that straight women have been pushed out of the women's movement by lesbian women," complained one heterosexual respondent, "and it's been pretty ugly.... The women's movement is the only place in the world where women have to come out of the closet as a heterosexual." Most of the heterosexual women I interviewed did not share this sentiment, but many felt left out of a predominantly lesbian movement. During the 1970s, the celebration of womanhood had made heterosexual women welcome as part of the mostly lesbian "women's community." But by the 1980s and 1990s, lesbians were increasingly unwilling to soft-pedal either their sexuality or their political demands. Both lesbian and heterosexual identity became more salient in the radical women's movement as a result.

At the same time, divisions among lesbians diminished. In the early and mid-1970s, lesbian feminists were often critical of longtime lesbians for "mimicking heterosexuality" in butch–fem roles, viewing women as sex objects, and not participating in feminist activities. For example, a fundraising talent show in Columbus attempted to bring the bar and political worlds together. A humorous skit in which a woman adopted a "ditzy" feminine character, enjoyed by bar women, was loudly protested by political women, who disrupted the performance arguing that it parodied women. The talent show ended prematurely, and the alliance between the two groups stalled. By the late 1970s and early 1980s, however, the local lesbian bar, Summit Station (commonly known as "Jack's"), sometimes hosted feminist fundraisers and became more of a hangout for lesbian feminists. At the same time feminists softened critiques of traditional butch–fem relationships and subculture and increasingly recognized political resistance by lesbians outside the formal women's movement. One longtime lesbian activist described the changes in relations between lesbian feminists and other groups of lesbians.

> [In the 1970s] the community was fairly well segregated, so that the political community was separate from the softball community and was separate from the community of teachers.... Over time those sort of walls came down, among those groups at least, as women aged.... [Now] there's a great deal of mix and less separation between and among those women that define themselves variously.

[...]

In addition to the lessening of distinctions among lesbians, the division between lesbians and gay men has become more permeable in the 1980s, particularly with the rise of acquired immune-deficiency syndrome (AIDS) and lesbians' extensive participation in the AIDS movement. One woman who had been part of Lesbian Peer Support commented that she had become involved with a local AIDS organization because

> for the first time I identified that this is happening to my tribe. These are my people, and I need to stand with them now, because this is important.

"My people" means lesbians and gay men for her now, whereas in the 1970s it meant women.

[...]

Another woman who has been active on gay and lesbian issues since the 1970s explained her continuing identification with gay men.

> It doesn't have to do as much with an identity of being a woman as of being a gay and lesbian sort of outcast.... That's more direct and more related to my own set of things than other kinds of issues like childcare or abortion.

Seeing lesbianism, rather than womanhood, as the defining element of her identity is a significant change.

A final notable pattern is illustrated by three participants who identified as lesbian but reported having sexual relationships with men in the 1980s for the first time in two decades. Two of the three continued to identify themselves as lesbians, whereas the third identified as bisexual. One lesbian, who described her affair with a man as "totally peculiar," saw affairs with men as a widespread phenomenon, commenting that she has "discovered since that a whole lot of us, lesbians, went through a phase like that." This "phase" occurred as lesbian feminist identity became more fluid, permitting sexual experimentation without the stigma of political betrayal. At the same time, it may be that as the feminist community weakened in the early 1980s, the ideal of being "woman-identified" came to seem less real and more difficult to maintain. In the early 1990s the counterintuitive notion of "lesbians who sleep with men" spread: The lesbian writer Jan Clausen published an article in a gay publication about her relationship with a man, singer Holly Near wrote in her autobiography about being a lesbian but having sex with men, and students at OSU (Ohio State University) formed a support group for "lesbians who just happen to be in relationships with politically correct men." Most of the women I interviewed still believed that sexuality was linked to politics and that the political implications of being a lesbian who slept with men were different from those of being a lesbian who did not. But the borders between lesbians and nonlesbians were undeniably blurred. The debate over whether one can identify as a lesbian and still be sexually involved with men is, at core, about collective identity: What behavior must one exhibit (or refrain from) in order to be considered a lesbian? A feminist?

The feminist network. Veterans of the Columbus women's movement have maintained an elaborate and meaningful network that makes them more than an abstract political generation; they are a community. The network is a material embodiment of group boundaries. Many participants kept in touch with each other, and even when they had not been in touch, often kept tabs on each other's locations and activities. One woman, for example, told me that each year she checked the new phone book listing for another activist to make sure that she was still at the same address, although they had not talked in years. Of course, not all women who were active in the Columbus radical women's movement have kept in touch with each other. More peripheral members, those who have become conservative, former lesbians, and those who were "trashed out" are all less likely to have retained contacts with others. But even though the network is partial and has many broken links, many women are integrated into it in some way.

In part, the network exists because women's political commitments still make them inclined to work together on social change issues. One woman who recently ran for political office noted that a former member of the Women's Caucus at OSU was the first person to send a contribution to her campaign. Another woman contacted a fellow activist who had established a new feminist organization and took publicity about the new organization to a local conference. A national feminist organization founded in the 1980s by a veteran of the Columbus women's movement now has a board of directors that includes several women who participated in feminist organizations together in the 1970s.

In addition, the network remains important because of the emotional and intellectual closeness that grows from sharing a common important experience. Many longtime feminists reported that friendships they formed in the women's movement of the 1970s have remained important in the 1980s and 1990s. One woman explained the quality of such relationships.

> Some of these people, I've known them for so long now that we can refer back to a certain event or series of events with just a word or two. It's that kind of communication you can have with someone you've known for a long time, so that we don't really discuss it, we know what we mean. And we get that kind of good feeling that you have with people that you've been through a lot with and you've known for so long.

Another woman described formalizing important relationships through the creation of what she terms "chosen kinship."

> I've been working on my own chosen family... [and] I run workshops for women on kinship and chosen kinship.... At this point, I have a ritual and I take people in only if they seem to be really staying powers in my life. I don't do this lightly.

Although her chosen family is not limited to women with whom she was active in the 1970s, several such women are part of her network. The formality of the notion of chosen kinship emphasizes the importance of a network for establishing group boundaries.

Such relationships serve to sustain commitment to feminist politics and collective identity. One woman who works in a non-feminist setting explained that in order to retain feminist commitment when social pressures urge her to be absorbed into the political mainstream, "I surround myself with all my friends... people that I think still have a political world ethic about them." Another woman who is in a committed relationship with a woman she met in the Columbus women's movement of the 1970s said simply:

> Without each other I don't know how we'd be surviving.... One of the things we are for each other more than anything else is a reality check. Without the reality check, we could fall off the edge. In the 1980s, I certainly could have fallen off the edge if [she] hadn't been here.

Perhaps, in the end, the "reality check" is the most important contribution of the network: the reminder that, despite opposition and sometimes invisibility, feminists are neither crazy nor alone.

The women who were the furthest removed from the organized women's movement and whose feminist identity was the least important to them were those who had lost contact with the feminist network. One woman, who had formerly identified as a lesbian and had later married a man, reported that her resulting loss of membership in the lesbian community made it difficult to remain a feminist activist at the same level. Three other women who had moved to conservative parts of the country similarly found it difficult to remain active feminists because of the loss of a feminist network.

Because the lesbian feminist movement remained vibrant and large in the 1980s and 1990s and built a social movement community and political culture, lesbians often were able to maintain their commitment more easily than heterosexual women. The lesbian feminist community has aided lesbians in maintaining a feminist collective identity and has provided support and opportunities for practicing political principles in daily life and mobilizing collective action. As a result, fewer of the lesbians than the heterosexual women I interviewed moved into mainstream careers or lifestyles, and more lesbians have continued to participate in organized collective efforts for social change. The four women I interviewed who have remained fulltime radical feminist activists are all lesbians. Even for lesbians, however, the highly politicized activist community of the 1970s no longer exists.

The loss of community that accompanied the decline of organized feminism in the early 1980s left all participants feeling a sense of loss, alienation, and nostalgia, and deprived them of the networks and culture that supported their collective identity and translated it into mobilization. Male participants in the civil rights and student movements of the 1960s described similar feelings of dislocation. Both in terms of the friendships they developed and the sense of shared political mission in life, participants felt that their experience in the women's movement of the 1970s in Columbus differed sharply from the communities of the 1990s. One woman expressed her nostalgia for the friendships she formed in the 1970s.

> I have never had the friendships, the significance, the meaning, everything that you could want in relationships, since then.... We saw ourselves as family. And I have never had that kind of family since, and I don't think I ever will.

Another woman compared the ease of making friends in a social movement culture with the difficulty she faces now.

> I find it very difficult to keep friends these days, because I don't run into anybody naturally. Like I used to just every day go into work [at WAC], you'd see all these people. You'd make plans to do things; it was just part of the flow. Now it's like you never see anybody, and you've got to call somebody up and make plans, it's this big effort.

The close-knit nature of women's movement culture fostered conflict, but it was nevertheless an important source of strength and continuing commitment for members, as this participant in WAC commented:

> We lived and worked together, literally.... It was just too much. You couldn't get away from anybody. And yet, the closeness of it was just not replicable.

Even in the absence of that "closeness," longtime feminists continued to rely on their connections to one another in the 1980s.

The clearest examples of how networks establish group boundaries come from separatist movements or those with separatist elements, such as utopian communes of the 1800s or the black nationalist movement of the 1960s. In such cases, movements create "a world apart" from the dominant culture in which participants can redefine their group. Feminists of the 1960s and 1970s have not created such a world apart in the present. Rather, they have dispersed, holding jobs where they may be one of only a few feminists. Yet friendship ties, political cooperation, and a sense of shared past bind them together.

The Survival of Feminist Commitment

The antifeminist backlash affected how longtime feminists understand themselves and their group. Changes in the external environment have not *determined* changes in feminist collective identity. They have, however, provided the context and events that feminists try to understand and interpret. Despite the hostility and opposition they encounter, the women's movement of the 1960s and 1970s forever marked participants' understanding of the world and their own place in it. Of course, not every participant in the women's movement has retained her radical feminist identity and beliefs to the same degree. A few women repudiate their earlier beliefs, and others vary in how much their outlooks have changed over the years.

Regardless of how women think of themselves and what they believe is true about the world, their daily lives have changed greatly. It is the conflict between this generation's enduring radical feminism and their limited opportunities for action in a constricting economy and hostile political climate that shaped feminist actions in the 1980s and early 1990s. This loss of political community, for most women, made it more difficult to continue externally oriented activism. Faced with the loss of the community that had sustained their activism, they turned to their jobs and their families, attempting to continue living their lives in a political way.

12 True Believers and Charismatic Cults

Janja Lalich

Systems of Control

The Democratic Workers Party had its beginnings in 1974. Full-time members, called "cadres" or "militants," typically numbered between 125 and 150, but in certain periods there were between 300 and 1,000 members at various grades of affiliation. In the early 1980s the DWP branched out into various locales around the United States, but the headquarters always remained in San Francisco. Throughout most of its existence, the DWP was a highly controversial organization. Marlene Dixon, the group's leader throughout its life span, was a former professor of sociology and a radical feminist of the sixties era. Through charisma and chutzpah, Dixon was able to gather around her extremely loyal followers, known throughout the Left for their obsessive devotion to her.

A feature that distinguished the DWP from so many other leftist groups at the time was its proudly feminist origins, as it had been founded and was led by women. In addition, the group was innovative and bold in its local, national, and international interventions and activities. Although most of the leadership personnel were women, the DWP was never solely a women's organization; almost from the beginning, the membership included both men and women, and throughout the years at least several men served in middle- and upper-level leadership positions.

As a Marxist-Leninist organization with a Maoist orientation, the DWP was part of the New Communist Movement (NCM), or the party-building movement. This movement was prominent in the Left in the 1970s and 1980s. Before I discuss the DWP's origins and evolution, I want to explain the roots of the NCM and describe its social milieu.

The NCM was a product of specific sociopolitical developments in the United States, as well as a direct by-product of the student movements of the 1960s. Historically, the movement was one outcome of the failures and inadequacies of the Old Left and the New Left, as well as a beneficiary of the perceived successes of certain international revolutionary movements. The New Communist Movement was, in fact, an umbrella term for a radical trend that tended to dominate U.S. leftist politics in the early 1970s. The movement itself was affected by political ideologies imported from abroad but also by events at home in the United States.

Organizations within the NCM drew on general feelings of social alienation, growing economic polarization, and political unrest and distrust. According to the *Encyclopedia of the American Left*, groups and activists in the NCM reached thousands through their political actions and publications. As a movement, however, it did not have staying power. In addition to the growing crisis in the world Communist movement and in many socialist countries, which began in the 1960s but took hold in the 1980s, most NCM groups could not withstand the turmoil in their own ranks. By the end of 1989, almost all NCM groups had either disbanded or splintered into practical invisibility.

[. . .]

It was in that environment—serious and searching—that a confluence of factors and personalities resulted in the birth of the DWP, which drew on elements of the NCM while also being a creative concoction that had a particular appeal to certain types of activists. Marlene Dixon, with the support of her first circle of devotees, blended the seriousness of the Marxist-Leninist fighting party with a feminist perspective. This unique feature allowed the group to draw radicals from leftist circles as well as the women's movement. Dixon's theoretical orientation also meant that the DWP was aligned with a variant of political theory called world-systems theory that not only was sophisticated but also distinguished the party from the so-called China-liners or Soviet-liners.

Sanctions. Given the emphasis on obedience and discipline, members understood that they could be sanctioned for not following rules or for in any way breaking the discipline. Militants were "punished" in a variety of ways besides submitting to collective criticism sessions and writing self-criticisms.

More practical sanctions, for example, were increased quotas, extra work duty, demotion from a particular position or function, removal from a practice, and instructions to leave a workplace or cease contact with a particular person. In more serious cases, there were periods of probation, suspension, or even house arrest (which could mean being confined and guarded by security forces).

Expulsion was the ultimate sanction. Most expulsions were handled privately between the member and the leaders. Other members learned about them by means of Branch announcements. Some expulsions came at the conclusion of trials, formal meetings at which a militant came before the rest of the members to be charged and publicly criticized. Sometimes in trials the accused was allowed to respond; sometimes, after a typically lengthy and harsh public denunciation, the accused militant was given the verdict and sent away without a chance to speak.

There were two types of expulsion—without prejudice and with prejudice. To be expelled *without prejudice* meant that the ex-member could be spoken to if seen, sometimes was allowed to work with one of the DWP front groups, often was expected to give a regular monthly "donation," and, in some cases, after a certain amount of time determined by leadership, was able to apply to rejoin. To be expelled *with prejudice* meant the person was declared an enemy and for all intents and purposes was considered to no longer exist. The expelled person was to be completely shunned; if members saw someone who had been expelled with prejudice—for example, in a store or on the street—they were to act as though the person was not there.

It was always the decision of top leaders as to who merited the extreme punishment of expulsion with prejudice. Dixon gave the final approval on all expulsions, with or without prejudice, even when recommendations came from Eleanor or the Discipline and Control Board, a cadre committee that handled such matters. Most often, to be handed such a severe sentence had nothing to do with the actual thoughts or actions of the individual who was about to be shunned and become nonexistent. Generally, by means of criticism, staged trials, threats, and, at times, acts of violence, expelled members were intimidated into years of silence and would not think of speaking about their Party experiences, much less take any action against the group.

Examples of the kinds of actions against expelled members are as follows: a founder being expelled was whisked from her house, everything taken from her, and put on a plane to her parents' home across the country; an expelled militant was thrown out of his house, all of his clothes and belongings discarded onto the street; a foreign-born, inner-circle militant was put on a plane to Europe without a penny in her pocket. Many of these actions were carried out by the Eagles, a special security force of select militants who received physical fitness training from a Party cadre who had been a Marine. Other expelled militants were threatened and extorted, given a schedule to repay the DWP for the "training" they had received—often an amount in the thousands of dollars.

That type of violence and isolationist technique contributed to an us-versus-them mentality, a feature found in many cults and certainly characteristic of this one. Declaring enemies drew battle lines and created a feeling of superiority and righteousness among members, as well as a sense of paranoia and hostility, as though these "enemies" truly posed a threat to the organization.

The Party's first purge. Because the first mass expulsion of members was central to the way in which the disciplinary structure took hold, it merits discussion here. Just after Christmas 1976, Dixon ordered the Party's first real purge. Formally, it was called the Campaign Against Lesbian Chauvinism and Bourgeois Feminism; in later years it was referred to simply as "the lesbian purge." Though the membership was always mixed (in both gender and sexual preference), in the early years there were quite a number of lesbian members because much of the recruiting had been done among friendship networks of the founders, eleven of whom were lesbians. The purge was carried out under the political pretext that a clique of lesbians in the Party were "bourgeois feminists"; Dixon provided a new theoretical line on homosexuality to support her actions. Overnight, a number of female members were gone, with no explanation, and an investigative panel was questioning the rest of the members about their activities and testing their loyalty; a strict seal of silence was imposed to control information. After about a week, a pamphlet was produced and all the members were called to meetings to learn about an internal campaign to root out enemies "in our midst"—a clique charged with being exploitative, oppressive, and preventing the Party's growth. The pamphlet explained that some female members had been expelled by the judgment of the leadership. Others, who had not yet been expelled (their fates were uncertain), were brought to stand before their comrades as they were formally charged with "crimes" and denounced collectively. This first purge served many purposes.

First, it established the Party's right to intervene in any aspect of members' personal lives and asserted its unmitigated power over their lives. The investigation that took place left nothing sacred; it included probing interviews (more like interrogations) and search-and-seizure tactics. In addition, because the purge happened so unexpectedly, it generated unspoken fear and uncertainty: someone could be in the group one day and gone the next—including a mate or a spouse. That uneasy feeling contributed to an ongoing atmosphere of watchfulness, terror, and condemnation.

Second, the purge helped to institute one of the DWP's main control mechanisms—the method of pitting people against each other so as to breed mistrust and foster loyalty only to Dixon. Actually, that precedent was begun in the first year when Virginia, Esther's best friend, was chosen to lead the investigation that culminated in the charges against Esther before her expulsion. Dixon reaffirmed the use of that tactic during the lesbian purge; eventually, over the years, every possible grouping or type within the DWP was subjected to such divisive treatment. There were campaigns against and purges of men, parents (i.e., militants with children), intellectuals, middle-level leaders, friendship networks, militants with political pasts, those from a middle-class (PB) background, and those with PB skills. In other words, not only were there no boundaries, but there were to be no bonds other than to the DWP. Such divisive tactics were implemented strategically throughout the years, ensuring that no one would trust anyone else.

Third, the Campaign Against Lesbian Chauvinism set the tone and style for future purges and mass trials. A booklet was produced almost overnight and distributed Party-wide for study and discussion. Accused militants were named, their "crimes" described, their punishments highlighted. Some were expelled without trial, never to be heard from again; others were ordered to come before their peers to face criticism and denunciation. After the trials, many women were suspended, unable to participate in any activity and cut off from contact with other members, for a period ranging from three weeks to six weeks.

And fourth, the purge served to break up a key friendship network. Among those named in the campaign were some of the founders and many who had been in the first ring of people to join soon after the founding. They were among the hardest workers, the most politically dedicated militants, and the most fervently loyal followers. Many were already in middle-level leadership positions. Perhaps Dixon thought they posed a threat to her, or perhaps she was testing the loyalty of her followers.

Forming Systems of Influence

Underlying the powerful systems of control in the DWP was what Dixon called unity of will. "Unity of will is the substance that harnesses us together," she wrote, "that creates our strength, endurance and flexibility. Unity of will is forged by discipline. *Discipline is the operation of the necessity of the party* ... demanding the surrender of individualism into the greater social whole; the transformation of our bourgeois independence into a collective interdependence; and the subordination of our individual will to the collective will of the organization."

In addition to this notion of collective will, another concept was taught in Party School, namely, that each individual's will was to merge with the Party. It was referred to as "bone of his bone and blood of his blood." That image was used to convey the idea that eventually cadres would reach a point at which their will was so united with the Party that the two would be inseparable: at that point, the organization was no longer external to each person but an integral part of each militant's being.

Cadre tension. Cadre life was not easy, nor was it meant to be. Indeed, the very tension of "the constant pressure of Party authority" butting up against the member's independent spirit was recognized as the center of crisis and, therefore, growth for each militant. Militants were taught that cadre development did not even really occur until the ideal was internalized—that is how long and hard the road was. At that point the hardship of daily life would become an accepted reality "because that is the way things must be if we are to achieve our purpose." Living with—and confronting—the tension between self and the Party was the heart of the struggle.

In practical terms, this meant that inner turmoil was standard fare; militants accepted that feeling stressed, feeling conflicted, feeling confused were indications not that something was wrong but that something was right. Such internal struggle indicated that the militant was engaged in the process of self-transformation. In the end, the militant was rewarded by understanding that "this is a cadre party": "The demands we make on ourselves come from us. It's not the Party doing it to you. ... We are agents of our own change." This idea was critical to each militant's sense of ownership and personal responsibility for the organization. At the same time, it meant that anxiety, fear, and guilt were everyday, seemingly self-generated emotions.

Integral to the DWP belief system, then, was crisis and struggle, testing, and a heightened awareness of the Party. Leadership militants responsible for training worked hard to implement such guidelines as "Don't break their spirit, but their individualism." At the same time, the militants did their part by living by the exhortations of an internal voice that repeated the lessons from their cadre training: "Submit but never break. Submission is not mindless, not blind; but submit without reservation. Submit with energy and commitment." Those challenging and somewhat contradictory mottos kept militants confused and on edge. Anxiety was embedded in the life of each cadre member. Like all other aspects, it was wrapped in a political aura and given a political justification. In cadre training, militants learned that to be a good Communist meant to be self-conscious, to be in constant tension with the Party. The idea was to be in continual struggle to shed old habits and attitudes so that the new cadre man or woman could emerge. The more that tension was felt, the more the person was engaged in the struggle. In that sense, anxiety became an accepted state of mind.

Peer pressure Meetings were one obvious place where peer pressure came into play. For example, the leaders would give a presentation on a change in the direction of some work or would open up a denunciation of a militant for some error. Each militant present was expected to say how much he or she agreed with what was just said. Ideally, each person said something different from what had already been said; but more to the point, each person was expected to agree with ("unite with") the thrust of what was happening and support the leadership position. Questions, should there be any, had to be couched within overall agreement. After years of this kind of participation, militants became quite incapable of creative or critical thinking, could only parrot each other, and had shrunken vocabularies riddled with arcane internal phraseology. For example, "bourgeois careerism," "PB self-indulgence," "need-to-know," "commandism," and "me-firstism" became everyday expressions. Afterward many members spoke of feeling "deadened" by this undemocratic experience and as though they lost a sense of themselves as thinking persons.

Reporting was another mechanism of peer pressure. The "one-help" system was a means by which members learned about, and were desensitized to, the practice of reporting on each other. This was a type of buddy system by which new members were assigned a helper (the one-help) to assist them in their integration into Party life. In weekly meetings, new members were to reveal to their one-help all thoughts, questions, or feelings about the organization. One-helps were supposed to help new members become "objective" about things, assist them in seeing things from "a Party point of view," and coach them in how to schedule their time so that they could figure out how to do even more for the organization.

Each one-help wrote detailed weekly reports about everything the new member said and did. Those reports were sent to Branch leadership, New Members teachers, Party School teachers, and Staff/New Members (the administrative team, who under Eleanor's direct guidance oversaw the training and development of all new members). To facilitate "breaking" the new member, these reports were used to monitor development and to identify an action or attitude that could serve as the basis of a group criticism in a future meeting. The more meat for criticism in the one-help report, the better the one-help. Just about every militant, at one time or another, was assigned to be a one-help to a new member. To be given that assignment was considered a sign of development and of the Party's trust. The one-help system helped to institutionalize incessant reporting on one another; it also helped to create an atmosphere of widespread fear of fellow comrades.

For example, I recruited a longtime friend, Stephanie, and we became housemates when she was still a relatively new member. (I needed a roommate because my two previous roommates had just been expelled during a campaign against middle-level leadership.) Although it was highly unusual to have a nonmember stay in a Party house, that summer Stephanie's mother was allowed to visit and stay with us for a week or two. This occurred while the Party was still completely clandestine. Shortly after her mother left, Stephanie was harshly denounced in her Branch meeting for having addressed me by my real name, instead of my Party name, during the time her mother was visiting. The short-sightedness exemplified here is twofold. First, Stephanie's mother already knew me (or at least knew of me) before she came to stay with us, as Stephanie and I had been friends for some time before we each joined the Party. Before moving in, she had told her mother that she was going to be my housemate (although she had not revealed our Party affiliation). Certainly, it would have seemed bizarre to her mother if suddenly I had a different name. Second, and perhaps even more startling, I was the one who reported Stephanie for the security violation of having used my real name in front of her mother. In retrospect, I view this as a classic example of what is sometimes called black-and-white thinking commonplace among cult members. And not only black-and-white, for its simplicity and lack of subtlety; but black-*is*-white, in what may be recognized by outsiders as ready acceptance of blatant contradictions.

Modeling. The top leaders were expected to be exemplary in terms of commitment, exhibited dedication, and willingness to struggle and be criticized. The motto was: "Don't ask of anyone what you yourself have not done." Certain members of the leadership circle underwent intense levels of criticism on a regular basis. Also, they were expected to make greater sacrifices and be willing to discuss them in meetings in order to be a model to lower-ranking militants.

The following is an example of the model/enforcer role. Frieda was the first parent in the Party. After some struggle, Frieda submitted to and united with the idea that she could raise her child on her time off, and she assured the Party that being a mother would not affect her commitment. In actuality, Frieda rarely had time off, and the child was raised primarily in a Party-run child care facility, where children received "superficial care but no real sustenance." Eventually, the Party adopted the attitude that it was "a selfish choice to have a child." Setting an example for others, Frieda, a true believer, modeled an exemplary attitude about the policy and helped to enforce the prevailing norms on parenting. At times, Frieda admitted later, she "was harder on others than necessary" to compensate for what she recognized as her own weak point.

Another major aspect of modeling behavior was reflected in the relationship between leadership and nonleadership militants and the growing patterns of corrupt behavior. Essentially, nothing was to be questioned and there was no criticism of leadership, except on occasions when Dixon called for a campaign against specific individuals. Total unity was expected, even while, concomitantly, militants were told to think for themselves and take initiative in their work. Yet anyone who disagreed or offered a criticism—member or nonmember—was labeled an enemy of the Party and hence an enemy of the working class. Disagreements were a rarity in the DWP. Typically, ones that were aired were handled swiftly, by the militant's capitulation or expulsion.

Commitment. There was an overriding sense that one's commitment to the Party was supposed to outweigh everything else. "A militant's first desire must be to serve, and not to lead," taught *The Militant's Guide*. Such intense dedication was routinely studied, often by using the example of Rubashov in *The Training of the Cadre*. Although the text names Rubashov as the protagonist, this was actually the story of the Soviet Communist leader and theoretician Nikolai Bukharin. In 1938, during the Stalin era, Bukharin signed a false confession knowing he would be found guilty of treason and shot. Militants learned that after much struggle and while imprisoned, Rubashov saw the light and united with his party. Ultimately, he said he was happy to be executed by the party. This was held up as exemplary devotion on the part of the cadre. Another historical example of the requisite depth of devotion was that of Chairman Mao allowing his closest friend and most beloved comrade, Lin Piao, to be shot.

The lesson was, Defend Communism and defend the Party to the end. In that vein, teachers asked militants in Party School, "Could you shoot someone?" Although a rhetorical question of sorts, the level of tension in the room during such a discussion was high. To give one's life for the Party was regarded as the highest honor.

Cult Formation: The Self-Sealing Social System

In general, humans are knowledgeable about their situations and their interactions with others. According to Giddens, in most cases, if you ask a person why he or she did something, he or she can give you reasons. Yet such a point of view does not preclude individuals from being limited in their knowledge or their power, both of which tend to have an effect on one's decision-making capabilities. All is not equal on most if not all playing fields.

Not only was power centralized in the DWP and Heaven's Gate, but knowledge was centralized, and access to it was limited or blocked in many ways. The degree and depth of knowledge available to group members were severely hampered in all four dimensions of the social structure:

- Charismatic authority: Leadership was secretive and inaccessible.
- Transcendent belief system: Group doctrine was inviolable and came down from on high.
- Systems of control: Rigid boundaries defined inaccessible space and topics closed to discussion or inquiry.
- Systems of influence: Internalized norms, all-pervasive modeling, and constant peer monitoring ruled out inappropriate questioning.

In both groups, then, the boundaries of knowledge were shut tight and reinforced in three specific ways—through the process of resocialization, through the use of ideology, and through social controls.

Resocialization into the cult identity

The works of Erik Erikson and Erving Goffman are critical to any understanding of resocialization. Giddens relied on these works in his description of the resocialization process as the systematic breaking down of the person in order to instill trust in the authority figure. He and others have pointed out that typical patterns of resocialization are found in specific situations, including the battlefield, prison camps, religious conversion, and forced interrogation. Known patterns of resocialization include launching a deliberate, sustained attack on ordinary routines; producing a high degree of anxiety in the person; stripping away socialized responses; and attacking the foundation of the basic security system grounded in the trust of others. In the target person, one can expect to see an upsurge in anxiety, regressive modes of behavior, succumbing to the pressures, and adopting a new attitude of trust in and identification with the authority figure(s). Giddens wrote: "The radical disruption of routine produces a sort of corrosive effect upon the customary behaviour of the actor, associated with the impact of anxiety or fear. This circumstance brings about heightened suggestibility, or vulnerability to the promptings of others; the correlate of such suggestibility is regressive behaviour. The outcome of these is a new process of identification—transitory in the mob case, more permanent in protracted critical situations—with an authority figure."

The goal of resocialization, then, is the reconstructed personality. This reconstruction often revolves around one aim, "to get the individual to *identify* with the socializing agent." The desired effect is a new self whose "actions will be dictated by the imagined will or purpose of the actor he has identified with.... It is then that will which generates the internal sanctions for future actions." Such a process of resocialization was a central facet of membership in both the DWP and Heaven's Gate. It was the essence of the DWP's cadre transformation and of Heaven's Gate's transition to the genderless creature. The ultimate effect of such processes is not only a "violation of territories of the self" but also, and perhaps more important, the generation of a state of personal closure, as the person closes himself off to outside knowledge or disconfirming evidence that might challenge this "new self."

Resocialization is a great reinforcer of the status quo within the group. Equally significant, it serves as a hindrance to independent information gathering and a barrier to accessing sources of knowledge. In this context, the purpose of resocialization is to create a true believer—not a curiosity seeker or a critical thinker.

Using ideology to enclose the system

The second reinforcer of the boundaries of knowledge resides in the ideological realm. In the two cases examined here, the belief system became quite purposefully an ideological barricade. The constant striving for an impossible ideal that was the linchpin of membership caused members to feel consistently inadequate about themselves and their accomplishments. This kept them in a self-recriminating and self-critical behavioral and attitudinal mode.

This stultifying dynamic worked to stave off questioning the system or the "truths" of the system. Adherents were too busy criticizing themselves for their incessant failures and too consumed with working harder to achieve their goals—either the short-term ones set by the group or leader or the long-term goal of freedom and self-fulfillment as promised by the leader. The result was self-denial, exhaustion, and guilt. All of that was held neatly in place by the serious commitment each member made to the cause—and to the leader and other members of the group.

External and internalized mechanisms of control

The third reinforcer of closed boundaries was the use of specific social controls. Given the invasive and all-pervasive nature of the systems of influence and control found in Heaven's Gate and the DWP, the sociological concept of total institutions is useful here. These closed social systems are recognized for their "totalizing discipline," reshaped identity, and constraint. The distinctive features of total institutions are interrogative procedures, removal of personal boundaries, forced and continual relations with others, and total control of time. Although many of the conditions of life in the DWP and Heaven's Gate are recognizably similar to those features, the differences must not be ignored. First, both groups were voluntaristic (except for children born or brought into the DWP), unlike the blatant confinement of the asylum, which was the locus of Goffman's class study on total institutions. Second, membership in the two groups involved an attraction to, affinity for, and eventual adoption of a belief system that undergirded the adherent's acquiescence to the systems of control. Again, that is quite a different milieu from that experienced by an inmate in a locked ward in a mental hospital.

However, Goffman's analysis was meant to have broader applications. Thus abbeys, monasteries, convents, cloisters, and other retreats from the world were included in the category of total institutions. Now this might work for the Heaven's Gate group, whose members at times even referred to themselves as monks. But it would be difficult to squeeze the DWP into that category, especially with its stated mission of mass practice and social change. Although it was seclusive, the DWP was quite involved in worldly matters and in that sense could not be described as a retreat from the world. Nonetheless, the extent to which DWP cadres created and lived in a world unto themselves revealed that on some level they were just as cut off from the larger society as nuns in a cloister.

Despite these differences from the classic definition of a total institution, the constraining features of the systems of control and influence kept DWP and Heaven's Gate members from obtaining certain key information or having access to certain knowledge. The dimension of power is most prominent here. Above all, these true believers knew that the systems of control ensured the continuity of the group and the ongoing special (charismatic) relationship between leader and followers. In that sense every rule had a context, and every demand on members was justified by the ideology and the normative system that flowed from it. The overriding power of group authority figures was accepted as a given. The normative system was understood as a necessary mechanism of commitment and change, ultimately for the good of each participant who was striving to meet the ideal. Power in such a situation is both very real and quite subtle. Giddens said it precisely when he wrote, "Power relations are often most profoundly embedded in modes of conduct which are taken for granted by those who follow them, most especially in routinized behaviour, which is only diffusely motivated." The success of these two groups was in their capacity to convince followers, who routinely convinced each other that they were acting of their own accord, for their own good.

Yet for all their efforts at good behavior, sanctions of all kinds existed in both groups. Members feared disapproval and punishment by means of a wide range of structural and social mechanisms—from slippage meetings and criticism sessions to ostracism and public trials and expulsion. DWP sanctions also included various forms of physical punishment, from double-duty work shifts to bodily harm. In effect, fully committed DWP cadres and Heaven's Gate students knew where the line was drawn. Their daily practice was the expression of their commitment. Any error was to be rooted out—with pleasure.

But the harshest sanction of all was internal—the devoted member's inner capacity to control urges, desires, actions, thoughts, and beliefs that were contrary to the group's teachings. Self-condemnation was everyday fare. These internalized sanctions were among the most powerful mechanisms of control. Ultimately, the individual cult member's ability to enact freedom of action was not restricted by lurking external forces or even by the confines of the system. Rather, at this point of the fusion of personal freedom and self-renunciation, at this point of personal closure, the individual may well become his own source of constraint.

The Social Psychology of the Individual Change Process

Heaven's Gate and the DWP had widely divergent ruling ideologies. But the overall character of these groups was not belief-specific. Rather, what is relevant to our understanding here is the manifestation of broader principles of charismatic influence and control within the confines of each group's totalistic system. The demands in this milieu led to an individual worldview shift. The foundation for this was a social structure in which personal freedom (e.g., salvation), as aspired to by each participant, could be gained only through self-renunciation (transformation) of the highest order. The charismatic commitment of each individual was stretched to mold the adherent into a deployable agent, or true believer. This was not achieved for every member of the group, however. For some, commitment was not that strong; they doubted major aspects of the belief system; they failed tests and either left or were ejected from the group; they did not have enough faith or lost faith in the leader—for one reason or another, they were not ready to take that leap. But for those who were, the parts were in place.

The interaction between the individual and the social structure is crucial at this stage. The four structural dimensions (charismatic authority, transcendent belief system, systems of control, and systems of influence) are interlocked and interdependent. They support and reinforce one another, creating the self-sealing system. For the person living within such a system, the conflation of these four dimensions generates an internal dualism, which, I believe, is the linchpin of a binding commitment and the genesis of the true believer. This internalized way of being becomes as much a part of the system as the mechanisms that engender it.

Let me explain what I mean by "internal dualism." Each of the structural dimensions creates a boundary inside and around the individual, and each dimension has a double-sided effect. These personal boundaries are grouped into four dualistic categories: purpose and commitment, love and fear, duty and guilt, and internalization and identification.

Purpose/commitment

The cult member responds to the power of the group's beliefs and enjoys the strength of collective commitment. She believes she has found meaning and purpose. Yet this requires a commitment that demands single-mindedness, a way of thinking characterized by dogmatism and rigidity, and no identity outside the context of the group.

Love/fear

As much as members love their leaders, so do they fear them because of the power they hold over the members' lives, the threat of disapproval, and the expressions of paranoia that raise the specter of the "evil" outside world. Members also enjoy group solidarity and feel a sense of personal power and elitism; yet, at the same time, they fear peer shunning or withdrawal of support. It is a tightrope walk, with little room for error.

Duty/guilt

The member's sense of duty shares space with guilt, always a forceful human motivator. Feeling duty-bound and obligated, members find themselves participating in activities that in other circumstances may have violated a personal ethical code. Now the leader is the only moral arbiter. In some cases, through repetition, ritual, and other group activities, the member becomes desensitized to behavior previously considered unthinkable or objectionable. The longer a person remains with a group, the more invested he is, and potentially all the more complicit with group-dictated actions and behaviors. Life outside the group seems less and less an option.

Identification/Internalization

Finally, by means of the processes of identification and internalization, the member feels in complete unity with the group and the leader. Although on occasion she may still experience dissonance or confusion over discrepancies, at the same time she has access to fewer and fewer outside sources of information and therefore little capacity for reality checks outside the bounds of the system. She feels completely separated from her own pregroup identities and cannot imagine life outside the group. Here the process has come full circle.

The State of Personal Closure

As these dualistic personal boundaries develop and strengthen, a state of personal closure begins to develop. We might think of personal closure as the individualized version of the self-sealing system on an organizational level. Closure is meant in the sense not of completion, which is one use of the term, but rather of a closing in of the self in a self-sealed world. Lifton described it as a "disruption of balance between self and the outside world." He wrote:

> Pressured toward a merger of internal and external milieus, the individual encounters a profound threat to his personal autonomy. He is deprived of the combination of external information and inner reflection which anyone requires to test the realities of his environment and to maintain a measure of identity separate from it. Instead, he is called upon to make an absolute polarization of the real (the prevailing

> ideology) and the unreal (everything else). To the extent that he does this, he undergoes a *personal closure* which frees him from man's incessant struggle with the elusive subtleties of truth.

The personal closure that is the culmination of cultic life is profoundly confining because one is closed to both the outside world and one's inner life. This phenomenon is quite different from cognitive dissonance because it involves all aspects of one's life. It is also much more all-encompassing than our understanding of the normal processes of conformity because of the depth and extent of the internalization and identification. The quality of the belief change actually shifts members' value structure—either temporarily or permanently. When such a shift occurs, individual choice is not an individual matter.

[...]

In a group such as this, individual decisions are not a matter of satisficing, of choosing the "good enough" alternative. Rather, options are limited even further by the combination of the self-sealing nature of the system and the participant's rigid adherence to the norms and near-total identification with the leader and the stated goals. [...] Through charismatic authority, the member has come to identify with the leader. Through the transcendent belief system, the member has adopted and internalized the utopian worldview. Through the systems of control, the member has accepted daily behavioral controls. And through the systems of influence, the member has internalized the group norms and attitudes. [...] But in a context of bounded choice, a person's perceptions and, hence, decision-making processes are constrained even further. [...] Not only are choices limited, but the actual decision-making process is hampered by the true believer's internal voices, which are in complete alignment with the self-sealing system. In this way, behaviors or actions that might look crazy or irrational to the outsider look completely rational from the perspective of the person inside the bounded reality of the cult.

13 Disengaging from Movements

Bert Klandermans

Maintaining Movement Commitment

Movement commitment does not last by itself. It must be maintained via interaction with the movement and any measure that makes that interaction gratifying helps to maintain commitment. Downton and Wehr (1991) discuss mechanisms of social bonding which movements apply to maintain commitment. Leadership, ideology, organization, rituals, and social relations which make up a friendship network each contribute to sustaining commitment and the most effective is, of course, a combination of all five. These authors refer to the 'common devotion' that results from shared leadership; to group pressure as the primary means of maintaining a social movement's ideology; to 'taking on a role within the organization itself' as a way of increasing people's investment in the organization; to rituals as patterns of behaviour that are repeated over time to strengthen core beliefs of the movement; and to circles of friends that strengthen and maintain individual commitment by putting an individual's beliefs and behaviour under greater scrutiny and social control.

Although not all of them are equally well researched, each of these five mechanisms are known from the literature on union and movement participation as factors which foster people's attachment to movements. For example, it is known from research on union participation that involving members in decision-making processes increases commitment to a union (Klandermans 1986; 1992). For such different groups as the lesbian movement groups (Taylor and Whittier 1995) and a group called Victims of Child Abuse Laws (Fine 1995) it was demonstrated how rituals strengthen the membership's bond to the movement. Unions and other movement organizations have developed all kind of services for their members to make membership more attractive. Selective incentives may seldom be sufficient reasons to participate in a movement, but they do increase commitment.

It is important to emphasize, that at least theoretically, affective, continuance, and normative commitment have different sets of determinants. Empirical support for these assumptions may not yet be conclusive, but certainly points in the hypothesized direction. To recapitulate, affective commitment relates to how gratifying the exchange relationship is between a movement and a participant; continuance commitment to the stakes someone has in a movement and the attractiveness of alternatives; and normative commitment refers to a congruence between one's values and those of the movement. Affective commitment more than the other two dimensions seems to be dependent on interactions with the organization one is a member of. The more satisfactory these interactions are, the stronger the affective commitment. Therefore, attempts to make contacts with the movement more satisfactory are instrumental to the maintenance of affective commitment. Continuance commitment is dependent on investments made and the perceived attractiveness of alternatives: the more members have invested and the less attractive alternatives appear to them the stronger their continuance commitment will be. Therefore, sacrifices required from members or other attempts to increase members' investments, derogation of alternatives, and attempts to convince members of the superiority of their own organization are ways to maintain continuance commitment. Normative commitment depends on long term processes of socialization. There is little a movement organization can do in terms of influencing processes of long term socialization, but through frame alignment (Snow et al. 1986) it can try to increase the degree of congruence between the values of the organization and those of the individual.

Despite its efforts, and with the possible exception of some religious sects and underground organizations, it is unlikely for a movement organization to be able to prevent participants from leaving the organization if they are determined to do so. Turnover of supporters is, thus, part and parcel of the life of every movement. Although it is hardly possible to estimate turnover rates in movements, because movements do not carry membership administrations, many movement organizations do administer their membership. In the Netherlands among organizations such as labour unions, Amnesty International, and Greenpeace annual turnover rates of 10 per cent are not unusual. Maintaining commitment may be an important resource to keep people within the movement, but there is of course more. Leaving – like joining – is a process which is controlled by a complex set of determinants and again there is reason to assume that the process will not be identical for various forms of participation. In an attempt to explain why people leave a social movement, I will in the next part of this chapter discuss evidence we collected in the context of research among former participants of the labour movement and the peace movement. What made them decide to leave?

Disengagement

Disengagement can take different forms and not every kind of participation can be discontinued in the same way. Sometimes it is enough to just stay away, sometimes disaffiliation requires some action, and sometimes an individual chooses to combine exit and voice and leave the organization in a highly vocal way. For example, those supporters of the Dutch peace movement who in June 1985 stated to our interviewers that they were prepared to sign the petition against cruise missiles the peace movement had announced to organize that fall, but changed their minds, needed not to take any action, it sufficed just to refrain from signing (Oegema and Klandermans 1994). On the other hand, those members of IKV-groups who were so disappointed after the Dutch government had decided in November 1985 to deploy cruise missiles, that they wanted to quit the movement, had to actually inform their fellow-activists that they were going to give up and may have encountered some attempts to make them stay. But with the movement being on the wane as witnessed, for example, by an increasing number of people who felt that the movement was declining (Oegema 1993), little of that kind may have occurred and groups may even have collapsed as a whole. Indeed, with some simplification one could say that two years after the government's decision, one third of the local peace groups had collapsed, and, of those groups that were still alive one third of the members had left, while the activity level was down to not even one third of what it had been before. Members of such organizations as Amnesty International, Greenpeace or a union, however, must formally resign by writing a letter to the organization and volunteers in these kind of organizations tend to be looked at almost as personnel with periods of advanced notice if they want to resign. And finally, in a chemical company where we conducted some research for the union, a working-group announced publicly that they were going to change to another union collectively because they disagreed with their union's stand in the negotiations, thus actually turning their defection into an act of protest.

Disengagement need not restrict itself to enduring forms of participation. In fact, movement participation often concerns taking part in a string of events (attending a meeting, taking part in a demonstration, signing a petition). In that context, defection can simply take the form of staying away, or as one could call it *passive defection* or *neglect*. Obviously, this is the form disaffiliation usually takes in the case of once-only activities. In the case of enduring forms of participation, however, disengagement requires explicit steps. Therefore, one could call it *active defection* or *exit*.

What makes people defect? Insufficient gratification in combination with lack of commitment seems the answer. For example, more than 70 per cent of the workers who left their unions did so because they were dissatisfied, frustrated or felt that they weren't treated well by their union (van de Putte 1995). But discontent is not a sufficient condition. Obviously, movement commitment must also decline. Indeed, Moreland and Levine (1982) hypothesized that the level of commitment of those members who eventually leave a group develops in a cyclical way. Initially, it increases until some peak level is reached, then it declines until the level is reached at which people decide to quit.

That raises, of course, the questions of what causes insufficient gratification, and of why commitment declines? Psychologically speaking, it is too simple to assume that disengagement is the opposite of engagement, if only because, in the course of participation, a certain level of commitment develops which interacts with levels of gratification. Moreover, the three forms of commitment do not necessarily reach the same degree. Similarly, they may decline at different rates and for different reasons. Taking the results with regard to union commitment into account, normative commitment presumably is the most stable of the three. Seeing that its roots are in long term socialization processes, this is what one would expect. Continuance commitment seems to be the next in terms of stability. Investments, of course, are made in the past and cannot be changed anymore, but new alternatives may appear and existing alternatives may become more attractive so that continuance commitment may decline. Affective commitment is the most variable of the three. It declines when interaction with the movement or its members becomes less gratifying. Note that under such circumstances the two other forms of commitment may restrain someone from quitting. Affective commitment, continuance commitment, and normative commitment balance each other out; and thus the more stable forms of commitment may compensate for a decline in those that are less stable. If a person sees no attractive alternatives, has invested heavily in the organization, and is truly committed to the values and goals of the movement, he or she may decide that, all things considered, he or she would rather continue to share the burden and make the necessary sacrifices than leave.

Thus disengagement, passive and active alike, results from the interaction of insufficient levels of gratification and commitment. In the next few sections, I will further elaborate on this assumption with the help of evidence from our research on the Dutch peace movement and labour movement.

Neglect: Erosion of Support

Neglect is difficult to observe. How to assess how many people could have been at an event staged by a movement? And then, far from all the no-shows are people who have turned away from the movement. Indeed, as I have argued previously there are all kinds of reasons why sympathizers end up being no-shows, which have nothing to do with defection. Yet sometimes people who initially support a movement change their minds and become unwilling to support the movement any longer. In this case, the problem isn't that sympathy is not converted into action, but rather that sympathy disappears. *Erosion of support*, as we defined it (Oegema and Klandermans 1994) is the nonparticipation of individuals who, though once prepared to participate, have changed their minds and lost their readiness to take action. Erosion, we hypothesized, occurs when individuals perceive the ratio of costs to benefits as *becoming* less favourable over time, and/or their grievances are no longer pressing, and/or their sympathy for the movement wanes.

Erosion of support occurs in the context of movement decline, changes in public opinion, and issue attention cycles. These settings have to do with the macro-context of movement participation. In fact, resignation in those contexts is most of the time not so much deliberate decisions to withdraw, but natural attrition. Erosion of support, however, can also occur in the context of action mobilization campaigns, as a reverse effect of mobilization. In that context erosion is not so much an additional symptom of movement decline, but a well-considered refusal to participate any longer. In the context of disaffiliation, it is this kind of erosion that I am interested in.

Mobilization campaigns polarize a population – cognitively and socially. *Cognitive* polarization takes place because, in the context of action mobilization, the mobilizing organization's features become especially distinct: Goals and means become pronounced, rhetoric changes, and interactions with opponents become confrontational. Opposing parties argue, previously mild debates sharpen, and latitudes of indifference become smaller and smaller. Opponents and countermovement organizations are often extremely skilled in creating caricatures of the movement and sowing doubt in the hearts of half-hearted sympathizers. In other words, action mobilization forces a shift in public discourse: In the media and in informal conversations among citizens, public discourse becomes increasingly focused on campaign issues. As a result, individual citizens and societal actors are forced to take sides.

Action mobilization implies *social* polarization, for it rearranges an individual's social environment into proponents and opponents of the movement. Most individuals live in a fairly homogeneous social environment and will find themselves unambiguously in one camp or the other, but some may discover that groups, organizations, or parties with which they identify are suddenly in their enemy's camp or that groups and people with whom they feel little affinity have become allies. If they don't like the social identity implied by these new arrangements, they may choose to detach themselves from the movement. In the context of election campaigns, Lazarsfeld, Berelson, and Gaudet (1948: 56–64) referred to this process of conflicting identifications as 'cross pressure' (see also Lane 1964: 197–203). Nothing can illustrate this argument about cross pressure put on individuals better than the following data from the petition-campaign of the peace movement in the Netherlands.

Peace Movement Sympathizers Under Cross Pressure

Close to one-fifth of those interviewees who were prepared to sign the People's Petition against the deployment of cruise missiles changed their minds and indicated that they no longer wanted to sign (I refer to these respondents as 'switchers'). They were predominantly sympathizers who identified with one of the two political parties in power in the government (Christian Democrats and Conservatives), that is to say, the government that was about to decide to deploy the missiles. These individuals reported that their social environments became less supportive during the anti-missile campaign, and because their support was only lukewarm to begin with, the increasingly negative environment undermined their motivation to sign (as shown by a less positive evaluation of the peace movement and less strong rejection of cruise missiles). Interestingly, these individuals reported an increase in the number of their personal conversations about cruise missiles. This increase and the fact that their decision *not* to sign evoked supportive reactions from significant others are evidence of social pressure. I must emphasize, however, that it is the *combined* impact of these factors that accounts for erosion. Identification with one of the two parties in government was not in itself sufficient to produce erosion – after all, a fair proportion of those who identified with one of the parties had wanted to sign and did indeed sign. Rather, the turnabout from sympathizer to switcher was the result of a combination of factors: identification with one of the two parties; the perception that one's environment did not support the movement; plus, initially, the expectation, and later, the experience, of negative reactions from significant others, which weakened an already halfhearted motivation. Comparison of the four communities where we conducted our research, furthermore, highlights the impact of countercampaigns in this regard: An intense countercampaign in one community produced high levels of erosion. But on the basis of our current discussion we may add now that apparently, countercampaigns have this effect especially in a context of a non-supportive social environment.

Important for my argument on the interaction of insufficient gratification and commitment is the observation that during the campaign the initially relatively positive feelings among switchers toward the people in the movement changed into strongly negative ones: by November switchers no longer felt any sympathy for the people in the movement. This factor, together with their already less than positive feelings toward other aspects of the peace movement, contributed to their change of mind.

Exit: Resigning as a Participant

In 1991 we interviewed some 3000 union members. Twenty months later 195 (6.5 per cent) of them had left their union; in that same period 25 (14 per cent) of the union activists stopped being activists. Resigning one's membership or quitting as a volunteer is different from erosion, if only because one must have entered the organization to begin with to be able to exit it – as a member of a group, a paid-up member of a movement organization, a volunteer, a paid official, and so on. Moreover, resignation is active withdrawal and therefore much more than passive defection or neglect seen as an evaluative move. Why do people resign from a movement that they entered more or less enthusiastically some longer or shorter time ago?

Disappointment, stressful experiences, burnout, attractive alternatives, changed life stage, or simply lost motivation, all may account for resignation. Depending on the position a person is exiting some of these processes and experiences may be more or less important. In this section I will draw from our research among ex-union members, ex-union activists, and ex-peace activists. How do their experiences differ from those who stayed? Although the process of resignation may be different for different movements, I do believe that understanding resignation from a labour union or the peace movement is informative in a more general sense.

Resigning one's union membership. In the Netherlands, union membership is voluntary and so is resigning as a member. As a consequence, being a union member is an individual choice determined by belief in unionism and in the instrumentality of a union membership, and a pro-union climate in one's company (van Rij 1994, 1995; van Rijn 1995). Most workers become union members within five years of entering the labour market. Chances that workers become members further on in their careers are much lower. Half of the new members have left the organization again within five years (van de Putte 1995). Doubts about the instrumentality of union membership, disappointing experiences with the union as a service-organization, and a change in career (becoming unemployed or disabled or changing jobs) were the main reasons given for their resignation. There appear to be two patterns of resignation: (a) 40 per cent of the members who had quit had already been considering leaving the union when we interviewed them a year and a half before. At the time when they still had been members, people who considered leaving had significantly lower levels of commitment than those who did not. Yet, only one-fifth of those who considered leaving, did eventually leave. (b) The remaining 60 per cent had no intention whatsoever of leaving the organization at the time of our first interview, but nevertheless resigned in the period between our two interviews. What happened in that period to both groups? Lack of contact seems to be the main cause of resignation among the first group. Nobody in the organization prevented them from carrying out their intentions. One of our interviewees complained that when he resigned nobody in the organization tried to persuade him to stay. Lack of contact or negatively experienced contacts seemed the main reasons for the second group. In sum, then, disappointment in the organization and low levels of commitment prepare people to resign, but negatively experienced contacts or lack of positively experienced contacts make them actually decide to leave. This evokes the spiral image of mutually reinforcing levels of commitment and participation. Low levels of commitment are, inter alia, caused by lack of positive contacts with the organization. Once levels of commitment are lowering and doubt is sown in the hearts, then, when gratifying contacts still fail to occur the step to resign as a member is easily taken.

Religious sects but also underground organizations are very much aware of these mechanisms, and therefore make serious efforts to maintain both levels of commitment and contacts with the organization very high (Richardson, van der Lans, and Derks, 1986; della Porta 1992b). Thus Richardson et al. observe that voluntary disaffiliation in communal religious groups is usually much more difficult for the individual than in non-communal groups (p. 105; see also Robbins 1988).

Resigning as a union activist. Becoming a union activist requires higher than average levels of union commitment (Barling et al. 1992), more frequent contact with the union, belief in unionism, feelings of responsibility, and a highly supportive social environment (Nandram 1995; Hoekstra 1994). Unlike their fellow-members, members who become activists find union activism an attractive job to take on. Indeed, many of them are activists for an extended period of time – up to ten years or more. Yet some 35 per cent considered quitting activism and 14 per cent actually did so. The question, of course, is why?

Being a union activist is a time-consuming job. On average activists spend 4 hours per week (half of it of their free time, half of it their working time) on their union, and a fair proportion even 5–10 hours a week. It is not only a time-consuming job, it is also stressful. Union activists can get caught between many fires, company management, union officials, members, colleagues, spouses. As a consequence, many of them report overload and role conflicts. One-third to half of the activists feel that they have more tasks than they can manage. Half to two-thirds report conflicting expectations from their employers and their unions. A quarter to one-third experience contradictory demands from their colleagues, fellow-activists, or constituencies. Yet interestingly, these are not sufficient reason to quit. But, for some activists such stressful experiences produce burnout and burnout *is* a reason to step down, especially in the context of an unsupportive environment (colleagues and/or family members who discourage continuation).

Burnout is a stress reaction typical of people who work with people. It is an overarching concept which covers loss of motivation, cynicism, and depersonalization (Maslach 1982). Burnout is typically observed among idealistically motivated volunteers, who start their job with unrealistically high expectations. The question remains, of course, why some activists experience burnout and quit while others don't and remain active. In fact, we do not know much about that subject. But our own research among union activists and peace activists and a modest but interesting study by Gomes and Maslach (1991) suggest some of the answers, that could perhaps stimulate more research into the dynamics underlying long-term commitment to activism.

Research in our own group suggests that a fair proportion of both union activists and peace movement activists experience burnout – up to 50 per cent if a loose measure of loss of motivation is used and some 10 per cent if a more elaborated but strict measure of burnout is used (Nandram 1995; Struik 1991). Interestingly, it is not so much the costs and tensions associated with participation that produce burnout. That at least is not what the scant research leads one to suspect. Costs, tensions, risks, and the like seem to be part of the game in the eyes of the participants. The results presented by both Gomes and Maslach and Struik, seem to suggest that it is high costs or high levels of psychological tension *in combination* with high levels of commitment that produce burnout. It is the inability to be flexible about their work as an activist and to take time to relax that seems to do the damage. In the words of one of Gomes and Maslach's (1991, p. 6) interviewees: 'You keep pushing yourself. There's no limit. It's like an anorexic getting thin – you're never quite thin enough. When you're an activist you're never working hard enough. So you're exhausted and feel like you've got nothing left to give.' Such observations have important implications. Activists are by definition the more committed members of a movement who feel a moral obligation to actively support the movement. In a way this makes them more vulnerable to burnout than other supporters. If on the top of that they are part of a movement culture which conveys the message that no periods of low motivation can be permitted, the already existing susceptibility to burnout is easily carried through. Indeed, Gomes and Maslach suggest that unreasonably high standards of unwavering commitment often backfires, leading eventually to complete withdrawal and that by living a more flexible life activists can increase their overall effectiveness and function as role models for other activists and enjoy their lives more along the way.

But movement organizations can have a salutary impact. From social psychology we know that social support plays a vital role in people's efforts to cope with stress (Lazarus and Folkman 1984). Our research among union activists suggests that the extent to which stress results in loss of motivation (burnout) also depends on the amount of social support activists experience that they receive from their unions (Hoekstra and Klandermans 1995). Being an activist *is* on many an occasion a taxing experience. Seeing that your movement organization appreciates your hardship and is prepared to support you in your efforts to cope with it, apparently makes a real difference.

Persisters, shifters, and terminators. Not every activist who leaves a movement is burned out, however. It is not uncommon to see movements lose momentum, whereupon certain categories of activist start to evacuate the arena. This process has been demonstrated time and again in accounts of movement decline (see for example Oberschall 1978 on the Students for a Democratic Society; Duffhues and Felling 1989 on the Dutch Catholic Movement; or Silverman 1991 on the Canadian Peace Movement). But, to my knowledge our study of defection among activists of the Dutch peace movement in its period of decline was the first attempt to map and understand who left at different times and who stayed and where those who left did go. We called them persisters, shifters, and terminators depending on their careers over the six years we investigated. *Persisters* were those who stayed behind as prophetic minorities to maintain the abeyance structure (Taylor 1989) of the peace movement. *Shifters* were those who left the peace movement to become active in another movement and *terminators* were those who gave up political activism altogether.

In 1991, six years after we interviewed our activists for the first time, 87.5 per cent were no longer active in the peace movement. The majority of those who quit did so in the years since our previous interviews in 1987. At that point 28 per cent of the people interviewed had left their group since our interviews in 1985, and 43 per cent of those who stayed had considered leaving. Who were the people who left and why did they leave? First of all, 16 per cent were members of groups that had ceased to exist and so discontinuation of participation in their case was not active defection. The remaining 44 per cent chose to quit while the group was still functioning. Some of them had already left the movement in 1987, while others quit between 1987 and 1991. In both cases we may rightly ask why.

But let me contextualize these dates a little bit first. The year 1985 was the year of the petition against the cruise missiles. The activists had worked themselves to a standstill for the petition, and the total disregard of the outcome by the government was a major blow to many of them, although paradoxically very few had expected a different outcome. Yet, what kept many of them going were the coming elections in 1987 and the confident expectation that the parties in government (Christian Democrats and Conservatives) would be punished for the stand they had taken on cruise missiles. To their dismay nothing of the kind took place and worse perhaps the IKV (the Interdenominational Peace Council, the core organization of the Dutch peace movement in those days) decided not to campaign against the parties in government because it did not want to estrange the churches any further by campaigning against the Christian Democratic Party.

Two blows in a row forced many activists to reconsider their participation in the peace movement. Yet there is no single answer to the question of why they eventually left or stayed. Some of those who left were marginal members to begin with: they had spent relatively little time in activism in 1985, they were less committed to the movement, and had already considered leaving the movement in 1985. Some of those who left were burned out, had lost their faith or felt estranged from the other people in the movement. Others radicalized when the movement refused to adopt more militant strategies. Again others shifted to other movements. And finally, some left for reasons which had nothing to do with any of these factors, but because of personal reasons (family responsibilities, studies, jobs, moved to another city and so on).

Note that none of these explain movement decline. These are reasons why people leave movements, but movement decline is the outcome of both exiting and entering. Indeed, movement decline results from the movement's inability to keep participants *and* its inability to attract new participants to replace those who leave (Cornfield 1986). There are always people leaving movements. Even in 1985 at the Dutch peace movement's peak, activists were leaving, but more activists were joining so the net result was growth. It was only in the years after 1985, after the movement's failure to have an impact on the government and after the start of the talks between Reagan and Gorbachev that the movement lost its attraction and that those quitting outnumbered those joining.

Unlike those who left, *persisters* consisted of activists who were somewhat older, politically less radical, more often active members of church organizations. For most of them the peace movement had been the first movement they had joined in their lives. They spent a relatively large amount of time in the movement and occupied formal positions. When asked why they remained active in the peace movement they referred predominantly to commitment to the group they were part of and the people in that group.

Those who left had lost much of their commitment to the movement when they did so and especially to the IKV, the movement organization they were members of. In their eyes the movement had lost much of its vitality and had little to offer any more.

Among those who left, however, *shifters* and *terminators* were of two different kinds and left for different reasons and with different destinations. Shifters had been active in other movements more often than terminators before they engaged in the peace movement. The movements mentioned were movements such as the anti-nuclear power movement, the anti-Vietnam war movement, the environmental movement, the student movement, third world support groups, the women's movement, and so on. Moreover, shifters had more often participated in more militant protests like blockades and site-occupations. Unlike the terminators, the shifters left the movement because they opted for more militant strategies against the policy of the IKV. Shifters spent the most hours a week on the movement, even more than persisters; terminators spent the least. Among shifters being an activist seems to have been a central part of their identity, whereas among terminators activism was a more external affair – though certainly more active than the average citizen, activism did not occupy their lives completely. Among those who stopped because their group ceased to exist, those who quit activism altogether reported feelings of burnout, unlike those who shifted to other movements.

In sum, *persisters* had no history in social movement participation. The peace movement was the first movement they had joined in their lives. They spent a relatively large amount of time in the movement, occupied formal positions in the movement, and continued to be active. They were more often committed to a church than the other types. Of the three they identified most strongly with the peace movement. *Shifters*, on the other hand, have a lifelong history as activists. They were active in other movements before they entered the peace movement and they continued to be active in other movements after they had left the peace movement. Of the three types they had spent the most time on movement activities in the past and in the present. They were active on a broad range of activities, which adds to their image as activists 'pur sang'. *Terminators* who had finally left a still existing group, had a more marginal position in their groups compared to the others. They spent less time, took less responsibility and identified less with the movement. Those who had stopped because their group had broken up however, quit political activism altogether because of feelings of burnout.

As an epilogue, the international peace movement attempted in 1991 to remobilize to protest the Gulf War, in the Netherlands with surprisingly little success. Persisters, shifters and terminators among the former activists alike took an extremely negative stand on the military intervention, much more so than the general population in the Netherlands. However, while 63 per cent of the persisters took part in actions against the war, this held for only 32 per cent of the shifters and 22 per cent of the terminators. Apparently chances were low that the latter two – disconnected from the peace movement networks as they were – were targeted and mobilized. This was evidenced by the fact that shifters and terminators not only were asked to participate less often, but hardly spoke about the war with any other person still active in the peace movement.

Radicalization. Our findings regarding the Dutch peace movement draw our attention to the fact that becoming inactive is not the only response to movement decline. Indeed, radicalization has been described as an alternative response to movement decline by several authors (cf. della Porta and Tarrow 1986; Kriesi, Koopmans, Duyvendak and Giugni 1995). Some of the peace activists we interviewed were young, militant, and frustrated by the movement's failure and its unwillingness to turn to more militant, strategies. They joined other more militant groups of the peace movement or left the peace movement altogether and joined some other more radical protest movement such as the antifascism movement. It is important to note that these activists were already more radical when, at the time, they entered the movement. Most of them joined the movement at its peak as what has been called the 'second generation' of activists. As such they seem to have followed the more general route to radicalization described in the literature on underground organizations (della Porta 1992b). According to this literature 'radicals' in a movement are more militant from the outset. They enter the movement at a later point in the cycle and, then, when the government becomes less responsive or even repressive they further radicalize.

Important for our discussion on sustained participation and defection is the observation that sustained participation can take the form of radicalization. Evidence collected thus far points to the vital role of social networks in this regard (see della Porta 1992a for a compilation). Loyalty to the peer group is an important motive as activists move towards ever-deepening political commitment and make the transition from non-militant groups to the underground. Yet it is important to emphasize that radicalization is not a self-induced process but a response to something, be it movement failure, decline or institutionalization, or state repression. The point is, however, that as a rule only a minority within the larger political subculture responds to such a course of events with radicalization. In della Porta's words, it is 'the second generation of activists, which was socialized to politics after violence has become accepted in larger or smaller wings of the social movement sector, [which] thus accepted radical action as routine' (p. 23). [...] Donatella della Porta (1992b) emphasizes that most participants in underground organizations started their movement careers with more moderate forms of movement participation. Underground organizations evolve when protest repertoires gradually escalate toward violence, because more moderate strategies are deemed to be ineffective or because state repression impresses people as 'absolute injustice'. Kriesi et al. (1995) make the interesting observation that institutionalization of a movement and radicalization often coincide. As movement organizations are co-opted by state agencies or become more moderate, more radical factions break away from the alliance and stage militant forms of protest. Movement cycles as Tarrow (1989a and b) argued, are triggered by tactical innovation. As long as authorities do not yet know the answer to the new tactics these innovations offset the balance of power between challengers and authorities with movement successes as the result. It is these early successes which not only make for rapid diffusion of protest but for a 'second generation' of activists flocking into the movement organizations associated with the initial successful strategy. As long as the strategy pays off, more militant activists are willing to abide by it, but as the novelty wanes and the authorities learn how to respond, the coalition of moderates and militants breaks down. The militants plead for more radical directions which the moderates are unwilling to take. The militants may then take over the organization and force the moderate majority out – as, for example, the Weathermen did in the case of SDS (Braungart and Braungart 1992) or leave the organization and establish separate groups that stage radical and sometimes violent protest – a process described for the Italian protest cycle of the late sixties and early seventies by della Porta and Tarrow (1986) and for the Dutch and German protest cycles in the seventies and eighties by Kriesi et al. (1995).

The Dutch peace movement provides a typical example of this dynamic. When the movement was in the upswing militant activists flocked into its ranks. This was not always to the enchantment of the original more moderate activists, who often felt overruled by this 'second generation.' As long as the moderate strategy of the movement seemed to be successful in mobilizing mass support the extremes could be held together, but once it became clear that the Dutch government was not impressed at all and key movement organizations such as the IKV were unwilling to resort to more militant strategies the militants started to abandon the ranks again (Klandermans 1994). For a short period they staged more confrontational protest events, but then the talks between Reagan and Gorbachev and the INF-treaty resulting from it meant the end of the Dutch peace movement as a manifest movement (Oegema 1991).

[. . .]

References

Barling, Julian, Clive Fullagar, and Kevin E. Kelloway. 1992. *The Union and Its Members. A Psychological Approach*. New York/Oxford: Oxford University Press.

Braungart, Richard and Margaret M. Braungart. 1992. 'From Protest to Terrorism: The Case of SDS and the Weathermen.' Pp. 45–78 in della Porta, Donatella (ed.). 'Social Movements and Violence: Participation in Underground Organizations.' *International Social Movement Research*, Vol. 4. Greenwich, Conn.: JAI-Press.

Cornfield, Daniel B. 1986. 'Declining Union Membership in the Post World War II Era: The United Furniture Workers, 1939–1982.' *American Journal of Sociology*.

Della Porta, Donatella (ed.). 1992a. 'Social Movements and Violence: Participation in Underground Organizations.' *International Social Movement Research*. Vol. 4. Greenwich, CT: JAI-Press.

Della Porta, Donatella. 1992b. 'Political Socialization in Left-Wing Underground Organizations: Biographies of Italian and German Militants.' Pp. 259–290 in della Porta, Donatella (ed.). 'Social Movements and Violence: Participation in Underground Organizations.' *International Social Movement Research*, Vol. 4. Greenwich, Conn.: JAI-Press.

Della Porta, Donatella and Sidney Tarrow. 1986. 'Unwanted Children: Political Violence and the Cycle of Protest in Italy: 1966–1973.' *European Journal of Political Research*, 14: 607–632.

Downton, James V. and Paul Wehr. 1991. 'Peace Movements: The Role of Commitment and Community in Sustaining Member Participation.' *Research in Social Movements, Conflicts and Change*. Vol. 13: 113–134.

Duffhues, Ton and Albert Felling. 1989. 'The Development, Change, and Decline of the Dutch Catholic Movement.' Pp. 95–117 in Organizing for Change: Social Movement Organizations in Europe and the United States. *International Social Movement Research,* Vol. 2, edited by Bert Klandermans. Greenwich, Conn.: JAI-Press.

Fine, Gary Alan. 1995. 'Public Narration and Group Culture: Discerning Discourse in Social Movements.' Pp. 127–143 in *Social Movements and Culture*, edited by Hank Johnston and Bert Klandermans, Minneapolis/London: University of Minnesota Press/UCL Press.

Gomes, Mary E. and Christina Maslach. 1991. Commitment and Burnout among Political Activists: An In-depth Study. Paper presented at the 14th Annual Meeting of the International Society of Political Psychology. Helsinki, Finland.

Hoekstra, Manon. 1994. *CNV-kaderleden: Recrutering en ondersteuning*. Amsterdam, Vrije Universiteit.

Hoekstra, Manon and Bert Klandermans. 1995. Role Conflicts of Union Activists: How Social Support Can Help. Paper presented at the Second International Conference on Emerging Union Structures. Stockholm, Sweden.

Klandermans, Bert. 1986. 'Psychology and Trade Union Participation: Joining, Acting, Quitting.' *Journal of Occupational Psychology*, 59: 189–204.

Klandermans, Bert. 1992. 'The Social Construction of Protest and Multi-organizational Fields.' In Aldon Morris and Carol Mueller (eds.) *Frontiers in Social Movement Theory*. New Haven, CT: Yale University Press.

Klandermans, Bert. 1994. 'Transient Identities? Membership Patterns in the Dutch Peace Movement.' Pp. 168–184 in *New Social Movements. From Ideology to Identity*, edited by Enrique Larana, Hank Johnston and Joseph R. Gusfield. Philadelphia: Temple University Press.

Kriesi, Hanspeter, Ruud Koopmans, Jan-Willem Duyvendak, and Marco G. Giugni. 1995. *The Politics of New Social Movements in Western Europe. A Comparative Analysis*. Minneapolis/London: University of Minnesota Press/UCL Press.

Lane, Robert E. 1964. *Political Life. Why and How People Get Involved in Politics*. New York: Free Press.

Lazarsfeld, Paul F., Bernard B. Berelson, and Hazel Gaudet. 1948. *The People's Choice*. New York: Columbia University Press.

Lazarus, R.S. and S. Folkman. 1984. *Stress Appraisal and Coping*. New York: Springer.

Maslach, C. 1982. *Burn-out. The Costs of Caring*. Englewood Cliffs: Prentice Hall.

Moreland, Richard L. and John Levine. 1982. 'Socialization in Small Groups: Temporal Changes in Individual-Group Relations', *Advances in Experimental Social Psychology*, 15: 137–192.

Nandram, Sharda. 1995. Het beredeneerd aan – en afmelden als kaderlid. Een studie naar het vrijwilligerswerk binnen de vakbond. Unpublished dissertation, Vrije Universiteit, Amsterdam.

Oberschall, Anthony. 1978. 'The Decline of the 1960's Social Movements.' *Research in Social Movements, Conflict and Change,* Vol. 1, Greenwich, Conn.: JAI Press.

Oegema, Dirk. 1991. 'The Dutch Peace Movement, 1977 to 1987.' Pp. 93–149 in *Peace Movements in Western Europe and the United States International Social Movement Research,* Vol. 3, edited by Bert Klandermans. Greenwich, Conn.: JAI-Press.

Oegema, Dirk. 1993. *Tussen petitie en perestroika. De nadagen van de Nederlandse vredesbeweging*. Dissertatie Vrije Universiteit.

Oegema, Dirk and Bert Klandermans. 1994. 'Why Social Movement Sympathizers Don't Participate: Erosion and Non-conversion of Support.' *American Sociological Review*, 59: 703–722.

Richardson, James T., Jan van der Lans, and Frans Derks. 1986. 'Leaving and Labeling: Voluntary and Coerced Disaffiliation from Religious Social Movements.' *Research in Social Movements, Conflicts and Change*, 9: 97–126.

Robbins, Thomas. 1988. *Cults, Converts and Charisma*. London: Sage.

Snow, David A., Rochford E. Burke Jr., Steve K. Worden, and Robert D. Benford. 1986. 'Frame Alignment Processes, Micro-mobilization and Movement Participation.' *American Sociological Review*, 51: 464–481.

Struik, Anne-Margriet. 1991. Stoppen of doorgaan? Redenen om te stoppen of door te gaan met participeren in de lokale afdelingen van de vredesbeweging. Unpublished thesis, Vrije Universiteit, Amsterdam.

Tarrow, Sidney. 1989a. *Struggle, Politics and Reform: Collective Action, Social Movements and Cycles of Protest*. Cornell University, Western Societies Paper No. 21.

Tarrow, Sidney. 1989b. *Democracy and Disorder; Protest and Politics in Italy. 1965–1975*. Oxford: Oxford University Press.

Taylor, Verta. 1989. 'Social Movement Continuity: The Women's Movement in Abeyance.' *American Sociological Review*, 54: 761–775.

Taylor, Verta and Nancy E. Whittier. 1995. 'Analytical Approaches to Social Movement Culture: The Culture of the Women's Movement.' Pp. 163–187 in *Social Movements and Culture*, edited by Hank Johnston and Bert Klandermans. Minneapolis/London: University of Minnesota Press/UCL Press.

Van de Putte, Bas. 1995. 'Uit de bond: Bedanken als vakbondslid.' Pp. 87–112 in *De vakbeweging na de welvaartsstaat*, edited by Bert Klandermans and Jelle Visser. Assen: van Gorcum.

Van Rij, Coen. 1994. To Join or Not to Join. An Event-History Analysis of Trade-Union Membership in the Netherlands. Unpublished Dissertion, Amsterdam: Nimmo.

Van Rij. Coen. 1995. 'Naar de bond: Vakbondsloopbanen en beroepsloopbanen.' Pp. 67–86 in *De vakbeweging na de welvaartsstaat*, edited by Bert Klandermans and Jelle Visser. Assen: van Gorcum.

Van Rijn, Ingrid. 1995. Why Workers Join Unions – and Leave Them. Matters of Money and Mind. Unpublished Dissertation, Free University, Amsterdam.

Part V

What Do Movement Participants Think and Feel?

Introduction

To most readers, the point of view of movement participants would seem to be the most important issue in understanding social movements. What do they want to accomplish? What do they demand? What kinds of emotions propel or draw them into the street? What goes through their minds? Are these people like the rest of us, or somehow different? In this part we try to get inside the heads—but also the hearts—of protestors, to see the world from their point of view. In the end, we all care about something deeply enough that, under the right circumstances, we could be drawn into a movement that addresses it.

One hundred years of scholarship thought this was an important goal, but unfortunately the same scholars assumed they knew what was inside protestors' heads without doing much empirical research to see if they were right. To them protest was such an unusual activity that protestors had to be either immature, mistaken, or irrational. For some of these early theorists, people could be driven mad by crowds, swept up into the motion of the crowd and led to do things they otherwise would not (LeBon 1895). Others assumed that people must be alienated from their societies in order to engage in such deviant behavior. Still others thought there must be some kind of strange psychological dynamics at work: people joined because they felt personally inadequate and wished to become part of something larger than themselves (Hoffer 1951); or young people used protest as a way to rebel against their fathers in an Oedipal dynamic (Smelser 1968). These theories were so dismissive of social movements that a new generation of scholars in the 1960s, who were sympathetic to many of the movements they saw around them, and sometimes participated in, virtually abandoned the effort to look inside the heads of protestors.

The mobilization and then process theorists simply assumed that protestors had rational goals, primarily the pursuit of their own economic, political, and legal interests. By assuming this, they did not have to investigate protestors' points of view any more than their predecessors had. To them, the idea that protestors had strong emotions seemed to admit that protestors were not rational; the idea that protestors needed to do some cultural work to "construct" their grievances and goals seemed to make these less important, more arbitrary. Besides, if a group's interests were structurally determined—by their economic class position, say, or by racism in the laws—it was easy to concentrate on the mobilization of resources and other opportunities for action that most interested these theorists. They assumed the willingness to protest was already there, and only needed an opportunity for expression.

But even at the height of these structural approaches, not all social scientists were willing to give up on the minds of protestors. Kristin Luker was one of these. We have excerpted a chapter of her book, *Abortion and the Politics of Motherhood*, which masterfully lays out the crux of the abortion debate: those on each side see the world in very different ways. They make conflicting assumptions about what motherhood means, about what a woman's life should be like, about what can be left to chance and what is a valid area for human planning and control. They live in different worlds, and are shocked and outraged when they find out about the other side's world. Luker describes the worldviews of the two sides in largely cognitive terms, but she is also trying to explain the emotional reactions—surprise, outrage, vindictiveness—that result. She does not explicitly theorize about emotions, perhaps afraid that this might make the protestors seem less rational. Her main contribution is to show that both sides are acting reasonably given their visions of the world. (Because of space limitations, we have only reproduced her analysis of the anti-abortion activists.)

In many debates, people on the two sides simply live in different social and cultural worlds, with contrasting experiences, moral values, and beliefs. Neither side is altogether irrational, although each may make claims or hold beliefs that can be tested—and potentially disproved—through scientific evidence. In the years since Luker wrote her book, there has been an explosion of research on the mental worlds of protestors. Frame alignment deals with different ways of viewing the world, different ways of cutting it up in order to put some aspects in the frame and leave others out of it. Collective identity is another tool for dividing up the world in a way that may spur action.

This cultural "constructionist" approach does not suggest that protestors are irrational. But protestors sometimes make mistakes, such as constructing visions of the world that hurt their own cause. These are strategic errors, from which they usually try to learn, rather than a form of irrationality. Jane Mansbridge examines one such malfunction in her chapter on the women's movement. Efforts to pass the ERA (Equal Rights Amendment) depended on volunteers who were there because of their strong beliefs and feelings. As a result they tended to divide the world into "us" (inside the movement) and "them" (everyone else). This is a common temptation for social movements (it was even stronger, Mansbridge says, among the ERA's opponents), but it encourages extreme claims out of touch with the broader public and legislators. It is a common cause of radicalization in movements. This is a dilemma for most movements: whether to rely on exclusivity, purity, and homogeneity in order to reach in, or whether to "water down" the message in order to reach out. Both strategies have their advantages and disadvantages.

In the next chapter, Ryan and Gamson also show how cultural framings are intertwined with strategic activities. Good frames don't do anything by themselves, but must be combined with organizations and networks and other sorts of mobilizing activities. Frames are not especially useful for reaching anonymous audiences through the mass media; they are better as a means for carrying on conversations with allies and components of your own coalition. They allow different groups to talk to one another about how to proceed. Of course, the news media matter a lot, but they contain individuals and organizations with whom activists must carry on a dialogue.

Almost all scholars now admit that cultural meanings are an important dimension of social movements, that we need to look at how protestors view the world, and the kind of rhetoric they use to present this vision to others. There are still two large gaps in the literature, however. For all the process theorists' emphasis on the state and other players in a movement's environment, they have done little work to understand these other people's points of view. State bureaucrats, politicians, and police officers also have distinctive worldviews, and also try to persuade others that their arguments and perspectives are valid. Few scholars have approached these others from a cultural point of view (for one exception, see Jasper 1990). This has been left to neighboring fields of research such as that on moral panics (e.g. Goode and Ben-Yehuda 1994).

Another big gap has been the emotions of protestors. Almost all the cultural work on social movements has been about their cognitive beliefs and moral principles, but an equally important part of culture consists of their feelings about the world, themselves, and each other. A variety of emotions are apparent in Luker's and Mansbridge's selections, as thoughts and feelings are not easily separated.

James Jasper has tried to outline the importance of emotions, especially arguing that many standard explanatory concepts in social-movement research have emotions hidden inside them, unexamined and untheorized. It is often these emotions that are doing the causal work for the concepts, as when "opportunities" provide, most of all, emotional inspiration for protestors. Some emotions, he argues, have to do with people's long-term feelings toward each other, while others are more immediate reactions to events and information. Social movements work hard to shape both of these. Jasper argues that emotions are a part of culture, just like beliefs and moral values. (For more on emotions, see Jasper 1997; and Goodwin, Jasper, and Polletta 2001.)

Nothing expresses the ideas of a movement or arouses the emotions of participants better than music. Songs have been crucial to the U.S. civil rights and labor movements, for instance, as well as the causes of the 1960s. So we provide a list of important songs that represent several different movements of the twentieth century. The list comes from *Contexts* magazine.

As Mansbridge shows, the views and feelings that maintain the enthusiasm of members may not advance a movement's cause with the external world: these are two very different audiences for a social movement's words and actions. In part VII we will examine the strategic uses of words and images—in other words, how movements employ words and images to attain their goals. There may be tradeoffs between their external effectiveness and their internal solidarity, enthusiasm, and ability to recruit new members.

Discussion Questions

1. What are the core elements of the anti-abortion worldview?
2. What is the tradeoff between reaching in and reaching out, as Mansbridge describes it?
3. How are frames and other ideas put into action? How do organizers actually use them in pursuing their ends?
4. What are reactive and affective emotions? What is the relationship between them?
5. Can you think of other examples of the role of emotions in social movements?
6. What favorite songs of yours express protest against some condition?

14 World Views of Pro- and Anti-Abortion Activists

Kristin Luker

[. . .] Different beliefs about the roles of the sexes, about the meaning of parenthood, and about human nature are all called into play when the issue is abortion. Abortion, therefore, gives us a rare opportunity to examine closely a set of values that are almost never directly discussed. Because these values apply to spheres of life that are very private (sex) or very diffuse (morality), most people never look at the patterns they form. For this reason the abortion debate has become something that illuminates our deepest, and sometimes our dearest, beliefs.

At the same time, precisely because these values are so rarely discussed overtly, when they are called into question, as they are by the abortion debate, individuals feel that an entire *world view* is under assault. An interesting characteristic of a world view, however, is that the values located within it are so deep and so dear to us that we find it hard to imagine that we even have a "world view" – to us it is just reality – or that anyone else could not share it. By definition, those areas covered by a "world view" are those parts of life we take for granted, never imagine questioning, and cannot envision decent, moral people not sharing.

When an event such as the abortion controversy occurs, which makes it clear that one's world view is not the only one, it is immediately apparent why surprise, outrage, and vindictiveness are the order of the day. Individuals are surprised because for most of them this is the first time their deepest values have been brought to explicit consciousness, much less challenged. They are outraged because these values are so taken for granted that people have no vocabulary with which to discuss the fact that what is at odds is a fundamental view of reality. And they are vindictive because denying that one's opponents are decent, honorable people is one way of distancing oneself from the unsettling thought that there could be legitimate differences of opinion on one's most cherished beliefs.

In the course of our interviews, it became apparent that each side of the abortion debate has an internally coherent and mutually shared view of the world that is tacit, never fully articulated, and, most importantly, completely at odds with the world view held by their opponents. This chapter will examine in turn the world views of first the pro-life activists, then the pro-choice activists to demonstrate the truth of what many of the activists we interviewed asserted: that abortion is just "the tip of the iceberg." To be sure, not every single one of those interrelated values that I have called a "world view" characterized each and every pro-life or pro-choice person interviewed. It is well within the realm of possibility that an activist might find some individual areas where he or she would feel more akin to the values expressed by their opponents than by those on their own side. But taken as a whole, there was enough consistency in the way people on each side talked about the world to warrant the conclusion that each side has its own particular "world view," that these world views tend to be isolated from competing world views, and that forced to choose, most activists would find far more in common with the world view of their side than that of their opponents.

Pro-Life Views of the World

To begin with, pro-life activists believe that men and women are intrinsically different, and this is both a cause and a product of the fact that they have different roles in life. Here are some representative comments from the interviews:

> The question is, what is natural for human life and what will make people happy? Now I deplore the oppression of any people, and so I would ipso facto deplore the oppression of women but a lot of things are being interpreted as oppression simply [out of] restless agitation against a natural order that should really be allowed to prevail. The feminist movement has wanted to, as it were, really turn women into men or to kind of de-sex them, and they [feminists] pretend that there are no important differences between men and women. Now when it comes to a woman doing a job, a woman being paid the same rate that a man gets for the same job, I'm very much in favor of all that. [What] I find so disturbing [about] the whole abortion mentality is the idea that family duties – rearing children, managing a home, loving and caring for a husband – are somehow degrading to women. And that's an idea which is very current in our society – that women are not going to find fulfillment until they get out there and start competing for a livelihood with men and talking like men, cursing and whatever, although not all men curse. I don't mean that to sound ... maybe that's beginning to have an emotional overtone that I didn't want it to have.
>
> [...]
>
> [Men and women] were created differently and we're meant to complement each other, and when you get away from our [proper] roles as such, you start obscuring them. That's another part of the confusion that's going on now, people don't know where they stand, they don't know how to act, they don't know where they're coming from, so your psychiatrists' couches are filled with lost souls, with lost people that for a long time now have been gradually led into confusion and don't even know it.
>
> [...]

Movement Culture Social movements often have, and self-consciously cultivate, an internal culture that is different from the larger culture in which they are embedded. In other words, participants in movements often share beliefs, norms, ways of working together, forms of decision-making, emotional styles, sexual practices, musical, literary, and sartorial tastes, etc., that are distinct from those of the larger culture. Sometimes movement cultures are warm, jovial, and inviting; sometimes they are austere, serious, and even intimidating. Some are cultivated to attract the greatest number of people; some are intended to attract, or produce, a relatively small number of highly committed people. Distinctive types of movement culture may prove politically effective in certain contexts, yet quite ineffectual in others.

Pro-life activists agree that men and women, as a result of these intrinsic differences, have different roles to play: men are best suited to the public world of work, and women are best suited to rear children, manage homes, and love and care for husbands. Most pro-life activists believe that motherhood – the raising of children and families – is the most fulfilling role that women can have. To be sure, they live in a country where over half of all women work, and they do acknowledge that some women are employed. But when they say (as almost all of them do) that women who work should get equal pay for equal work, they do not mean that women *should* work. On the contrary, they subscribe quite strongly to the traditional belief that women should be wives and mothers *first*. Mothering, in their view, is so demanding that it is a full-time job, and any woman who cannot commit herself fully to it should avoid it entirely.

> Well, if that's what you've decided in life, I don't feel that there's anything wrong with not being a wife or mother. If someone wants a career, that's fine. But if you are a mother I think you have an important job to do. I think you're responsible for your home, and I think you're responsible for the children you bring into the world, and you're responsible, as far as you possibly

> can be, for educating and teaching them; obviously you have to teach them what you believe is right – moral values and responsibilities and rights.... It's a huge job, and you never know how well you're doing until it's too late.

Because pro-life activists see having a family as an emotionally demanding, labor-intensive project, they find it hard to imagine that a woman could put forty hours a week into an outside job and still have time for her husband and children. Equally important, they feel that different kinds of emotional "sets" are called for in the work world and in the home.

[...]

For a woman to shift gears from her emotional role in the home to a competitive role in the office is not only difficult, they argue, but damaging to both men and women, and to their children.

These views on the different nature of men and women and the roles appropriate to each combine to make abortion look wrong three times over. First, it is intrinsically wrong because it takes a human life and what makes women special is their ability to nourish life. Second, it is wrong because *by giving women control over their fertility*, it breaks up an intricate set of social relationships between men and women that has traditionally surrounded (and in the ideal case protected) women and children. Third and finally, abortion is wrong because it fosters and supports a world view that deemphasizes (and therefore *downgrades*) the traditional roles of men and women. Because these roles have been satisfying ones for pro-life people and because they believe this emotional and social division of labor is both "appropriate and natural," the act of abortion is wrong because it plays havoc with this arrangement of the world. For example, because abortion formally diminishes male decision-making power, it also diminishes male responsibility. Thus, far from liberating women, pro-life people argue, abortion oppresses them.

[...]

> I think I like men enough to know that men still want women to be a little bit feminine and all the rest of it, and I think [pro-choice people] have helped destroy that, I think they've made women into something like the same as men, and we're not. I think we're totally different. I don't think that means that we can't do some jobs they do, but I think we're totally different. I think that they've helped destroy the family because they want to make it so free for the woman to go to work, like with the childcare centers and all the rest of it. You know, now, evidently they're thinking up Social Security for the woman who works in the home and all the rest of it, and I just think that's ridiculous.

Because pro-life people see the world as inherently divided both emotionally and socially into a male sphere and a female sphere, they see the loss of the female sphere as a very deep one indeed. They see tenderness, morality, caring, emotionality, and self-sacrifice as the exclusive province of women; and if women cease to be traditional women, who will do the caring, who will offer the tenderness? A pro-life doctor argued that although women may have suffered from the softening influence they provided for men and for the society as a whole, they had much to gain as well.

> I think women's lib is on the wrong track. I think they've got every [possible] gripe and they've always been that way. The women have been the superior people. They're more civilized, they're more unselfish by nature, but now they want to compete with men at being selfish. And so there's nobody to give an example, and what happens is that men become *more* selfish. See, the women used to be an example and they had to take it on the chin for that ... but they also benefited from it because we don't want to go back to the cavemen, where you drag the woman around and treat her like nothing. Women were to be protected, respected, and treated like something important.

In this view, everyone loses when traditional roles are lost. Men lose the nurturing that women offer, the nurturing that gently encourages them to give up their potentially destructive and aggressive urges. Women lose the protection and cherishing that men offer. And children lose full-time loving by at least one parent, as well as clear models for their own futures.

These different views about the intrinsic nature of men and women also shape pro-life views about sex. The nineteenth century introduced new terms to describe the two faces of sexual activity, distinguishing between "procreative love," whose goal is reproduction, and "amative love," whose goal is sensual pleasure and mutual enjoyment.

[...]

For the pro-life people we talked with, the relative worth of procreative sex and amative sex was clear. In part this is because many of them, being Catholic, accept a natural law doctrine of sex, which holds that a body part is destined to be used for its physiological function. As one man put it: "You're not just given arms and legs for no purpose.... There must be some cause [for sex] and you begin to think, well, it must be for procreation ultimately, and certainly procreation in addition to fostering a loving relationship with your spouse."

In terms of this view, the meaning of sexual experiences is distorted whenever procreation is not intended. Contraception, premarital sex, and infidelity are wrong not only because of their social consequences but also because they strip sexual experience of its meaning. The man just quoted continued to spell out the implications of this position:

> Most pro-lifers think that people, regardless of their station in life, ought to be chaste – this means chaste also for married people.... I think this is because [pro-lifers], much more than pro-abortion people, are in reverence of sexuality and believe it literally to be a sacred thing. I really think pro-abortion people have a hard time arguing that they think that. [But] if you do think this way, [sex is] something very special, it's the means by which two people can express their union with one another, spiritual and physical. Then you see that it must be protected somehow, by certain forms and conventions, including marriage. [...]

[...]

Because many pro-life people see sex as literally sacred, they are disturbed by values that seem to secularize and profane it. The whole constellation of values that supports amative (or "recreational") sex is seen by them as doing just that. Values that define sexuality as a wholesome physical activity, as healthy as volleyball but somewhat more fun, call into question everything that pro-life people believe in. Sex is sacred because in their world view it has the capacity to be something transcendent – to bring into existence another human life. To routinely eradicate that capacity through premarital sex (in which very few people seek to bring a new life into existence) or through contraception or abortion is to turn the world upside down.

As implied by our discussion so far, the attitudes of pro-life people toward contraception are rooted in their views about the inherent differences between men and women and about the nature and purpose of sexuality. Although the activists we interviewed often pointed out that the pro-life movement is officially neutral on the topic of contraception, this statement does not fully capture the complexity of their views and feelings. Virtually all of them felt very strongly that the pill and the IUD are abortifacients (they may cause the death of a very young embryo) and that passage of a human life law against abortion would also ban the pill and the IUD. Most of them, furthermore, refused to use traditional contraceptives on moral grounds. As a pro-life doctor said:

> I think it's quite clear that the IUD is abortifacient 100 percent of the time and the pill is sometimes an abortifacient – it's hard to know just when, so I think we need to treat it as an abortifacient. It's not really that much of an issue with me, [but] I think there's respect for germinal life that is equivalent to a respect for individual life,

and if one doesn't respect one's [own] generative capacity, I think one will not respect one's own life or the progeny that one has. So I think there's a spectrum there that begins with one's self and one's generative capacity.

Their stance toward other people's use of contraception is therefore ambivalent. They disapprove of "artificial" contraception, by which they mean use of the condom, the diaphragm, and vaginal spermicides. Many of them feel that the only acceptable "natural" method of birth control is natural family planning (NFP), the modern version of the rhythm method. As one woman said:

I know that some Catholics are split on the contraceptive issue, but I feel contraception is a stopping of the consequences of a natural act, so therefore I don't believe in it. And I have a certain faith [that] if the Lord has sent this problem, He'll send a solution, and so [here is] this natural family planning thing which is beginning to be perfected – well, it's just like I was telling a priest who was beginning to believe in contraceptives, I said there's going to be an answer through natural law.

Developed in large part by Drs. John and Evelyn Billings of Australia, NFP improves upon the older rhythm method by teaching couples to recognize changes in the woman's body that signal the onset of ovulation. NFP is morally acceptable to Catholics because, at least in the original formulation of the method, individuals abstain from sex right before, during, and right after ovulation. Pro-life people who practice NFP argue that it has secular benefits as well. Here is what one woman [...] had to say:

It's really a whole new way of life for a married couple because it demands very close communication, to have to communicate with one another every day about their fertility. I think that's so beautiful. They both learn about one another's bodies, and it creates a tremendous closeness, and I think it demands a very mature love. Because, you know, a husband sees that he can't just demand love from his wife if she is not feeling good, if she is sick. So the same thing applies if she's fertile and they just can't afford to have another child right then. They have to postpone... making love in that fashion during those few days of the cycle.... It creates a completely new closeness and respect for one another, and devotion, and they live very much closer and happier, with much more love in their lives.

[...]

Again, several factors interact to reinforce the belief that "artificial" contraception is wrong. To begin with, if the goal of sex is procreation, then contraceptives are by nature wrong, and this is the starting point for many pro-life people. But it is important to remember that this is a personal choice for them, not a matter of unquestioning obedience to doctrine. Many will say that they do not use contraception because their church does not approve; but, in fact, Catholics are increasingly using contraception in patterns similar to those of non-Catholics, and their families (and family ideals) are becoming increasingly hard to distinguish from those of the population at large. Moreover, some data suggest that the most direct representative of the church, the parish priest, is also likely to be tacitly in favor of birth control. Most pro-life people are therefore part of an institution that proclaims a value that most of its members and some of its officials ignore.

When pro-life people use NFP as a form of fertility control, they have not only a different moral rationale but also a different goal than pro-choice people have when they use contraception. They are using it *to time the arrival of children, not to foreclose entirely the possibility of having them.* For them, the risk of pregnancy while using NFP is not only *not a* drawback, it is a positive force that can enhance the marriage. As one man said:

I'll tell you, when you're using a so-called natural method... you can be incredibly perceptive as to when the fertile period is. But you're not going to be so perceptive that you're going to shut off every pregnancy. You know, there are a lot of things

> that people just simply do not understand because they've had no experience with them. It's like people who eat in restaurants all the time and have never been on the farm and had a natural meal – you know, where the food comes from the freshly killed animals the same day, from the fields. They don't have any concept of what a natural meal is like, and I think the same thing is true in the sexual area. I think that when you take the step of cutting off all possibility of conception indefinitely, it puts emotional and physical restraints on a relationship that remove some of its most beautiful values.... The frame of mind in which you know there might be a conception in the midst of a sex act is quite different from that in which you know there could not be a conception.... I don't think that people who are constantly using physical, chemical means of contraception really ever experience the sex act in all of its beauty.

Thus the one thing we commonly assume that everyone wants from a contraceptive – that it be 100 percent reliable and effective – is precisely what pro-life people do *not* want from their method of fertility control.

Pro-life values on the issue of abortion – and by extension on motherhood – are intimately tied to the values we have just illustrated. But they also draw more directly on notions of motherhood (and fatherhood) that are not shared by pro-choice people. This might seem obvious from the fact that pro-life people often account for their own activism by referring to the notion that babies are being murdered in their mothers' wombs. But pro-life feelings about the nature of parenthood draw on other more subtle beliefs as well.

Pro-life people believe that one becomes a parent by *being* a parent; parenthood is for them a "natural" rather than a social role. One is a parent by virtue of having a child, and the values implied by the in-vogue term *parenting* (as in *parenting classes*) are alien to them. The financial and educational preparations for parenthood that pro-choice people see as necessary are seen by pro-life people as a serious distortion of values. Pro-life people fear that when one focuses on job achievement, home owning, and getting money in the bank *before* one has children, children will be seen as barriers to these things. As one pro-life woman put it:

> There has been a very strong attitude that the child represents an obstacle to achievement. Not just that the child is something desirable that you add further down the line... but that the child is an obstacle to a lifestyle that will include the yacht and weekend skiing.... A great many couples are opting not to have any children at all because of the portrayal of the child as an obstacle, especially to a woman's career and a two-salary family.

It is worth noting, in this context, that several pro-life women said that few people actually *enjoy* the state of being pregnant. [...]

> I think it's a normal thing [not to enjoy pregnancy]. I think it's also kind of built into the system because everything changes in your body and very often you're sick and... you kind of hate the thought that things are changing, but after you start feeling a little better, you start looking forward to the baby. [But] a lot of the abortions are already done by that time.

> I never wanted to have a baby, I never planned to have five children, I never felt the total joy that comes from being pregnant. I mean I was *sick* for nine months. I mean my general attitude was, "Hell, I'm pregnant again." But I thought pregnancy was a natural part of marriage, and I believed so much in the word *natural*, and so I loved the babies when they were born. I realized that a lot of women have abortions in that first trimester out of the... physical and psychological fear that they experience, and the depression.... A lot of them will regret having that abortion later on. They work too fast, the doctors advise them too fast. They can outgrow that feeling of fear if they give themselves a chance.

[...]

Clearly, pro-life activists are concerned about the fact that women may seek abortions before they have had a chance to accommodate themselves to the admittedly unpleasant reality of being pregnant.

Pro-life people tacitly assume that the way to upgrade motherhood is to make it an *inclusive* category, that all married people should be (or be willing to be) parents. In particular, women who choose to be in the public world of work should eschew the role of wife and mother, or, if they marry, should be prepared to put the public world of work second to their role as wife and mother. If a man or woman is to be sexually active, they feel, he or she should be married. And if married, one should be prepared to welcome a child whenever it arrives, however inopportune it may seem at the time. In their view, to try to balance a number of competing commitments – especially when parenthood gets shuffled into second or fourth place – is both morally wrong and personally threatening.

Pro-life people also feel very strongly that there is an anti-child sentiment abroad in our society and that this is expressed in the strong cultural norm that families should have only two children.

> Well, I think there's always been a problem with kids. But it doesn't seem to me that they're looked on as positively as they used to be. People look down on someone who wants to have more than two kids. Kids are looked on as a burden, [as] work. And they are. [People aren't] looking at the fun side of it and the nice side of it.

[...]

Since one out of every five pro-life activists in this study had six or more children, it is easy to see how these values can seem threatening. In the course of our interviews, a surprising number of activists said they did not feel discriminated against because of their pro-life activities, including their opposition to abortion, but that they did feel socially stigmatized because they had large families. As one woman with several children said: "[My husband,] being a scientist, gets a lot [of questions]. You know, having a large family, it's just for the poor uneducated person, but if you have a doctor's degree and you have a large family, what's wrong with you?" The pro-choice argument that parents must plan their families in order to give their children the best emotional and financial resources therefore sounds like an attack on people with large families. "[People think] children can't possibly make it and be successful if they come from a large family... because you can't give them all the time and energy that they need. Well, first of all, I'm here [at home], I'm not out working, which adds to the amount of time that I can give."

Pro-life values on children therefore represent an intersection of several values we have already discussed. Because pro-life people believe that the purpose of sexuality is to have children, they also believe that one should not plan the exact number and timing of children too carefully, for it is both wrong and foolish to make detailed life plans that depend upon exact control of fertility. Because children will influence life plans more than life plans will influence the number of children, it is also wrong to value one's planned accomplishments – primarily the acquisition of the things money can buy – over the intangible benefits that children can bring. Thus, reasoning backwards, pro-life people object to every step of the pro-choice logic. If one values material things too highly, one will be tempted to try to make detailed plans for acquiring them. If one tries to plan too thoroughly, one will be tempted to use highly effective contraception, which removes the potential of childbearing from a marriage. Once the potential for children is eliminated, the sexual act is distorted (and for religious people, morally wrong), and husbands and wives lose an important bond between them. Finally, when marriage partners who have accepted the logic of these previous steps find that contraception has failed, they are ready and willing to resort to abortion in order to achieve their goals.

This is not to say that pro-life people do not approve of planning. They do. But because of their world view (and their religious faith) they see human planning as having very concrete limits. To them it is a matter of priorities: if individuals want fame, money, and worldly success, then they have every right to pursue them. But if they are sexually active (and married, as they should be if they are sexually active), they have an obligation to subordinate other parts of life to the responsibilities they have taken on by virtue of that activity.

These views about the nature of parenthood and the purpose of sexuality also come together to shape attitudes about premarital sex, particularly among teenagers. Not surprisingly, people who feel that sex should be procreative find premarital sex disturbing. Since the purpose of sex is procreation (or at least "being open to the gift of a new life"), people who are sexually active before marriage are by definition not actively seeking procreation; and in the case of teenagers, they are seldom financially and emotionally prepared to become parents. So for pro-life people, premarital sex is both morally and socially wrong. As one man put it:

> One of my pet peeves is the words *sexually active young person* because I don't equate being sexually active with having sex – that's not my value system. "Sexually active" [sounds like what] any nice Christian teen-aged girl and guy ought to be. I trust that my sexuality is broader than the act of sex.... I want young people to be reinforced so they don't think of themselves as some kind of neuter because [they are not having sex]. And that's what we're doing with sex.

Although they agree that there is a very real problem with teen-aged pregnancy in the United States today, pro-life people believe that the availability of contraception is what encourages teens to have sex in the first place, so they feel that sex education and contraception simply add fuel to the fire.

> I don't think that we would have as many sexually active teenagers, first of all, if contraception weren't readily available and acceptable. And when they use the term *responsible sex*, they don't mean the same thing I do, or that many of us do. *Responsible sex* to people who are in the contraceptive world means use contraception so you don't get pregnant [or catch a] venereal disease, which I've been reading is a false security they've been given.... So there's possibly more of a temptation to participate in sex than we had when we were young, aside from morality, because you just knew that if you were sexually active you might well get pregnant.

[...]

For most pro-life people, the answer to the problems of teen-aged sexuality is *moral* rather than practical: teenagers should be taught that sex before marriage is wrong. For example: "There is really only going to be one way to avoid the tremendous increase in teen-age pregnancies, abortion, unwed mothers, and venereal disease. And that is to try very hard to promote and go back to an ethic that makes a strong standard of abstinence for the unwed – I guess I can't just say teens."

Providing contraception (and abortion) services for teenagers represents a clear threat to pro-life views. A series of legal and policy decisions in the United States as a whole have put teenagers in a rather peculiar situation. A person under the age of eighteen, as a minor, cannot have medical treatment without parental consent, but there are three exceptions to this doctrine. Teenagers may seek contraceptive services, may have an abortion, and may seek treatment for venereal disease without parental consent. As a matter of public policy, the social benefits to these treatments are considered to outweigh the social benefits of requiring parental consent.

Pro-life people believe that this policy acts to cut off parental support and resources precisely when children need them most. They feel that children underestimate how accepting and supportive parents will be and therefore make hasty (and irrevocable) decisions alone. They also think the policy serves to loosen the ties between parent and child. They argue that families have enough pressures on them anyway and that this policy in effect gives children permission to engage in activities whose consequences they cannot fully appreciate – and more to the point, activities their parents disapprove of.

Equally important, pro-life people see public policy in this realm as intruding the state into areas where it does not belong, namely, within the family. From their point of view, the family is both beleaguered and sacred, and any policy that seeks to address the members of a family as separate entities, rather than as an organic whole, is a priori harmful. As one woman put it:

> Even this... family planning is sexual education. It's planned downtown with Planned Parenthood, it's not planned with the parents. So [under] the laws which exist now, the children get contraceptives without parental consent. What it's doing is [creating] a gap in family relationships. And the home and the family... should be the primary source of moral values. Well, if some parents don't take responsibility, then I think it's the responsibility of education *to encourage parents to do it, rather than take it away from them* – which is what has happened [emphasis added].

This pro-life opposition to sex education, however, springs from feelings that are even deeper than a concern about the state intruding itself between members of a family. Their opposition draws on certain strongly felt but rarely articulated beliefs about the nature of morality. Pro-life people as a group subscribe to explicit and well-articulated moral codes. (After all, many of them are veterans of childhood ethics and religion classes.) Morality, for them, is a straightforward and unambiguous set of rules that specify what is moral behavior. Since they believe that these rules originate in a Divine Plan, they see them as transcendent principles, eternally valid regardless of time, cultural setting, and individual belief. "Thou shalt not kill," they argue, is as valid now as it was 2,000 years ago, and the cases to which it applies are still the same. They tend to locate their morality in traditional, ancient codes such as the Ten Commandments and the "Judeo-Christian" law, which have stood the test of time and exist as external standards against which behavior should be judged.

Thus, abortion offends the deepest moral convictions of pro-life people in several ways. To begin with, it breaks a divine law. The Commandment says "Thou shalt not kill." The embryo is human (it is not a member of another species) and alive (it is not dead). Thus, according to the reasoning by syllogism they learned in childhood religion classes, the embryo is a "human life," and taking it clearly breaks one of the Commandments.

Moreover, the logic used by pro-choice advocates (and the Supreme Court) to justify abortion affronts the moral reasoning of pro-life people. For them, either the embryo is a human life or it is not; the concept of an intermediate category – a *potential* human life – seems simply inadmissible. Further, the argument that individuals should arrive at a *personal* decision about the moral status of this intermediate category is as strange to most of them as arguing that individual soldiers in wartime should act according to their own judgment of the wisdom of the army's battle plan.

A professed unwillingness to deviate from a strict moral code naturally has its repercussions in private life. Pro-life people, their rhetoric notwithstanding, do have abortions. Among pro-choice people who were associated with organizations that arrange abortions, it was something of a cliché that pro-life people were believers only until they found themselves with an unwanted pregnancy, which made them more than willing to seek an abortion. When pressed for proof, however, these pro-choice activists retreated behind medical ethics, claiming they could not invade a patient's privacy by actually naming names. Later in the study, however, more persuasive evidence was offered by pro-life people active in Life Centers. These centers, staffed and funded by the pro-life movement, are located in hospitals or other medical settings and offer free pregnancy tests and pregnancy counseling should the pregnancy test prove positive. Although counselors in Life Centers actively encourage women to continue their pregnancies, they do not openly advertise their pro-life stand; they explain only that they provide free pregnancy tests and counseling. But since most places that offer free tests and counseling are also abortion referral centers, many women come to Life Centers in order to get such a referral. Life Center counselors estimate that as many as a third of the women they see go on to have an abortion, even after having had pro-life counseling. Since Life Centers are by definition pro-life, when people who work in them say that pro-life members (and in particular the children of pro-life members) have come into their centers seeking abortions, we can probably believe them. After all, they have nothing to gain by admitting that their own members (and their own children), like the rest of us, sometimes have trouble living up to their ideals.

Thus, pro-life people, like the pro-choice people we will examine shortly, have a consistent, coherent view of the world, notwithstanding the fact that like anyone else, they cannot always bring their behavior in line with their highest ideals. The very coherence of their world view, however, makes clear that abortion, and all it represents, is profoundly unsettling to them. By the same token, the values that pro-life people bring to bear on the abortion issue are deeply threatening to those people active in the pro-choice movement.

[...]

World Views

All these different issues that divide pro-life and pro-choice activists from one another – their views on men and women, sexuality, contraception, and morality – in turn reflect the fact that the two sides have two very different orientations to the world and that these orientations in turn revolve around two very different moral centers. The pro-life world view, notwithstanding the occasional atheist or agnostic attracted to it, is at the core one that centers around God: pro-life activists are on the whole deeply committed to their religious faith and deeply involved with it. A number of important consequences follow.

Because most pro-life people have a deep faith in God, they also believe in the rightness of His plan for the world. They are therefore skeptical about the ability of individual humans to understand, much less control, events that unfold according to a divine, rather than human, blueprint. From their point of view, human attempts at control are simply arrogance, an unwillingness to admit that larger forces than human will determine human fate. One woman made the point clearly: "God is the Creator of life, and I think all sexual activity should be open to that [creation]. That does not mean that you have to have a certain number of children or anything, but it should be open to Him and His will. The contraceptive mentality denies his will, 'It's my will, not your will.' And here again, the selfishness comes in."

This comment grew out of a discussion on contraception, but it also reveals values about human efficacy and its role in a larger world. While individuals can and should control their lives, pro-life people believe they should do so with a humility that understands that a force greater than themselves exists and, furthermore, that unpredicted things can be valuable. A woman who lost two children early in life to a rare genetic defect makes the point: "I didn't plan my son, my third child, and only because I was rather frightened that I might have a problem with another child. But I was certainly delighted when I became pregnant and had him. That's what I mean, I guess I feel that you can't plan everything in life. Some of the nicest things that have happened to me have certainly been the unplanned." Another woman went further: "I think people are foolish to worry about things in the future. The future takes care of itself."

Consequently, from the pro-life point of view, the contemporary movement away from the religious stand, what they see as the "secularization" of society, is at least one part of the troubles of contemporary society.

By this they mean at least two things. First, there is the decline in religious commitment, which they feel keenly. But, second, they are also talking about a decline of a common community, a collective sense of what is right and wrong. From their viewpoint, once morality is no longer codified in some central set of rules that all accept and that finds its ultimate justification in the belief in a Supreme Being, then morality becomes a variation of "do your own thing."

For pro-life people, once the belief in a Supreme Being (and by definition a common sense of culture) is lost, a set of consequences emerge that not only creates abortion per se but creates a climate where phenomena such as abortion can flourish. For example, once one no longer believes in an afterlife, then one becomes more this-worldly. As a consequence, one becomes more interested in material goods and develops a world view that evaluates things (and, more importantly, people) in terms of what Marxists would call their "use value." Further, people come to live in the "here-and-now" rather than thinking of this life – and in particular the pain and disappointments of this life – as spiritual training for the next life. When the belief in God (and in an afterlife) are lost, pro-life people feel that human life becomes selfish, unbearably painful, and meaningless.

> I think basically a secular nature of our society, that we basically lost our notion of God as being important in our lives... it's hard at times to see that suffering can make you a better person, so people don't want any part of it.

> I think there's a decline in our civilization. Bracken, Dr. Julius Bracken, said that the problem used to be why does God allow suffering or pain or things like that, and now the problem is man's own existence, you know, man believes that he's in a circle of nothingness and therefore there is no such thing as a moral or immoral act.

One of the harshest criticisms pro-life people make about pro-choice people, therefore, which encapsulates their feeling that pro-choice people are too focused on a short-term pragmatic view of the present world rather than on the long-term view of a transcendent world, is that pro-choice people are "utilitarian."

In part, pro-life people are right: the pro-choice world view is not centered around a Divine Being, but rather around a belief in the highest abilities of human beings. For them, reason – the human capacity to use intelligence, rather than faith, to understand and alter the environment – is at the core of their world; for many of them, therefore, religious or spiritual beliefs are restricted only to those areas over which humans have not yet established either knowledge or control: the origin of the universe, the meaning of life, etc. As one pro-choice activist, speaking of her own spiritual beliefs, noted: "What should I call it? Destiny? A Supreme Being? I don't know. I don't worship anything, I don't go anyplace and do anything about it, it's just an awareness that there's a whole area that might be arranging something for me, that I am not arranging myself – though every day I do more about arranging things myself."

Whatever religious values pro-choice people have are subordinated to a belief that individuals live in the here and now and must therefore make decisions in the present about the present. Few pro-choice people expressed clear beliefs in an afterlife so that their time frame includes only the worldly dimension of life. Thus, the entire articulation of their world view focuses them once again on human – rather than divine – capacities and, in particular, on the capacity for reason.

There are important implications to the fact that reason is the centerpiece of the pro-choice universe. First, they are, as their opponents claim, "utilitarian." Without explicitly claiming the heritage of the Scottish moralists, utilitarianism is consonant with many of the pro-choice side's vaguely Protestant beliefs and, more to the point, with their value of rationality and its extensions: control, planning, and fairness. Second, as this heritage implies, they are interventionists.

From their point of view, the fact of being the only animal gifted with intellect means that humans should use that intellect to solve the problems of human existence. What the pro-life people see as a humility in the face of a God whose ways are unknowable to mere humans, pro-choice people see as a fatalistic reliance upon a Creator whom humans wishfully endow with magical powers. These same values lead pro-choice people to be skeptical of the claim that certain areas are, or should be, sacrosanct, beyond the reach of human intervention. *Sacred* to them is too close to *sacred cow*, and religion can merge imperceptibly into dogma, where the church could persecute Galileo because science was too threatening both to an old way of thinking of things and an established power structure. Truth, for pro-choice people, must always take precedence over faith.

Because of their faith in the human ability to discover truth, pro-choice people are on the whole optimistic about "human nature." While in their more despairing moments they can agree with the pro-life diagnosis of malaise in contemporary American life – that "things fall apart and the center does not hold" in Yeats' terms – they emphatically disagree upon the solution. Rather than advocate what they see as a retreat from the present, an attempt to re-create idealized images of the past, they would argue that "the Lord helps those who help themselves" and that people should rally to the task of applying human ingenuity to the problems that surround us.

In consequence, pro-choice people do not see suffering as either ennobling or as spiritual discipline. In fact, they see it as stupid, as a waste, and as a failure, particularly when technology exists to eliminate it. While some problems are not at present amenable to human control, pro-choice people will admit, they are sure to fall to the march of human progress. Thus, not only can humans "play God," it is, in an ironic sort of way, what they owe their Creator, if they have one: given the ability to alter Nature, it is immoral not to do so, especially when those activities will diminish human pain.

All of these values come home for pro-choice people when they talk about the *quality of life*. By this term they mean a number of things. In part they use this phrase as a short-hand way of indicating that they think of *life* as consisting of social as well as biological dimensions. The embryo, for example, is only a potential person to them in large part because it has not yet begun to have a social dimension to its life, only a physical one. In corollary, a pregnant woman's rights, being both social and physical, transcend those of the embryo. This view is rooted in their values about reason: biological life is physical and of the body. Humans share physical life with all other living beings, but reason is the gift of humans alone. Thus social life, which exists only by virtue of the human capacity for reason, is the more valuable dimension of life for pro-choice people. (This viewpoint explains in part why many pro-choice people find unfathomable the question of "when does life begin?" For them it is obvious: physical life began only once, most probably when the "cosmic soup" yielded its first complex amino acids, the forerunners of DNA; social life begins at "viability" when the embryo can live – and begin to form social relationships – outside of the womb.)

But for pro-life people, this line of reasoning is ominous. If social life is more important than physical life, it then follows that people may be ranked by the value of their social contributions, thus making invidious distinctions among individuals. In contrast, if physical life is valued because it is a gift from the Creator, then no mere human can make claim to evaluate among the gifts with which various individuals are born. A view that the physical or genetic dimension of life is paramount – that all who are born genetically human are, a priori, persons – means that at some level all are equal. A hopelessly damaged newborn is, on this level, as equally deserving of social resources as anyone else. What pro-life people fear is that if the pro-choice view of the world is adopted, then those who are less socially *productive* may be deemed less socially *valuable.* For pro-life people, many of whom have situational reasons to fear how pro-choice people would assign them a social price tag, such a prospect is a nightmare.

The phrase *quality of life* evokes for pro-choice people a pleasing vista of the human intellect directed to resolving the complicated problems of life – the urge for knowledge used to tame sickness, poverty, inequality, and other ills of humankind. To pro-life people, in contrast, precisely because it is focused on the here and now and actively rejects the sacred and the transcendent, it evokes the image of Nazi Germany where the "devalued" weak are sacrificed to enlarge the comfort of the powerful.

Thus, in similar ways, both pro-life and pro-choice world views founder on the same rock, that of assuming that others do (or must or should) share the same values. Pro-life people assume that all good people should follow God's teachings, and moreover they assume that most good-minded people would agree in the main as to what God's teachings actually are. (This conveniently overlooks such things as wars of religion, which are usually caused by differences of opinion on just such matters.) Pro-choice people, in their turn, because they value reason, assume that most reasonable people will come to similar solutions when confronted with similar problems. The paradox of utilitarianism, that one person's good may be another person's evil, as in the case of the pro-life belief that a too-effective contraceptive is a bad thing, is not something they can easily envisage, much less confront.

What neither of these points of view fully appreciates is that neither religion nor reason is static, self-evident, or "out there." Reasonable people who are located in very different parts of the social world find themselves differentially exposed to diverse realities, and this differential exposure leads each of them to come up with different – but often equally reasonable – constructions of the world. Similarly, even deeply devout religious people, because they too are located in different parts of the social world and, furthermore, come from different religious and cultural traditions, can disagree about what God's will is in any particular situation. When combined with the fact that attitudes toward abortion rest on these deep, rarely examined notions about the world, it is unambiguously clear why the abortion debate is so heated and why the chances for rational discussion, reasoned arguments, and mutual accommodation are so slim.

Biography – Joan Andrews, Living Martyr

Social movements get an enormous boost from martyrs who give their lives for the cause. They testify to the importance of the issue, as important to them as life itself. Plus they demonstrate how viciously repressive and brutal the other side, or the police, are. Death raises deep emotions, and forces people to ask what their deepest values are, what they might consider dying for. Short of these literal martyrs are figurative martyrs whose sacrifices fall somewhat this side of death, but are severe enough to earn them wide recognition in their social movement. In the anti-abortion movement, Joan Andrews was a person like this.

An anti-abortion protestor for some years, Andrews was convicted of third-degree burglary for entering the Ladies Center clinic in Pensacola, Florida in 1986 and damaging abortion equipment she found there. She was sentenced to five years in Florida state prisons. She protested her sentence by refusing to stand at her sentencing or to cooperate with the guards, who had to carry her out. She spent twenty months in a small cell in solitary confinement, with no church services and few visitors.

Despite her own plea to "focus on the babies," Andrews became a rallying cry for the anti-abortion movement, living proof of how the government ignored and repressed the movement. She also helped to bring the abortion issue, until then mostly of concern to Catholics, to Protestant fundamentalists, as her situation became a regular topic on Christian radio and television. Although she herself was Catholic, she was from the rural South, and mostly she was a victim of the evils of secular America – a threat to both Catholics and Protestants. She helped join these two wings of the anti-abortion movement.

Joan had an unusual religious background. Her mother was fervidly Catholic and raised her six children that way – the only Catholics in their part of rural Tennessee. Born in 1948, Joan grew up getting into fights in defense of her religious beliefs. An even more memorable event, when Joan was twelve, was her mother's miscarriage three or four months into another pregnancy. Mrs. Andrews put the tiny fetus in holy water, had it blessed by the local priest, and let her children see and hold it before they named and buried it (along with a lock of hair from each child). The image of her tiny brother, wrapped up in Catholic ceremony, strongly shaped Joan's view of the world.

Like many others who would flood into the anti-abortion movement, Andrews was shocked by the *Roe v. Wade* decision in January 1973. Outraged at how widespread the practice was as well as its legitimation by the Supreme Court, she decided to devote her life to the anti-abortion cause. She was soon available for any anti-abortion protest, anywhere, anytime. She never had a job, and only needed bus fare. She and a handful of others also pushed the movement into more radical tactics, spray-painting clinic walls, putting superglue in their locks, and pouring foul-smelling liquids in their waiting rooms. Andrews' nomadic activism was an inspiration to the growing movement, and at the same time she helped link local networks with each other. She also brought plenty of practical know-how to each city she visited. The conflict over abortion escalated in the mid-1980s, with shouting and pushing in front of clinics, vandalism and bombings of clinics, and lawsuits against the movement for a national conspiracy to shut down the clinics.

In Pensacola in March 1986, Andrews managed to sneak in the back entrance of a clinic while a large confrontation was unfolding in front. Before police could stop her, she had destroyed some machinery. As soon as she was out of jail on bond, she went right back to the same clinic. But her timing was bad; the protest occurred several months after three local abortion clinics had been bombed. Public and judicial opinion were not favorable. Yet even after her conviction in a nonjury trial in July, she was offered probation in exchange for agreeing to stay away from that same clinic. She refused, on the theory that total noncooperation with the justice system would bring more attention and gum up the works more than additional protest. The judge sentenced her to five years in prison.

She perfected noncooperation in jail. She slept on the floor and refused blankets. She stopped taking showers or exercising. She went limp and forced guards to carry her whenever she was supposed to leave her cell. She ate only the bare minimum amount of food she thought necessary to keep herself alive. She refused to accept the voluminous mail, tens of thousands of letters, that were sent her. Because everyone in the anti-abortion movement knew her, and had prayed and protested beside her, they rallied to her defense. She became an issue almost as prominent as that of abortion!

Most anti-abortionists are conservatives who favor prisons, and often think not enough is being done to fight crime. So the image of Joan Andrews in jail, while – they were convinced – most real felons were not, was shocking. Said one televangelist, "For nine months, she's been in solitary confinement. It seems it's a worse crime today to save a life than it is to take one." Florida's new law-and-order governor Bob Martinez couldn't simply grant

Andrews clemency, but Florida decided to ship her out to Pennsylvania, where she had an outstanding warrant. She was released on probation after serving more than two years in prison. By then, October 1988, the anti-abortion movement was solidly fundamentalist, with the spotlight on Randall Terry and Operation Rescue. Andrews did not feel comfortable in this milieu and quickly dropped out of sight. But it was a movement that she, through her conscientious objection, had helped to create.

15 Ideological Purity in the Women's Movement

Jane J. Mansbridge

Like all social movements, both American feminism and Schlafly's brand of political fundamentalism faced a basic tension between reaching out and reaching in. To change the world, a movement must include as many people as possible. But to attract devoted activists, a movement must often promote a sense of exclusivity – "we few, we happy few, we band of brothers."

If many forces in the ERA movement promoted inclusivity, other forces promoted the separatism, concern with purity, and homogeneity of thought associated with exclusivity. Despite their inclusive ideals, activists working for the ERA tended to maintain their own morale by dividing the world into "us" and "them," seeking doctrinal purity, and rejecting interpretations of reality that did not fit their preconceptions. The fundamentalist churches were, if anything, even more subject to this kind of tension, since they believed that impurity could lead not just to social exclusion but to personal damnation.

Us Against Them

Rosabeth Moss Kanter's study of nineteenth-century communes found that when communes institutionalized exclusivity they were more likely to survive. The most successful communes discouraged relationships outside the group through geographic isolation, economic self-sufficiency, a special language and style of dress, and rules that controlled members' and outsiders' movements across the boundaries of the community. Three-quarters of Kanter's successful communes did not recognize the traditional American patriotic holidays. Half read no outside newspapers. More than a quarter specifically characterized the outside world as wicked.

Although social movements are usually inclusive in their conscious aims, building an organization on belief in a principle can, when the world refuses to go along with that principle, produce a deep sense of "us" against "them." When two movements organized with ideological incentives are pitted against each other, reality will provide plenty of temptations to see the opposition as evil incarnate. For an opponent of the ERA, a photograph of two lesbians in cut-off shorts embracing in the middle of an ERA demonstration triggered the perception of evil. For proponents, a legislator's characterization of them as "bra-less, brain-less broads," patronizingly repeated time after time, called forth equally intense hatred. Opponents' images of "libbers" and an "East Coast Establishment media blitz," and proponents' images of "right-wing crazies" or legislators conniving to kill the ERA in "smoke-filled rooms" all had elements of truth in them. The process of struggle accentuated the gulf. As a proponent, I found it impossible to sit in a legislative gallery, hear even a few legislators joke as they voted down equal rights for women, and not hate. And I have rarely seen such concentrated hate as I saw on the faces of some women in red when I stepped into an elevator in the state capitol on lobbying day wearing my green "ERA YES" button.

Like nationalism and some forms of religious conversion, some kinds of political activity engender a transformation of self that requires reconfiguring the world into camps of enemies and friends. Running for office or campaigning for social legislation is likely to have this effect. Other kinds of political activity, like holding political office, require people to break down such boundaries, or at least make them more subtle. The movements for and against the ERA had the same effects on participants as most struggles over social legislation, solidifying in-group ties without creating lines of dialogue with the "other." Political comradeship within the groups arose from mutual dependence and mutual respect, as proponents worked together late into the night preparing testimony or opponents piled into rented vans at 6:00 in the morning to negotiate icy roads to the state capitol. Both sides also demanded sacrifice. The conviction that "if I don't do this, the cause may fail" brought many women for the first time in their lives to write out checks for fifty, one hundred, five hundred, or even a thousand dollars for a political cause. The people who experienced that solidarity and made that sacrifice often began to think of themselves as political beings, helping produce – not simply consume – the politics that affected them. But this admirable result frequently depended on a Manichaean vision of "us" and "them" to bring it about.

Cross-Cutting Ties In some social contexts (institutions, cities, countries), people who belong to one social group (e.g., an economic class, ethnicity, religion, gender, etc.) have ongoing and even intimate social ties or connections with people in other types of groups. Irish-Americans, for example, may have friends, lovers, co-workers, roommates, and so forth who are Italian-American, African-American, etc. Their social ties, in other words, "cut across" two or more groups or categories of people. Other things being equal, these cross-cutting ties tend to reduce the likelihood that incompatible or contradictory identities, ideas, values, or interests will form among the groups in question; these ties thereby reduce the likelihood of group conflict. It is difficult (although not impossible) to feel that a group of people with whom you regularly and intimately associate are your enemies; you may have disagreements with such people, but you are likely to feel that such disagreements can be resolved through dialogue and compromise. By contrast, when no such cross-cutting ties exist, and religious groups (for example) only associate "with their own kind," then distinctive identities, ideas, values, and interests are more likely to emerge among such religious groups, with the result that sectarian conflict is also more likely. Groups with whom one seldom if ever associates are likely to seem more different, foreign, and inscrutable. In extreme cases, some groups may not even be considered human beings by others. In such instances, obviously, disagreements are likely to result in open conflict and even violence.

Doctrinal Purity

Once the necessary distinction has been made between "us" and "them," it follows that the less you are like "them," the more you are one of "us." Becoming "us" involves purifying your beliefs. The dynamic that binds activists to the movement entails idealism, radicalism, and exclusion. It works against the inclusive policy of accommodation and reform.

In organizations that have chosen ideological exclusivity as a means for building community, leaders are likely to be even more radical than their followers, for the leaders now serve not as intermediaries and ambassadors to the outside world but as moral exemplars whose function is inspiration. While traditional organizational theory predicts that leaders will grow more conservative than the rank and file, both Ellie Smeal of NOW and Phyllis Schlafly of STOP ERA – although undoubtedly less radical than some of their most active volunteers – were almost certainly further apart in their views than were the majority of people who gave time or money to their respective movements.

Neither the pro- nor the anti-ERA movement seems to have pushed its adherents strongly toward internal disputes over purity, but some pressures were there on both sides. Among the proponents, for example, these pressures came out in the lawyers' decisions on combat and abortion.

Homogeneity

In groups that are building a sense of community, like attracts like, and potential deviants try to suppress their differences in order to belong. The internal homogeneity that the members create binds them to one another more fully.

The very inclusivity of a social movement paradoxically accentuates homogeneity. A social movement, unlike an organization, has no formal entrance requirements or certification of membership; its members define themselves and identify themselves to one another solely in terms of their ideology. You are a member of a movement to the degree that you believe what the other people in the movement believe. Once you stop so believing you are, by definition, no longer "in" the movement. All members know this, at least subconsciously. They also know that they have "joined" the movement in part to have the support of like-minded people – to make and keep friends. If deviating too far from the movement's current ideology will cause you to lose your friends, you will only move in this direction when you already feel estranged, or when you feel you have "no choice."

Among proponents, the pressure to conform was probably strongest in the radical women's movement, where "betraying the women's movement" by not taking the correct ideological line could be "as terrifying as betrayal of your family, your closest friends." But even in the most conservative branch of the ERA movement in Illinois, ERA Illinois, I felt nervous about suggesting that we include in our 1982 testimony before the Illinois legislature a statement supporting the "deferential" interpretation on the military, which I had just discovered. As it turned out, the board of directors had no problem with my suggestion. My nervousness came from self-censorship and from fantasies of rejection, not from an accurate projection of what would happen. But inchoate fears of this kind are common among those whose particular access to information or experience leads them to contemplate deviations from "the party line." I have no direct evidence regarding such pressures among opponents, but it is hard to imagine that they were not equally intense. Indeed, since active opponents were by and large more rooted in small communities where they expected to spend the rest of their lives, and many were often more committed to their churches than feminists were to "the movement," the costs of challenging their co-workers were probably even higher.

Turning Inward: An Iron Law?

If social movements cannot reward their members materially, and if the activists must find their rewards in ideology and solidarity, we might expect such movements to follow an "iron law of involution," by which "every social movement tends to splinter into sects, unless it wins quickly, in which case it turns into a collection of institutions."

The socialist movement in America illustrates this iron law. As Daniel Bell argues, it foundered on the tension between inclusion and exclusion. The labor movement turned into an institution, while the Communist party turned into a sect. The party became ideologically exclusive, the very commitment of its members stemming in part from "that inward dread of not proving sufficiently revolutionary which hounds us all." Its members also became social isolates, cut off from others, not only because others ostracized them but also because they needed isolation to avoid confronting the wide gap between their revolutionary expectations and their actual achievements. Their intense political commitment left little room for their jobs or families, and they felt uncomfortable with people who did not share their mission. Said one member,

> When you are in the party for many years, as I have been, you develop warm bonds with your comrades. I have had a few friends outside the party, but they can never be as close friends. They can't be

> friends at all if they are hostile to the party. You never feel as comfortable with an outsider as you do with your comrades.

All committed activists sense that their political commitment sets them apart from the great majority of citizens. The extreme case occurs when activism requires illegal action – as in Resist, a draft resistance group founded in 1967–1968, whose members had all committed the illegal act of burning or turning in a draft card. With that one act the resisters became outlaws. But processes more common to all activists intensified their estrangement from the outside world. The resisters tended to feel both moral superiority and anger at having risked a great deal for the welfare of others without personally receiving anything in return. As politics took up more of their identities, ideological disagreements with their former friends became harder to stand. Finally, their decreasing interest in nonpolitical activities slowly eroded any ties outside the movement world, while they built up an almost religious sense of community within.

In the Black Power movement, activists struggled over the extent to which blacks should work with whites; in the Pentecostal movement, religious groups struggled over "whether or not a 'Spirit-filled' Christian should come out of the 'whore of Babylon' or remain within and try to redeem her." In the women's movement, one activist concluded sadly of another group, "We saw them as not being as pure as we. They still exist, and we don't."

The strengths of exclusivity are the strengths of a committed cadre. Exclusivity can produce a personal life that is intense, deep, and meaningful. Shared commitment and assumptions can also engender penetrating intellectual discourse, for the very intensity of the commitment urges one beyond both platitude and party line. Organizationally, an exclusive group can count on its members to do what needs doing.

By contrast, the strength of inclusivity is "the strength of weak ties." Personally, a loose and inclusive organization makes possible the ego-strengthening retreat into apolitical sanctuaries like the family. Intellectually, it allows friendships that run the "whole gamut of political views." Organizationally, it allows a host of different ties to the larger community. William Kornhauser, comparing the political and personal lives of liberal political activists affiliated with Americans for Democratic Action to those of Communist party members, concludes that "a liberal group finds strength in the multiple ties its members establish in the community." Mark Granovetter, comparing two communities resisting urban renewal – one a tightly knit Italian neighborhood of long standing, the other a more loosely organized aggregation – argues that one reason the loose aggregation succeeded while the tightly knit community failed may have been that members of less exclusive and less tightly knit neighborhoods could use their many weak contacts with diverse organizations and individuals outside the neighborhood to further the neighborhood's interests. As with contacts, so with information. Granovetter demonstrates that there is a

> structural tendency for those to whom one is only *weakly* tied, to have better access to... information one does not already have. Acquaintances, as compared to close friends, are more prone to move in different circles than one's self. Those to whom one is closest are likely to have the greatest overlap in contact with those one already knows, so that the information to which they are privy is likely to be much the same as that which one already has.

So too with thinking itself. Acquaintances with different views and different structural roles can force us to articulate our hidden expectations and understandings, and even, on occasion, to negotiate, reflect, and make choices – all processes central to thinking well.

Escaping the Iron Law

What conditions tend to turn a movement into a sect? Or, if we assume that the dynamics of recruiting are such as to turn every movement inward, what conditions impede this natural tendency toward exclusivity? The history of the ERA movement suggests three conditions: the likelihood of winning, the dependence of the movement on actors in different structural roles, and an explicitly inclusive ideology.

The ERA came extremely close to being ratified. Although no state ratified after 1977, the votes came so close in several states between 1977 and 1982 that even the sponsors were not able to predict beforehand which way the legislature would go. These conditions should have maximized the impact of political realism, by reducing both overconfidence and the temptation of the loser to retreat to purity. Because the goal of this particular social movement was to ratify a U.S. constitutional amendment, which requires a supermajority, the usual pressures for inclusivity – and therefore heterogeneity – in membership were increased.

The decentralized nature of the ERA movement also led to a division of labor between different states, between different communities within each state and between different constituencies on both the local and state levels. One organization within the movement would attract a more conservative membership, another a more radical one. Internally, this decentralization let members of each group feel more comfortable with one another. Externally, the division of labor made possible a "Mutt and Jeff" (or "good cop/bad cop") act, in which the more conservative organization could tell relevant power holders that if certain concessions were not forthcoming it could not hold back the radicals much longer. But most important, the division of labor fostered distinctive perspectives that had the effect of undermining any unifying ideology. "Hydra-headed" organizationally, the movement was also "fly-eyed." It depended on many different kinds of individual actors – homemakers, secretaries, executives, writers, lawyers, academics, and politicians – almost all of whom remained in their other roles while working for the ERA. The distinctive incentives and exposures of their other roles gave these different members of the movement slightly different views of the common struggle, and these views produced different insights.

Finally, the ideology of the women's movement itself is inclusive, stressing the sisterhood of women of differing classes, ethnicities, regions, and traditional politics. That ideology requires women to listen to one another, on the grounds that each woman's story has its own validity and right to be heard. The first, simple statement of that ideology is that all women are sisters and fundamentally "on the same side." They are on the same side no matter what their class, their upbringing, or their politics, because structurally they have similar relationships to the world, and particularly to men. The "consciousness-raising group" of the women's movement typically did its work by allowing women who habitually sorted themselves by class, mores, and politics to see their similarities as women. It allowed each woman to hear other women talking about their lives as they had lived them, and to feel compassion for scenes never lived through, joy for memories mutually held but previously thought trivial, and the anger of recognition at events not shared until that moment. The movement's assertion that the "personal is political" means, among other things, that when women speak of what is important to them, those experiences often derive from common experiences in a world where men have most of the power. This means that it is a mistake not to listen and try to make sense of what other women say, even when one disagrees with them. In the ERA movement, no matter how involved any particular set of activists became with trying to persuade a legislator, organize a demonstration, or write a brief, the inclusive ideology of the broader women's movement was always there to push, gently, toward a strategy of listening to what other women – even in the opposition – had to say.

These forces in the ERA movement meant that if any movement could escape the iron law of involution, this would have been the one. That it did not fully escape means that no organization based on voluntary membership is likely to do so.

Social movements become "movements" only by building on common values and common dreams. They may hope to include everyone someday, but they cannot, by definition, do so today. To survive, they must balance the conflicting claims of pragmatism and purity, reaching out and turning in. Perhaps no social movement can maintain this balance for long, which may be why social movements are usually transitory. But some certainly maintain it longer than others, and exert more influence as a result. While the feminist movement that began in the late 1960s was often out of touch with middle-of-the-road legislators and with the millions of Americans whom they represented, it maintained a far better balance between reaching out and turning in than any of the other movements that began in the 1960s. This may help explain its longevity. Whether the conservative antifeminist movement of the 1970s and 1980s, with its renewed emphasis on traditional family values and sexual behavior, will prove equally resilient remains to be seen.

16 Are Frames Enough?

Charlotte Ryan and William A. Gamson

"What is power? Power is the ability to say what the issues are and who the good guys and bad guys are. That is power."

—*Conservative pundit Kevin Phillips*

Social movements in the United States have long recognized "framing" as a critical component of political success. A frame is a thought organizer, highlighting certain events and facts as important and rendering others invisible. Politicians and movement organizations have scurried to framing workshops and hired consultants who promise to help identify a winning message. In the current political climate, demoralized social movements and activists find this promise appealing.

After two decades of conducting framing workshops at the Media/Movement Research and Action Project (MRAP), which we codirect, we have concluded that framing is necessary but not sufficient. Framing is valuable for focusing a dialogue with targeted constituencies. It is not external packaging intended to attract news media and bystanders; rather, it involves a strategic dialogue intended to shape a particular group into a coherent movement. A movement-building strategy needs to ground itself in an analysis of existing power relations and to position supporters and allies to best advantage. Used strategically, framing permeates the work of building a movement: acquiring resources, developing infrastructure and leadership, analyzing power, and planning strategy. The following success story illustrates this approach.

October 2003: The setting was unusual for a press conference—a pristine, cape-style house surrounded by a white picket fence. The mailbox in front read A. Victim. The car in the driveway had a Rhode Island license plate, VICTIM. The crowd in front of the makeshift podium included film crews, photographers, and reporters from every major news outlet in Rhode Island.

The young woman at the podium wore a T-shirt and carried a coffee mug, both reading, "I'm being abused." Her mouth was taped shut. As the crowd grew silent, she pulled off the tape and began to speak. "Domestic violence is never this obvious. This could be any neighborhood, any community. But as victims, we don't wear signs to let you know we're being abused." After a pause, she continued, "Look around you to your left and right. We are everywhere, in all walks of life." At that, the cameras swiveled around to capture a sea of faces in the audience. Scattered throughout the crowd were other survivors of domestic violence, each with her mouth taped shut. That evening and the following day, the press carried the words and images.

The press conference was the beginning of a campaign by the Rhode Island Coalition Against Domestic Violence (RICADV) in collaboration with its survivor task force, Sisters Overcoming Abusive Relations (SOAR). The campaign was part of a continuing effort to reframe how domestic violence is understood—as a widespread problem requiring social, not individual, solutions. Follow-ups to the press conference included events at schools and churches, soccer tournaments, and softball games involving police, firefighters, and college teams, dances, fashion shows, health fairs, self-defense classes, marches, and candlelight vigils, culminating in a Halloween party and open house sponsored by SOAR.

The campaign was a new chapter in a multiyear effort not only to reframe public understanding of domestic violence but to translate into practice this call for social, not private, responses. RICADV promoted a seven-point plan to close gaps in the safety net of domestic violence services and, along with SOAR and other allies, shepherded the plan through the Rhode Island legislature.

As recently as the mid-1990s, when RICADV began working with MRAP on using the media for social change, the media coverage and public understanding of domestic violence issues was very different. The Rhode Island media, like the media in general, framed domestic violence issues as private tragedies. A typical story told of a decent man who had lost control, cracking under life's burdens: "A model employee whose life fell apart," read one *Providence Journal* headline (March 22, 1999). Or neighbors say that they could never imagine their friendly neighbor shooting his wife and child before turning the gun on himself: "They seemed nice, you know. They always seemed to get along as far as I could see" (*Providence Journal,* April 29, 1996). The media coverage of domestic violence a decade later reflects a successful effort to reframe the political debate.

Why Framing Matters

Like a picture frame, an issue frame marks off some part of the world. Like a building frame, it holds things together. It provides coherence to an array of symbols, images, and arguments, linking them through an underlying organizing idea that suggests what is essential—what consequences and values are at stake. We do not see the frame directly, but infer its presence by its characteristic expressions and language. Each frame gives the advantage to certain ways of talking and thinking, while it places others "out of the picture."

Sociologists, cognitive psychologists, political scientists, and communications scholars have been writing about and doing frame analysis for the past 30 years. With the help of popular books such as psychologist George Lakoff's *Don't Think of an Elephant!,* the idea that defining the terms of a debate can determine the outcome of that debate has spread from social science and is rapidly becoming part of popular wisdom.

A Few Things We Know about Frames

- Facts take on their meaning by being embedded in frames, which render them relevant and significant or irrelevant and trivial. The contest is lost at the outset if we allow our adversaries to define what facts are relevant. To be conscious of framing strategy is not manipulative. It is a necessary part of giving coherent meaning to what is happening in the world, and one can either do it unconsciously or with deliberation and conscious thought.

  The idea dies hard that the truth would set us free if only the media did a better job of presenting the facts, or people did a better job of paying attention. Some progressives threw up their hands in dismay and frustration when polls showed that most Bush voters in 2004 believed there was a connection between al-Qaeda and Saddam Hussein. The "fact" was clear that no connection had been found. If these voters did not know this, it was because either the news media had failed in their responsibility to inform them, or they were too lazy and inattentive to take it in.

  But suppose one frames the world as a dangerous place in which the forces of evil—a hydra-headed monster labeled "terrorism"—confront the forces of good. This frame depicts Saddam Hussein and al-Qaeda as two heads of the same monster. In this frame, whether or not agents actually met or engaged in other forms of communication is nit-picking and irrelevant.

- People carry around multiple frames in their heads. We have more than one way of framing an issue or an event. A specific frame may be much more easily triggered and habitually used, but others are also part of our cultural heritage and can be triggered and used as well, given the appropriate cues. For example, regarding the issue of same-sex marriage, witness the vulnerability of the Defense of Marriage frame. What it defends is an idea—in the minds of its advocates, a sacred idea. The idea is that a man and a woman vow commitment to each other until death parts them and devote themselves to the raising of a new generation.

  Same-sex couples can and do enter into relationships that, except for their gender, fit the sacred idea very well—they are committed to each other for life and to raising a new generation. Part of the ambivalence that many traditionalists feel about the issue comes from their uneasy knowledge that same-sex couples may honor this idea as much or more than do opposite-sex couples. In the alternative frame, the focus of the issue is not on gender, but on the question Why should two people who are committed for life be denied legal recognition of their commitment, with all of the attendant rights and responsibilities, just because they are of the same sex?

  One important reframing strategy involves making the issue less abstract and more personal. Sociologist Jeffrey Langstraat describes the use of this strategy in the debate in the Massachusetts State House. A generally conservative legislator, who somewhat unexpectedly found himself supporting same-sex marriage, called it "putting a face on the issue." He pointed to a well-liked and respected fellow legislator involved in a long term, same-sex relationship. "How can we say to her," he asked his colleagues, "that her love and commitment [are] less worthy than ours?"
- Successful reframing involves the ability to enter into the worldview of our adversaries. A good rule of thumb is that we should be able to describe a frame that we disagree with so that an advocate would say, "Yes, this is what I believe." Not long ago, a reporter at a rare George Bush press conference asked the president why he keeps talking about a connection between Saddam Hussein and al-Qaeda when no facts support it. When the president responded, "The reason why I keep talking about there being a connection is because there is a connection," he was not lying or being obtuse and stupid, he was relying on an unstated frame. Frames are typically implicit, and although Bush did not explicitly invoke the metaphor of the hydra-headed monster or the axis of evil, we can reasonably infer that he had something like this in mind—the forces of evil are gathering, and only America can stop them.
- All frames contain implicit or explicit appeals to moral principles. While many analysts of conflicts among frames emphasize how frames diagnose causes and offer prognoses about consequences, Lakoff usefully focuses on the moral values they invoke. Rather than classifying frames into those that emphasize causes and consequences and those that emphasize moral values, however, it is even more useful to think of all frames as having diagnostic, prognostic, and moral components.

Why Framing Is not All that Matters

Too much emphasis on the message can draw our attention away from the carriers of frames and the complicated and uneven playing fields on which they compete. Successful challenges to official or dominant frames frequently come from social movements and the advocacy groups they spawn. Although they compete on a field in which inequalities in power and resources play a major role in determining outcomes, some movements have succeeded dramatically against long odds in reframing the terms of political debate. To succeed, framing strategies must be integrated with broader movement-building efforts. This means building and sustaining the carriers of these frames in various ways—for example, by helping them figure out how to gain access where it is blocked or how to enable groups with similar goals to collaborate more effectively.

Too narrow a focus on the message, with a corresponding lack of attention to movement-building, reduces framing strategy to a matter of pitching metaphors for electoral campaigns and policy debates, looking for the right hot-button language to trigger a one-shot response. Adapted from social marketing, this model ignores the carriers and the playing field, focusing only on the content of the message. In isolation from constituency-building, criticism of the media, and democratic media reform, framing can become simply a more sophisticated but still ungrounded variation on the idea that "the truth will set you free." The problem with the social-marketing model is not that it doesn't work—in the short run, it may—but that it doesn't help those engaged in reframing political debates to sustain collective efforts over time and in the face of formidable obstacles.

Political conservatives did not build political power merely by polishing their message in ways that resonate effectively with broader cultural values. They also built infrastructure and relationships with journalists and used their abundant resources to amplify the message and repeat it many times. Duane Oldfield shows how the Christian Right built media capacity and cultivated relationships with key political actors in the Republican Party, greatly expanding the carriers of their message beyond the original movement network. Wealthy conservatives donated large amounts of money to conservative think tanks that not only fine-tuned this message but also created an extended network of relationships with journalists and public officials.

Participatory Communication

The Rhode Island Coalition Against Domestic Violence did not succeed because it found a better way to frame its message but because it found a better model than social marketing to guide its work. Call it the participatory communication model. The social marketing model treats its audience as individuals whose citizenship involves voting and perhaps conveying their personal opinions to key decision makers. The alternative model treats citizens as collective actors—groups of people who interact, who are capable of building long-term relationships with journalists and of carrying out collaborative, sustained reframing efforts that may involve intense conflict.

Widely used in the Global South, this alternative approach—inspired by Paulo Freire—argues that without communications capacity, those directly affected by inequalities of power cannot exercise "the right and power to intervene in the social order and change it through political praxis." The first step is to map the power relations that shape structural inequalities in a given social and historical context. This strategic analysis informs the next phase, in which communities directly affected by structural inequalities cooperate to bring about change. This is empowerment through collective action. Finally, participatory communication models include a third, recurring step—reflection.

By encouraging reflection about framing practices, participatory communicators foster ongoing dialogues that build new generations of leaders and extend relational networks. "Everyone is a communicator," says RICADV, and all collective action embodies frames. SOAR's staging of the bit of street theater described at the beginning of this article did not come out of the blue.

SOAR was part of the Rhode Island Coalition, which had been building communication infrastructure during a decade of collaboration with MRAP.

MRAP and RICADV began working together in 1996, but to begin our story there would be historically inaccurate. RICADV explains to all new members that they "stand on the shoulders" of the women who founded the domestic violence movement in the 1970s. The Rhode Island Coalition against Domestic Violence began in 1979 and, until 1991, operated roughly on a feminist consensus model. At this point an organizational expansion began that resulted in the hiring of new staff in 1995. The framing successes we describe, therefore, grew out of one of the more successful initiatives of the U.S. women's movement. Groups working to end domestic violence during the last three decades can claim significant progress, including the establishment of research, preventive education, support systems, and the training of public safety, social service, and health care providers.

History matters. In this case, the efforts on which RICADV built had already established many critical movement-building components:

- Activists had established a social movement organization committed to a mission of social change—to end domestic violence in the state of Rhode Island.
- They had established a statewide service network with local chapters in each region of the state.
- They had created a statewide policy organization to integrate the horizontal network into focused political action at the state and national legislative levels.
- They had obtained government funding for part of RICADV's education and service work, protecting the organization against fluctuation in other revenue sources such as fundraisers, corporate sponsors, donations, and grants.
- On the grassroots level, RICADV had supported the growth of an organization that encouraged victims of domestic violence to redefine themselves as survivors capable of using their experience to help others.
- Finally, they had created a physical infrastructure—an office, staff, computerized mailing lists, internal communication tools such as newsletters, and institutionalized mechanisms for community outreach. The most prominent of these was Domestic Violence Awareness Month in October, during which stories about domestic violence are commonly shared.

In short, RICADV's framing successes were made possible by the generous donations of people who had formed a social movement that encouraged internal discussion, decision making, strategic planning, focused collective action, resource accumulation, coalition-building, reflection, and realignment. The conscious use of framing as a strategic tool for integrating its worldview into action ensured that the organization could consistently "talk politics" in all its endeavors.

By the mid-1990s, the organization had made great strides on the national framing front regarding the public portrayal of domestic violence. In the wake of several high-profile domestic violence cases, made-for-TV movies, and star-studded benefits, domestic violence was positioned as an effective wedge issue that cut across hardening Right–Left divisions. The Family Violence Prevention Fund headed a national public education effort, working hard through the 1990s to frame domestic violence as a public as opposed to a private matter. High visibility had gained recognition of the issue, but much work remained to be done on the grassroots level and in legislative circles.

Changing Media Frames and Routines

When MRAP and RICADV began to collaborate in 1996, we had a running start. Already, RICADV routinely attracted proactive coverage, particularly during Domestic Violence Awareness Month. But all was not rosy. RICADV and other state coalitions across the nation had discovered that, despite media willingness to cover domestic violence awareness events, reporters covering actual incidents of domestic violence ignored the movement's framing of domestic violence as a social problem. Their stories reverted to sensationalized individual framings such as "tragic love goes awry."

In part, such stories represented the institutionalized crime beat tradition that tended to ignore deeper underlying issues. Crime stories about domestic violence routinely suggested that victims were at least partially responsible for their fate. At other times, coverage would focus on the perpetrator's motive, while the victim would disappear. News beats created split coverage: a reporter might sympathetically cover an event sponsored by a domestic violence coalition and yet write a crime story that ignored the movement's framing of domestic violence as social. All these effects were intensified if the victims were poor or working-class women and/or women of color.

At the beginning of our joint effort, RICADV routinely experienced this split-screen coverage: in covering coalition events, the media routinely reported that domestic violence was everyone's business and that help was available. On the front page and in the evening news, however, these coverage patterns isolated the victim, implying complicity on her part (more than 90 percent of victims in this study were female):

- She was a masochistic partner in a pathological relationship.
- She provoked her batterer.
- She failed to take responsibility for leaving.

Such stories undermined efforts to change policy and consciousness. They portrayed isolated victims struggling for protection while obscuring the social roots of domestic violence.

To address these and other framing issues systematically, RICADV Executive Director Deborah DeBare urged her board to hire a full-time communication coordinator in the spring of 1996. They chose Karen Jeffreys, a seasoned community organizer, who took a movement-building approach to communications. Jeffreys had previously drawn our MRAP group into framing projects on housing and welfare rights.

With MRAP support, she began an effort to make RICADV an indispensable source for news and background information about domestic violence in the Rhode Island media market. Gaining media standing was not an end in itself but a means to promote the reframing of domestic violence as a social problem requiring social solutions. By 2000, RICADV had published a handbook for journalists summarizing recommendations from survivors, reporters, advocates, and MRAP participants. Local journalists actively sought and used it, and it has been widely circulated to similar groups in other states.

To help implement the participatory communications model, Jeffreys worked out an internal process called a "media caucus" to ensure widespread participation in media work. Participants discussed how to respond to inquiries from reporters and how to plan events to carry the message. The media caucus conducted role-playing sessions, in which some participants would take the part of reporters, sometimes hardball ones, to give each other practice and training in being a spokesperson on the issue. RICADV encouraged the development and autonomy of SOAR, a sister organization of women who had personally experienced domestic violence. They worked to ensure that the voices of abused women were heard.

The press conference in 2003 was the culmination of years of work with reporters that succeeded in making the conference a "must attend" event for journalists. They had not only learned to trust RICADV and the information it provided but perceived it as an important player. RICADV and SOAR jointly planned the press conference, choosing the setting, talking about what clothes to wear, and planning the order in which people would speak. Without Karen Jeffreys' knowledge, but to her subsequent delight, the two spokespersons from SOAR, Rosa DeCastillo and Jacqueline Kelley, had caucused again and added visual effects, including the tape over the mouths. The planning and support gave the SOAR women the courage and the skills to innovate and helped make the press conference an effective launching pad for the campaign that followed.

Conclusion

Framing matters, but it is not the only thing that matters. There is a danger in "quick fix" politics—the sexy frame as the magic bullet. Framing work is critical, but framing work itself must be framed in the context of movement-building. If those who aim to reframe political debates are to compete successfully against the carriers of official frames, who have lots of resources and organization behind them, they must recognize power inequalities and find ways to challenge them. This requires them to recognize citizens as potential collective actors, not just individual ones.

The participatory communication model appeals to people's sense of agency, encouraging them to develop the capacity for collective action in framing contests. You cannot transform people who feel individually powerless into a group with a sense of collective power by pushing hot buttons. Indeed, you cannot transform people at all. People transform themselves through the work of building a movement—through reflection, critique, dialogue, and the development of relationships and infrastructure that constitute a major reframing effort.

In the spirit of the communication model that we are advocating, it is only fitting to give our RICADV partners the last words. The collaborative process inside the organization allows them to finish each other's sentences:

Alice: Each concerned group is a small stream. RICADV's job is to make the small streams come together, to involve the whole community and make social change for the whole state. And that's our mission—to end domestic violence in Rhode Island. But to do this, all RICADV's work—lobbying, policy, services, public relations—had to come together. We were moving... (pause)

Karen: ... moving a mountain. As organizers, we think strategically. Organizers think of social justice, and social justice is always about changing systems. So we were trained to read situations differently, to see gaps in institutional layers and links. We saw the potential of... (pause)

Alice: ... of social justice, of making that change. Whereas a traditional publicist thinks, "Let's get publicity for our organization's work," as organizers, we saw systems and movements. We were definitely going to move the domestic violence issue to another place!

Karen: It's our instinct to... (pause)

Alice: ... to get the community involved and fix this. We saw a whole movement.

Recommended Resources

David Croteau, William Hoynes, and Charlotte Ryan, eds. *Rhyming Hope and History: Activist, Academics, and Social Movements* (University of Minnesota Press, 2005). Essays on the joys and frustrations involved in collaborations between academics and activists.

George Lakoff. *Don't Think of an Elephant! Know Your Values and Frame the Debate* (Chelsea Green Publishing, 2004). Popularizes many of the most important insights of frame analysis, but implicitly adopts a social-marketing model that ignores movement-building and power inequalities.

Duane M. Oldfield. *The Right and the Righteous: The Christian Right Confronts the Republican Party* (Rowman and Littlefield, 1996). Describes the methodical movement-building process that helped the Christian Right succeed in its reframing effort.

Rhode Island Coalition Against Domestic Violence (RICADV). *Domestic Violence: A Handbook for Journalists* (www.ricadv.org, 2000). Offers succinct and practical lessons for journalists on the reporting of domestic violence.

Charlotte Ryan, Michael Anastario, and Karen Jeffreys. "Start Small, Build Big: Negotiating Opportunities in Media Markets." *Mobilization* 10 (2005):111–128. Detailed discussion of how the RICADV built its media capacity and systematic data on how this changed the framing of domestic violence in the Rhode Island media market.

17 The Emotions of Protest

James M. Jasper

Emotions have disappeared from models of protest. When crowds and collective behavior, not social movements and collective action, were the lens for studying protest, emotions were central. Frustration, anger, alienation, and anomie were not merely an incidental characteristic but the motivation and explanation of protest. Such images were displaced 30 years ago by metaphors of rational economic calculators and purposive formal organizations, for whom social movements were just one more means of pursuing desired ends. In the last 15 years, these instrumental metaphors have themselves been challenged from a cultural perspective in which protestors have a variety of reasons for pursuing a range of goals, not all of them material advantages for individuals or groups. Goals, interests, even strategies and political opportunities are increasingly viewed as embedded in and defined by cultural meanings and practices.

In this wave of culturally oriented research, considerable respect has still been paid to the rationality of protestors. They know what they want, varied though this may be, and they set out to get it. This respect may be the reason that most cultural researchers, although harking back to collective-behavior traditions in some ways, have avoided the issue of emotions. A variety of key cultural concepts – identity, injustice frames, cognitive liberation, and others – have been treated as though they were entirely cognitive, as though their highly charged emotional dimensions hardly mattered. If protestors are emotional, does that make them irrational? Recent researchers seem to fear – wrongly – that it does.

Emotions pervade all social life, social movements included. The most prosaic daily routines, seemingly neutral, can provoke violent emotional responses when interrupted. Unusual actions probably involve even more, and more complex, feelings. Not only are emotions part of our responses to events, but they also – in the form of deep affective attachments – shape the goals of our actions. There are positive emotions and negative ones, admirable and despicable ones, public and hidden ones. Without them, there might be no social action at all. To categorize them as rational or irrational (much less to dismiss them all as interferences with rationality) is deeply wrongheaded. We can categorize protestors' actions, usually *post hoc*, as strategically effective or mistaken, but rarely as irrational or rational. Even the proverbial Southern sheriff who flies into a rage and hits a peaceful civil rights demonstrator, although acting upon hateful and extreme emotions, has probably made a strategic error (at least when caught on camera) more than he has acted irrationally.

Emotion Management Political activists typically try hard to induce emotions that they think are good for their movement or cause and to prevent emotions or moods that they think are bad. At their planning meetings and at protest events themselves, activists often work hard at generating such emotions as outrage, excitement, joy, guilt, hope for the future, solidarity, and/or commitment to the cause. Emotion management may also involve attempts to mitigate fear, depression, hopelessness, and boredom. Activists may also try to calm down especially angry people, whose behavior may cause problems for the movement, especially if it professes nonviolent principles.

Emotions are as much a part of culture as cognitive understandings and moral visions are, and all social life occurs in and through culture. We are socialized (or not socialized) into appropriate feelings in the same way we learn or do not learn our local culture's beliefs and values. There is some individual variation in all three aspects of culture, and we recognize deviant emotional reactions and attachments as readily as deviant beliefs. As with the rest of culture, there is tension between the public, systematic expectations concerning emotional expression, and the individual innovations and idiosyncrasies that diverge from them. Emotions are learned and controlled through social interaction, although never with complete effectiveness.

In what follows, I argue for the centrality of emotions for understanding one corner of social life: the collective, concerted efforts to change some aspect of a society that we label social movements. I first discuss what emotions are, in particular the degree to which they are defined by context and culture in the same way that cognitive meanings are. I distinguish emotions that are transitory responses to external events and new information (such as anger, indignation, or fear) from underlying positive and negative affects (such as loyalties to or fears of groups, individuals, places, symbols, and moral principles) that help shape these responses. Then I distinguish emotions according to the social context that creates and shapes them, especially between those that form outside an organized movement and those that occur inside it. The former group primarily includes emotions that might lead individuals to join or even found protest groups; the latter, emotions that spur action, maintain the group, or lead to its demise.

[...]

What Are Emotions?

Emotions do not merely accompany our deepest desires and satisfactions, they constitute them, permeating our ideas, identities, and interests. They are, in Collins' words (1990:28), "the 'glue' of solidarity – and what mobilizes conflict." Recently, sociologists have rediscovered emotions, although they have yet to integrate them into much empirical research outside of social psychology. One aspect of this renewal has been an emphasis on how emotions are culturally constructed (and hence linked to cognitive appraisals) rather than being automatic somatic responses (and hence potentially less controllable, or less "rational"). To the extent that emotions depend on cognitions, they more clearly allow learning and adaptation to one's environment, i.e., rationality.

Older schools of thought viewed emotions as natural sensations – "feelings" – originating in the body, beyond the control of those experiencing them. In common parlance, people are said to be "seized by emotion," to be "in the grip" of passions such as jealousy or anger. The irrefutable bodily symptoms of emotions, whether increased adrenaline or redness in the face, are taken to be the emotions themselves, to which we then attach names. Emotions, in this view, thwart our wiser intentions and prevent effective actions. No doubt this sometimes happens, as in the case of the Southern sheriff. But people make cognitive mistakes as easily as emotional ones, and more strategic battles have been lost, in all likelihood, by mistaken cognitions than by mistaken emotions. Mistakes, furthermore, are not necessarily irrational, just mistaken.

Constructionists respond by pointing to the considerable interpretation that our bodily states require as well as to the cross-cultural diversity of emotions. Rather than being a simple set of inner sensations (are the physical sensations that accompany annoyance and indignation, for example, distinguishable?), an emotion is an action or state of mind that makes sense only in particular circumstances. Averill (1980:308) describes emotions as transitory social roles, which he in turn defines as "a socially prescribed set of responses to be followed by a person in a given situation." The rules governing the response consist of "social norms or shared expectations regarding appropriate behavior."

In the constructionist view, then, emotions are constituted more by shared social meanings than automatic physiological states. Some theorists argue that bodily changes are there, but must be interpreted before they can become emotions; others take the more extreme view that bodies change only in response to cultural settings associated with particular emotions. Evidence of the many cross-cultural differences in emotions seems to support the latter position. Nonetheless, the apparent existence of several universals, especially facial expressions of surprise, anger, and fear, suggests a weaker constructionist model in which, while some or most of any emotion is socially constructed, there is some natural expression involved as well. Thoits (1989:320) distinguishes a strong version of constructionism – there are no basic, universal emotions – from a weaker version – basic emotions may exist but explain little. Primary emotions such as anger and surprise may be more universal and tied directly to bodily states, whereas complex secondary ones such as compassion or shame may depend more on cultural context. It is possible as well that primary emotions are more important in face-to-face settings – of the kind many symbolic interactionists study – than in ongoing political processes, where secondary emotions such as outrage or pride may be more influential.

Both the strong and the weak forms of constructionism tie emotions to cognition in several ways. Emotions involve beliefs and assumptions open to cognitive persuasion. We often can be talked out of our anger on the grounds that it is too extreme a response, or that we are misinformed. The plots of many plays or novels, from Shakespeare to Hardy, depend on "mistaken" emotions derived from incorrect information. Because emotions normally have objects (we are afraid *of* something), they depend at least partly on cognitive understandings and appraisals of those objects. This allows learning and adaptation. If emotions are tied to beliefs and contexts, they are also partly open to debate as to whether they are appropriate or not at a given time. Because there are cultural rules governing them, emotions can usually be labeled as normal or deviant. Even our gut-level emotions, if they exist, are conditioned by our expectations, which in turn are derived from knowledge about appropriate conditions in the world.

Emotions are also tied to moral values, often arising from perceived infractions of moral rules. According to Harré (1986:6), "the study of emotions like envy (and jealousy) will require careful attention to the details of local systems of rights and obligations, of criteria of value and so on. In short, these emotions cannot seriously be studied without attention to the local moral order." One context in which emotions unfold is that of common human narratives, or what de Sousa (1987) calls "paradigm scenarios." Just as the death of a friend leads one through several predictable emotional stages, other unexpected and unpleasant events – such as a proposal for a nearby nuclear power plant – may lead to surprise, sadness, anger, then outrage. Solomon (1976) even describes the roles that accompany these plots: with anger, you are the judge and the other person is the defendant; with contempt, you are pure and blameless while the other person is vile and despicable. Each emotion implies a family of terms to hurl at your opponent. A social movement organizer deploys different language and arouses different emotions in her listeners if she paints her opponents as inherently malevolent or well-meaning but ignorant.

Most constructionists focus on emotions that represent temporary responses to events and information, since these are so clearly tied to cognition. But emotions also cover more permanent feelings of the type normally labeled affect or sentiment: love for one's family and other selected individuals; a sense of identification with a group and loyalty to its members; fondness for places and objects, perhaps based on memories;

positive responses to symbols of various kinds; and negative versions of each of these. To Heise (1979), affect is a central component of social life: all actions, actors, and settings have an affective component, involving not only a good-bad dimension but a potency dimension and a dimension capturing level of activity (lively–quiet). Humans act, according to Heise, in order to confirm their underlying sentiments. If "neighborhood" has positive connotations of safety and quiet, Heise's affect control theory would predict that a resident would fight to keep her neighborhood that way. Much political activity, no doubt, involves the reference to or creation of positive and negative affects toward groups, policies, and activities.

Trust and respect are examples of affects with an enormous impact on political action. We have deep tendencies to trust certain individuals, groups, and institutions but not others, and many of our allegiances, alliances, and choices follow from this pattern. Past experience or observation, agreement over goals or values or styles, collective identities, maybe even abstract deductions from principles: all these affect whom we trust. We tend to trust those we agree with and agree with those we trust. Generalized trust in the political system, furthermore, affects political behavior, usually dampening protest because of an assumption that the government will fix things without public pressure.

Affects and reactive emotions are two ends of a continuum with a grey area in the middle. At one end, love for a parent or loyalty to a country are usually strong and abiding affects, in the context of which many specific emotional reactions can come and go. Anger over a decision, at the other extreme, is usually a short-term response. In between are cases such as respect for a political leader, which can be an ongoing affect or a response to a particular action or a combination of the two. Fear, for instance, can slide along the continuum, depending on whether it is fear of abstract entities such as war or radiation or it is fear of more concrete embodiments such as a specific war or proposed nuclear reactor. Also in the middle are what are frequently labeled "moods": chronic or recurring feelings that do not always have a direct object. They may begin as, and are shaped by, reactions, but they linger.

General affects and specific emotions are a part of all social life as surely as cognitive meanings and moral values are. What is more, they are relatively predictable, not accidental eruptions of the irrational. The transitory emotional responses, it seems to me, are a function of both external context (or, more precisely, interpreted information about that context) and deeper affective states, for the latter help explain why people respond differently to the same information. Those who feel positively about their neighborhood, for instance, may respond with greater outrage to proposals to change it. Parallel loyalties to professional ethics might determine who becomes a whistle-blower when asked by one's boss to break certain rules (Bernstein and Jasper, 1996). The affects help shape the responses.

The relationship between these two kinds of emotions varies, perhaps, also along a continuum. At one extreme, rigid affective loyalties dominate all responses, potentially leading to paranoia or rigid ideologies. At the other extreme, these affects are flexible or weak, and emotional responses are dominated more by immediate context. The responses might themselves be weaker as a result, or they might simply consist of the kind of reaction that almost anyone would have in the same situation.

At stake in the constructionist debate is the rationality of emotions: to the extent that they are collectively shaped, depend on context, and are based on cognitions (themselves changeable through learning), they do not appear irrational. The dismissal of emotions as irrational comes in part from the tendency of Freudian psychological theories, especially earlier in the 20th century, to explain emotions through personality, in other words as a result of individual idiosyncrasies fixed early in life rather than as responses to changing cultural contexts. Works such as Lasswell's *Psychopathology and Politics* (1930) were filled with discussions of narcissism, latent homosexuality, oral dependence, and anal retention – often aimed at showing protest participation to be an immature activity. Freudians emphasized processes of ego-defense, which Greenstein (1987:3) defines as "the means through which individuals, often without realizing it, adapt their behavior to the need to manage their inner conflicts." According to Greenstein, the development in the 1960s of a post-Freudian ego psychology, which stressed the cognitive strengths and adaptive resources of the ego, discouraged the view that political participation arose from psychopathologies. The ego was adapting to external realities, not simply projecting internal conflicts.

The apparent threat to rationality remains, though, in any model of the unconscious. Conflicts, urges, or affects that we cannot understand or control, may prevent us from learning or adapting to new circumstances – processes that might be thought of as a minimal requirement for rationality. Such psychodynamics certainly exist. But it may be unfair to label them as emotions, in contrast to cognition, for they encompass both. They are part of the many limits on human reasoning power, with emotional limits alongside the many cognitive limitations documented by psychologists and others. Neurotic patterns derived from childhood interfere with our processing of cognitive information as much as they do with our emotional responses. Paranoia, for instance, is largely a problem of giving too much credence to irrelevant cognitive cues.

There is a difference between emotions as transitory social roles, which are publicly defined and shaped as much as cognitive meanings are, and the emotions attendant to individual idiosyncrasies, personalities, and affective loyalties. The latter may occasionally thwart the well-defined emotional expectations of those around one. But the issue here is not that of emotions, but of how individuals relate to social expectations. There is always some individual variation in behavior, cognition, and emotional responses. This makes social-scientific generalizations difficult, but no more so for emotions than for other aspects of social life. We recognize structured systems of cognitive meanings that, like language, can be defined independently of individuals. That some individuals use these improperly or substitute their own meanings on occasion does not invalidate the systems or ruin their explanatory power. The same is true for emotions. There are systematic pressures to have well-defined emotional responses and affective ties in certain contexts. When individuals fail to meet these expectations, we can explain why without questioning the logic of the emotional system. Even patterns of affect have rules.

Beliefs can be mistaken, emotions inappropriate. But irrational? Either beliefs or emotions can be irrational if they cause actions that consistently lead to a deterioration in one's resources or strategic position or if they prevent learning and improvement. Affective loyalties such as love might blind us in this way, for they are more likely to frame the interpretation of new information than to change in response to that information, making us less adaptable and thus perhaps less rational. But since these affects are very close to moral values and basic goals, a commitment to them is hard to dismiss simply as irrational. They make nonsense of the very means/ends distinction that allows us to judge actions as ineffective for certain goals. Shorter term emotional responses, such as the sheriff's anger, can hurt one's strategic position, but learning and improvement are possible even here. One learns, as other angry sheriffs have, not to strike peaceful protestors. Or not to strike them when cameras are rolling. If a fear of irrationality has prevented students of social movements from incorporating emotions into their models, the time has come to rethink this stance.

Emotions in Protest

As an integral part of all social action, affective and reactive emotions enter into protest activities at every stage. Some help explain why individuals join protest events or groups, ranging from emotional responses they can have as individuals to those that recruiters can stir in them. Others are generated during protest activities, including both affective ties among fellow members and feelings toward institutions, people, and practices outside the movement and its constituent groups. These affect whether a movement continues or declines, and when. In all stages, there are both preexisting affects and shorter term emotional responses to events, discoveries, and decisions.

Our world is patterned by affect. Our relationships with other humans, even fleeting ones, are charged with emotions. Those intimates whom we know well are wrapped in a complex web of emotions that we can never fully sort out. Affection or resentment toward our parents gives many activities associated with them (even symbolically) a positive or negative affective charge; we may protest in order to shock them, gain their respect, or replicate some childhood dynamic. Admiration for others also influences our choices, as we follow their examples or strive for their approval. We also have many emotional attachments to places and fight fiercely when we feel certain locales are threatened. We often have simple feelings even about strangers: attraction or repulsion, for example. Sexual desire, fulfilled or merely aroused, affects many of our choices of how to spend our time – or more precisely, with whom. Through group stereotypes, we also have emotions toward those we have never met.

But that is not all. On top of these affects, and often based on them, we have transitory feelings about all our activities. As Harold Garfinkel showed, even relatively thoughtless habits, when disrupted, release a torrent of emotions. We have feelings about our lives, whether boredom or excitement, about politics, no matter how remote it sometimes seems, even about events on the other side of the globe. There would be no social movements if we did not have emotional responses to developments near and far. Sometimes emotional responses are strong enough that people search out protest groups on their own. It is affects and emotional responses that political organizers appeal to, arouse, manipulate, and sustain to recruit and retain members. Table 17.1 lists some of the emotions that help lead people into social movements, keep them there, and drive them away. Some are primarily affects, others mostly reactive emotions, still others share aspects of each. In this latter category are the emotions often labeled "moods." In many cases, the same emotions – in different contexts, or with different objects – that lead people into social movements can lead them out again.

Just to list these emotions should suggest their prevalence in social movements, but we can categorize them further. Table 17.2 provides examples of emotions according to the two basic distinctions I have mentioned: affects vs. reactive emotions, and the social settings where they are developed and sustained. It is the interaction between the affects and responses outside the movement that may propel someone to join an organization, participate in an event, contribute money, or be receptive to a recruiter's plea. The right side of the table suggests a number of internal movement dynamics: affects about one's fellow members may lead to either continued allegiance or defection; responses to the decisions and actions of other players in a conflict help explain strategic choices, including whether to continue or not. Although many emotions can only fall in the right-hand column or in the left, many others can be created or sustained in either setting; most of the affects and reactive emotions that would draw someone to a movement would also help keep her there.

Every extensive study of a social movement is filled with emotions like those that fill these tables, but they almost never receive theoretical attention or even appear in indices [...]. There seem to be two main exceptions, in which scholars have addressed the emotions of social movements.

Certain social movements aim at changing the broader culture of their society, including

Table 17.1 Some emotions potentially relevant to protest

Primarily affective

Hatred, Hostility, Loathing: Powerful step in the creation of outrage and the fixing of blame. Can alter goals from practical results to punishment of opponents.

Love: One can have erotic and other attachments to people already in a movement; love also shapes one's affective map of the world.

Solidarity, Loyalty: Positive feelings toward others can lead to action on behalf of that group or category.

Suspicion, Paranoia: Often lead to indignation and articulation of blame.

Trust, Respect: Basic positive affects that influence other emotional and cognitive responses, patterns of alliances, and credibility.

Primarily reactive

Anger: Can have many sources, and can be channeled in many directions, including both rage and outrage. Can interfere with effective strategies.

Grief, Loss, Sorrow: Loss, especially of a loved one, can bring on life passage and raise issues of the meaning of life.

Outrage, Indignation: These build on other emotions, largely by providing a target for analysis.

Shame: Can lead to anger and aggressive reactions.

Moods and others in between

Compassion, Sympathy, Pity: One can imagine the plight of others and develop a desire to help them.

Cynicism, Depression: They discourage protest by dampening hopes for change.

Defiance: Stance that encourages resistance.

Enthusiasm, Pride: Positive emotions that protest leaders try to encourage: enthusiasm for the movement and cause, pride in the associated collective identity, as in Black Power, gay and lesbian rights.

Envy, Resentment: Exaggerated by early crowd theorists, these are emotions that few admit to and which usually lead to actions other than protest; yet they may also appear among protestors.

Fear, Dread: These can arise from a sense of threat to one's daily routines or moral beliefs. They can paralyze but also be developed into outrage.

Joy, Hope: One can be attracted by the joys of empowerment, a sense of "flow" in protest and politics, or the anticipation of a better state of affairs in the future.

Resignation: Like cynicism, can dampen perceived possibility for change.

Table 17.2 Examples of emotions by social setting

	Settings where developed and sustained	
Types	*Outside movement*	*Inside movement*
Ongoing affects, loyalties	Love for family members. Fondness for neighborhood. Reassuring security of home. Fears of radiation, war. Trust in certain public figures, mistrust of others. Racial or other prejudices.	Love, attraction to other members. Loyalty to shared symbols, identity. Respect, trust for leaders. Jealousy of leaders, others. Trust or mistrust of allies. Trust or mistrust of government officials, politicians.
Responses to events, information	Shock at loved one's death. Anger at government decision. Outrage at plans for nuclear plant. Indignation over siting of waste dump. Resignation over government inaction.	Anger, outrage, indignation over government actions, reactions to movement demands, responses of media.

the acceptability and display of certain emotions. These are often movements fighting against the stigmatization of some group. And since emotions are often defined as "women's work," such efforts have frequently been part of the women's movement. In the late 1960s thousands of consciousness-raising groups helped women learn to feel less guilty about their resentment toward husbands, fathers, employers, and other men. Anger was not only considered positive, it was almost a requirement for membership, argues Hochschild (1975:298), who continues, "Social movements for change make 'bad' feelings okay, and they make them useful. Depending on one's point of view, they make bad feelings 'rational.' They also make them visible." According to Taylor and Whittier (1995), women's groups regularly try to transform the negative feelings many women have because of their structural positions, including depression, fear, and guilt. Taylor (1996) has examined self-help groups for mothers suffering from postpartum depression, an emotion widely stigmatized as "inappropriate," not part of the mother role. In this paper I do not examine such cases, where changes in emotions are among a movement's explicit goals, but rather I examine emotions as part of a movement's own dynamics.

The other exception is the collective-behavior approach, which traditionally acknowledged the importance of emotions – but by linking the anger of organized protestors to the fears of panics. For example John Lofland (1985:32), in describing the joys of crowds, recognizes the problematic emotions emphasized in the collective-behavior tradition, summed up in the image of a crowd: "with all the emotional baggage of irrationality, irritability, excess, fickleness, and violence." Lofland seems to imply that negative emotions such as fear and anger are closer to irrationality than positive ones such as joy. And organized social movements, as opposed to crowds, still appear free from emotions. There is still a taint or suspicion of irrationality surrounding most emotions.

[...]

Movements are themselves a distinct setting in which emotions can be created or reinforced. In contrast to emotions that grow out of existing moral frameworks such as religious systems or professional ethics, the emotions created within social movements are attempts, often explicit, to elaborate intuitive visions into explicit ideologies and proposals. The anger of a farmer living near a proposed site for a nuclear plant is the intuition that the antinuclear movement tries to build into a systematic ideology of opposition. What the farmer sees first as "meddlesome outsiders" develops into "technocracy"; fear develops into outrage. Each cognitive shift is accompanied by emotional ones.

Some of the emotions generated within a social movement – call them *reciprocal* – concern participants' ongoing feelings toward each other. These are the close, affective ties of friendship, love, solidarity, and loyalty, and the more specific emotions they give rise to. Together they create what Goodwin (1997) calls the "libidinal economy" of a movement, yielding many of the pleasures of protest, including erotic pleasures. Other emotions – call them *shared* – are consciously held by a group at the same time, but they do not have the other group members as their objects. The group nurtures anger toward outsiders, or outrage over government policies. Reciprocal and shared emotions, although distinct, reinforce each other – thereby building a movement's culture. Each measure of shared outrage against a nuclear plant reinforces the reciprocal emotion of fondness for others precisely because they feel the same way. They are like us; they understand. Conversely, mutual affection is one context in which new shared emotions are easily created. Because you are fond of others, you want to adopt their feelings. Both kinds of collective emotion foster solidarity within a protest group. They are key sources of identification with a movement.

Collective emotions, the reciprocal ones especially, are linked to the pleasures of protest. Most obvious are the pleasures of being with people one likes, in any number of ways. Other pleasures arise from the joys of collective activities, such as losing oneself in collective motion or song. This can be satisfying even when done with strangers – who of course no longer feel like strangers. And articulating one's moral principles is always a source of joy, pride, and fulfilment – even when it is also painful.

Emotions are one of the products of collective action, especially internal rituals. Collective rites remind participants of their basic moral commitments, stir up strong emotions, and reinforce a sense of solidarity with the group, a "we-ness." Rituals are symbolic embodiments, at salient times and places, of the beliefs and feelings of a group. Singing and dancing are two activities often found in rituals, providing the requisite emotional charge through music, coordinated physical activity, and bodily contact (McNeill, 1995). Since Durkheim first described "collective effervescence," it has been clear that these activities were crucial in creating it, by transporting participants onto another plane, into what they feel is a more ethereal, or at any rate different, reality. In many ways, singing and dancing are the kernel of truth in older crowd theories, the one moment when a large group can attain a certain coordination and unity, can silence the small groups talking among themselves, can concentrate the attention of all. Of course, this coordination does not emerge spontaneously, since participants must know the dances and the lyrics. And it is hard to imagine *all* participants joining in (McPhail, 1991). But Durkheim was pointing to important processes that reinforce emotions in predictable ways.

Singing was especially important to the civil rights movement (Morris, 1984). Lyrics such as "Onward Christian Soldiers," "There's a great day coming," and "We shall overcome" lent biblical authority to the campaign with specific references to fundamental beliefs and narratives (Watters, 1971). Deliverance through a great leader – Moses, Jesus, Martin Luther King, Jr. – was a reassuring emotional message. Extensive religious training meant that almost all African American participants knew the music, loudly generating a moving feeling of solidarity. Lyrics are a form of shared knowledge that helps one feel like an insider. Morris (1984:47) quotes King: "The opening hymn was the old familiar 'Onward Christian Soldiers,' and when that mammoth audience stood to sing, the voices outside (the church building could not accommodate the large gatherings) swelling the chorus in the church, there was a mighty ring like the glad echo of heaven itself.... The enthusiasm of these thousands of people swept everything along like an onrushing tidal wave." It is hard to imagine more powerful emotional materials.

[...]

References

Averill, James R. 1980 "A constructivist view of emotion." In Robert Plutchik and Henry Kellerman (eds.), *Emotion: Theory, Research, and Experience, vol. 1: Theories of Emotion.* New York: Academic Press.

Bernstein, Mary and James M. Jasper 1996 "Interests and credibility: Whistle-blowers in technological conflicts." *Social Science Information* 35:565–589.

Collins, Randall 1990 "Stratification, emotional energy, and the transient emotions." In Theodore D. Kemper (ed.), *Research Agendas in the Sociology of Emotions.* Albany: SUNY Press.

de Sousa, Ronald 1987 *The Rationality of Emotion.* Cambridge: MIT Press.

Goodwin, Jeff 1997 "The libidinal constitution of a high-risk social movement. Affectual ties and solidarity in the Huk Rebellion." *American Sociological Review* 62:53–69.

Greenstein, Fred I. 1987 *Personality and Politics*, new ed. Princeton: Princeton University Press.

Harré, Rom 1986 "An outline of the social constructionist viewpoint." In Rom Harré (ed.), *The Social Construction of Emotions.* Oxford: Basil Blackwell.

Heise, David R. 1979 *Understanding Events.* Cambridge: Cambridge University Press.

Hochschild, Arlie Russell 1975 "The sociology of feeling and emotion: Selected possibilities." In Marcia Millman and Rosabeth Moss Kanter

(eds.), *Another Voice*. Garden City NY: Anchor Books.
Lasswell, Harold D. 1930 *Psychopathology and Politics*. Chicago: University of Chicago Press.
Lofland, John 1985 *Protest*. New Brunswick, NJ: Transaction Publishers.
McNeill, William H. 1995 *Keeping Together in Time: Dance and Drill in Human History*. Cambridge, MA: Harvard University Press.
McPhail, Clark 1991 *The Myth of the Madding Crowd*. New York: Aldine de Gruyter.
Morris, Aldon D. 1984 *The Origins of the Civil Rights Movement*. New York: Free Press.
Solomon, Robert C. 1976 *The Passions*. New York: Doubleday-Anchor.
Taylor, Verta 1996 *Rock-a-by Baby*. New York: Routledge.
Taylor, Verta and Nancy Whittier 1995 "Analytical approaches to social movement culture: The culture of the women's movement." In Hank Johnston and Bert Klandermans (eds.), *Social Movements and Culture*. Minneapolis: University of Minnesota Press.
Thoits, Peggy A. 1989 "The sociology of the emotions." *Annual Review of Sociology* 15:317–342.
Watters, Pat 1971 *Down to Now*. New York: Pantheon.

18 Classic Protest Songs: A List

Joe Hill, the legendary labor activist and songwriter, once wrote, "A pamphlet, no matter how good, is never read more than once. But a song is learned by heart and repeated over and over." Music has indeed been a rich source of political ideas and social analysis—an important popular form of public sociology. But which songs have moved Americans the most over the past century or offered the richest political insights? After consulting widely, we offer the following hit parade, in rough chronological order. —The Editors

"Lift Every Voice and Sing." Lyrics by James Weldon Johnson; music by J. Rosamand Johnson. Key lyric: "*We have come over a way that with tears has been watered / We have come, treading our path through the blood of the slaughtered.*" Known as the "Black National Anthem"—the antidote to "America, the Beautiful."

"Which Side Are You On?" By Florence Reece. "*Don't scab for the bosses, don't listen to their lies / Us poor folks haven't got a chance unless we organize.*" Written during the labor struggles in Harlan County, Kentucky, in the 1930s, it was later adopted by the civil rights movement.

"Strange Fruit." Performed by Billie Holiday. By Abel Meeropol (who later adopted the children of Julius and Ethel Rosenberg). "*Pastoral scene of the gallant south / The bulging eyes and the twisted mouth.*" A chilling protest against lynching. Maybe the greatest protest song of all time.

"Pastures of Plenty." By Woody Guthrie. "*Every state in this union us migrants has been / 'Long the edge of your cities you'll see us, and then / We've come with the dust and we're gone in the wind.*" Guthrie's ode to America's migrant workers.

"The Times They Are A-Changin'." By Bob Dylan. "*There's a battle outside and it's raging / It'll soon shake your windows and rattle your walls.*" Tough call between this and Dylan's "Blowin' in the Wind," "Only a Pawn in Their Game," "Masters of War," "With God on Our Side," etc., etc.

"We Shall Overcome." Adapted from a gospel song, the anthem of the civil rights movement. "*Deep in my heart, I do believe / We shall overcome some day.*" Infinitely adaptable.

"Ain't Gonna Let Nobody Turn Me 'Round." Also adapted from a Negro spiritual. "*I'm gonna keep on walkin', keep on talkin' / Fightin' for my equal rights.*" Another powerful civil rights anthem.

"I Ain't Marching Anymore." By Phil Ochs. "*It's always the old to lead us to the war / It's always the young to fall / Now look at all we've won with the saber and the gun / Tell me is it worth it all?*" An antiwar classic, complete with a revisionist history of American militarism.

"For What It's Worth." Performed by Crosby, Stills, and Nash. By Stephen Stills. "*There's something happening here / What it is ain't exactly clear / There's a man with a* *gun over there / Telling me I've got to beware.*" Eerily foreboding.

"Say It Loud (I'm Black and I'm Proud)." By James Brown. "*Now we demand a chance to do things for ourself / We're tired of beatin' our head against the wall and workin' for someone else.*" A Black Power anthem by the Godfather of Soul.

"Respect." Performed by Aretha Franklin. By Otis Redding. "*I ain't gonna do you wrong while you're gone / Ain't gonna do you wrong 'cause I don't wanna / All I'm askin' is for a little respect when you come home.*" The personal is political.

"Redemption Song." By Bob Marley. "*Emancipate yourselves from mental slavery / None but ourselves can free our minds.*" Marley's "Get Up, Stand Up" is also a contender.

"Imagine." By John Lennon. "*Imagine no possessions / I wonder if you can / No need for greed or hunger / A brotherhood of man.*" Lennon as utopian socialist.

"Fight the Power." By Public Enemy. "*Got to give us what we want / Gotta give us what we need / Our freedom of speech is freedom or death / We got to fight the powers that be.*" An exuberant hip-hop call to arms.

Part VI

How Are Movements Organized?

Introduction

Forty years ago, social movements were thought to be extremely disorganized affairs. Individuals were believed to drift into them for personal rather than political reasons; crowds were thought to be irrational and shifting in their focus, hence easily manipulated by demagogues. This is why movements were categorized as a form of "collective behavior," which implies less purpose and intention than the term collective "action." If politics occurred outside normal institutional channels such as parties and voting, then it was thought not to have any form of organization at all.

Perhaps the biggest breakthrough in the field of social movements beginning in the late 1960s was to show that social movements are thoroughly organized, both formally and informally. The informal organization consists of social networks through which individuals are recruited: it turns out they are not isolated and alienated but well integrated into society (see part III). Networks like these also shape what movements can do once they emerge. On the formal dimension, movements usually create, even consist of, formal organizations, which are often legal entities recognized by the state. This section examines these formal organizations (usually dubbed "SMOs" for social movement organizations) and the way they are related to each other in a social movement.

SMOs vary enormously. Some have a great deal of formal structure and rules, while others have nothing but informal traditions and habits. Some are centralized and hierarchical, others decentralized and egalitarian. Some require a lot of money to function and survive, while others subsist on nothing more than the hours contributed by volunteers. They also differ in their sources of funding: some get grants from philanthropic foundations, others from broad direct-mail efforts; members themselves support some, governments actually support others. There are great differences as well in the commitment required of members. For revolutionary cells, protest is a full-time job that usually entails cutting ties with non-members. Other protest groups require nothing more than a Saturday afternoon every few months—or even just an occasional contribution (many SMOs have different kinds of members, ranging from financial supporters to those who volunteer their labor, to full-time staff).

Most of the "new" social movements that began to emerge in the 1960s, including student movements, the New Left, and later environmental, feminist, and antinuclear movements, thought it important to avoid bureaucratic organizations. They preferred egalitarian groups that encouraged everyone to participate in decisionmaking. Joyce Rothschild and Allen Whitt (1986) described these alternative organizations as avoiding the traditional trappings of bureaucracy: paid staff, experts, hierarchy, impersonal rules, and a permanent division of labor. In other words, organizational forms are one area in which many protestors have tried to change the way their societies do things, in anticipation of the kind of future they envision (Breines 1982; Polletta 2002). One of the purposes of avoiding traditional bureaucracy is to foster "free spaces" in which creative alternatives to mainstream practices can be imagined, discussed, and tried out (Evans and Boyte 1986).

Social movements also vary in how many component organizations they have, and in how these are related to each other. At one extreme there may be a single organization that directs the movement, as with some revolutionary movements. At the other there may be many organizations with little coordination among them: each may be reassured by the existence of others but have little direct need for them. Most movements fall somewhere between these extremes. No matter how many SMOs they contain, movements still vary in the degree of coordination among them. Gerlach and Hine (1970) once described social movements as segmented, polycephalous, and reticulate: each group is relatively autonomous from the others, there is no definite head, and yet they have loose links among the parts.

John McCarthy and Mayer Zald, in a famous article excerpted in this section (1977), looked at social movement organizations as though they were like business firms in a market. If an SMO is like a firm, then a movement is like an industry. The important implication is that SMOs may have to compete with each other over the same volunteers and contributors, even when they are in the same movement and thus have the same goals. The economic metaphor focuses our attention on the financing of SMOs, including the many different kinds of relationships they can have with contributors—who are not necessarily the beneficiaries. Paid staff, the "entrepreneurs" who put SMOs together, are crucial. This emphasis on resources helped create the "resource mobilization" approach to social movements. Their approach seems to work well in understanding moderate, well-behaved groups, such as mainstream environmental organizations, that employ professional staffs and raise most of their funds through direct-mail solicitations.

Another tradition of research, exemplified by Charles Tilly (1978), used political rather than economic metaphors to understand social movement organizations. Research on labor unions and other groups that pursued economic and political benefits at the same time helped inspire what has come to be called the "political process" school. Researchers in this tradition view protest groups as being like political parties, except operating outside the electoral system. SMOs are a normal part of politics, whatever form they take. They are instrumental vehicles for the pursuit of group interests.

The weakness of these traditions emphasizing formal organizations was to depict protestors as invariably self-interested and indeed selfish. Having rejected the psychology of older traditions, these scholars inadvertently embedded the assumptions of neoclassical economics in

Indigenous Organization In order to sustain protest, people need to communicate with one another, strategize, advertise, recruit new protestors, and generally coordinate their activities. It often helps, accordingly, if would-be protestors already belong to the same (or linked) political or social organizations, churches, friendship networks, schools, sports clubs, work places, neighborhoods, and so on. Sometimes entire organizations or networks are recruited into a movement, a process known as **bloc recruitment**. If such "indigenous organization" (sometimes called **mobilizing structures**), whether formal or informal, does not already exist, would-be protestors have to create their own protest organizations. Self-organization or self-recruitment to movements, in other words, is sometimes as important as pre-existing organization. These connections are helpful not only for coordinating action and spreading information, but also for building affective ties and loyalties.

Participatory Democracy In the early 1960s, the New Left promoted what it called participatory democracy (sometimes called "direct democracy"), as opposed to the regular channels of representative democracy. Instead of voting for those who would make the ultimate decisions, a basic goal was to allow people to make decisions directly. Participatory democracy was meant to involve everyone in discussions of an issue before voting on it as a group. Better yet, a consensus might emerge so that a formal vote would not be necessary. Needless to say, this approach, popular with social movements of the 1960s through the 1980s and beyond, works best with small groups, and no one has yet quite figured out how to extend the principle to national decisionmaking or link it to traditional representative democracy. Critics have pointed to the seemingly endless discussions it entails in practice, as well as to the possibility that golden-tongued informal leaders can dominate a group without the accountability they would face if they were formal leaders. Participatory democracy reveals some of the core values of the New Left, especially the idea that individuals should control the world around them by making decisions about issues that directly shape their lives.

their models: people were rational pursuers of their own narrow interests. These scholars ignored one of the central issues of social movements: how people come to perceive a shared grievance or interest, especially in something remote from their daily lives, such as global warming, nuclear energy, or human rights abuses in distant lands. There are many emotional and cognitive processes that go into the construction of movement goals. We can't lose sight of what people want from their protest organizations.

We can go further. Organizations themselves are more than instruments for attaining goals. They also carry symbolic messages in their very structures. Protestors want to attain their goals, to be sure, but they also want to show that they are certain kinds of people (e.g., compassionate, objective, outraged, maybe even dangerous). With certain kinds of organizational forms, they can show they mean business, or that they are radically different from existing organizations. A school of thought called the "new institutionalism" has arisen in organizational theory to show that organizational structures are never simply the most efficient means to given ends, but also reflect their surrounding cultures' assumptions about the world. An organization's structure often reflects cultural fads popular at the time of its founding.

Elisabeth Clemens, in an article excerpted below, applies this school of thought to social movement organizations. Focusing on women's groups, she suggests that marginalized populations typically adapt culturally familiar forms of organization (e.g., clubs, unions, parliaments, even armies) for political purposes. The "repertoire" or models of organization available to a population shape the ways in which it may organize itself for collective action. When choosing a model from this organizational repertoire, moreover, normative considerations are typically more important than efficiency.

The excerpt by Paul Wapner argues that many movements, including the environmental and human rights movements, increasingly organize across national boundaries. Transnational forms of organization, of course, make sense in an increasingly integrated world. Many contemporary social problems simply cannot be addressed at a national level. In this sense, transnational organization is a response to "globalization." Transnational environmental activist groups (TEAGs, as Wapner calls them) pressure governments, but they do much more than this. They have been instrumental in disseminating an ecological sensibility to new groups, pressuring multinational corporations, and empowering local communities. Thus, they are an important component of an emerging "world civic politics" or "global civil society" that is independent of national states.

Jackie Smith, in the final excerpt in this section, describes the complex transnational network of activists and organizations that has mobilized in recent years for "global justice" or for what Smith calls "democratic globalization." Smith sees this network as a potentially powerful tool that allows people to act effectively beyond their local and even national communities. The formation and coordination of the global justice movement, which some have called a "movement of movements," has been facilitated by technological changes, including the Internet. Smith shows that the number of transnational social movement organizations (TSMOs) has increased dramatically in recent years, even as these have adopted decentralized forms of organization. In fact, paradoxically, as movements have taken on global issues, many have drawn upon small-scale, face-to-face forms of organization, including the "affinity group." Affinity groups are small, semi-independent groups of like-minded activists (they may live in the same neighborhood or have similar political or aesthetic tastes) which typically coordinate their actions with other, similar affinity groups. The affinity-group model of organization has some similarities with anarchism, including a distaste for all forms of hierarchy. Coalitions based on affinity groups typically display a great deal of tactical flexibility, but they are inherently more difficult to direct and control than more centralized forms of organization.

There have been debates over the effects of formal organization on social movements. William Gamson (1990) found that social movements with more-bureaucratic organizations were more successful. They are certainly likely to survive longer, as the point of rules and formality is to persist. However, Frances Fox Piven and Richard Cloward (1979), looking at a number of poor people's movements, argued that the most powerful tool of the oppressed is their ability to disrupt things. Bureaucratic organization usually interferes with this, as bureaucrats begin to develop an interest in maintaining the organization and their own positions and status, even if this means ignoring or suppressing the demands of the organization's rank and file. This debate continues.

Discussion Questions

1. In what ways do SMOs differ from each other?
2. When would SMOs have an advantage in being formal, when informal? When hierarchical, when egalitarian?
3. What are some of the symbolic messages that SMOs might wish to convey through their formal structures? To whom?
4. If you joined a movement, what type of organization would you find appealing? What would turn you off?
5. In what ways is transnational or cross-border organizing easier than it might have been, say, one hundred years ago? What are some of the difficulties involved in organizing a transnational movement?
6. What are the advantages of the affinity-group model of organization? What are its disadvantages?

19 Social Movement Organizations

John D. McCarthy and Mayer N. Zald

For quite some time a hiatus existed in the study of social movements in the United States. In the course of activism leaders of movements here and abroad attempted to enunciate general principles concerning movement tactics and strategy and the dilemmas that arise in overcoming hostile environments. Such leaders as Mao, Lenin, Saul Alinsky, and Martin Luther King attempted in turn to develop principles and guidelines for action. The theories of activists stress problems of mobilization, the manufacture of discontent, tactical choices, and the infrastructure of society and movements necessary for success. At the same time sociologists, with their emphasis upon structural strain, generalized belief, and deprivation, largely have ignored the ongoing problems and strategic dilemmas of social movements.

Recently a number of social scientists have begun to articulate an approach to social movements, here called the resource mobilization approach, which begins to take seriously many of the questions that have concerned social movement leaders and practical theorists. Without attempting to produce handbooks for social change (or its suppression), the new approach deals in general terms with the dynamics and tactics of social movement growth, decline, and change. As such, it provides a corrective to the practical theorists, who naturally are most concerned with justifying their own tactical choices, and it also adds realism, power, and depth to the truncated research on and analysis of social movements offered by many social scientists.

The resource mobilization approach emphasizes both societal support and constraint of social movement phenomena. It examines the variety of resources that must be mobilized, the linkages of social movements to other groups, the dependence of movements upon external support for success, and the tactics used by authorities to control or incorporate movements. The shift in emphasis is evident in much of the work published recently in this area (J. Wilson 1973; Tilly 1973, 1975; Tilly, Tilly, and Tilly 1975; Gamson 1975; Oberschall 1973; Lipsky 1968; Downs 1972; McCarthy and Zald 1973). The new approach depends more upon political, sociological, and economic theories than upon the social psychology of collective behavior.

This paper presents a set of concepts and propositions that articulate the resource mobilization approach. It is a partial theory because it takes as given, as constants, certain components of a complete theory. The propositions are heavily based upon the American case, so that the impact of societal differences in development and political structure on social movements is unexplored, as are differences in levels and types of mass communication. Further, we rely heavily upon case material concerning organizations of the left, ignoring, for the most part, organizations of the right.

The main body of the paper defines our central concepts and presents illustrative hypotheses about the social movement sector (SMS), social movement industries (SMI), and social movement organizations (SMO).

However, since we view this approach as a departure from the main tradition in social movement analysis, it will be useful first to clarify what we see as the limits of that tradition.

Perspectives Emphasizing Deprivation and Beliefs

Without question the three most influential approaches to an understanding of social movement phenomena for American sociologists during the past decade are those of Gurr (1970), Turner and Killian (1972), and Smelser (1963). They differ in a number of respects. But, most important, they have in common strong assumptions that shared grievances and generalized beliefs (loose ideologies) about the causes and possible means of reducing grievances are important preconditions for the emergence of a social movement in a collectivity. An increase in the extent or intensity of grievances or deprivation and the development of ideology occur prior to the emergence of social movement phenomena. Each of these perspectives holds that discontent produced by some combination of structural conditions is a necessary if not sufficient condition to an account of the rise of any specific social movement phenomenon. Each, as well, holds that before collective action is possible within a collectivity a generalized belief (or ideological justification) is necessary concerning at least the causes of the discontent and, under certain conditions, the modes of redress. Much of the empirical work which has followed and drawn upon these perspectives has emphasized even more heavily the importance of understanding the grievances and deprivation of participants. (Indeed, scholars following Gurr, Smelser, and Turner and Killian often ignore structural factors, even though the authors mentioned have been sensitive to broader structural and societal influences, as have some others.)

Recent empirical work, however, has led us to doubt the assumption of a close link between preexisting discontent and generalized beliefs in the rise of social movement phenomena. A number of studies have shown little or no support for expected relationships between objective or subjective deprivation and the outbreak of movement phenomena and willingness to participate in collective action (Snyder and Tilly 1972; Mueller 1972; Bowen et al. 1968; Crawford and Naditch 1970). Other studies have failed to support the expectation of a generalized belief prior to outbreaks of collective behavior episodes or initial movement involvement (Quarantelli and Hundley 1975; Marx 1970; Stallings 1973). Partially as a result of such evidence, in discussing revolution and collective violence Charles Tilly is led to argue that these phenomena flow directly out of a population's central political processes instead of expressing momentarily heightened diffuse strains and discontents within a population (Tilly 1973).

Moreover, the heavy focus upon the psychological state of the mass of potential movement supporters within a collectivity has been accompanied by a lack of emphasis upon the processes by which persons and institutions from outside of the collectivity under consideration become involved; for instance, Northern white liberals in the Southern civil rights movement, or Russians and Cubans in Angola. Although earlier perspectives do not exclude the possibilities of such involvement on the part of outsiders, they do not include such processes as central and enduring phenomena to be used in accounting for social movement behavior.

The ambiguous evidence of some of the research on deprivation, relative deprivation, and generalized belief has led us to search for a perspective and a set of assumptions that lessen the prevailing emphasis upon grievances. We want to move from a strong assumption about the centrality of deprivation and grievances to a weak one, which makes them a component, indeed, sometimes a secondary component in the generation of social movements.

We are willing to assume (Turner and Killian [1972] call the assumption extreme)

"... that there is always enough discontent in any society to supply the grass-roots support for a movement if the movement is effectively organized and has at its disposal the power and resources of some established elite group" (p. 251). For some purposes we go even further: grievances and discontent may be defined, created, and manipulated by issue entrepreneurs and organizations.

We adopt a weak assumption not only because of the negative evidence (already mentioned) concerning the stronger one but also because in some cases recent experience supports the weaker one. For instance, the senior citizens who were mobilized into groups to lobby for Medicare were brought into groups only after legislation was before Congress and the American Medical Association had claimed that senior citizens were not complaining about the medical care available to them (Rose 1967). Senior citizens were organized into groups through the efforts of a lobbying group created by the AFL-CIO. No doubt the elderly needed money for medical care. However, what is important is that the organization did not develop directly from that grievance but very indirectly through the moves of actors in the political system. Entertaining a weak assumption leads directly to an emphasis upon mobilization processes. Our concern is the search for analytic tools to account adequately for the processes.

Resources To sustain themselves over time, social movements need resources: money and the physical or professional capacities it can buy. Today, organizers need telephones, FAX machines, computers, direct-mail fundraising services, paid lobbyists, photocopiers, and postage. They need to rent offices and hire staff. They devote considerable time to raising the funds for such purposes. Some resources are "lumpy": you don't need a second bullhorn if your first works fine. And in all cases, there needs to be the know-how to put physical capacities to work. What is more, resources are not fixed in amount: activists work hard to mobilize more resources, to see their existing capacities in new and imaginative ways, and to find ways to protest that are within their means.

Resource Mobilization

The resource mobilization perspective adopts as one of its underlying problems Olson's (1965) challenge: since social movements deliver collective goods, few individuals will "on their own" bear the costs of working to obtain them. Explaining collective behavior requires detailed attention to the selection of incentives, cost-reducing mechanisms or structures, and career benefits that lead to collective behavior (see, especially, Oberschall 1973).

Several emphases are central to the perspective as it has developed. First, study of the aggregation of resources (money and labor) is crucial to an understanding of social movement activity. Because resources are necessary for engagement in social conflict, they must be aggregated for collective purposes. Second, resource aggregation requires some minimal form of organization, and hence, implicitly or explicitly, we focus more directly upon social movement organizations than do those working within the traditional perspective. Third, in accounting for a movement's successes and failures there is an explicit recognition of the crucial importance of involvement on the part of individuals and organizations from outside the collectivity which a social movement represents. Fourth, an explicit, if crude, supply and demand model is sometimes applied to the flow of resources toward and away from specific social movements. Finally, there is a sensitivity to the importance of costs and rewards in explaining individual and organizational involvement in social movement activity. Costs and rewards are centrally affected by the structure of society and the activities of authorities.

We can summarize the emerging perspective by contrasting it with the traditional one as follows:

1. Support base
   A. Traditional. Social movements are based upon aggrieved populations which provide the necessary resources and labor. Although case

studies may mention external supports, they are not incorporated as central analytic components.

B. Resource mobilization. Social movements may or may not be based upon the grievances of the presumed beneficiaries. Conscience constituents, individual and organizational, may provide major sources of support. And in some cases supporters – those who provide money, facilities, and even labor – may have no commitment to the values that underlie specific movements.

2. Strategy and tactics

A. Traditional. Social movement leaders use bargaining, persuasion, or violence to influence authorities to change. Choices of tactics depend upon prior history of relations with authorities, relative success of previous encounters, and ideology. Tactics are also influenced by the oligarchization and institutionalization of organizational life.

B. Resource mobilization. The concern with interaction between movements and authorities is accepted, but it is also noted that social movement organizations have a number of strategic tasks. These include mobilizing supporters, neutralizing and/or transforming mass and elite publics into sympathizers, achieving change in targets. Dilemmas occur in the choice of tactics, since what may achieve one aim may conflict with behavior aimed at achieving another. Moreover, tactics are influenced by interorganizational competition and cooperation.

3. Relation to larger society

A. Traditional. Case studies have emphasized the effects of the environment upon movement organizations, especially with respect to goal change, but have ignored, for the most part, ways in which such movement organizations can utilize the environment for their own purposes (see Perrow 1972). This has probably been largely a result of the lack of comparative organizational focus inherent in case studies. In analytical studies emphasis is upon the extent of hostility or toleration in the larger society. Society and culture are treated as descriptive, historical context.

B. Resource mobilization. Society provides the infrastructure which social movement industries and other industries utilize. The aspects utilized include communication media and expense, levels of affluence, degree of access to institutional centers, preexisting networks, and occupational structure and growth.

Theoretical Elements

Having sketched the emerging perspective, our task now is to present a more precise statement of it. In this section we offer our most general concepts and definitions. Concepts of narrower range are presented in following sections.

A *social movement* is a set of opinions and beliefs in a population which represents preferences for changing some elements of the social structure and/or reward distribution of a society. A *countermovement* is a set of opinions and beliefs in a population opposed to a social movement. As is clear, we view social movements as nothing more than preference structures directed toward social change, very similar to what political sociologists would term issue cleavages. (Indeed, the process we are exploring resembles what political scientists term interest aggregation, except that we are concerned with the margins of the political system rather than with existing party structures.)

The distribution of preference structures can be approached in several ways. Who holds the beliefs? How intensely are they held? In order to predict the likelihood of preferences being translated into collective action, the mobilization perspective focuses upon the preexisting organization and integration of those segments of a population which share preferences. Oberschall (1973) has presented an important synthesis of past work on the preexisting organization of preference structures, emphasizing the opportunities and costs for expression of preferences for movement leaders and followers. Social movements whose related populations are highly organized internally (either communally or associationally) are more likely than are others to spawn organized forms.

Social Movement Organizations (SMOs) Some analysts have studied social movements as though they were composed primarily of formal organizations that act much as businesses do. This is partly just a metaphor and partly a reflection of the fact that many social movements are indeed composed largely of formal organizations. This means that one of their main activities is raising funds (or "mobilizing resources") to keep themselves afloat and their staffs paid. They compete with each other for contributions, especially from those who support the movement in no way other than financially. This development reflects modern laws governing nonprofit organizations, the affluence of societies in which many people have discretionary income to contribute to their favorite causes, and the ability of activists to find professional careers in social change organizations. In addition to social movement organizations (often abbreviated SMOs), scholars have also analyzed "social-movement industries," in which different SMOs compete for resources and attention, as well as the entire "social-movement sector" of societies.

A *social movement organization* (SMO) is a complex, or formal, organization which identifies its goals with the preferences of a social movement or a countermovement and attempts to implement those goals. If we think of the recent civil rights movement in these terms, the social movement contained a large portion of the population which held preferences for change aimed at "justice for black Americans" and a number of SMOs such as the Student Non-Violent Coordinating Committee (SNCC), the Congress of Racial Equality (CORE), the National Association for the Advancement of Colored People (NAACP), and Southern Christian Leadership Conference (SCLC). These SMOs represented and shaped the broadly held preferences and diverse subpreferences of the social movement.

All SMOs that have as their goal the attainment of the broadest preferences of a social movement constitute a *social movement industry* (SMI) – the organizational analogue of a social movement. A conception paralleling that of SMI, used by Von Eschen, Kirk, and Pinard (1971), the "organizational substructure of disorderly politics," has aided them in analyzing the civil rights movement in Baltimore. They demonstrate that many of the participants in a 1961 demonstration sponsored by the local chapter of CORE were also involved in NAACP, SCLC, the Americans for Democratic Action (ADA), or the Young People's Socialist Alliance (YPSA). These organizations either were primarily concerned with goals similar to those of CORE or included such goals as subsets of broader ranges of social change goals. (The concept employed by Von Eschen et al. is somewhat broader than ours, however, as will be seen below.)

Definitions of the central term, social movement (SM), typically have included both elements of preference and organized action for change. Analytically separating these components by distinguishing between an SM and an SMI has several advantages. First, it emphasizes that SMs are never fully mobilized. Second, it focuses explicitly upon the organizational component of activity. Third, it recognizes explicitly that SMs are typically represented by more than one SMO. Finally, the distinction allows the possibility of an account of the rise and fall of SMIs that is not fully dependent on the size of an SM or the intensity of the preferences within it.

Our definitions of SM, SMI, and SMO are intended to be inclusive of the phenomena which analysts have included in the past. The SMs can encompass narrow or broad preferences, millenarian and evangelistic preferences, and withdrawal preferences.

Organizations may represent any of these preferences.

The definition of SMI parallels the concept of industry in economics. Note that economists, too, are confronted with the difficulty of selecting broader or narrower criteria for including firms (SMOs) within an industry (SMI). For example, one may define a furniture industry, a sitting-furniture industry, or a chair industry. Close substitutability of product usage and, therefore, demand interdependence is the theoretical basis for defining industry boundaries. Economists use the *Census of Manufacturers* classifications, which are not strictly based on demand interdependence. For instance, on the one hand various types of steel are treated as one industry, though the types (rolled, flat, wire) are not substitutable. On the other hand, some products are classified separately (e.g., beet sugar, cane sugar) when they are almost completely substitutable (Bain 1959, pp. 111–18).

Given our task, the question becomes how to group SMOs into SMIs. This is a difficult problem because particular SMOs may be broad or narrow in stated target goals. In any set of empirical circumstances the analyst must decide how narrowly to define industry boundaries. For instance, one may speak of the SMI which aims at liberalized alterations in laws, practices, and public opinion concerning abortion. This SMI would include a number of SMOs. But these SMOs may also be considered part of the broader SMI which is commonly referred to as the "women's liberation movement" or they could be part of the "population control movement." In the same way, the pre-1965 civil rights movement could be considered part of the broader civil liberties movement.

Economists have dealt with this difficulty by developing categories of broader inclusiveness, sometimes called sectors. Even this convention, however, does not confront the difficulties of allocating firms (SMOs) which are conglomerates, those which produce products across industries and even across sectors. In modern America there are a number of SMOs which may be thought of as conglomerates in that they span, in their goals, more narrowly defined SMIs. Common Cause, the American Friends Service Committee (AFSC), and the Fellowship of Reconciliation (FOR) are best treated in these terms as each pursues a wide variety of organizational goals which can only with difficulty be contained within even broadly defined SMIs. The *social movement sector* (SMS) consists of all SMIs in a society no matter to which SM they are attached. (The importance of this distinction will become apparent below.)

Let us now return to the resource mobilization task of an SMO. Each SMO has a set of *target goals*, a set of preferred changes toward which it claims to be working. Such goals may be broad or narrow, and they are the characteristics of SMOs which link them conceptually with particular SMs and SMIs. The SMOs must possess resources, however few and of whatever type, in order to work toward goal achievement. Individuals and other organizations control resources, which can include legitimacy, money, facilities, and labor.

Although similar organizations vary tremendously in the efficiency with which they translate resources into action, the amount of activity directed toward goal accomplishment is crudely a function of the resources controlled by an organization. Some organizations may depend heavily upon volunteer labor, while others may depend upon purchased labor. In any case, resources must be controlled or mobilized before action is possible.

From the point of view of a SMO the individuals and organizations which exist in a society may be categorized along a number of dimensions. For the appropriate SM there are adherents and nonadherents. *Adherents* are those individuals and organizations that believe in the goals of the movement. The *constituents* of a SMO are those providing resources for it.

At one level the resource mobilization task is primarily that of converting adherents into constituents and maintaining constituent involvement. However, at another level the task may be seen as turning nonadherents into adherents. Ralph Turner (1970) uses the term bystander public to denote those nonadherents who are not opponents of the SM and its SMOs but who merely witness social movement activity. It is useful to distinguish constituents, adherents, bystander publics, and opponents along several other dimensions. One refers to the size of the resource pool controlled, and we shall use the terms mass and elite to describe crudely this dimension. Mass constituents, adherents, bystander publics, and opponents are those individuals and groups controlling very limited resource pools. The most limited resource pool which individuals can control is their own time and labor. Elites are those who control larger resource pools.

Each of these groups may also be distinguished by whether or not they will benefit directly from the accomplishment of SMO goals. Some bystander publics, for instance, may benefit directly from the accomplishment of organizational goals, even though they are not adherents of the appropriate SM. To mention a specific example, women who oppose the preferences of the women's liberation movement or have no relevant preferences might benefit from expanded job opportunities for women pursued by women's groups. Those who would benefit directly from SMO goal accomplishment we shall call *potential beneficiaries*.

In approaching the task of mobilizing resources a SMO may focus its attention upon adherents who are potential beneficiaries and/or attempt to convert bystander publics who are potential beneficiaries into adherents. It may also expand its target goals in order to enlarge its potential beneficiary group. Many SMOs attempt to present their goal accomplishments in terms of broader potential benefits for ever-wider groupings of citizens through notions of a better society, etc. (secondary benefits). Finally, a SMO may attempt to mobilize as adherents those who are not potential beneficiaries. *Conscience adherents* are individuals and groups who are part of the appropriate SM but do not stand to benefit directly from SMO goal accomplishment. *Conscience constituents* are direct supporters of a SMO who do not stand to benefit directly from its success in goal accomplishment.

William Gamson (1975) makes essentially the same distinction, calling groups with goals aimed at helping nonconstituents universalistic and those whose beneficiaries and constituents are identical, nonuniversalistic. Gamson concludes, however, that this distinction is not theoretically important, since SMOs with either type of constituents have identical problems in binding them to the organization. It is not more "irrational," in Olson's sense, to seek change in someone else's behalf than in one's own, and in both cases commitment must be gained by other means than purposive incentives. The evidence presented by Gamson suggests that this dimension does not bear much relationship to SMO success in goal accomplishment or in the attainment of legitimacy. We argue below, however, that the distinction should be maintained: it summarizes important attachments and social characteristics of constituents. The problems of SMOs with regard to binding beneficiary and conscience constituents to the organization are different, not with regard to the stakes of individual involvement relative to goal accomplishment (the Olson problem) but with regard to the way constituents are linked to each other and to other SMOs, organizations, and social institutions.

A SMO's potential for resource mobilization is also affected by authorities and the delegated agents of social control (e.g., police). While authorities and agents of control groups do not typically become constituents of SMOs, their ability to frustrate (normally termed social control) or to enable resource mobilization is of crucial importance. Their action affects the readiness of bystanders, adherents, and constituents to alter their own status and commitment. And they themselves may become adherents and constituents. Because they do not always act in concert, Marx (1974) makes a strong case that authorities and delegated agents of control need to be analyzed separately.

The partitioning of groups into mass or elite and conscience or beneficiary bystander publics, adherents, constituents, and opponents allows us to describe more systematically the resource mobilization styles and dilemmas of specific SMOs. It may be, of course, to the advantage of a SMO to turn bystander publics into adherents. But since SMO resources are normally quite limited, decisions must be made concerning the allocation of these resources, and converting bystander publics may not aid in the development of additional resources. Such choices have implications for the internal organization of a SMO and the potential size of the resource pool which can be ultimately mobilized. For instance, a SMO which has a mass beneficiary base and concentrates its resource mobilization efforts toward mass beneficiary adherents is likely to restrict severely the amount of resources it can raise. Elsewhere (McCarthy and Zald 1973) we have termed a SMO focusing upon beneficiary adherents for resources a classical SMO. Organizations which direct resource appeals primarily toward conscience adherents tend to utilize few constituents for organizational labor, and we have termed such organizations professional SMOs.

Another pattern of resource mobilization and goal accomplishment can be identified from the writings of Lipsky (1968) and Bailis (1974). It depends upon the interactions among beneficiary constituency, conscience adherents, and authorities. Typical of this pattern is a SMO with a mass beneficiary constituency which would profit from goal accomplishment (for instance, the Massachusetts Welfare Rights Organization) but which has few resources. Protest strategies draw attention and resources from conscience adherents to the SMO fighting on behalf of such mass groups and may also lead conscience elites to legitimate the SMO to authorities. As a result of a similar pattern, migrant farmworkers benefited from the transformation of authorities into adherents.

But a SMO does not have complete freedom of choice in making the sorts of decisions to which we have alluded. Such choices are constrained by a number of factors including the preexisting organization of various segments of the SM, the size and diversity of the SMI of which it is a part, and the competitive position of the SMS. Also, of course, the ability of any SMO to garner resources is shaped by important events such as war, broad economic trends, and natural disasters.

The Elements Applied: Illustrative Hypotheses

Let us proceed to state hypotheses about the interrelations among the social structure, the SMS, SMIs, and SMOs. Occasionally, we introduce specifying concepts. Because the levels of analysis overlap, the subheadings below should be viewed as rough organizing devices rather than analytic categories.

Resources, the SMS, and the Growth of SMIs

Over time, the relative size of the SMS in any society may vary significantly. In general it will bear a relationship to the amount of wealth in a society. Hence, hypothesis 1: *As the amount of discretionary resources of mass and elite publics increases, the absolute and relative amount of resources available to the SMS increases.* This hypothesis is more of an orienting postulate than a directly testable hypothesis, but it is central to our perspective. And some related supporting evidence can be given.

By discretionary resources we mean time and money which can easily be reallocated, the opposite of fixed and enduring commitments of time and money. In any society the SMS must compete with other sectors and industries for the resources of the population. For most of the population the allocation of resources to SMOs is of lower priority than allocation to basic material needs such as food and shelter. It is well known that the proportion of income going to food and shelter is higher for low-income families, while the proportion of income going to savings and recreation increases among high-income families. The SMOs compete for resources with entertainment, voluntary associations, and organized religion and politics.

There is cross-sectional evidence that the higher the income the larger the average gift to charitable activities and the greater the proportion of total income given (see Morgan, Dye, and Hybels 1975). Moreover, Morgan et al. (1975) show that (1) the higher the education the more likely the giving of time, and (2) people who give more time to volunteer activities also give more money. As the total amount of resources increases, the total amount available to the SMS can be expected to increase, even if the sector does not increase its relative share of the resource pool. However, as discretionary resources increase relative to total societal resources, the SMS can be expected to gain a larger proportional share. This argument is based upon our belief that, except in times of crisis, the SMS is a low-priority competitor for available resources – it benefits from the satiation of other wants.

Of course, the validity of this hypothesis depends upon a *ceteris paribus* proviso. What might the other factors be? First, the existing infrastructure, what Smelser (1963) terms structural conduciveness, should affect the total growth of the SMS. Means of communication, transportation, political freedoms, and the extent of repression by agents of social control, all of which may affect the costs for any individual or organization allocating resources to the SMS, serve as constraints on or facilitators of the use of resources for social movement purposes. Also, the technologies available for resource accumulation should affect the ability of SMOs within the sector to mobilize resources. For instance, the advent of mass-mailing techniques in the United States has dramatically affected the ability of the SMS to compete with local advertising in offering a product to consumers. The organization of the SMIs will support or hinder the growth of the sector as additional resources become available. The greater the range of SMOs, the more different "taste" preferences can be transformed into constituents.

Hypothesis 2: *The greater the absolute amount of resources available to the SMS the greater the likelihood that new SMIs and SMOs will develop to compete for these resources.* This and the previous proposition contain the essence of our earlier analysis (McCarthy and Zald 1973). That study accounts in part for the proliferation in SMOs and SMIs in the 1960s in the United States by demonstrating both the relative and the absolute increases of resources available to the SMS. The major sources of increase in financial resources were charitable giving among mass and elite adherents and government, church, foundation, and business giving among organizational adherents.

These two propositions attempt to account for the total growth of the SMS. They ignore variations in the taste for change over time. They imply nothing about which SMI will reap the benefits of sector expansion. Nor do they imply what types of SMOs will lead the growth of an expanding SMI. They explicitly ignore the relationship between the size of the SMS and the intensities of preferences within a SM.

Parallel hypotheses could be stated for the relationship of resources amongst different categories of SM adherents and SM growth. For instance, hypothesis 3: *Regardless of the resources available to potential beneficiary adherents, the larger the amount of resources available to conscience adherents the more likely is the development of SMOs and SMIs that respond to preferences for change.* The importance of this hypothesis in our scheme hinges upon the growing role of conscience constituents in American social movements. First, the greater the discretionary wealth controlled by individuals and organizations the more likely it is that some of that wealth will be made available to causes beyond the direct self-interest of the contributor. An individual (or an organization) with large amounts of discretionary resources may allocate resources to personal comfort and to the advancement of some group of which he or she is not a member. Second, those who control the largest share of discretionary resources in any society are also those least likely to feel discontentment concerning their own personal circumstances.

In a sense, hypothesis 3 turns Olson (1965) on his head. Though it may be individually irrational for any individual to join a SMO which already fights on behalf of his preferences, the existence of a SM made up of well-heeled adherents calls out to the entrepreneur of the cause to attempt to form a viable organization. To the extent to which SM beneficiary adherents lack resources, SMO support, if it can be mobilized, is likely to become heavily dependent upon conscience constituents.

This argument is also important in understanding the critique of interest group pluralism as a valid description of modern America. Many collectivities with serious objective deprivations, and even with preexisting preferences for change, have been highly underrepresented by social movement organizations. These SMs tend to be very limited in their control of discretionary resources. It is only when resources can be garnered from conscience adherents that viable SMOs can be fielded to shape and represent the preferences of such collectivities.

Organization Structure and Resource Mobilization

How do the competitive position of the SMS, processes within a SMI, and the structure of a SMO influence the task of resource mobilization? Some aspects of these questions have been treated by Zald and Ash (1966). To discuss SMOs in detail we need to introduce assumptions about relevant SMO processes and structures.

Assume that SMOs operate much like any other organization (J. Q. Wilson 1973), and consequently, once formed, they operate as though organizational survival were the primary goal. Only if survival is insured can other goals be pursued. Second, assume that the costs and rewards of involvement can account for individual participation in SMOs and that, especially, selective incentives are important since they tend to raise the rewards for involvement. Gamson (1975) and Bailis (1974) provide impressive evidence that selective material incentives operate to bind individuals to SMOs and, hence, serve to provide continuous involvement and thus resource mobilization.

For a number of reasons the term member has been avoided here. Most important, membership implies very different levels of organizational involvement in different SMOs. The distinction between inclusive and exclusive SMOs has been utilized in the past to indicate intensity of organizational involvement (Zald and Ash 1966), but intensity of involvement actually includes several dimensions, usefully separated. Let us attempt to partition constituent involvement in any SMO. First there is the *cadre*, the individuals who are involved in the decision-making processes of the organization. Cadre members may devote most of their time to matters of the organization or only part of their time. Those who receive compensation, however meager, and devote full time to the organization, we term professional cadre; those who devote full time to the organization, but are not involved in central decision making processes, we term professional staff; those who intermittently give time to organizational tasks, not at the cadre level, we term workers. (Remember, constituents are those who give time *or* money.)

A *transitory team* is composed of workers assembled for a specific task, short in duration. Transitory teams are typically led by cadre members. Members of transitory teams and cadre have more extensive involvement than other segments of a SMO constituency. What distinguishes these constituents from others is that they are directly linked to the organization through tasks – they are involved directly in the affairs of the SMO. Since involvement of this sort occurs in small face-to-face groups, workers, whether through transitory teams or through continuous task involvement, can be expected to receive solidary incentives from such involvement – selective benefits of a nonmaterial sort.

Federated and Isolated Structure

A SMO which desires to pursue its goals in more than a local environment may attempt to mobilize resources directly from adherents or to develop federated chapters in different local areas. Federation serves to organize constituents into small local units. The SMOs which develop in this manner may deal with constituents directly as well as through chapters or only through chapters. But many SMOs do not develop chapters. These deal directly with constituents, usually through the mails or through traveling field staff. The important point is that constituents in nonfederated SMOs do not normally meet in face-to-face interaction with other constituents and hence cannot be bound to the SMOs through solidary selective incentives. We term these constituents, isolated constituents.

Federation may occur in two ways. One strategy assigns professional staff the task of developing chapters out of isolated adherents or constituents. To some extent SDS and CORE utilized this approach during the 1960s. Common Cause seems to have used it recently. Another strategy relies upon preexisting nonmovement local groups which have heavy concentrations of adherents or isolated constituents. This latter style, termed group mobilization by Oberschall (1973), was typical of several waves of recruitment by the Ku Klux Klan. Federation developing out of preexisting groups can occur quite rapidly, while organizing unattached individuals probably requires more time and resources. To the extent that it utilized mass involvement in the South, SCLC operated through preexisting groups. We have argued elsewhere (McCarthy and Zald 1973) that nonfederated SMOs dealing with isolated constituents accounted for much of the SMS growth during the burst of SMO activity during the decade of the 1960s.

Empirically, SMOs will combine elements of the two major organizational forms we have identified here. The manner in which the organization garners the bulk of its resources should be used to characterize it during any time period. For instance, CORE would be deemed federated until the early 1960s, nonfederated at its peak during the early 1960s, and then federated again. It maintained a set of federated chapters during this entire period, but during the interim period its major resource flow was provided by isolated conscience constituents.

Hypothesis 4: *The more a SMO is dependent upon isolated constituents the less stable will be the flow of resources to the SMO.* Because isolated constituents are little involved in the affairs of the SMO, support from them depends far more upon industry and organizational (and counter-industry and counterorganizational) advertising than does support from constituents who are involved on a face-to-face basis with others. Advertising and media attention provide information about the dire consequences stemming from failure to attain target goals, the extent of goal accomplishment, and the importance of the particular SMO for such accomplishment.

Strickland and Johnston's (1970) analysis of issue elasticity is useful in understanding isolated constituent involvement in SM activities. At any time a number of target goals are offered to isolated adherents to any SM by one or more SMOs (and by other SMIs). Isolated adherents may choose to become constituents by allocating resources to one or another SMO based upon the goals propounded. The SMOs within any SMI will tend to compete with one another for the resources of these isolated adherents. If they allocate resources, but remain isolated, their ties to the SMO remain tenuous. To the extent that any individual is an adherent to more than one SM, various SMIs will also be competing for these resources.

Treating SMO target goals as products, then, and adherence as demand, we can apply a simple economic model to this competitive process. Demand may be elastic, and its elasticity is likely to be heavily dependent upon SMO advertising. Products may be substitutable across SMIs. For example, while various SMOs may compete for resources from isolated adherents to the "justice for black Americans" SM, SMOs representing the "justice for American women" SM may be competing for the same resources (to the extent that these two SMs have overlapping adherent pools). Some adherents may have a high and inelastic demand curve for a SMO or SMI, others' demand curves may show great elasticity.

This suggests that effective advertising campaigns may convince isolated adherents with high-issue elasticity to switch SMOs and/or SMIs. Issue elasticity relates to what Downs (1972) terms "issue attention cycles." These apparent cycles, he observes, include the stages of a problem discovered, dramatic increases in adherence as advertising alerts potential adherents, attempts at problem solution, lack of success of such attempts, and a rapid decline in adherence and advertising. Isolated adherents may purchase a target goal product when offered but can be expected to base decisions about future purchases upon their conception of product quality. Tullock (1966) has argued that the consumption of such products is vicarious, not direct; thus, perceived product quality is not necessarily related to actual goal accomplishment. Much publicity is dependent upon a SMO's ability to induce the media to give free attention, as most SMOs cannot actually afford the high costs of national advertising. They do, however, use direct-mail advertising. The point is that the media mediate in large measure between isolated constituents and SMOs.

Perceived lack of success in goal accomplishment by a SMO may lead an individual to switch to SMOs with alternative strategies or, to the extent that products are substitutable, to switch to those with other target goals. It must be noted, however, that there is also an element of product loyalty in this process. Some isolated constituents may continue to purchase the product (to support a SMO) unaware of how effective or ineffective it may be.

One could treat individual SMO loyalty in the same way as political party loyalty is treated by political sociologists, but most SMOs do not command such stable loyalties from large numbers of people. Certain long-lasting SMOs, the NAACP and the AFSC, for instance, may command stable loyalties, and the process of socializing youth into SMO loyalty could be expected to be similar to that of socialization into party loyalty. This process, however, most probably occurs not among isolated constituents, but among those who are linked in more direct fashion to SMOs.

Advertising by SMOs recognizes that isolated constituents have no direct way of evaluating the product purchased; therefore it may stress the amount of goal accomplishment available to the isolated constituent for each dollar expended. The AFSC, for instance, informs isolated potential constituents in its mass mailings that its overhead costs are among the lowest of any comparable organization, and hence the proportion of each donation used for goal accomplishment is higher. Within an industry SMO products are normally differentiated by conceptions of the extremity of solutions required (Killian 1972) and by strategies of goal accomplishment (passive resistance, strikes, etc.). When products are not differentiated in either of these ways, we can expect differentiation in terms of efficiency.

These considerations lead to a subsidiary hypothesis, 4*a*: *The more dependent a SMO is upon isolated constituents the greater the share of its resources which will be allocated to advertising*. As indicated, SMO advertising can take the form of mailed material which demonstrates the good works of the organization. Media bargaining (Lipsky 1968) can also be conceptualized as SMO advertising. By staging events which will possibly be "newsworthy," by attending to the needs of news organizations, and by cultivating representatives of the media, SMOs may manipulate media coverage of their activities more or less successfully. Some kind of information flow to isolated constituents including positive evaluation is absolutely essential for SMOs dependent upon them.

The foregoing reasoning, combined with hypotheses 1 and 2, leads us to hypothesis 4*b*: *The more a SMO depends upon isolated constituents to maintain a resource flow the more its shifts in resource flow resemble the patterns of consumer expenditures for expendable and marginal goods.* Stated differently, if a SMO is linked to its major source of constituent financial support through the advertising of its products, isolated constituents will balance off their contributions with other marginal expenditures. Time of year, state of the checkbook, mood, and product arousal value will influence such decision making.

The more attractive the target goal (product) upon which such a solicitation is based, the more likely that isolated adherents will become isolated constituents. Consequently, SMOs depending heavily upon such resource mobilization techniques must resort to slick packaging and convoluted appeal to self-interest in order to make their products more attractive. This should be especially true within competitive SMIs. The behavior in the early 1970s of environmental groups, which depend heavily upon isolated constituents, appears to illustrate this point. Many of those SMOs took credit for stalling the Alaskan pipeline and attempted to link that issue to personal self-interest and preferences in their direct-mail advertising. Slick packaging is evident in the high quality of printing and the heavy use of photogravure.

Another technique advertisers utilize to appeal to isolated adherents is the linking of names of important people to the organization, thereby developing and maintaining an image of credibility. In the same way that famous actors, sports heroes, and retired politicians endorse consumer products, other well-known personalities are called upon to endorse SMO products: Jane Fonda and Dr. Spock were to the peace movement and Robert Redford is to the environmental movement what Joe Namath is to pantyhose and what William Miller is to American Express Company credit cards.

The development of local chapters helps bind constituents to SMOs through networks of friendships and interpersonal control. But, hypothesis 5: *A SMO which attempts to link both conscience and beneficiary constituents to the organization through federated chapter structures, and hence solidary incentives, is likely to have high levels of tension and conflict.* Social movement analysts who have focused upon what we have termed conscience constituency participation normally call it outsider involvement. Von Eschen et al. (1971), for instance, show that for a local direct action civil rights organization involvement on the part of geographical outsiders (both conscience and beneficiary) created pronounced internal conflict in the organization. Marx and Useem (1971) have examined the record of the recent civil rights movement, the abolitionist movement, and the movement to abolish untouchability in India. In these movements, "... outsiders were much more prone to be active in other causes or to shift their allegiances from movement to movement" (p. 102). Ross (1975) has argued the importance of friendship ties based upon geographical and generational lines to the internal conflict of SDS. The more unlike one another workers are, the less likely there is to be organizational unity, and the more likely it is that separate clique structures will form. If conscience constituents are more likely to be active in other SMOs and to be adherents of more than one SM, we would expect their involvement to be less continuous.

Now we can combine our earlier discussion of conscience and beneficiary constituents with our analysis of SMI and SMO processes. First, conscience constituents are more likely to control larger resource pools. Individuals with more resources exhibit concerns less directly connected with their own material interests. Consequently, conscience constituents are more likely to be adherents to more than one SMO and more than one SMI. Though they may provide the resources for an SMO at some point, they are likely to have conflicting loyalties.

This provides an account for why SMO leaders have been skeptical of the involvement of conscience constituents – intellectuals in labor unions, males in the women's liberation movement, whites in the civil rights movements. Conscience constituents are fickle because they have wide-ranging concerns. They may be even more fickle if they are isolated constituents – they are less likely to violate personal loyalties by switching priority concerns. But organizations which attempt to involve them in face-to-face efforts may have to suffer the consequences of the differences in backgrounds and outside involvements from those of beneficiary constituents. On the one hand, involving only conscience constituents in federated chapters, which might be a method of avoiding such conflict, forces the SMO to pay the price of legitimacy – how can a SMO speak for a beneficiary group when it does not have any beneficiary constituents? On the other hand, depending exclusively upon mass beneficiary constituents reduces the potential size of the resource pool which can be used for goal accomplishment.

Not only may the involvement of conscience and beneficiary constituents lead to interpersonal tensions, it also leads to tactical dilemmas. Meier and Rudwick (1976) document the extent to which the question of whether the NAACP should use black or white lawyers to fight its legal battles has been a continuous one. Especially in the early days, the symbolic value of using black lawyers conflicted sharply with the better training and court room effectiveness of white lawyers. W. E. B. Du Bois came out on the side of court room effectiveness.

Rates of Resource Fluctuation and SMO Adaptation

We have focused thus far upon the development of resource flows to SMOs, primarily in terms of how they link themselves to their constituents and the size of the resource pool controlled by constituents. What are the implications of larger or smaller resource flows for the fate of SMOs, for careers in social movements, and for the use of different types of constituencies?

An interesting question concerns the staying power of new and older entries into a SMI. Hypothesis 6: *Older, established SMOs are more likely than newer SMOs to persist throughout the cycle of SMI growth and decline*. This is similar to the advantage of early entry for a firm in an industry: A structure in place when demand increases improves the likelihood of capturing a share of the market. Stinchcombe (1965, p. 148) points out that "as a general rule, a higher proportion of new organizations fail than old. This is particularly true of new organizational *forms*, so that *if an alternative requires new organization*, it has to be much more beneficial than the old before the flow of benefits compensates for the relative weakness of the newer social structure." All the liabilities of new organizational forms which Stinchcombe elaborates – new roles to be learned, temporary inefficiency of structuring, heavy reliance upon social relations among strangers, and the lack of stable ties to those who might use the organization's services – beset new organizations of established forms as well, if to a lesser degree. Moreover, a history of accomplishment is an important asset, and, as Gamson (1975) shows for his sample of SMOs, longevity provides an edge in the attainment of legitimacy. Older organizations have available higher degrees of professional sophistication, existing ties to constituents, and experience in fund-raising procedures. Thus, as factors conducive to action based upon SM preferences develop, older SMOs are more able to use advertising to reach isolated adherents, even though new SMOs may of course benefit from the experience of older ones. The NAACP, for instance, already had a fund-raising structure aimed at isolated adherents before the increase in demand for civil rights goals increased in the 1960s. And CORE had the advantage of a professional staff member who was committed to the development of such techniques, but it took time for him to convince the decision makers of the organization to pursue such resource mobilization tactics (Meier and Rudwick 1973). Newer SMOs may capture a share of the isolated constituent market, but they will be disadvantaged at least until they establish a clear image of themselves and a structure to capitalize upon it. J. Q. Wilson (1973) cogently argues that competition between SMOs for resources occurs between organizations offering the most similar products, not between those for which competition in goal accomplishment produces conflict. Since SMOs within the same SMI compete with one another for resources, they are led to differentiate themselves from one another. The prior existence of skilled personnel and preexisting images are advantages in this process. In the same way that name recognition is useful to political candidates it is useful to SMOs when issue campaigns occur.

Hypothesis 7: *The more competitive a SMI (a function of the number and size of the existing SMOs) the more likely it is that new SMOs will offer narrow goals and strategies.* We have alluded to the process of product differentiation. As the competition within any SMI increases, the pressure to specialize intensifies. The decision of George Wiley to present the National Welfare Rights Organization as an organization aimed at winning rights for black welfare recipients was apparently made partially as a result of the preexisting turf understandings of other civil rights organizations.

Hypothesis 8: *The larger the income flow to a SMO the more likely that cadre and staff are professional and the larger are these groups.* This proposition flows directly from an economic support model. It is obvious that the more money is available to an organization, the more full-time personnel it will be able to hire. Though this is not a necessary outcome, we assume that SMOs will be confronted with the diverse problems of organizational maintenance, and as resource flows increase these will become more complex. As in any large organization, task complexity requires specialization. Specialization is especially necessary in modern America, where the legal requirements of functioning necessitate experienced technicians at a number of points in both resource mobilization and attempts to bring influence to bear. The need for skills in lobbying, accounting, and fund raising leads to professionalization.

It is not that SMOs with small resource flows do not recognize the importance of diverse organizational tasks. In them, a small professional cadre may be required to fulfill a diverse range of tasks such as liaison work with other organizations, advertising, accounting, and membership service. Large resource flows allow these functions to be treated as specialties, though organizations of moderate size may have problems of premature specialization. Economies of scale should be reached only at appropriate levels of growth. In CORE we have a good example of this process: early specialization required constant organizational reshuffling in order to combine functions and staff members in what seemed to be the most efficient manner (Meier and Rudwick 1973).

Hypothesis 9: *The larger the SMS and the larger the specific SMIs the more likely it is that SM careers will develop.* A *SM career* is a sequence of professional staff and cadre positions held by adherents in a number of SMOs and/or supportive institutions. Such a career need not require continuous connection with a SMI, though the larger the SMI the more likely such continuous involvement ought to be. Supportive institutions might be universities, church bodies, labor unions, governmental agencies and the like (Zald and McCarthy 1975). Moreover, target institutions sometimes develop positions for SM cadre, such as human-relation councils in local governments. Corporations have affirmative-action offices and antitrust lawyers.

When the SMI is large, the likelihood of SMI careers is greater simply because the opportunity for continuous employment is greater, regardless of the success or failure of any specific SMO. Though many of the skills developed by individuals in such careers (public relations, for instance) may be usefully applied in different SMIs, our impression is that individuals typically move between SMIs which have similar goals and hence have overlapping constituencies. While we might find individuals moving between civil rights and labor SMOs, we would be unlikely to find movement from civil rights SMOs to fundamentalist, anticommunist ones. (But it should be remembered that communists have become anticommunists, and that an antiwar activist such as Rennie Davis later took an active role in the transcendental meditation movement.) The relevant base for SMO careers, then, is usually SMIs or interrelated SMIs.

Funding strategies affect not only careers but also the use of beneficiary constituents as workers. Hypothesis 10: *The more a SMO is funded by isolated constituents the more likely that beneficiary constituent workers are recruited for strategic purposes rather than for organizational work.* This proposition is central to the strategy of the professional SMO. It leads to considering the mobilization of beneficiary constituent workers as a rational tool for attempts to wield influence, rather than as an important source of organizational resources. Earlier we mentioned the creation of senior citizen groups for purposes of bargaining by the AFL-CIO in the Medicare fight. The use of some poor people for strategic purposes by the Hunger Commission, a professional SMO, also illustrates the point. Also germane is the fact that of the groups in Gamson's study (1975) none that were heavily dependent upon outside sponsors provided selective material incentives for constituents. Binding beneficiary constituents to a SMO with incentives is not so important to an organization which does not need them in order to maintain a resource flow.

Much of our discussion has been framed in terms of discretionary money, but discretionary time is also of importance.

[...]

Conclusion

The resource mobilization model we have described here emphasizes the interaction between resource availability, the preexisting organization of preference structures, and entrepreneurial attempts to meet preference demand. We have emphasized how these processes seem to operate in the modern American context. Different historical circumstances and patterns of preexisting infrastructures of adherency will affect the strategies of SMO entrepreneurial activity in other times and places. Our emphasis, however, seems to be useful in accounting for parallel activity in different historical contexts, including peasant societies, and in explaining the processes of growth and decline in withdrawal movements as well.

The history of the Bolshevik SMO (Wolfe 1955) shows how important stable resource flows are to the competitive position of a SMO. The Bolsheviks captured the resource flow to the Russian Social Revolutionary movement and, at certain points in their history, depended heavily upon isolated conscience constituents. Free media are probably necessary to mass isolated constituent involvement in resource flows, so isolated adherents with control over large resource pools are probably more important to SMI growth in societies without mass media. Leites and Wolf (1970) make a similar analysis of the revolutionary SMI in its relationship to the constant rewards of participation by the peasants in Vietnam. Of course, the extent of discretionary resources varies considerably between that case and the modern American case, but so did the ability of authorities to intervene in the manipulation of costs and rewards of individual involvement in the revolutionary

SMO. The flow of resources from outside South Vietnam was important in the SMO's ability to manipulate these costs and rewards. Extranational involvement in the American SMS seems almost nonexistent.

Moreover, Oberschall (1973) has shown how important communal associations may be for facilitating mobilization in tribal and peasant societies. Although the number of SMOs and hence the size of the SMI may be smaller in peasant societies, resource mobilization and SM facilitation by societal infrastructure issues are just as important.

Withdrawal movements are typically characterized primarily by the way in which constituents are bound to the SMO (Kanter 1972). But SMOs in withdrawal SMs also encounter difficulties in developing stable resource flows, and they use a variety of strategies similar to those of other SMOs in response to their difficulties. The recent behavior of the Unification Church of America (led by the Rev. Sun Myung Moon) in the United States illustrates processes close to those we have focused upon for modern reform movements: heavy use of advertising and emphasis upon stable resource flows in order to augment the development of federated constituencies. The Father Divine Peace Mission (Cantril 1941) utilized rather different strategies of resource mobilization, including a heavier dependence upon the constituents themselves, but the importance of maintaining flows for continued viability was recognized in both of these withdrawal movements.

Our attempt has been to develop a partial theory; we have only alluded to, or treated as constant, important variables – the interaction of authorities, SMOs, and bystander publics; the dynamics of media involvement; the relationship between SMO workers and authorities; the impact of industry structure; the dilemmas of tactics. Yet, in spite of the limitations of our brief statement of the resource mobilization perspective, we believe it offers important new insights into the understanding of social movement phenomena and can be applied more generally.

References

Bailis, L. 1974. *Bread or Justice*. Springfield, Mass.: Heath-Lexington.

Bain, J. S. 1959. *Industrial Organization*. New York: Wiley.

Bowen, D., E. Bowen, S. Gawiser, and L. Masotti. 1968. "Deprivation *Mobility*, and Orientation toward Protest of the Urban Poor." Pp. 187–200 in *Riots and Rebellion: Civil Violence in the Urban Community*, edited by L. Masotti and D. Bowen. Beverly Hills, Calif.: Sage.

Cantril, H. 1941. *The Psychology of Social Movements*. New York: Wiley.

Crawford, T. J., and M. Naditch. 1970. "Relative Deprivation, Powerlessness and Militancy: The Psychology of Social Protest." *Psychiatry* 33 (May): 208–23.

Downs, A. 1972. "Up and Down with Ecology – the Issue Attention Cycle." *Public Interest* 28 (Summer): 38–50.

Gamson, W. A. 1975. *The Strategy of Protest*. Homewood, Ill.: Dorsey.

Gurr, T. R. 1970. *Why Men Rebel*. Princeton, N.J.: Princeton University Press.

Kanter, R. M. 1972. *Commitment and Community: Communes and Utopias in Sociological Perspective*. Cambridge, Mass.: Harvard University Press.

Killian, L. 1972. "The Significance of Extremism in the Black Revolution." *Social Forces* 20 (Summer): 41–48.

Leites, N., and C. Wolf, Jr. 1970. *Rebellion and Authority*. Chicago: Markham.

Lipsky, M. 1968. "Protest as a Political Resource." *American Political Science Review* 62: 1144–58.

McCarthy, J. D., and M. N. Zald. 1973. *The Trend of Social Movements in America: Professionalization and Resource Mobilization*. Morristown, N.J.: General Learning Press.

Marx, G. T. 1970. "Issueless Riots." *Annals* 391 (September): 21–33.

Marx, G. T. 1974. "Thoughts on a Neglected Category of Social Movement Participant: The Agent Provocateur and the Informant." *American Journal of Sociology* 80 (September): 402–42.

Marx, G. T., and M. Useem. 1971. "Majority Involvement in Minority Movements: Civil Rights, Abolition, Untouchability." *Journal of Social Issues* 27 (January): 81–104.

Meier, A., and E. Rudwick. 1973 *CORE: A Study in the Civil Rights Movement, 1942–1968*. New York: Oxford University Press.

——. 1976. "Attorneys Black and White. A Case Study of Race Relations within the NAACP." *Journal of American History* 62 (March): 913–46.

Morgan, J. N., R. F. Dye, and J. H. Hybels. 1975. *A Survey of Giving Behavior and Attitudes: A Report to Respondents*. Ann Arbor, Mich.: Institute for Social Research.

Mueller, E. 1972. "A Test of a Partial Theory of Potential for Political Violence." *American Political Science Review* 66 (September): 928–59.

Oberschall, A. 1973. *Social Conflict and Social Movements*. Englewood Cliffs, N.J.: Prentice-Hall.

Olson, M., Jr. 1965. *The Logic of Collective Action*. Cambridge, Mass.: Harvard University Press.

Perrow, C. 1972. *Complex Organizations: A Critical Essay*. Glenview, Ill.: Scott, Foresman.

Quarantelli, E. L., and J. R. Hundley. 1975. "A Test of Some Propositions about Crowd Formation and Behavior." Pp. 317–86 in *Readings in Collective Behavior*, edited by R. R. Evans. 2d ed. Chicago: Rand McNally.

Rose, A. 1967. *The Power Structure*. New York: Oxford University Press.

Ross, R. 1975. "Generational Change and Primary Groups in a Social Movement." Unpublished paper. Clark University, Worcester, Mass.

Smelser, N. 1963. *Theory of Collective Behavior*. New York: Free Press.

Snyder, D., and C. Tilly. 1972. "Hardship and Collective Violence in France." *American Sociological Review* 37 (October): 520–32.

Stallings, R. A. 1973. "Patterns of Belief in Social Movements: Clarifications from Analysis of Environmental Groups." *Sociological Quarterly* 14 (Autumn): 465–80.

Stinchcombe, A. L. 1965. "Social Structure and Organizations." Pp. 142–93 in *Handbook of Organizations*, edited by James March. Chicago: Rand-McNally.

Strickland, D. A., and A. E. Johnston. 1970. "Issue Elasticity in Political Systems." *Journal of Political Economy* 78 (September/October): 1069–92.

Tilly, C. 1973. "Does Modernization Breed Revolution?" *Comparative Politics* 5 (April): 425–47.

——. 1975. "Revolution and Collective Violence." Pp. 483–555 in *Handbook of Political Science*, edited by F. Greenstein and N. Polsky. Vol. 3. *Macro Political Theory*. Reading, Mass.: Addison-Wesley.

Tilly, C., L. Tilly, and R. Tilly. 1975. *The Rebellious Century: 1830–1930*. Cambridge, Mass.: Harvard University Press.

Tullock, G. 1966. "Information without Profit." Pp. 141–60 in *Papers on Non-Market Decision Making*, edited by G. Tullock. Charlottesville: University of Virginia, Thomas Jefferson Center for Political Economy.

Turner, R. H. 1970. "Determinants of Social Movement Strategies." Pp. 145–64 in *Human Nature and Collective Behavior: Papers in Honor of Herbert Blumer*, edited by Tamotsu Shibutani. Englewood Cliffs, N.J.: Prentice-Hall.

Turner, R. N., and L. Killian. 1972. *Collective Behavior*. 2d ed. Englewood Cliffs, N.J.: Prentice-Hall.

Von Eschen, D., J. Kirk, and M. Pinard. 1971. "The Organizational Sub-Structure of Disorderly Politics." *Social Forces* 49 (June): 529–43.

Wilson, J. 1973. *Introduction to Social Movements*. New York: Basic.

Wilson, J. Q. 1973. *Political Organizations*. New York: Basic.

Wolfe, B. 1955. *Three Who Made a Revolution*. Boston: Beacon.

Zald, M. N., and R. Ash. 1966. "Social Movement Organizations: Growth, Decline and Change." *Social Forces* 44 (March): 327–40.

Zald, M. N., and J. D. McCarthy 1975. "Organizational Intellectuals and the Criticism of Society." *Social Service Review* 49 (September): 344–62.

20 Organizational Repertoires

Elisabeth S. Clemens

Although we commonly think of social movements as agents of change, the dominant accounts of the relation of movements to politics lead to the opposite conclusion. While movements are often credited with limited substantive achievements – the passage of legislation or the defeat of a particular politician – at an organizational level we have come to expect co-optation, conservative goal transformation, and the "iron law of oligarchy," all operating to minimize differences between a challenging social movement and existing political institutions (Jenkins 1977; Michels [1911] 1962). Even in the case of social revolution, as Tocqueville ([1856] 1955) argued, insurgent movements may only intensify already emergent patterns of state authority. In each of these contests between established political institutions and oppositional social movements, the existing institutions endure even if the substance of policy is altered. But analytically, we are left with the question of how political institutions change. What accounts for transformations in the basic models or conventions that inform political organization and action?

Such a broad question is most easily approached in a specific context. In the decades immediately before and after the turn of the century, the institutions of American politics underwent "one of the more significant governmental transformations in American history – the emergence of meaningful regulatory and administrative policies" along with "a series of lasting changes in the nature and structure of political participation; party voting declined and interest-group politics became more important" (McCormick 1986, p. 83). These changes in the basic models of political participation came in the wake of efforts by agrarian groups and organized labor to secure greater leverage in a polity where the formal equality of white male citizens seemed increasingly irrelevant. At the same time, women mobilized to secure the vote for the one half of the adult population that was formally disenfranchised. But the connections between changing political institutions and the wave of popular political mobilization remain unclear.

In the scholarly division of labor, these two problems have been addressed by separate literatures: the study of social movements and the history of party systems or electoral regimes. Of late, however, women's historians have questioned this partitioning of inquiry, arguing that as more "is learned of the magnitude and centrality of women's contributions in these years, the more likely it seems that understanding them will provide a basis for the comprehensive analysis of progressivism that has eluded historians until now" (DuBois 1991, pp. 162–63). In order to arrive at such an analysis, however, two theoretical assumptions that have led us to discount social movements as sources of change must be reconsidered.

First, some movement organizations may be comparatively immune to pressures to adapt to the existing institutional environment. To establish this possibility, I will identify the logics of political incorporation implicit in the classic models of political sociology – specifically those of Robert Michels and Max Weber – and then apply them to a set of social movement groups known collectively as the "woman movement" of the late 19th and early 20th centuries in the

United States. This movement was rooted in the antebellum proliferation of female benevolent societies and abolitionist activities. When the Civil War amendments failed to provide for their enfranchisement, women gradually regrouped around the causes of temperance and woman suffrage, while constructing an impressive network of nationwide, federated women's organizations (Scott 1991). By the 1880s, women's organizations and causes were established alongside, but largely apart from, the nation's formal political institutions. The next decades saw increasing political mobilization of women as well as a series of legislative gains that compared favorably not only with the successes of women in other nations but also with the victories of labor and agrarian insurgents in the United States (Clemens 1990; Skocpol and Ritter 1991). The ability of women's groups to enter the political arena without being fully co-opted suggests that processes of conservative organizational transformation are conditioned by both the social identity of those organized and the character of existing political institutions.

Second, at least some of the interactions between social movements and existing political institutions must be capable of producing changes in those conventions that inform political action and organization. After presenting an alternative model of the interaction of movements and institutions, I will argue that the organizational dynamics of the American woman movement help to explain one of the most important institutional changes in U.S. political history: the shift from the 19th-century "state of courts and parties" to a political regime grounded in legislative activity and interest-group bargaining (Skowronek 1982; McCormick 1986). While internal struggles and electoral tactics were central forces in the decline of the parties and the preeminent position of electoral politics (McGerr 1986; Shefter 1983), voluntary associations played a key role in elaborating a new style of politics focused on specific issues, interests, and legislative responses. A rapidly growing literature now documents the widespread involvement of women's groups in a political project that moved from the "municipal housekeeping" of the 1890s to the development of formidable state and national lobbies during the 1910s and the 1920s. While rarely producing a pure expression of womanhood, these efforts did span lines of race, ethnicity, class, and region (Baker 1991; Frankel and Dye 1991; Muncy 1991; Scott 1991). Women's groups were not alone in this organizational innovation, but because of their marginal position with respect to electoral politics, their efforts to create an institutional alternative are particularly clear.

The central point, then, is to replace the focus on bureaucratization that characterizes work in the Michels-Weber tradition with a recognition that the social world offers multiple models of organization as well as conventions concerning who may use what models for what purposes. Models of organization comprise both templates for arranging relationships within an organization and sets of scripts for action culturally associated with that type of organization. Thus, models may be thought of as being intermediate to abstract dimensions of organizational form (e.g., degree of hierarchy) and to examples of specific organizations. Models can refer to "organizations of that type" or to "organizations that do that type of thing." Mention of either an attribute or an action may invoke a shared model or form of organizing.

Women's groups, along with others, were politically successful insofar as they adapted existing nonpolitical models of organization for political purposes. Rather than adopting a single bureaucratic form, these groups made use of multiple models of organization – unions, clubs, parliaments, and corporations – each of which articulated in different ways with existing political institutions. This finding requires that the scope of the standard Michels-Weber account of social movement development be delimited by a more elaborated analysis of social organization. Drawing on current debates in organization theory, I will argue that our understanding of the relation of social movements to political change has been handicapped by the twin assumptions that the choice of organizational form is governed primarily by considerations of efficacy and that classic bureaucratic hierarchies are the most effective form for achieving political goals. The choice of organizational models may also be governed by "logics of appropriateness" (March and Olsen 1989, pp. 23–24) or institutional norms (DiMaggio and Powell 1983) and, given variations in environment, composition, and organizational goals, bureaucratic forms may well prove less effective than network arrangements, solidary groups, or other conceivable alternatives (Powell 1990). Finally, when deployed in novel ways by unfamiliar groups, even the most familiar organizational models can have unsettling consequences for political institutions.

The set of organizational models that are culturally or experientially available may be thought of as an "organizational repertoire." This concept integrates the theoretical vocabulary of organization theorists sensitive to diversity of form with the cognitive or cultural framework of "repertoires of collective action" put forward by social movement scholars attuned to historical variation (Tilly 1978, 1986). As in social constructionist accounts, institutionalization, and by extension institutional change, is understood as the product of habitualization, the self-reproduction (or failure thereof) of a particular social pattern (Jepperson 1991). But rather than focusing on a "shared history" of interaction as the primary source of reciprocal typifications (Berger and Luckmann 1966, pp. 53–67), this analysis argues that consensus may also result as actors make use of a common, culturally available (rather than situationally constituted) repertoire of alternative models for interpreting a situation or acting in it. By deploying multiple organizational models in diverse institutional fields, social movements can be a source of institutional change even if they themselves undergo transformations of a more or less conservative nature.

In developing a model of institutional change, this argument draws on contemporary organization theory while requiring a shift in focus away from the centers of institutionalized organizational fields and toward their peripheries. Rather than attributing the disruption of organizational fields to various exogenous shocks, this account suggests that strategic political action as well as the search for collective identities produces migrations of organizational models and, potentially, the disruption of organized fields of action. The institutions of modern society are understood to be "potentially contradictory and hence make multiple logics available to individuals and organizations" (Friedland and Alford 1991, p. 232). These movements of organizational models are patterned in at least two ways: by the distribution of multiple memberships in organizational fields – the Simmelian web of group affiliations – and by the cultural logics informing the deployment of organizational repertoires. In developing a theory of organizational choice, James March pointed to the role of imitation as a component of "sensible foolishness," arguing that "in order for imitation to be normatively attractive we need a better theory of who should be imitated" (1979, pp. 75–76). Earlier generations of political actors found just such a theory embedded in their repertoires of organization, the cultural understandings linking organizational models to actors and purposes.

The Woman Movement: Scope and Sources

The potential of social movements or voluntary associations to transform institutional politics is evident in a striking – although, until recently, underappreciated – case of political organization by a comparatively disadvantaged group. The American "woman movement" of the late 19th and early 20th centuries drew together women who were relatively privileged in terms of economic standing and education (Blair 1980; Sklar 1985), yet suffered from formal and informal exclusionary practices that limited their ability to cultivate political skills or to exercise those skills if they were somehow acquired. Notwithstanding their formal disenfranchisement in much of the nation (the Nineteenth Amendment was not ratified until 1920), middle-class and upper-middle-class women constructed an impressive array of voluntary associations that were a significant force in the public life of the nation. Eighteen years after its founding in 1874, the Women's Christian Temperance Union (WCTU) numbered 150,000 members (Bordin 1981, pp. 3–4) and exerted influence on legislation ranging from temperance to woman suffrage. The General Federation of Women's Clubs (GFWC) was founded in 1890 and had perhaps 500,000 members by 1905 and over 1 million by the end of the decade. In addition to these groups, associated charities, civic clubs, auxiliaries to fraternal orders, and suffrage associations filled out a dense network of women's organizations. As a key element of the era's social reform constituency, these groups contributed to the founding of America's distinctively "maternalist" welfare state, a policy regime emphasizing programs such as mothers' pensions rather than unemployment and old age insurance (Gordon 1990; Skocpol 1992).

At an institutional level, women's groups were central to a broader reworking of the organizational framework of American politics: the decline of competitive political parties and electoral mass mobilization followed by the emergence of a governing system centered on administration, regulation, lobbying, and legislative politics. This change involved the invention of new models of political participation outside the established parties and the articulation of interests and demands that could be addressed by legislation and the active intervention of state agencies. Although the invention of modern interest-group politics may not have been intended by women activists, it was one of the most important consequences of this period of experimentation with political organization.

Although women's organizations of the period realized that some form of political action would be needed to advance many of their causes, politics as usual was out of the question. In addition to their formal exclusion from electoral activity, women's associations joined in a broader cultural attack on political methods. According to Mrs. Croly, the first president of the GFWC: "If I were to state what seems to me to be the great hindrance to club life and growth, it would be the employment of political methods, of political machinery and wire-pulling to bring about results. Politics can never be purified until its methods are changed, while its introduction into our club life subverts the whole intention and aims of club organization" (Croly 1898, p. 128).

Politics itself was not rejected, only the existing forms of political organization, the models of the electoral party and patronage machines. To construct an alternative, women's groups drew on models of organization that were culturally or experientially available in other areas of social life. Borrowing from this broader repertoire of social organization, these groups helped transform the repertoire of political action in the Progressive Era.

[...]

Focusing on repertoires of organization, the analysis seeks to establish mechanisms for such changes by locating the interaction of social movements and politics within a broader social system that embraces alternative models of organization and multiple institutions that may promote organizational conformity or isomorphism (DiMaggio and Powell 1983). While applications of the neo-institutionalist model that examine a single focal institution (usually the state or the professions) tend to emphasize how isomorphic processes promote stability and homogeneity, the opposite outcome is also possible. When familiar organizational forms are deployed in unfamiliar ways, insurgent groups may well destabilize existing institutions and ultimately contribute to the institutionalization of new conventions for political action. Organizational heterogeneity is reflected in the repertoires of organization; this is an account of cultural "tool kits" whose potential to create change flows from the complex organization of modern societies rather than from "unsettled" times (Swidler 1986). Rather than rejecting the classic Michels-Weber model, I will use the case of the woman movement to identify scope conditions for that model and, by extension, to provide criteria for identifying the types of movements most likely to contribute to significant institutional change in the political arena.

The Iron Law Reconsidered

Political organization can have profoundly ironic effects. As Robert Michels argued in his classic study of the Social Democratic Party in Wilhelmine Germany, "Organization is the weapon of the weak in the struggle with the strong." But this leverage is gained at a high price: "Organization is ... the source from which the conservative currents flow over the plain of democracy, occasioning there disastrous floods and rendering the plain unrecognizable" ([1911] 1962, pp. 61–62). Hierarchical bureaucratic organization is necessary to compete effectively in the formal political arena, yet the processes of competition and organization distance the leadership from the interests of their followers and from the organization's initial commitment to the transformation of the political system.

Although the inevitability of such conservative transformations has been challenged within the literature on social movements, immunity is associated with forms of insulation – economic independence, membership exclusivity, and ideological or professional purity (Jenkins 1977; Selznick 1960, pp. 23, 77, 153; Zald and Ash 1966). Furthermore, these studies have tended to focus on the internal dynamics of voluntary organizations rather than on their interactions with political institutions. For Michels, however, these may well be the exceptions that prove the rule. In his original analysis, ongoing interaction of radical political organizations with the institutions of formal politics and the economic environment was the primary engine of conservative transformation. Thus, we are left with a paradox, one that has been central to critiques of political pluralism (McAdam 1982, pp. 5–6, 18–19). To the extent that organized groups committed to political change seek to secure change through political processes – the give-and-take of coalition building and electoral mobilization – they seem doomed to fail as their goals of social change are sacrificed to the constraints of political process.

In this article, my central claim is that turn-of-the-century women's organizations – along with other associations – did cause substantial changes within American politics. Therefore, my first task must be to explain why women's organizations were comparatively immune from the logics of conservative transformation described in Michels's analysis. In *Union Democracy* (1956), the famous deviant case analysis of the International Typographical Union, Lipset, Trow, and Coleman argued that the "internal politics" of the union (the organization of work, the strength of locals, and a distinctive history of political conflict) contributed to its relative immunity from Michels's iron law. To understand the transformative potential of the women's groups of the Progressive Era, however, three aspects of external politics must be examined. The first two concern the relation of an organizational model to broader social structures. Michels's argument builds on two distinctive logics of incorporation – economic and political – that assume an organizational membership of enfranchised heads of households. Consequently, the effects of organization may vary with the social identity of those who are organized. The third point involves the symbolic rather than instrumental aspects of organizational models; the appropriation of an established model by marginal groups may have consequences that are less than entirely conservative. Given the economic and political situations of their members, women's groups were less likely to be drawn into established forms of political organization. Insofar as they did adopt these established models, however, heightened contradiction rather than effective co-optation was often the result.

The Logic of Economic Incorporation

One of the rules of investigative journalism is to follow the money. This rule also plays an important part in political sociology, receiving its classical form in Weber's analysis of the routinization of charismatic authority. The "administrative staff" of a movement or organization have: "an interest in continuing it in such a way that both from an ideal and a material point of view, their own position is put on a stable everyday basis. This means, above all, making it possible to participate in normal family relationships or at least to enjoy a secure social position in place of the kind of discipleship which is cut off from ordinary worldly connections, notably in the family and in economic relationships" (Weber 1978, p. 246).

This familiar passage identifies two distinct mechanisms by which economic imperatives shape the relation of the administrative staff to the organization: the interest in the continuation of the organization itself and the assurance of their own economic situation "making it possible to participate in normal family relations." Both of these imperatives play a prominent role in Michels's account of the iron law of oligarchy. The administrative staff will be unwilling to challenge the leadership from within: "Financial dependence upon the party, that is to say upon the leaders who represent the majority, enshackles the organization as with iron chains" (Michels 1962, pp. 140, 138). The status of party officials as breadwinners for their families also pushes the organization's goals in a conservative direction. For that fraction of the bourgeoisie who cast their lot with the working class, "no backward path is open. They are enchained by their own past. They have a family, and this family must be fed" (Michels 1962, p. 208). Family responsibilities and social position produce similar effects on leaders recruited from among the workers, who will be reluctant to abandon their improved status as officials of a labor organization (1962, p. 259). This account is generalizable, therefore, only to the extent that alternative forms of organizational support (e.g., personal or institutional patronage, see Jenkins [1977]) are unavailable and that staff or members are responsible for their own economic well-being and that of their dependents.

These dynamics continue to figure prominently in contemporary discussions of social movements, although a conservative outcome is no longer assumed to be inevitable. Analyses of funding stress the dangers of co-optation posed by a reliance on outside funding or patronage, while noting the limitations of resources within various communities marginalized by established political institutions (Jenkins 1977; McAdam, McCarthy, and Zald 1988). The constraints of everyday life have also been recognized in less narrowly economic terms as "biographical availability" (McAdam 1986); career and family responsibilities may constrain one's ability or inclination to participate in politics.

As I will argue below, the impact of these resource constraints is mediated by the form of organization. The more obvious point, however, is that the Michels-Weber account overlooks the gendered division of labor within households. Many of the leading figures in the woman movement were subject to a different set of constraints. At the most general level, changes in the division of labor and the growth of a market for consumer commodities left middle-class and upper-middle-class women of the late 19th century with increasing amounts of time free from household responsibilities (Wood 1912, pp. 24–25). Among those most active in the women's associations, many were supported financially by their husbands, and others came from families of considerable wealth and education (Blair 1980; Sklar 1985). The imperatives of the breadwinner, so central to both Weber and Michels, were clearly less relevant for these groups. For the less privileged, the women's groups themselves might provide a community – such as the settlement houses (Deegan 1988, pp. 40–45) – or activist careers might be funded by either broad constituencies or prominent patrons. The fact that many educated women remained single or childless – along with many mothers active in these associations having the help of a household staff – lessened the constraints of biographical availability.

The Logic of Political Incorporation

Just as the logic of economic incorporation is mediated by the forms of social organization and family life, the logic of political incorporation is structured by specific institutions. In Michels's terms, political participation leads to the conservative transformation of oppositional organizations by way of the system of electoral competition and the identification of movement leaders with the political establishment. Foreshadowing Anthony Downs's analysis of party systems (1957), Michels argued that by competing in elections, oppositional parties would be drawn toward the political center and, thereby, moderate their radical goals (1962, pp. 334–35). But if electoral competition does not produce favorable outcomes, even formal political parties may adopt alternative organizational models and strategies that emphasize ideological purity or solidary incentives rather than electoral advantage (Kitschelt 1989, p. 41). Furthermore, sheer numbers are less closely linked to victory in other systems of political contestation. For a revolutionary party, the requirements of training cadres may well outweigh the advantages of a large membership. For lobbying groups, as for all those engaged in "symbolic politics," resources, status, and style may matter more than numbers.

Women's formal disenfranchisement obviously distanced them from the logic of electoral incorporation. Although their groups frequently sought to persuade male voters to support woman suffrage or temperance or some other cause – and often moderated the radicalism of these claims for strategic ends – these efforts were only loosely coupled to the internal life of most women's associations. Barred from efforts to mobilize members directly as a voting bloc – with the consequent need to acquire majority, if not unanimous, consent to the organization's goals – women's associations typically developed internal "departmental" structures that allowed individual members to focus their efforts on a variety of goals, from visiting the sick to agitating for social legislation. Combined with a political mission summed up in the WCTU motto "Do Everything!" the departmental structure allowed factions or local organizations to experiment in advance of any consensus by the national membership. The organizational arrangements of the woman movement often freed it from the conservative consequences of consensual decision making (Baker 1991, pp. 20–21); when the Woman's Joint Congressional Committee was established in 1920, "procedure held that whenever three of the WJCC's organizations voted to support or oppose a piece of legislation, they formed a subcommittee to do their lobbying" (Muncy 1991, p. 103). Such systems of "loose coupling" (Thompson 1967) provided an additional source of insulation, buffering the internal life of the organization from both environmental constraints that might favor centralized bureaucratic forms directed toward discrete instrumental goals and from the veto of conservative factions within a given group.

The Instrumental Claim for Bureaucratic Organization

The claim for the efficacy of hierarchical bureaucratic organization was the first substantive argument made by Michels (1962) and remains widely accepted, even among his critics:

> It is indisputable that the oligarchical and bureaucratic tendency of party organization is a matter of technical and practical necessity. It is the inevitable product of the very principle of organization. Not even the most radical wing of the various socialist parties raises any objection to this retrogressive evolution, the contention being that democracy is only a form of organization and that where it ceases to be possible to harmonize democracy with organization, it is better to abandon the former than the latter. Organization, since it is the only means of attaining the ends of socialism, is considered to comprise within itself the revolutionary content of the party, and this essential content must never be sacrificed for the sake of form. [p. 72]

While it is possible to imagine circumstances in which oppositional groups will be immune from the economic and political logics of conservative incorporation, this claim is the bedrock of Michels's assertion that "who says organization says oligarchy" and, by extension, that organization entails both internal and external conservative transformations. In its most simple form, the argument runs as follows: (1) hierarchical, centralized bureaucracies are the most effective form of organization; (2) consequently, existing political parties and institutions have adopted this form of organization; (3) in the course of pursuing their ends, oppositional parties will adopt the same organizational form for strategic reasons, even at the expense of their ideological commitments; (4) therefore, growing organizational isomorphism will lead oppositional parties to become like established political groups, precluding the possibility of meaningful political change.

This argument may be challenged on at least two points. I will discuss the first, the assumption that there is a single form of bureaucratic hierarchy toward which all organizations evolve in the pursuit of efficacy, in the context of an alternative model to be developed below. The second, however, concerns the assumption that the adoption of existing organizational forms by an oppositional group necessarily has a conservative or moderating influence on its critical stance toward existing political institutions and endangers "internal" democracy. Since politics is structured by intersecting rules – how to organize, who should organize, and for what – it is possible that the adoption of conventional organizational models may be destabilizing as it exposes contradictions within the existing system.

Many early efforts by politically active women accepted both the institutionalized models of American politics and the traditional cultural division of the social world into "separate spheres" for men and women. Yet this borrowing revealed incompatibilities between the organizational systems of politics and gender. Attempts by women to use recognizably political methods eventually necessitated a denial of the dual system of separate spheres. Initially, women's political institutions were largely self-directed. In 1848 the Women's Rights Convention at Seneca Falls issued a formal "Declaration of Principles" and Elizabeth Cady Stanton declared that "woman herself must do this work; for woman alone can understand the height, the depth, the length, the breadth of her degradation" (quoted in Flexner 1970, p. 77). By the second half of the century, women's organizations were promoting "Women's Parliaments" as forums in which women could debate and publicize their views. Through the rest of the 19th century, women drew on this model of separate polities parallel to the separate spheres. In 1892, for example, the Southern California Womans Parliament met for "the full and free discussion of reforms necessary to the progress of women's work in the church, home and society" (1892, p. 1). Women's work was redefined in public terms rather than traditional religious terms, but retained its identity as a distinct feminine realm. Yet by the end of the century, the appeal of this form of political organization had been undermined, in part by its own success. By establishing a common ground for public involvement and domestic ideals, the parliaments helped to make the idea of political involvement by women more widely acceptable. But because the parliaments were so easily linked with the highly contentious issue of woman suffrage, women frequently faced less opposition when they pursued their goals through organizational models that were not derived directly from the existing political system.

But what would such organizational models be like? For women's associations, and for the suffrage organizations in particular, the immediate dilemma was that any instrumental advantages of hierarchical, centralized bureaucratic form counted against one of the central goals of these groups: the demonstration that women were capable of being independent citizens rather than subject to undue direction by priests, husbands, or other authorities. Consequently, it was not enough to replace hierarchical organizations headed by men with bureaucratic voluntary associations led by elite women. From the level of local parlor meetings to national conventions, attention was paid to the form – if not always the substance – of participatory organization and proper procedure. In San Francisco, the Richelieu club was "mostly composed of the presidents of other clubs. ... The club's aim is to carry on the drill of parliamentary usage with a view of having a more accurate knowledge of one's rights upon the floor and one's duty in the chair of an assembly" (*Club Life*, October 1902, p. 3). Women's papers regularly featured drills on parliamentary procedure. Although some organizations were dominated by a single national figure (such as the WCTU under Frances Willard), the GFWC regularly elected new presidents and, in almost all cases, the federated structure and complex departmental divisions of these associations provided for considerable opportunity and flexible participation within the woman movement. Although an organizational chart of any of the major women's groups would possess many traits of a classical bureaucracy, individual careers rarely involved a regular progression through a hierarchy of offices, suggesting that these groups accommodated the shifting familial and economic obligations of activists (Clemens and Ledger 1992). While embracing the internal specialization of the modern corporation, women were much more ambivalent about establishing a clear hierarchy of authority. Although studies of interest-group politics and social movements have both viewed organization in terms of its contribution to instrumental goals of policy change and legislation, the advantages of centralization and specialization may be tempered by the meanings attributed to organizational models and the differing ability of organizational forms to sustain involvement.

This brief overview of women's organizations does, however, establish the premises upon which an alternative account of political organization and institutional change must be fashioned. The first point is that the choice of organizational models is not governed solely by instrumental considerations. Cultures have rules about who should organize in what way and for what purposes; consequently, the choice of a conventional model by an unconventional group may produce neither the efficacy nor the conservative transformations suggested by Michels's analysis. Second, complex societies present many possible models of organization – multiple combinations of hierarchy, centralization, authority, and exchange – which may be simultaneously "legitimate" and incompatible. Americans of the late 19th century were familiar with both the centralized hierarchical forms of the patronage party and the modern corporation, yet the period's politics are often portrayed as a conflict between these two models of organizing public life. To the extent that a challenging group is immune to the processes of incorporation discussed above, both its potential to cause institutional change and the character of that change will reflect the range of alternative models available in its members' repertoires of organization.

Repertoires of Organization: An Alternative Approach

For much of political sociology, organizations matter as resources; they make coordinated action possible and success more likely. The role of organizations in blocking action has also been demonstrated; prior commitments and established networks can make new patterns of mobilization difficult (Connell and Voss 1990). But organization has consequences beyond the process of mobilization itself. As a group organizes in a particular way, adopts a specific model of organization, it signals its identity both to its own members and to others. Models of organization are part of the cultural tool kit of any society and serve expressive or communicative as well as instrumental functions. In addition, the adoption of a particular organizational form influences the ties that an organized group forms with other organizations. The chosen model of collective action shapes alliances with other groups and relations with political institutions. At both cultural and institutional levels, models of organization and collective activity are central mechanisms in the transformation of political systems. Once organizational form is viewed as being simultaneously a statement of identity and constitutive of broader institutional fields, social movements appear as not only vehicles of preexisting interests and causes of specific political outcomes, but as critical sources of institutional change.

In order to make sense of such change, the language of cultural analysis is helpful. If a society's cultural heritage constitutes a set of "models of" and "models for" action (Geertz 1973), an organizational repertoire, the appropriation of each of these possible models is not equally probable. Instead, certain models are privileged by the existing distributions of power, status, and wealth as well as by established institutional arrangements. At the most basic level, there are certain advantages to familiarity: "Even government officials and industrial managers of our own time generally behave as though they preferred demonstrations and strikes to utterly unconventional forms of collective action" (Tilly 1986, p. 391). Organization theorists have emphasized this process, exploring the ways in which conformity to institutional rules produces increasing homogeneity within organizational fields (DiMaggio and Powell 1983; Meyer and Rowan 1977). But if one recognizes an established *repertoire* of acceptable forms instead of a single institutional rule, processes of institutional isomorphism can also promote change within a social system.

Consider the following possibilities. A group finds itself in a situation where the established models of organization and paths of action are inadequate. This may occur for many reasons: existing models may be tactically or culturally discredited (as wire-pulling and other "methods of politics" were for Mrs. Croly); existing models may be unavailable or off-limits (as electoral politics were for most American women); or no established models of action may be associated with that situation (e.g., methods of holding legislators accountable for specific votes prior to the development of preelection pledges and legislative roll-call reporting). Confronted with analogous situations, organization and decision theorists have developed accounts of search procedures. These accounts typically establish some relation – either purposive or stochastic – between an environment that provides multiple potential "solutions" and some selection criteria or procedures (e.g., Heclo 1974; Kingdon 1984; March and Olsen 1989; Meyer and Rowan 1977). Once selected, the choice of a particular solution or organizational model then has consequences for both the environment and the system of relations among organizations. Certain choices may produce organizations that make sufficient demands on their environment to induce new organizations to form (Westney 1987). At the same time, the choice of a model may draw an organization closer to some groups while weakening other interorganizational ties. For example, teachers may choose to affiliate with an occupational group based on the model of the labor union or one modeled on the professions. This difference, in turn, sets up distinctive alliance patterns with other organizations such as the AFL-CIO or the American Medical Association (Hess 1990).

Applied to the study of political change, this account highlights the significance of the available set of organizational models and the process of selection. The repertoire of organization both reflects and helps to shape patterns of social organization. As it is mastered by any given individual or group, a repertoire is largely constituted through experience or awareness of existing forms of social organization. We know what it is to be part of a committee or a commune or a platoon because we have participated in, observed, or heard of these different forms of organization. Similarly, we know what different organizational models signify with respect to the expectations and behaviors of members as well as the collective identity presented to others. Thus, the initial use of familiar forms by unfamiliar groups will have a destabilizing effect on existing conventions of organization. For example, the clubwomen, now quaint and moderate figures, named themselves in violation of established feminine conventions. While the term "club" was rejected by some as a "masculine" label, more daring groups such as the New England Women's Club "deliberately chose *club* to indicate a break with tradition; it did not want to be associated with good-works societies" (Martin 1987, p. 63; emphasis in source; see also Ruddy 1906, p. 24). For outsiders, organizational form was a signal of these groups' novel qualities and aims. " 'What is the object?' was the first question asked of any organization of women, and if it was not the making of garments, or the collection of funds for a church, or philanthropic purpose, it was considered unworthy of attention, or injurious doubts were thrown upon its motives" (Croly 1898, p. 9).

By distancing themselves from religious associations and charitable societies, women's clubs constituted themselves as "absolutely a new thing under the sun" (Wood 1912, p. 188). And in defining itself through the appropriation of organizational models not traditionally associated with female groups, the women's club movement is a clear example of innovation grounded in the materials at hand. This process of organizational change through the rearrangement of existing repertoires characterized the woman movement as a whole.

Once one group has pioneered the use of an organizational model in a new arena, that model may then be adopted for use by other groups. Although the rationale for adoption may flow from momentary strategic advantages, widespread adoption is a source of fundamental change in the organizing categories of the political system. Returning to the specific case of political change in the United States, I argue that the shift from the electoral regime of highly competitive parties to the legislative and administrative focus of interest-group bargaining can be understood by examining the organizational experiments of groups that were comparatively disadvantaged under the first of these regimes. The subsequent shift in the available repertoire of organization – the recognized set of political options – then gave way to a system in which this form of mobilization became part of the taken-for-granted. Writing in 1907, John R. Commons, a prominent economist and social reformer, observed that "there is no movement of the past twenty years more quiet nor more potent than the organization of private interests. No other country in the world presents so interesting a spectacle" ([1907] 1967, p. 359). With respect to the conventions of political action and organization, this new system entailed a focus on legislative rather than electoral politics and a consequent organization on the basis of stakes in particular issues rather than broad political philosophies. As one commentator complained by the 1920s:

> The present unionized era of leagues, societies, alliances, clubs, combines and cliques offers confederation for mutual support of

> almost any interest conceivable except for the diversified interests of the humble in the application of general law. With united front the bankers, the brokers, the dairy men, the detectives, the sportsmen, the motorists, the innkeepers, the barbers, the mintgrowers, the Swiss bell ringers, *et al.*, may and do present their complaints to the legislature for adjustment. [Wismer 1928, p. 172]

Although manufacturers organized nonpartisan trade associations in both the United States and Europe, only in the United States did "interest" – rather than party, class, language, or religion – become the primary idiom of political life, a *legitimate* if not necessarily welcome form of political organization (see also Clemens 1990; Maier 1981; McCormick 1986; Reddy 1987; Rodgers 1987). The making of specific claims on legislatures was not in itself new, but previously took the form of petitions, private bills directed at individuals, or the considerable bribery of the Gilded Age (Thompson 1985). What was new was the exertion of issue-specific pressure through political education, public opinion, expert testimony, and the increasingly sophisticated legislative tactics of issue- or constituency-based organizations.

This new system of political organization grew out of an eclectic process of reorganization. Rather than accepting a single model for political action, groups drew on both traditional models and the most modern good government groups as well as imitating what worked for their frequent opponents, the corporations and political machines. By the 1890s, for example, temperance associations and women's groups had set up their own precinct organizations and departmental organizations to exert focused pressure on specific government institutions (Bordin 1981; Kerr 1980). In California, the Women's Christian Temperance Union "exerted an influence out of proportion to its size, because of its strong church support, its unique ability to cooperate easily with all other temperance organizations, and because, unlike the fraternal societies, it devoted its energies almost entirely to agitation and reform work. On the model of the national W.C.T.U. the state organization set up many departments, thirty in all, each concentrating on a separate phase of temperance work" (Ostrander 1957, p. 58).

Recognizing the need to create a political counterweight and a vehicle for shaping public opinion, the liquor industry responded by appropriating an organizational model then unfamiliar in business politics: "The liquor dealers formed an organization which, to outward appearances at least, was based on an idea new to California. They formed what was publicized as a liquor-men's temperance association. Following the example of many temperance organizations before them, the liquor dealers patterned themselves after Masonic design. The new organization was called the Knights of the Royal Arch, and in April, 1902, the Grand Lodge of the Knights of the Royal Arch was formed in San Francisco" (Ostrander 1957, p. 100).

Complete with exotically titled officials, and, no doubt, secret handshakes, this innovation by the liquor interests appears retrograde, a move away from the modern politics of interest based on public opinion and expertise rather than fraternal solidarity. But to conceive of institutional change as the product of novel applications of existing organizational repertoires is not to claim that all such applications will be effective. If California's liquor dealers engaged in a retrospective form of organizational borrowing, temperance advocates and especially women's groups helped to transform the meaning of corporate political models such as the lobby. In the process, a model that had been associated with corrupt practices was now transformed and legitimated as a taken-for-granted component of political action.

This account of changes in the forms of political organization generates a series of propositions quite different from those associated with the Michels-Weber model. *First*, rather than identifying a unilinear trend toward hierarchical, bureaucratic forms, this alternative account suggests that we should expect to find a lot of cultural work around the questions of What kind of group are we? and What do groups like us do? The links between organizational and cultural analysis are clear; models of organization are not only conventions for coordinating action but also statements of what it means for certain people to organize in certain ways for certain purposes (Kanter 1972). *Second*, we should expect that both the substance of these debates and the subsequent patterns of mobilization should vary by the set of organizational models that are culturally and experientially available to a given group at a particular point in time. *Third*, patterns of organization in response to novel or ambiguous situations should be shaped by a group's existing or desired ties to other groups committed to a particular model of organization. The selection of a specific organizational form should then strengthen ties between some organizations while weakening others.

[...]

References

Baker, Paula. 1991. *The Moral Frameworks of Public Life: Gender, Politics, and the State in Rural New York, 1870–1930*. New York: Oxford University Press.

Berger, Peter L., and Thomas Luckmann. 1966. *The Social Construction of Reality: A Treatise in the Sociology of Knowledge*. Garden City, N.Y.: Anchor.

Blair, Karen J. 1980. *The Clubwoman as Feminist: True Womanhood Redefined, 1868–1914*. New York: Holmes & Meier.

Bordin, Ruth. 1981. *Woman and Temperance: The Quest for Power and Liberty, 1873–1900*. Philadelphia: Temple University Press.

Clemens, Elisabeth S. 1990. "Organizing as Interests: The Transformation of Social Politics in the United States, 1890–1920." Ph.D. dissertation. University of Chicago, Department of Sociology.

Clemens, Elisabeth S., and Patrick Ledger. 1992. "Careers of Activism in the Woman Suffrage Movement." Paper presented at the meetings of the American Sociological Association, Pittsburgh.

Commons, John R. (1907) 1967. *Proportional Representation*. New York: Augustus M. Kelley.

Connell, Carol, and Kim Voss. 1990. "Formal Organization and the Fate of Social Movements: Craft Association and Class Alliance in the Knights of Labor." *American Sociological Review* 55 (2): 255–69.

Croly, Mrs. J. C. 1898. *The History of the Women's Club Movement in America*. New York: Henry G. Allen.

Deegan, Mary Jo. 1988. *Jane Addams and the Men of the Chicago School, 1892–1918*. New Brunswick, N.J.: Transaction.

DiMaggio, Paul, and Walter W. Powell. 1983. "The Iron Cage Revisited: Institutional Isomorphism and Collective Rationality in Organizational Fields." *American Sociological Review* 48 (2): 147–60.

Downs, Anthony. 1957. *An Economic Theory of Democracy*. New York: Harper & Row.

DuBois, Ellen C. 1991. "Harriot Stanton Blatch and the Transformation of Class Relations among Woman Suffragists." Pp. 162–79 in *Gender, Class, Race, and Reform in the Progressive Era*, edited by Noralee Frankel and Nancy S. Dye. Lexington: University Press of Kentucky.

Flexner, Eleanor. 1970. *Century of Struggle: The Woman's Rights Movement in the United States*. New York: Atheneum.

Frankel, Noralee, and Dye, Nancy S., eds. 1991. *Gender, Class, Race and Reform in the Progressive Era*. Lexington: University Press of Kentucky.

Friedland, Roger, and Robert R. Alford. 1991. "Bringing Society Back In: Symbols, Practices, and Institutional Contradictions." Pp. 232–63 in *The New Institutionalism in Organizational Analysis*, edited by Walter W. Powell and Paul DiMaggio. Chicago: University of Chicago Press.

Geertz, Clifford. 1973. *The Interpretation of Cultures*. New York: Basic.

Gordon, Linda, ed. 1990. *Women, the State, and Welfare*. Madison: University of Wisconsin Press.

Heclo, Hugh. 1974. *Modern Social Politics in Britain and Sweden*. New Haven, Conn.: Yale University Press.

Hess, Carla. 1990. "The Construction of Boundaries and Divisions of Labor: Teachers, Workers, and Professionals." Paper presented at the annual meetings of the American Political Science Association, San Francisco.

Jenkins, J. Craig. 1977. "Radical Transformation of Organizational Goals." *Administrative Science Quarterly* 22 (4): 568–86.

Jepperson, Ronald L. 1991. "Institutions, Institutional Effects, and Institutionalism." Pp. 143–63 in *The New Institutionalism in Organizational Analysis*, edited by Walter W. Powell and Paul DiMaggio. Chicago: University of Chicago Press.

Kanter, Rosabeth Moss. 1972. *Commitment and Community: Communes and Utopias in Sociological Perspective*. Cambridge, Mass.: Harvard University Press.

Kerr, K. Austin. 1980. "Organizing for Reform: The Anti-Saloon League and Innovation in Politics." *American Quarterly* 32 (1): 37–53.

Kingdon, John W. 1984. *Agendas, Alternatives, and Public Policies*. Boston: Little, Brown.

Kitschelt, Herbert. 1989. *The Logics of Party Formation: Ecological Politics in Belgium and West Germany*. Ithaca, N.Y.: Cornell University Press.

Lipset, Seymour Martin, Martin A. Trow, and James S. Coleman. 1956. *Union Democracy: The Internal Politics of the International Typographical Union*. Glencoe, Ill.: Free Press.

Maier, Charles S. 1981. " 'Fictitious bonds . . . of wealth and law': On the Theory and Practice of Interest Representation." Pp. 27–61 in *Organizing Interests in Western Europe: Pluralism, Corporatism, and the Transformation of Politics*, edited by Suzanne Berger. New York: Cambridge University Press.

March, James G. 1979. "The Technology of Foolishness." Pp. 69–81 in *Ambiguity and Choice in Organizations*, 2d ed. Edited by J. G. March and J. P. Olsen. Bergen: Universitetsforlaget.

March, James G., and Johan P. Olsen. 1989. *Rediscovering Institutions: The Organizational Basis of Politics*. New York: Free Press.

Martin, Theodora Penny. 1987. *The Sound of Our Own Voices: Women's Study Clubs, 1860–1910*. Boston: Beacon.

McAdam, Doug. 1982. *Political Process and the Development of Black Insurgency, 1930–1970*. Chicago: University of Chicago Press.

——. 1986. "Recruitment to High-Risk Activism: The Case of Freedom Summer." *American Journal of Sociology* 92: 64–90.

McAdam, Doug, John McCarthy, and Mayer Zald. 1988. "Social Movements." pp. 695–737 in *Handbook of Sociology*, edited by Neil Smelser. Newbury Park, Calif.: Sage.

McCormick, Richard P. 1986. *The Party Period and Public Policy: American Politics from the Age of Jackson to the Progressive Era*. New York: Oxford University Press.

McGerr, Michael. 1986. *The Decline of Popular Politics: The American North, 1865–1928*. New York: Oxford University Press.

Meyer, John W., and Bryan Rowan. 1977. "Institutionalized Organizations: Formal Structure as Myth and Ceremony." *American Journal of Sociology* 83 (2): 340–63.

Michels, Robert. (1911) 1962. *Political Parties: A Sociological Study of the Oligarchical Tendencies of Modern Democracy*. New York: Free Press.

Muncy, Robyn. 1991. *Creating a Female Dominion in American Reform, 1890–1935*. New York: Oxford University Press.

Ostrander, Gilman M. 1957. "The Prohibition Movement in California, 1848–1933." *University of California Publications in History*, vol. 57. Berkeley: University of California Press.

Powell, Walter W. 1990. "Neither Market nor Hierarchy: Network Forms of Organization." *Research in Organizational Behavior* 12: 295–336.

Reddy, William M. 1987. *Money and Liberty in Modern Europe: A Critique of Historical Understanding*. New York: Cambridge University Press.

Rodgers, Daniel. 1987. *Contested Truths: Keywords in American Politics since Independence*. New York: Basic Books.

Ruddy, Ella Giles, ed. 1906. *The Mother of Clubs, Caroline M. Seymour Severance: An Estimate and Appreciation*. Los Angeles: Baumgardt.

Scott, Anne Firor. 1991. *Natural Allies: Women's Associations in American History*. Urbana: University of Illinois Press.

Selznick, Philip. 1960. *The Organizational Weapon: A Study of Bolshevik Strategy and Tactics*. Glencoe, Ill.: Free Press.

Shefter, Michael. 1983. "Regional Receptivity to Reform: The Legacy of the Progressive Era." *Political Science Quarterly* 98 (3): 459–83.

Sklar, Kathryn Kish. 1985. "Hull House in the 1890s: A Community of Women Reformers." *Signs* 10: 658–77.

Skocpol, Theda. 1992. *Protecting Soldiers and Mothers: The Politics of Social Provision in the United States, 1870s–1920s*. Cambridge, Mass.: Harvard University Press, Belknap.

Skocpol, Theda, and Gretchen Ritter. 1991. "Gender and the Origins of Modern Social Policies in Britain and the United States." *Studies in American Political Development* 5 (1): 36–93.

Skowronek, Stephen. 1982. *Building a New American State: The Expansion of National Administrative Capacities, 1877–1920*. New York: Cambridge University Press.

Swidler, Ann. 1986. "Culture in Action: Symbols and Strategies." *American Sociological Review* 51 (2): 273–86.

Thompson, James. 1967. *Organizations in Action*. New York: McGraw-Hill.

Thompson, Margaret. 1985. *The "Spider Web": Congress and Lobbying in the Age of Grant*. Ithaca: N.Y.: Cornell University Press.

Tilly, Charles. 1978. *From Mobilization to Revolution*. Reading, Mass.: Addison-Wesley.

——. 1986. *The Contentious French*. Cambridge, Mass.: Harvard University Press, Belknap.

Tocqueville, Alexis de. (1856) 1955. *The Old Regime and the French Revolution*, translated by Stuart Gilbert. New York: Anchor.

Weber, Max. 1978. *Economy and Society*, edited by Guenther Roth and Claus Wittich. Berkeley: University of California Press.

Westney, D. Eleanor. 1987. *Imitation and Innovation: The Transfer of Western Organizational Patterns to Meiji Japan*. Cambridge, Mass.: Harvard University Press.

Wismer, Otto G. 1928. "Legal Aid Organizations: 'Lobbyists for the Poor.' " *Annals of the American Academy of Political and Social Science* 136 (March): 172–76.

Wood, Mary I. 1912. *The History of the General Federation of Women's Clubs: For the First Twenty-Two Years of Its Organization*. New York: General Federation of Women's Clubs.

Zald, Mayer N., and Roberta Ash. 1966. "Social Movement Organizations: Growth, Decay and Change." *Social Forces* 44: 327–41.

21 Transnational Environmental Activism

Paul Wapner

Interest in transnational activist groups such as Greenpeace, European Nuclear Disarmament (END), and Amnesty International has been surging. [. . .] Recent scholarship demonstrates that Amnesty International and Human Rights Watch have changed state human rights practices in particular countries. Other studies have shown that environmental groups have influenced negotiations over environmental protection of the oceans, the ozone layer, and Antarctica and that they have helped enforce national compliance with international mandates. Still others have shown that peace groups helped shape nuclear policy regarding deployments in Europe during the cold war and influenced Soviet perceptions in a way that allowed for eventual superpower accommodation. This work is important, especially insofar as it establishes the increasing influence of transnational nongovernmental organizations (NGOs) on states. Nonetheless, for all its insight, it misses a different but related dimension of activist work – the attempt by activists to shape public affairs by working within and across societies themselves.

Transnational Advocacy Network (TAN) Some activists live in different societies and yet collaborate and assist one another across borders. These activists share common beliefs and concerns (e.g., the environment, human rights, international trade and investment), and they exchange information and resources in pursuit of common goals. Transnational networks of activists and organizations sometimes arise because certain problems can only be addressed at a transnational level. In some cases, these networks arise because activists or organizations in one society reach out to those in other societies who have more resources or more political clout. See Keck and Sikkink (1998).

Recent studies neglect the societal dimension of activists' efforts in part because they subscribe to a narrow understanding of politics. They see politics as a practice associated solely with government and thus understand activist efforts exclusively in terms of their influence upon government. Seen from this perspective, transnational activists are solely global pressure groups seeking to change states' policies or create conditions in the international system that enhance or diminish interstate cooperation. Other efforts directed toward societies at large are ignored or devalued because they are not considered to be genuinely political in character.

Such a narrow view of politics in turn limits research because it suggests that the conception and meaning of transnational activist groups is fixed and that scholarship therefore need only measure activist influence on states. This article asserts, by contrast, that the meaning of activist groups in a global context is not settled and will remain problematic as long as the strictly societal dimension of their work is left out of the analysis. Activist efforts within and across societies are a proper object of study and only by including them in transnational activist research can one render an accurate understanding of transnational activist groups and, by extension, of world politics.

This article focuses on activist society-oriented activities and demonstrates that activist organizations are not simply transnational pressure groups, but rather are political actors in their own right. The main argument is that the best way to think about transnational activist societal efforts is through the concept of "world civic politics." When activists work to change conditions without directly pressuring states, their activities take place in the civil dimension of world collective life or what is sometimes called global civil society. Civil society is that arena of social engagement which exists above the individual yet below the state. It is a complex network of economic, social, and cultural practices based on friendship, family, the market, and voluntary affiliation. Although the concept arose in the analysis of domestic societies, it is beginning to make sense on a global level. The interpenetration of markets, the intermeshing of symbolic meaning systems, and the proliferation of transnational collective endeavors signal the formation of a thin, but nevertheless present, public sphere where private individuals and groups interact for common purposes. Global civil society as such is that slice of associational life which exists above the individual and below the state, but also across national boundaries. When transnational activists direct their efforts beyond the state, they are politicizing global civil society.

[...]

Amnesty International, Friends of the Earth, Oxfam, and Greenpeace target governments and try to change state behavior to further their aims. When this route fails or proves less efficacious, they work through transnational economic, social, and cultural networks to achieve their ends. The emphasis on world civic politics stresses that while these latter efforts may not translate easily into state action, they should not be viewed as simply matters of cultural or social interest. Rather, they involve identifying and manipulating instruments of power for shaping collective life. Unfortunately, the conventional wisdom has taken them to be politically irrelevant.

In the following I analyze the character of world civic politics by focusing on one relatively new sector of this activity, transnational environmental activist groups (TEAGs). As environmental dangers have become part of the public consciousness and a matter of scholarly concern in recent years, much attention has been directed toward the transboundary and global dimensions of environmental degradation. Ozone depletion, global warming, and species extinction, for instance, have consequences that cross state boundaries and in the extreme threaten to change the organic infrastructure of life on earth. Responding in part to increased knowledge about these problems, transnational activist groups have emerged whose members are dedicated to "saving the planet." World Wildlife Fund, Friends of the Earth, Greenpeace, Conservation International, and Earth Island Institute are voluntary associations organized across state boundaries that work toward environmental protection at the global level. TEAGs have grown tremendously since the 1970s, with the budgets of the largest organizations greater than the amount spent by most countries on environmental issues and equal to, if not double, the annual expenditure of the United Nations Environment Program (UNEP). Furthermore, membership in these groups has grown throughout the 1980s and 1990s to a point where millions of people are currently members of TEAGs. This article demonstrates that, while TEAGs direct much effort toward state policies, their political activity does not stop there but extends into global civil society. In the following, I describe and analyze this type of activity and, in doing so, make explicit the dynamics and significance of world civic politics.

[...]

Disseminating an Ecological Sensibility

Few images capture the environmental age as well as the sight of Greenpeace activists positioning themselves between harpoons and whales in an effort to stop the slaughter of endangered sea mammals. Since 1972, with the formal organization of Greenpeace into a transnational environmental activist group, Greenpeace has emblazoned a host of such images onto the minds of people around the world. Greenpeace activists have climbed aboard whaling ships, parachuted from the top of smokestacks, plugged up industrial discharge pipes, and floated a hot air balloon into a nuclear test site. These direct actions are media stunts, exciting images orchestrated to convey a critical perspective toward environmental issues. Numerous other organizations, including the Sea Shepherds Conservation Society, Earth-First! and Rainforest Action Network, engage in similar efforts. The dramatic aspect attracts journalists and television crews to specific actions and makes it possible for the groups themselves to distribute their own media presentations. Greenpeace, for example, has its own media facilities; within hours it can provide photographs to newspapers and circulate scripted video news spots to television stations in eighty-eight countries. The overall intent is to use international mass communications to expose anti-ecological practices and thereby inspire audiences to change their views and behavior vis-à-vis the environment.

Direct action is based on two strategies. The first is simply to bring what are often hidden instances of environmental abuse to the attention of a wide audience: harpooners kill whales on the high seas; researchers abuse Antarctica; significant species extinction takes place in the heart of the rain forest; and nuclear weapons are tested in the most deserted areas of the planet. Through television, radio, newspapers, and magazines transnational activist groups bring these hidden spots of the globe into people's everyday lives, thus enabling vast numbers of people to "bear witness" to environmental abuse. Second, TEAGs engage in dangerous and dramatic actions that underline how serious they consider certain environmental threats to be. That activists take personal risks to draw attention to environmental issues highlights their indignation and the degree of their commitment to protecting the planet. Taken together, these two strategies aim to change the way vast numbers of people see the world – by dislodging traditional understandings of environmental degradation and substituting new interpretive frames.

[...]

Raising awareness through media stunts is not primarily about changing governmental policies, although this may of course happen as state officials bear witness or are pressured by constituents to codify into law shifts in public opinion or widespread sentiment. But this is only one dimension of TEAG direct action efforts. The new age envisioned by Hunter is more than passing environmental legislation or adopting new environmental policies. Additionally, it involves convincing all actors – from governments to corporations, private organizations, and ordinary citizens – to make decisions and act in deference to environmental awareness. Smitten with such ideas, governments will, activists hope, take measures to protect the environment. When the ideas have more resonance outside government, they will shift the standards of good conduct and persuade people to act differently even though governments are not requiring them to do so. In short, TEAGs work to disseminate an ecological sensibility to shift the governing ideas that animate societies, whether institutionalized within government or not, and count on this to reverberate throughout various institutions and collectivities.

[...]

Consider the following. In 1970 one in ten Canadians said the environment was worthy of being on the national agenda; twenty years later one in three felt not only that it should be on the agenda but that it was the most pressing issue facing Canada. In 1981, 45 percent of those polled in a U.S. survey said that protecting the environment was so important that "requirements and standards cannot be too high and continuing environmental improvements must be made regardless of cost"; in 1990, 74 percent supported the statement. This general trend is supported around the world. In a recent Gallup poll majorities in twenty countries gave priority to safeguarding the environment even at the cost of slowing economic growth; additionally, 71 percent of the people in sixteen countries, including India, Mexico, South Korea, and Brazil, said they were willing to pay higher prices for products if it would help to protect the environment.

These figures suggest a significant shift in awareness and concern about the environment over the past two decades. It is also worth noting that people have translated this sentiment into changes in behavior. In the 1960s the U.S. Navy and Air Force used whales for target practice. Twenty-five years later an international effort costing $5 million was mounted to save three whales trapped in the ice in Alaska. Two decades ago corporations produced products with little regard for their environmental impact. Today it is incumbent upon corporations to reduce negative environmental impact at the production, packaging, and distribution phases of industry. When multilateral development banks and other aid institutions were established after the Second World War, environmental impact assessments were unheard of; today they are commonplace. Finally, twenty years ago recycling as a concept barely existed. Today recycling is mandatory in many municipalities around the world, and in some areas voluntary recycling is a profit-making industry. (Between 1960 and 1990 the amount of municipal solid waste recovered by recycling in the United States more than quintupled.) In each of these instances people are voluntarily modifying their behavior in part because of the messages publicized by activists. If one looked solely at state behavior to account for this change, one would miss a tremendous amount of significant world political action.

A final, if controversial, example of the dissemination of an ecological sensibility is the now greatly reduced practice of killing harp seal pups in northern Canada. Throughout the 1960s the annual Canadian seal hunt took place without attracting much public attention or concern. In the late 1960s and throughout the 1970s and 1980s the International Fund for Animals, Greenpeace, the Sea Shepherds Conservation Society, and a host of smaller preservation groups saw this – in hindsight inaccurately, according to many – as a threat to the continued existence of harp seals in Canada. They brought the practice to the attention of the world, using, among other means, direct action. As a result, people around the globe, but especially in Europe, changed their buying habits and stopped purchasing products made out of the pelts. As a consequence, the market for such merchandise all but dried up with the price per skin plummeting. Then, in 1983, the European Economic Community (EEC) actually banned the importation of seal pelts. It is significant that the EEC did so only after consumer demand had already dropped dramatically. Governmental policy, that is, may have simply been an afterthought and ultimately unnecessary. People acted in response to the messages propagated by activist groups.

When Greenpeace and other TEAGs undertake direct action or follow other strategies to promote an ecological sensibility, these are the types of changes they are seeking. At times, governments respond with policy measures and changed behavior with respect to environmental issues. The failure of governments to respond, however, does not necessarily mean that the efforts of activists have been in vain. Rather, they influence understandings of good conduct throughout societies at large. They help set the boundaries of what is considered acceptable behavior.

When people change their buying habits, voluntarily recycle garbage, boycott certain products, and work to preserve species, it is not necessarily because governments are breathing down their necks. Rather, they are acting out of a belief that the environmental problems involved are severe, and they wish to contribute to alleviating them. They are being "stung," as it were, by an ecological sensibility. This sting is a type of governance. It represents a mechanism of authority that can shape widespread human behavior.

Multinational Corporate Politics

In 1991 the multinational McDonald's Corporation decided to stop producing its traditional clamshell hamburger box and switch to paper packaging in an attempt to cut back on the use of disposable foam and plastic. In 1990 Uniroyal Chemical Company, the sole manufacturer of the apple-ripening agent Alar, ceased to produce and market the chemical both in the United States and abroad. Alar, the trade name for daminozide, was used on most kinds of red apples and, according to some, found to cause cancer in laboratory animals. Finally, in 1990 Starkist and Chicken of the Sea, the two largest tuna companies, announced that they would cease purchasing tuna caught by setting nets on dolphins or by any use of drift nets; a year later Bumble Bee Tuna followed suit. Such action has contributed to protecting dolphin populations around the world.

In each of these instances environmental activist groups – both domestic and transnational – played an important role in convincing corporations to alter their practices. To be sure, each case raises controversial issues concerning the ecological wisdom of activist pressures, but it also nevertheless demonstrates the effects of TEAG efforts. In the case of McDonald's, the corporation decided to abandon its foam and plastic containers in response to prodding by a host of environmental groups. These organizations, which included the Citizens Clearinghouse for Hazardous Waste, Earth Action Network, and Kids against Pollution, organized a "send-back" campaign in which people mailed McDonald's packaging to the national headquarters. Additionally, Earth Action Network actually broke windows and scattered supplies at a McDonald's restaurant in San Francisco to protest the company's environmental policies. The Environmental Defense Fund (EDF) played a mediating role by organizing a six-month, joint task force to study ways to reduce solid waste in McDonald's eleven thousand restaurants worldwide. The task force provided McDonald's with feasible responses to activist demands. What is clear from most reports on the change is that officials at McDonalds did not believe it necessarily made ecological or economic sense to stop using clamshell packaging but that they bent to activist pressure.

Uniroyal Chemical Company ceased producing Alar after groups such as Ralph Nader's Public Interest Research Group (PIRG) and the Natural Resources Defense Council (NRDC) organized a massive public outcry about the use of the product on apples in the U.S. and abroad. In 1989 NRDC produced a study that found that Alar created cancer risks 240 times greater than those declared safe by the U.S. Environmental Protection Agency (EPA). This was publicized on CBS's *60 Minutes* and led to critical stories in numerous newspapers and magazines. Moreover, activists pressured supermarket chains to stop selling apples grown with Alar and pressured schools to stop serving Alar-sprayed apples. The effects were dramatic. The demand for apples in general shrank significantly because of the scare, lowering prices well below the break-even level. This led to a loss of $135 million for Washington State apple growers alone. Effects such as these and continued pressure by activist groups convinced Uniroyal to cease production of the substance not only in the U.S. but overseas as well. Like McDonalds, Uniroyal changed its practices not for economic reasons nor to increase business nor because it genuinely felt Alar was harmful. Rather, it capitulated to activist pressure. In fact, there is evidence from nonindustry sources suggesting that Alar did not pose the level of threat publicized by activists.

Finally, in the case of dolphin-free tuna, Earth Island Institute (EII) and other organizations launched an international campaign in 1985 to stop all drift-net and purse seine fishing by tuna fleets. For unknown reasons, tuna in the Eastern Tropical Pacific Ocean swim under schools of dolphins. For years tuna fleets have set their nets on dolphins or entangled dolphins in drift nets as a way to catch tuna. While some fleets still use these strategies, the three largest tuna companies have ceased doing so. TEAGs were at the heart of this change. Activists waged a boycott against all canned tuna, demonstrated at stockholders' meetings, and rallied on the docks of the Tuna Boat Association in San Diego. Furthermore, EII assisted in the production of the film *Where Have All the Dolphins Gone?* which was shown throughout the United States and abroad; it promoted the idea of "dolphin-safe" tuna labels to market environmentally sensitive brands; and it enlisted Heinz, the parent company of Starkist, to take an active role in stopping the slaughter of dolphins by all tuna companies. Its efforts, along with those of Greenpeace, Friends of the Earth, and others, were crucial to promoting dolphin-safe tuna fishing. One result of these efforts is that dolphin kills associated with tuna fishing in 1993 numbered fewer than 5,000. This represents one-third the mortality rate of 1992, when 15,470 dolphins died in nets, and less than one-twentieth of the number in 1989, when over 100,000 dolphins died at the hands of tuna fleets. These numbers represent the effects of activist efforts. Although governments did eventually adopt domestic dolphin conservation policies and negotiated partial international standards to reduce dolphin kills, the first such actions came into force only in late 1992 with the United Nations moratorium on drift nets. Moreover, the first significant actions against purse seine fishing, which more directly affects dolphins, came in June 1994 with the United States International Dolphin Conservation Act. As with the Canadian seal pup hunt, government action in the case of tuna fisheries largely codified changes that were already taking place.

In each instance, activist groups did not direct their efforts at governments. They did not target politicians; nor did they organize constituent pressuring. Rather, they focused on corporations themselves. Through protest, research, exposés, orchestrating public outcry, and organizing joint consultations, activists won corporate promises to bring their practices in line with environmental concerns. The levers of power in these instances were found in the economic realm of collective life rather than in the strictly governmental realm. Activists understand that the economic realm, while not the center of traditional notions of politics, nevertheless furnishes channels for effecting widespread changes in behavior; they recognize that the economic realm is a form of governance and can be manipulated to alter collective practices.

Perhaps the best example of how activist groups, especially transnational ones, enlist the economic dimensions of governance into their enterprises is the effort to establish environmental oversight of corporations. In September 1989 a coalition of environmental, investor, and church interests, known as the Coalition for Environmentally Responsible Economies (CERES), met in New York City to introduce a ten-point environmental code of conduct for corporations. One month later CERES, along with the Green Alliance, launched a similar effort in the United Kingdom. The aim was to establish criteria for auditing the environmental performance of large domestic and multinational industries. The code called on companies to, among other things, minimize the release of pollutants, conserve nonrenewable resources through efficient use and planning, utilize environmentally safe and sustainable energy sources, and consider demonstrated environmental commitment as a factor in appointing members to the board of directors. Fourteen environmental organizations, including TEAGs such as Friends of the Earth and the International Alliance for Sustainable Agriculture, publicize the CERES Principles (formerly known as the Valdez Principles, inspired by the Exxon *Valdez* oil spill) and enlist corporations to pledge compliance. What is significant from an international perspective is that signatories include at least one Fortune 500 company and a number of multinational corporations. Sun Company, General Motors, Polaroid, and a host of other MNCs have pledged compliance or are at least seriously considering doing so. Because these companies operate in numerous countries, their actions have transnational effects.

The CERES Principles are valuable for a number of reasons. In the case of pension funds, the code is being used to build shareholder pressure on companies to improve their environmental performance. Investors can use it as a guide to determine which companies practice socially responsible investment. Environmentalists use the code as a measuring device to praise or criticize corporate behavior. Finally, the Principles are used to alert college graduates on the job market about corporate compliance with the code and thus attempt to make environmental issues a factor in one's choice of a career. Taken together, these measures force some degree of corporate accountability by establishing mechanisms of governance to shape corporate behavior. To be sure, they have not turned businesses into champions of environmentalism, nor are they as effectual as mechanisms available to governments. At work, however, is activist discovery and manipulation of economic means of power.

Via the CERES Principles and other forms of pressure, activists thus influence corporate behavior. McDonald's, Uniroyal, and others have not been changing their behavior because governments are breathing down their necks. Rather, they are voluntarily adopting different ways of producing and distributing products. This is not to say that their actions are more environmentally sound than before they responded to activists or that their attempt to minimize environmental dangers is sincerely motivated. As mentioned, environmental activist groups do not have a monopoly on ecological wisdom, nor is corporate "greening" necessarily well intentioned. Nonetheless, the multinational corporate politics of transnational groups are having an effect on the way industries do business. And to the degree that these enterprises are involved in issues of widespread public concern that cross state boundaries, activist pressure must be understood as a form of world politics.

Empowering Local Communities

For decades TEAGs have worked to conserve wildlife in the developing world. Typically, this has involved people in the First World working in the Third World to restore and guard the environment. First World TEAGs – ones headquartered in the North – believed that Third World people could not appreciate the value of wildlife or were simply too strapped by economic pressures to conserve nature. Consequently, environmental organizations developed, financed, and operated programs in the field with little local participation or input.

While such efforts saved a number of species from extinction and set in motion greater concern for Third World environmental protection, on the whole they were unsuccessful at actually preserving species and their habitats from degradation and destruction. A key reason for this was that they attended more to the needs of plants and especially animals than to those of the nearby human communities. Many of the earth's most diverse and biologically rich areas are found in parts of the world where the poorest peoples draw their livelihood from the land. As demographic and economic constraints grow tighter, these people exploit otherwise renewable resources in an attempt merely to survive. Ecological sustainability in these regions, then, must involve improving the quality of life of the rural poor through projects that integrate the management of natural resources with grassroots economic development.

Often after having supported numerous failed projects, a number of TEAGs have come to subscribe to this understanding and undertake appropriate actions. World Wildlife Fund (WWF) or World Wide Fund for Nature, as it is known outside English-speaking countries, is an example of such an organization. WWF is a conservation group dedicated to protecting endangered wildlife and wildlands worldwide. It originated in 1961 as a small organization in Switzerland, making grants to finance conservation efforts in various countries. Over the past thirty years it has grown into a full-scale global environmental organization with offices in over twenty countries. Within the past decade, WWF has established a wildlands and human needs program, a method of conservation to be applied to all WWF projects linking human economic well-being with environmental protection. It structures a game management system in Zambia, for example, which involves local residents in antipoaching and conservation efforts, and the channeling of revenues from tourism and safaris back into the neighboring communities that surround the preserves. It informs a WWF-initiated Kilum Mountain project in the Cameroon that is developing nurseries for reforestation, reintroducing indigenous crops, and disseminating information about the long-term effects of environmentally harmful practices. Finally, it is operative in a project in St. Lucia, where WWF has lent technical assistance to set up sanitary communal waste disposal sites, improved marketing of fish to reduce overfishing, and protected mangroves from being used for fuel by planting fast-growing fuel-wood trees. WWF is not alone in these efforts. The New Forests Project, the Association for Research and Environmental Aid (AREA), the Ladakh Project, and others undertake similar actions.

In these kinds of efforts, TEAGs are not trying to galvanize public pressure aimed at changing governmental policy or directly lobbying state officials; indeed, their activity takes place far from the halls of congresses, parliaments, and executive offices. Rather, TEAGs work with ordinary people in diverse regions of the world to try to enhance local capability to carry out sustainable development projects. The guiding logic is that local people must be enlisted in protecting their own environments and that their efforts will then reverberate through wider circles of social interaction to affect broader aspects of world environmental affairs.

[...]

World Civic Politics

The predominant way to think about NGOs in world affairs is as transnational interest groups. They are politically relevant insofar as they affect state policies and interstate behavior. In this article I have argued that TEAGs, a particular type of NGO, have political relevance beyond this. They work to shape the way vast numbers of people throughout the world act toward the environment using modes of governance that are part of global civil society. [...]

I suggested that the best way to think about these activities is through the category of "world civic politics." When TEAGs work through transnational networks associated with cultural, social, and economic life, they are enlisting forms of governance that are civil as opposed to official or state constituted in character. Civil, in this regard, refers to the quality of interaction that takes place above the individual and below the state yet across national boundaries. The concept of world civic politics clarifies how the forms of governance in global civil society are distinct from the instrumentalities of state rule.

At the most foundational level, states govern through legal means that are supported by the threat or use of force. To be sure, all states enjoy a minimum of loyalty from their citizens and administrate through a variety of nonlegal and noncoercive means. Ultimately, however, the authority to govern per se rests on the claim to a monopoly over legitimate coercive power. By contrast, civic power has no legally sanctioned status and cannot be enforced through the legitimate use of violence. It rests on persuasion and more constitutive employment of power in which people change their practices because they have come to understand the world in a way that promotes certain actions over others or because they operate in an environment that induces them to do so. Put differently, civic power is the forging of voluntary and customary practices into mechanisms that govern public affairs. When TEAGs disseminate an ecological sensibility, pressure corporations, or empower local communities, they are exercising civic power across national boundaries.

[...]

Biography – Lois Gibbs, Housewife Warrior

Compared to many social movements, the American environmental movement has created few nationally prominent leaders. Much of the movement's work is not flamboyant enough to attract media attention, but many groups have consciously tried to avoid the kind of celebrity leaders who rose to fame in the 1960s, like Abbie Hoffman. What is more, most environmental groups since the 1980s have been local, not national, efforts. Lois Gibbs is an exception, thanks to the intense media attention that came her way. She lived in a housing development called Love Canal.

Love Canal was a neighborhood in the town of Niagara Falls, in upstate New York. The land had been owned by the Hooker Chemical Company from 1946 until 1953, when it sold it to the Niagara Falls Board of Education for one dollar. The condition was that the company not be held liable for the chemical wastes (22,000 tons) it had buried there. The city built an elementary school on the site, then sold the remainder to real estate developers.

In the mid-1970s, Lois Gibbs' attention was focused on raising a family. She had a normal suburban existence, amidst tree-lined streets and weekend do-it-yourselfers. She and her husband, a chemical worker, had high-school degrees. When she was 26, they had bought their own modest three-bedroom house. They had two children, and Lois stopped working when they were born. Neither she nor her husband were interested in politics or active in any community organizations. Lois thought of herself as painfully shy, incapable of public speaking.

Gibbs began to see articles about Love Canal's health hazards in the *Niagara Falls Gazette*; at first she didn't realize it was her neighborhood. When she did, she grew alarmed, as her son Michael had just completed kindergarten in the school built right on top of the old canal. Could this, she wondered, explain the seizures he had begun having right after he started school, or the sudden drop in his white blood count during the winter? She turned to her brother-in-law, a biologist at the Buffalo campus of the State University of New York, who confirmed what the articles said: many of the chemicals buried in Love Canal are known to damage the central nervous system. They decided Michael should no longer go to the 99th Street School.

Concern for her own children quickly developed into a moral shock. The superintendent of schools for the district refused to allow Michael to attend a different elementary school, despite two doctor's letters pointing to his special sensitivities. The president of the PTA seemed uninterested as well. Shy Lois Gibbs began carrying a petition door to door, beginning with her own friends and acquaintances. She was surprised to hear about so many mysterious illnesses, crib deaths, and other cases of children suffering. When the New York Department of Health held a meeting in June 1978, she heard more: a pet dog had burned its nose just sniffing the ground, a toddler could not walk in her own backyard without burning her feet, basements with chemicals oozing through the walls. By now, she had the courage to ask questions, although she did not get serious answers.

Lois Gibbs was soon testifying before government hearings, addressing rallies of local residents, and leading a surging movement angry with the government for not doing enough to help. The Love Canal Homeowners Association, which she helped found, was a major reason that government eventually did respond, paying to relocate those residents who wished to move. It was their frequent, and frustrating, interactions with government bureaucrats which helped the Love Canal residents coalesce as a group, with considerable collective spirit and identity.

The New York State Health Department declared a health emergency, recommending that pregnant women and children under two leave the area closest to the old dump site. Eventually President Jimmy Carter declared it a federal disaster area. The state and federal government would spend nearly $300 million over the next twelve years studying and cleaning up the land, before declaring it safe again in 1990. Many homes in the most affected areas were purchased by the government. Love Canal helped inspire Congress to pass the Superfund cleanup program for toxic waste in 1980.

The battle also propelled Gibbs into an activist career. She left Love Canal, and her husband, moving to the Washington, D.C. area to establish the Citizens' Clearinghouse for Hazardous Waste. Its purpose was to provide information and advice to other local groups facing toxic waste and other hazards, just as the Love Canal neighbors had. Within a few years, there were thousands of groups associated with Gibbs' new organization, forming one of the most vital wings of the environmental movement in the 1980s.

22 The Transnational Network for Democratic Globalization

Jackie Smith

The network concept integrates the understanding that a wide variety of actors participate in social movements at various times and places. Analysts have used the concept of mobilizing structures to refer to the many different formal and informal entities that tend to be involved in a wide variety of different movements. A key idea here is that, as modern societies become increasingly bureaucratic, or formally and professionally organized, they generate many different spaces that have the potential to be appropriated for social change efforts. [. . .]

At the same time, most broad-based and long-term movements contain a number of formal organizations whose primary goal is to advance movement-specific aims. But movements are not only made up of formal organizations, and some would argue that they are becoming increasingly decentralized and informal in their structure, as individuals and loosely defined networks become more common. McCarthy (1996) uses the concept of mobilizing structures to describe the variation in who participates in typical social movements. Table 22.1 draws from this work to describe the mobilizing structures that characterize transnational social movement networks.

The top, left-hand cell of table 22.1 displays some of the *informal, non-movement structures* through which transnational movements can mobilize influence. National mobilizing structures are likely to include friendship and professional networks, or informal collections of individuals and/or organizations that because of social or work routines have either incidental or deliberate contact on a regular basis. However, their transnational importance has expanded with the greater ease of travel and communication. In addition, officials in international agencies and delegates on national missions to international governmental organizations can be important channels of transnational mobilization. There are also distinctly transnational networks of people likely to be responsive to movement goals, such as refugees, immigrant workers, or international students, who might bring pressure on their state of occupancy (or of their birth) to modify policies vis-à-vis their home (or host) states.

The *formal, non-movement* cell lists societal organizations that often support nascent movements or join broader social change campaigns. Some of these groups—including some labor unions and many service-providing organizations—may have grown out of earlier social movements. In transnational settings, this category may include large organizations working on development projects, resettling refugees, and undertaking other humanitarian initiatives. In some countries, unions are more likely to be considered movement than non-movement actors, given their more confrontational approach to governments and capitalists.

[. . .]

The *informal movement* dimension of mobilizing structures may be the most dynamic and important one for contemporary global change. This category consists of networks of activists or like-minded individuals. Sometimes these networks take the form of affinity groups, which are informal structures characterized by clearly defined norms and shared expectations that emerged from early anarchist and direct action protests in the West. These were also important

Table 22.1 Transnational Mobilizing Structures

	Non-movement	*Movement*
Informal	Friendship networks Professional networks Expatriate networks Individuals in intergovernmental bureaucracies or national delegations	Activist networks Affinity groups Refugee/exile networks
Formal	Churches Unions* Professional associations Regional cooperative associations Service organizations Intergovernmental and state bureaucracies National delegations Foundations	TSMOs Unions* SMOs (national and local) Protest committees (of other NGOs) Transnational NGO coalitions Movement research institutes

Sources: Adapted from McCarthy (1996: 145); Smith et al. (1997: 62).
*In some national contexts, unions may be more appropriately considered movement structures because their key operations challenge fundamental power structures. But in most Western societies their principal strategies and formal organizational missions do not include broad social change goals, and in other countries they are controlled by governments. Thus they are included in the non-movement column.

in the protests of the late 1990s and early twenty-first century against global financial institutions. These more informal networks might be even more important for transnational movements than they are for national ones. [...] Perhaps because social movements are most clearly engaged in "information politics" and communication-based political work, scholars have emphasized the importance of informal and fluid networks of actors to global social change processes.

Finally, the *formal movement* actors in transnational movements include transnational social movement organizations as well as increasing numbers of national and locally organized social movement organizations. They can also include protest committees of other formal organizations such as professional associations or unions. Increasingly, movement activity generates formal transnational organizations that help coordinate action on particular issues or campaigns over time. And because modern politics involves extensive amounts of information and deliberation of a variety of scientific evidence and political viewpoints, think tanks and research institutes established to promote the aims of particular social movements are increasingly common and important.

Movement networks will vary over time in terms of which actors they integrate and how extensively different types of actors are involved in network activity. But an analysis of the mobilizing structures available in a given context helps us identify the possibilities for broadening support for the more particular goals of global justice activists as well as for the more encompassing aim of enhancing global democracy in a given social setting. Also, it can help us assess the organizational, political, cultural, and technical capacities of the network.

Organizations and Episodes

Mobilizing structures help link people, ideas, and resources, but the essence of social movements is collective action in public spaces. Such actions might be called "episodes of contention," or instances where opponents mobilize public, collective challenges to authorities (McAdam et al. 2001: 85). Often these episodes involve mass demonstrations, civil disobedience, and even violence against property or (far less frequently) persons. Typical protest episodes today are shaped in important ways by social movement organizations, which devote extensive efforts to spreading particular understandings of problems and encouraging public support for social change ideas.

Social movement organizations facilitate demonstrations by specifying and publicizing the date and location of action, arranging with public authorities for permission to use public spaces, providing marshals and other facilities to accommodate protesters, and building alliances with social networks outside the movement in order to generate large numbers of demonstrators. [...]

Contemporary transnational activism tends to involve a more diverse array of actors and a more complex and multilayered analysis of political issues than most local or national protests. Thus, we would expect that episodes of transnational contention would involve a different constellation of mobilizing structures than we are likely to see in more localized contexts. Table 22.2 illustrates some of the key organizations mobilizing around the 1999 World Trade Organization protests in Seattle. It examines how different mobilizing structures contributed to that particular protest episode.

Table 22.2 illustrates the varying roles different movement actors played in one of the more prominent confrontations in the contemporary movement for global economic justice. A key idea this map reveals is that the groups with the least formal and routine transnational ties were more likely to be engaged in the important work of grassroots-level education and mobilization. [...]

In contrast, groups with more routine transnational ties and formal transnational structures were better able to monitor developments in international policy and to help people make connections between locally experienced grievances and global processes. Starhawk, a U.S.-based feminist/ecology/peace activist, defended the importance of this division of labor in her response to a "Manifest of Anti-capitalist Youth against the World Social Forum":

> I do think the NGOs serve a useful and necessary purpose—they're like a different part of an ecosystem, that simply does a different job. But they wouldn't have much impact without people in the streets. We know that—they do too even if they don't always admit it publicly. They also have resources and information that can help our work, as long as we don't let them dictate our politics or our strategies.
>
> (Starhawk 2001)

[...]

The key point of this discussion of mobilizing structures is to demonstrate the range of different social actors that can become involved in social movement activities and to identify some of the actors that can be important to global movements or to global civic engagement more broadly. The strength of any movement will depend largely upon the extensiveness and range of different mobilizing structures it includes. Strong movements are those that can reach people in the *spaces of their everyday lives*, namely in the more informal and non-movement spaces where people socialize, recreate, worship, and nurture their families and communities.

The strongest democracies are ones where political spaces articulate with those of people's everyday routines. Where government policies and employers' practices help enable people to learn about and remain attentive to political issues and to participate in politics, we can expect to find strong democracies. Providing effective political education in public schools, promoting the emergence of spaces for public discourse about politics (such as labor unions or more participatory political parties), and scheduling elections at times and places that do not conflict with voters' life and work routines are examples of pro-democracy policies. [...]

Many governments and economic elites do not have much direct interest in seeing broader public participation in the political

Table 22.2 Mobilizing Structures and Divisions of Labor in the "Battle of Seattle"

Intensity of Transnational Tie	*Movement of Mobilizing Structures**	*Major Roles*
No formal transnational ties	Local chapters of national SMOs (e.g., NOW) Neighborhood committees United for a Fair Economy	Public education Mobilizing participation in protest Localizing global frames
Diffuse transnational ties	Direct Action Network Reclaim the Streets Ruckus Society Coalition for Campus Organizing	Public education Mobilizing participation in protest Localizing global frames Tactical innovations and diffusion
Routine transnational ties	Public Citizen Global Exchange Rainforest Action Network United Students Against Sweatshops Council of Canadians Sierra Club	Public education Facilitating local mobilization by others Tactical innovations and diffusion Articulating and disseminating global strategic frames Research/publication of organizing materials Facilitating transnational exchanges Monitoring international institutions Public education
Formal transnational ties	Greenpeace Friends of the Earth International Forum on Globalization Third World Network Peoples' Global Action 50 Years Is Enough Network Women's Environment and Development Organization	Facilitating local mobilization by others Articulating and disseminating global strategic frames Research/publication of organizing materials Monitoring of international institutions Coordinating transnational cooperation Cultivating and maintaining global constituency Global symbolic actions

Source: From Smith (2005).

Note: The list of structures and divisions of labor in this table is illustrative, not comprehensive.

*Organizations vary a great deal in their levels of formalization and hierarchy. For instance, Friends of the Earth and Greenpeace have well-defined organizational structures and institutional presences while groups like Peoples' Global Action resist forming an organizational headquarters, and Reclaim the Streets seeks to sustain a loose, network-like structure relying heavily on electronic communications.

life of society. In fact, they may see their interests as directly threatened by a more participatory system of governance. Thus, those actors with the most power tend to see their interests as preserving the status quo rather than the democratic ideals of contemporary political institutions. Herein lies the challenge for social movements and their pro-democracy alliance networks. Efforts to bring political education, discussion, and action into the places where people engage in their everyday routines of reproducing social life will expand the possibilities for people with fewer resources and less leisure time to be active participants in politics. Without such connections, only those individuals with the most resources, free time, and skills can enjoy full rights of participation in political life. [...]

Transnational Connections

Episodes of contention, such as the UN global conferences or the "battle of Seattle," have been important for generating new relationships and action by the transnational democratic globalization network. These episodes can also trigger the spread of new collective identities and relational forms. They help introduce activists from different countries who would otherwise never meet, and they challenge activists to conceptualize their concerns in broader terms. They also create spaces that encourage the formation of new interpersonal and interorganizational relationships that can generate new transnational alliances. [...]

As should be clear in this discussion, transnational connections among activists take a range of different forms, networks, campaigns, and organizations that reflect varying degrees of coordination and shared ways of thinking. Communication may be more or less frequent and more or less defined by explicit rules and procedures. Table 22.3 reproduces Jonathan Fox's useful scheme for analyzing variation in the density and content of transnational ties.

Table 22.3 introduces three interconnected forms of transnational association: networks, coalitions, and formal transnational organizations. At one end of the spectrum are networks, which involve the lowest density, fewest connections, and least commitment to transnational alliances. Networks themselves vary considerably in the extent to which they reflect a coherent and unified collection of actors. [...]

Compared to networks, coalitions involve more routine communications, more clearly defined expectations and efforts at mutual support, and more explicit commitment to specific campaigns, such as the abolition of third world debt (as is the case of the coalition called Jubilee 2000). However, many of these tend to be defined around short-term goals, with few long-term commitments to *sustained* transnational cooperation. To minimize the need to engage in difficult discussions about collective decision making or otherwise to devote time to coordinate action and thinking, many coalitions tend to adopt very specific and limited objectives. They agree to promote only those specific aims as a collective, and they have varying levels of organization that can integrate coalition participants into decision making. The limited scope of coalitions makes it less necessary that the group have formal mechanisms for participation by members and for the resolution of conflicting interests within the coalition.

The most intense and integrated forms of transnational cooperation are formal transnational organizations, which reflect more frequent communication and cooperation across different political campaigns and a commitment to shared ideologies and cultures. A key difference here is that relations in transnational organizations are more explicitly or formally defined, meaning that structures for regular communication and cooperation are clearly established and actors can operate around shared sets of expectations and commitments. There are explicit guidelines for resolving disputes within the organization and most groups have mechanisms to incorporate input and participation from members. This helps generate trust among participants and helps sustain long-term transnational relationships that are needed to support multifaceted political actions that go beyond single-issue campaigns. Because behaviors are routinized within the organization, there is space for the emergence of a shared organizational culture marked by common political understandings, collective identities, and styles of communicating and engaging in political action.

As is true of most typologies, table 22.3 may overstate the differences between networks, coalitions, and organizations. But

Table 22.3 Transnational Networks, Coalitions, and Movements

Shared Characteristics	*Transnational Networks*	*Transnational Coalitions*	*Transnational Movement Organizations*
Exchange of information and experiences	Yes	Yes	Yes
Organized social base	Sometimes more, sometimes less or none	Sometimes more, sometimes less or none	Yes
Mutual support	Sometimes, from afar and possibly strictly discursive	Yes	Yes
Joint actions and campaigns	Sometimes loose coordination	Yes, based on mutually agreed minimum goals, often short-term tactical	Yes, based on shared long-term strategy
Shared ideologies	Not necessarily	Not necessarily	Generally yes
Shared political cultures	Often not	Often not	Shared political values, styles and identities

Source: Fox (2002: 352).

the essence of these conceptual distinctions is that the extent to which transnational relations are routinized or defined as part of the regular practices of activists will affect the character of transnational alliances and their possibilities for generating collective action over the long term. Enduring and dense transnational alliances depend upon the cultivation of shared understandings of political realities and of mutual trust and respect. Not all transnational efforts seek or demand that quality of tie. For instance, some coalitions may simply come together to promote a particular aim, after which they find it most advantageous to return to their other priorities. In the short run, they may or may not generate more formalized transnational ties. However, they do generate interpersonal and inter-organizational connections that can, over the long term, stimulate future transnational networking, campaigning, or organizing efforts.

[...]

There is an uneasy relationship between social movements and formal organizations that surfaces frequently in social science analyses and in discussions among activists themselves. Key features of social movements are their fluidity, adaptability, and decentralization, while formal organizations require structure, stability, predictability, and some degree of centralization. Thus, activists face a constant tension between the need for more formalized and predictable decision-making processes and structures and the demand for flexibility and openness to participatory politics. More informal structures can also make movements more resistant to efforts by their adversaries to repress them. Although these conflicting demands for some level of formal organization and for flexibility are not unique to transnational movements, they seem especially daunting in struggles that bring together activists of widely varying cultural, political, and economic backgrounds to confront a complex and uncertain global political environment. An important response to this tension in the democratic globalization network is to encourage hybrid, network-like organizational structures that seek (with varying degrees of success) to allow coordination while maintaining decentralized and participatory relations within the organization (Chesters 2004).

Formal organizations provide predictability and stability needed for long-term campaigns, and they help secure steady flows of resources, ideas, and skills for movements.

They also provide opportunities for organizers to make a living by doing the work of the movement, thereby supporting and cultivating personnel who help with mobilizing and supporting popular participation in movements as well as with the more detail-oriented tasks of monitoring political developments and "translating" international legal documents for the activist community. They also have been at the heart of heated debates among activists, some of whom decry the influence of nongovernmental organizations (NGOs)—a catch-all term used in the UN to include all civil society groups, including those created by business interests as well as the vast majority of organizations doing work outside the realm of political advocacy—in transnational movements. Some critics see these groups as preferring reformist to more transformative goals, reflecting the interests of more privileged activists, as largely based in the global North, and as placing the needs of organizational maintenance over the promotion of the movement's aims.

In the following section I summarize the broad outlines of what we might call the "organizational fraction" of the democratic globalization network, or the population of more-or-less formally organized transnational social movement organizations (TSMOs). While some may see a fundamental incompatibility between organization and movement, most people with experience in activism recognize that movements need to adopt some structure to allow for predictable and regular communication and joint decision making. They must do so even as they resist organizational forms that promote hierarchy and reduce flexibility and spontaneity. Movements are made up of networks of formal organizations, individuals, and many informal associations and alliances that interact in a variety of ways. As table 22.2 shows, formal transnational organizations play a particular role in a global division of labor within the network. Understanding this subset of network actors can help us better understand the makeup and capacities of the broader collection of actors.

The Transnational Social Movement Sector

Using data from the *Yearbook of International Organizations*, I have mapped the population of TMSOs working to promote social change. This will help us assess how social movement actors have responded to broad global political and economic changes and to assess some of the strengths and weaknesses of transnational movements. While these organizations often rely on the popular mobilizing potential of both formal and informal associations working at local and national levels, they help activists relate global forces to local conditions, and they help broker connections between local actors and transnational settings.

The predominant trend in this analysis is that we see rapid and dramatic growth in the population of TSMOs. Figure 22.1 charts this growth, from just around a hundred groups in the early 1950s to over a thousand by 2003. The most rapid growth occurred during the decade of the 1980s, probably in response to new openings created by the ending of the Cold War and the renewed hopes for multilateral problem solving this generated, hopes that helped launch a series of global conferences on issues ranging from the environment to development to human rights. Figure 22.1 shows that the last few decades of the twentieth century were marked by the expansion of an organizational infrastructure for transnational social change activism. This growth appears to mirror that of other forms of transnational association, and may both support and respond to expansions in the numbers and intensity of intergovernmental organizations.

What issues have generated this kind of transnational organizational response? Certainly we would not expect people to organize transnationally around all possible issues, but we do anticipate that they would organize around problems that require international responses for their solution. The top issues attracting the attention

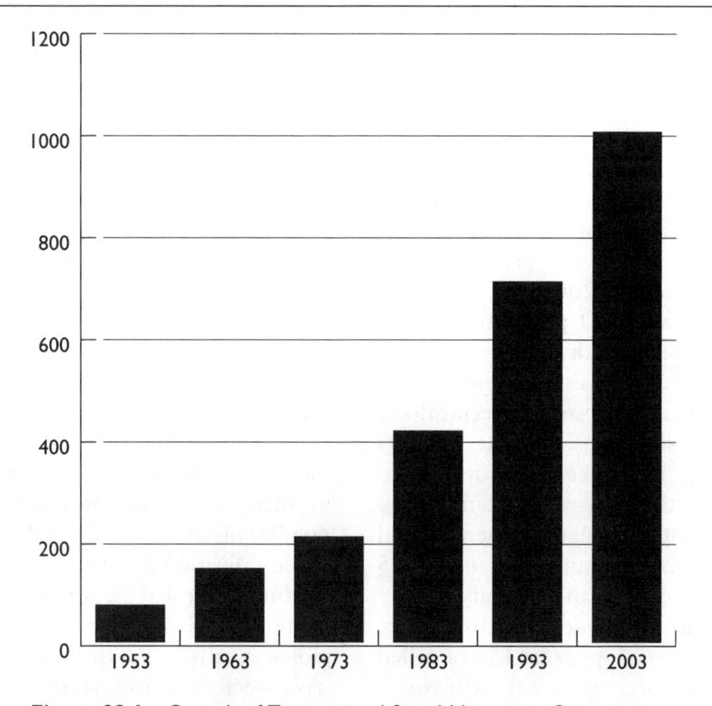

Figure 22.1 Growth of Transnational Social Movement Organizations
Source: Yearbook of International Organizations.

Table 22.4 Issue Focus of TSMOs, 1963, 1983, 2003: Percent of all Groups with Primary Focus on Issue

	1963 Total No. TSMOs = 179	*1983 Total No. TSMOs = 429*	*2003 Total No. TSMOs = 1031*
Human rights	34%	32%	33%
Environment	2	8	18
Peace	27	18	16
Women's rights	11	8	10
Development	4	5	8
Global economic justice	3	5	11
Multi-issue	18	18	28

Source: *Yearbook of International Organizations.*
Notes: These figures exclude labor unions. Figures do not total 100% because categories are not mutually exclusive (e.g., groups working on "human rights and peace" or "women and development" are counted in each of those issue categories as well as the multi-issue category).

of transnational social movement organizations were human rights, the environment, women's rights, peace, and economic justice. Table 22.4 displays these changes.

Throughout the late twentieth century, roughly a third of all TSMOs focused on human rights. About 10 percent focused on peace and another 10 percent addressed women's rights issues. Environmental issues attracted growing attention from TSMOs, with the percentage of groups rising from just 2 percent in the early 1960s (before the first major global environmental conference) to nearly 20 percent of all TSMOs in

2003. Economic justice also attracted growing support, rising from 3 percent to 11 percent of all TSMOs between the 1960s and 2000. Finally, groups adopting complex, multi-issue frames—often ones explicitly advocating for international law and multilateralism—expanded from around 17 percent of all groups in the 1960s to 28 percent in 2000.

Reviewing the TSMO population in the latter part of the twentieth century, we notice two important and consistent trends. First, there is a shift toward more decentralized organizational structures. Second, TSMOs are expanding their networks of ties to other groups in their environment, including both international nongovernmental and governmental organizations. Table 22.5 summarizes the data on these trends.

In the earliest decades of this study, TSMOs tended to adopt what I have called the "federated organizational structure." This structure has an international secretariat that retains the authority to grant or withhold affiliates' rights to use the organization's name, and that otherwise regulates the activities of member groups, which tend to be organized into national sections. Amnesty International is a prominent example of this more centralized structure. While this sort of federated structure might have proved effective in earlier times, technological change has reduced the need for such centralized and hierarchical structures. To sustain the voluntary participation of members, activist groups needed to find ways to satisfy a desire for more local autonomy. Moreover, a changing political environment demands new ideas and flexible responses, and more decentralized structures better accommodate such needs. Not surprisingly, we find an almost directly parallel rise in the percentages of TSMOs adopting a more decentralized, coalitional structure alongside a precipitous decline in the percentage of groups maintaining more centralized, federated structures. Whereas about half of all TSMOs were coalitions in the 1970s, by the 2000s, there were twice as many coalitions as federations in the population of TSMOs. A related pattern of decentralization is reflected in the fact that, starting in the 1980s, we find more TSMOs forming *within* either the region of the global North or South than was true in the past, when most groups crossed this regional divide. [. . .]

The second pattern we find in this analysis is a distinct tendency for TSMOs to be active networkers, forming ties to both nongovernmental and intergovernmental organizations as they pursue their social change activities. The average number of ties transnational social change groups reported to other organizations increased during the past two decades. Whereas in the early 1980s TSMOs reported an average of fewer than two ties either to other inter-

Table 22.5 Changes in TSMO Network Ties, 1973–2003

	1973	*1983*	*1993*	*2003*
Number of TSMOs	236	429	735	1031
Ratio coalition/federation structure	.62	.93	1.38	1.82
% TSMO headquarters in global South	11%	18%	24%	23%
% with UN consultative status	56%	49%	38%	42%
Average # NGO ties (st. dev)	1.00	1.62	4.26	3.54
	(1.36)	(2.69)	(5.06)	(4.53)
Average # IGO ties (st. dev)	1.43	1.42	2.19	2.30
	(1.81)	(1.97)	(3.32)	(3.07)

Source: *Yearbook of International Organizations.*

Notes: Counts exclude labor organizations. The reported average numbers of ties to IGOs and NGOs have been calculated using a maximum value of 10 for IGOs and 20 for NGOs, since a very small percentage of groups report unusually large numbers of contacts.

national NGOs or to intergovernmental organizations, by 2000 these organizations reported an average of 2.3 ties to intergovernmental bodies and about 3.5 ties to other international NGOs. These figures, moreover, do not reflect what are likely to be substantial increases in ties to national and local organizations.

In sum, the evidence available here shows a distinctive shift in the late twentieth century toward higher levels of transnational association by citizens advocating social and political change. Over time, the organizational structures of TSMOs have become both more decentralized and more densely connected to other organizations in the political environment. This evidence supports my contention that the network concept is useful for analyzing the collections of actors involved in social change efforts. Below I explore the implications of the trends discussed in this chapter for our understandings of how transnational networks for global democracy operate in the contemporary global system.

Toward a "New Global Politics"?

The discussion thus far has demonstrated relationships between social movements, organizations, and broader institutions and processes. Social movements, while attempting to alter relations of power, are shaped in important ways by the political and economic institutions that reflect and seek to preserve existing power relations. At the same time, social movements are seeking to bring new actors and claims into the political arena in order to generate changes in those institutional rules and relationships. Over time, they help democratize these spaces by bringing new actors and issues to political agendas and by helping to give political voice to groups that are excluded by existing institutional arrangements.

Social movement actors have adopted the technologies used by states and private-sector actors and applied these technologies in new ways as they sought to mobilize new groups of people. [...] Few activists in recent (and not-so-recent) protests would deny the importance of new information technologies to their work. Over the last decade especially, these technologies have dramatically transformed possibilities for transnational political organization and action in an increasingly global polity. Moreover, innovations in the subversive use of technologies are being met with new challenges as political and corporate elites seek to control and to better exploit their commercial potential.

Transnational social movement networks have clearly become more decentralized and more closely connected with the everyday routines of greater numbers of people. Local and national groups can more readily relate to transnational organizations and campaigns and can participate more directly in transnational political processes than they could in the past. Advances in information technologies as well as the professionalization and global integration of the global workforce have facilitated this decentralization (Smith and Fetner 2007). While the former process facilitates rapid and extensive information flows, the latter facilitates the ready interpretation and mobilization of information by diverse groups working at local levels. These changes have led growing numbers of activists to speak of a new global politics that is more participatory and innovative than that of earlier decades. [...]

Because social movements are most clearly engaged in information politics and communication-based political work, scholars have emphasized the importance of informal and fluid networks of actors to global social change processes. Our notion emphasizes a complex multilateralism, global politics as increasingly made up of interactive networks of state, non-state, and intergovernmental actors. By facilitating communication and translation across different political spaces and levels of action, transnational networks help relate the practices and ideas in local contexts to global-level institutions and processes.

[...]

Table 22.6 Changing Structures and "Generations" of Transnational Activism

Generation	*(1) Multilateralist*	*(2) Transitional Advocacy Networks*	*(3) Direct Action*
Timeframe	*Pre-1980*	*Late 1980s–1990s—UN Conference Era*	*Late 1990s–Seattle/Post-Seattle Era*
Geographic Scope	Mostly Northern	Mostly Northern—growing participation from South	Rapidly growing Southern participation
Organizational Structure	Small networks, strong role for individual leaders, transnational organizations central	NGO-centered issue networks, transnational organizations central but more national groups	More informal and polycentric; multi-issue/multi-sectors; More national and sub-national organizations in addition to transnational
Scale of Action	Mostly in global forums—limited mass mobilizing efforts	Mostly in global forums or focused on UN conferences or summits	More autonomous from inter-governmental agenda Connecting local problems/actions to global conditions—domestication of issues
Major Strategies	Elite lobbying Formal lobbying	*Strategic campaigns:* Limited political goals Turned on and off by lead organizations Maintained organizational identities	*Permanent campaigns:* Diverse political goals Decentralized control and leadership Organizational and tactical innovation Foster movement identities
Capacity		Problem- and campaign-focused networking, some popular mobilization	Mass protest, value change Technological adaptations/innovation

Source: Adapted from Bennett (2005: 214).
Note: Activities to shape cultural and social spaces are common to all three "generations," and to most social movement activism generally, but they are more pronounced in the latest period.

Table 22.6 shows several important shifts in transnational activism. First, the scope of transnational activism has expanded, including growing numbers of actors from the global South. Economic disadvantages and higher levels of political repression in the South are no longer preventing people in those countries from cultivating transnational activist networks that aim to remedy the problems they face. A second change is in the structure of transnational organizations, which has become less centralized and more connected to local and national activist networks. Third, the scale of transnational action has changed as well, moving from global to more locally oriented sites. In other words, transnational organizing efforts are becoming more connected to the daily routines of larger numbers of people. Fourth, strategies have shifted from a focus on global institutions in the earliest generation of activism toward the cultivation of issue-based campaigns led by key organizations to more permanent and Internet-based forms of mobilization with more decentralized leadership and individualized identities. [...]

A final conclusion from table 22.6 is that the capacities of transnational collections of activists have changed from more limited, elite-level lobbying toward increasingly mass-based political action. This has fundamentally altered the organizational demands of transnational movements, and more established organizations like Greenpeace are finding that they risk being "outflanked" by new movement actors, and they have adopted new strategies to respond to these developments (Chesters 2004). Chesters argues that the kinds of shifts documented here signal a need for analysts to adopt an approach that focuses less on specific organizations and more on the *processes* and *relations* among diverse actors. While some of these may indeed be captured within our more traditional understandings of organizations, many may be taking on new forms. The increasingly common reference to the idea of a "new politics" by transnational activists suggests that many are noticing important changes in the character of global political organization and action.

[...]

Conclusion

This chapter presents evidence of the social infrastructure for an evolving democratic globalization network that is expanding possibilities for people to act collectively beyond their immediate local and national settings. We see some significant trends that are likely to generate more participation in the democratic globalization network over time, as expanding global institutions and interdependence strengthen demands for transnational cooperation. First, transnational social movement organizations have expanded in recent decades, adopting more decentralized organizational structures. They also increasingly cultivate more ties to both nongovernmental and intergovernmental actors. Information technologies have allowed more local and national groups to connect to transnational networks, limiting the need for formally structured transnational movement organizations. These trends help explain the expanding representation of people from outside the global North. We also find that more leadership and innovation in transnational campaigns has been coming from national and local levels of action rather than from transnational sites, and at the same time we have seen more mass mobilizations around global issues. This decentralized, network pattern, moreover, mirrors a trend in governmental and corporate sectors, which have also seen a trend toward decentralization in the face of globalization forces. [...]

The expansion of a more formally organized and more densely networked global civil society might contribute to the democratization of the global political system. First, it helps increase flows of information between global and local contexts, thereby enhancing public awareness and debate on global problems and policies. Second, by helping empower groups that are marginalized by formal political processes and by structuring opportunities for them to participate in global politics, it increases the openness and representativeness of international institutions. Third, by expanding capacities for rapid transnational communication and public participation, it can enhance the transparency and accountability of governments to both their citizens and to other governments. Fourth, by cultivating transnational identities and shared organizational bonds, it can generate global notions of fairness that become a yardstick against which various proposals and policies can be evaluated. And finally, by providing for the sustained public attention to global problems, transnational organizations and networks can increase the effectiveness of global institutions through ongoing efforts to monitor and to mobilize pressure for compliance with international agreements.

References

Bennett, W. Lance. 2005. "Social Movements Beyond Borders: Understanding Two Eras of Transnational Activism." Pp. 203–226 in *Transnational Protest and Global Activism*, edited by D. della Porta and S. Tarrow. Lanham, MD: Rowman & Littlefield.

Chesters, Graeme. 2004. "Global Complexity and Global Civil Society." *Voluntas: International Journal of Voluntary and Non-Profit Organizations* 15:323–342.

Fox, Jonathan. 2002. "Assessing Binational Civil Society Coalitions: Lessons from the Mexico-U.S. Experience." Pp. 341–417 in *Cross-Border Dialogues: U.S.-Mexico Social Movement Networking*, edited by D. Brooks and J. Fox. La Jolla, CA: Center for U.S.-Mexican Studies, University of California–San Diego.

McAdam, Doug, Sidney Tarrow, and Charles Tilly. 2001. *Dynamics of Contention*. New York: Cambridge University Press.

McCarthy, John D. 1996. "Constraints and Opportunities in Adopting, Adapting and Inventing." Pp. 141–151 in *Comparative Perspectives on Social Movements: Political Opportunities, Mobilizing Structures and Cultural Framings*, edited by D. McAdam, J. McCarthy, and M. Zald. New York: Cambridge University Press.

Smith, Jackie. 2005. "Building Bridges or Building Walls? Explaining Regionalization among Transnational Social Movement Organizations." *Mobilization* 10:251–270.

Smith, Jackie, Charles Chatfield, and Ron Pagnucco, eds. 1997. *Transnational Social Movements and Global Politics: Solidarity Beyond the State*. Syracuse: Syracuse University Press.

Smith, Jackie, and Tina Fetner. 2007. "Structural Approaches in the Study of Social Movements." In *Handbook of Social Movements: Social Movements Across Disciplines*, edited by B. Klandermans and C. Roggeband. New York: Springer.

Starhawk. 2001. "Response to 'Manifest of Anticapitalist Youth against the World Social Forum.'" Electronic Communication.

Part VII

What Do Movements Do?

Introduction

If you are in a social movement, the most pressing question you face is: what is to be done? How do you choose tactics that will help your cause? How do you recruit more people, attract the news media, favorably impress decisionmakers? Tactical decisions are the real "stuff" of social movements. Yet, oddly, few scholars have taken a serious look at how these decisions are made, how or when protestors innovate in their tactics, or what the tradeoffs are between different kinds of tactics. Most of those who have written about issues like these have been practitioners rather than academics.

One reason scholars have avoided the question of tactical choice may be that movements have a hard enough time simply surviving. For researchers in the mobilization tradition, this was a serious accomplishment for movement organizations. As a result, they examined how these organizations raised funds, took advantage of tax laws, and recruited members. Similarly, process theorists concentrated on movements (workers, civil rights) that faced considerable repression from the state, so again simple survival was an accomplishment.

Scholars have also avoided questions of tactics because choices made in the heat of conflict are hard to explain in a rigorous fashion. Much depends on the instincts of movement leaders, who themselves may not always be able to explain why they made one choice rather than another. Decisions are sometimes made fast, and it may be difficult to reconstruct the process later—when being interviewed by researchers, for instance.

Tactical choices are usually made during the course of interaction with other decisionmakers: with one's opponents, of course, but also with the police, the media, legislators, potential allies, and many others. To take just one example: before many rallies or marches in the U.S. today, leaders negotiate with the police over where they will go, what they will do, how many will be arrested, and so on. Leaders must also make tactical choices with regard to their own followers: how to placate disaffected factions, how to keep members coming back to future events, how to increase the membership. As a result, any given action will probably be designed for several different audiences at the same time. An action that satisfies one may not please another.

In regard to their opponents, protestors hope to change behavior through persuasion or intimidation, and to undermine their opponents' credibility with the public, media, and the state. With state agencies, protestors hope to change laws, policies, regulatory practices, administrative rules,

Civil Society Civil society refers to the sphere of association and conversation which falls outside the direct control of the state and other authorities. Civil society encompasses the dialogues and interactions through which political views are formed and through which groups come to understand their interests vis-à-vis those of other groups and the state. Civil society includes voluntary associations, friendship networks, religious groups, independent newspapers, and the like. Social movements generally emerge out of civil society and often attempt to expand it, and movements are themselves an important component of civil society.

Repertoires of Protest What do protestors do to further their cause? In any given society, there are a handful of routine ways in which people protest. In modern Western societies, for example, most social movements choose from a surprisingly small number of tactics, especially petitions, demonstrations, marches, vigils, and sit-ins (and similar forms of civil disobedience). This is our "repertoire of protest." Widespread knowledge of one or more of these routines both facilitates protest and constrains the tactical options available. At the same time, expectations about what protestors are likely to do may also help authorities contain or suppress protestors. A repertoire is learned, shared, and occasionally modified. Innovative forms of protest are not easy to invent, even when they would seem to be helpful or necessary. According to Charles Tilly, who first coined the term, a repertoire is shaped by a society's sense of justice (which a tactic must appeal to or at least not violate), the daily routines and social organization of the population (a tactic should fit with these), their prior experience with collective action (so they have the know-how), and the patterns and forms of repression they are likely to face (which a good tactic will minimize). Tactics endure because they are relatively successful and/or deeply meaningful to people.

and to avoid repression. In the courts protestors typically strive to have unfavorable laws struck down. With both courts and police, they hope for tolerance of their own protests. Social movements seek to use the news media to spread their message, and sometimes to undermine their opponents. Protestors may also approach professional groups, such as engineers, to change their standards. They may seek allies in other protest groups. And from the public at large, they may hope for sympathy, contributions, changes in awareness. Finally, they even have goals for their own members: personal transformations and continued fervor for the cause. In other words, movements have a lot of goals to balance in their tactics.

As a result of this complexity, scholars have usually dealt with strategy and tactics by trying to make them a structural issue. Charles Tilly developed the concept of a repertoire of collective action to explain the range of tactics available to protestors in any given society in a particular period. Most social movements in that society will then draw on the same repertoire, because it is largely structurally determined. But this concept says little about how any given leader applies the existing repertoire: why a march rather than a letter-writing campaign?; why wait a week before responding to your opponents' actions rather than acting immediately?; why choose one cultural frame rather than another for a speech?

But Tilly's instincts are solid: protestors adapt their tactics to their resources, opportunities, and daily life. James Scott (1985, 1990) has described what resistance looks like in slave and peasant societies, where there is close surveillance and few legal and political freedoms. He calls these tactics "weapons of the weak." Only with industrialization and urbanization did protestors have newspapers and (later) television at their disposal. Workers lived and worked more closely together, so planning and coordination were easier than they had been for peasants. Large numbers of people could be mobilized. A broad range of tactics—from the formation of national organizations to mass rallies—became available to movements in industrial society which had not been to peasants.

Protestors in different societies face different political structures within which they must operate, even controlling for level of economic development. In an article that helped define the process approach, Herbert Kitschelt (1986) argued that antinuclear protestors in Europe and the United States chose different strategies because their countries contained different kinds of political machinery. French protestors could not bring lawsuits as their American counterparts did, in part because they lacked the grounds on which to sue. French political parties are also less open to new grassroots issues, compared to American parties, and so French antinuclear protestors could not

Free Spaces Most efforts at change face resistance or repression, so it is often helpful to have a safe setting in which to meet, exchange ideas, and make plans—a space sheltered from the prying eyes of opponents and authorities. Churches played this important role in the U.S. civil rights movement, although schools, recreational facilities, and other organizations can also function as free spaces. The most influential free space of the twentieth century was, ironically, a prison. On Robben Island, in the bay off Cape Town, hundreds of South African political prisoners were put together, isolated from outside networks but permitted to converse freely with one another. As Mandela biographer Anthony Sampson puts it, "It was like a protracted course in a remote left-wing university."

work through the electoral system either. As a result, they took to the streets more quickly than the Americans did, forced to work outside the system because that system lacked openings for input.

Our first reading is by one of the greatest community organizers of the twentieth century, Saul Alinsky. His tactical principles are not unlike those of theorists of war: try to take your opponents by surprise, try to make them think you are more powerful than you are. Try to use tactics your own followers enjoy and are familiar with. The idea of keeping the pressure on is important, because you never know where and when your opponent will be vulnerable or will make a blunder. The greater the pressure, the greater the chance you will trip them up. Alinsky also recognizes that it is usually necessary to portray your enemy as an utter villain, a real flesh-and-blood person who can be blamed, not an abstract principle. This can lead to strong emotions and polarization. Alinsky's rules are quite general, but they can be helpful reminders to social movement leaders.

If tactical choice is a difficult topic to model rigorously, that of tactical innovation is even more so. In describing civil-rights sit-ins, Aldon Morris exemplifies the resource-mobilization approach to tactics. He is not so much concerned with the origins of this tactic, nor the strategic thinking behind its use. Rather, he is concerned to show the indigenous organizations and social networks through which it rapidly spread, primarily arguing against a view of protest as spontaneous eruptions. In this excerpt Morris also touches on another important issue: the emergence of "movement centers" with resources, social ties (especially preachers and NAACP activists), and regular meetings (usually at churches). Other theorists have called these "free spaces," places relatively free from surveillance where oppositional ideas and tactics can develop.

Mary Bernstein examines the use of identity claims as a form of strategy, inserting culture into a political process framework. She contrasts "identity deployment" that emphasizes the differences between a group and the majority with those that emphasize the similarities. The major determinants of which kind of identity rhetoric a group will favor are the group's political interactions with their opponents and with the state, as well as the group's own organizational structure. In the process tradition, her concentration is on external audiences, who may favor very different messages from the ones movement members prefer.

Gay Seidman and Robert Brym look at the use of violent strategies by social movements and try to dispel some of the myths surrounding these. They point out that guerrilla warfare and terrorism are rational political responses to state violence and conflicts over territory, not the handiwork of psychopaths or religious fanantics, as the media often suggest—though religion may play an important role in political violence. Scholars as well as journalists, Seidman points out, are often hesitant to emphasize the rationality or achievements of political violence, in part because of their moral discomfort with it. In the case of the anti-apartheid movement in South Africa, this has led some scholars to avoid discussing violence altogether and to portray the movement, misleadingly, as a nonviolent civil rights struggle like that in the United States. But political violence, like war, is routine politics by other means.

Javier Auyero, in the final excerpt of the section, emphasizes the connections between routine politics and protest strategies. By closely examining a protest in Argentina, Auyero shows how this protest grew out of the routine politics familiar to people with a specific local history. In so doing, Auyero also shows how political strategy is shaped by the biography of activists—by their experiences, memories, cultural understandings, and identities.

We should note, finally, that even though social movements are defined, in part, by their use of "extra-institutional" means to pursue political goals, protest can also take place *within* institutions. Mary Fainsod Katzenstein, in her book *Faithful and Fearless* (1998), looks at how feminists have worked within religious institutions to pursue gains for women. She focuses on the kinds of language feminists use, the rhetorical claims they make, but at the same time she precisely describes the settings in which they make these claims. She calls these feminists' "habitats" in the institutions they hope to change. "Free spaces" *outside* normal organizations, in other words, are not always necessary for movements to flourish; sometimes they can thrive *within* dominant institutions. Movement messages (in both words and actions) and the audiences they are aimed at remain the essence of what social movements do.

The choice of strategies and tactics is certainly an area in which additional research is needed. One limitation has been that most scholars have thought about movements as their unit of analysis: how each grows, operates, and affects the world around it. But tactical choices are made in close interaction with others in the same "field of conflict." Similarly, the internal structure of movements may affect their ability to innovate and choose the most effective courses of action.

Discussion Questions

1. Why do social movements in different societies and different periods of history have different repertoires of collective action available to them?
2. How and why do new tactics spread?
3. What roles do "movement centers" and other "free spaces" play in social movements?
4. In what ways can identity claims be seen as strategic?
5. Why do some movements use violence to obtain their objectives? Under what conditions do you think this is justifiable?
6. How are the strategies activists employ connected to more routine politics, and to activists' everyday lives?

23 Protest Tactics

Saul D. Alinsky

We will either find a way or make one.
— *Hannibal*

Tactics means doing what you can with what you have. Tactics are those consciously deliberate acts by which human beings live with each other and deal with the world around them. In the world of give and take, tactics is the art of how to take and how to give. Here our concern is with the tactic of taking; how the Have-Nots can take power away from the Haves.

For an elementary illustration of tactics, take parts of your face as the point of reference; your eyes, your ears, and your nose. First the eyes; if you have organized a vast, mass-based people's organization, you can parade it visibly before the enemy and openly show your power. Second the ears; if your organization is small in numbers, then do what Gideon did: conceal the members in the dark but raise a din and clamor that will make the listener believe that your organization numbers many more than it does. Third, the nose; if your organization is too tiny even for noise, stink up the place.

Weapons of the Weak Today, social movements are one common way in which people protest against something they fear or dislike. But organized movements are rare in many other kinds of societies, especially where those in power are likely to repress any organized efforts. In most agricultural societies, like those of feudal Europe, peasants or slaves have been watched carefully by landlords or overseers. In situations of close surveillance, people find other ways to resist. They may work very slowly or poorly when doing tasks for their lord or master. They may do the wrong thing and "play dumb" when confronted by their bosses. They may subtly sabotage a construction project. At night they may poach or pilfer from local elites. They also tell jokes or spread gossip about their superiors as a way of undermining their power. For thousands of years, slaves and serfs have used "weapons of the weak" like these to get back at those exploiting them. See Scott (1985).

Always remember the first rule of power tactics:

Power is not only what you have but what the enemy thinks you have.

The second rule is: *Never go outside the experience of your people.* When an action or tactic is outside the experience of the people, the result is confusion, fear, and retreat. It also means a collapse of communication, as we have noted.

The third rule is: *Wherever possible go outside of the experience of the enemy.* Here you want to cause confusion, fear, and retreat.

General William T. Sherman, whose name still causes a frenzied reaction throughout the South, provided a classic example of going outside the enemy's experience. Until Sherman, military tactics and strategies were based on standard patterns. All armies had fronts, rears, flanks, lines of communication, and lines of supply. Military campaigns were aimed at such standard objectives as rolling up the flanks of the enemy army or cutting the lines of supply or lines of communication, or moving around to attack from the rear. When Sherman cut loose on his famous March to the Sea, he had no front or rear lines of supplies or any other lines. He was on the loose and living on the land. The South, confronted with this new form of military invasion, reacted with confusion, panic, terror, and collapse. Sherman swept on to inevitable victory. It was the same tactic that, years later in the early days of World War II, the Nazi Panzer tank divisions emulated in their far-flung sweeps into enemy territory, as did our own General Patton with the American Third Armored Division.

The fourth rule is: *Make the enemy live up to their own book of rules.* You can kill them with this, for they can no more obey their own rules than the Christian church can live up to Christianity.

The fourth rule carries within it the fifth rule: *Ridicule is man's most potent weapon.* It is almost impossible to counterattack ridicule. Also it infuriates the opposition, who then react to your advantage.

The sixth rule is: *A good tactic is one that your people enjoy.* If your people are not having a ball doing it, there is something very wrong with the tactic.

The seventh rule: *A tactic that drags on too long becomes a drag.* Man can sustain militant interest in any issue for only a limited time, after which it becomes a ritualistic commitment, like going to church on Sunday mornings. New issues and crises are always developing, and one's reaction becomes, "Well, my heart bleeds for those people and I'm all for the boycott, but after all there are other important things in life" – and there it goes.

The eighth rule: *Keep the pressure on*, with different tactics and actions, and utilize all events of the period for your purpose.

The ninth rule: *The threat is usually more terrifying than the thing itself.*

The tenth rule: *The major premise for tactics is the development of operations that will maintain a constant pressure upon the opposition.* It is this unceasing pressure that results in the reactions from the opposition that are essential for the success of the campaign. It should be remembered not only that the action is in the reaction but that action is itself the consequence of reaction and of reaction to the reaction, and infinitum. The pressure produces the reaction, and constant pressure sustains action.

The eleventh rule is: *If you push a negative hard and deep enough it will break through into its counterside*; this is based on the principle that every positive has its negative. We have already seen the conversion of the negative into the positive, in Mahatma Gandhi's development of the tactic of passive resistance.

One corporation we organized against responded to the continuous application of pressure by burglarizing my home, and then using the keys taken in the burglary to burglarize the offices of the Industrial Areas Foundation where I work. The panic in this corporation was clear from the nature of the burglaries, for nothing was taken in either burglary to make it seem that the thieves were interested in ordinary loot – they took only the records that applied to the corporation. Even the most amateurish burglar would have had more sense than to do what the private detective agency hired by that corporation did. The police departments in California and Chicago agreed that "the corporation might just as well have left its fingerprints all over the place."

In a fight almost anything goes. It almost reaches the point where you stop to apologize if a chance blow lands *above* the belt. When a corporation bungles like the one that burglarized my home and office, my visible public reaction is shock, horror, and moral outrage. In this case, we let it be known that sooner or later it would be confronted with this crime as well as with a whole series of other derelictions, before a United States Senate Subcommittee Investigation. Once sworn in, with congressional immunity, we would make these actions public. This threat, plus the fact that an attempt on my life had been made in Southern California, had the corporation on a spot where it would be publicly suspect in the event of assassination. At one point I found myself in a thirty-room motel in which every other room was occupied by their security men. This became another devil in the closet to haunt this corporation and to keep the pressure on.

The twelfth rule: *The price of a successful attack is a constructive alternative.* You cannot risk being trapped by the enemy in his sudden agreement with your demand and saying "You're right – we don't know what to do about this issue. Now you tell us."

The thirteenth rule: *Pick the target, freeze it, personalize it, and polarize it.*

In conflict tactics there are certain rules that the organizer should always regard as universalities. One is that the opposition must be singled out as the target and "frozen." By this I mean that in a complex, interrelated, urban society, it becomes increasingly difficult to single out who is to blame for any particular evil. There is a constant, and somewhat legitimate, passing of the buck. In these times of urbanization, complex metropolitan governments, the complexities of major interlocked corporations, and the interlocking of political life between cities and counties and metropolitan authorities, the problem that threatens to loom more and more is that of identifying the enemy. Obviously there is no point to tactics unless one has a target upon which to center the attacks. One big problem is a constant shifting of responsibility from one jurisdiction to another – individuals and bureaus one after another disclaim responsibility for particular conditions, attributing the authority for any change to some other force. In a corporation one gets the situation where the president of the corporation says that he does not have the responsibility, it is up to the board of trustees or the board of directors, the board of directors can shift it over to the stockholders, etc., etc. And the same thing goes, for example, on the Board of Education appointments in the city of Chicago, where an extra-legal committee is empowered to make selections of nominees for the board and the mayor then uses his legal powers to select names from that list. When the mayor is attacked for not having any blacks on the list, he shifts the responsibility over to the committee, pointing out that he has to select those names from a list submitted by the committee, and if the list is all white, then he has no responsibility. The committee can shift the responsibility back by pointing out that it is the mayor who has the authority to select the names, and so it goes in a comic (if it were not so tragic) routine of "who's on first" or "under which shell is the pea hidden?"

The same evasion of responsibility is to be found in all areas of life and other areas of City Hall Urban Renewal departments, who say the responsibility is over here, and somebody else says the responsibility is over there, the city says it is a state responsibility and the federal government passes it back to the local community, and on ad infinitum.

It should be borne in mind that the target is always trying to shift responsibility to get out of being the target. There is a constant squirming and moving and strategy – purposeful, and malicious at times, other times just for straight self-survival – on the part of the designated target. The forces for change must keep this in mind and pin that target down securely. If an organization permits responsibility to be diffused and distributed in a number of areas, attack becomes impossible.

[...]

One of the criteria in picking your target is the target's vulnerability – where do you have the power to start? Furthermore, any target can always say, "Why do you center on me when there are others to blame as well?" When you "freeze the target," you disregard these arguments and, for the moment, all the others to blame.

Then, as you zero in and freeze your target and carry out your attack, all of the "others" come out of the woodwork very soon. They become visible by their support of the target.

The other important point in the choosing of a target is that it must be a personification, not something general and abstract such as a community's segregated practices or a major corporation or City Hall. It is not possible to develop the necessary hostility against, say, City Hall, which after all is a concrete, physical, inanimate structure, or against a corporation, which has no soul or identity, or a public school administration, which again is an inanimate system.

John L. Lewis, the leader of the radical C.I.O. labor organization in the 1930s, was fully aware of this, and as a consequence the C.I.O. never attacked General Motors, they always attacked its president, Alfred "Ice-water-In-His-Veins" Sloan; they never attacked the Republic Steel Corporation but always its president, "Bloodied Hands" Tom Girdler, and so with us when we attacked the then-superintendent of the Chicago public school system, Benjamin Willis. Let nothing get you off your target.

With this focus comes a polarization. As we have indicated before, all issues must be polarized if action is to follow. The classic statement on polarization comes from Christ: "He that is not with me is against me" (Luke 11:23). He allowed no middle ground to the money-changers in the Temple. One acts decisively only in the conviction that all the angels are on one side and all the devils on the other. A leader may struggle toward a decision and weigh the merits and demerits of a situation which is 52 per cent positive and 48 per cent negative, but once the decision is reached he must assume that his cause is 100 per cent positive and the opposition 100 per cent negative. He can't toss forever in limbo, and avoid decision. He can't weigh arguments or reflect endlessly – he must decide and act. Otherwise there are Hamlet's words:

> And thus the native hue of resolution
> Is sicklied o'er with the pale cast of thought,
> And enterprises of great pith and moment
> With this regard their currents turn awry,
> And lose the name of action.

Many liberals, during our attack on the then-school superintendent, were pointing out that after all he wasn't a 100 per cent devil, he was a regular churchgoer, he was a good family man, and he was generous in his contributions to charity. Can you imagine in the arena of conflict charging that so-and-so is a racist bastard and then diluting the impact of the attack with qualifying remarks such as "He is a good churchgoing man, generous to charity, and a good husband"? This becomes political idiocy.

[...]

- *The real action is in the enemy's reaction.*
- *The enemy properly goaded and guided in his reaction will be your major strength.*
- *Tactics, like organization, like life, require that you move with the action.*

24 Tactical Innovation in the Civil Rights Movement

Aldon Morris

Roots of a Tactical Innovation: Sit-Ins

During the late 1950s activists associated with direct action organizations began experimenting with the sit-in tactic. The 1960 student sit-in movement followed naturally from the early efforts to mobilize for nonviolent direct action that took place in black communities across the South. Analysis of sit-ins of the late 1950s will reveal the basic components of the internal organization that was necessary for the emergence of the massive sit-ins of 1960.

In earlier chapters it was demonstrated that the NAACP Youth Councils, CORE chapters, and the SCLC affiliates were the main forces organizing the black community to engage in nonviolent protest. It was emphasized that these groups were closely tied to the black church base. The adult advisers of the NAACP Youth Councils were often women, who supervised the activities of fifteen to twenty young people, but it was not unusual to find men functioning as advisers also. Some of the Youth Councils felt a kinship with the direct action movement and were not rigidly locked into the legal approach of the NAACP.

The Southern CORE chapters, operating primarily in South Carolina and several border states, were organized by James McCain and Gordon Carey, were headed largely by local ministers, and had a disproportionate number of young people as members. These groups were preparing the way for the massive sit-ins of 1960 by conducting sit-ins between 1957 and 1960 at segregated facilities, including lunch counters.

Tactical Innovation Sometimes people may have intense grievances, they may be fairly well organized, and they may even believe that some authorities might be willing to listen to them, yet they do not protest because they are not quite sure how to do so effectively. The types of protest with which they are familiar may seem too difficult to carry out or may not strike them as likely to make a difference. However, certain tactical innovations – the discovery (or rediscovery) of new forms of protest – may spread very quickly and mobilize many people if these new tactics are relatively easy to adopt, resonate with people's moral views, and seem likely to succeed. The rapid spread of the sit-in tactic in 1960 is an example of how a tactical innovation can sometimes lead to an explosion of protest.

Early Sit-ins: Forerunners

On February 1, 1960, four black college students initiated a sit-in at the segregated lunch counter of the local Woolworth store in Greensboro, North Carolina. That day has come to be known as the opening of the sit-in movement. Civil rights activists, however, had conducted sit-ins between 1957 and 1960 in at least sixteen cities: St. Louis, Missouri; Wichita and Kansas City, Kansas; Oklahoma City, Enid, Tulsa, and Stillwater, Oklahoma; Lexington and Louisville, Kentucky; Miami, Florida; Charleston, West Virginia; Sumter, South Carolina; East St. Louis, Illinois; Nashville, Tennessee; Atlanta, Georgia; and Durham, North Carolina. The Greensboro sit-ins are important as a unique link in a long chain of sit-ins. Although this book will concentrate on the uniqueness of the Greensboro link, there were important similarities in the entire chain. Previous studies have presented accounts of most of the earlier sit-ins, but without due appreciation of their scope, connections, and extensive organizational base.

The early sit-ins were initiated by direct action organizations. From interviews with participants in the early sit-ins and from published works, I found that civil rights organizations initiated sit-ins in fifteen of the sixteen cities I have identified. The NAACP, primarily its Youth Councils, either initiated or co-initiated sit-ins in nine of the fifteen cities. CORE, usually working with the NAACP, played an important initiating role in seven. The SCLC initiated one case and was involved in another with CORE and FOR. Finally, the Durham Committee on Negro Affairs, working with the NAACP, initiated sit-ins in Durham. From these data we can conclude that the early sit-ins were a result of a multifaceted organizational effort.

Those sit-ins received substantial backing from their respective communities. The black church was the chief institutional force behind the sit-ins; nearly all of the direct action organizations that initiated them were closely associated with the church. The church supplied those organizations with not only an established communication network but also leaders and organized masses, finances, and a safe environment in which to hold political meetings. Direct action organizations clung to the church because their survival depended on it.

Not all black churches supported the sit-ins, and many tried to keep their support "invisible." Clara Luper, the organizer of the 1958 Oklahoma City sit-ins, wrote that the black church did not want to get involved, but church leaders told organizers "we could meet in their churches. They would take up a collection for us and make announcements concerning our worthwhile activities." Interviewed activists revealed that clusters of churches were usually directly involved with the sit-ins. In addition to community support generated through the churches, the activists also received support from parents of those participating in demonstrations.

The early sit-ins were organized by established leaders of the black community. The leaders did not spontaneously emerge in response to a crisis but were organizational actors in the fullest sense. Some sit-in leaders were also church leaders, taught school, and headed the local direct action organization; their extensive organizational linkages gave them access to a pool of individuals to serve as demonstrators. Clara Luper wrote, "The fact that I was teaching American History at Dungee High School in Spencer, Oklahoma, and was a member of the First Street Baptist Church furnished me with an ample number of young people who would become the nucleus of the Youth Council." Mrs. Luper's case is not isolated. Leaders of the early sit-ins were enmeshed in organizational networks and were integral members of the black community.

Rational planning was evident in this early wave of sit-ins. As we have seen, during the late 1950s the Reverends James Lawson and Kelly Miller Smith, both leaders of Nashville Christian Leadership Council, formed what they called a "nonviolent workshop." In them Lawson meticulously taught local college students the philosophy and tactics of nonviolent protest. In 1959 those students held "test" sit-ins in two department stores. Earlier, in 1957, members of the Oklahoma City NAACP Youth Council created what they called their "project," whose aim was to eliminate segregation in public accommodations. The project comprised various committees and groups that planned sit-in strategies. After a year of planning, the project group walked into the local Katz Drug Store and initiated a sit-in. In 1955 William Clay organized an NAACP Youth Council in St. Louis. Through careful planning and twelve months of demonstrations, its members were able to desegregate dining facilities at department stores. In Durham, North Carolina, in 1958 black activists of the Durham Committee on Negro Affairs conducted a survey of "five-and-dime" stores in Durham. It revealed that such stores were heavily dependent on black trade. Clearly, the sit-ins in Durham were based on rational planning.

Rational planning was evident in CORE's sit-ins during the late 1950s. CORE prepared for more direct action, including sit-ins, by conducting interracial workshops in Miami in September 1959 and January 1960. Dr. King assisted in the training of young people in one of the CORE workshops. In April 1959 a newly formed Miami CORE group began conducting sit-ins at downtown variety store lunch counters. In July 1959 James Robinson, writing to affiliated CORE groups and others, stated: "You have probably read in the newspaper about the dramatic all-day sit-ins which Miami CORE has conducted at a number of lunch counters. Up to 50 people have participated at many of these sit-ins." In early September 1959 CORE conducted a sixteen-day workshop on direct action in Miami, called the September Action Institute. Robinson wrote of it: "The discussion of the theory and techniques of nonviolent direct action will become understandable to all Institute members precisely because their actual participation in action projects will illuminate what otherwise might remain intangible." While the institute was in session, sit-ins were conducted at the lunch counters of Jackson's–Byrons Department Store. According to Gordon Carey of CORE, "Six days of continuous sit-ins caused the owners of the lunch counter concession to close temporarily while considering a change of policy." Immediately following that store's closing, CORE activists began sitting in at Grant's Department Store. Carey wrote: "We sat at the lunch counter from three to six hours daily until the 2-week Institute ended on September 20." On September 19, 1959, officials of the Jackson's–Byrons Store informed CORE that Negroes would be served as of September 21. Four black CORE members went to the store on September 21 but were refused service. Carey's account continues:

> Miami CORE determined to return to Jackson's–Byrons every day. The lunch counter has about 40 seats: On September 23 we had 40 persons sitting-in. It is not easy to get 40 persons on a weekday to sit-in from 10 A.M. till 3 P.M., but we maintained the demonstrations throughout the week. One woman who sat with us daily, works nights from 10 P.M. to 6 A.M. Cab drivers and off-duty Negro policemen joined us at the counter.

On September 25, 1959, city officials in Miami began arresting CORE members, and local whites physically attacked the protesters. Carey was told to be "out of Miami by Monday." Yet, Carey reports, "That day we had 80 persons sitting-in – half of them at Grant's." The Grant's store closed rather than serve blacks. On November 12, 1959, CORE made plans to sit in at the "white" waiting room of the Greenville, South Carolina, airport. The action was planned to protest the fact that the black baseball star Jackie Robinson had been ordered to leave the "white" waiting room a few days earlier. On January 23, just ten days before the famous sit-in at Greensboro, North Carolina, the CORE organization in Sumter, South Carolina, reported that its teenage group was "testing counter service at dime store: manager says he plans to make a change." Again, the action in Sumter had long-range planning behind it: A year earlier, at CORE's National meeting of 1959, the Sumter group had reported that students were involved in its activities. The Sumter CORE organization also had expressed the opinion that "emphasis should be on students and children. In future projects [we] hope to attack employment in 10¢ stores, food stores and chain stores."

In the summer of 1959 the SCLC, CORE, and FOR jointly held a nonviolent workshop on the campus of Spelman College in Atlanta. When the conference ended, James Robinson, Executive Secretary of CORE, along with the Reverend Wyatt Walker, James McCain, Professor Guy Hershberger, and Elmer Newfield, headed for Dabbs, a segregated restaurant in Atlanta. This interracial group shocked everyone by sitting down and eating. In a CORE news release, James Robinson humorously wrote: "We all had agreed that it was the best coffee we had ever had – the extra tang of drinking your coffee interracially across the Georgia color bar is highly recommended!" Besides providing an example for the other workshop participants, these acts of defiance showed everyone how to protest. Marvin Rich of CORE explained: "They were being demonstrated in a public form, so people would just walk by and see it. And people who didn't think things were possible saw that they were possible, and six months later, in their own home town, they may try it out."

Finally, the early sit-ins were sponsored by indigenous resources of the black community; the leadership was black, the bulk of the demonstrators were black, the strategies and tactics were formulated by blacks, the finances came out of the pockets of blacks, and the psychological and spiritual support came from the black churches.

Most of the organizers of the early sit-ins knew each other and were well aware of each other's strategies of confrontation. Many of the activists belonged to the direct action wing of the NAACP. That group included such activists as Floyd McKissick, Daisy Bates, Ronald Walters, Hosea Williams, Barbara Posey, and Clara Luper, who thought of themselves as a distinct group because the national NAACP was usually disapproving or at best ambivalent about their direct action approach.

The NAACP activists built networks that bypassed the conservative channels and organizational positions of their superiors. At NAACP meetings and conferences they sought out situations where they could freely present their plans and desires to engage in confrontational politics and exchange information about strategies. Once acquainted, the activists remained in touch by phone and mail.

Thus it is no accident that sit-ins occurred between 1957 and 1960. Other instances of "direct action" also occurred during this period. Daisy Bates led black students affiliated with her NAACP Youth Council into the all-white Little Rock Central High School and forced President Eisenhower to send in federal troops. CORE, beginning to gain a foothold in the South, had the explicit goal of initiating direct action projects. We have already noted that CORE activists were in close contact with other activists of the period. Although the early sit-ins and related activities were not part of a grandiose scheme, they were tied together through organizational and personal networks.

The Sit-in Cluster of the Late 1950s

Organizational and personal networks produced the first cluster of sit-ins in Oklahoma in 1958. In August 1958 the NAACP Youth Council of Wichita, Kansas, headed by Ronald Walters, initiated sit-ins at the lunch counters of a local drug store. At the same time Clara Luper and the young people in her NAACP Youth Council were training to conduct sit-ins in Oklahoma City. The adult leaders of the two groups knew each other: They worked for the same organization, so several members of the two groups traded numerous phone calls to exchange information and discuss mutual support. Direct contact was important, because the local press often refused to cover the sit-ins. Less than a week after Wichita, Clara Luper's group in Oklahoma City initiated its planned sit-ins.

Shortly thereafter sit-ins were conducted in Tulsa, Enid, and Stillwater, Oklahoma. Working through CORE and the local NAACP Youth Council, Clara Luper's friend Shirley Scaggins organized the sit-ins in Tulsa. Mrs. Scaggins had recently lived in Oklahoma City and knew the details of Mrs. Luper's sit-in project. The two leaders worked in concert. At the same time the NAACP Youth Council in Enid began to conduct sit-ins. Mr. Mitchell, who led that group, knew Mrs. Luper well. He had visited the Oklahoma Youth Council at the outset of its sit-in and had discussed sit-in tactics and mutual support. The Stillwater sit-ins appear to have been conducted independently by black college students.

The network that operated in Wichita and several Oklahoma communities reached as far as East St. Louis, Illinois. Homer Randolph, who in late 1958 organized the East St. Louis sit-ins, had previously lived in Oklahoma City, knew Mrs. Luper well, and had young relatives who participated in the Oklahoma City sit-ins.

In short, the first sit-in cluster occurred in Oklahoma in 1958 and spread to cities within a 100-mile radius through established organizational and personal networks. The majority of these early sit-ins were (1) connected rather than isolated, (2) initiated through organizations and personal ties, (3) rationally planned and led by established leaders, and (4) supported by indigenous resources. Thus, the Greensboro sit-ins of February 1960 did not mark the movement's beginning but were a critical link in the chain, triggering sit-ins across the South at an incredible pace. What happened in the black community between the late 1950s and the early 1960s to produce such a movement?

In my view the early sit-ins did not give rise to a massive sit-in movement before 1960 because CORE and the NAACP Youth Council did not have a mass base. The SCLC, which did have a mass base, had not developed fully. Besides, direct action was just emerging as the dominant strategy during the late 1950s.

As the SCLC developed into a Southwide direct action organization between 1957 and 1960, it provided the mass base capable of sustaining a heavy volume of collective action. It augmented the activities of CORE and the NAACP Youth Councils, because they were closely tied to the church. Thus the SCLC, closely interlocked with NAACP Youth Councils and CORE chapters, had developed solid movement centers by late 1959. The centers usually had the following seven characteristics:

1. A cadre of social change-oriented ministers and their congregations. Often one minister would become the local leader of a given center, and his church would serve as the coordinating unit.
2. Direct action organizations of varied complexity. In many cities local churches served as quasi-direct action organizations, while in others ministers built complex church-related organizations (e.g. United Defense League of Baton Rouge, Montgomery Improvement Association, Alabama Christian Movement for Human Rights of Birmingham, Petersburg Improvement Association). NAACP Youth Councils and CORE affiliates also were components of the local centers.
3. Indigenous financing coordinated through the church.
4. Weekly mass meetings, which served as forums where local residents were informed of relevant information and strategies regarding the movement. These meetings also built solidarity among the participants.
5. Dissemination of nonviolent tactics and strategies. The leaders articulated to the black community the message that social change would occur only through nonviolent direct action carried out by masses.
6. Adaptation of a rich church culture to political purposes. The black spirituals, sermons, and prayers were used to deepen the participants' commitment to the struggle.
7. A mass-based orientation, rooted in the black community, through the church.

From the perspective of this study, the period between the 1950s bus boycotts and the 1960 sit-ins provided pivotal resources for the emerging civil rights movement. My analysis emphasizes that the organizational foundation of the civil rights movement was built during this period, and active local movement centers were created in numerous Southern black communities.

25 The Strategic Uses of Identity by the Lesbian and Gay Movement

Mary Bernstein

> [The organizers of the 1993 lesbian and gay march on Washington] face a dilemma: how to put forward a set of unsettling demands for unconventional people in ways that will not make enemies of potential allies. They do so by playing down their differences before the media and the country while celebrating it in private.
>
> (*Tarrow* 1994, p. 10)

Sidney Tarrow's portrayal of the 1993 lesbian and gay march on Washington highlights a central irony about identity politics and the decline of the Left: Critics of identity politics decry the celebration of difference within contemporary identity movements, charging them with limiting the potential for a "politics of commonality" between oppressed peoples that could have potential for radical social change (Gitlin 1995). On the other hand, the lesbian and gay movement seems largely to have abandoned its emphasis on *difference from* the straight majority in favor of a moderate politics that highlights *similarities to* the straight majority.

Over time, "identity" movements shift their emphasis between celebrating and suppressing differences from the majority. For example, the Civil Rights movement underscored similarities to the majority in order to achieve concrete policy reforms. At other times, movements that assert radical racial identities to build communities and challenge hegemonic American culture take center stage. The American feminist movement has alternately emphasized innate gender differences between men and women and denied that such differences exist or that they are socially relevant. Under what political conditions do activists celebrate or suppress differences from the majority? Why does the stress on difference or similarity change over time?

To answer these questions, this article draws on evidence from several campaigns for lesbian and gay rights ordinances. The lesbian and gay movement was chosen because it is considered the quintessential identity movement (Melucci 1989; Duyvendak 1995; Duyvendak and Giugni 1995). The cultural barriers to acceptance of homosexuality and the challenge of self-acceptance for lesbians and gay men require cultural struggle. However, the lesbian and gay movement has been altered from a movement for cultural transformation through sexual liberation to one that seeks achievement of political rights through a narrow, ethnic-like (Seidman 1993) interest-group politics. This well-documented transition has yet to be explained.

This research will show that celebration or suppression of differences within political campaigns depends on the structure of social movement organizations, access to the polity (Tilly 1978), and the type of opposition. By specifying the political conditions that explain variation in strategies within movements, one can better understand differences in forms of collective action across movements.

Identity and Movement Types

Attempts to classify social movements have typically centered around the distinction between "strategy-oriented" and "identity-oriented" movements (Touraine 1981). Abandoning this distinction, Duyvendak and Giugni argue instead that "the real difference is, however, the one between movements pursuing goals in the outside world, for which the action is instrumental for goal realization, and identity-oriented movements that realize their goals, at least partly, in their activities" (1995, pp. 277–78). Social movements, then, are classified on "their logic of action," whether they employ an identity or instrumental logic of action, and whether they are internally or externally oriented. Movements such as the lesbian and gay movement are internally oriented and follow an identity logic of action. Instrumental movements, by contrast, engage in instrumental action and are externally oriented (Duyvendak and Giugni 1995, pp. 84–85).

This mechanical bifurcation of movement types, reflected in the division between identity theory on the one hand and resource mobilization and political process theory on the other, has left the literature on contentious politics unable to explain changes in forms of collective action. First, the casual use of the term "identity" obscures fundamental distinctions in meaning (e.g., Gitlin 1995). Second, I argue that theorists must abandon the *essentialist* characterization of social movements as expressive or instrumental because it impairs the study of all social movements. This essentialist characterization stems from the conflation of goals and strategies (i.e., that instrumental strategies are irrelevant to cultural change, while expressions of identity cannot be externally directed) apparent in resource mobilization, political process, and new social movement theories. Finally, attempts to integrate these theories have been unsuccessful.

Subsumed under the rubric of new social movements, "identity movements" have been defined as much by the goals they seek, and the strategies they use, as by the fact that they are based on a shared characteristic such as ethnicity or sex. According to new social movement theorists, identity movements seek to transform dominant cultural patterns, or gain recognition for new social identities, by employing expressive strategies.

New social movement theory suggests that movements choose political strategies in order to facilitate the creation of organizational forms that encourage participation and empowerment. Thus strategies that privilege the creation of democratic, nonhierarchical organizations would be chosen over strategies narrowly tailored to produce policy change.

For resource mobilization and political process theorists, identity may play a role in mobilization through solidary incentives but once the "free rider" problem is overcome all other collective action is deemed instrumental, targeted solely at achieving concrete (i.e., measurable) goals. Resource mobilization and political process theorists have neglected the study of identity movements with their seemingly "nonpolitical," cultural goals. Even when culture is recognized as an integral part of sustaining activist communities, changing or challenging mainstream culture is rarely considered a goal of activism. Strategies are seen as rationally chosen to optimize the likelihood of policy success. Outcomes are measured as a combination of policy change ("new advantages") and access to the structure of political bargaining (Jenkins and Perrow 1977; Tilly 1978; McAdam 1982; Gamson 1990). Such a narrow framing of social movement goals can lead to erroneous assumptions about the reasons for collective action and for strategy choice (Turner and Killian 1972; Jenkins 1983). Where goals are cultural and therefore harder to operationalize, theorists assume collective action has no external dimension but is aimed simply at reproducing the identity on which the movement is based (see Duyvendak 1995; Duyvendak and Giugni 1995). This leaves theorists unable to explain social movement action that seems to be working at cross purposes to achieving policy change. Furthermore, it relegates "prefigurative" (Polletta 1994) politics – a politics that seeks to transform observers through the embodiment of alternative values and organizational forms – to the realm of the irrational.

Although political opportunity or political process models share resource mobilization's assumptions about the relationship between strategies and goals, they provide a more useful starting point for understanding how political strategies are chosen. According to Tilly (1978), forms of collective action will be affected by "political coalitions and . . . the means of actions built into the existing political organization" (p. 167). These short- and medium-term "volatile" (Gamson and Meyer 1996) elements of "political opportunity" include the opening of access to participation, shifts in ruling alignments, the availability of influential allies, and cleavages among elites. As the political context changes, strategies should also change. Yet political opportunity models lack specificity in analyzing why or under what political conditions movements choose particular forms of collective action.

Attempts to reconcile the disjuncture between new social movement and resource mobilization or political process theory center on the relationship between forms of collective action and the movement's life cycle. The emergent "new social movements" of the 1960s and 1970s seemed so striking because they utilized innovative, direct action tactics. According to Calhoun (1995):

> As Tarrow (1989) has remarked, this description confuses two senses of *new:* the characteristics of all movements when they are new, and the characteristics of a putatively new sort of movement.
>
> It is indeed generally true that any movement of or on behalf of those excluded from conventional politics starts out with a need to attract attention; movement activity is not just an instrumental attempt to achieve movement goals, but a means of recruitment and continuing mobilization of participants. (p. 193)

In this view, a lack of historical perspective has mistakenly led new social movement theorists to label behavior "distinctive" when it is simply behavior indicative of an emergent social movement.

This criticism of new social movement theory glosses over important empirical and theoretical distinctions. First, not every emergent social movement employs novel or dramatic tactics in order to gain new recruits. Religious right organizations that arose in the 1970s drew on the dense network of conservative churches as well as direct mail lists to mobilize; they did not employ innovative or novel tactics. Rather than misattributing certain forms of collective action to the newness of social movements, one should ask what accounts for different forms of mobilization. Furthermore, attributing certain forms of collective action to the newness of social movements precludes an understanding of why such forms of collective action may emerge at later points in a movement's protest cycle.

Second, the glib dismissal of the sorts of political action attributed to new social movements as simply expressive, or unrelated to political structure, ignores the external or instrumental dimensions of seemingly expressive action. If putatively new social movements do challenge dominant cultural patterns, then theorists must take seriously the political nature of such collective action. Social movement theory must examine the challenges all social movements present to dominant cultural patterns.

This research seeks to provide a more complete understanding of the role of identity in collective action. I build in part on political process theory, while incorporating new social movement theory's emphasis on the importance of cultural change to movement activism. I argue that the concept of "identity" has at least three distinct analytic levels, the first two of which have been developed in the social movement literature. First, a shared collective identity is necessary for mobilization of *any* social movement, including the classic labor movement (Calhoun 1995). Second, identity can be a goal of social movement activism, either gaining acceptance for a hitherto stigmatized identity or deconstructing categories of identities such as "man," "woman," "gay," "straight" (Gamson 1995), "black," or "white." Finally, this research argues that expressions of identity can be deployed at the collective level as a political strategy, which can be aimed at cultural or instrumental goals.

Once the concept of identity is broken down into these three analytic dimensions, then one can explore the political conditions that produce certain identity strategies. [...]

Three Analytic Dimensions of Identity

The creation of communities and movement solidarity, which the bulk of research on collective identity examines (Williams 1995), is necessary for mobilization. I define *identity for empowerment* to mean the creation of collective identity and the feeling that political action is feasible (see table 25.1). In other words, some sort of identity is necessary to translate individual to group interests and individual to collective action. All social movements require such a "political consciousness" (Morris 1992) to create and mobilize a constituency (Taylor and Whittier 1992; Calhoun 1995).

Identity for empowerment is not necessarily a consciously chosen strategy, although it is a precursor to collective action. If a movement constituency has a shared collective identity and the institutions or social networks that provide a cultural space from which to act, then community building and empowerment will be forfeited to "instrumental" goals of policy attainment. In the absence of visibility or movement organizations, more work must be done to build organizations and recruit activists.

Collective identity can also have an external dimension in mobilization. Beckwith (1995) argues that an actor can use her or his identity to gain "political standing" (i.e., to legitimate participation) in a social movement in which she or he is not directly implicated. So, for example, women involved in coal mining strikes who are not miners can justify participation based on their relations to the miners, such as mother, sister, or wife. The choice of identity (e.g., wife of miner vs. working-class woman) can have implications for future activism.

Identity can also be a goal of collective action (*identity as goal*). Activists may challenge stigmatized identities, seek recognition for new identities, or deconstruct restrictive social categories. New Left organizations of the 1960s, for example, sought not only concrete policy reform, but thought that the creation of alternative cultural forms could foster structural change. Polletta (1994) asserts that "student-organizers of the Student Nonviolent Coordinating Committee (SNCC) saw their task as to mobilize and secure recognition for a new collective

Table 25.1 The three analytic dimensions of "identity"

Dimension	*Description*
Identity for empowerment	Activists must draw on an existing identity or construct a new collective identity in order to create and mobilize a constituency. The particular identity chosen will have implications for future activism.
Identity as goal	Activists may challenge stigmatized identities, seek recognition for new identities, or deconstruct restrictive social categories as goals of collective action.
Identity as strategy	Identities may be deployed strategically as a form of collective action. *Identity deployment* is defined as expressing identity such that the terrain of conflict becomes the individual person so that the values, categories, and practices of individuals become subject to debate. *Identity for critique* confronts the values, categories, and practice of the dominant culture. *Identity for education* challenges the dominant culture's perception of the minority or is used strategically to gain legitimacy by playing on uncontroversial themes.

identity – poor, 'unqualified' southern blacks – in a way that would transform national and local politics by refashioning criteria of political leadership" (p. 85). Feminists influenced American culture by challenging and altering conventional usage of sexist terms in the English language. Gamson (1995) argues that social movement theory must take seriously the goal of contemporary "queer politics" to deconstruct social categories, including "man," "woman," "gay," and "straight." Without a broader understanding of the goals of collective action and their relationship to the structural location of the actors, social movement theory cannot adequately explain strategy choices made by activists.

In addition to influencing motivations and goals of collective action, "cultural resources also have an external, strategic dimension" (Williams 1995, p. 125). I define *identity deployment* to mean expressing identity such that the terrain of conflict becomes the individual person so that the values, categories, and practices of individuals become subject to debate. What does it mean to "deploy identity" strategically? Taylor and Raeburn (1995) view identity deployment as a way to contest stigmatized social identities for the purposes of institutional change. Yet contesting stigma to change institutions is not the only reason for identity deployment. The goal of identity deployment can be to transform mainstream culture, its categories and values (and perhaps by extension its policies and structures), by providing alternative organizational forms. Identity deployment can also transform participants or simply educate legislators or the public.

Identity deployment can be examined at both the individual and collective level along a continuum from education to critique. Activists either dress and act consistently with mainstream culture or behave in a critical way. *Identity for critique* confronts the values, categories, and practices of the dominant culture. *Identity for education* challenges the dominant culture's perception of the minority or is used strategically to gain legitimacy by playing on uncontroversial themes. Although the goals associated with either identity strategy can be moderate or radical, identity for education generally limits the scope of conflict by not problematizing the morality or norms of the dominant culture.

Identity deployment should be understood dramaturgically as the collective portrayal of the group's identity in the political realm, whether that be in city council hearings or at sit-ins in segregated restaurants. The strategic deployment of identity may differ from the group's (or individuals') private understanding of that identity. In this research, I examine identity deployment at the collective level.

It is important not to conflate the goals of identity deployment with its form (i.e., critical or educational). Both can be part of a project of cultural challenge or a strategy to achieve policy reform. Whether these strategies are associated with organizational forms that encourage participation and empowerment by privileging the creation of democratic, nonhierarchical organizations, as new social movement theory would suggest, or with narrow interest group strategies designed to achieve policy change, as resource mobilization and political process perspectives would suggest, then becomes an empirical question, not an essentialist assumption based on movement types.

Understanding identity as a tool for mobilization, as a goal, and as a strategy will lead to a more comprehensive understanding of social movements. Instead of asking whether identity plays a role in a given movement, we can ask several questions: What role does identity play in mobilization? To what extent is identity a goal of collective action? Why or under what political conditions are identities that celebrate or suppress differences deployed strategically?

General Model

I argue that identity strategies will be determined by the configuration of political access, the structure of social movement organizations, and the type and extent of opposition. In addition to affecting political outcomes, the characteristics of movement organizations should also influence political strategies. I define *inclusive* movement organizations to be those groups whose strategies, in practice, seek to educate and mobilize a constituency or maximize involvement in political campaigns. *Exclusive* organizations actively discourage popular participation, choosing strategies unlikely to mobilize a movement constituency. Changes in the political context should also influence political strategies. I consider that a movement has *access* to the polity if candidates respond to movement inquiries, if elected officials or state agencies support and work toward the movement's goals, or if movement leaders have access to polity members (e.g., through business affiliations, personal contacts, or official positions in political parties). Organized opposition is also an important part of the political context. Most contemporary American social movements eventually face organized opposition to their goals, and this should influence the types of identities deployed. *Routine opposition* will refer to polity insiders (Tilly 1978); that is, those who by virtue of their institutional position (such as a cardinal of the Catholic Church) have the ear of policy makers. *Opposing movements* will refer to groups outside the polity mobilized around the issues of contention.

The role of identity in mobilization will differ across movements, but not because of some abstract essentialism of movement types. For example, identity for empowerment may play a smaller role in mobilizing movements sparked by a "moral shock" – such as the antiwar movement, the antinuclear movement, or the animal rights movement – than in mobilizing movements based on a shared characteristic or identity. But once a movement has emerged, I suggest that the same conditions that determine identity deployment should also apply to movements started by moral shocks.

In order to emerge, a social movement requires a base from which to organize and some sort of collective identity to translate individual into group interests. Movements with access to the structure of political bargaining *or* strong organizational infrastructures that have fostered a shared identity will tend to seek policy change, emphasize sameness rather than difference, and will use identity for education rather than identity for critique (see figure 25.1, paths 1, 2a). However, if the movement faces organized opposition from outside the political establishment, and if the movement is led by exclusive, narrowly focused groups uninterested in movement building, the movement may split, with some groups emphasizing differences and community building, while the exclusive groups continue to emphasize sameness and narrowly focused policy change (a mixed model; see figure 25.1, path 2b). In such cases, critical identities may be deployed as much in reaction to movement leadership as to the opposition.

When an emergent movement lacks both political access and an organizational infrastructure or collective identity, then an emphasis on difference will be needed to build solidarity and mobilize a constituency (figure 25.1, path 3). Such movements will tend to focus on building community and celebrating difference, as will those sectors of a movement marginalized by exclusive groups encountering nonroutine opposition (figure 25.1, path 4b).

Once a movement has been established – with constituency and organizational actors – then movement between the cells in figure 25.1 may take place as organized opposition emerges or declines, political coalitions shift, and the structures of movement organizations change over time.

After a movement's emergence, the types of identity deployment will be related to the structure of social movement organizations, access to the polity and whether opposition is routine, deriving from polity insiders, or external, arising from organized opposing movements. Changes in short- or medium-term elements of the political context should have a determining effect on forms of collective action such that greater access

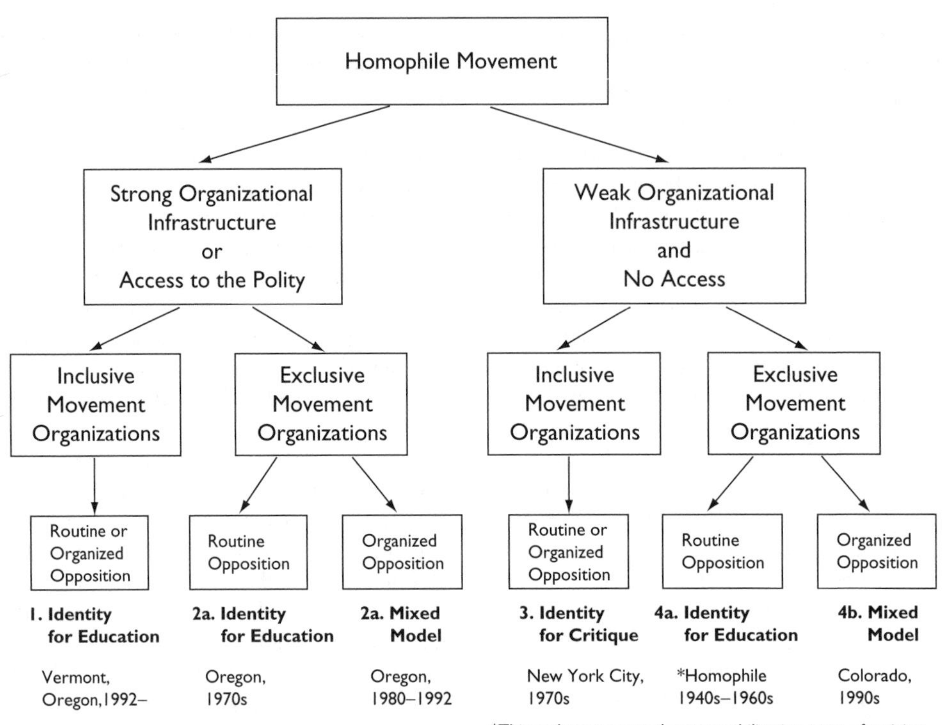

Figure 25.1 Identity deployment in the lesbian and gay movement

produces more moderate forms of collective action and identity for education strategies, while closing opportunities will lead to an emphasis on identity for critique. When the polity is relatively open and diverse segments of the activist community are represented in movement organizations or are included in political campaigns, there will be less emphasis on criticizing normative values. Because identity is deployed in the context of concrete interactions, the baseline against which activists define themselves will be influenced by opposing movements. Exclusive social movement organizations, the presence of a strong opposition, and negative interactions with the state will likely result in greater dissension within the community. That dissension will lead to factionalization and will produce moderates who will focus more on education and traditional lobbying tactics and radicals who will focus on criticizing dominant values (a "mixed model"). Radicalization in the movement can stem as much from reaction to movement leaders as from reactions to the political context. In short, identity deployment in the political realm will depend on the structure of and relations among movement organizations, the extent of political access, and the type of opposition.

[...]

When lesbians and gay men deploy their identity strategically, debates may center around whether sexual orientation is immutable, what constitutes "homosexual practices," or whether pedophilia is the same as homosexuality. Lesbian and gay lives become the subject of conflict. Nothing about the lesbian and gay movement dictates the strategic use of identity at the collective level. For example, activists could draw attention to discriminatory employment practices, with a universal appeal to everyone's right to a job based on their skills. That is different than disclosing one's sexual orientation to legislators or neighbors, saying "Here I am, know me."

In the case of the lesbian and gay movement, identity for education challenges negative stereotypes about lesbians and gay men, such as having hundreds of sexual partners a year or struggling with uncontrollable sexual urges, while identity for critique challenges dominant cultural assumptions about the religious or biological "naturalness" of gender roles and the heterosexual nuclear family. Arguably the greatest success of the women's movement has been to break down the division between public and private through challenging traditional notions of gender. Both identity for critique and identity for education can be part of broader projects seeking cultural change or policy reform.

Although many have looked at the relationship between lesbian and gay culture and individual-level identity strategies, few have examined this phenomena empirically, as a collective, consciously chosen political strategy. The rest of this article explores identity strategies along the continuum from critique to education at the collective level. As Seidman (1993, pp. 135–36) argues, we must "relate the politics of representation to institutional dynamics" rather than reducing cultural codes to textual practices abstracted from institutional contexts. The lesbian and gay movement has challenged a variety of institutions in American society, but I will restrict my analysis to interactions with the state because, with the onslaught by the Religious Right, the state has become one of the central loci of identity deployment. Future research will have to determine the ways diverse institutional dynamics (e.g., the church or psychiatry) influence the creation and deployment of identities.

The Homophile Movement

A collective identity among lesbians and gay men emerged prior to the strategic recruitment of a constituency by organizational actors, as long-term structural changes brought increasing numbers of gay men and lesbians together in urban settings. The secretive nature of the early homophile organizations, however, precluded mass mobilization. The only public meeting places for lesbians and gay men – cruising places and Mafia-run bars – were ill-suited for mobilization. Cherry Grove, Fire Island, a visible lesbian and gay summer community, may have provided a more hospitable avenue for mobilization but was not linked to a broader organizational infrastructure.

The predominantly underground homophile movement of the 1940s and 1950s has been well documented. Groups such as the Daughters of Bilitis and the Mattachine Society had exclusive organizational structures, lacked access to the polity, and faced routine opposition from the state (see figure 25.1, path 4a). The goals of the homophile movement varied over the years as some sought assimilation while others thought homosexuality was a distinctive and positive trait that should not be subsumed by mainstream culture. Yet both sides agreed on strategies: homophile activists would educate professionals (in particular medical professionals) about the realities of homosexuality; those professionals would in turn advocate for changes in state policies on behalf of homosexuals.

As the social strictures against homosexuality loosened, the lesbian and gay movement became more public through the 1960s. Much of the emergent movement's activism appeared to be "expressive," aimed for and at lesbians and gay men. In part, that perception was strengthened by the connection of many activists in post-Stonewall organizations to the New Left (e.g., RadicaLesbians, the Furies, and the Gay Liberation Front)[1] who felt that alternative cultural forms would lead to a revolutionary restructuring of society. The visible and outspoken nature of 1960s and 1970s activists accounts for the perception by scholars that the lesbian and gay movement was fundamentally different from other social movements.

But this perception is misguided because it ignores the diversity within the lesbian and gay movement, even around the time of

Stonewall. The development of these local movements and the strategies they chose depended on their access to the polity, on their organizational structure, and on the type of opposition they faced. For example, where movement leaders had access to the polity, usually in smaller cities where gay white businessmen had contacts in government or where earlier movement activities had created political access, as in Washington, D.C., expressive action was minimal. In most cases, local movements lacked access to the polity and had to create a constituency. To do so, they had to locate others like themselves. The lack of lesbian and gay institutions, such as churches or bookstores, forced leaders to construct those spaces as well as to launch political campaigns.

When groups lack their own institutions and a political consciousness, they will concentrate on identity for empowerment and community growth. Over time, as institutions and opportunities to act develop, what was once seen as an expressive movement will come to be seen as instrumental as political representation increases and the emphasis on empowerment decreases. Once a movement has been established, forms of collective action will depend on access to decision makers, the extent of opposition, and the degree of inclusiveness of movement organizations.

New York City and Oregon

In 1971, New York City's Gay Activists Alliance (GAA) launched a campaign to add "sexual orientation" to the list of protected categories in the city's human rights ordinance. Although GAA engaged political authorities in the public realm, it emphasized identity for critique, seeking to increase publicity and refusing to compromise for the sake of policy change (figure 25.1, path 3). Activists borrowed freely from the tactics of other contemporary movements, turning sit-ins into "kiss-ins" at straight bars to protest bans on same-sex displays of affection. They held peaceful demonstrations protesting police brutality and infiltrated local political clubs to "zap" public officials with questions about police raids on gay bars, entrapment, and support for antidiscrimination policies. Activists consistently refused to dress in accordance with mainstream culture, using their identity to criticize gender roles and heterosexual norms. In short, they used theatrical tactics that increased the scope of the conflict, demanding publicity, regardless of its potentially dilatory effect on achieving policy change. For example, Eleanor Holmes Norton, chair of New York City's Commission on Human Rights, offered GAA members the option of holding private hearings on the ordinance. GAA refused, declaring that it would only participate in open hearings, although that was less likely to achieve policy change. GAA finally secured public hearings after a demonstration – intended to be peaceful – outside General Welfare Committee chair Saul Sharison's apartment building turned bloody when Tactical Police Force officers taunted and then beat demonstrators with their clubs. Despite dissension within GAA, drag queens were ultimately allowed to participate in the hearings. City council members would subsequently exploit the confusion between transvestism and homosexuality to defeat the ordinance.

The fight for antidiscrimination legislation in Oregon contrasted sharply with the battle in New York City. Activists in Portland and Eugene in the 1970s – primarily gay white men – had easy access to the polity because of their status as business persons. The Portland Town Council (PTC), an informal coalition of gay-oriented businesses and organizations, was founded in 1970. Due largely to the lack of opposition and the semi-insider status of its members, the PTC won a series of incremental victories culminating in Portland's passage of a law to prohibit discrimination against city employees on the basis of sexual orientation. In Eugene, activists also capitalized on their insider status by choosing strategies that discouraged mass participation, including secret meetings with council members. In

1977, Eugene passed a lesbian and gay rights ordinance.

The PTC also spearheaded efforts to add sexual orientation to the state's human rights statute. Despite agonizingly narrow defeats of statewide antidiscrimination bills (by one vote in 1975), activists continued to work with state officials. In 1976, at the PTC's request, Oregon Governor Straub created the Ad Hoc Task Force on Sexual Preference to conduct factual research and to make policy recommendations to the Oregon legislature. The PTC served as an advisory board, recommended areas for research, and facilitated interactions between lesbian and gay communities and the task force.

The strategies employed in New York City and Oregon contrasted sharply. When given the choice, New York City activists consistently privileged strategies that challenged dominant cultural values over those that would maximize the likelihood of policy success. By refusing to hold private hearings with the Human Rights Commission, activists increased the scope of conflict. Rather than allaying the fears of legislators and the public by reassuring them of the incremental nature of the policy reform, activists exacerbated those fears by having transvestites testify at public hearings. In Oregon, activists were content to hold secret meetings with lawmakers in order to gain legal change.

What accounts for these diverse approaches to political change? The early stage of New York City's lesbian and gay liberation movement appears to be consistent with a new social movement interpretation. At the time, movement theorists stated explicitly that the battle was over ending oppressive gender roles and the restrictive categories of heterosexuality and homosexuality that inhibited everyone's true bisexual nature. Thus activists chose strategies that highlighted differences from the straight majority, seeing themselves as the embodiment of the liberation potential. Uncompromising strategies that reproduced the identity on which the movement was based and created participatory organizations took priority over goals of achieving policy reform. Creating a sense that gay was good and should be expressed publicly, with pride, would not come through secretive meetings with city officials or concealing drag queens.

In Oregon, on the other hand, little emphasis was placed on creating democratic organizations. The goals in Eugene, Portland, and at the state level were to obtain narrow legal protections. Rather than focus on mobilization, the PTC hired a lobbyist to advocate for the new antidiscrimination legislation. The comparison of Oregon to New York City suggests that newly emerging social movements will only emphasize differences through expressive tactics to the extent that they lack access to the polity and a strong organizational infrastructure.

Political access and differing resources explain in part the different orientations of the Oregon and New York City activists to cultural and legal change. In New York City, activists faced a closed polity. New York State retained an antisodomy statute, which effectively criminalized the status of being lesbian or gay and was used to justify police entrapment and bar raids. The New York City police routinely used violence to quell peaceful lesbian and gay demonstrations and were unresponsive to lesbians and gay men who were the victims of violence.

Lesbians and gay men needed to become a political minority. To do so, they had to increase visibility at the expense of losing short-term policy battles. Influenced as well by other contemporary movements (e.g., the Civil Rights, New Left, and feminist movements) activists had little to lose and much to gain by radical political action. Although deploying identity for critique may have had long-term political benefits, many saw the goal of a political battle in terms of empowering the lesbian and gay communities. In short, the political battle was an opportunity to create a cultural shift in sensibilities among lesbians and gay men (Marotta 1981).

Despite the importance of the political context, it was in interactions with the state that identities were formed and deployed. Although activists' analysis of the relationship between political and cultural change – either that political campaigns served the purpose of empowering activists or that political reforms would enable cultural change – produced and reinforced critical identities, negative interactions with the state entrenched an oppositional dynamic. The New York City Council's initial refusal to hold public hearings, in addition to the police repression that included the attack on demonstrators outside Sharison's building, cemented the antagonistic relationship between activists and the state. Because organizations were inclusive and the lesbian and gay social movement sector was relatively undifferentiated, a cultural critique could only be expressed in the political realm. There was nothing about the movement per se that dictated the deployment of critical identities. Activists' interpretations of the relationship between culture and politics and the types of identities deployed were contingent on interactions with the state.

A second part of the formation of a critical identity was the absence of an organized opposition. Because opposition was routine, lesbians and gay men had only to define themselves against mainstream cultural views in order to criticize the dominant culture. Identities were constructed through interactions with the state, in the absence of organized third parties. In short, inclusive movement organizations, lack of access to the polity, negative interactions with the state, and routine opposition produced critical identities.

Activists in Oregon had greater resources than did activists in New York City, due in part to class and gender differences. The unique access to government officials facilitated by business connections enabled quick passage of local legislation and almost won passage of statewide legislation. Unlike GAA, the PTC had had mostly positive relations with state authorities in Portland, Eugene, and the state capitol. So after narrow losses in the state legislature, rather than respond in a critical way through dramatic demonstrations, the PTC approached Governor Robert Straub for redress. Had Governor Straub not been responsive to lesbian and gay demands, or, similarly, had the Eugene City Council initially rebuffed the gay activists, critical identities would have been deployed, as much in reaction to the elite gay leadership as to the state (which is what happened in Oregon more than a decade later).

Critical identities, however, were not deployed in Eugene, and success came easily as a result of political access and the low-key tactics of the gay activists. The elitist attitude and nonparticipatory stance of the gay leadership, however, created antagonisms between different lesbian and gay communities. But because interactions with the state had been positive, as shown by the bill's relatively quick passage, these tensions lay dormant. When newly organized religious right groups placed a referendum to repeal Eugene's lesbian and gay rights ordinance on the ballot, the dissension within the lesbian and gay communities made it difficult for them to present a united front, and the antilesbian and antigay referendum ultimately passed.

By the end of the 1970s, the lesbian and gay movement had undergone profound internal change. Activists no longer placed the same emphasis on challenging gender roles and the construction of heterosexuality in state-oriented lesbian and gay rights campaigns. As many have observed, an ethnic- or interest-group model that sought achievement of rights replaced the liberation model that sought freedom from constraining gender roles and sexual categories. Institutionalized, professionally led organizations often supplanted the grassroots groups of the early 1970s in leading campaigns directed at the state. The gay liberation fronts and the gay activists' alliances had all but disappeared. In addition to internal changes within the lesbian and gay movement, by the end of the 1970s the religious right emerged and worked to oppose all of the changes sought by lesbian and gay activists.

The next section explains why these changes within the lesbian and gay movement occurred and what accounts for the continued variation in forms of collective action across the United States. Access to political decision makers produced identity for education, as in Vermont (figure 25.1, path 1). However, where exclusive groups faced organized opposition, as in Colorado, a mixed model of identity deployment was produced as marginalized groups within the lesbian and gay movement reacted to the lesbian and gay leadership and to the opposition (path 4b). In Oregon, exclusive leadership and intense opposition would later produce a mixed model (path 2b). But as activists realized that sustaining a prolonged campaign against the religious opposition required cooperation among diverse lesbian and gay communities, organizations became more inclusive and an educational model prevailed (path 1).

[...]

Implications

This approach to understanding the strategic deployment of identity has potential applications to other movements based on a shared characteristic. For example, the Southern Civil Rights movement that emerged in the 1950s followed path 1 as shown in figure 25.2. The complex organizational infrastructure of the South, which included black colleges, black churches, and even beauty parlors, provided a locus from which to organize (Morris 1984). Thus when federal policies began to change, leaders were able to mobilize from an existing base. Emergent, inclusive civil rights organizations underscored sameness rather than difference and sought concrete policy goals.

Over time, the focus on identity for education often gave way to identity for critique as the black power movement gained momentum (figure 25.2, path 3). According to Robert Scheer (1970, p. 202), black power, or "black *revolution* [is] the statement of an alternative system of values, the move to acquire power to assert those values, and the express willingness to respond with revolutionary violence to the violence inherent in established power." By fostering an identity based on differences from the majority, black nationalism was a way to challenge dominant cultural values, to build communities, and to create revolutionary change. Leaders hoped that deploying critical identities based on perceived cultural differences would be a crucial step toward economic independence and political power.

I suggest that local variations in political access and organizational infrastructures, as well as the degree of exclusivity of African-American leadership would also account, in part, for the relative stress placed on deploying critical or educational identities. In short, local conditions (political access and the type of opposition) as well as the relationships among African-American political organizations should help explain the vicissitudes in the deployment of radical racial identities on the one hand and educational identities on the other.

When the feminist movement began to emerge in the 1960s, two activist factions were identified. Older professional women appointed to state governmental commissions on the status of women created formal organizations and began to lobby (Evans 1979; Freeman 1984). What came to be known as the liberal wing of feminism stressed similarities to the majority, deployed identity for education (i.e., that there were no socially significant differences between men and women), and focused attention on gaining formal policy reforms (figure 25.2, path 1). Because of their political access, older feminists stressed similarities to men.

The other wing of the emergent feminist movement was dominated by college-age women. Lacking the political access of the older wing, and of course influenced by the New Left, these women stressed identity for critique and their activism followed a dramatically different path from that of the older wing (figure 25.2, path 3). The younger wing, which eventually became

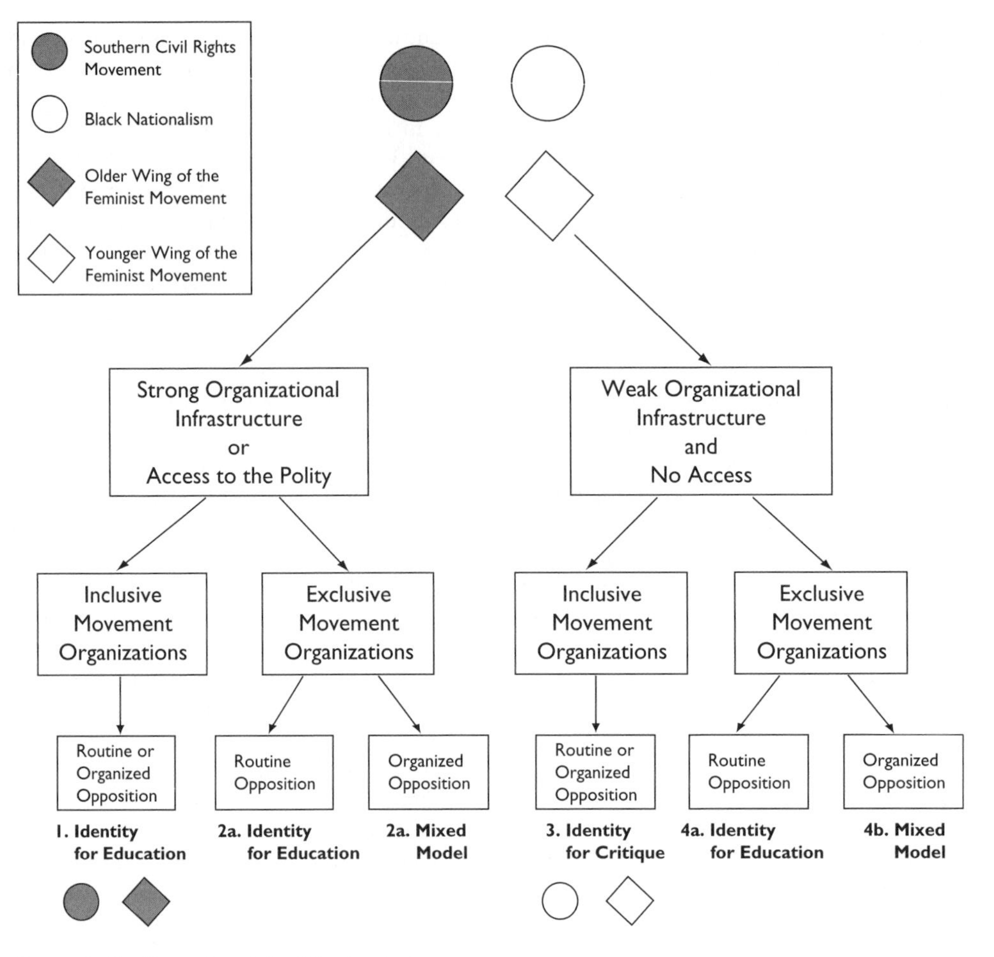

Figure 25.2 General model of identity deployment

identified with radical feminism, drew attention to "women's values" deriving from motherhood as a positive and distinct characteristic that set women apart from men in socially meaningful ways. Rather than devaluing these traits, critical female identities were deployed to criticize problematic manifestations of male dominance (such as violence and nuclear arms).

Reforming policy and challenging culture was a goal of both strategies. Suppressing differences to denaturalize categories such as "family" challenged the cultural underpinnings of existing policies based on an allegedly natural, gender-based public/private distinction. Stressing differences was also a part of a broader project of normative challenge. Over time, the relative emphasis on stressing similarities or differences changed as local conditions varied.

This brief overview of the feminist and Civil Rights movements broadly suggests how the differing structural locations of the actors, the extent of political access, and the strength of the organizational base from which these movements could mobilize influenced the types of identities deployed. This cursory overview of the movements cannot (and is not meant to) capture their complexity, but only to suggest the importance of understanding identity deployment and *why* certain movements *appear to be* internally or externally directed, and why they seem to seek "instrumental" or "identity" goals.

[...]

Note

1 "Stonewall" refers to the 1969 riots that took place in New York City when patrons of the gay afterhours club, the Stonewall Inn, fought back during a police raid. The weekend of rioting that ensued sparked national publicity for the movement, and dozens of new gay liberationist organizations formed, accelerating the trend toward radicalism that had begun earlier in the 1960s.

References

Beckwith, Karen. 1995. "Women's Movements and Women in Movements: Political Opportunity in Context." Paper presented at the meetings of the American Political Science Association, August 31–September 3, Chicago.

Calhoun, Craig. 1995. " 'New Social Movements' of the Early Nineteenth Century." Pp. 173–215 in *Repertoires and Cycles of Collective Action*, edited by Mark Traugott. Durham, N.C.: Duke University Press.

Duyvendak, Jan Willem. 1995. "Gay Subcultures between Movement and Market." Pp. 165–80 in *New Social Movements in Western Europe: A Comparative Analysis*, edited by Hanspeter Kriesi, Ruud Koopmans, Jan Willem Duyvendak, and Marco G. Giugni. Minneapolis: University of Minnesota Press.

Duyvendak, Jan Willem, and Marco G. Giugni. 1995. "Social Movement Types and Policy Domains." Pp. 82–110 in *New Social Movements in Western Europe: A Comparative Analysis*, edited by Hanspeter Kriesi, Ruud Koopmans, Jan Willem Duyvendak, and Marco G. Giugni. Minneapolis: University of Minnesota Press.

Evans, Sara. 1979. *Personal Politics: The Roots of Women's Liberation in the Civil Rights Movement and the New Left*. New York: Vintage Books.

Freeman, Jo. 1984. "The Women's Liberation Movement: Its Origins, Structure, Activities, and Ideas." Pp. 543–56 in *Women: A Feminist Perspective*, edited by Jo Freeman. Palo Alto, Calif.: Mayfield.

Gamson, Joshua. 1995. "Must Identity Movements Self Destruct? A Queer Dilemma." *Social Problems* 42 (3): 390–407.

Gamson, William. 1990. *The Strategy of Social Protest*, 2d ed. Belmont, Calif.: Wadsworth.

Gamson, William A., and David S. Meyer. 1996. "The Framing of Political Opportunity." Pp. 275–90 in *Comparative Perspectives on Social Movements: Political Opportunities, Mobilizing Structures, and Cultural Framings*, edited by John McCarthy, Doug McAdam, and Meyer N. Zald. Cambridge: Cambridge University Press.

Gitlin, Todd. 1995. *The Twilight of Common Dreams: Why America Is Wracked by Culture Wars*. New York: Metropolitan Books.

Jenkins, J. Craig. 1983. "Resource Mobilization Theory and the Study of Social Movements." *Annual Review of Sociology* 9: 527–53.

Jenkins, J. Craig, and Charles Perrow. 1977. "Insurgency of the Powerless: Farm Worker Movements (1946–1972)." *American Sociological Review* 42 (2): 249–68.

Marotta, Toby. 1981. *The Politics of Homosexuality*. Boston: Houghton Mifflin.

McAdam, Doug. 1982. *Political Process and the Development of Black Insurgency, 1930–1970*. Chicago: University of Chicago Press.

Melucci, Alberto. 1989. *Nomads of the Present*. London: Hutchinson Radius.

Morris, Aldon D. 1984. *The Origins of the Civil Rights Movement: Black Communities Organizing for Change*. New York: Free Press.

——. 1992. "Political Consciousness and Collective Action." Pp. 351–73 in *Frontiers in Social Movement Theory*, edited by Aldon D. Morris and Carol McClurg Mueller. New Haven, Conn.: Yale University Press.

Polletta, Francesca. 1994. "Strategy and Identity in 1960s Black Protest." *Research in Social Movements, Conflicts and Change* 17: 85–114.

Scheer, Robert. 1970. "Editor's note to 'The Biography of Huey P. Newton' by Bobby Seale in *Ramparts*." Pp. 202–6 in *The Movement toward a New America: The Beginnings of a Long Revolution*, edited by Mitchell Goodman. New York: United Church Press and Alfred A. Knopf.

Seidman, Steven. 1993. "Identity and Politics in a 'Postmodern' Gay Culture: Some Historical and Conceptual Notes." Pp. 105–42 in *Fear of a Queer Planet: Queer Politics and Social*

Theory, edited by Michael Warner. Minneapolis: University of Minnesota Press.

Tarrow, Sidney. 1989. *Struggle, Politics, and Reform: Collective Action, Social Movements and Cycles of Protest.* Ithaca, N.Y.: Cornell University Press.

Tarrow, Sidney. 1994. *Power in Movement: Social Movements, Collective Action and Politics.* New York: Cambridge University Press.

Taylor, Verta, and Nicole C. Raeburn. 1995. "Identity Politics as High-Risk Activism: Career Consequences for Lesbian, Gay, and Bisexual Sociologists." *Social Problems* 42 (2): 252–73.

Taylor, Verta, and Nancy E. Whittier. 1992. "Collective Identity in Social Movement Communities; Lesbian Feminist Mobilization." Pp. 104–29 in *Frontiers in Social Movement Theory*, edited by Aldon D. Morris and Carol McClurg Mueller. New Haven, Conn.: Yale University Press.

Tilly, Charles. 1978. *From Mobilization to Revolution.* Reading, Mass.: Addison Wesley.

Touraine, Alain. 1981. *The Voice and the Eye: An Analysis of Social Movements.* Cambridge: Cambridge University Press.

Turner, Ralph, and L. Killian. 1972. *Collective Behavior.* Englewood Cliffs, N.J.: Prentice-Hall.

Williams, Rhys H. 1995. "Constructing the Public Good: Social Movements and Cultural Resources." *Social Problems* 42 (1): 124–44.

26 Armed Struggle in the South African Anti-Apartheid Movement

Gay Seidman

An odd silence marks recent discussions of social movements. If writers in the past sometimes glorified armed struggle, treating it as the highest stage of resistance to colonial authority (Fanon 1968), in the last twenty years social movement theorists have generally avoided the subject entirely. Recent social movement analysts appear reluctant to engage directly with movements' use of violent tactics, remaining silent about the interplay between violent and nonviolent tactics, or about how the clandestine presence of armed activists might affect processes within a larger social movement. With rare exceptions, recent social movement analysts fail to ask a glaringly obvious question: what difference does the adoption of armed struggle make to the internal dynamics of above-ground social movements?

Nowhere is the silence around violence more deafening than in discussions of South Africa's anti-apartheid movement of the 1980s. All too frequently, the anti-apartheid movement is presented as a victory for peaceful protest, as if the movement directly paralleled the mainstream American civil rights movement of the late 1950s. The truth, of course, is very different: South Africa's visible popular movement was deeply entwined with a clandestine guerrilla struggle. The anti-apartheid movement was as much an anti-colonial movement for national self-determination as a civil rights movement working within an existing legal framework. In South Africa, the armed struggle played a key role: it attracted popular support to the anti-apartheid movement, it demonstrated the persistence of resistance to white supremacy despite repression, and it served as a complicated badge of commitment for anti-apartheid activists.

[...]

Social movement theorists tend to treat armed struggle either as the unproblematic extension of ordinary social movement processes (McAdam, Tarrow, and Tilly 2001), or conversely, as a pathological effect of competition or decline within social movements (Braungart and Braungart 1992; della Porta and Tarrow 1986). Several recent studies of clandestine movements in industrialized countries see the shift to armed struggle as both cause and symptom of movement decline, as isolated small networks of activists move away from their communities and become distant from above-ground activists (della Porta 1992; della Porta 1995; Moyano 1992; Neidhardt 1992). Even when social movement analysts consider the possibility that clandestine activists might sustain links to above-ground social movements, they generally suggest that the very fact of working underground prompts activists to privilege military concerns over popular mobilization, thereby undermining the possibility that clandestine activists could retain leadership positions in open social movements.

Perhaps reflecting that theoretical vision, many scholars of South Africa try to fit the anti-apartheid movement into the framework of Western social movement theory—a framework that focuses on the mobilization of popular protest, ignoring questions of recruitment to clandestine networks, military supply, and training, or how activists'

A Chronology of the South African Anti-Apartheid Movement

1912: the Native National Congress is founded, later renamed the African National Congress (ANC)

1913–1914: civil disobedience campaign led by Indian activist Mohandas Gandhi

1948: the National Party takes power and enacts policy of apartheid ("separateness") aimed at continued white domination of the black majority

1950: the Group Areas Act segregates blacks and whites; the multiracial Communist Party is banned

1952: the ANC begins a campaign of civil disobedience—the Defiance Campaign—led by Nelson Mandela; over 8000 are arrested

1955: the multiracial Congress of the People adopts the Freedom Charter, based on the UN Universal Declaration of Human Rights; its signers (including Mandela) are later charged with treason, but eventually acquitted

1959: the Pan-Africanist Congress (PAC) splits from the ANC over the issue of collaborating with whites

1960: protests against the "pass laws" (requiring blacks to carry passbooks to regulate their movement); 69 black demonstrators are killed at Sharpeville and thousands are arrested; the ANC and PAC are banned and go underground

1961: South Africa leaves the British Commonwealth; Mandela and activists from the ANC and Communist Party establish a military wing, *Umkhonto we Sizwe* ("Spear of the Nation"), which launches a sabotage campaign; the PAC also establishes a military wing

1962–1963: Mandela and other ANC and *Umkhonto we Sizwe* leaders are arrested

1964: Mandela and seven other ANC leaders are sentenced to life imprisonment

1970s: over 3 million blacks are forcibly resettled in "homelands"

1976: Soweto uprising; over 600 people are killed in clashes between black protesters and security forces; some flee to ANC camps in nearby African countries

1977: Steve Biko, leader of the "Black Consciousness" movement, dies in police custody; thousands attend his funeral; the UN enacts a mandatory arms embargo against South Africa

1984–1989: general uprising in black townships; government declares a state of emergency

1984: Anglican Bishop Desmond Tutu is awarded the Nobel Peace Prize

1986: South African military attacks ANC camps in Botswana, Zambia, and Zimbabwe; Dutch Reformed Church declares apartheid an error

1989: F. W. de Klerk becomes president and secretly meets with Mandela; many ANC activists are released from prison; public facilities are desegregated

1990: Mandela is released after 27 years in prison; the ANC is unbanned and declares an end to armed struggle

1991: start of multi-party talks; de Klerk repeals remaining apartheid laws, including Group Areas Act; international sanctions against South Africa are lifted; bloody clashes occur between the ANC and the Zulu Inkatha movement

1993: Mandela and de Klerk receive Nobel Peace Prize

1994: the ANC wins South Africa's first elections based on universal suffrage; Mandela becomes president (1994–1999); South Africa's Commonwealth membership is restored, and South Africa rejoins the United Nations after a 20-year absence

1996: Truth and Reconciliation Commission, led by Archbishop Tutu, begins hearings on human rights abuses committed by former government and liberation movements during the apartheid era

involvement in armed struggle or underground networks affects their participation in public debate. Generally, descriptions of anti-apartheid activism stress the role of student groups, political activists, unions, and women's groups, rarely mentioning the way these groups interacted and cooperated with armed activists within the national liberation movement. Some descriptions virtually ignore the armed struggle (Marx 1991); others mention only its symbolic importance, relegating to footnotes any mention of concrete links between clandestine ANC strategies and open tactics (Murray 1994;

Seidman 1994; Wood 2000). Even the rare description which acknowledges that armed struggle mattered (Younis 2000) generally mentions it almost apologetically, neglecting questions about the impact of choices of military targets or sources of military supply and training on movement processes, or how armed struggle might have been consciously integrated with popular mobilization.

The failure to fully engage the clandestine side of the anti-apartheid movement involves a theoretical parallel: the silence around South Africa's armed struggle echoes a broader silence in contemporary social movement theory, whose recent focus on peaceful mass protest virtually excludes or dismisses all other forms of mobilization. Especially for anti-colonial movements, however, a broadly-supported armed struggle introduces a host of complex social processes: the construction of a "national" project across disparate ethnic groups or social classes; the decision to take up arms and the mobilization of popular support for an impossible undertaking; the problems of maintaining discipline and control in a guerrilla army; the logistics involved in providing supplies and infiltrating guerrillas; the relation between guerrillas and local populations.

[...]

Practical and Ethical Considerations

Obviously, much of the deafening silence about the dynamics of armed struggle stems from immediate concerns about safety and practicality, both for researchers and their subjects. Above all, while an authoritarian regime is still in place, it is almost impossible to research the dynamics of armed struggle in any objective way. Access to clandestine activities is obviously difficult; researchers considered sympathetic enough to gain access to clandestine armed-struggle processes are unlikely to be able then to claim objectivity.

But even beyond the access problem, ethical concerns limit any researcher's ability to talk openly about armed struggle. In South Africa, for example, naming any links between popular collective mobilization and armed struggle during the 1980s would have seriously endangered participants in each, giving an authoritarian regime access to information it could use against its opponents, and an excuse to ban above-ground popular organizations because of their links to clandestine guerrilla activities.

Specific problems confronted foreign researchers who wanted to explore the ANC's clandestine role within the above-ground popular movement, especially within the legal and open coalition called the United Democratic Front (UDF) during the 1980s. First, of course, the government denied visas to anyone who expressed an interest in underground ANC activity or clandestine links. In the mid-1980s, for example, Pretoria refused a research visa to an American researcher because he said he hoped to write a history of white activism within the non-racial movement—and then, the American Fulbright committee withdrew promised funding because he could not enter South Africa.

But even more frequently, foreign researchers were kept in the dark by their South African informants. Of course, many South Africans were themselves unaware of the presence of people with clandestine ANC links in above-ground activist groups. White South African progressives, who often served as important social and political links for outside researchers because of their academic connections, were perhaps especially likely to be kept out of clandestine loops; South Africa's linguistic diversity and racial divisions made it relatively easy for those activists aware of clandestine links—activists who were generally though not invariably black—to restrict knowledge of underground activities. But even activists or South African academics who were "witting" were unlikely to tell outside researchers about any illegal connections they might know about. They simply lied, protecting the clandestine links between armed networks and open, legal groups. By the late 1980s, the hints were becoming ever broader, but even then, most above-ground activists continued to maintain a plausible facade, distancing their organizations from any activities that could jeopardize their group. One prominent activist who served as a key informant for an American social scientist writing about the "internal" struggle for freedom in the 1980s, for example, explicitly denied that the anti-apartheid UDF had any ANC links; but when the ANC was unbanned in 1990, that same informant was immediately named ANC treasurer, a trusted position that supports his claim that he had been working with clandestine networks for years (VK, interview, Harare 1989).

Nevertheless, the practical problems of studying armed struggle can be exaggerated. There are many ways that researchers might discuss armed struggle without endangering informants, and without going into any details about specific links between "internal" protests and guerrilla activity. In the South African case, two examples demonstrate that the ANC was not, in fact, completely off-limits. American political scientist Stephen Davis (1987) was able to research and write about the ANC's guerrilla structures, although he was unable to link them directly to "internal" activities in the 1980s. Even more impressively, South African sociologist Jacklyn Cock (1991) was able to complete the research for an excellent book on the gender dynamics of the ANC's guerrilla forces at a time when a conviction for "furthering the aims of a banned organization" could have landed her in jail.

The problem is not simply that researchers were worried about protecting sources, although those concerns were very real. The deeper difficulty lies in our inability to incorporate questions about the dynamics of armed struggle and clandestine networks into the theoretical prisms through which we view social movements. Some of that silence can be attributed to the Cold War: for decades, many theorists felt little need to ask how armed struggle worked, or how it mattered, because the Cold War seemed to explain everything. In the context of the great conflict between the communist East and the capitalist West, questions about the local dynamics of armed conflict were overshadowed and virtually irrelevant. In the South African case, the fact that the ANC received weapons and military training from the Soviet bloc often defined researchers' vision of the armed struggle. Western researchers who saw Africa as a Cold War battleground tended to support the South African government against the Communist threat, viewing apartheid's racial exclusion as a lesser evil (e.g., Crocker and Lewis 1979). Even Western researchers who opposed apartheid frequently dismissed the ANC's guerrillas as irrelevant, or feared that Soviet-influenced agitators might subvert the anti-apartheid movement's noble goals (Murray 1987).

The Cold War apparently meant that researchers faced a dichotomous choice in their approach to armed struggle. Those who supported a guerrilla movement's aims frequently emphasized its indigenous character, naturalizing the participation of local racially-defined communities, ignoring divisions and conflicts within the "national" support base, and steadfastly ignoring evidence of external support for specific strategies or specific definitions of "national liberation." Those who were less sympathetic, on the other hand, tended to emphasize the role of outside support and guidance, and in the process, to overlook questions about why and how local participants were drawn into the struggle, or what kind of support the "armed struggle" received internally.

In the South African case, at least, this dichotomous vision impoverished our description and understanding of the dynamics of popular protests as well as of the guerrilla struggle itself. Throughout the 1970s and 1980s, the link between armed struggle and township protests begged discussion, but researchers consistently avoided asking questions, refusing to consider obvious evidence that the popular resistance inside the country was directly aware of, and concerned with, guerrilla campaigns, or that the ANC's persistent popularity stemmed precisely from its engagement in an almost-suicidal armed struggle.

Throughout the 1980s, although street protests frequently included symbols and references to the armed struggle, journalists or researchers rarely mentioned them or explored the clandestine relationship between above-ground protest and clandestine activism. Symbols of the armed struggle pervaded anti-apartheid protests: songs and slogans celebrated guerrilla efforts, while signs welcoming "Comrade Joe" Slovo and his MK cadres were as common as cardboard cut-outs of bazookas at political events. Journalists in the 1980s consistently described the *toyi-toyi*—the high-stepping dance performed at township funerals and protests throughout the 1980s—as a traditional African dance; but whatever the truth of its origins, in the mid-1980s activists in several different locations claimed that they danced the *toyi-toyi* in explicit imitation of guerrilla military training exercises (interviews, Johannesburg and Durban 1987). When activists' coffins were draped in the ANC colors, everyone understood that the dead person had been part of what activists referred to as the ANC's "underground structures."

Similarly, researchers rarely acknowledged the importance of specific guerrilla attacks in mobilizing popular protests, or explored how township activists learned of these events despite newspaper censorship, or how township youths contacted underground ANC networks before they left the country to join the guerrilla struggle. We never asked what resources flowed from the external ANC leadership to the "grassroots" groups inside the country, and what other links existed between clandestine networks and above-ground popular protest—or if we did, we stayed silent about the answers in our academic work, hoping to protect activists or to preserve the cover of an appropriately dispassionate stance.

But surely now some of these questions can be reopened. In the aftermath of decolonization and the Cold War, it should be possible to go back to re-examine some of these processes as a basis for better understanding the legacies of armed struggle and their implications for post-colonial politics. How did popular movements decide to take up strategies involving armed struggle? How did activists mobilize support for that decision or quash opposition to it? What were the organizational links between guerrillas and their supporters? How do national liberation movements manage to garner resources from impoverished colonial populations and sustain popular support in the face of repeated defeats by superior forces? How were strategic choices made about targets and campaigns of armed struggle, and what were the implications of those choices for post-colonial politics?

Blurring the Line

Aside from practical considerations, however, the fact that so many researchers have avoided discussing the recurrent evidence of popular South African support for, and involvement in, the "external" armed struggle—from the township songs and slogans calling on the ANC's guerrilla army to march across the border, to the heroic stature accorded leaders of the ANC's armed wing, *Umkhonto we Sizwe* or Spear of the Nation—begs further consideration. Some of the reluctance to deal with armed struggle, I suspect, comes from an unconscious moral distinction, between "good" popular grassroots mobilization and "bad"—or at least ambiguous—armed struggle: as researchers, do we perhaps fear tarnishing the moral righteousness of the anti-apartheid struggle if we admit that some of the heroic popular struggles of the townships might have been linked directly to clandestine networks involved in armed attacks? Throughout the 1980s, Amnesty International refused to adopt Nelson Mandela or any other South African convicted of belonging to the ANC as a prisoner of conscience, because of the ANC's persistent support for armed struggle; has a similar distinction unconsciously shaded descriptions of the anti-apartheid movement? Most researchers in the late twentieth century feel far more ambivalent about armed struggle than they do about unarmed protestors in the street. In contrast to the way some Western student protestors glorified anti-imperialist guerrilla struggles in the late 1960s, most social movement analysts writing after the early 1980s seem to be drawn, consciously or not, to idealize non-violent popular mobilization, linking it in some vague way to Gandhian non-violence or to the passive resistance of the American civil rights movement.

At least in the case of South Africa's anti-apartheid movement, the lines between different types of collective action may be more blurred than this distinction implies. As is well known, the turn to armed struggle in South Africa came after several decades in which anti-apartheid protests seemed to have had little impact. Passive resistance relies heavily on appeals to the oppressor's humanity; by 1960, many South African activists believed the apartheid regime would not listen. The South African government—elected in 1948 by less than half the electorate, in an election basically restricted to the 20 percent of South Africans legally classified as white—was firmly committed to maintaining white domination. The government viewed as subjects the 80 percent of South Africans who were not racially classified "white," refusing to recognize their claims to political rights or inclusion. [...]

In the early 1950s, anti-apartheid activists sought to imitate Gandhi's recent successes in India. In 1952, thousands of volunteers joined the ANC's Defiance Campaign, refusing to obey segregationist rules at bus stops, train stations, post offices and so on, generally in an orderly and non-violent manner. In terms of mass mobilization, the campaign was a huge success. Eight thousand people were arrested between June and November, 1952; popular enthusiasm for the campaign swelled the ANC's membership, from about 7000 to about 100,000. In terms of political achievement, however, the campaign was a dismal failure: the government made no concessions, and took firm steps to crush the campaign. Thousands of volunteers were jailed, and when jails grew overcrowded, the government rushed through new laws allowing judges to sentence resisters to floggings as well as to three-year jail terms. Meetings were outlawed, leaders were placed under house arrest. Drawing on the language of the Cold War, the government redefined resistance to racial segregation as communism, and then charged the campaign's leaders with treason; repression disorganized resistance and immobilized the campaign (Kuper 1957; Lodge 1983: 33–66; Mandela 1994: 176–227).

Over the next decade, repeated attempts to engage in non-violent tactics—bus boycotts, demonstrations, petitions, pass-burning campaigns—provoked violent reactions. The 1960 massacre outside the Sharpeville police station, where 69 people were killed and 178 wounded, shot in the back as they tried to run from a police attack, symbolized the government's refusal to permit any kind of peaceful protest. In an earlier era, South African prime minister Jan Smuts released Gandhi from jail when he led non-violent demonstrations. After 1948, however, South Africa's leaders explicitly rejected compassion; regretfully, a prominent South African proponent of non-violence concluded that it seemed unlikely that South Africa's rulers could "be converted by extreme suffering when they are so strongly confirmed in the ideologies of white domination" (Kuper 1957: 94).

Faced with an intransigent regime at home, South Africans looked beyond their borders for help. From the early 1960s, black South Africans repeatedly appealed to the international community to impose economic sanctions, arguing that South Africans would take up arms unless political and economic pressure from the outside offered a peaceful way to undermine the powerful and repressive apartheid state. But again, South Africans found no audience. In India and in the American South,

London and Washington had each sought to avoid embarrassment on the international stage, intervening on the side of resisters to overcome the intransigence of local colonial officials, states' rights advocates and white elites. But by the mid-1960s, no Western power had direct colonial or federal links to Pretoria, and no Western power appeared to feel much moral responsibility for ending apartheid. From 1960 to 1990, Britain and the United States routinely vetoed efforts at the United Nations to impose sanctions on South Africa, allowing only a loophole-riddled arms embargo in 1976. [...]

In the intervening decades, however, anti-apartheid leaders argued they could no longer ask their followers to risk their lives in unarmed confrontation. In the aftermath of the Sharpeville massacre, when the government arrested 20,000 political activists and banned political parties that demanded political rights for all South Africans, anti-apartheid leaders concluded they had no choice but to establish armed wings. Despite the arrest in the early 1960s of most major anti-apartheid figures—including Nelson Mandela, a popular political organizer who served as the ANC's first military commander—the ANC managed over the next fifteen years to establish a network of cells and arms caches, linked to camps of guerrillas located farther north, in Angola, Tanzania, and Uganda.

It is important to place the ANC's "turn to armed struggle" in its historical context. Discussions in South Africa were clearly influenced by prominent examples of contemporary nationalist struggles, including Algeria and Kenya; parallel discussions were going on in nationalist movements in Angola, the then-Congo, Zimbabwe, and Mozambique. Obviously, the willingness of Eastern European countries and Libya to support armed nationalist movements with resources and training helped persuade ANC leaders that this turn was a logical one. Conversely, in the months immediately after the Sharpeville massacre, the decision by U.S. banks to extend a very large loan to shore up South Africa's capital reserves undermined those ANC activists who preferred appeals to the West. But again, these are questions that future researchers will have to ask: what were the internal dynamics of this discussion? How did activists understand the choices facing them? How did leaders evaluate their chances of success through armed struggle, and how were opponents of this strategy either persuaded or excluded? These questions have pragmatic correlates: how were decisions made about specific alliances and types of military training, or about sites for guerrilla camps? Who was recruited for armed struggle, and how, and through what networks were they spirited out of South Africa? What were their experiences in traveling north through different parts of the continent and in training camps and schools spread across Eastern Europe, and how did these experiences shape their vision of South Africa's future?

In terms of social movement theory, perhaps the most important question revolves around how the existence of an exiled guerrilla army affected popular protests inside the country. Especially as decolonization proceeded down the continent, politically aware South Africans recognized both the difficulties confronting a struggling guerrilla army, and the possibility that some day, guerrilla campaigns might intensify. For example, although the 1976 Soweto uprising was of course primarily a protest against Afrikaans as medium of instruction, student protestors at the time also celebrated the recent collapse of Portuguese control in Angola and Mozambique, a collapse which removed colonial buffer zones which had protected South Africa's borders from guerrilla incursion. Thousands of black South Africans had left the country after 1960, living for years in guerrilla camps in the forests of independent African countries, or traveling to Eastern Europe for military training. From the late 1960s on, small groups of ANC soldiers tried to infiltrate through Angola, Mozambique, or Rhodesia, but they were usually imprisoned or killed by colonial police before they even reached South Africa. In 1976, student protestors recognized new possibilities for guerrilla infiltration—possibilities that were given substance when thousands of young South Africans left the country to join the ANC's "external" army.

By the early 1980s, the ANC's armed wing could claim to have attained some real visibility (Davis 1987), especially after some of its most dramatic attacks: the 1977 down-town shoot-out between South African police and Solomon Mahlangu, a student protestor who had left the country for military training after 1976, returning with a highly-symbolic AK-47; the 1980 attack on a coal-into-oil refinery, Sasol, which created a three-day smoke-plume that could be seen from Johannesburg; a 1983 explosion that destroyed the South African Air Force intelligence headquarters; or the 1984 rocket attack on an army camp near Pretoria. None of these attacks came close to bringing down the state, but they provided physical evidence of a tangible *potential* threat to the regime—reinforcing the sense, as Nadime Gordimer (1984) put it, that "something out there" represented a shadowy threat to the long-term future of white supremacy.

It did not hurt the ANC's popularity, either within the country or internationally, that the ANC's armed wing was believed to follow unusually principled rules. Where guerrillas linked to the PLO, for example, chose to attack civilians in Israel/Palestine, and to attack Israeli targets outside of the Middle East, the ANC leadership claimed it pursued a more restrained approach. From the early 1960s, South African guerrillas were supposed to concentrate on sabotage and military attacks, avoiding civilian targets. In a deeply segregated society, it would have been easy to kill random whites. Segregated white schools, segregated movie theaters, segregated shopping centers meant that if white deaths were the only goal, potential targets could be found everywhere. But Oliver Tambo, the ANC's leader in exile, insisted that a Christian like himself could not condone a single unnecessary death. Only a handful of ANC attacks caused civilian deaths, white or black. For the most part, ANC guerrillas limited their targets to military installations and economic sabotage, to electric pylons, military installations, power plants—and when they did not, the ANC leadership could always deny responsibility, since guerrillas cut off from their base might be described as acting outside instructions.

While highly principled, this strategy was not particularly successful militarily: despite the rhetoric, most anti-apartheid activists concluded by the mid-1970s that in a highly urbanized, industrialized society, facing a well-equipped and sophisticated enemy army, a guerrilla insurrection could not succeed. Instead, anti-apartheid activists put their energy into political organizing, bringing people together around local issues, and looking for ways to protest which would not provoke immediate repression. [...] By 1976, more than half of black South Africans lived in urban areas and worked in industrial settings—sites which offered new possibilities for organization. Especially as more experienced activists began to be released from the jail terms which began in the early 1960s, they began to look at how black students could paralyze urban school systems, black workers could paralyze production, black communities could demand better urban services. Like poor people elsewhere, anti-apartheid activists discovered the power of disruption: black South Africans learned that by mobilizing collective protests at school, at work, or in segregated black townships, they could disrupt the smooth functioning of apartheid, through boycotts, strikes, and demonstrations—without exposing individual leaders to arrest, or provoking immediate police attacks.

Through the 1970s and 1980s, South Africa moved into a period of rolling insurgency. In 1973, a scattering of illegal wildcat strikes among black factory workers showed that some employers would rather negotiate than fire and replace striking workers; by 1985, South Africa had one of the world's most militant labor movements, and employers often begged police to release trade unionists so they could have someone with whom to negotiate. Similarly, the 1976 Soweto uprising revealed the capacity of high school students to disrupt township life; by the late 1980s, black high schools and universities were regularly disrupted by boycotts, to such an extent that employers and even white government officials expressed concerns about future shortages of skilled workers. From the early 1980s, township activists began to organize community groups around local issues, ranging from bus fares to high rents; by the mid-1980s, these township "civic associations" organized rent and consumer boycotts, funerals for activists killed by police, and other forms of protest. In all these cases, activists focused on local issues; but beneath all the various demands and tactics was a common demand for political rights, democracy, and human dignity (Marx 1991; Price 1991; Seidman 1994). As these community protests escalated, most ANC activists came to believe any real prospect of bringing down the South African government by force had been postponed indefinitely. By the early 1980s, the ANC was putting most of its resources and energy into supporting popular mobilization in townships, with clandestine networks linking activists across the country with the ANC leadership-in-exile.

Yet although most published accounts continue to treat these unions, community organizations, and student groups as strictly separate from the ANC's military efforts, the links between above-ground protests and clandestine guerrilla campaigns were far stronger than activists or researchers generally acknowledged at the time. Through the mid-1980s, the ANC leadership called its attacks "armed propaganda," describing their aim in terms of raising black South Africans' morale, rather than a full-scale war. Public accounts regularly understated the symbolic importance of even small guerrilla actions—or even the way the well-publicized capture and trial of yet another ANC guerrilla often seemed to reinforce activists' determination. [...]

Guerrilla attacks held a prominent place in the culture of the anti-apartheid movement. In the 1980s, although most ANC activists had abandoned the idea that a guerrilla movement would ever manage a military overthrow of the highly organized South African state, many township activists' commitment to armed struggle—and respect for those who participated actively in it—was almost visceral. Almost certainly, at least some part of Nelson Mandela's extraordinary popularity stems from his role as first commander of "MK"—as *Umkhonto*, the ANC's armed wing, was popularly nicknamed. Twenty-seven years later, Mandela garnered even more admiration in the townships when the government revealed that Mandela had repeatedly rejected government offers to release him from prison if only he would renounce armed struggle (Sparks 1994: 49). Even when ANC resources had shifted to emphasize popular organization and protests over military attack, it retained its rhetorical commitment to armed struggle, describing its strategy as one that used "the hammer of armed struggle on the anvil of mass action." Indeed, as the anti-apartheid movement moved into a phase marked by popular unrest in 1985, the exiled ANC leadership announced intensification of its guerrilla efforts—a shift from what it called "armed propaganda" to "people's war." Even government data suggest that this announcement was in fact followed by a marked increase in attacks involving landmines, hand-grenades, or AK-47s (SAIRR 1986: 542).

Of course, few South Africans ever participated actively in the armed struggle, or were even touched by it directly. Moreover, it will be difficult to tease out retroactively how many people really participated, or who knew even sketchy details of underground activity. The government routinely rejected any distinction between peaceful support for the ANC and clandestine involvement, construing even so mild an act as scraping "Free Nelson Mandela" on the side of an enamel mug as support for armed struggle. Student activists, trade unionists, community organizers were all detained without charges, tortured, and convicted under security legislation that treated them as "terrorists." Throughout the 1980s, "above-ground" activists routinely denied any connection to illegal organizations in hopes of finding some legal space in which to mobilize anti-apartheid resistance.

Ironically, however, just as security police insisted on blurring the line between different kinds of anti-apartheid resistance, many black South Africans also considered these categories intertwined: the struggle against apartheid, as activists often repeated, continued on many fronts. And the symbolic importance of the armed struggle even for those anti-apartheid activists who retained a strong moral commitment to non-violence should not be underestimated. Even someone as explicitly pacifist as Archbishop Desmond Tutu avoided condemnation of those who had chosen armed struggle. Throughout the 1980s, the ANC was regularly named by over half of black South Africans as the party they would vote for if allowed to vote, partly because of its history as the oldest anti-apartheid organization, but also, almost certainly, because of a popular perception in black townships that the ANC embodied armed resistance to an oppressive regime.

But aside from the symbolic importance of the armed struggle, we do not yet have a clear picture of how far clandestine guerrilla networks extended, nor of the role played by activists linked to clandestine ANC networks in coordinating mass mobilization. Many of the "non-violent" protests of the 1980s were coordinated by activists who were secretly linked to the ANC, and whose understanding of the anti-apartheid strategy embraced the armed struggle—even if they personally chose to focus on work in unions, community groups, or other forms of collective action. Many anti-apartheid activists avoided learning anything about guerrilla activities, hoping to protect mass protest and themselves from the kind of repression invited by participation in guerrilla activities, and to protect clandestine guerrilla networks by reducing their visibility to the police. But some seepage was inevitable: a guerrilla needing help, including shelter or money, would frequently turn first to township activists whose statements suggested they might have ANC loyalties, even if they had no direct involvement in the armed wing, and frequently, those activists responded with support and aid.

Perhaps more importantly, through the 1980s ANC military strategists frequently planned attacks that would be popularly understood in terms of links to on-going mass mobilization. "Armed propaganda" boosted activists' morale, and reminded them that an army of clandestine guerrillas might already have infiltrated the country from their bases farther north on the African continent. As the popular uprising intensified after 1984, even smaller, less-dramatic attacks had an immediate impact on the conversations in union meetings, church groups, and student groups the following day, raising morale among activists and providing proof that resistance would continue despite repression. Small attacks made large impressions when they were linked to popular struggles: where police had cordoned off a township, a postoffice might be hit by a hand-grenade; in the middle of a bus boycott, an empty bus might be bombed. Press censorship meant that these attacks were rarely reported in the national press, but activists' networks spread the news rapidly, often adding exaggerated details for good measure. [...]

As future historians re-examine the relationship between the "internal" opposition, the ANC's political leadership, and the ANC's military wing, they will also have to explore links between ANC underground networks and the violence that often accompanied township protests during the 1980s—episodes which should not be seen as somehow tarnishing the moral claims of the anti-apartheid movement, but rather as underscoring how problematic it can be to grade political protest against an absolutist moral score card. The strategy of disrupting apartheid from below required that nearly all black South Africans participate in campaigns entailing personal risk and daily difficulties; strikes, consumer boycotts, bus and rent boycotts, were generally called by groups affiliated to the UDF, but were often enforced by groups of young militants who identified explicitly with the ANC. Efforts to initiate and extend such campaigns often provoked violent conflict between black South Africans who thought ending apartheid was worth any sacrifice, and those who felt that in the short term at least, they had more to lose than to gain. While nationally-visible leaders often dismissed acts like "necklacing"—placing a burning tire on a suspected informer—as the work of police provocateurs, such behavior was often widely condoned in townships. This kind of violent enforcement of mass mobilization was probably not centrally planned, but it reflected and reinforced the ANC's strategy of making the townships ungovernable—a coordinated strategy that underscores the importance of re-examining the role of a clandestine network of activists linked across the country to each other and to the ANC leadership-in-exile.

The Impact of Armed Struggle

Almost certainly, South Africa's armed struggle was more important in shaping the "above-ground" anti-apartheid movement than is generally acknowledged in contemporary scholarly analysis, and its legacies continue to play out in post-apartheid politics. In this section, I briefly suggest some ways in which a more integrated understanding of the anti-apartheid movement would alter our vision of the movement's internal dynamics. I then suggest that our silence about armed struggles in the past may undermine our ability to understand South African contention in the present.

A more integrated vision of the anti-apartheid movement would rearrange any description of the internal dynamics of above-ground protest. Evidence, of course, remains sketchy; if, on the one hand, the legacy of repression and danger makes most activists—and even more, most scholars—nervous about admitting knowledge of clandestine activities even twenty years later, there remains the converse danger that respondents will exaggerate their past links to underground activities. But there is significant evidence suggesting that clarifying the role of armed campaigns will require that we re-examine the anti-apartheid movement as a whole—specifically, re-examining the networks on which the anti-apartheid movement was built, the resources on which anti-apartheid groups relied, and the culture, identity, and emotions involved in mobilizing resistance to the apartheid regime.

There is a great deal of evidence suggesting that activists' persistent support for the armed struggle played an important role in the associational networks of the anti-apartheid movement more broadly—not only in terms of recruiting young activists to leave the country for military training and supporting guerrillas when they returned, but also in terms of linking activists' strategies in different parts of the country to overall ANC strategy. Often built around veteran ANC activists or prominent activist families, these clandestine networks were frequently involved in coordinating campaigns in different parts of the country, and perhaps even more importantly, in coordinating guerrilla attacks with above-ground campaigns. Written descriptions of open protest meetings rarely mention the frequency with which speakers would allude to their participation in clandestine networks: by the late 1980s it was not unusual for activists to indirectly acknowledge links to illegal cells by opening their remarks with references to "the line," indicating special knowledge and implying direct communication with the exiled ANC leadership.

Needless to say, many of these activists probably exaggerated reality, since the very fact of clandestinity meant that most listeners could not check the claimants' true status; moreover, activists claiming access to "the line" often contradicted each other, since there were many different voices and opinions even within the networks. Nevertheless, especially in UDF groups or in a few specifically ANC-linked unions, individuals' links to clandestine networks often gave a special status to their knowledge or suggestions.

That status was probably invisible to most outside researchers, revealed only if the activist was arrested for involvement in military activities; but it may well have been known or guessed by many listeners in township groups. Glenn Adler, an American researcher in the 1980s, has written movingly of his realization that a key informant, Themba Dyassi, was widely known to fellow unionists as a footsoldier in a clandestine MK cell. Apparently, the union shop stewards asked Dyassi to be Adler's first interviewee, to investigate Adler while Adler interviewed him. Although Dyassi and other MK members in the factory held no formal role in the union leadership—in a conscious effort to insulate the union from the legal repression that would have accompanied any discovery of union ties to MK—their status among politically aware activists in the factory was linked to their status in clandestine networks (Adler 1992; Adler 1994).

I do not mean to suggest that the links between underground networks and above-ground groups were entirely clear or straightforward: tensions plagued above-ground groups, revolving around their relation to clandestine networks, their relationship to activists known to be involved in illegal activities, and the extent to which their organizational strategies should reflect specifically local issues as well as national ones (Seekings 2000). Similarly, MK activists were constantly engaged in discussion about whether or not specific targets were appropriate, or would alienate popular sentiment (interview, TM, Botswana 1987). Perhaps now that activists can discuss their clandestine roles more openly, more researchers can re-examine the way the concerns of secret networks played out in above-ground discussions, and give a fuller picture of the interaction between clandestine and above-ground debates.

If we know little about networks, we know even less about how material resources coming from clandestine networks may have affected the anti-apartheid movement as a whole. Obviously, the military resources provided by Eastern Europe to the exiled ANC played an important role in ideological discussions within the ANC; countries that provided military support and training became special allies for the ANC, strengthening the weight of the South African Communist Party within the ANC alliance. But we have very little understanding of how clandestine resources funneled to internal, above-ground groups may have shaped strategic choices and ideological debates within the open anti-apartheid movement. In impoverished black communities, the anti-apartheid movement struggled to find money to sustain protests. Organizing in the townships required money not only for leaflets, gasoline and cars, and meeting spaces, but, especially in the repressive 1980s, for housing and feeding activists who were hiding from the police, for lawyers' fees to support detainees, for sustaining families during consumer boycotts, strikes, and stayaways. Through the early 1980s, the UDF received much of its funding from church groups and other international supporters. Some of these, like the prominent British anti-apartheid organization International Defence and Aid or the Dutch anti-apartheid movement, took advice directly from the exiled ANC about which South African groups to fund. But the UDF also received clandestine funding from the exiled ANC, sometimes smuggled into the country by the same methods used to smuggle guns and explosives (interview, FS, Botswana, 1984).

How did access to donor funds and to smuggled cash alter the dynamics of debates within above-ground groups? What difference did it make to the strategies of above-ground groups that activists linked to clandestine networks could sometimes draw on additional resources, providing support for one kind of protest organization rather than another? In the early 1980s, for example, debates over whether activists should pursue "non-racialism" compared to a separatist black consciousness approach were frequently described in purely ideological terms; but clandestine resources gave greater visibility to "Charterist," or non-racial, approaches—and probably attracted new recruits more easily to non-racial organizations than might have otherwise been the case.

Neither networks nor resources alone would have sustained township support, however, if the idea of armed struggle had not retained a place at the symbolic core of the national liberation struggle. This strong symbolic role was neither natural nor accidental: ANC-affiliated activists worked hard through the 1980s to construct a culture of support for MK's guerrillas, in which those who chose to join the armed struggle—a choice that obviously involved enormous risks and sacrifice—were often considered heroes, even by activists who explicitly avoided clandestine work. Broad public campaigns like the 1981 campaign to "Unban the Freedom Charter," which used a loophole in South Africa's press censorship to discuss the ANC's goals and strategies, were conscious efforts to promote the ANC's visibility above ground. At the same time, however, more secretive efforts built community support for the ANC's armed struggle. Above-ground activists frequently traveled, legally and illegally, to neighboring states, where they met exiled ANC activists, sharing ideas and information, and discussing strategy. Some of these meetings are described in trial transcripts, when in-country activists were charged with "furthering the aims"; but many more went unnoticed, and undiscussed in public forums. In some of these discussions—including the very visible 1982 "Culture and Resistance" conference held in Botswana, where several hundred in-country, above-ground activists met ANC exiles and each other—ANC supporters worked hard to reinforce a township discourse that treated the armed struggle as a legitimate, perhaps essential, part of the anti-apartheid movement.

At the beginning of the 1980s, the ANC was only one of several parties within the anti-apartheid movement; by 1990, it had emerged as the government's primary negotiating partner. In those rare social movement discussions that mention armed struggle, some ethnic support for armed struggle tends to be portrayed as natural (e.g., Waldmann 1992); but in the case of South Africa, the construction of community support for the ANC's guerrilla efforts was slow and painstaking. The growth of support did not reflect an innate black South African community consensus, but required movement resources and energy, and careful efforts to create a culture affirming the armed struggle.

As social movement analysts re-examine the 1980s anti-apartheid movement, perhaps we should explore more carefully how the actual armed struggle intersected with the construction of a culture of support for that struggle. In the definition of a militant national project, how and to what extent did support for the armed struggle express an oppositional national identity, challenging settler domination and racial supremacism and symbolically linking the anti-apartheid struggle to other anti-colonial struggles for self-determination?

Finally, it is worth noting that the armed struggle within the anti-apartheid movement is not important only for its historical symbolism: its legacy remains deeply embedded in Southern African politics, shaping collective memories and national aspirations as well as individual careers. Collective memories of nationalist struggles often give special place to guerrillas, as heroes and martyrs whose commitment went beyond the ordinary. Such glorification of armed struggle lends legitimacy to particular political claims in the present. It could be argued, for example, that the ANC's popular commitment to a "non-racial" ideology, which welcomes white participation, was greatly shored up by the visible participation of several key whites in the guerrilla command structure, some of whom still serve in the ANC cabinet. [...]

References

Adler, Glenn. 1992. "The Politics of Research during a Liberation Struggle: Interviewing Black Workers in South Africa," in *Subjectivity and Multiculturalism in Oral History*, ed. Ronald J. Grele. Westport, CT: Greenwood Press.

Adler, Glenn. 1994. *The Factory Belongs to All Who Work in it: Race, Class and Collective Action in the South African Motor Industry, 1967–1986*. PhD dissertation, Columbia University.

Braungart, Richard G., and Margaret M. Braungart. 1992. "From Protest to Terrorism: The Case of SDS and the Weathermen." *International Social Movement Research* 4: 45–78.

Cock, Jacklyn. 1991. *Colonels & Cadres: War and Gender in South Africa*. New York: Oxford University Press.

Crocker, Chester, and William Lewis. 1979. "Missing Opportunities in Africa." *Foreign Policy* 35: 142–161.

Davis, Stephen. 1987. *Apartheid's Rebels: Inside South Africa's Hidden War*. New Haven, CT: Yale University Press.

Della Porta, Donatella. 1992. "Introduction: On Individual Motivations in Underground Political Organizations." *International Social Movement Research* 4: 3–28.

Della Porta, Donatella. 1995. *Social Movements, Political Violence, and the State*. Cambridge: Cambridge University Press.

Della Porta, Donatella, and Sidney Tarrow, 1986. "Unwanted Children: Political Violence and the Cycle of Protest in Italy, 1966–1973." *European Journal of Political Research* 14: 607–632.

Fanon, Frantz, 1968. *The Wretched of the Earth*. Trans. Constance Farrington. New York: Grove Press.

Gordimer, Nadine. 1984. "Something Out There." *Salmagundi* 62 (Winter 1984): 118–192.

Kuper, Leo. 1971 (1957). *Passive Resistance in South Africa*. New Haven, CT: Yale University Press.

Lodge, Tom. 1983. *Black Politics in South Africa since 1945*. Johannesburg: Ravan Press.

Mandela, Nelson. 1994. *Long Walk to Freedom*. Boston: Little, Brown and Co.

Marx, Anthony. 1991. *Lessons of Struggle*. Oxford: Oxford University Press.

McAdam, Doug, Sidney Tarrow, and Charles Tilly. 2001. *Dynamics of Contention*. Cambridge: Cambridge University Press.

Moyano, Maria Jose. 1992. "Going Underground in Argentina: A Look at the Founders of a Guerrilla Movement." *International Social Movement Research* 4: 105–129.

Murray, Martin. J. 1987. *South Africa: Time of Agony, Time of Destiny*. London: Verso.

——. 1994. *Revolution Deferred: The Painful Birth of Post-Apartheid South Africa*. London: Verso.

Neidhardt, Freidhelm. 1992. "Left-Wing and Right-Wing Terrorist Groups: A Comparison for the German Case." *International Social Movement Research* 4: 215–235.

Price, Robert. 1991. *The Apartheid State in Crisis: Political Transformation in South Africa, 1975–1990*. New York: Oxford University Press.

Seekings, Jeremy. 2000. "The Development of Strategic Thought in South Africa's Civic Movements, 1977–90," in Glenn Adler and Johnny Steinberg (eds.), *From Comrades to Citizens: The South African Civics Movement and the Transition to Democracy*. London: Macmillan.

Seidman, Gay. 1994. *Manufacturing Militance: Workers' Movements in Brazil and South Africa, 1970–1985*. Berkeley: University of California Press.

South African Institute of Race Relations (SAIRR). 1986. *Race Relations Survey 1985*. Johannesburg: Institute of Race Relations.

Sparks, Alistair. 1994. *Tomorrow is Another Country*. Johannesburg: Struik Books.

Waldmann, Peter. 1992. "Ethnic and Sociorevolutionary Terrorism: A Comparison of Structures. *International Social Movement Research* 4: 237–257.

Wood, Elisabeth. 2000. *Forging Democracy from Below*. Cambridge: Cambridge University Press.

Younis, Mona, 2000. *Liberation and Democratization: The South African and Palestinian National Movements*. Minneapolis: University of Minnesota Press.

Biography – Nelson Mandela: "I am prepared to die"

Nelson Mandela must be reckoned as one of the greatest leaders—real and symbolic—of the twentieth century. Mandela came to lead the movement against white supremacy (known as apartheid or "separateness") in South Africa. He spent 27 years in prison for those efforts, becoming a symbol of defiance against injustice. Upon his release from prison, Mandela helped negotiate South Africa's transition to democracy. He won the Nobel Peace Prize and became South Africa's first president to be elected under universal suffrage.

Rolihlahla Mandela was born on July 18, 1918, to an elite family in the Transkei region of South Africa. He attended a Christian mission school and later the College of Fort Hare. He was given the name Nelson, after the British admiral, by a primary school teacher who had trouble pronouncing his given name. Mandela eventually chose to become a lawyer and opened a law practice with Oliver Tambo, another important anti-apartheid leader.

Mandela joined the Youth League of the African National Congress (ANC) in 1944 and soon rose to the top leadership of the ANC. The ANC, which advocated "non-racialism" (or what would today be called "multiracialism"), was the main black anti-apartheid organization in South Africa, although it did not engage in mass politics or movement activities (demonstrations, civil disobedience, and the like) before 1949.

Like many "Africanists" in the ANC Youth League, Mandela was initially wary of collaborating with whites, and he supported the expulsion of Communists from the ANC. The Communist Party was a multiracial group, but it was viewed by some in the ANC as an essentially white organization with ulterior motives. However, Mandela later embraced the ANC's non-racialism and abandoned his earlier anti-Communism. The Africanists left the ANC in 1959 and established the Pan-Africanist Congress (PAC).

Mandela led the nonviolent Defiance Campaign of 1952 and helped coordinate the multiracial Congress Alliance that brought together black, white, and South Asian opponents of apartheid. The Alliance issued the "Freedom Charter" in 1955, which declared that "South Africa belongs to all who live in it, black and white, and . . . no government can justly claim authority unless it is based on the will of all the people." The government arrested 156 members of the Alliance, charging them with treason. The subsequent Treason Trial concluded in 1961 with the acquittal of all the defendants against whom the government had not already dropped its charges, including Mandela.

Mass protests in 1960 against the government's hated pass laws, which required non-whites to carry a passbook in order to control their movements, resulted in the massacre of 69 protestors in the town of Sharpeville. The government then banned the ANC and PAC. Both organizations went underground and decided to form military wings. Mandela and activists from the ANC and the Communist Party established Umkhonto we Sizwe ("Spear of the Nation"), which launched a campaign of sabotage and began preparations for guerrilla warfare.

Mandela and other leading anti-apartheid activists were arrested in 1962 and 1963; many more fled into exile. In June 1964, Mandela and seven others were convicted of various charges and sentenced to life imprisonment. At the trial, Mandela declared:

> During my lifetime I have dedicated myself to this struggle of the African people. I have fought against white domination, and I have fought against black domination. I have cherished the ideal of a democratic and free society in which all persons live together in harmony and with equal opportunities. It is an ideal which I hope to live for and to achieve. But if needs be, it is an ideal for which I am prepared to die.

Mandela would spend most of his 27 years in prison at Robben Island, a prison off Cape Town that became home—and a kind of university or think-tank—for many black political prisoners. During his years in prison, Mandela became an internationally recognized symbol of defiance to apartheid. Activists in Europe, North America, and elsewhere demanded Mandela's release as well as strict sanctions on trade and investment in South Africa.

Following more years of renewed protest and labor strikes during the mid-1980s, many businesspeople and white politicians came slowly to conclude that apartheid was probably doomed. Strikes paralyzed the economy and black townships became virtually ungovernable by the white regime. Secret talks with exiled ANC officials, and eventually with Mandela, were begun, especially after F. W. de Klerk became president. De Klerk began to release ANC activists from prison. Finally, on February 11, 1990, Mandela himself was released, an event broadcast live around the world. He addressed a huge rally in Cape Town that day, concluding with his famous pledge that he was prepared to die for a free and democratic South Africa.

Over the next several years, and despite many obstacles and setbacks, Mandela helped negotiate South Africa's transition to democracy. This was no easy task. The apartheid economy had created a wealthy class of whites and a huge mass of impoverished blacks. Whites feared that democracy would empower black politicians who would expropriate their wealth. The presence of the Communist Party in the anti-apartheid coalition seemed foreboding, despite the collapse of the Soviet bloc after 1989. Mandela played a conspicuous role in allaying the fears of whites. Eventually, a deal was struck: The white minority agreed to accept democracy; in return, white wealth and property would be respected. For their efforts, Mandela and de Klerk jointly received the Nobel Peace Prize in 1993.

In South Africa's first elections with universal suffrage, in April 1994, the ANC predictably swept into power, and Mandela was easily elected president. During his term in office (1994–99), racial reconciliation continued to be a major preoccupation. A Truth and Reconciliation Commission was established, led by Archbishop Desmond Tutu, to hold hearings on human rights abuses committed by both former government officials and anti-apartheid activists. Controversially, individuals who admitted to human rights abuses before the commission received amnesty from prosecution.

South Africa continues to be a land of vast inequalities and human misery. But thanks to Mandela and the anti-apartheid movement, it is much closer to the ideal of a democratic and free society to which Mandela dedicated his life.

27 Suicide Bombing

Robert J. Brym

In October 1983, Shi'a militants attacked the military barracks of American and French troops in Beirut, killing nearly 300 people. Today the number of suicide attacks worldwide has passed 1,000, with almost all the attacks concentrated in just nine countries: Lebanon, Sri Lanka, Israel, Turkey, India (Kashmir), Russia (Chechnya), Afghanistan, Iraq, and Pakistan. Israel, for example, experienced a wave of suicide attacks in the mid-1990s when Hamas and the Palestinian Islamic Jihad (PIJ) sought to undermine peace talks between Israel and the Palestinian Authority. A far deadlier wave of attacks began in Israel in October 2000 after all hope of a negotiated settlement collapsed. Altogether, between 1993 and 2005, 158 suicide attacks took place in Israel and the occupied Palestinian territories, killing more than 800 people and injuring more than 4,600.

Over the past quarter century, researchers have learned much about the motivations of suicide bombers, the rationales of the organizations that support them, their modus operandi, the precipitants of suicide attacks, and the effects of counterterrorism on insurgent behavior. Much of what they have learned is at odds with conventional wisdom and the thinking of policymakers who guide counterterrorist strategy. This chapter draws on that research, but I focus mainly on the Israeli/Palestinian case to draw six lessons from the carnage wrought by suicide bombers. In brief, I argue that (1) suicide bombers are not crazy, (2) nor are they motivated principally by religious zeal. It is possible to discern (3) a strategic logic and (4) a social logic underlying their actions. Targeted states typically react by repressing organizations that mount suicide attacks, but (5) this repression often makes matters worse. (6) Only by first taking an imaginative leap and understanding the world from the assailant's point of view can we hope to develop a workable strategy for minimizing suicide attacks. Let us examine each of these lessons in turn.

Lesson 1: Suicide Bombers Are not Crazy

Lance Corporal Eddie DiFranco was the only survivor of the 1983 suicide attack on the U.S. Marine barracks in Beirut who saw the face of the bomber. DiFranco was on watch when he noticed the attacker speeding his truck full of explosives toward the main building on the marine base. "He looked right at me [and] smiled," DiFranco later recalled.

Was the bomber insane? Some Western observers thought so. Several psychologists characterized the Beirut bombers as "unstable individuals with a death wish." Government and media sources made similar assertions in the immediate aftermath of the suicide attacks on the United States on September 11, 2001. Yet these claims were purely speculative. Subsequent interviews with prospective suicide bombers and reconstructions of the biographies of successful suicide attackers revealed few psychological abnormalities. In fact, after examining many hundreds of cases for evidence of depression, psychosis, past suicide attempts, and so on, Robert Pape discovered only a single person who could be classified as having a psychological problem (a Chechen woman who may have been mentally retarded).

On reflection, it is not difficult to understand why virtually all suicide bombers are psychologically stable. The organizers of suicide attacks do not want to jeopardize their missions by recruiting unreliable people. A research report prepared for the Danish government a few years ago noted: "Recruits who display signs of pathological behaviour are automatically weeded out for reasons of organizational security." It may be that some psychologically unstable people want to become suicide bombers, but insurgent organizations strongly prefer their cannons fixed.

Lesson 2: It's Mainly about Politics, not Religion

In May 1972, three Japanese men in business suits boarded a flight from Paris to Tel Aviv. They were members of the Japanese Red Army, an affiliate of the Popular Front for the Liberation of Palestine. Eager to help their Palestinian comrades liberate Israel from Jewish rule, they had packed their carry-on bags with machine guns and hand grenades. After disembarking at Lod Airport near Tel Aviv, they began an armed assault on everyone in sight. When the dust settled, 26 people lay dead, nearly half of them Puerto Rican Catholics on a pilgrimage to the Holy Land.

Israeli guards killed one of the attackers. A second blew himself up, thus becoming the first suicide bomber in modern Middle Eastern history. The Israelis captured the third assailant, Kozo Okamoto.

Okamoto languished in an Israeli prison until the mid-1980s, when he was handed over to Palestinian militants in Lebanon's Beka'a Valley in a prisoner exchange. Then, in 2000, something unexpected happened. Okamoto apparently abandoned or at least ignored his secular faith in the theories of Bakunin and Trotsky, and converted to Islam. For Okamoto, politics came first, then religion.

A similar evolution occurs in the lives of many people. Any political conflict makes people look for ways to explain the dispute and imagine a strategy for resolving it; they adopt or formulate an ideology. If the conflict is deep and the ideology proves inadequate, people modify the ideology or reject it for an alternative. Religious themes often tinge political ideologies, and the importance of the religious component may increase if analyses and strategies based on secular reasoning fail. When religious elements predominate, they may intensify the conflict.

For example, the Palestinians have turned to one ideology after another to explain their loss of land to Jewish settlers and military forces and to formulate a plan for regaining territorial control. Especially after 1952, when Gamal Abdel Nasser took office in Egypt, many Palestinians turned to Pan-Arabism, the belief that the Arab countries would unify and force Israel to cede territory. But wars failed to dislodge the Israelis. Particularly after the Six-Day War in 1967, many Palestinians turned to nationalism, which placed the responsibility for regaining control of lost territory on the Palestinians themselves. Others became Marxists, identifying wage-workers (and, in some cases, peasants) as the engines of national liberation. The Palestinians used plane hijackings to draw the world's attention to their cause, launched wave upon wave of guerrilla attacks against Israel, and in the 1990s entered into negotiations to create a sovereign Palestinian homeland.

Yet Islamic fundamentalism had been growing in popularity among Palestinians since the late 1980s—ironically, without opposition from the Israeli authorities, who saw it as a conservative counterweight to Palestinian nationalism. When negotiations with Israel to establish a Palestinian state broke down in 2000, many Palestinians saw the secularist approach as bankrupt and turned to Islamic fundamentalism for political answers. In January 2006, the Islamic fundamentalist party, Hamas, was democratically elected to form the Palestinian government, winning 44 percent of the popular vote and 56 percent of the parliamentary seats. In this case, as in many others, secular politics came first. When secularism failed, notions of "martyrdom" and "holy war" gained in importance.

This does not mean that most modern suicide bombers are deeply religious, either among the Palestinians or other groups. Among the 83 percent of suicide attackers worldwide between 1980 and 2003 for whom Robert Pape found data on ideological background, only a minority—43 percent—were identifiably religious. In Lebanon, Israel, the West Bank, and Gaza between 1981 and 2003, fewer than half of suicide bombers had discernible religious inclinations. In its origins and at its core, the Israeli–Palestinian conflict is not religiously inspired, and suicide bombing, despite its frequent religious trappings, is fundamentally the expression of a territorial dispute. In this conflict, many members of the dominant group—Jewish Israelis—use religion as a central marker of identity. It is hardly surprising, therefore, that many Palestinian militants also view the struggle in starkly religious terms.

The same holds for contemporary Iraq. As Mohammed Hafez has recently shown, 443 suicide missions took place in Iraq between March 2003 and February 2006. Seventy-one percent of the identifiable attackers belonged to al-Qaeda in Iraq. To be sure, they justified their actions in religious terms. Members of al-Qaeda in Iraq view the Shi'a who control the Iraqi state as apostates. They want to establish fundamentalist, Sunni-controlled states in Iraq and other Middle Eastern countries. Suicide attacks against the Iraqi regime and its American and British supporters are seen as a means to that end.

But it is only within a particular political context that these ambitions first arose. After all, suicide attacks began with the American and British invasion of Iraq and the installation of a Shi'a-controlled regime. And it is only under certain political conditions that these ambitions are acted upon. Thus, Hafez's analysis shows that suicide bombings spike (1) in retaliation for big counterinsurgency operations and (2) as a strategic response to institutional developments which suggest that Shi'a-controlled Iraq is about to become more stable. So although communal identity has come to be religiously demarcated in Iraq, this does not mean that religion per se initiated suicide bombing or that it drives the outbreak of suicide bombing campaigns.

Lesson 3: Sometimes It's Strategic

Suicide bombing often has a political logic. In many cases, it is used as a tactic of last resort undertaken by the weak to help them restore control over territory they perceive as theirs. This political logic is clear in statements routinely released by leaders of organizations that launch suicide attacks. Characteristically, the first communiqué issued by Hamas in 1987 stated that martyrdom is the appropriate response to occupation, and the 1988 Hamas charter says that jihad is the duty of every Muslim whose territory is invaded by an enemy.

The political logic of suicide bombing is also evident when suicide bombings occur in clusters as part of an organized campaign, often timed to maximize strategic gains. A classic example is the campaign launched by Hamas and the PIJ in the mid-1990s. Fearing that a settlement between Israel and the Palestinian Authority would prevent the Palestinians from gaining control over all of Israel, Hamas and the PIJ aimed to scuttle peace negotiations by unleashing a small army of suicide bombers.

Notwithstanding the strategic basis of many suicide attacks, we cannot conclude that strategic reasoning governs them all. More often than not, suicide bombing campaigns fail to achieve their territorial aims. Campaigns may occur without apparent strategic justification, as did the campaign that erupted in Israel after negotiations between Israel and the Palestinian Authority broke down in 2000. A social logic often overlays the political logic of suicide bombing.

Lesson 4: Sometimes It's Retaliatory

On October 4, 2003, a 29-year-old lawyer entered Maxim restaurant in Haifa and detonated her belt of plastic explosives. In addition to taking her own life, Hanadi Jaradat killed 20 people and wounded dozens of others. When her relatives were later interviewed in the Arab press, they explained her motives as follows: "She carried out the attack in revenge for the killing of her brother and her cousin [to whom she had been engaged] by the Israeli security forces, and in revenge for all the crimes Israel is perpetrating in the West Bank by killing Palestinians and expropriating their land." Strategic calculation did not inform Jaradat's attack. Research I conducted with Bader Araj shows that, like a majority of Palestinian suicide bombers between 2000 and 2005, Jaradat was motivated by the desire for revenge and retaliation.

Before people act, they sometimes weigh the costs and benefits of different courses of action and choose the one that appears to cost the least and offer the most benefits. But people are not calculating machines. Sometimes they just don't add up. Among other emotions, feelings of anger and humiliation can trump rational strategic calculation in human affairs. Economists have conducted experiments called "the ultimatum game," in which the experimenter places two people in a room, gives one of them $20, and tells the recipient that she must give some of the money—as much or as little as she wants—to the other person. If the other person refuses the offer, neither gets to keep any money. Significantly, in four out of five cases, the other person refuses to accept the money if she is offered less than $5. Although she will gain materially if she accepts any offer, she is highly likely to turn down a low offer so as to punish her partner for stinginess. This outcome suggests that emotions can easily override the rational desire for material gain. (Researchers at the University of Zürich have recently demonstrated the physiological basis of this override function by using MRI brain scans on people playing the ultimatum game.) At the political level, research I conducted with Bader Araj on the events precipitating suicide bombings, the motivations of suicide bombers, and the rationales of the organizations that support suicide bombings shows that Palestinian suicide missions are in most cases prompted less by strategic cost–benefit calculations than by such human emotions as revenge and retaliation. The existence of these deeply human emotions also helps to explain why attempts to suppress suicide bombing campaigns sometimes do not have the predicted results.

Lesson 5: Repression Is a Boomerang

Major General Doron Almog commanded the Israel Defense Forces Southern Command from 2000 to 2003. He tells the story of how, in early 2003, a wealthy Palestinian merchant in Gaza received a phone call from an Israeli agent. The caller said that the merchant's son was preparing a suicide mission, and that if he went through with it, the family home would be demolished, Israel would sever all commercial ties with the family, and its members would never be allowed to visit Israel again. The merchant prevailed upon his son to reconsider, and the attack was averted.

Exactly how many suicide bombers have been similarly deterred is unknown. We do know that of the nearly 600 suicide missions launched in Israel and its occupied territories between 2000 and 2005, fewer than 25 percent succeeded in reaching their targets. Israeli counterterrorist efforts thwarted three-quarters of them using violent means. In addition, Israel preempted an incalculable number of attacks by assassinating militants involved in planning them. More than 200 Israeli assassination attempts took place between 2000 and 2005, 80 percent of which succeeded in killing their main target, sometimes with considerable "collateral damage."

Table 27.1 Insurgency, repression, and perceptions by party

	HAMAS/PIJ	FATAH/Other
Number of successful suicide attackers, 2000–5	85	48
Number of attempted state assassinations, 2000–5	124	82
Percentage of leaders never willing to recognize Israel	100%	10%
How has Israel's assassination policy affected the ability of your organization to conduct suicide bombing operations?	increased 33% not affected 42% decreased 25%	increased 9% not affected 5% decreased 86%
In comparison with other tactics used by your organization, how costly has suicide bombing been in terms of the human and material resources used, damage to your organization, etc.?	as or less costly 53% more costly 20% don't know 27%	as or less costly 11% more costly 86% don't know 4%

The first two rows of data in this table were calculated from a systematic analysis of newspapers (the *New York Times*, *ha-Aretz*, *al-Quds*, and *al-'Arabi*) by Robert Brym and Bader Araj. The remainder of the data is based on a survey of 45 Palestinian insurgent leaders conducted by Bader Araj in the West Bank and Gaza during the spring and summer of 2006.

Common sense suggests that repression should dampen insurgency by increasing its cost. By this logic, when state organizations eliminate the people who plan suicide bombings, destroy their bomb-making facilities, intercept their agents, and punish the people who support them, they erode the insurgents' capabilities for mounting suicide attacks. But this commonsense approach to counterinsurgency overlooks two complicating factors. First, harsh repression may reinforce radical opposition and even intensify it. Second, insurgents may turn to alternative and perhaps more lethal methods to achieve their aims.

Consider the Palestinian case (see table 27.1). Bader Araj and I were able to identify the organizational affiliation of 133 Palestinian suicide bombers between September 2000 and July 2005. Eighty-five of them (64 percent) were affiliated with the Islamic fundamentalist groups Hamas and the PIJ, while the rest were affiliated with secular Palestinian groups such as Fatah. Not surprisingly, given this distribution, Israeli repression was harshest against the Islamic fundamentalists, who were the targets of 124 Israeli assassination attempts (more than 60 percent of the total).

Yet after nearly five years of harsh Israeli repression—involving not just the assassination of leaders but also numerous arrests, raids on bomb-making facilities, the demolition of houses belonging to family members of suicide bombers, and so on—Hamas and PIJ leaders remained adamant in their resolve and much more radical than Palestinian secularist leaders. When 45 insurgent leaders representing all major Palestinian factions were interviewed in depth in the summer of 2006, 100 percent of those associated with Hamas and PIJ (compared to just 10 percent of secularist leaders) said they would never be willing to recognize the legitimacy of the state of Israel. That is, the notion of Israel as a Jewish state was still entirely unacceptable to each and every one of them. When asked how Israel's assassination policy had affected the ability of their organization to conduct suicide bombing operations, 42 percent of Hamas and PIJ respondents said that the policy had had no effect, while one-third said the policy had increased their organization's capabilities (the corresponding figures for secularist leaders were 5 percent and 9 percent, respectively).

And when asked how costly suicide bombing had been in terms of human and organizational resources, organizational damage, and so on, 53 percent of Hamas and PIJ leaders (compared to just 11 percent of secularist leaders) said that suicide bombing was less costly or at least no more costly than the alternatives. Responses to such questions probably tell us more about the persistent resolve of the Islamic fundamentalists than their actual capabilities. And that is just the point. Harsh Israeli repression over an extended period apparently reinforced the anti-Israel sentiments of Islamic fundamentalists.

Some counterterrorist experts say that motivations count for little if capabilities are destroyed. And they would be right if it were not for the substitutability of methods: increase the cost of one method of attack, and highly motivated insurgents typically substitute another. So, for example, Israel's late prime minister, Yitzhak Rabin, ordered troops to "break the bones" of Palestinians who engaged in mass demonstrations, rock throwing, and other nonlethal forms of protest in the late 1980s and early 1990s. The Palestinians responded with more violent attacks, including suicide missions. Similarly, after Israel began to crack down ruthlessly on suicide bombing operations in 2002, rocket attacks against Israeli civilians sharply increased in frequency. In general, severe repression can work for a while, but a sufficiently determined mass opposition can always design new tactics to surmount new obstacles, especially if its existence as a group is visibly threatened (and unless, of course, the mass opposition is exterminated in its entirety). One kind of "success" usually breeds another kind of "failure" if the motivation of insurgents is high.

Lesson 6: Empathize with Your Enemy

In October 2003, Israeli Chief of Staff Moshe Ya'alon explicitly recognized this conundrum when he stated that Israel's tactics against the Palestinians had become too repressive and were stirring up potentially uncontrollable levels of hatred and terrorism. "In our tactical decisions, we are operating contrary to our strategic interests," he told reporters. Ya'alon went on to claim that the Israeli government was unwilling to make concessions that could bolster the authority of moderate Palestinian Prime Minister Mahmoud Abbas, and he expressed the fear that by continuing its policy of harsh repression, Israel would bring about the collapse of the Palestinian Authority, the silencing of Palestinian moderates, and the popularization of more radical voices like that of Hamas. The head of the General Security Service (Shabak), the defense minister, and Prime Minister Ariel Sharon opposed Ya'alon. Consequently, his term as chief of staff was not renewed, and his military career ended in 2005. A year later, all of Ya'alon's predictions proved accurate.

Ya'alon was no dove. From the time he became chief of staff in July 2002, he had been in charge of ruthlessly putting down the Palestinian uprising. He had authorized assassinations, house demolitions, and all the rest. But 15 months into the job, Ya'alon had learned much from his experience, and it seems that what he learned above all else was to empathize with the enemy—not to have warm and fuzzy feelings about the Palestinians, but to see things from their point of view in order to improve his ability to further Israel's chief strategic interest, namely, to live in peace with its neighbors.

As odd as it may sound at first, and as difficult as it may be to apply in practice, exercising empathy with one's enemy is the key to an effective counterterrorist strategy. Seeing the enemy's point of view increases one's understanding of the minimum conditions that would allow the enemy to put down arms. An empathic understanding of the enemy discourages counterproductive actions such as excessive repression, and it encourages tactical moves that further one's strategic aims. As Ya'alon suggested, in the Israeli case such tactical moves might include (1) offering meaningful rewards—for instance, releasing hundreds of millions of Palestinian tax dollars held in escrow by Israel, freeing selected Palestinians from Israeli prisons, and shutting down remote and costly Israeli settlements in the northern West Bank—in exchange for the renunciation of suicide bombing, and (2) attributing the deal to the intercession of moderate Palestinian forces so as to buttress their popularity and authority. (From this point of view, Israel framed its unilateral 2005 withdrawal from Gaza poorly because most Palestinians saw it as a concession foisted on Israel by Hamas.) Once higher levels of trust and stability are established by such counterterrorist tactics, they can serve as the foundation for negotiations leading to a permanent settlement. Radical elements would inevitably try to jeopardize negotiations, as they have in the past, but Israel resisted the temptation to shut down peace talks during the suicide bombing campaign of the mid-1990s, and it could do so again. Empathizing with the enemy would also help prevent the breakdown of negotiations, as happened in 2000; a clear sense of the minimally acceptable conditions for peace can come only from an empathic understanding of the enemy.

Conclusion

Political conflict over territory is the main reason for suicide bombing, although religious justifications for suicide missions are likely to become more important when secular ideologies fail to bring about desired results. Suicide bombing may also occur for strategic or retaliatory reasons—to further insurgent aims or in response to repressive state actions.

Cases vary in the degree to which suicide bombers are motivated by (1) political or religious and (2) strategic or retaliatory aims. For example, research to date suggests that suicide bombing is more retaliatory in Israel than in Iraq, and more religiously motivated in Iraq than in Israel. But in any case, repression (short of a policy approaching genocide) cannot solve the territorial disputes that lie at the root of suicide bombing campaigns. As Zbigniew Brzezinski, President Jimmy Carter's national security adviser, wrote a few years ago in the *New York Times*, "to win the war on terrorism, one must … begin a political effort that focuses on the conditions that brought about [the terrorists'] emergence." These are wise words that Israel—and the United States in its own "war on terror"—would do well to heed.

Recommended Resources

Hany Abu-Hassad. *Paradise Now*. This movie sketches the circumstances that shape the lives of two Palestinian suicide bombers, showing that they are a lot like us and that if we found ourselves in similar circumstances, we might turn out to be a lot like them. (Nominated for the 2005 Oscar for best foreign-language film.)

Robert J. Brym and Bader Araj. "Suicide Bombing as Strategy and Interaction: The Case of the Second Intifada." *Social Forces* 84 (2006): 1965–82. Explains suicide bombing as the outcome of structured interactions among conflicting and cooperating parties and organizations.

Mohammed M. Hafez. "Suicide Terrorism in Iraq: A Preliminary Assessment of the Quantitative Data and Documentary Evidence." *Studies in Conflict and Terrorism* 29 (2006): 591–619. The first systematic analysis of suicide bombing in Iraq demonstrates the strategic and retaliatory aims of the assailants.

Errol Morris. *The Fog of War*. Robert McNamara's extraordinarily frank assessment of his career as secretary of defense in the Kennedy and Johnson administrations. This film is a profound introduction to strategic thinking and a valuable lesson on how to learn from one's mistakes. His first lesson: empathize with your enemy. (Winner of the 2003 Oscar for best documentary.)

Robert A. Pape. *Dying to Win: The Strategic Logic of Suicide Terrorism* (Random House, 2005). In support of the view that suicide bombing takes place mainly for rational, strategic reasons, Pape analyzes all suicide attacks worldwide from 1980 to 2003.

Christoph Reuter. *My Life Is a Weapon: A Modern History of Suicide Bombing*. Trans. H. Ragg-Kirkby (Princeton University Press, 2004). A succinct overview of the past 25 years of suicide attacks.

28 Everyday Life, Routine Politics, and Protest

Javier Auyero

Contentious Snapshot

June 26, 1996. Governor Sapag and picketer Laura Padilla sign a public agreement in the city of Cutral-co, province of Neuquén, Argentina. The whole country watches the event on TV, reads about it in newspapers, or hears about the details on the radio. That agreement puts an end to a protest of thousands of residents of Cutral-co and Plaza Huincul who blocked all the access roads to the area, effectively halting the movement of people and goods for seven days and six nights. It all begins on June 20 with the news of the cancellation of a deal between the provincial government and Agrium, a Canadian company, to build a fertilizer plant in the region, a plant that will provide, at best, 50 full-time jobs. A few hours after local radio stations spread the bad news, five main barricades and dozens of smaller pickets, with varying numbers of women, men, and children in each, isolate this oil and gas region from the rest of the province and the country. During days and nights, one slogan unites the hundreds of protesters: "Nobody comes in, nobody gets out. We want Governor Sapag to come here. We want jobs."

It is below 30 degrees on the morning of June 25, when a federal judge in command of 200 soldiers of the Gendarmería Nacional *comes to Plaza Huincul with the intention of clearing the National Road 22 of demonstrators. With the help of tear gas and rubber bullets the gendarmes clear out the first barricade less than a mile from the main blockade at* Torre Uno *(the oil derrick that memorializes the discovery of petroleum in the region) but as they attempt to move forward, they notice that approximately 20,000 people (close to half of the total population of both towns) are awaiting them. From the roof of a van, her arm held by a masked picketer, the judge addresses the crowd with a megaphone, recuses herself from the case, and tells protesters that she, and the gendarmes at her command, are leaving town. The crowd cheers her, sings the national anthem, and shouts: "The people won, the people won!"*

On the morning of the protest's seventh day, Governor Sapag meets with the "Committee of Pickets' Representatives" (a recently formed organization of which Laura Padilla is now the main spokesperson) in Cutral-co. The handwritten agreement signed by the governor and the picketer states that the protest was a "clear demonstration of the hunger suffered by the population" of both cities, and promises public works that will provide locals with jobs, delivery of food, the reconnection of gas and electricity for approximately 2500 families whose service was cut off due to lack of payment. The agreement also states that the governor will declare both communities in "occupational and social emergency," specifies some of the projects that the provincial government will begin and/or support to create jobs, promises that the provincial bank will assist local businesses with new credit lines, assures that no punitive measures will be taken against those who took active part in the protest, and, finally, guarantees that new investors will be sought to build the fertilizer plant.

Five years later, I am sitting in the living room of Laura's modest house in General Roca (in the neighboring province of Rio Negro) when she hands me the notebook she carried during the seven days of the protest that came to be nationally known as la pueblada*: "You can have it, take it with you ... Part of what we, the picketers, did is in this notebook." In one of our last conversations, Laura, a 44-year-old mother of three, currently unemployed, tells me that, when she signed the agreement with*

> *the Governor, "I was signing against all the injustices, the humiliations, that I suffered throughout my life."*

In one simple statement, Laura alerted me about a key dimension of popular contention, a dimension that (I realized when back from the field) figures prominently in Charles Tilly's notion of repertoire of collective action, i.e. the intimate relationship of everyday life with protest.[1] This key, though understudied, aspect of contentious politics constitutes the object of this chapter. Based on archival research and ethnographic fieldwork, this article draws upon the theatrical metaphor of "repertoire" to examine the continuities between everyday life, routine politics, and contentious joint action. Focusing on a case study, the six-day road blockade in the Argentine Patagonia known as *la pueblada*, the article scrutinizes these connections through a thick description of (a) the intersection of this episode of popular protest with the life history of one of its key participants, paying particular attention to the ways in which Laura's biography (i.e. her social trajectory not merely as a picketer but as a woman, a wife, a mother, and a worker) shapes her actions, thoughts, and feelings during the uprising, and (b) the modes in which routine politics affect the origins and shape of the protest.

Everyday Life at the Crossroads

At the time of the protest, Laura is working as a private tutor teaching language and social studies in a house she rents with her friend Jorge, who teaches math. The few students she has barely help her to make ends meet. What follows is an excerpt from Laura's diary covering the first day of the protest (the original version mixes past and present tenses):

> *Thursday, June 20, 1996. I woke up early. My same duties were awaiting me. No work was forthcoming, but I had to go and wait for it. Everything was as usual. I had to go to Court to check the paperwork for the child allowance I was claiming from my husband; that was tedious, tiring, humiliating ... [At noon my neighbor told me to tune to* Radio Victoria*] I listened to the radio but I didn't understand what was going on: "they will blockade the roads, stores will close for the day." There were phone calls to the radio station in which people expressed all their anger. [When I got back to work, Jorge] told me the history of Agrium, the fertilizer plant, the different factions within the governing party (Movimiento Popular Neuquino, hereafter MPN) and all the things I had to know [...] I went back home and I turned on the radio again and I listened to all the angry comments that the people were making: "Another political promise was vanishing." Unemployment, "father YPF" was gone, hunger, nothing to do [...] I went to bed with the radio on my side, by then I had begun to identify with that poverty [the radio was talking about]. And I cried for the three years of solitude [since she got divorced in 1993], the three years of efforts, of struggles for my three kids ... three years of fights against a humiliating court system [...] That night I cried a lot ... And I cried and I felt identified with the comments that people were making on the radio [...] I am poor, with no possibilities, with no hope, 36 years old, alone [...] I don't receive child support [...] The morning of the 21st every store was closed ... I never participated in something like this ... What shall I do? I talked to my neighbor and we decided to go to the road, the radio was announcing big barbecues, and they were saying that the cabs were free if you wanted to go. In other words, it was like a day in the country, and with that mentality, I went to the road, [I went] to have a barbecue with my neighbors [...] The reality: unemployment and poverty, injustice. My reality: unemployment, poverty, injustice. That was my life.*

Laura is certainly not the sole recipient of those radio messages. Early that June 20th, Radio Victoria airs the cancellation of the deal between the provincial government and Agrium, and "opens its microphones to listen to the people's reaction ... A neighbor called saying that the people should show its discontent ... [another one] said that we should get together in the road," Mario

Fernández, director and owner of the radio station, recalls. All my interviewees mention those radio messages as central in their recollections, not only in terms of the ways in which the radio calls on people but also in terms of the way in which the local radio *frames* the cancellation of the fertilizer plant project.[2] On Radio Victoria, the former mayor Grittini and his political ally, the radio station owner and director Fernández, depict the cancellation of the deal with Agrium as a "final blow to both communities," as the "last hope gone," as an "utterly arbitrary decision of the provincial government." Daniel remembers that: "there was a lot of anger ... the radio said that we should go out and demonstrate, they were saying that it was the time to be courageous." "I learned about the blockade on the radio ... they were talking about the social situation," Zulma says. Laura, Daniel, Zulma and the rest point towards both the same framing articulator and its similar functions: The radio both makes sense of the "social situation" and persuades people to go to the road.

As the radio broadcasts "the ire that we felt"—as Daniel explains to me—and calls people to the *Torre Uno* in Route 22, cabs bring people there free of charge. Is this a sudden eruption of indignation? Are radio reporters and taxi drivers merely the first to spontaneously react? Hardly so. The factionalism within the governing party, the MPN, and particularly, the actions of the former mayor Grittini who is waging his own personal fight against Mayor Martinasso and Governor Sapag,[3] are at the root of both the "injustice framing"[4] and the veritable mobilization of resources.[5] In an interview that he prefers not to tape—"because the truth cannot be told to a tape recorder"—Daniel Martinasso tells me: "Grittini backed the protest during the first couple of days. How? Well, in the first place buying a couple of local radio stations so that they call people to the route." "Is it that easy to buy a radio station?" I innocently ask him. "I myself paid Radio Victoria so that they broadcast nice things about my administration. The radio's reception area was built with the money I paid to the owner ... that's how politics work in Cutral-co." Grittini's and his associates' efforts (Radio Victoria's owner Fernández being a key figure at this stage) don't stop there. Although there is not firm evidence, many sources (journalists, politicians, and picketers) indicate that he also sends the trucks that bring hundreds of tires to the different pickets and some of the bulldozers to block the traffic. He is also behind the free distribution of food, gasoline, firewood, and cigarettes in the barricades. Some even say that Grittini pays $50 per night to hundreds of young picketers and that his associates provide them with wine and drugs.

Thus, while the radio airs its angry messages (telling people that "something has to be done" and calling them to go to the *Torre Uno*), cabs drive people there and to the other barricades for free, tires are brought to the pickets, food, cigarettes, and other essentials are distributed free of charge ("We even get diapers for the babies!" Laura and other women recall). This *mobilization of resources* and this *framing process* do not, however, operate in a vacuum but under background conditions that are ripe for a large-scale protest.

State Dismantling

Both Plaza Huincul and Cutral-co were born of and developed through oil activity. Since their inception in 1918 and 1933 respectively, both towns grew with the rhythm of (and became highly dependent on) the benefits provided by oil production and by the activities of the state oil company, YPF (the first government company, founded in 1922). With the discovery of petroleum in the area came its territorial occupation and settlement carried out under the aegis of state action. The rapid population growth of both towns reflects the expansion of YPF's activities. From 1947 to 1990, the total population increased from 6452 to 44,711, an impressive demographic growth by all accounts. The cradle-to-grave enterprise welfare of YPF benefited its workers with higher than average salaries, modern housing serviced by the very same company personnel ("anything that was broken in the house was fixed by YPF," I was repeatedly told by former YPF workers), access to a very good hospital and health plan, and paid vacations ("once a year, we had free plane tickets and two weeks in a hotel in Buenos Aires or anywhere in the country"). YPF's welfare extended well beyond the confines of the company: It was the whole social and economic life of the region that was boosted by its presence. YPF built entire neighborhoods, provided others with sewers and lighting, erected a local high-quality hospital, a movie theater, a sports center, and provided school buses for most of the population.

In less than two years an economic system and a form of life that had lasted more than four decades was literally shattered. The privatization of YPF was passed as law by the National Congress on September 24, 1992, and soon enough the devastating effects were felt in the region. YPF not only cut back its personnel from 4,200 employees to 600 in less than a year; it also ceased to be the welfare enterprise around which the life of both towns evolved (the company even moved its headquarters out of Plaza Huincul), and became an enclave industry functioning under strict capitalist guidelines.

Headlines of the major regional newspaper captured the general mood as the first effects of the privatization began to be felt in Cutral-co and Plaza Huincul: "Uncertain future awaits Cutral-co and Plaza Huincul," "Alarming unemployment in the oil region," "The struggle against becoming a ghost town." As massive layoffs were taking place, the articles described a "general feeling of uncertainty" about the beginnings of the process that is now in its mature form: hyper-unemployment. In Cutral-co, 30 percent of the economically active population (25,340 residents) was unemployed (1997). More than half the population of both towns lives below the official poverty line.

In her diary, Laura speaks in very general terms about the widespread joblessness and misery. It would not be possible to understand the meanings that *la pueblada* has for residents and picketers without a grasp of the bigger historical picture, i.e. on the structural adjustment process and its local translation, the privatization of YPF. As relevant as the background structural conditions are to understanding the lived protest, they are not the sole source of the meanings that Laura ascribes to this massive mobilization. The emergence of the protest finds Laura at a very difficult moment in her life. Her diary describes her own deprivations since the time of her divorce and the humiliations suffered at the hands of a callous court system. It would be equally difficult to grasp her participation in the protest without delving into some aspects of her biography.

Herstory

The reconstruction of Laura's life-story took me more than 20 hours of taped interviews, and innumerable conversations and letters. Let me here mention four main themes that I deem crucial to understand both her life and her contentious experience: Laura was born and raised in a family where politics was considered a bad word and politicians seen as "dirty and corrupt fellows" ("my father never became a member of the then governing party and for that we suffered a lot ... he never got a secure job in the oil company, they kept transferring him from one place to the next ... politics screwed us up"). She married quite young, and sooner than later she became the victim of her husband's violence. She describes her marriage as "a jail" in which she was repeatedly beaten, abused, and (once) raped. She went through a tortuous divorce (that included having to "look for a punch" from her husband so that she could file a domestic violence complaint and not lose the custody of her children; and "tedious, tiring, and humiliating" paperwork at the courts claiming child support from her ex-husband), and last, through a painful, and at the beginning hesitant, participation in therapy groups for domestic violence victims. "In all of the separation process," she told me "going to the domestic violence groups, I learned about the cycle of violence, I learned about the honeymoon period which is when the beater repents and the woman has hope again, believes again that the story will change, that everything is going to be different, I learned how the beater goes along accumulating tension that ends with an explosion ... I also realized what happened in one of the reconciliations, the time he put the gun on the nightstand (and asked her to have sex), that was rape. I took a long time to overcome it, it gave me a shock, it was like taking on being a single mother, with all the violence that signifies, abused woman, with all the humiliations, and on top of all that a rape. It took me a long time to process that; I cooked and would cry, I went to take a bath and would cry, or I went to go to sleep and would cry. I had to go to psychologists all over again, because it was something that, after being in groups for a long time, I asked again: What happened to me in my life? How did I fall so far? How did I fail to defend myself? I wouldn't forgive myself for it. Until, little by little, through conversations in the groups ... I discovered that there were others who had been through the same."

By June 1996, Laura was barely making ends meet by teaching private lessons, as she describes in her diary. She was suing her husband to obtain child support, but without a private lawyer, the lawsuit was making little, if any, progress. These were her worries on the morning of June 21, when she listened to Radio Victoria broadcasting the angry comments of the residents of Cutralco; they were speaking in terms painfully familiar to her: poverty, unemployment, hopelessness, injustice.

A Barbecue on the Barricade

It came as a surprise to me that Laura (the symbol of *la pueblada*, the nationally known picketer) did not attend the road blockade in order to complain. Early in the morning of the 21st, she tunes to Radio Victoria to follow the news. "On local radio, they were saying that the pickets needed grill broilers. They didn't have enough of them to cook the incredible amount of meat they had. And so there I was, at home, and I told my neighbor: 'What a boring day! What if we go to the road to have a barbecue? With the grill I have, we will be able to get into one of the groups' ... Life was so tedious in Cutralco," Laura evokes, "going to the road blockade was like an excursion. Through the radio, I found out that in Añelo (northern barricade) picketers were in need of grill broilers. That was 19 kilometers away from home. I went there in a free cab to have a barbecue, to spend a day in the countryside with my children." By now, Laura is aware of the political character of the protest. Yesterday, her friend Jorge told her that the factionalism within the MPN was behind the demonstration. "I had needs, that's true. But that was my story. My story would never become associated with anything political.[6] Politicians were in the road blockade at *Torre Uno*. I would never go there. I went to a less important barricade, with fewer people, and lots of food." More recently, in her job as a private teacher she learned more about the dark side of local political life: "Most of my students were the sons of local politicians and officials. Their families were breaking apart; parents didn't pay any attention to their kids, they were on drugs; their parents would buy them expensive stuff but not listen to them ... "

"We arrive at Añelo around 10.30 am with my neighbor. There are close to 200 people," Laura explains to me. In the picket, Laura explains to me, "the motto is: 'nobody comes in, nobody goes out.'" No vehicle or person is allowed to go through Añelo (and, from the available evidence, through none of the other barricades). Around noon, the radio informs the people in Añelo and in the rest of the pickets that there will be a meeting at *Torre Uno*, delegates from each picket should attend. Since Laura is "the teacher," the one who, for the rest of the picketers, "knows how to speak," they choose her and Raúl (a 40-year-old man who has been in the picket since the night before) to be their delegates. Raúl, however, refuses to go: "He says he doesn't know how to speak in public," Laura remembers.

The meeting at the *Torre Uno* is an impressive gathering with more than 5000 people. Laura is amazed by the amount of people and astonished with the lack of attention paid to the pickets' delegates. This is how she describes what happens in the meeting:

> When we get there, surprise! Those holding the microphone are reading their speeches, they are not improvising, they are using foul language, they are asking for the resignation of the governor. The people in my picket are not like that, they are there because they are hungry ... They don't want the governor to resign. Those holding the microphone never call upon us, the representatives of the pickets. They don't even say that we are there, they ignore us.

Those "holding the microphone" are, in Laura's mind, the local politicians. "I just can't stand this. It's too much, it's all politics. I ask myself: what the hell am I doing in this meeting? I better go back to Añelo." Her suspicions are shared by other picketers. Less than a month after *la pueblada*, Rubén recalls: "When I went to the *Torre*, I realized that it was like a political rally, there were as always three or four politicians making promises ..."

As Laura arrives at her picket, "people from *Torre Uno* are telling the other picketers that the trucks carrying oil and gasoline have to go through our barricade, that we shouldn't be blocking the oil traffic.[7] And the people from my picket are mad, indignant, our motto is 'nobody comes in, nobody goes out', not even the trucks carrying gasoline. People go ballistic!" Here is where the trouble begins.

Disrespect

After hours of conversation with Laura I accidentally come across one incident that, minor as it seems, and unrelated to the structural roots of the uprising as it is, appears to be crucial to understand her involvement in the protest. The following is Laura's reconstruction of the dialogue that takes place in the middle of the chaos when picketers are angrily telling the envoys from *Torre Uno* that nobody, "not even the oil trucks" will pass through Añelo:

> **Raúl** (talking to Laura): Didn't you go to the meeting at *Torre Uno* and tell them that nobody will pass through the picket?
> **Laura**: Listen to me. They didn't pay us any attention. That meeting was a farce. They didn't call us, they didn't care for our opinions ... they didn't even want to know what's going on in the pickets.
> **Raúl** (talking to the people around): *See, this shit happened because we sent a woman ...*
> **Laura** (angry): Stop there, hang on there ... You were supposed to come with me. And you convinced me to go. And now you say that a woman is good for nothing. You are the one who's useless because you didn't want to come with me ...
> **Raúl** (dismissive): *See, she is like all women, she loudly bitches inside her home but outside ...*
> **Laura** (now very angry, on the verge of tears): Look ... we are now going to the radio. I will get all the pickets' delegates together and I will show you that I am telling the truth. After that, I hope I don't see you in my fucking life again!

Laura is now joined by Omar, another picketer who was present at the meeting at *Torre Uno*, who tries to persuade Raúl: "Laura is telling the truth," Omar says, but Raúl keeps saying that Laura is useless. And so Laura asks Omar to take her to Radio Victoria. The microphones of the radio are opened to each and every resident to express his or her point of view on the current situation. But Laura uses that outlet to call for a meeting of the picketers, in the *Aeropuerto*, "at the other end of the city, at the extreme opposite of *Torre Uno*, without politicians. On the radio, I say: 'This meeting is for the representatives of the pickets. No politicians should come.'"

Laura has no history of prior activism, and a deep distrust of anything political. When did she decide to stay in the road, with all the risks and suffering implied (it is the middle of the winter in the Patagonia and it is very cold and windy, and rumors about the imminent arrival of the gendarmes had run rampant since the very beginning) and no benefits for herself in sight? After days of talking with her, of driving her around the main pickets and listening to her stories, of watching videos and reading newspapers, I realized that the question is misleading. *Pace* rational action theorists, so fond of instances of calculation and decision-making, there is no moment in which Laura made a plain, make or break, choice to stay on the road, no occasion in which she ran the costs and benefits of possible action plans through a psychic adding machine to decide on a plan that will maximize her investment of energy, both physical and emotional. She was actually *sucked into* the role of picketer by the interactions she had on the road; interactions deeply shaped by elements of her own biography. To be blunt, she stayed on the road because she felt disrespected first by the politicians at *Torre Uno* and second, and most important at this stage, by a man. True, her last three years were years of poverty and immiseration, years that would give her or anybody else enough reasons to protest. But she wasn't there for that, "that was my story, never to be associated with anything political." Those three years, "three years of efforts, of struggles" as she writes in her diary, were also years of "breathing the air of liberty"—as she puts it when referring to the absence of her husband. With the help of others in the groups against domestic violence, they were years of learning about the respect that women deserve from men—something that, given her history of domestic abuse and violence, was not at all clear in her mind. They were, in other words, *years of material decay but also of moral empowerment.* That day on the road, Raúl touched a nerve, giving Laura the looked-for chance to obtain the esteem and recognition she had learned about during those three years: "I was mad with Raúl ... it really bothered me; he treated me badly, as if I was stupid because I was a woman. I was offended, as if we women are useless. No way." And thus she became a picketer, in part, out of a gender trouble.

And so begins Laura's six-day career as a picketer [...] The picketer's biography informs her actions on the road in an additional way. "If I have to define what I did I'd say this: my aim was to protect people," Laura tells me when I first meet her. And she comes back to this issue of protection and of the nonviolent character of the protest oftentimes. Her remarks reflect, to some extent, part of the picketers' discussions at that time. But they also reflect her personal anxiety about safety. She tells me, "We wanted to protect people. I said that on radio: we, the picketers, are here to protect people." Her caring and protective actions were directed toward one main group in the pickets: young people (*los pibes*). Laura sheds tears every time she describes the moment when she convinced the more than 50 youngsters in her picket, who were getting violent after hours of heavy drinking, to throw the cartons of cheap wine into the burning tires. Laura comes back to this issue of wine, violence, and protection repeatedly, obsessively I would say, during the time we spend together. And there is a reason for that; a reason that has to do with how deeply her protective and caring actions are linked with the story of her own life, and particularly, with "the three years of suffering" that preceded the contentious episode:

> We had to protect the people; we had to protect ourselves. How so? We had to take care of the violent people. How did we calm them down? *In the groups* (against domestic violence), *I learned* that you have

> to approach the violent person smoothly, put your arm around him, and touch him. When someone is irritated, you have to approach him tenderly; the first thing you have to tell him is that you understand him. People told me that in the groups. *Those were the techniques that we learned to placate the violent husband ... That's what we did in the pickets* [...] *The things I learned in the groups against domestic violence were very useful those days.* In order to calm down the violent kids, you have to be kind to them, touch them ... *pretty much in the same way I did with my husband when he got mad* (my emphasis).

Although the way she becomes involved in the protest is highly singular, the way she begins to understand the collectivity of those protesting, the way she defines who she and her fellow picketers are, is hardly unique: it is a shared understanding that begins to take shape at that meeting in the barricade of *Aeropuerto*, where the first picketers' organization is born. This collective dimension deserves closer analytical attention.[8]

Concluding Remarks

C. Wright Mills would say that when episodes of collective contention take place, a private tutor like Laura becomes a picketer.[9] Wright Mills would then add that neither the protesters' lives nor the history of the uprisings can be understood without understanding them both. "Understanding them both" is the task of the sociological imagination. This chapter has examined the intersection of one episode of popular protest with the life history of Laura, a woman living in a neglected region of Argentina, paying particular attention to the ways Laura's biography shapes her actions and words during the uprising.

The embeddedness of contention in local context gives protest its power and meaning. Existing scholarship insists on the rootedness of collective action in "normal" social relations, on the multifarious ways joint struggle takes place embedded, and often hidden, in the mundane structures of everyday life and usual politics.[10] Contentious gatherings, writes Tilly, "obviously bear a coherent relationship to the social organization and routine politics of their settings. But what relationship? That is the problem."[11] In this chapter, I have examined this relationship by dissecting the ways one protester's actions, thoughts, and feelings during the uprising were deeply informed by the history of her life, her towns' history, current condition, and prevailing political routines. The way Laura lived this popular revolt was not only informed by her singular history but by the interactions she had with other fellow protesters and with authorities, and by the shared understandings forged jointly on the cold roads of Cutral-co and Plaza Huincul. Further work should examine the relationship between this collective identity and the history and current predicament of both towns. Further work should also scrutinize the manifold ways these shared self-understandings were constructed in opposition to local politicians and officials—some of whom, to end with a paradox, we can find at the origins of this contentious episode where everyday life, routine politics, and protest meet and mesh.

Notes

1 See Charles Tilly, *The Contentious French* (Cambridge, MA: Harvard University Press, 1986); "Contentious Repertoires in Great Britain," in Mark Traugott, ed., *Repertoires and Cycles of Collective Action* (Durham, NC: Duke University Press, 1995).

2 On framing (and its critics) as a central element in the emergence and course of mobilization, see Robert Benford and David Snow, "Framing Processes and Social Movements: An Overview and Assessment," *Annual Review of Sociology* 26 (2000): 611–39; David Snow and Robert Benford, "Ideology, Frame Resonance, and Participant Mobilization," in Bert Klandermans, Hanspeter Kriesi, and Sidney Tarrow, eds., *From Structure to Action: Comparing Social Movement Research* (Greenwich, CN: JAI Press, 1988), 197–217; Francesca Polletta, "Contending Stories:

Narrative in Social Movements," *Qualitative Sociology* 21(4) (1998a): 419–46; Mark Steinberg, *Fighting Words: Working-Class Formation, Collective Action, and Discourse in Early Nineteenth-Century England* (Ithaca, NY: Cornell University Press, 1999).

3 Months before, in the party primaries (*internas*) current Governor Sosbisch allied with Cutral-co former mayor Grittini against the then current Governor Sapag. Sapag won the primaries and Mayor Martinasso, who initially sided with Sosbisch-Grittini, switched factions and join Sapag's group.

4 An "injustice frame" is a mode of interpretation—prefatory to protest—produced and adopted by those who classify the actions of an authority as unjust. See William Gamson, "The Social Psychology of Collective Action," in Aldon Morris and Carol McClurg Mueller, eds., *Frontiers in Social Movement Theory* (New Haven, CT: Yale University Press, 1992).

5 For the classic statement on resource mobilization theory, see John McCarthy and Mayer Zald, "Resource Mobilization and Social Movements," *American Journal of Sociology* 82 (1977): 1212–41; J. Craig Jenkins, "Resource Mobilization Theory," *Annual Review of Sociology* 9 (1983): 527–53.

6 Laura's personal troubles are indeed political in the sense that feminism, broadly understood, speaks of the term "political" but not in the sense that Laura herself gives it. When speaking of "politics" and "political" I am referring to indigenous categories, i.e., to the definitions that actors themselves adopt: Politics, in this sense, mean "party politics."

7 Apparently (and this has been confirmed by many local sources), some of the organizers of the protest did not want protesters to interrupt the distribution of gasoline and oil to nearby areas (former mayor Grittini, for one, was the owner of many gas stations in the area).

8 See my *Contentious Lives* (Durham, NC: Duke University Press, 2003).

9 C. Wright Mills, *The Sociological Imagination* (London: Oxford, 1959).

10 See, among others, James Rule, *Theories of Civil Violence* (Berkeley: University of California Press, 1988) and Beth Roy, *Some Trouble with Cows* (Berkeley: California University Press, 1994).

11 Charles Tilly, "How to Detect, Describe, and Explain Repertoires of Contention," Center for the Study of Social Change, New School for Social Research, *The Working Paper Series* 150 (1992): 6.

Part VIII

How Do Institutions Influence Movements?

Introduction

Any social movement must deal with a range of powerful institutions. Among them, the state is usually the most important. Many movements make demands directly of the state, primarily through demands for changes in policies or laws. Sometimes it is state actions that are the focus of the grievance. If nothing else, the state lays down the rules of the game within which protestors maneuver, and if they choose to break those rules they are likely to encounter punitive action from the police or armed forces. Another major institution with which social movements usually come into contact are the news media, which can be used to purvey a movement's message, portray opponents in an unfavorable light, and influence state decisions. In this section we examine these major players in a social movement's environment.

In the political process school, the state is the major influence on social movements, even to the extent of very often causing movements to arise in the first place. In part II we saw that, according to this theory, it is changes in the state ("political opportunities" like the lessening of repression, divisions among elites, etc.) which often allow movements to form.

There are different ways of understanding the term "opportunity." One is in a more structural fashion, in which large changes occur without much intervention by movements themselves. Sociologists Craig Jenkins and Charles Perrow represent this point of view in the excerpts below, from a 1977 article that helped define the process approach. For one thing, they argue that the same factors explain both the rise of farmworker insurgency and its outcomes. Those factors center squarely on political and economic elites. When they are divided, such that some of them provide resources and political support to a social movement, then that movement has a much better chance of both establishing itself and attaining its goals (we'll see in part X that these are both seen as forms of success in the process model). In another argument typical of the process approach, Jenkins and Perrow dismiss the explanatory importance of discontent, which they say "is ever-present for deprived groups." Jenkins and Perrow also exemplify the process school's focus on those social movements composed of people with little or no political and economic power, groups who normally face severe repression when they try to organize and make demands on the system.

Celebrities Most social movements try to publicize their cause by attracting media coverage. They seek to stage protest events that will be considered newsworthy, perhaps because they are flamboyant or represent a new twist on old tactics. But certain people are also newsworthy, attracting attention simply because they are celebrities. When they call a news conference, reporters come. Social movement groups often try to get well-known actors, musicians, singers, and athletes to support their causes, knowing they will get more publicity this way. This strategy can backfire, however, when a celebrity has her own view of a social issue which may be at odds with that of the protest group.

Moral Panics Students of deviance, social problems, and politics have used the concept of a moral panic to describe sudden concern over a group or activity, accompanied by calls for control and suppression. Out of an infinite range of potential perceived threats, one—which may be neither new nor on the rise—suddenly receives considerable attention. Marijuana use, motorbikes, and rock and roll music are common examples. The news media, public officials, religious leaders, and private "moral entrepreneurs" are key in focusing public attention on the issue, typically by identifying some recognizable group as "folk devils"—usually young people, racial and ethnic minorities, or other relatively powerless groups—responsible for the menace. New political or legal policies are sometimes the result, as are new symbols and sensibilities (available as the raw materials for future panics). Some moral panics inspire grassroots protest groups, but others are manipulated by interested elites to undo the work of social movements. For instance, a series of moral panics over the "black underclass" in American cities—having to do with crime, teenage pregnancy, drugs, and so on—were used to scale back affirmative action programs in the 1980s.

Another way to understand opportunities is shorter term. During any conflict, there will be moments when quick action can have a big effect. The media suddenly notice your cause, perhaps because of a crisis or accident, or maybe because of an event you have organized. You must move quickly to use them to get your message across. Or there may be a crisis in government that gives your social movement room to maneuver and make the government concede to your demands just to keep the peace. Social movements are constantly looking for these openings in the state, as well as for sympathetic politicians. But many of these windows of opportunity can hurt as well as help, reshaping, curtailing, or channeling movement demands in the very process of recognizing them. "Opportunities" are also "constraints."

A third way to envision opportunities (or a third kind of opportunity) is as relatively permanent features of a country's political landscape. Administrative structures, legal systems, electoral rules, and constitutions all constrain what social movements can achieve. We might call these "horizons" of opportunity, since they define what is possible within that system, in contrast to "windows" of opportunity that open and shut quickly.

The mass media are of course another important institution that shapes and constrains movements and which movements seek to shape and constrain as well. Modern social movements can hardly be imagined without the media to amplify their messages. The cheap newspapers that appeared in the nineteenth century, for instance, helped larger, more national movements form for the first time in the industrialized countries. Today, hardly any movement can afford to ignore the media, which can reach much larger numbers than can the movement itself through personal networks or its own publications. These anonymous audiences can be especially important in contributing funds and in affecting state policies.

Movement activists devote considerable time to figuring out events that will attract news coverage—in other words, events which editors and reporters will consider "newsworthy" (Gans 1979). Especially flamboyant marches and rallies, new twists on old themes, and clever incantations can all help events to get on the evening news. Abbie Hoffman was a genius at attracting this kind of attention, with events such as the "levitation" of the Pentagon. But social movements challenging the status quo often face media that are not entirely sympathetic, and which sometimes are hostile to the movement's message. What is more, movements' opponents often have better access to the news media. Movements have little control over how they are ultimately portrayed.

Choice Points Protestors and their opponents make numerous choices in the course of their varied engagements. In doing so they face many strategic dilemmas, in which each course of action has potential benefits but also costs and risks. The creativity of movements is evident when a choice is made to do something differently from what is expected or what has been done in the past. Not all choices are consciously faced, as many people—following routines—do what other protest groups usually do because that "is just the way it is done." Even when they are not faced, the strategic dilemmas still exist as tradeoffs, shaping the outcomes of conflict. Scholarly analysts can often see alternatives activists themselves do not.

Perhaps the best analysis of the complex interaction between a movement and the media is Todd Gitlin's book about the New Left of the 1960s, *The Whole World Is Watching*, parts of which appear below. He first shows some of the ways that the media "framed" the protest at its height (in other words, when it was most threatening to mainstream institutions) by concentrating on its more extreme ideas and actions and at the same time trivializing the threat it posed. At the same time, this loosely organized movement began thinking about itself in the terms laid out by the media! As the next part of Gitlin's excerpt shows, one hazard of media coverage is the creation of media stars from among movement leaders. These are not always the actual organizational or intellectual leaders, but usually people who are flamboyant and photogenic—in other words, with a talent for attracting media attention. This creation of spokespersons whose power comes from their ability to attract media coverage further distorts a movement's message. Many potential leaders simply abdicate this role in the face of media dynamics.

It is clear from Gitlin's account that one effect of the media can be to give undue prominence to radical or illegal wings of movements, or to segments that are further outside mainstream culture: the "kooks" in a movement. Governments, too, often radicalize a movement by indiscriminately repressing moderates and radicals (in which case there is little incentive to be a moderate), or simply by repressing a movement too heavy-handedly. In the end, these interactions with media and the state deeply affect a movement's ability to change its society.

The media have had a significant influence on the human rights movement in the West, as detailed by James Ron, Howard Ramos, and Kathleen Rodgers. The media are generally uninterested in (and often incapable of) reporting human rights abuses in poor and "obscure" countries, even when those abuses are extensive. So human rights organizations, which generally prize media visibility, tend to focus on abuses in wealthier and more accessible countries, even if the abuses there are less severe. Media visibility also makes it easier for rights organizations to raise funds, an important incentive for focusing their efforts on wealthier and better-known countries. The media's priorities, in short, encourage the human rights movement to pay less attention to abuses in poorer countries than would be merited in a fairer world.

The opposite side of this coin, as Clifford Bob shows, is a tendency for movements in poorer countries to adjust their own goals and strategies to match the concerns of potential allies in richer countries. Bob notes how the Ogoni ethnic group in Nigeria, led by Ken Saro-Wiwa (see the short biography that follows Bob's article), reframed its conflict with multinational oil companies from one of ethnic domination to "environmental warfare." This strategic shift was instrumental in winning the support of Western environmental organizations. But worthy movements that lack savvy, charismatic leaders attuned to Western audiences (including highly participatory movements) are likely to suffer in isolation. Movements that seem complex, unfashionable, or hopeless are unlikely to attract international support.

Corporations are another important institution with which movements contend. The changing character of corporations and the capitalist economy has altered the playing field on which movements—especially labor and environmental movements—have mobilized in recent years.

Corporations are increasingly powerful and global in scale. As Stephen Lerner points out, most of the 100 largest economies in the world today are not countries, but global corporations. Accordingly, Lerner suggests, labor unions need to focus their organizing efforts on corporations, not countries, which in turn means organizing on the same global scale as corporations. (Lerner is an official of the Service Employees International Union [SEIU], the fastest-growing union in the U.S.) Multinational corporations may be increasingly powerful, but they are also dependent on service workers whose jobs cannot be relocated or "off-shored." (A janitor in Manila cannot clean an office in Los Angeles; a maid in Calcutta cannot make a bed in Miami.) So even low-wage workers have some potential leverage in the global economy. Global capitalism has certainly created daunting challenges for labor movements, but it has not changed the need for or possibility of them. As we have seen, in fact, it has even spurred a transnational movement for democratic globalization.

Discussion Questions

1. What kinds of "opportunities" affect the efficacy of social movements?
2. What are the benefits and risks of having allies among prominent politicians or other celebrities?
3. To what extent was the farmworkers' movement successful because of a shifting political environment? To what extent was its success a product of specific strategies?
4. As a political activist, how would you go about getting media attention for your cause? What are some of the risks of that attention?
5. What factors shape how the media will portray a social movement and its ideas?
6. Corporations are increasingly global in their operations. In what ways does this make them more or less vulnerable to pressure from workers and their allies?

29 Farmworkers' Movements in Changing Political Contexts

J. Craig Jenkins and Charles Perrow

From about 1964 until 1972, American society witnessed an unprecedented number of groups acting in insurgent fashion. By insurgency we mean organized attempts to bring about structural change by thrusting new interests into decision-making processes. Some of this insurgency, notably the civil rights and peace movements, had begun somewhat earlier, but after 1963 there were organized attempts to bring about structural changes from virtually all sides: ethnic minorities (Indians, Mexican-Americans, Puerto Ricans), welfare mothers, women, sexual liberation groups, teachers and even some blue-collar workers. The present study isolates and analyzes in detail one of these insurgent challenges – that of farmworkers – in an effort to throw light on the dynamics that made the 1960s a period of dramatic and stormy politics.

Our thesis is that the rise and dramatic success of farmworker insurgents in the late 1960s best can be explained by changes in the political environment the movement confronted, rather than by the internal characteristics of the movement organization and the social base upon which it drew. The salient environment consisted of the government, especially the federal government, and a coalition of liberal support organizations. We shall contrast the unsuccessful attempt to organize farmworkers by the National Farm Labor Union from 1946 to 1952 with the strikingly successful one of the United Farmworkers from 1965 to 1972.

The immediate goals of both movements were the same – to secure union contracts. They both used the same tactics, namely, mass agricultural strikes, boycotts aided by organized labor, and political demands supported by the liberal community of the day. Both groups encountered identical and virtually insurmountable obstacles, namely, a weak bargaining position, farmworker poverty and a culture of resignation, high rates of migrancy and weak social cohesion, and a perpetual oversupply of farm labor, insuring that growers could break any strike.

The difference between the two challenges was the societal response that insurgent demands received. During the first challenge, government policies strongly favored agribusiness; support from liberal organizations and organized labor was weak and vacillating. By the time the second challenge was mounted, the political environment had changed dramatically. Government now was divided over policies pertaining to farmworkers; liberals and organized labor had formed a reform coalition, attacking agri-business privileges in public policy. The reform coalition then furnished the resources to launch the challenge. Once underway, the coalition continued to fend for the insurgents, providing additional resources and applying leverage to movement targets. The key changes, then, were in support organization and governmental actions. To demonstrate this, we will analyze macro-level changes in the activities of these groups as reported in the *New York Times Annual Index* between 1946 and 1972.

Repression Armies and police are almost always better armed than social movements. If political leaders retain control over the military and police, accordingly, then they can suppress almost any social movement that they choose. Such repression will be constrained primarily by public opinion or by disagreements among elites. While repression generally works to dampen protest, however, it sometimes "backfires," provoking greater levels of protest, including armed resistance, by people who are angry and outraged by the repression, in addition to whatever grievances prompted them to protest in the first place. Even armed revolutionaries, however, rarely succeed against a unified state. But the likelihood that (or at least the speed with which) a state will move to suppress a social movement varies enormously. Movements aimed at seizing state power receive the fastest attention. Those that are disruptive or which challenge economic elites can also expect a powerful repressive response. But many moderate movements, asking for reforms within the existing political and economic order, may escape repression. In fact, this is usually a prerequisite for their survival, given the enormous imbalance in power between the state and most social movements.

The Classical Model

In taking this position, we are arguing that the standard literature on social movements fails to deal adequately with either of two central issues – the formation of insurgent organizations and the outcome of insurgent challenges. Drawing on Gusfield's (1968) summary statement, the classical literature holds in common the following line of argument.

Social movements arise because of deep and widespread discontent. First, there is a social change which makes prevailing social relations inappropriate, producing a strain between the new and the old. Strain then generates discontent within some social grouping. When discontent increases rapidly and is widely shared, collective efforts to alleviate discontent will occur. Though there is disagreement about how to formulate the link between strain and discontent, e.g., subjective gaps between expectations and satisfactions versus emotional anxiety induced by anomie, the central thrust is consistent. Fluctuations in the level of discontent account for the rise of movements and major changes in movement participation.

Recent research, though, has cast doubt on the classic "discontent" formulations. Disorders do not arise from disorganized anomic masses, but from groups organizationally able to defend and advance their interests (Oberschall, 1973; Tilly et al., 1975). As for relative deprivation, Snyder and Tilly (1972) and Hibbs (1973) have failed to find it useful in accounting for a wide variety of collective disruptions. Nor is it clear that we can use the concept without falling into post hoc interpretations (cf. Wilson, 1973:73–9).[1]

In this study, we do not propose to test each of the various "discontent" formulations currently available. *A priori*, it is rather hard to believe that farmworkers' discontent was, for example, suddenly greater in 1965, when the Delano grape strike began, than throughout much of the 1950s when there was no movement or strike activity. Indeed, it seems more plausible to assume that farmworker discontent is relatively constant, a product of established economic relations rather than some social dislocation or dysfunction. We do not deny the existence of discontent but we question the usefulness of discontent formulations in accounting for either the emergence of insurgent organization or the level of participation by the social base. What increases, giving rise to insurgency, is the amount of social resources available to unorganized but aggrieved groups, making it possible to launch an organized demand for change.

As for the outcome of challenges, the importance of resources is obvious. Though the classical literature has rarely dealt with the issue directly, there has been an implicit position. The resources mobilized by movement organizations are assumed to derive from the aggrieved social base. The outcome of the challenge, then, whether or not one adopts a "natural history" model of movement development, should depend primarily upon internal considerations, e.g., leadership changes and communication dynamics among the membership.

However, are deprived groups like farmworkers able to sustain challenges, especially effective ones, on their own? We think not. Both of the movements studied were, from the outset, dependent upon external groups for critical organizational resources. Nor, as the history of agricultural strikes amply attests, have farmworker movements proven able to mobilize numbers sufficient to wring concessions from employers. For a successful outcome, movements by the "powerless" require strong and sustained outside support.

If this line of argument is correct, we need to contest a second thesis frequently found in the classical literature – the assertion that the American polity operates in a pluralistic fashion (Kornhauser, 1959; Smelser, 1962). A pluralistic polity is structurally open to demands for change. As Gamson (1968; 1975) has put it, the political system should be structurally "permeable," readily incorporating new groups and their interests into the decision-making process. Once organized, groups redressing widely-shared grievances should be able to secure at least some part of their program through bargaining and compromise. Yet our evidence shows that farmworker challenges have failed, in part, because of the opposition of public officials, and that a successful challenge depended upon the intervention of established liberal organizations and the neutrality of political elites.

We can then summarize the classical model as follows. (1) Discontent, traced to structural dislocations, accounts for collective attempts to bring about change. (2) The resources required to mount collective action and carry it through are broadly distributed – shared by all sizeable social groupings. (3) The political system is pluralistic and, therefore, responsive to all organized groups with grievances. (4) If insurgents succeed, it is due to efforts on the part of the social base; if they do not, presumably they lacked competent leaders, were unwilling to compromise, or behaved irrationally (e.g., used violence or broke laws).

In contrast, we will argue that (1) discontent is ever-present for deprived groups, but (2) collective action is rarely a viable option because of lack of resources and the threat of repression. (3) When deprived groups do mobilize, it is due to the interjection of external resources. (4) Challenges frequently fail because of the lack of resources. Success comes when there is a combination of sustained outside support and disunity and/or tolerance on the part of political elites. The important variables separating movement success from failure, then, pertain to the way the polity responds to insurgent demands.

Structural Powerlessness of Farmworkers

The major impediment to farmworker unionization has been the oversupply of farm labor, undercutting all attempted harvest strikes. There are few barriers of habit or skill that restrict the entry of any applicant to work in the fields. The result is an "unstructured" labor market, offering little job stability and open to all comers. The fields of California and Texas are close enough to the poverty-stricken provinces of Mexico to insure a steady influx of workers, many of whom arrive by illegal routes. Continuous immigration not only underwrites the oversupply of labor, but complicates mobilization by insuring the existence of cultural cleavages among workers.

Furthermore, there are reasons to believe that a significant number of workers have only a limited economic interest in the gains promised by unionization. The majority of farmworkers, both domestic and alien, are short-term seasonal workers. During the early 1960s, farm employment in California averaged less than three months of the year. This means that a majority of workers are interested primarily in the "quick dollar." Imposition of union restrictions on easy access to jobs would conflict with that interest. And for the vast majority of farmworkers, regardless of job commitment or citizenship status, income is so low as to leave little economic reserve for risk-taking. Since a major portion of the year's income comes during the brief harvest period, workers are reluctant to risk their livelihood on a strike at that time.

In addition to these structural restraints on collective action, there were the very direct restraints of the growers and their political allies. The California Department of Employment and the U.S. Department of Labor have long operated farm placement services that furnish workers for strike-bound employers. Insurgent actions that directly threaten growers, like picket lines and mass rallies, consistently have been the target of official harassment. Though never returning to the scale of the "local fascism" of the 1930s grower vigilante actions are not uncommon.

Bringing these considerations to bear on the comparison of farmworker challenges, there is reason to believe that circumstances were slightly more conducive to the mobilization efforts of the UFW. Between 1946 and 1965 farm wage rates rose slightly and a few public welfare benefits were extended, at least within California. Presumably, farmworkers were slightly more secure economically by the mid-1960s. More significant, though, were changes in the social composition of the farm labor force. During the late 1940s farmworkers in California were either "dustbowlers" or Mexican *braceros* (government-imported contract workers); by the mid-1960s the California farm labor force was predominantly Mexican-descent, short-term workers, most of whom only recently had migrated across the border. Not only were linguistic-cultural cleavages somewhat less pronounced, but these new immigrants were more likely to settle and develop stable community ties than their "Okie" predecessors.

Also, the United Farmworkers pursued a mobilization strategy better designed than that of the NFLU to sustain the participation of farmworkers. From its inception, the UFW was an Alinsky-styled community organization. The primary advantage was that it offered a program of services and social activities that did not depend upon first securing a union contract. Members developed an attachment to the organization independent of the immediate gains that might derive from any strike. Though the National Farm Labor Union had taken limited steps in a similar direction, its program remained primarily that of the conventional "business" union, promising wage gains and better working conditions rather than social solidarity and community benefits.

But the critical issue is whether differences in either the structural position of farmworkers or the mobilization strategy adopted by the movements affected either dependent variable. As we shall see, the impetus for both of the challenges came from the interjection, into an otherwise placid situation, of a professionally-trained cadre backed by outside sponsors. Farmworker discontent remained unexpressed in any organized way until outside organizers arrived on the scene.

As for the question of challenge outcome, despite the UFW's advantages, it experienced no more success in strike efforts than did the NFLU. Where the NFLU had to contend with the semi-official use of *braceros* as strikebreakers, the UFW had to deal with vastly increased numbers of illegal aliens and short-term workers crossing the picket lines. The combination of structural constraints and direct controls insured that neither union was able to mobilize a sufficiently massive social base to be effective.

What separated the UFW success from the NFLU failure was the societal response to the challenges. The NFLU received weak and vacillating sponsorship; the UFW's backing was strong and sustained. Under the pressure of court injunctions and police harassment, the NFLU boycott collapsed when organized labor refused to cooperate. By contrast, the UFW boycotts became national "causes," receiving widespread support from organized labor and liberal organizations; though official harassment remained, the UFW did not deal with the same systematic repression confronted by the NFLU. The success of a "powerless" challenge depended upon sustained and widespread outside support coupled with the neutrality and/or tolerance from the national political elite.

[...]

Our analysis centers on the comparison of three time periods. The first, 1946–1955, spans the challenge of the National Farm Labor Union. Chartered to organize farmworkers at the 1946 American Federation of Labor convention, the NFLU launched a strike wave in the Central Valley of California that ended with the abortive Los Baños strike of 1952. The selection of 1955 as the end point of the period was somewhat arbitrary.

By comparison, the third period, 1965–1972, covers the sustained and successful challenge of the United Farmworkers. The 1965 Coachella and Delano strikes announced the UFW challenge; in 1970, after two years of nation-wide boycott efforts, the UFW brought table-grape growers to the bargaining table and began institutionalizing changes in the position of farmworkers. (The Teamster entry in 1973 is not dealt with in this paper.)

During the period intervening between the two challenges, 1956–1964, important changes took place in the political system that set the stage for a successful challenge. In the absence of a major "push" from insurgents, issues pertaining to farm labor received a different treatment in the hands of established liberal organizations and government officials. We will argue that these years constituted a period of germination and elite reform that made possible the success of the late 1960s.

[...]

Period I: The NFLU Conflict (1946–1955)

The first period illustrates in classical terms the obstacles to a sustained and successful farmworker challenge. In addition to the structural constraints restricting farmworker activity, the political environment confronting the insurgents was unfavorable. Government officials at all levels and branches came into the conflict predominantly on the side of the growers, despite the mandate of agencies such as the Department of Labor or the Education and Labor Committees in Congress to protect the interests of deprived groups like farmworkers. Though external support was decisive in launching the challenge, it was weak and frequently ill-focused, dealing with the consequences rather than the causes of farmworker grievances. When support was withdrawn, the challenge soon collapsed.

Chartered at the 1946 convention of the American Federation of Labor, the National Farm Labor Union set out to accomplish what predecessors had been unable to do – successfully organize the farmworkers of California's "industrialized" agriculture. The leadership cadre was experienced and resourceful. H. L. Mitchell, President of the NFLU, was former head of the Southern Tenant Farmers Union; the Director of Organizations, Henry Hasiwar, had been an effective organizer in several industrial union drives during the 1930s; Ernesto Galarza, who assumed prime responsibility for publicity efforts, had served as political liaison for Latin American unions and had a Ph.D. in economics from Columbia University.

Initially, the strategy was quite conventional: enlist as many workers as possible from a single employer, call a strike, demand wage increases and union recognition, and picket to keep "scabs" out of the fields. American Federation of Labor affiliates would then provide strike relief and political support to keep the picket line going. An occasional church or student group would furnish money and boost morale.

But the government-sponsored alien labor or *braceros* program provided growers with an effective strike-breaking weapon. According to provisions of the law, *braceros* were not to be employed except in instances of domestic labor shortage and *never* to be employed in fields where domestic workers had walked out on strike. Yet in the two major tests of union power, the DiGiorgio strike of 1948 and the Imperial Valley strike of 1951, the flood of *braceros* undermined the strike effort of domestic workers. In the Imperial strike, the NFLU used citizen's arrests to enforce statutes prohibiting employment of *braceros* in labor disputed areas. However, local courts ruled against the tactic and the Immigration Service refused to remove alien "scabs" from the fields. Nor were affairs changed when the *bracero* administration was transferred to the U.S. Department of Labor in 1951. Domestic workers were pushed out of crops by *braceros,* and *braceros* reappeared in the Los Baños strike of 1952 to break the challenge.

In response, the NFLU launched a two-pronged political challenge – a demand for termination of the *bracero* program and, to get around the problem of ineffective strikes, requests for organized labor's support of boycotts. Neither demand found a favorable audience. Lacking strong labor or liberal support, the demand for an end to the *bracero* traffic ended in minor reforms in the *bracero* administration. As for the boycott, despite initial success, it collapsed when a court injunction was issued (improperly) on the grounds that the NFLU was covered by the "hot cargo" provisions of the Taft-Hartley Act. The National Labor Relations Board initially concurred and reversed its position over a year later. By then the Union's resources were exhausted and organized-labor support had long since collapsed.

Figure 29.1 charts the level of favorable actions by selected groups, allowing us to gauge the societal response to insurgency. The curves delineating government, liberal, and farmworker activities move roughly in concert. (Organized labor, though, played little public role in this or the next period.) [...]

The main issue for the period was labor supply. [...] The union attempted, through court actions, lobby efforts and public protest, to pressure government to end the *bracero* program since it was so central to the control of the labor supply. The official response, however, was largely symbolic. Though government tended to respond to concrete insurgency with favorable concrete actions, the majority of favorable governmental actions were actually symbolic (58%). Nor did many of these concrete moves decisively aid the farmworker cause. Key actions, such as pulling strikebreaking *braceros* out of the fields, did not occur.

What, then, are we to make of the fact that 50% of reported governmental actions were coded as favorable to the interest of farmworkers? Was government responding to the conflict between insurgents and growers in some even-handed "pluralist" way? Here it is necessary to recall that we are using news media reportage on a social problem and efforts to redress that problem. The news media will be more sensitive to efforts attempting to define or solve that problem than to efforts to maintain the *status quo*. Consequently, unfavorable actions by government and growers are underrepresented in our data. If only 50% of news-reported government actions can be coded as favorable, then the full universe of governmental activities should, in the balance, be more favorable to growers.

The strength of this assertion is borne out by information on actions favorable to growers. Figure 29.2 charts these actions for government and growers. [...] In quantitative terms, government was more responsive to agribusiness interests. Clearly, in critical instances, e.g., leaving *braceros* in struck fields, government policies favored growers over workers.

In addition to the predominantly unfavorable response of government, the NFLU failed to receive sustained, solid support from the liberal community. The major problem was the type of activities in which liberals engaged. When they acted, liberals consistently supported farmworkers over growers but they rarely moved beyond symbolic proclamations. Only 24% of liberal actions during the period were concrete. By

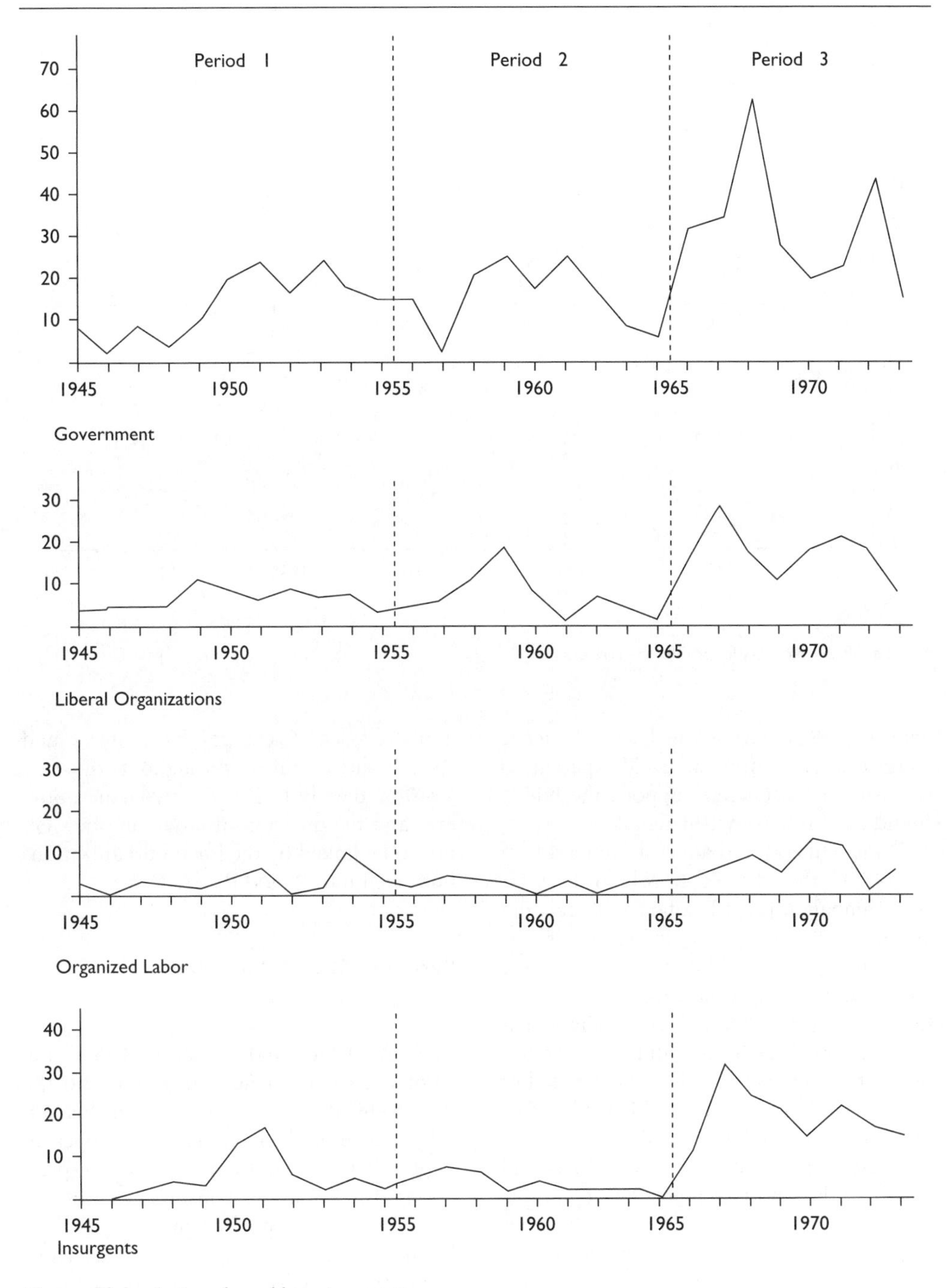

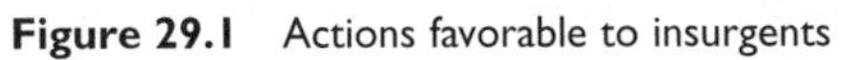

Figure 29.1 Actions favorable to insurgents

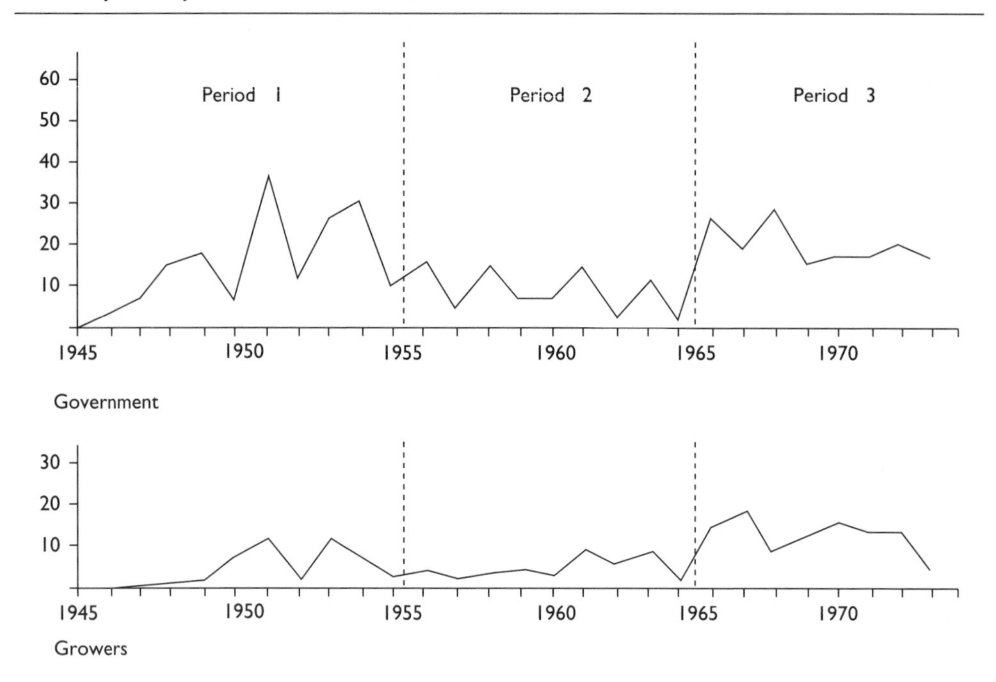

Figure 29.2 Actions favorable to growers

contrast, 38% during the UFW challenge were so. [...] Where the UFW experienced consistent and concrete support, the NFLU found itself relatively isolated.

Though liberals did not rush to the side of the NFLU, they did play a role in the pressure campaign. [...] Insofar as liberals did act alongside insurgents, apparently it was in the presence of public officials. But there were problems even with this limited-scale liberal support. Liberals focused almost exclusively on the working and living conditions of farmworkers. Following the lead of Progressive Party candidate Henry Wallace in 1948, several religious and "public interest" associations sponsored conferences and issued study reports publicizing deplorable camp conditions and child labor. In what might be considered a typical pattern of liberalism of the time, they were concerned with the plight of the workers rather than the fact of their powerlessness or the role of the *bracero* program in underwriting that powerlessness. It was a humanitarian, nonpolitical posture, easily dissipated by "red baiting" in Congressional investigations and "red scare" charges by growers and their political allies throughout the late 1940s and early 1950s. The two issues, poverty and the question of labor supply, were not to be linked by the liberal organizations until well into Period II.

Period II: Elite Reform and Realignment (1956–1964)

The late 1950s and the early 1960s, the second Eisenhower administration and the brief Kennedy period emerge from this and other studies in the larger project as a period of germination. Contrary to some interpretations, the remarkable insurgencies of the late 1960s did not originate with the Kennedy administration, but with developments that initially began to appear during Eisenhower's second term. Nor did the Kennedy years witness a dramatic escalation of insurgent activity. Indeed, in the case of farmworkers, insurgency showed a decline (figure 29.1). For our purposes, the two presidential administrations can be treated as a single period, one that witnessed important realignments and shifts in political resources in the national polity, culminating in a supportive environment for insurgent activity.

Farmworker insurgency during the reform period was at a low ebb. Actions by farmworker insurgents dropped from 16% to 11% of all pro-worker activity. In 1956–1957 the NFLU, now renamed the National Agricultural Workers Union (NAWU), secured a small grant from the United Auto Workers, enabling it to hang on as a paper organization. Galarza, by then the only full-time cadre member, launched a publicity campaign to reveal maladministration and corruption within the *bracero* administration. Aside from a brief and ineffective organizing drive launched in 1959 by the Agricultural Workers Organizing Committee (AWOC), generating only one reported strike (in 1961), this was the sum of insurgent activity for the nine-year Period II (figure 29.1). Growers remained publicly inactive and seemingly secure in their position, aroused only at renewal time for the *bracero* program to lobby bills through Congress. Until the insurgency of Period III began, growers retained a low profile in the *Times* (figure 29.2).

With the direct adversaries largely retired from the public arena, affairs shifted into the hands of government and the liberals. Despite the absence of significant insurgency, the balance of forces in the national polity had begun to shift. Actions favorable to the interests of farmworkers increased from 50% to 73%, remaining on the same plane (75%) throughout the following UFW period. Beginning during the last years of the Eisenhower administration, three interrelated developments brought about this new supportive environment: (1) policy conflicts within the political elite that resulted in a more "balanced," neutral stance toward farmworkers; (2) the formation of a reform coalition composed of liberal pressure groups and organized labor that, in the midst of elite divisions, was able to exercise greater political influence; (3) the erosion of the Congressional power-base of conservative rural interests, stemming immediately from reapportionment.

The concern of liberal pressure groups initially was focused on the need to improve housing and educational conditions of migrant workers. In 1956, the Democratic National Convention included a plank for increased welfare aid to migrants. The next year, the National Council of Churches, already involved in the early civil rights movement in the South, began a study of migrant camp conditions and child labor. In early 1958, the Council brought public pressure to bear on Secretary of Labor James Mitchell to enforce existing laws regarding migrant camps throughout the nation. In late 1958, several liberal pressure groups were joined by the AFL-CIO in attacking the *bracero* program, scoring administrative laxity, and arguing that federal labor policies were the origin of social problems. The two as yet unrelated issues – poverty and labor policies – were now firmly linked in the public debate.

The fusion of these two issues was significant. Of course, economic conditions already had been linked with social deprivations in public parlance, but the concern of liberal groups in the past had been with inspection of housing, assurances of educational opportunity, and public health measures. To argue now that a public program of importing foreign labor perpetuated the list of conditions deplored by liberals was a substantial change. As later happened more generally with the New Left, the advocates of reform had begun to look at the source of problems in terms of a system.

About the same time, organized labor took a new interest in farmworkers. In 1959, the AFL-CIO Executive Council abolished the NAWU and created the Agricultural Workers Organizing Committee (AWOC), headed by Norman Smith, a former UAW organizer. Despite strong financial backing, the AWOC produced little results. Concentrating on 4 a.m. "shake-ups" of day laborers, the AWOC managed to sponsor a number of "job actions" but only one major strike and little solid organization. Like the

NFLU, the AWOC had to confront the problem of *braceros*. In the one reported strike, the Imperial Valley strike of February, 1961, the AWOC used violence to intimidate strikebreaking *braceros* and create an international incident over their presence. Officials quickly arrested the cadre, and the AWOC ceased to exist except on paper. Though the AWOC drive consumed over one million dollars of AFL-CIO funds, it produced neither contracts nor stable membership. Yet, and this indicates the shift, this type of financial support had never before been offered by organized labor.

The final element in the formation of a supportive environment was a shift in governmental actions. Actions favorable to farmworkers increased from the unfavorable 50% prevailing during Period I to a more "balanced" 68% of all governmental actions. Of these, the portion coded "concrete," and therefore more likely to have impact, increased from 40% in Period I to 65%. Indicative of the change taking place in official views, the focus of governmental attentions shifted from the labor supply issue (56% of favorable actions during Period I) to the question of farmworkers' living and working conditions (73% during Period II).

The change in official actions stemmed, in part, from internal conflicts within the national political elite. Secretary of Labor James Mitchell was a surprise Eisenhower appointee from the Eastern wing of the Republican Party, a former labor consultant for New York department stores and a future protege of Nelson Rockefeller. Mitchell took the Department of Labor in a more pro-union direction than was thought possible, at the time becoming a "strong man" in the cabinet because of his success in mollifying unions. In 1958, an open fight between the Taft and Eastern wings of the Republican Party developed, with the conservatives favoring a national "right-to-work" law. Mitchell, as an advocate of unionism and apparently jockeying for position for the Republican Vice-Presidential nomination, became a figure of elite reform within Republican circles.

A second factor contributing to the shift in official actions was the pressure campaign launched by the reform coalition. [...]

Tangible effects of the pressure campaign appeared almost immediately. In 1957, under pressure from the liberal reform coalition, the Department of Labor under Mitchell's guidance carried out an internal review of farm labor policies. The upshot was a series of executive orders to tighten up enforcement of regulations covering migrant camps. When the economic recession of 1958–1959 arrived, sensitivity within the Administration to rising unemployment levels increased. In response, Mitchell vowed to enforce more fully the 1951 statutes requiring farm employment to be offered to domestic workers prior to importation of *braceros*. Growers, long accustomed to having their *bracero* requests met automatically, rebelled when asked to provide more justification. In February, 1959, Mitchell took an even stronger step, joining the liberal reformers in support of legislation to extend minimum-wage laws to agriculture and to impose new restrictions on the use of *braceros*.

The following year, the division within the Eisenhower Administration opened up into a full-scale, cabinet-level battle over renewal of the *bracero* program. The Farm Bureau and the state grower associations engaged that other administration "strong man," Secretary of Agriculture Ezra Taft Benson, to defend the program. In testimony before the House Committee on Agriculture, the White House took a neutral stance; Benson defended the program, while Mitchell argued that the program exerted demonstrable adverse effects upon domestic workers and should be abolished. Into this breach in the political elite stepped the liberal-labor support coalition. At the same time, the House Committee on Public Welfare opened hearings on health and camp conditions, giving the Cotton Council and the Meatcutters Union a chance to air opposing views.

Initially, the reform effort failed. In March, 1960, Secretary Mitchell withdrew his program, resolving the dispute on the cabinet level. The next month, agribusiness pushed a two-year renewal of the *bracero* program through Congress. But, for the first time, the issue had been debated seriously and a loose coalition of liberal pressure groups (e.g., National Council of Churches, National Advisory Committee of Farm Labor, NAACP) and organized labor had formed. Though the eventual termination of the *bracero* program did not undermine growers' ability to break strikes (there were other substitutes, e.g., "green card" commuters, illegal aliens), the fight against the program did refocus the concern of liberals and organized labor on the structural problem of farmworker powerlessness.

The reform coalition sustained the campaign over the next three years. In 1960, the Democratic platform condemned the *bracero* program. Once in office, the New Frontiersmen, though demanding no important statutory changes, did vow to enforce fully the laws restricting *bracero* use. By renewal time in 1963, the Kennedy Administration was in the pursuit of a public issue ("poverty") and courting minority-group votes. For the first time, the White House went formally on record against the program. Only at the last minute was a pressure campaign, mounted by Governor Pat Brown of California and the Department of State, responding to Mexican diplomatic pressure, able to save the program temporarily. Amid promises from Congressional farm bloc leaders that this was the last time the program would be renewed, a one-year extension was granted.

In addition to the efforts of the reform coalition, which played a critical role in other reforms of the same period, and the new elite-level neutrality, the fall of the *bracero* program stemmed from the narrowing power base of the Congressional farm bloc. Congressional reapportionment had visibly shaken the conservative farm bloc leaders. Searching for items in the farm program that could be scuttled without damaging the main planks, the farm bloc leaders fixed on the *bracero* program. The mechanization of the Texas cotton harvest had left California growers of specialty crops the main *bracero* users. When the test came, *bracero* users, as a narrow, special interest, could be sacrificed to keep the main planks of the farm program intact.

Period II, then, emerges from this analysis as a period of reform and political realignment that dramatically altered the prospective fortunes of insurgents. Reforms, stemming from elite-level conflicts and a pressure campaign conducted by liberal public-interest organizations and organized labor, came about in the virtual absence of activity by farmworker insurgents. The activism of several key liberal organizations depended, in turn, upon broad economic trends, especially the growth of middle-class disposable income that might be invested in worthy causes (McCarthy and Zald, 1973). Insurgents did not stimulate these changes in the national polity. Rather, they were to prove the beneficiaries and, if anything, were stimulated by them.

Period III: The UFW Success (1965–1972)

During the NFLU period, the number of insurgent actions reported totaled 44. Most of these were symbolic in character, only 27% being concrete. Insurgency was brief, concentrated in a four-year period (1948–1951). However, in the third period, insurgency became sustained. Insurgent actions reached a new peak and remained at a high level throughout the period. A total of 143 actions conducted by farmworker insurgents were recorded. Significantly, 71% of these were concrete in character. By the end of the period, the success of the United Farmworkers was unmistakable. Over a hundred contracts had been signed; wages had been raised by almost a third; union hiring halls were in operation in every major agricultural area in California; farmworkers, acting through ranch committees set up under each contract, were exercising a new set of powers.

The key to this dramatic success was the altered political environment within which the challenge operated. Though the potential for mobilizing a social base was slightly more favorable than before, the UFW never was able to launch effective strikes. Though the UFW cadre was experienced and talented, there is little reason to believe that they were markedly more so than the NFLU leadership; neither did the tactics of the challenge differ. The boycotts that secured success for the UFW also had been tried by the NFLU, but with quite different results. What had changed was the political environment – the liberal community now was willing to provide sustained, massive support for insurgency; the political elite had adopted a neutral stance toward farmworkers.

As before, external support played a critical role in launching the challenge. The initial base for the United Farmworkers was César Chávez's National Farmworkers Association (NFWA) and remnants of the AWOC still receiving some support from the AFL-CIO. During the 1950s, Chávez had been director of the Community Service Organization, an Alinsky-styled urban community-organization with strong ties to civil rights groups, liberal churches and foundations. Frustrated by the refusal of the CSO Board of Directors to move beyond issues salient to upwardly-mobile urban Mexican-Americans, Chávez resigned his post in the winter of 1961 and set out to organize a community organization among farmworkers in the Central Valley of California. Drawing on his liberal contacts, Chávez was able to secure the backing of several liberal organizations which had developed a new concern with poverty and the problems of minority groups. The main sponsor was the California Migrant Ministry, a domestic mission of the National Council of Churches servicing migrant farmworkers. During the late 1950s, the Migrant Ministry followed the prevailing policy change within the National Council, substituting community organization and social action programs for traditional evangelical ones. By 1964, the Migrant Ministry had teamed up with Chávez, merging its own community organization (the FWO) with the NFWA and sponsoring the Chávez-directed effort.

By summer, 1965, NFWA had over 500 active members and began shifting directions, expanding beyond economic benefit programs (e.g., a credit union, cooperative buying, etc.) to unionization. Several small "job actions" were sponsored. Operating nearby, the remaining active group of the AWOC, several Filipino work-crews, hoped to take advantage of grower uncertainty generated by termination of the *bracero* program. The AWOC launched a series of wage strikes, first in the Coachella Valley and then in the Delano-Arvin area of the San Joaquin Valley. With the AWOC out on strike, Chávez pressed the NFWA for a strike vote. On Mexican Independence Day, September 16th, the NFWA joined the picket lines.

Though dramatic, the strike soon collapsed. Growers refused to meet with union representatives; a sufficient number of workers crossed the picket lines to prevent a major harvest loss. Over the next six years, the same pattern recurred – a

Political Opportunities Some groups are eager and sufficiently organized to protest, yet are fearful that they will be ignored or even repressed if they do. These groups may not engage in protest, accordingly, until (1) they have at least some access to authorities, or they see signs that (2) repression is declining, (3) elites are divided, or (4) elites or other influential groups are willing to support them. Such shifts in the political environment diminish the risks associated with protest and amplify the political influence of protesters. The appearance or "expansion" of these types of "political opportunities" may be a necessary precondition for – and may explain the precise timing of – the emergence of a protest movement. The same political opportunities, whether or not their participants are even aware of them, may also help movements to change laws and public policies. Of course, when they are willing to take sufficient risks, movements sometimes create opportunities for themselves, rather than simply waiting for changes among elites.

dramatic strike holding for a week, grower intransigence, police intimidation, gradual replacement of the work force by playing upon ethnic rivalries and recruiting illegal aliens. What proved different from the NFLU experience was the ability of the insurgents, acting in the new political environment, to secure outside support.

Political protest was the mechanism through which much of this support was garnered. By dramatic actions designed to capture the attention of a sympathetic public and highlight the "justice" of their cause, insurgents were able to sustain the movement organization and exercise sufficient indirect leverage against growers to secure contracts. The UFW's use of protest tactics departed from that of rent strikers analyzed by Lipsky (1968; 1970). Though the basic mechanism was the same (namely, securing the sympathy of third parties to the conflict so that they would use their superior resources to intervene in support of the powerless), the commitments of supporting organizations and the uses to which outside support was put differed. Lipsky found that protest provided unreliable resources, that the news media and sympathetic public might ignore protestors' demands and that, even when attentive they often were easily satisfied with symbolic palliatives. Though the UFW experienced these problems, the presence of sustained sponsorship on the part of the Migrant Ministry and organized labor guaranteed a stable resource base.

Nor were the uses of protest-acquired resources the same. Lipsky's rent-strikers sought liberal pressure on public officials. For the UFW, protest actions were used to secure contributions and, in the form of a boycott, to exercise power against growers. Marches, symbolic arrests of clergy, and public speeches captured public attention; contributions from labor unions, theater showings and "radical chic" cocktail parties with proceeds to "*La Causa*" supplemented the budget provided by sponsors and membership dues.

Given the failure of strike actions, a successful outcome required indirect means of exercising power against growers. Sympathetic liberal organizations (e.g., churches, universities, etc.) refused to purchase "scab" grapes. More important, though, major grocery chains were pressured into refusing to handle "scab" products. To exercise that pressure, a combination of external resources had to be mobilized. Students had to contribute time to picketing grocery stores and shipping terminals; Catholic churches and labor unions had to donate office space for boycott houses; Railway Union members had to identify "scab" shipments for boycott pickets; Teamsters had to refuse to handle "hot cargo"; Butchers' union members had to call sympathy strikes when grocery managers continued to stock "scab" products; political candidates and elected officials had to endorse the boycott. The effectiveness of the boycott depended little upon the resources of mobilized farm-workers; instead, they became a political symbol. It was the massive outpouring of support, especially from liberals and organized labor, that made the boycott effective and, thereby, forced growers to the bargaining table.

The strength of liberal-labor support for the UFW is indicated by the high level of concomitant activity between insurgents and their supporters. [...] Given the fact that liberal activities rarely occurred jointly with pro-worker government activities, it is clear that liberals directed their efforts toward supporting insurgents rather than pressuring government.

The more "balanced," neutral posture of government that was the product of the reform period continued. Sixty-nine percent of all official actions were favorable to farmworkers (as against 50% and 68% in Periods I and II). Concretely, this meant that court rulings no longer routinely went against insurgents; federal poverty programs helped to "loosen" small town politics; hearings by the U.S. Civil Rights Commission and Congressional committees publicized "injustices" against farmworkers; welfare legislation gave farmworkers more economic security and afforded insurgents a legal basis to contest grower employment practices.

National politicians, such as Senators Kennedy and McGovern, lent their resources to the cause.

The most striking changes in official actions took place on the federal level. Actions favorable to farmworkers rose from 46% of federal level activity in the first period, to 63% in the second and 74% in the third. State and local government, more under the control of growers, followed a different pattern. In Period I, when growers had opposition only from insurgents, only 26% of official actions were judged favorable to workers. In Period II, when farmworkers were acquiescent but the liberal-labor coalition was experiencing growing influence in national politics, 67% were favorable, slightly more than on the federal level. But when insurgency reappeared in Period III, the percent favorable dropped to 45%, far lower than the federal level. Government divided on the question, federal actions tending to be neutral, if not supportive, of insurgents while state actions, still under grower dominance, continued to oppose insurgents.

Significantly little of the pro-worker trend in governmental actions during the UFW period is associated with either insurgent or liberal activities. [...] Only organized labor appeared to be performing a pressure function. [...] Official positions had already undergone important changes during the reform period. The termination of the *bracero* program had left government in a neutralized position. No longer a key player in the conflict, but still under the influence of the reform policies, government preserved its neutral stance despite less visible pressure from any of the partisans.

There was, of course, opposition on the part of growers and allied governmental actors. There were numerous instances of police harassment, large-scale purchases of boycotted products by the Department of Defense, and outspoken opposition from Governor Reagan and President Nixon.

However, growers had lost their entrenched political position. Public officials no longer acted so consistently to enhance grower interests and to contain the challenge. [...] By the time the United Farmworkers struck in 1965, agricultural employers were no longer able to rely upon government, especially at the federal level, to be fully responsive to their interest in blocking unionization.

Conclusion

The critical factor separating the National Farm Labor Union failure from the United Farmworker success was the societal response to insurgent demands. In most respects, the challenges were strikingly similar. In both instances, the leadership cadre came from outside the farmworker community; external sponsorship played a critical role in launching both insurgent organizations; both movements confronted similar obstacles to mobilizing a social base and mounting effective strikes; both resorted to political protest and boycotts. What produced the sharp difference in outcome was the difference in political environment encountered. The NFLU received token contributions, vacillating support for its boycott and confronted major acts of resistance by public authorities. In contrast, the UFW received massive contributions, sustained support for its boycotts and encountered a more "balanced," neutral official response.

The dramatic turnabout in the political environment originated in economic trends and political realignments that took place quite independent of any "push" from insurgents. During the reform period, conflicts erupted within the political elite over policies pertaining to farmworkers. Elite divisions provided the opening for reform measures then being pressed by a newly active coalition of established liberal and labor organizations. Though the reforms did not directly effect success, the process entailed by reform did result in a new political environment, one which made a successful challenge possible.

If this analysis is correct, then several assumptions found in the classic literature are misleading. Rather than focusing on fluctuations in discontent to account for the emergence of insurgency, it seems more fruitful to assume that grievances are relatively constant and pervasive. Especially for deprived groups, lack of collective resources and controls exercised by superiors – not the absence of discontent – account for the relative infrequency of organized demands for change. For several of the movements of the 1960s, it was the interjection of resources from outside, not sharp increases in discontent, that led to insurgent efforts.

Nor does the political process centered around insurgency conform to the rules of a pluralist game. The American polity had not been uniformly permeable to all groups with significant grievances (Gamson, 1975). Government does not act as a neutral agent, serving as umpire over the group contest. Public agencies and officials have interests of their own to protect, interests that often bring them into close alignment with well-organized private-interest groups. When insurgency arises threatening these private interests, public officials react by helping to contain insurgency and preserve the *status quo*. But if an opposing coalition of established organizations decides to sponsor an insurgent challenge, the normal bias in public policy can be checked. Sponsors then serve as protectors, insuring that the political elite remains neutral to the challenge.

The implications for other challenges are rather striking. If the support of the liberal community is necessary for the success of a challenge by a deprived group, then the liberal community is, in effect, able to determine the cutting edge for viable changes that conform to the interests of those groups still excluded from American politics. Moreover, there is the possibility of abandonment. Since liberal support can fade and political elites shift their stance, as has happened to the UFW since 1972, even the gains of the past may be endangered. The prospects for future insurgency, by this account, are dim. Until another major realignment takes place in American politics, we should not expect to see successful attempts to extend political citizenship to the excluded.

Note

1 Shifts in perceptions, treated as central by relative deprivation theorists, in our view would be secondary to the main process – changes in social resources.

References

Gamson, William 1968 "Stable unrepresentation in American society." *American Behavioral Scientist* 12:15–21.

—— 1975 *The Strategy of Social Protest*. Homewood, Il.: Dorsey.

Gusfield, Joseph 1968 "The study of social movements." Pp. 445–52 in David Sills (ed.), *International Encyclopedia of the Social Sciences*, Volume 14. New York: Macmillan.

Hibbs, Douglas 1973 *Mass Political Violence*. New York: Wiley.

Kornhauser, William 1959 *The Politics of Mass Society*. Glencoe, Il.: Free Press.

Lipsky, Michael 1968 "Protest as political resource." *American Political Science Review* 62:1144–58.

——1970 *Protest in City Politics*. Chicago: Rand McNally.

McCarthy, John and Mayer Zald 1973 *The Trend of Social Movements in America*. Morristown, N.J.: General Learning Corporation.

Oberschall, Anthony 1973 *Social Conflict and Social Movements*. Englewood Cliffs, N.J.: Prentice-Hall.

Smelser, Neil J. 1962 *The Theory of Collective Behavior*. New York: Free Press.

Snyder, David and Charles Tilly 1972 "Hardship and collective violence in France, 1830 to 1960." *American Sociological Review* 37:520–32.

Tilly, Charles, Louise Tilly and Richard Tilly 1975 *The Rebellious Century*. Cambridge, Ma.: Harvard University Press.

Wilson, John 1973 *Introduction to Social Movements*. New York: Basic Books.

Biography — César Chávez and the UFW

César Estrada Chávez, born in Yuma, Arizona, in 1927, led the most successful union of farmworkers in U.S. history. Chávez himself worked as a migrant farmworker from the age of ten, after his family lost their land during the Great Depression. César, who was forced to attend dozens of elementary schools as his family moved about, quit school after the eighth grade to help support his family. After serving in the navy during World War II, Chávez married and settled in the San Jose, California, *barrio* called *Sal Si Puedes* ("Get out if you can").

While working in the orchards outside San Jose, Chávez met Fred Ross, an Anglo organizer for the Community Service Organization (CSO), which was sponsored by the Chicago-based Industrial Areas Foundation led by the famous community organizer, Saul Alinsky (see chapter 20). Chávez was soon working full time for the CSO, registering farmworkers to vote and organizing chapters of the CSO across California and Arizona. He once registered more than two thousand voters in just two months.

Chávez's wife, Helen, worked in the fields to support her husband and family during these years. (During his lifetime, Chávez never earned more than five thousand dollars a year.) In 1962 Chávez decided to leave the CSO to organize a union of farmworkers, the National Farm Workers Association (NFWA), later renamed the United Farm Workers of America (UFW). Farmworkers had tried to organize unions before, but none had been successful, even though most farmworkers earned little more than a dollar an hour during this time.

Chávez roamed from one migrant camp to the next during the mid-1960s, tirelessly organizing a few followers in each. By 1964 the NFWA had about one thousand members in fifty locales. Chávez once said that "A movement with some lasting organization is a lot less dramatic than a movement with a lot of demonstrations and a lot of marching and so forth. The more dramatic organization does catch attention quicker. Over the long haul, however, it's a lot more difficult to keep together because you're not building solid.... A lasting organization is one in which people will continue to build, develop and move when you are not there."

In 1965, the NFWA joined in a strike against California grape growers, who brought in scabs and thugs who beat up the strikers. The strikers took a pledge of nonviolence, and Chávez himself conducted a 25-day fast in 1968 (a tactic he utilized often, like his hero Mahatma Gandhi) which attracted national media attention. Senator Robert Kennedy was at his side when he broke his fast, calling Chávez "one of the heroic figures of our time." Chávez also organized a nationwide boycott of grapes, forging a broad support coalition that included other unions, churches, and student and civil rights groups. Most of the major growers finally signed contracts with the union by 1970, and in 1975 the Agricultural Labor Relations Act was passed in California, which provided for secret ballot elections, guaranteed the right to boycott, and oversaw collective bargaining between growers and farmworkers. Tens of thousands of farmworkers covered by UFW contracts enjoyed better wages, health insurance, and pension benefits.

The UFW lost much of its momentum during the early 1980s, confronting a new conservative state government in California. Chávez announced a new grape boycott in 1984, emphasizing how pesticides were harming both farmworkers and consumers. In 1988 Chávez conducted a 36-day "Fast for Life" to protest growers' use of harmful pesticides.

Chávez was president of the UFW when he died on April 23, 1993. Tens of thousands of mourners attended his funeral. The following year, President Bill Clinton posthumously awarded him the Presidential Medal of Freedom, the highest civilian honor.

30 The Media in the Unmaking of the New Left

Todd Gitlin

With the SDS March on Washington on April 17, 1965, student antiwar protest – and SDS activity in particular – became big news. Now reporters began to seek out SDS leaders and to cover protest events. That spring, major articles on the New Left appeared in newsmagazines (*Newsweek, Time, U.S. News & World Report*), large-circulation weeklies (the *Saturday Evening Post*, the *New York Times Magazine*), and liberal weeklies (the *Nation*, the *New Republic*, the *Reporter*); and television news produced its own survey pieces. The movement was amplified.

But which movement? The observer changed the position of the observed. The amplification was already selective: it emphasized certain themes and scanted others. Deprecatory themes began to emerge, then to recur and reverberate. The earliest framing devices were these:

- *Trivialization* (making light of movement language, dress, age, style, and goals);
- *Polarization* (emphasizing *counter*demonstrations, and balancing the antiwar movement against ultra-Right and neo-Nazi groups as equivalent "extremists");
- *Emphasis on internal dissension*;
- *Marginalization* (showing demonstrators to be deviant or unrepresentative);
- *Disparagement by numbers* (under-counting); and
- *Disparagement of the movement's effectiveness.*

In the fall, as parts of the antiwar movement turned to more militant tactics, new themes and devices were added to the first group:

- *Reliance on statements by government officials and other authorities*;
- *Emphasis on the presence of Communists*;
- *Emphasis on the carrying of "Viet Cong" flags*;
- *Emphasis on violence in demonstrations*;
- *Delegitimizing use of quotation marks* around terms like "peace march"; and
- *Considerable attention to right-wing opposition to the movement*, especially from the administration and other politicians.

Some of this framing can be attributed to traditional assumptions in news treatment: news concerns the *event*, not the underlying condition; the *person*, not the group; *conflict*, not consensus; the fact that "*advances the story*," not the one that explains it. Some of this treatment descends from norms for the coverage of deviance in general: the archetypical news story is a crime story, and an opposition movement is ordinarily, routinely, and unthinkingly treated as a sort of crime. Some of the treatment follows from organizational and technical features of news coverage – which in turn are not ideologically neutral. Editors assign reporters to beats where news is routinely framed by officials; the stories then absorb the officials' definitions of the situation. And editors and reporters also adapt and reproduce the dominant ideological assumptions prevailing in the wider society. All these practices are anchored in organizational policy, in recruitment and promotion: that is to say, in the internal structure of institutional power and decision. And when all these sources are taken into account, some of the framing will still not be explained unequivocally; some must be understood as the product of specifically political transactions, cases of editorial judgment and the interventions of political elites. The proportion of a given frame that emanates from each of these sources varies from story to story; that is why stories have to be scrutinized one by one, as concretely as possible, before we can begin to compose general theories.

When we examine stories closely, we discover that there were exceptional moments of coverage within both the *Times* and CBS News. Not only was there – within the boundaries of the norms – some latitude for expressions of individual idiosyncrasy, for random perturbations within the general terms of the code; there were also larger conflicts within the news organizations about how to cover the movement, conflicts that were fought and resolved in different ways at different times. The overall effect of media coverage was blurred and contradictory; there was not a single voice. But increasingly the impression was conveyed that extremism was rampant and that the New Left was dangerous to the public good.

In short, the media were far from mirrors passively reflecting facts found in the real world. The facts reported were out there in the real world, true: out there *among others*. The media reflection was more the active, patterned remaking performed by mirrors in a fun house.

As media actively engaged the movement, an adversary symbiosis developed. Within the movement, arguments emerged about how best to cope with the new situation. Some groupings within the movement stayed on the defensive; others turned to the offense. In neither case was it possible to ignore the media spotlight, or to turn it at will to the movement's own uses.

Some movement organizers responded casually, at first, to the media's attentions. Their commitment to face-to-face organization remained primary; in their view, the press would play a secondary role in transmitting news and images to uncommitted publics. They were working within a pre-spotlight organizational form; they were eager to maintain the movement's own distinct communication channels. But in the fall of 1965, media attention and right-wing attacks caught them by surprise. The strategy they improvised called for a sort of judo operation: using the weight of the adversary to bring him down. They would use the unsought media attention to amplify the antiwar message. They began to speak into the symbolic microphone.

Others, committed to an antiwar movement before all else, and operating mostly outside SDS, began to organize symbolic events deliberately to attract the media spotlight. Very small groups of draft-card burners could leap to national prominence. Three pacifists, trying to awaken a national conscience, immolated themselves and died. Some within SDS proposed attention-getting actions – later called "media events" – that would, they hoped, place the issue of the war at the focus of national politics. Galvanizing opposition, even repression, from the administration or from the political Right could be a means to that end.

As the spotlight kept on burning, media treatment entered into the movement's internal life. The media helped recruit into SDS new members and backers who expected to find there what they saw on television or read in the papers. The flood of new members tended to be different from the first SDS generation – less intellectual, more activist, more deeply estranged from the dominant institutions. Politically, many of them cared more about antiwar activity than about the broad-gauged, long-haul, multi-issued politics of the earlier SDS. They were only partially assimilated into the existing organization; they viewed the SDS leaders, the remnants of the founding generation, with suspicion. The newcomers overwhelmed SDS's fragile institutions, which had been created for a tiny organization, a network of so-called Old Guard elite clusters living in intense political and personal community. The fragile person-to-person net of organizational continuity was torn.

This new generation coursed into SDS in the wake of the April 1965 antiwar march, and by June 1966 they had moved into the key positions of leadership. They were known as the Prairie Power people, underscoring – and at times exaggerating – their non-Northeastern, non-elite origins. True, this generation *did* differ from the founders in many ways; the distinction cannot be laid purely and simply at the door of the media and their selectivities. For one thing, the Old Guard elite had already graduated from college, many from elite colleges at that; many had moved into Northern ghettoes as community organizers. Most of the new leaders, by contrast, were still students at state universities. Coming from more conservative regions, Texas and the Great Plains primarily, many of the new generation had become radical quickly, because even mild rebellion against right-wing authority – hair grown slightly long, language grown obscene, or the like – provoked repression. If one were to be punished for small things, it was only a small step to declaring oneself an outlaw in earnest, a communist, a revolutionary: as soon be hanged for a sheep as a goat. So, as cultural rebels, they tended to skip the stage of consciousness that marked the Old Guard generation and informed its politics: a *radical disappointment* with existing liberal institutions, liberal promises, and liberal hopes. In style, too, they declared their deep disaffection from the prevailing culture: many were shaggy in appearance, they smoked dope, they had read less, they went for broke. Even Northeastern members of the Prairie Power leadership shared the new style.

The media not only helped produce and characterize this sharp break within SDS, but they proceeded to play it up; in so doing, they magnified its importance – both to the outside world and inside the organization. When it happened that, as the former SDS National Secretary wrote in December 1965, "chapters, regional offices, and members find out what the organization is doing by reading the newspapers," mass-mediated images were fixing (in the photographic sense) the terms for internal debate; they were helping define the organization's situation for it. Again, none of this happened in a vacuum. The drastic escalation in the war was at the same time pushing many people, both in and out of SDS, toward greater militancy, greater estrangement from dominant American values. The default of liberal forces isolated the whole generation of radical youth, pushing them toward the left. Larger cultural forces were nourishing the possibility of a deviant counterculture. But the media blitz, by amplifying and speeding all these processes, prevented SDS from assimilating them. The organization tried – and failed. Thus the internal frailties that were later to undo the organization were already built in at the moment of its greatest growth and vigor. In its beginning as a mass organization was its end.

[...]

Celebrity as Career: Performing

The career of Jerry Rubin personifies another course, another variant of pyramiding and a greater, typically American success: the slide toward inflated rhetoric that followed from the celebrity conferred by the mass media. Rubin had been involved in the Free Speech Movement of 1964 and had headed the Vietnam Day Committee of 1965; each had been made to appear both trivial and outlandish by the media. So when Rubin was subpoenaed by the House Un-American Activities Committee (HUAC) in the summer of 1966, he was inventive enough to try to devise a stratagem which would permit him to make a political critique of HUAC despite the interference of the image-transmitting process. He thus situated himself in the avant-garde artistic tradition of straining for effect.

R. G. Davis, then the director of the San Francisco Mime Troupe (and no relation to Rennie), remembers talking with Rubin in the Café Mediterraneum in Berkeley about tactics for his impending appearance before HUAC: "What image was good for him? We talked about the variable of what you could dress like. And we talked about it a lot. I suggested that he come up in an American Revolutionary costume.... It seemed to me that *they might not report what he had to say, but they would take a picture of him*. It was unlikely that the press would have listened to his statement."

Experienced activists had learned that they could not determine which of their words, if any, would end up on the air. A twenty-minute interview or speech might be recorded, and a fifteen-second clip would end up on the evening news. So R. G. Davis and Rubin applied themselves to the judo tack: turning the unavoidable spotlight to some political advantage. Davis goes on:

> I think there was general agreement that if you had a long statement and you answered questions, they still would distort.... I don't know how we got there, but I remember firmly saying, "The American Revolution was an easy [image] to get, and it would be a great statement about freedom of speech." Here was a solid image that everyone would recognize as a real contradiction. A House Committee that is investigating what people think and say! And the contradiction would be obvious if you could get it across that way. It felt to me like the dollar, you know, the straight image of America. He thought that was a good idea. He said he was going to do it.

Rubin did wear the American Revolutionary costume before HUAC, and his image was broadcast far and wide. Rubin's act of devout derision helped discredit the Committee on campuses. On top of the small fame of the Vietnam Day demonstrations of 1965, Rubin's appearance gave him a national reputation not only within the movement but outside it; it launched his career as a purveyor of conspicuous symbols. *Because of the media's procedures for identifying and confirming leaders, and his skill in manipulating them, and because of the weakness of the movement's organizations*, he was able to operate for years as a freelance broadcaster of symbols, outside any sizable organization, speaking for "youth," for "the movement," and for any action he thought represented his shadow Yippie group.

This made him a celebrity if not a leader; after he left Berkeley to organize the March on the Pentagon in 1967, he had no organized base. Many of his peers disliked what they saw as his egotism, and many resented him as a usurper of the spotlight; this resentment probably drove him still further toward flamboyance and unaccountability. His own desire for the spotlight, undoubtedly the product of several political and personal purposes, matched the media's need for quotable, eccentric, engagingly wacky personalities. Again, though, the issue is not simply personality but the structure of movement assumptions, tolerances, and vulnerabilities. One of Rubin's co-workers in the Berkeley antiwar movement, Michael P. Lerner, recalls a widespread feeling in the movement there that Rubin's "ego was so offensive they had to smash it." Lerner argues that this antagonism explains "not only why Jerry left Berkeley, but...why Jerry then moved toward the politics which he didn't really believe in. And he moved toward it for opportunistic reasons." By Lerner's account, only a few months before Jerry helped found the Youth International Party in 1967, "Jerry wasn't a Yippie":

> His reaction at first to the hip phenomenon was curiosity, interest, but not identification. So what was happening was that as the more straight-line political people were giving him less and less place to be a political person, presumably because of his great sin of wanting to have his name in the paper, or his face on TV,... he began to move more and more to trying to find a politics that would give him a space for ... getting some kind of personal recognition and allowing for him to be who he was.

Deprived by resentful constituents of the chance to use the media *legitimately* as political amplification, but still committed to that use of both media and themselves, Rubin and other such leaders were isolated. As Lerner puts it, "they were driven to the media as their base when their own base abandoned them."

But sustained media performance requires a recognizable persona, an objectified quasi-identity like a newscaster's or a comedian's. Lerner's theory draws support from a notion proposed by the old Berkeley movement hand Michael Rossman: that Rubin's Yippie show was a willed fusion of hippie and politico styles for media consumption. In an open letter of March 1968, Rossman – himself an anti-leader partial to the styles and projects that for shorthand can be called "hippie" – wrote to Rubin: "Years ago I asked one of my students what she thought of Leary and his League of Spiritual Discovery, traveling pitchman selling the Way. 'Leary,' she said, 'is a Harvard professor who dropped acid.' Don't become known as a politico who dropped acid, Jerry."

Rubin acquired a *following* instead of a face-to-face political base. His following was organized precisely as a mass media audience: atomized, far-flung, episodic, not alive politically except when mobilized in behalf of centralized symbols of revolt. Among all the movement leader-celebrities of the late sixties, Rubin enjoyed the quintessential notoriety, moving from the leadership of one improvised, occasional organization to another: from the Berkeley mayoral race of April 1966 to the San Francisco Be-In of January 1967, to the March on the Pentagon in October 1967, to Yippie and the Chicago demonstrations of August 1968. By then, he and the rest of the Yippie handful were almost automatically news. He learned that he could make news by playing the role "Jerry Rubin." With Abbie Hoffman, Paul Krassner, and occasional others, he could call press conferences and infuse the Youth International Party with a solid reputation for size and significance. As Michael Rossman wrote to him, "In our developing theology of organizing, you're into the Leadership Heresy; Yippie is a hippy bureaucracy that decrees." Although his media-summoned constituency failed to descend on Chicago for the demonstrations in 1968, Rubin's celebrity status remained untouched, for the Chicago city government, the police, and the national apparatus of repression took his media reputation at face value and thereby ratified it. In the fall of 1968, he dressed up again for the cameras in a confused uniform of Indian war paint, hippie beads, Vietnamese sandals, and a toy machine gun – a living emblem of the confusion of iconographic realms in the late days of the New Left, and of the counterculture's insensitive, mechanical appropriation of the insignia of oppressed peoples. The underground papers, themselves severed from day-to-day political life and growing wild with revolutionism, joined the national media in amplifying this mishmash.

And then the Chicago Conspiracy trial of 1969–70, which Rubin construed as a sort of reward for his rebellion and revelry, provided him an almost daily stage for his continuing show. Stanhope Gould, the field producer who supervised much of CBS's coverage of the trial, remembers accompanying Rubin and Abbie Hoffman with a camera crew on their speaking engagements. Why Rubin and Hoffman rather than, say, Rennie Davis, Tom Hayden, or Dave Dellinger? I asked Gould. "Because they were the most colorful and symbolic of the [Chicago] Seven," Gould said. By contrast, Gould had earlier produced and edited a takeout on Rennie Davis when Rennie had been subpoenaed by HUAC before the Nixon inauguration ("in-hog-uration") protest of January 1969. Replete with "lots of long-lens, artsy-craftsy stuff," by Gould's account, this "mood piece" of five or six minutes meant to explain how Rennie Davis, the son of one of President Truman's Council of Economic Advisors, had grown into a radical leader; and thus Gould intentionally omitted a balancing spokesman of the HUAC type. Because the piece wasn't balanced, Gould's superior, Russ Bensley, the top CBS News producer in charge of takeouts, canceled it. Over the ten years that Gould worked for the Cronkite News, this was one of the very few pieces he completed that was not aired; he had violated an outer limit which had not been drawn clearly until after the fact. But the standard that ruled out a respectful investigation of Rennie Davis's political evolution permitted coverage of more "colorful and symbolic" – and more easily dismissible – movement celebrities. Yippie avant-garde defiance was permissible as entertainment; sympathetic treatment of a would-be organizer of communities was not.

Rubin's performances were not devoid of method or strategy; rather, they were justified by an explicit theory of revolution. Rubin believed that his self-dramatizations, and the spectacular events they accompanied, mobilized oppositional consciousness and revolutionary action. His concept of mass organization mirrored the mass media's theory of itself. The mass media try to turn the audience into replicas of the ideal consumer; Jerry Rubin believed he could turn part of his audience, youth, into replicas of himself, and inspire them to reproduce the symbolic events he and the media could define as revolutionary actions. Ché Guevara had called for "two, three . . . many Vietnams" throughout the Third World; in the spring of 1968, Tom Hayden had called for "two, three . . . many Columbias." If "two, three . . . many Columbias," why not two, three . . . many Chicagos, Yippies, Rubins? In January 1970, on a day off from the Conspiracy trial in Chicago, R. G. Davis taped a discussion with Rubin in which Rubin articulated his theory of media effect:

> The year after Chicago, there were more demonstrations on college and high school campuses than any other year. And I would say it was directly and psychologically related to Chicago, the memory and myth of Chicago. People sang, "I miss Chicago." There was a riot in Berkeley the week after Chicago. Chicago reached people through the media. It became a myth in their own heads, it became exaggerated way out of proportion. And they tried to act it out in their own situation thanks to Chicago.

Rubin went on to argue that "FSM [the Free Speech Movement] created Columbia, thanks to the media." Davis objected: "But Columbia was so many years after FSM." Rubin responded:

> But dig this: the kids who watched FSM were ten, eleven years old. Five years later, campuses were up all over the country. And it wasn't through traditional political organizing – reading books, and getting leaflets and hearing arguments. It was through being turned on by something they saw on television.

Rubin argued that mobilization through media "doesn't negate the micro" level of local organizing; "we were just on a macro level." But his contempt for the written word spoke more loudly. Rubin's confusion between image and reality was shared by much of his youthful audience, raised on television as it had been; Rubin's genius was to transpose that confusion into a theory of revolutionary mobilization. In his conception, the revolutionary mass was just that: a *mass*, to be "turned on" by media buttons. Since in this view the revolutionary task reduced itself to mobilizing that passive mass for a specific action – an assumption similar to conventional marketing assumptions – the problem of the mobilizer was simply instrumental: not whether or why to mobilize for a newsworthy action, but *how*?

Of course, Rubin could only have thrived as a celebrity if the media reported him. That he was "colorful and symbolic" *even when he explicitly violated approaches more legitimate in the movement* was the basis of his success as a celebrity. *It was precisely the isolated leader-celebrities, attached indirectly to unorganized constituencies reached only through mass media, unaccountable to rooted working groups, who were drawn toward extravagant, "incidental," expressive actions – actions which made "good copy" because they generated sensational pictures rich in symbolism.* They were repelled by the movement and attracted by the media at the same time. This logic of symbiosis was to reach one culmination, appropriately enough, in the Symbionese

Liberation Army of 1973: a tiny group with no actual political base kidnapped a newspaper heiress and hijacked the spotlight with a memorable hydra-headed logo, some extravagant rhetoric ("Death to the fascist insect!"), and a political program that, only a few years later, no one remembers.

Celebrity as Trap: Abdicating

One distinct alternative to the pyramiding process in the movement was to refuse leadership altogether. A leader abdicated if he or she was no longer willing or able to withstand the conflicting demands of the media world and the movement base, and was unwilling to step up the tension (double or nothing) by leaping further into the glittering, envy-provoking, fickle world of celebrity. Since the movement was not clear about the difference between legitimate leadership and authoritarianism, leaders were reluctant to lead; and at the same time, internal criticism veered into ad hominem attacks. The resulting binds stepped up the pressure on leaders who were already deeply unsure of the basis of their authority. And so abdication was a strikingly common way out. Staughton Lynd was one of the better-known leaders who chose that route; Mario Savio of the Berkeley Free Speech Movement was another; a third was Robert Moses of the Student Nonviolent Coordinating Committee.

Moses was perhaps the most inspiring of the early SNCC leaders, one of the first to organize in dangerous Mississippi, a man whose courage, clarity, and stature in the movement were extraordinary. But especially as SNCC formalized its structure, Bob Moses could not believe in the authority he exercised. At a tumultuous meeting of the SNCC staff in February 1965, Moses renounced not only his leadership but his very name. One SNCC worker wrote this account at the time:

> Bob Moses came in Monday night after the structure and the elections were done, drunk. He had been fighting all weekend, fairly or unfairly, rightly or wrongly, for the voice of the silent people – the Negroes in Mississippi, the quiet bewildered staff. He had been saying that "if you want to have slaves, you had better give them the-vote and call them free men, because that's the only way the world will let you do it." So now he was drunk. First he shared cheese, bread, and an empty bottle of wine. Then he spoke.... First he announced that he had changed his name – he was no longer Robert Parris Moses, but Robert Parris [his mother's name]. He didn't want to be, and he wasn't the myth we had created. He wanted to be a person again. No one had shouted him down in the past few days, because he was Robert Moses. Now he would be Robert Parris.

Bob Moses soon left SNCC altogether, worked in early antiwar projects, and then abandoned the United States for over a decade in Africa.

Mario Savio, the most visible FSM leader, also rejected his own leadership in the course of criticizing the movement's "excessively undemocratic character." His parting words were strikingly close to Bob Moses's: "If the action isn't organized by you," he told a noon rally on the steps of Sproul Hall, April 26, 1965, "it's not worth being organized." "Lest I feel deserving of the charge of 'Bonapartism' which even I sometimes have made against myself, I'd like to wish you good luck and goodbye." Not only did the media assign Savio a power that his own political base did not, to make matters worse, the same media which granted him celebrity also flayed him unmercifully. The status conferred by the media was an ambiguous gift – and for a sensitive person, wrenching.

Indeed, all the celebrated movement leaders suffered from an enormous breach between the status conferred by the media and the support they could not muster from co-leaders and constituents. Breach easily became tension, and the tension could be devastating. The abdicators refused to be the victims of the conflicting demands made upon them; to save themselves from the dissociation of the looking glass, they removed themselves from leadership altogether. And then the movement suffered from the loss of its more sensitive leaders; the field was left to those less vulnerable to peer criticism, less accountable to base.

Alternatives for Leadership

Between abdication and the pyramiding of celebrity, there remained one slender choice: to try to use the media straightforwardly to broadcast ideas, without getting trapped in celebrity's routines. Many counted this the ideal choice; most spotlit leaders believed this was, in fact, what they were doing, and often they were making the attempt. But resisting the temptation of converting celebrity to outright stardom – playing court jester on the campus circuit or on talk shows, trying to slip one's few sentences about racism or war between commercials and Hollywood gossip – took enormous self-discipline. Experience was not sufficient guide. The inconsistent anti-authoritarianism of the white radical movement worked havoc on Paul Booth, on Rennie Davis, on Mario Savio, and on a good number of others.

The question arises then: in what circumstances could movements succeed in holding their leaders accountable, keep them from departing into the world of celebrity, and encourage them instead to use the media for political ends while minimizing damage to leaders and movement both? For one thing, a youth movement in a culture that celebrates youth is probably especially prone to the pressures and consequences of celebrity. Its leaders, lacking the adult rewards of career and family, are more dependent on the media for esteem; youth amidst the mass culture market feels entitled to fame, whether as rock star, athlete, or activist. Each way, the personal importance of access to media gets inflated. But more, a movement that could agree on goals and positions would permit its leaders less discretion to create policy in front of the cameras. The New Left, again, refused the self-discipline of explicit programmatic statement until too late – until, that is, the Marxist-Leninist sects filled the vacuum with dogmas, with clarity on the cheap. And finally, a movement organization could agree on formal procedures to review a leader's mass-mediated presentations. The movement would struggle to align its leaders with its policies, while leaders and constituents would agree on the prerogatives and obligations of each role. The issue, at bottom, is whether a movement can develop clear standards for what it expects from leaders, standards which do not jam its leaders into double binds; and whether leaders can avert celebrity's traps without abandoning leadership altogether.

The New Left met none of these conditions; thus its peculiar vulnerability to the spotlight. The pressure of political events intensified the strain on its structural weaknesses. And so it was difficult for any leader to maintain a plain, consistent, utilitarian approach to the media: to use the spotlight without getting burned up. Even more so because on the seemingly revolutionary wave of the late sixties, it seemed more and more that the way to be assured of access to that spotlight was to look and sound ever more extravagant.

[...]

Implications for Movements

Straining to take advantage of the media's interest in "exciting" or "important" news, opposition movements step into this web of conflicting yet interdependent corporate and State powers. One core task of opposition movements is to contest the prevailing definitions of things, the dominant frames. They must "rectify names," they must change the way people construe the world, they must penetrate and unmask what they see as the mystification sustained by the powers that be. In this sense, all insurgent movements must be empirical in their approach to the conventional definitions of objective reality; they must probe to discover *in practice* how far the principles of news "objectivity" can be severed both from the disparaging codes and from the corporate and State interests that sustain and delimit them.

Since the sixties, opposition movements have become still more sensitive to the impact of the media on their messages and their identities. At one extreme, the Symbionese Liberation Army learned how to manage an exercise in total manipulation, commandeering the media for a moment of spurious glory. At the other, the women's liberation movement, recognizing some of the destructive and self-destructive consequences of the spotlight, has learned from the experience of the New Left and worked with *some* success to decentralize leadership and "spokespersonship," avoiding *some* (not all) of the agonies of the single-focused spotlight. This is after much trial and much error. The results are uneven.

To what extent have the terms of hegemony been renegotiated? Hegemony exists in historical time, and its boundaries are adjustable as the media adjust to new social realities. *The more closely the concerns and values of social movements coincide with the concerns and values of elites in politics and in media, the more likely they are to become incorporated in the prevailing news frames*. Since the sixties, for example, consumer organizations have been elevated to the status of regular news makers; they and their concerns are reported with sympathy, sufficiently so as to inspire corporate complaints and counter-propaganda in the form of paid, issue-centered advertising. Ralph Nader and other public-interest lawyers have become respected celebrities, often interviewed for response statements, photographed in suits and ties and sitting squarely behind desks or in front of bookshelves, embodying solid expertise and mainstream reliability. They have learned to make the journalistic code work for them, while journalists have extended them the privilege of legitimacy. At times, environmentalist groups like the Sierra Club have been adept at using the media to publicize particular issues and to campaign for particular reforms. In the seventies, the prestigious media policymakers have legitimized some political values of their ecologically-minded peers in class and culture. These concerns have been institutionalized in government agencies like the Environmental Protection Agency and the Council on Environmental Quality, which now serve as legitimate news sources. The more radical wings of the environmental movement – those which challenge the raison d'être of centralized mass production and try to join the concerns of labor and environmentalists – are scanted.

Indeed, the very concept of a *movement* has been certified; an *activist*, left or right, is now a stereotyped persona accorded a right to parade quickly through the pageant of the news. Consumer activists, environmentalists, gay activists, feminists, pro- and antibusing people, as well as anti-abortionists, Jarvis-Gann supporters, Laetrile legalizers, angry loggers, farmers, and truck drivers – many movements which can be presented as working for (or against) concrete assimilable reforms have become regular, recognizable, even stock characters in newspapers and news broadcasts. The media spread the news that alternative opinions exist on virtually every issue. They create an impression that the society is full of political vitality, that opinions and interests contend freely – that the society, in a word, is pluralist. But in the process, they do extend the reach of movements that agree, at least for working purposes, to accept the same premise – and are willing to pay a price.

It is hard to know in advance what that price will be, hard to generalize about the susceptibilities of movements to the publicity process and its internal consequences. Of internal factors, two seem bound to increase a movement's *dependency* on the mass media: (1) the narrowness of its social base; and (2) its commitment to specific society-wide political goals. And then two other factors, when added onto the first two, seem to produce the most destructive *consequences* of media dependency: (3) the movement's turn toward revolutionary desire and rhetoric in a nonrevolutionary situation; and (4) its unacknowledged political uncertainties, especially about the legitimacy of its own leaders. Thus, in the case of the New Left: (1) It was contained within a relatively narrow social base: students and the young intelligentsia. (2) It had a specific political purpose, to end the war. These two factors in combination were decisive in forcing the movement into dependency on the media, although they did not by themselves generate destructive consequences. Proceeding into national reform politics from its narrow social base, the movement could hope to end the war only by mobilizing wider constituencies. Attempting to affect government policy in a hurry, it was forced to rely upon the mass media to broadcast the simple fact that opposition existed. And then the other factors came into play. (3) The New Left, in its revolutionary moment, allowed itself to believe it was in a revolutionary situation. In this mood, which flowed from (though it also contradicted!) the reformist antiwar moment, much of the New Left determined to muscle its way through to a political transformation so far beyond its means that it hurled itself into a politics of spurious amplification. Now mass-mediated images, and metaphors borrowed from the histories of previous revolutions, were dragooned into the Leninist role of vanguard organization – with consequences predictably ludicrous and self-destructive. And at the same time, (4) the New Left's ambivalence about criteria for leadership, especially when coupled with its inability to engender a coherent political ideology and organization, left all parties damaged: leaders were vulnerable to the temptations of celebrity, while the rank and file were stranded without means of keeping their leaders accountable. On the face of it, the black movement of the sixties and seventies shared these vulnerabilities, and for the same reasons. For the black movement also began with a narrow social base, the black population and students; it campaigned for the specific purpose of ending de jure segregation; it failed to give clear signals to its leaders; and a significant portion ended up committed to a revolutionary project within a nonrevolutionary situation.

But each factor is powerful insofar as it reinforces the previous factor or factors. If the chain can be broken, then the consequences of the previous factors can be minimized. If a movement is committed to working for specific political goals but refuses to devote itself to revolutionary politics, it may avoid the most severe dependency on the media; it is more likely, too, to be able to control the content of its publicity. The United Farm Workers, for example, are entrenched within a narrow social base and are committed to specific goals; but they have an undisputed leader whose media presence is (I am told) heralded with pride rather than envy; and by avoiding revolutionism, they have been able to occupy the media spotlight without subjecting themselves to its most destructive glare.

Reformist movements, then, are less vulnerable to structural deformation in the publicity process than are revolutionary ones. Reformists can achieve media standing by getting *their* experts legitimated; the standard frames are equipped to show them – and their class – to relatively good advantage. Revolutionaries, by contrast, can achieve media standing only as deviants; they become "good copy" as they become susceptible to derogatory framing devices; and past a certain point, precisely what made them "good copy" may make them dangerous to the State and subject, directly or indirectly, to blackout. But to say that reformist movements are less vulnerable to disparagement is not to say that they are immune. They, too, must confront the spotlight's tendency to convert leadership to celebrity, to highlight extravagant rhetoric (if not action), and to help induce transitional crises of generations. Likewise, the standard journalistic frames persist in marginalizing the most radical aspects of movements and setting them against the more moderate. They cover single-issue movements, but frame them in opposition to others: feminists against blacks, blacks against chicanos. *The routine frames that I examined earlier endure for reformist as well as deeply oppositional movements.* Even reformist movements must work industriously to broadcast their messages without having them discounted, trivialized, fragmented, rendered incoherent. Awareness of the media's routines and frames is no guarantee that a movement will be able to achieve publicity for its analysis and program on its own terms; the frames remain powerful, processing opposition into hegemonic order. But surely ignorance of the media's codes condemns a movement to marginality.

Biography – Abbie Hoffman: "Marx with Flowers in his Hair"

Born in Worcester, Massachusetts, in 1936, Abbie Hoffman became one of the most famous revolutionaries of the 1960s, embodying the playful side of the period better than anyone else. He graduated from Brandeis in 1959 with a B.A. in psychology, but soon embarked on a lifetime of political and cultural activism. He became a civil rights organizer, then moved to Manhattan's Lower East Side to market the products of Mississippi cooperatives. When black nationalism came to dominate the Student Nonviolent Coordinating Committee (SNCC) in the mid-1960s, he turned to the antiwar movement. He later said that he had tried "to bring the hippie movement into a broader protest," in other words to combine cultural expression with political protest. The "Yippies," which he founded with Jerry Rubin, were an effort to do just that.

Media events were Hoffman's specialty, based on his belief that "a modern revolutionary heads for the television station, not for the factory." In April 1967, Hoffman and a handful of companions threw dollar bills from the visitors' gallery of the New York Stock Exchange, causing a pause in trading while brokers scrambled for the money. That fall he organized an "exorcism" of the Pentagon, using incantations to try to levitate the building. (It did not work.) He and his friends planted a soot bomb at Con Edison headquarters, and mailed joints to three thousand people selected randomly from the phone book. In 1968 he traveled around with a pig, which he tried to nominate for President. Abbie later explained his approach: "Recognizing the limited time span of someone staring at a lighted square in their living room, I trained for the one-liner, the retort jab, or sudden knockout put-ons."

Hoffman's fame peaked in the aftermath of the Chicago Democratic convention in 1968, when he and seven other defendants went on trial for conspiracy in organizing the protests. (The "Chicago Eight" became the "Chicago Seven" when Black Panther Bobby Seale was bound and gagged and imprisoned for contempt of court.) Hoffman especially turned the trial into a form of guerrilla theater to express the ideas of the left. He even claimed, at one point, to be the illegitimate son of the judge presiding over the trial.

Hoffman had his critics. He had begun by using the media to get his message across, but the media in turn had made him a star. This came with a cost, as he and a handful of other celebrity-protestors came more and more to define the whole movement. Egalitarian efforts to avoid formal leaders had left a vacuum in which the media could place their own favorite spokespersons, inevitably those who were the most flamboyant.

Many protestors of the 1960s continued political activity alongside later jobs, but Hoffman devoted his adult life to full-time activism. He went underground in 1973 after being arrested in the sale of cocaine to undercover police, for which he faced a mandatory fifteen-year sentence. Using the name Barry Freed, he was active in environmental protest even while in hiding. In 1980 he turned himself in to authorities and served one year in prison. After that, he was a popular campus speaker and returned to writing. (*Steal This Book*, 1971, was his most memorable title.) He continued his political activities until 1989, when he committed suicide. In pain from an automobile accident the previous year, and on drugs for manic depression, he took a large dose of alcohol and phenobarbital on April 12. "Marx with flowers in his hair," one of Hoffman's phrases, described him well.

31 What Shapes the West's Human Rights Focus?

James Ron, Howard Ramos, and Kathleen Rodgers

In spring 2005, Amnesty International published a hard-hitting report on human rights violations by a host of abusive governments. The media, however, focused on the group's stinging critique of the United States and its Guantanamo prison. These accounts infuriated American officials, who claimed they were excessive and misplaced.

The Bush administration's response was disingenuous, but may still have contained a grain of truth. Human rights abuses by some countries get more media attention than others, and even the most fair-minded activist devotes more resources to some areas than others. Why does this happen? Are nefarious biases at work, or are structural forces at play? The question is crucial, since respect for human rights has become a leading indicator of state legitimacy.

Look closely, and human rights terminology is everywhere. From asylum laws to development policies, "human rights" promotion, vaguely defined, has assumed pride of place alongside such standard policy phrases as "structural adjustment," "good governance," and "democratization." Western countries increasingly insert human rights conditions into their trade and aid agreements, and even their military interventions. For example, the campaigns in Kosovo, East Timor, and Iraq all cited human rights justifications.

Human rights rhetoric enjoys strong public support. In 2003, a Gallup poll of U.S. respondents found 86 percent support for policies friendly to human rights, while a survey of Western opinion leaders found more confidence in Amnesty International's "brand" than in that of many major corporations. Today, Western publics, journalists, and governments regard Amnesty and Human Rights Watch as trustworthy information sources.

The long-term effect of all this is unclear, since much of the rhetoric is empty verbiage. In fact, one recent study argues that abusive governments are more likely than others to sign international human rights treaties.

Still, human rights pressures can and do make a difference, especially when governments are ripe for change, including those with competent bureaucracies, democratic leanings, and strong Western ties. Western influence per se does not help, but it often facilitates alliances between local human rights groups, journalists, international activists, and sympathetic Western officials.

Policy efficacy aside, the rhetoric of human rights is likely to be with us for some time, if only because a number of newly created training programs are educating an emerging group of officials, journalists, and activists. In 1981, there were only six such programs globally, but by 2005, there were at least 56 (figure 31.1).

Shaping the Human Rights Agenda

Yet, like economic globalization, the wave of rights talk has not spread evenly around the world. Some countries attract intense attention, while others languish in obscurity. The result is an imbalanced portfolio of Western human rights concern.

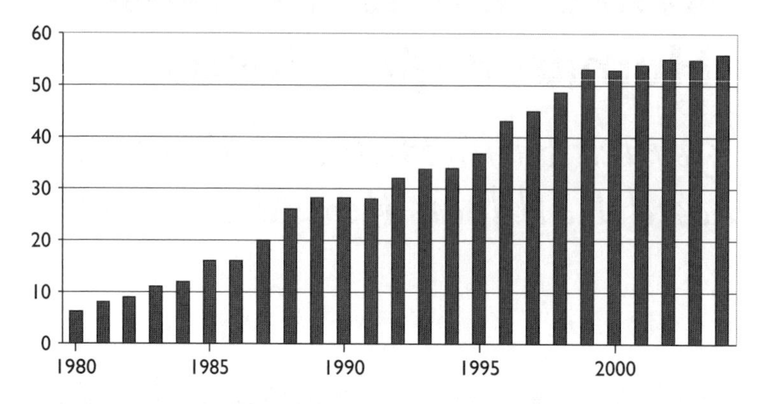

Data obtained from the Center for the study of Human Rights at Columbia University's catalog of university- and non-university-based human rights training programs

Figure 31.1 Human rights training programs, 1980–2005

Consider ethnic cleansing and massacres, two acute human rights violations that spurred much reporting and institution-building over the last decade, including the creation of a standing international criminal court. During 1991–93, Serbian abuses in Croatia and then Bosnia attracted Western compassion and policy interest, including thousands of media stories, Security Council resolutions, NGO fact-finding missions, and a special, UN-backed war crimes tribunal.

By 1998, this human rights machinery was large, effective, and focused on Serbian security-force violations. When Serbian agents began abusing civilians again in Kosovo, the human rights wheels began furiously turning. NGOs and UN monitors reported on Serbian abuses in intimate detail, Western journalists diligently covered the events, and in the spring of 1999, NATO mounted a massive air assault. Although the war initially exacerbated Serbian ethnic cleansing and indirectly killed thousands, Serbian troops were ultimately forced to withdraw, and many refugees returned home. Ever since, an international force has ruled the region, with mixed results for all.

Compare this to the West's relative indifference to events in Congo-Brazzaville, a small country bordering on the larger Congo-Kinshasa. Civil war raged there throughout the 1990s, claiming thousands of lives and rape victims, and displacing one-third of the country's 2.1 million residents. These figures rivaled Kosovo's, but the Balkans attracted far more human rights scrutiny. Bosnia and Kosovo are run by international peacekeepers and receive substantial assistance, while Congo-Brazzaville has neither.

The legal ramifications can also be profound. Serbian paramilitaries and nationalists still hide their wartime experiences, fearing international war crime indictments from the Hague. In Congo-Brazzaville, by contrast, former fighters speak freely of their misdeeds, even while queuing for post-conflict aid in UN-supported camps. Abuses in the two regions were similar, but no one issued international arrest warrants for Brazzaville's warlords.

Is it Racism?

Some argue that an anti-African racism underlies these disparities, prompting the Western-dominated international community to focus more on European victims. These claims gained credence in 1994 and again in 2005, when the Rwandan and

Darfur massacres unfolded without Kosovo-style interventions. But there are problems with this argument. True, Western militaries rarely intervene to stop African wars, but Western journalists, NGOs, and policymakers devote substantial attention to some African crises.

Consider Zimbabwe, a favorite site for contemporary human rights scrutiny. Western disgust with President Robert Mugabe's authoritarianism has skyrocketed in recent years, heaping opprobrium on the former guerrilla leader's increasingly brutal regime. In summer 2005, Western criticism peaked over the government's violent squatter evictions. Yet forced slum clearances are discouragingly common in the developing world, and similar abuses have occurred in Delhi, Jakarta, Beijing, and Lagos. Still, Western human rights attention has focused more on Mugabe's misdeeds, prompting the *Guardian*'s John Vidal to note that Zimbabwe's strongman, like Slobodan Milosevic and Saddam Hussein before him, is the "international monster of the moment."

Politics and Human Rights

These and other disparities crop up regularly across the globe, infuriating governments over alleged distortions of their records. Conspiracy theories and backlash politics abound, and many argue that the Western human rights agenda is neocolonial and self-interested.

In Israel, nationalists find anti-Semitism lurking behind critiques of their policies regarding Palestine; in Pakistan, traditionalists detect racist paternalism in Western concern for women's rights; in Turkey, critics see human rights reporting as covert support for Kurdish separatism. These complaints are largely misguided since abusive governments rarely acknowledge evil deeds. Still, the severity of human suffering alone rarely explains levels of Western scrutiny, and profound imbalances exist in the deployment of human rights criticisms.

In Turkey, Western European concern with violations against Kurdish civilians is linked, in part, to Turkey's bid for European Union membership, a controversial move that many oppose. European officials say Turkey's membership depends on its human rights record, giving interested parties incentives to probe allegations of abuse. Large Turkish and Kurdish diasporas highlight the issue, as does advocacy by Armenian activists exasperated by Turkey's refusal to acknowledge their own genocide.

Other political factors are also at play. As the third largest recipient of U.S. military aid from 1981 to 2000, Turkey forms an integral part of NATO's southern flank, using American weapons to fight Kurdish rebels. Given U.S. laws against aiding abusive regimes, American journalists, NGOs, and lobbyists are keen to probe Turkey's record. Everyone wants to be "policy-relevant" and effective, and Turkey's behavior, combined with existing U.S. laws, creates the potential for impact. Thus, Turkey's Western ties have transformed its human rights record into a topical issue for Western journalists, activists, and lawmakers.

Uzbekistan is another recent example. Since the breakup of the Soviet Union, an increasingly abusive regime has repressed extremists and nonviolent protesters. In spring 2005, a demonstration in the city of Andijan was brutally put down by Uzbek security forces, who killed some 500 civilians. Although some protestors did use violence, the army's response was massively disproportionate.

The Andijan events triggered a wave of reporting by Western media and NGOs, fueled largely by the presence of a U.S. military base supporting America's Afghan operations. Embarrassed by the massacre and the resulting media furor, the United States vigorously condemned the crackdown; Uzbekistan is a staunch ally in the "war on terror," but the massacre was a public relations liability. Shortly thereafter, Uzbekistan angrily instructed America to close its base within six months.

Human Rights and the United States

The "Washington connection" to violations in the developing world has provoked debate ever since the 1970s, when Jimmy Carter committed America to human rights-friendly policies. During the Cold War, the political left argued that abuses by Western allies attracted less attention than those of their enemies. As Noam Chomsky claimed, Western governments and media focused intensely on abuses by the likes of Nicaragua and the Soviet Union, but ignored violations by anticommunist allies.

These claims have merit, but they do not hold up over time. After all, U.S. Cold War allies such as El Salvador and Israel were heavily criticized by journalists and others during the 1980s. Indeed, the more U.S. officials defended these allies, the more the debate over their records intensified. U.S. government representatives were often slow to condemn allies, but the Western media and many NGOs were not.

A more plausible theory is that any connection to the United States or other powerful Western governments creates incentives for greater human rights scrutiny. Western officials are keen to protect their allies' reputations, but overt ties to the West facilitate unofficial investigations and lobbying. Activists, journalists, and interest groups of all kinds want to be heard and to shape policy, and they do this best when speaking out on countries that are relevant to Western foreign policy.

Interestingly, this claim should hold true for major Western adversaries such as Russia, Cuba, or China, whose policy relevance comes from their challenger status. The more Western allies are criticized, the more Western officials address their enemies' misdeeds. These duels feed on each another, pushing for greater scrutiny of friend and foe alike. In the process, abuses in countries deemed irrelevant to the Western policy agenda are often ignored.

A Systematic Study

To investigate these and other theories, we studied the coverage of human rights criticism by two elite Western media sources, the U.K.-based *Economist*, and the U.S. magazine *Newsweek*. We assumed that these two magazines would reflect and help shape government and activist agendas. More important, we believed they would lend insight into the type of human rights reports consumed by the West's internationally oriented reading public.

As English-language weeklies covering domestic and foreign affairs, the two magazines share some important qualities, but they differ in crucial ways. While the *Economist*'s readers are financially better off and better educated, *Newsweek*'s readers are far more numerous. Together, the two provide a useful indicator of Western reporting.

Our team read all articles appearing in either publication that included the phrase "human rights," and then selected all stories with specific mention of an abuse in a particular country. Although this omits reports of abuse without the keywords "human rights," it does provide a consistent measure of the way in which the human rights discourse is used. We coded articles from 1981 to 2000, but due to other data limitations, confined our statistical models to 148 countries from 1986 to 2000. Our study focused on 1027 articles published in the *Economist*, and 810 in *Newsweek*.

Our first observation was the dramatic growth in the number of articles containing any use of the phrase "human rights." In 1986, the *Economist* and *Newsweek* published 63 and 88 articles, respectively, with this keyword phrase. But in 2000, these figures had risen to 251 and 172 (see figure 31.2). The number of countries described as "human rights" abusers also grew. In 1986, the two sources jointly cited 24 countries for specific violations, while also mentioning "human rights"; by 2000, that pool had expanded to 61. As we suspected,

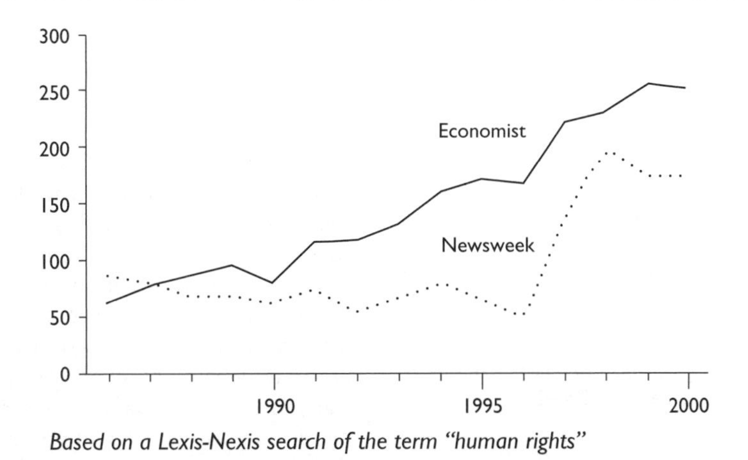

Figure 31.2 Articles on human rights in the *Economist* and *Newsweek*, 1986–2000

journalists used the term more frequently, and applied it more broadly.

We then developed a "top ten" list of abusers appearing in stories with the human rights keywords (figure 31.3). Two American adversaries, China and Russia (and the former Soviet Union), headed the list, lending credence to the left's suspicion that concern for human rights was a weapon used against Western enemies. Yet we could draw the opposite conclusion from the countries tied for third place: U.S. anticommunist ally Indonesia, and the United States itself. Of the remaining countries on the list, some, such as Turkey, Colombia, Chile, and the United Kingdom, were Western countries or their allies, while others, such as Serbia and Cuba, were adversaries. The only apparent outlier is Nigeria. Although it was not a major political ally of the West, it is an important economic ally, since its massive oil reserves are heavily exploited by Western petroleum companies.

The "most cited" list, in other words, lends support to the notion that Western policy relevance boosts media interest in the human rights records of both friends and enemies. Yet the list is also intriguing because of the countries that are absent. Missing are North Korea and Iraq, for example, two countries ranked during the 1986–2000 period as "very repressive" by Steven Poe's Political Terror Scale, a widely used indicator of government violations of civil and political rights. Similarly, the two countries with the most war-related deaths during 1986–2000—Sudan and Rwanda—received only marginal "human rights" attention. While the sheer magnitude of a country's suffering may matter, other factors are clearly at work.

Statistical Findings

Our list suggests that Western policy relevance matters, but our statistical analysis helps probe for other possibilities. Violations of civil and political rights do affect media coverage. A high Political Terror Score raised a country's media coverage, as did the intensity of armed conflict, measured by the percentage of the population directly killed in war. Moreover, the more closed a government's political rules and institutions were, the more likely the media were to report on its abuses.

Yet other factors also mattered, and it is here that the statistical story becomes interesting. Poverty, for example, has negative effects on media coverage. The poorer a country, the less likely are *Newsweek* and

1	China	244
2	Russia/USSR	127
3	Indonesia & East Timor	89
3	USA	89
4	Chile	60
5	Turkey	53
6	Serbia and Montenegro	51
7	Colombia	50
8	UK	48
9	Cuba	45
10	Nigeria	43

Figure 31.3 Top recipients of *Economist* and *Newsweek* human rights coverage, 1986–2000

the *Economist* to report on its abuses while citing "human rights." Controlling for actual levels of abuse, wealth seems to attract critical scrutiny.

This finding is counterintuitive, since poverty increases the likelihood of government abuse and civil war. Many feel that poverty itself is a human rights abuse because it violates essential economic and social rights. Why, then, were *Newsweek* and the *Economist* reluctant to mention abuses in poor countries?

We are not certain, but we have some plausible theories. Rich countries have better communications facilities and higher levels of education, both of which generate more information about government misdeeds. Wealthy countries also wield more influence internationally and may therefore be of greater interest to journalists. Historically, moreover, the West (and especially the United States) has downplayed respect for economic and social rights, seeing them as linked to a discredited communist agenda. This, too, may limit the media's willingness to define poverty-related problems as "human rights" violations.

A second intriguing finding was that human rights coverage increased with the number of NGOs formally registered in a given country. Like our finding on wealth, this was surprising, as countries bedeviled by civil war, government terror, or political extremism tend to have smaller NGO communities. Like wealth, however, such groups increase political participation, advocacy, and information about government behavior, and these may translate into greater media coverage.

Our findings on wealth and civil society highlight the information paradox noted by scholars of transnational activism. Countries with lower levels of actual abuse often produce more information about violations within their borders, since press freedoms, democratic norms, and vigorous activism all promote debate and exposure. Thus, politically open and wealthy countries attract more human rights attention, even though their abuses are comparatively less severe.

The Activists' Impact

Statistically, the advocacy of Amnesty International also makes a difference. When we included that group's press advocacy in our models, we discovered that Amnesty press releases boosted media coverage in general. This is good news for the organization, since its work depends on the ability to publicly name and shame abusers.

Without doubt, international human rights activism has come a long way since the 1970s, when a handful of small groups used part-time volunteers to protest abuses in Latin America and Eastern Europe. Today, Amnesty International's London staff numbers 400, and its $46 million budget is only one-quarter of the group's overall resources. New York's Human Rights Watch is equally influential, although its staff and budget are only half as large. Amnesty's activists engage with grassroots members as well as elites, but Human Rights Watch's media-savvy team focuses more heavily on the media and top policymakers.

Together, the two have achieved remarkable results. When governments shoot Uzbek protesters or bomb Afghan villagers, Amnesty and Human Rights Watch researchers appear soon after, using satellite links, media-savvy methods, and powerful legal arguments to broadcast their concerns. Abusive governments control bureaucracies and security forces, but their credibility is often shaky, and their information often stale. Global activists regularly use their information to discredit authoritarian rulers in weak countries. On occasion, they even make the most powerful Western official eat humble pie.

The Activists' Dilemma

Yet the activists' growing media influence has been a mixed blessing. The more they hone their message for the Western media, the more they must cater to Western journalistic tastes. Journalists increasingly call on activists for information and comment, but they ask more questions about some countries than others.

This places Amnesty, Human Rights Watch, and others in a painful bind. Although they are committed to exposing abuses wherever they occur, reports on "obscure" countries evoke little response. As one senior Amnesty manager noted, "You can work all you like on Mauritania, but the press couldn't give a rat's ass." As a result, activists are forced to adjust the flow of reporting to match media concerns. Consider again Kosovo and Congo-Brazzaville, two small regions with similar levels of violence during the 1990s. Amnesty issued 69 press releases on Kosovo during the relevant decade, compared to only two for Congo-Brazzaville. The media worried far more about the Balkans, and Amnesty's press officers were obliged to respond in kind.

Overall, the four countries most cited for their abuses in Amnesty press releases during 1986–2000 were the United States and three of its allies, Israel, Indonesia, and Turkey. Cumulatively, these countries earned a total of 502 press releases. Compare this to the 148 press releases issued about violations in the four countries considered "most repressive" by the Political Terror Scale (North Korea, Colombia, Iraq, and Sri Lanka), or to 126 press releases about abuses in the four countries with the worst armed conflicts (Sudan, Rwanda, Afghanistan, and Mozambique).

A similar picture emerges for Amnesty's background papers, which are aimed at more specialized, practitioner audiences. Here, the four countries most targeted were Turkey, Russia and the Soviet Union, China, and the United States, which cumulatively earned 1474 reports. This compares poorly to the 441 papers Amnesty wrote about violations in the four countries with the worst Political Terror Scores, or the 259 papers on abuses in the four most war-torn societies.

We must interpret these figures cautiously, since Amnesty engages in other types of advocacy efforts. For example, its representatives participate in UN meetings and briefing sessions, which promote human rights concerns in less visible ways. Indeed, these methods are often used with countries with low media profiles. And as Amnesty officials note, many politically repressive countries refuse to grant research visas, making it difficult to report on their abuses. Statistically, moreover, we found that Amnesty's papers are less sensitive to media reports, suggesting that the group has a somewhat diversified portfolio of written products.

Still, the trends are clear, and they are not unique to Amnesty International. Human Rights Watch's record-keeping is not as detailed, but a survey of their catalogued reports during the 1990s shows that the United States, Turkey, Indonesia, and China topped their list. Indeed, Human Rights Watch is probably even more media-savvy than Amnesty, enmeshed as it is in the fast-paced environment of elite New York and Washington politics. The group is intensely strategic, and its written reports are always part of a broader lobbying strategy in which press visibility plays a key role. As the group's director noted, Human Rights Watch's job is to influence public debates, and this often requires "seizing moments of public attention—usually whatever is in the news—to make human rights points." In many ways, this is an excellent strategy. Still, the relevant "public attention" is often Western, shaped by parochial policies and interests.

NGO fundraising is also at stake, since media visibility boosts charitable giving. According to one Amnesty manager, the group raises funds through work on high-profile venues, but then spends some revenue on less visible countries. Still, countries that attract little Western policy or media interest pose a huge challenge for activists. With many abuses occurring in high-profile countries, it is tempting to let "obscure" locales drift to the back burner.

These challenges have not escaped NGO attention. At Amnesty, some say they are concerned that the group is becoming too concerned with media impact; as one staffer noted, "Perhaps ... we are not conscious enough of swimming with the tide." At Human Rights Watch, employees criticize the attention given high-profile emergencies in Iraq and Afghanistan, arguing that other, equally deserving countries get fewer resources. In both groups, senior managers readily acknowledge the risks of a media-savvy strategy, but remain sensitive to the need for policy relevance and visibility.

These dilemmas are not easy to resolve. To grow and make a difference, Amnesty, Human Rights Watch, and others must work with elite Western journalists. Yet even as activists struggle to boost public engagement with little-noticed countries and conflicts, Western media tastes and the potential for policy influence exert strong, countervailing pressures. In the years to come, NGOs may yet conclude that their media-savvy strategy was a Faustian bargain.

Recommended Resources

Clifford Bob. 2005. *The Marketing of Rebellion: Insurgents, Media, and International Activism* (Cambridge University Press). Argues that the Western media and non-governmental organizations bestow attention on an isolated number of deserving cases.

Emilie M. Hafner-Burton and Kiyoteru Tsutsui. 2005. "Human Rights in a Globalizing World: The Paradox of Empty Promises," *American Journal of Sociology* 110:1372–1411. Uses statistical methods to argue that while global human rights treaties do not have an independent effect on abusive governments, mobilization by global civil society activists can make a difference.

James Ron, Howard Ramos, and Kathleen Rodgers. 2005. "Transnational Information Politics: Human Rights NGO Reporting, 1986–2000," *International Studies Quarterly* 49: 557–587. Argues that the volume of Amnesty International country reporting is shaped by actual human rights conditions as well as other factors, including previous reporting efforts, state power, U.S. military aid, and a country's media profile.

Human Security Report: War and Peace in the 21st Century (Oxford University Press, 2005), available online at http://www.humansecurityreport.info/index.php?option=com_frontpage&Itemid=1. Review of the methods used to measure the human cost of violence, including a discussion of the Political Terror Scale.

The websites of the world's two largest human rights organizations, Amnesty International (www.amnesty.org) and Human Rights Watch (www.hrw.org), contain a wealth of information on human rights conditions in dozens of countries.

32 The Quest for International Allies

Clifford Bob

For decades, Tibet's quest for self-determination has roused people around the world. Inspired by appeals to human rights, cultural preservation, and spiritual awakening, tens of thousands of individuals and organizations lend moral, material, and financial support to the Tibetan cause. As a result, greater autonomy for Tibet's 5.2 million inhabitants remains a popular international campaign despite the Chinese government's 50-year effort to suppress it.

However, while Tibet's light shines brightly abroad, few outsiders know that China's borders hold other restive minorities: Mongols, Zhuang, Yi, and Hui, to name only a few. Notable are the Uighurs, a group of more than 7 million located northwest of Tibet. Like the Tibetans, the Uighurs have fought Chinese domination for centuries. Like the Tibetans, the Uighurs face threats from Han Chinese in-migration, communist development policies, and newly strengthened antiterror measures. And like the Tibetans, the Uighurs resist Chinese domination with domestic and international protest that, in Beijing's eyes, makes them dangerous separatists. Yet the Uighurs have failed to inspire the broad-based foreign networks that generously support and bankroll the Tibetans. International celebrities—including actors Richard Gere and Goldie Hawn, as well as British rock star Annie Lennox—speak out on Tibet's behalf. But no one is planning an Uighur Freedom Concert in Washington, D.C. Why?

Optimistic observers posit a global meritocracy of suffering in which all deserving causes attract international support. Howard H. Frederick, founder of the online activist network Peacenet, has argued that new communications technologies help create global movements in which individuals "rise above personal, even national self-interest and aspire to common good solutions to problems that plague the entire planet." And Allen L. Hammond of the World Resources Institute recently wrote that the combination of global media, new technologies, and altruistic nongovernmental organizations (NGOs) may soon empower the have-nots of the world, bringing them "simple justice" by creating a "radical transparency" in which "no contentious action would go unnoticed and unpublicized."

But even while a handful of groups such as the Tibetans have capitalized on the globalization of NGOs and media to promote their causes, thousands of equally deserving challengers, such as the Uighurs, have not found their place in the sun. While the world now knows about East Timor, similar insurrections in Indonesian Aceh and Irian Jaya remain largely off the international radar screen. Among environmental conflicts, a small number of cases such as the Brazilian rubber tappers' struggle to "save" the Amazon, the conflict over China's Three Gorges Dam, and the recent fight over the Chad–Cameroon pipeline have gained global acclaim. But many similar environmental battles, like the construction of India's Tehri Dam, the destruction of the Guyanese rain forests, and the construction of the Trans Thai–Malaysia gas pipeline are waged in anonymity. Whole categories of other conflicts—such as landlessness in Latin America and caste discrimination in South Asia—go likewise little noticed. To groups challenging powerful opponents in these conflicts, global civil society is not an open forum marked by altruism, but a harsh, Darwinian marketplace where legions of desperate groups vie for scarce attention, sympathy, and money.

In a context where marketing trumps justice, local challengers—whether environmental groups, labor rights activists, or independence-minded separatists—face long odds. Not only do they jostle for attention among dozens of equally worthy competitors, but they also confront the pervasive indifference of international audiences. In addition, they contend against well-heeled opponents (including repressive governments, multinational corporations, and international financial institutions) backed by the world's top public relations machines. Under pressure to sell their causes to the rest of the world, local leaders may end up undermining their original goals or alienating the domestic constituencies they ostensibly represent. Moreover, the most democratic and participatory local movements may garner the least assistance, since Western NGOs are less likely to support groups showing internal strife and more inclined to help a group led by a strong, charismatic leader. Perhaps most troubling of all, the perpetuation of the myth of an equitable and beneficent global civil society breeds apathy and self-satisfaction among the industrialized nations, resulting in the neglect of worthy causes around the globe.

Pitching the Product

The ubiquity of conflict worldwide creates fierce competition for international support. In a 2001 survey, researchers at Leiden University in the Netherlands and the Institute for International Mediation and Conflict Resolution in Washington, D.C., identified 126 high-intensity conflicts worldwide (defined as large-scale armed conflicts causing more than 1000 deaths from mid-1999 to mid-2000), 78 low-intensity conflicts (100 to 1000 deaths from mid-1999 to mid-2000), and 178 violent political conflicts (less than 100 deaths from mid-1999 to mid-2000). In these and many other simmering disputes, weak challengers hope to improve their prospects by attracting international assistance.

Local movements usually follow two broad marketing strategies: First, they pitch their causes internationally to raise awareness about their conflicts, their opponents, and sometimes their very existence. Second, challengers universalize their narrow demands and particularistic identities to enhance their appeal to global audiences.

Critical to the success of local challengers is access to major Western NGOs. Many groups from low-profile countries are ignored in the developed world's key media centers and therefore have difficulty gaining visibility among even the most transnational of NGOs. Moreover, despite the Internet and the much-ballyhooed "CNN effect," repressive regimes can still obstruct international media coverage of local conflicts. In the 1990s, for example, the government of Papua New Guinea did just that on Bougainville island, site of a bloody separatist struggle that cost 15,000 lives, or roughly 10 percent of the island's population. During an eight-year blockade (1989–97), foreign journalists could enter the island only under government guard, while the rebels could dispatch emissaries abroad only at great risk. India has used similar tactics in Kashmir, prohibiting independent human rights monitors from entering the territory and seizing passports of activists seeking to plead the Kashmir: case before the U.N. General Assembly and other bodies. Less effectively, Sudan has tried to keep foreigners from entering the country's vast southern region to report on the country's 19-year civil war.

Even for causes from "important" countries, media access—and therefore global attention—remains highly uneven. Money makes a major difference, allowing wealthier movements to pay for media events, foreign lobbying trips, and overseas offices, while others can barely afford places to meet. For example, long-term support from Portugal helped the East Timorese eventually catch the world's attention; other Indonesian separatist movements have not had such steady friends. And international prizes such as the Goldman Environmental Prize, the Robert F. Kennedy Human Rights Award, and the Nobel Peace Prize have become important vehicles of internationalization. In addition to augmenting a leader's resources, these awards raise a cause's visibility, facilitate invaluable contacts with key transnational NGOs and media, and result in wider support. For instance, Mexican "farmer ecologist" Rodolfo Montiel Flores's receipt of the $125,000 Goldman Prize in 2000 boosted the campaign to release him from prison on false charges stemming from his opposition to local logging practices. Not surprisingly, such prizes have become the object of intense salesmanship by local groups and their international champions.

Local challengers who have knowledge of global NGOs also have clear advantages. Today's transnational NGO community displays clear hierarchies of influence and reputation. Large and powerful organizations such as Human Rights Watch, Amnesty International, Greenpeace, and Friends of the Earth have the resources and expertise to investigate claims of local groups from distant places and grant them legitimacy. Knowledge of these key "gatekeeper" NGOs—their identities, goals, evidentiary standards, and openness to particular pitches—is crucial for a local movement struggling to gain support. If homegrown knowledge is scarce, local movements may try to link themselves to a sympathetic and savvy outsider, such as a visiting journalist, missionary, or academic. Some Latin American indigenous groups, including Ecuador's Huaoroni and Cofán, Brazil's Kayapó, and others, have benefited from the kindness of such strangers, who open doors and guide their way among international networks.

Small local groups with few connections or resources have more limited options for raising international awareness and thus may turn to protest. Yet domestic demonstrations often go unseen abroad. Only spectacular episodes—usually violent ones—draw international media coverage. And since violence is anathema to powerful international NGOs, local groups who use force as an attention-grabbing tactic must carefully limit, justify, and frame it. For example, the poverty and oppression that underlay the 1994 uprising by Mexico's Zapatista National Liberation Army went largely unnoticed at home and abroad for decades. In the face of such indifference, the previously unknown Zapatistas resorted to arms and briefly seized the city of San Cristóbal on January 1, 1994. Immediately tarred by the Mexican government as "terrorists," the Zapatistas in fact carefully calibrated their use of force, avoiding civilian casualties and courting the press. Other tactics also contributed to the Zapatistas' international support, but without these initial dramatic attacks, few people beyond Mexico's borders would now know or care about the struggles of Mexico's indigenous populations.

The NGO Is Always Right

To improve their chances of gaining support, local movements also conform themselves to the needs and expectations of potential backers in Western nations. They simplify and universalize their claims, making them relevant to the broader missions and interests of key global players. In particular, local groups try to match themselves to the substantive concerns and organizational imperatives of large transnational NGOs.

Consider Nigeria's Ogoni ethnic group, numbering perhaps 300,000 to 500,000 people. Like other minorities in the country's southeastern Niger delta, the Ogoni have long been at odds with colonial authorities and national governments over political representation. In the late 1950s, as Royal Dutch/Shell and other multinationals began producing petroleum in the region, the Ogoni claimed that the Nigerian federal government was siphoning off vast oil revenues yet returning little to the minorities who bore the brunt of the drilling's impact. In the early 1990s, an Ogoni movement previously unknown outside Nigeria sought support from Greenpeace, Amnesty International, and other major international NGOs. Initially, these appeals were rejected as unsubstantiated, overly complex, and too political. Ogoni leaders responded by downplaying their contentious claims about minority rights in a poor, multiethnic developing state and instead highlighting their environmental grievances, particularly Shell's "ecological warfare" against the indigenous Ogoni. Critical to this new emphasis was Ogoni leader Ken Saro-Wiwa's recognition of "what could be done by an environment group [in the developed world] to press demands on government and companies."

The Ogoni's strategic shift quickly led to support from Greenpeace, Friends of the Earth, and the Sierra Club. These and other organizations provided funds and equipment, confirmed and legitimated Ogoni claims, denounced the Nigerian dictatorship, boycotted Shell, and eased Ogoni access to governments and media in Europe and North America. In the summer of 1993, as the Ogoni's domestic mobilizations brought harsh government repression, human rights NGOs also took notice. The 1994 arrest and 1995 execution of Saro-Wiwa ultimately made the Ogoni an international symbol of multinational depredation in the developing world, but it was their initial repositioning as an environmental movement that first put them on the global radar screen. (For its part, Shell countered with its own spin, attacking Saro-Wiwa's credibility as a spokesman for his people and denying his allegations against the company.)

Similar transformations have helped other local causes make global headway. In drumming up worldwide support for Guatemala's Marxist insurgency in the 1980s, activist Rigoberta Menchú projected an indigenous identity that resonated strongly with left-leaning audiences in Western Europe and North America. Her book *I, Rigoberta Menchú* made her an international symbol of indigenous oppression, helping her win the Nobel Peace Prize in 1992, year of the Columbus quincentenary, despite her association with a violent rebel movement. As anthropologist David Stoll later showed, however, Menchú and the guerrillas may have enjoyed more backing among international solidarity organizations than among their country's poor and indigenous peoples. According to Stoll, external support may have actually delayed the guerrillas' entry into domestic negotiations by several years, prolonging the war and costing lives.

Mexico's Zapatistas have also benefited abroad from their indigenous identity. At the beginning of their 1994 rebellion, the Zapatistas issued a hodgepodge of demands. Their initial call for socialism was quickly jettisoned when it failed to catch on with domestic or international audiences, and their ongoing demands for Mexican democratization had mainly domestic rather than international appeal. But it was the Zapatistas' "Indianness" and their attacks first on the North American Free Trade Agreement (NAFTA) and then on globalization that found pay dirt in the international arena. (Little coincidence that the day they chose to launch the movement—January 1, 1994—was also the day NAFTA went into effect.) Once the appeal of these issues had become clear, they took center stage in the Zapatistas' contacts with external supporters. Indeed, the Zapatistas and their masked (non-Indian) leader Subcomandante Marcos became potent symbols for antiglobalization activists worldwide. In February and March 2001, when a Zapatista bus caravan traversed southern Mexico and culminated in a triumphant reception in the capital's central square, dozens of Italian *tute bianche* ("White Overalls"), activists prominent in antiglobalization protests in Europe, accompanied the Zapatistas as bodyguards. Even the French farmer and anti-McDonald's campaigner José Bové was present to greet Marcos.

Focusing on an internationally known and notorious enemy (such as globalization or NAFTA) is a particularly effective way of garnering support. In recent years, multinational corporations and international financial institutions have repeatedly served as standins for obscure or recalcitrant local enemies. Even when a movement itself is little known, it can project an effective (if sometimes misleading) snapshot of its claims by identifying itself as the anti-McDonald's movement, the anti-Nike movement, or the anti-Unocal movement. Blaming a villain accessible in the developed world also forges strong links between distant social movements and the "service station on the block," thus inspiring international solidarity.

Such strategies are not aimed only at potential supporters on the political left. The recent growth of a well-funded Christian human rights movement in the United States and Europe has helped many local groups around the world. One major beneficiary is John Garang's Sudan People's Liberation Army, made up mostly of Christians from southern Sudan fighting against the country's Muslim-dominated north. Rooted in ethnic, cultural, and religious differences, the conflict has been aggravated by disputes over control of natural resources. Since fighting broke out in 1983, the war has attracted little attention, despite the deaths of an estimated 2 million people. As late as September 1999, then Secretary of State Madeleine Albright reportedly stated that "the human rights situation in Sudan is not marketable to the American people." However, in the mid-1990s, "slave redemptions" (in which organizations like Christian Solidarity International buy back Christians from their Muslim captors) as well as international activism by Christian human rights organizations began to raise the conflict's profile. The start of oil extraction by multinationals provided another hook to attract concern from mainstream human rights and environmental organizations. Joined by powerful African-American politicians in the United States angered over the slave trade, conservative NGOs have thrown their support behind Garang's group, thereby feeding perceptions of the conflict as a simple Christian-versus-Muslim clash. These NGOs have also found a receptive audience in the administration of U.S. President George W. Bush, thus boosting Garang's chances of reaching a favorable settlement.

By contrast, failure to reframe obscure local issues (or reframing them around an issue whose time has passed) can produce international isolation for a struggling insurgent group. Two years after the Zapatista attacks, another movement sprang from the poverty and oppression of southern Mexico, this time in the state of Guerrero. The Popular Revolutionary Army attacked several Mexican cities and demanded an old-style communist revolution. But these rebels drew little support or attention, particularly in contrast to the Zapatistas and their fashionable antiglobalization rhetoric. Meanwhile, Brazil's Landless Peasants Movement and smaller movements of the rural poor in Paraguay and Venezuela have suffered similar fates both because their goals seem out of step with the times and because their key tactic—land invasions—is too controversial for many mainstream international NGOs. In the Niger delta, radical movements that have resorted to threats, sabotage, and kidnappings have also scared off international support despite the similarity of their grievances to those of the Ogoni.

Leaders for Sale

If marketing is central to a local movement's gaining international support, a gifted salesman, one who identifies himself completely with his "product," is especially valuable. Many individual leaders have come to embody their movements: Myanmar's (Burma) Aung San Suu Kyi, South Africa's Nelson Mandela, as well as the Dalai Lama, Menchú, and Marcos. Even when known abroad only through media images, such leaders can make a host of abstract issues seem personal and concrete, thus multiplying a movement's potential support. For this reason, international tours have long been a central strategy for domestic activists. In the late-19th and early-20th centuries, for example, Sun Yat-sen crisscrossed the world seeking support for a nationalist revolution in China. Attracting international notice when he was briefly kidnapped by the Manchus in London, Sun found himself in Denver, Colorado, on another lobbying trip when the revolution finally came in 1911. Today, for well-supported insurgents, such roadshows are highly choreographed, with hard-charging promoters; tight schedules in government, media, and NGO offices; and a string of appearances in churches, college lecture halls, and community centers. In November 2001, for example, Oronto Douglas, a leader of Nigeria's Ijaw minority, embarked on a six-city, seven-day tour throughout Canada, where he promoted the Ijaw cause along with his new Sierra Club book *Where Vultures Feast: Shell, Human Rights, and Oil in the Niger Delta.*

What transforms insurgent leaders into international icons? Eloquence, energy, courage, and single-mindedness can undeniably create a charismatic mystique. But transnational charisma also hinges on a host of pedestrian factors that are nonetheless unusual among oppressed groups. Fluency in a key foreign language, especially English; an understanding of Western protest traditions; familiarity with the international political vogue; and expertise in media and NGO relations—all these factors are essential to giving leaders the chance to display their more ineffable qualities. Would the Dalai Lama appear as charismatic through a translator? For his part, Subcomandante Marcos has long insisted that he is but an ordinary man, whose way with words just happened to strike a responsive chord at an opportune moment.

Most of these prosaic characteristics are learned, not innate. Indeed, many NGOs now offer training programs to build advocacy capacity, establish contacts, and develop media smarts. The Unrepresented Nations and Peoples Organization in The Hague regularly holds intensive, week-long media and diplomacy training sessions for its member "nations," replete with role plays and mock interviews, helping them put their best foot forward in crucial venues. (Among others, Ken Saro-Wiwa praised the program for teaching him nonviolent direct action skills.) One of the most elaborate programs is the Washington, D.C.-based International Human Rights Law Group's two-year Advocacy Bridge Program, which aims to "increase the skills of local activists to amplify their issues of concern globally" and to "facilitate their access to international agenda-setting venues." Under the program, dozens of participants from around the world, chosen to ensure equal participation by women, travel to Washington for one week of initial training and then to Geneva for three weeks of on-site work at the U.N. Human Rights Commission. In their second year, "graduates" help train a new crop of participants.

Successful insurgent leaders therefore often look surprisingly like the audiences they seek to capture, and quite different from their downtrodden domestic constituencies. Major international NGOs often look for a figure who neatly embodies their own ideals, meets the pragmatic requirements of a "test case," or fulfills romantic Western notions of rebellion—in short, a leader who seems to mirror their own central values. Other leaders, deaf to the international zeitgeist or simply unwilling to adapt, remain friendless and underfunded.

The High Price of Success

Many observers have trumpeted global civil society as the great last hope of the world's have-nots. Yet from the standpoint of local challengers seeking international support, the reality is bleak. The international media is often myopic: Conflicts attract meager reporting unless they have clear relevance, major importance, or huge death tolls. Technology's promise also remains unfulfilled. Video cameras, Web access, and cellular phones are still beyond the reach of impoverished local challengers. Even if the vision of "radical transparency" were realized—and if contenders involved in messy political wrangles in fact desired complete openness—international audiences, flooded with images and appeals, would have to make painful choices. Which groups deserve support? Which causes are more "worthy" than others?

Powerful transnational NGOs, emblematic of global civil society, also display serious limitations. While altruism plays some role in their decision making, NGOs are strategic actors who seek first and foremost their own organizational survival. At times this priority jibes nicely with the interests of local clients in far-flung locations, but often it does not. When selecting clients from a multitude of deserving applicants, NGOS must be hard-nosed, avoiding commitments that will harm their reputations or absorb excessive resources. Their own goals, tactics, constituencies, and bottom lines constantly shape their approaches. Inevitably, many deserving causes go unsupported.

Unfortunately, the least participatory local movements may experience the greatest ease in winning foreign backing. Charismatic leadership is not necessarily democratic, for instance, yet external support will often strengthen a local leader's position, reshaping the movement's internal dynamics as well as its relations with opponents. Among some Tibetan communities today, there are rumblings of discontent over the Dalai Lama's religiously legitimated leadership, but his stature has been so bolstered by international support that dissident elements are effectively powerless. Indeed, any internal dissent—if visible to outsiders—will often reduce international interest. NGOS want their scarce resources to be used effectively. If they see discord instead of unity, they may take their money and clout elsewhere rather than risk wasting them on internal disputes.

The Internet sometimes exacerbates this problem: Internecine feuds played out on public listservs and chat rooms may alienate foreign supporters, as has happened with some members of the pro-Ogoni networks. And although much has been made about how deftly the Zapatistas used the Internet to get their message out, dozens of other insurgents, from Ethiopia's Oromo Liberation Front to the Western Sahara's Polisario Front have Web sites and use e-mail. Yet they have failed to spark widespread international enthusiasm. As the Web site for Indonesia's Papua Freedom Organization laments, "We have struggled for more than 30 years, and the world has ignored our cause." Crucial in the Zapatistas' case was the appeal of their message (and masked messenger) to international solidarity activists, who used new technologies to promote the cause to broader audiences. In fact, for most of their conflict with the Mexican government, the Zapatistas have not had direct access to the Internet. Instead, they have sent communiqués by hand to sympathetic journalists and activists who then publish them and put them on the Web. Thus the Zapatistas' seemingly sophisticated use of the Internet has been more a result of their appeal to a core group of supporters than a cause of their international backing.

Perhaps most worrisome, the pressure to conform to the needs of international NGOS can undermine the original goals of local movements. By the time the Ogoni had gained worldwide exposure, some of their backers in the indigenous rights community were shaking their heads at how the movement's original demands for political autonomy had gone understated abroad compared to environmental and human rights issues. The need for local groups to click with trendy international issues fosters a homogeneity of humanitarianism: Unfashionable, complex, or intractable conflicts fester in isolation, while those that match or—thanks to savvy marketing—appear to match international issues of the moment attract disproportionate support. Moreover, the effort to please international patrons can estrange a movement's jet-setting elite from its mass base or leave it unprepared for domestic responsibilities. As one East Timorese leader stated after international pressure moved the territory close to independence, "We have been so focused on raising public awareness about our cause that we didn't seriously think about the structure of a government."

The quest for international support may also be dangerous domestically. To gain attention may require risky confrontations with opponents. Yet few international NGOs can guarantee a local movement's security, leaving it vulnerable to the attacks of enraged authorities. If a movement's opponent is receptive to rhetorical pressure, the group may be saved, as the Zapatistas were. If not, it will likely face its enemies alone. The NATO intervention in Kosovo provides a rare exception. But few challengers have opponents as notorious and strategically inconvenient as Slobodan Milosevic. Even in that case, Albanian leader Ibrahim Rugova's nonviolent strategies met years of international inaction and neglect; only when the Kosovo Liberation Army brought the wrath of Yugoslavia down on Kosovo and after Milosevic thumbed his nose at NATO did the intervention begin.

Historically, desperate local groups have often sought support from allies abroad. Given geographical distance as well as political and cultural divides, they have been forced to market themselves. This was true not only in the Chinese Revolution but also in the Spanish Civil War, the Indian nationalist movement, and countless Cold War struggles. But the much-vaunted emergence of a global civil society was supposed to change all that, as the power of technologies meshed seamlessly with the good intentions of NGOs to offset the callous self-interest of states and the blithe indifference of faraway publics.

But for all the progress in this direction, an open and democratic global civil society remains a myth, and a potentially deadly one. Lost in a self-congratulatory haze, international audiences in the developed world all too readily believe in this myth and in the power and infallibility of their own good intentions. Meanwhile, the grim realities of the global morality market leave many local aspirants helpless and neglected, painfully aware of international opportunities but lacking the resources, connections, or know-how needed to tap them.

Recommended Resources

The leaders of local movements around the world have authored numerous first-person chronicles of their battles and causes. For a fascinating account of the Ogoni struggle, see Ken Saro-Wiwa's *A Month and a Day: A Detention Diary* (New York: Penguin, 1995). José Ramos-Horta describes the early years of East Timor's struggle for international support in *Funu: The Unfinished Saga of East Timor* (Trenton: Red Sea Press, 1987). Aung San Suu Kyi explains her experiences in Burma in *Freedom from Fear* (New York: Penguin, 1991). Many of Subcomandante Marcos's communiqués are available in Spanish and English on the Web site of the nonprofit group *¡Ya Basta!*

For a critical account of Rigoberta Menchú's projection of the Guatemalan revolution, see David Stoll's *Rigoberta Menchú and the Story of All Poor Guatemalans* (Boulder: Westview Press, 1999). Donald S. Lopez's *Prisoners of Shangri-La: Tibetan Buddhism and the West* (Chicago: University of Chicago Press, 1998) explores the price Tibet has paid for going international. Alison Brysk explains how Latin American indigenous groups deal with the global community in *From Tribal Village to Global Village: Indian Rights and International Relations in Latin America* (Stanford: Stanford University Press, 2000). See Clifford Bob's *The Marketing of Rebellion: Insurgents, Media, and International Activism* (Cambridge: Cambridge University Press, 2005) for a discussion of how the Ogoni and Zapatista movements fit into the academic literature on civil society and nonstate actors.

Margaret Keck and Kathryn Sikkink examine global nongovernmental organization (NGO) networks in *Activists Beyond Borders: Advocacy Networks in International Politics* (Ithaca: Cornell University Press, 1998). P.J. Simmons describes the growing role of activist groups in world affairs in "Learning to Live With NGOs" (*Foreign Policy*, Fall 1998). For recent comprehensive surveys of the global influence of nongovernmental activism, see Helmut Anheier, Marlies Glasius, and Mary Kaldor, eds., *Global Civil Society 2001* (Oxford: Oxford University Press, 2001) and Sudipta Kaviraj and Sunil Khilnani, eds., *Civil Society: History and Possibilities* (Cambridge: Cambridge University Press, 2001).

A special issue of *Peace Review: A Transnational Quarterly* (Vol. 13, No. 3, September 2001) examines the Internet's impact on social justice movements. For the role of media in global politics, see Royce J. Ammon's *Global Television and the Shaping of World Politics: CNN, Telediplomacy, and Foreign Policy* (London: McFarland & Company, 2001).

Biography – Ken Saro-Wiwa, Cultural Broker

Kenule Beeson Saro-Wiwa was born in 1941 to a chief of the Ogoni, an ethnic minority in the Niger Delta region of Nigeria. Saro-Wiwa, always known as Ken, built on this promising foundation by studying English at Government College Umuahia, the University of Ibadan, and then the University of Lagos. By the time the bloody Nigerian civil war broke out in 1967, he had a government post and supported the federal side against the insurgent Biafrans.

Ken Saro-Wiwa was a gifted and prolific writer. Through novels, memoirs, and a newspaper column he reached a wide audience in Africa and—significantly—beyond. *Sozaboy: A Novel in Rotten English* (1994) dealt with the civil war and the corruption of the regime, providing a moral shock for Western readers in the seductive form of a good read. Saro-Wiwa also produced a popular television series, *Basi & Co.*, which satirized the local customs and corruption of the emerging urban classes. His ability to understand and reach out to Western, English-speaking audiences would become a huge political advantage.

Increasingly active on behalf of Ogoni rights, Saro-Wiwa was dismissed from government service in 1973. He now devoted his time not only to television and writing, but also to business ventures, especially real estate, that provided him resources for his political work. In 1987 he again briefly joined the government when a new dictator promised a return to democracy. Saro-Wiwa, quickly realizing the promise was deceitful, resigned.

Saro-Wiwa helped Ogoni activists develop a strategy of reaching out to international groups. They founded the Movement for the Survival of the Ogoni People (MOSOP), tapping into the idea of indigenous peoples at risk. This attracted the attention of the UNPO (the Unrepresented Nations and Peoples Organization), which in turn gave MOSOP legitimacy with other international organizations. Through a process of trial and error, documented by Clifford Bob in *The Marketing of Rebellion* (2005) (see chapter 32 for Bob's general argument), movement leaders settled on two additional ways of framing their struggle in a way that would garner international attention. Their success was remarkable.

One frame was human rights, a discourse often seen as originating in and especially appealing to citizens of the developed world. (On these dynamics, see chapter 31 by James Ron et al.) To gain new support, MOSOP had to move away from presenting itself as an indigenous culture under threat from development, linking the threat instead to the dictatorial government of Nigeria. Basic human rights rather than cultural specificity sold well. A number of international human-rights groups, Amnesty International among them, eventually came to the aid of MOSOP and Saro-Wiwa.

Ogoni activists also framed their struggle as environmental. Their region contains oil, although virtually all the revenues from its exploitation are siphoned off by the federal government. Yet the local population suffers from the spills, blowouts, fires, and other accidents, from the resulting air and water pollution, and from the disruption from boomtown migrants. Shell Oil dominates production, providing MOSOP with a visible player to

Brokers Individuals who bring together previously unconnected groups and organizations are known as brokers. Brokerage is often very important for the development of movements, which cannot grow rapidly if they rely upon recruiting new members one at a time. Brokerage is closely connected to movement leadership. Individuals who are effective brokers often become leaders, and leaders are often in the best position to become effective brokers. Some influential brokers, however, may not become well known to the public. Belinda Robnett (1997) has shown that African-American women were important "bridge leaders" in the civil rights movement, helping to connect ordinary people in local communities with the formal organizations of the movement. These women did not become as famous as Martin Luther King Jr. or Ralph Abernathy, but they were essential to the movement's growth and success.

demonize, a player interested in its international reputation and subject to pressure from Western publics (especially in its home country, the Netherlands). Shell denied many of the Ogoni charges, but photos and videos often caught the company in lies—devastating blunders that opened opportunities for protestors (Jasper and Paulsen 1993). With their environmental frame, the Ogoni attracted support from environmental giants such as Greenpeace, Friends of the Earth, and the Sierra Club.

Saro-Wiwa's adept English allowed him to speak directly to non-Nigerians, especially wealthy protest organizations in the United States and elsewhere. Able to finance his own travel, he visited numerous international organizations in the early 1990s, pitching his case in vivid language. He almost single-handedly catapulted his tiny group into prominence in the world of international activism. Out of the hundreds of causes around the world, the Ogoni managed to gain enormous publicity and sympathy (and resources) in the West.

Framing is not everything, of course: mobilization is also crucial (see chapter 16 by Charlotte Ryan and William A. Gamson). In January 1993, MOSOP managed to put 300,000 Ogoni into the streets for "Ogoni Day," representing more than half the group's total population—an astounding turnout. In 1993 there were also riots when government troops fired on peaceful crowds and when police arrested MOSOP leaders. Such events were "newsworthy," as was the involvement of a prominent multinational like Shell.

The Nigerian government reacted with characteristic brutality. It jailed Saro-Wiwa, without a trial, for several months in 1992 and a month in the spring of 1993. This repression further increased international sympathy for Saro-Wiwa and his cause, as he was now a kind of celebrity capable of attracting media attention. A group like Amnesty International, which according to its mission cannot intervene unless someone has been killed, attacked, or jailed, now began to monitor and support the MOSOP cause.

The Nigerian regime responded by increasing its pressure. In May 1994, Saro-Wiwa and nine others were arrested on patently false charges of murdering four Ogoni elders. Many of the prosecution witnesses later admitted to having been bribed for their testimony. International indignation resulted in a Right Livelihood Award and a Goldman Environmental Prize for Saro-Wiwa, but these could not prevent a guilty verdict from the tribunal. The Ogoni Nine were hanged in a secret military procedure on November 10, 1995. The main cost to the government was Nigeria's suspension from the Commonwealth, but there were no economic sanctions (although the U.S. and other governments considered these).

After the death of Saro-Wiwa and many others, the movement declined. But its international campaign had some victories. Shell Oil devoted resources to local community development, cleaned up its environmental record, and began to hire more employees from the local population. The Nigerian government created more states, a reform which, at least on paper, might have entailed more autonomy to the many regions and tribes of the country. But the continuing instability of the regimes has nullified most of these changes.

Saro-Wiwa's son, in a book about his father published in 2000, reveals some of the tradeoffs involved in a life devoted primarily to political activity. *In the Shadow of a Saint: A Son's Journey to Understanding his Father's Legacy* is a powerful memoir about a family that was always second (or lower) in the patriarch's priorities. Ken Wiwa, now a journalist in Canada, resented his father's absences and infidelities, but also recognized that what made him a bad father also made him a great protest leader.

33 Global Corporations, Global Unions

Stephen Lerner

In November 2006 a group of Latino immigrant janitors won a historic strike in Houston, Texas—doubling their income, gaining health benefits, and securing a union contract for 5300 workers with the Service Employees International Union (SEIU). At a critical moment in the strike, 1000 janitors marched on the police station to protest the illegal arrests of two strikers. The next day, when the charges were dropped and the workers released, a local newspaper reported the crowd's chant as "*Arriba Revolución*!" The article got it wrong—workers were actually chanting "*Arriba La Unión*!" But it got the mood right. It looked and felt like a revolution in Houston. Thousands of immigrant workers and their supporters had successfully challenged the corporate power structure and its allies. They stood up to the police, blocked streets, garnered widespread support, and prevailed against enormous odds.

To many observers, a union fight in the heart of Texas seemed like a shot in the dark. But to workers toiling in poverty for the wealthiest corporations on earth, Houston was a shot heard around the world.

The SEIU janitors' month-long strike exposed a global economy addicted to cheap labor. Immigrant workers challenged a system that paid them $20 a night to clean toilets and vacuum the offices of global giants like Chevron and Shell Oil. They stood up to the global real estate interests that own and manage the office buildings where they work and the national cleaning companies that stay competitive by paying workers next to nothing.

Supported by activists from religious, civil rights, and community movements, janitors marched through Houston's most exclusive neighborhoods and shopping districts, into the lives of the rich and powerful. These disruptions forced Houston's elite, normally insulated from the workers who keep the city functioning, to face up to the human downside of the low-wage economy. Invoking the legacy of the civil rights movement, more than 80 union janitors and activists from around the country flew to Houston on "freedom flights" to support the strikers. They chained themselves to buildings, blocked streets, and were arrested for nonviolent acts of civil disobedience.

The city's corporate and political establishment tried to thwart the strikers. Twenty years ago they had successfully resisted an SEIU-led organizing drive among the city's janitors. So when workers took to the streets, the gloves came off again. Police helicopters circled, mounted police moved in, and protesters nursed broken bones in jail, while the district attorney demanded $40 million in combined bond, nearly $900,000 for each person arrested.

If the strike had been only a local affair, the civic elite would probably have won. But the campaign went global, arising in front of properties controlled by the same firms in cities around the world. As the strike spread, janitors in Chicago, New York, Washington, Mexico City, London, Berlin, and other cities honored picket lines or sponsored demonstrations. These protests and the negative publicity they drew put the struggle of 5000 workers in Texas in the international spotlight. Houston's business leaders intervened to end the dispute, and the workers secured their historic victory. The strike, the tension and passion it generated, and the reaction of the power structure explain why a reporter hearing "*Arriba La Unión*" thought he heard "*Revolución*."

Such a victory in anti-union Texas is worth attention. During the past four decades, union membership has steadily shrunk, first in the United States and now increasingly around the world. As unions have declined, we have seen greater inequality, cuts in social welfare benefits, and a redistribution of wealth to giant multinational corporations around the globe. Trade unions, laws, and social policies that benefited workers have been gutted in country after country. Corporations and newly minted private-equity billionaires boast of their ability to operate anywhere in the world without challenges from workers, unions, or governments to their increasing dominance of the global economy.

Given these trends, many observers have written the labor movement's obituary. But the Houston victory and successes by janitors elsewhere around the world signal a new upsurge of labor activism in America and beyond. Contrary to conventional wisdom, the spread of multinational corporations and the increasing concentration of capital have created the conditions that can turn globalization on its head and lift people out of poverty.

A Turning Point

SEIU's Building Services Division, like many U.S. unions, declined dramatically in the 1970s and 1980s. It lost a quarter of its members, work was part-timed, and benefits were cut. Through its Justice for Janitors campaign in the 1980s and 1990s, the SEIU grappled with how to respond to outsourcing within the United States; as large-contract cleaning companies consolidated on a national basis, so too co-workers in far-flung cities consolidated their efforts to win campaigns and contracts. By 2006, the SEIU had figured out how to use this national scope for growth and power, and members around the country used their sway with national employers and building owners to help the Houston janitors win their strike. Cleaners across the globe bore witness to the struggle and put Houston's real estate leaders under an international microscope.

But the conditions that allowed for success in Houston are already changing. Again the ground is shifting under our feet as the service industry and its clients continue to globalize. Just as the SEIU moved from organizing in single buildings to organizing whole cities and extending that strength to new regions like the South, it must respond to these new changes by developing a deeper global strategy. The largest property owners and service contractors are becoming global companies that operate in dozens of countries and employ or control the employment conditions of hundreds of thousands of workers. Simple solidarity will no longer suffice. Without a global union that unites U.S. workers with their counterparts across the world, workers' power to influence these corporations will continue to wane. Such corporations may threaten workers' way of life, but they also present an opportunity.

It is ironic that a great opportunity to organize global unions comes among the poorest, least skilled workers in one of the least organized and wealthiest sectors of the world economy. Contract janitors, security officers, and others who clean, protect, and maintain commercial property (most of them immigrants) perform site-specific work that is local by nature; their jobs cannot be moved from country to country. Workers who follow global capital from country to country in search of jobs have the power to demand and win better working and living standards. It is among the most invisible and seemingly powerless workers—whose labor is nonetheless essential to the economic success of the most powerful corporations—that we can build a global movement to reinvigorate trade unions, stop the race to the bottom, and lift workers out of poverty. Far from an isolated event, the Houston strike demonstrates how the extraordinary reorganization and realignment of the world's economy has opened up the opportunity to unite workers around the globe in a movement to improve their lives by redistributing wealth and power.

Understanding Globalization

The world is tilting away from workers and unions and the traditional ways they have fought for and won justice—away from the power of national governments, national unions, and national solutions developed to facilitate and regulate globalization. It is tilting toward global trade, giant global corporations, global solutions, and toward Asia—especially China and India. We cannot depend on influencing bureaucratic global institutions, like the International Labor Organization, or fighting entities that are ultimately under the control of global corporations, like the World Trade Organization. Workers and their unions need to use their still-formidable power to counter the power of global corporations before the world tilts so far that unions are washed away, impoverishing workers who currently have unions and trapping those who lack them in ever-deeper poverty. The power equation needs to be balanced before democratic institutions are destroyed.

As multinationals have grown, wealth and capital have become increasingly concentrated. Of the 100 largest economies in the world, 52 are not nations—they are global corporations. The top five companies, Wal-Mart, General Motors, Exxon Mobil, Royal Dutch/Shell, and BP, are each financially larger than all but 24 of the world's nations. The problem is not that corporations operate in more than one country—it is that multinational corporations are so powerful they increasingly dominate what happens in whole countries, hemispheres, and the entire globe.

As global corporations grow and state power declines, national unions are shrinking in membership and power. Union density is down across the globe. Though many countries experienced an increase in unionization during the 1970s and 1980s, density declined in the 1990s. From 1970 to 2000, 17 out of 20 wealthy countries surveyed by the Organisation for Economic Co-operation and Development had a net decline in union density. While the specifics and timing are different in each country, what is remarkable over the last 30 years is the similarity of the results.

No country, no matter how strong its labor movement or progressive its history, is immune to these global trends. Density is starting to decline in Scandinavia, South Africa, Brazil, and South Korea, countries that until recently had stable or growing labor movements. In France, general strikes and mass worker and student mobilizations have slowed the rollback of workers' rights, but these are defensive strikes by workers desperately trying to maintain standards that those in surrounding countries are losing.

The Antidote: Global Unions

For 150 years the argument for global unions was abstract, theoretical, and ideological: in brief, capitalism is global, therefore worker organizations should be too. However, even though capitalism was global, most employers were not. Theoretically, workers were stronger if united worldwide, but the day-to-day reality of unionized workers enabled them to win through the power of national governments. Unionized workers saw workers in other countries as potential competition for their jobs rather than allies. There was no immediate, compelling reason to act beyond national boundaries.

Now, globalization itself is creating the conditions to organize global unions in the service economy. The infrastructure of the FIRE sector (finance, insurance, and real estate) and the millions of service jobs needed to support it are concentrated in some 40 global cities, while manufacturing and mobile jobs—aided by new technology—are being shifted and dispersed around the globe. Global unions could certainly be formed in manufacturing or other sectors characterized by mobile jobs, but right now the opportunity is greatest in service jobs concentrated in the cities that drive the world economy.

Global cities—like New York, Hong Kong, London, and São Paulo—are economic hubs that rely on service jobs to function. Multinational corporations and their executives increasingly depend on these cities because they physically work, live, and play in them. Deeply embedded in each of these cities are hundreds of thousands of janitors, security guards, maintenance, hotel, airport, and other service workers whose labor is essential and cannot be off-shored. And, unlike the jobs in manufacturing and the garment industry, there is no threat of relocation.

The coexistence of immense wealth and low-wage service jobs concentrated in these global economic "engine rooms" dramatically increases the potential power of service workers to build a global movement.

The Houston Victory

Houston's janitors won because the five cleaning contractors that employ them clean more than 70 percent of the office space in the city and operate throughout the United States. Real estate companies like Hines and major tenants like Chevron and Shell operate around the world, allowing union allies to organize actions in places like Mexico City, Moscow, London, and Berlin. The unquenchable thirst of real estate companies for capital to finance their global expansion allowed pension funds like the California Public Employment Retirement fund to intervene, saying that conditions for janitors were both unacceptable and bad for their investment. If Houston's janitors had confronted a local oligarchy of cleaning contractors, building owners, and corporations, they would likely have stood alone and again been crushed.

The union worked among janitors in downtown commercial office buildings in the major northern cities of the United States. But even as the SEIU expanded to organize service workers in other sectors, the gains among janitors were severely threatened by the wave of outsourcing in the 1970s and 1980s.

The union's own structure—dozens of local unions, often competing and undercutting each other in the same city—constrained its ability to fight back, and it needed to build strong local unions that could bargain across a geographic jurisdiction. The SEIU learned the hard way that it could not make gains by organizing building by building; even if a contractor allowed its workers to unionize, the union was likely to be undercut when the contract next went out to bid.

So the SEIU scaled its strategy upwards, reckoning that the resources needed to wage a fight in a single building could be more efficiently deployed in winning a contractor's entire portfolio across a city, and by doing this with multiple contractors in a citywide campaign, it could unionize the entire commercial office-cleaning industry. Crucial to this was developing the "trigger": after a contractor agreed to go union, SEIU would not raise wages until a majority of its competitors also went union, ensuring that no contractor was put at a competitive disadvantage. It began to untangle the complicated relationships between the janitors' direct employers—the contractors—and their secondary employers, the building owners. It also worked to understand the latter's financial, regulatory, political, and operational situation and their key relationships, especially with investors.

The union also learned that the janitors had hidden power: their critical—though invisible—position in the FIRE industry meant they could not be off-shored. As a result, powerful constituencies in these cities rallied to demand justice for janitors in their communities who earned poverty wages while cleaning the offices of multibillion-dollar companies.

These formed the core elements of an integrated strategy that allowed the Justice for Janitors campaign to reestablish or win master agreements for janitors in commercial office markets in the largest U.S. cities, bringing 100,000 new members into the union. In turn that strength allowed the campaign to spread to cities such as Houston, where the same owners operated. Master agreements that included the right to honor picket lines meant that a contractor's unfair labor practices in one city could trigger strike action by SEIU locals in other cities.

There is no geographic limit to this strategy—as the key owners and contractors globalize, so do workers. Their victories demonstrate that in many ways multinationals are becoming more—not less—vulnerable as they spread across the globe.

Global Movement

In the face of the ascendancy of neoliberal policies, it may sound preposterous to argue that we are entering a moment of incredible opportunity for workers and their unions. But sometimes an unplanned combination of events may unleash social forces and contradictions that create the possibility—not the guarantee, the possibility—of creating a movement that lets us accomplish things we had never imagined possible. We are now in such a time.

How do we mount a campaign to organize workers into trade unions strong enough to raise wages and unite communities into organizations powerful enough to win decent housing, schools, and medical care? How do we build on the critical lessons and challenges of Houston, where janitors were far stronger than they would have been if they had focused their efforts on one building, company, or group of workers?

1. Organize Globally

Most trade unions still focus their resources and activity in one country. Despite one hundred years of rhetoric about the need for workers to unite across borders, most global work is symbolic solidarity action and not part of a broader strategy. As the economy has become interrelated and global, organizing work must do the same.

2. Corporations not Countries

A campaign to change the world needs to focus on the corporations that increasingly dominate the global economy. To raise wages and living standards, we must force the largest corporations in the world to negotiate a new social compact that addresses human rights and labor rights in enforceable agreements that could lift tens of millions out of poverty. This campaign must be grounded in the work sites of the corporations that drive the economy and the cities in which they are located and from which they get much of their capital.

Unions as well as community, religious, and political leaders need to lead a campaign calling on the 300 largest pension funds in the world to adopt responsible investment policies covering their 6.9 trillion Euros (US$9 trillion) in capital. If corporations want access to the capital in workers' pension funds, they ought to develop responsible policies that govern how workers' money is to be invested and used.

3. Global Workers, Global Unions, Global Cities

We must create truly global unions, whose mission and focus is on the new global economy, spread across six continents. But they do not need to be in every country or major city in order to have the breadth and reach to tackle the largest global corporations. The challenge of building global unions is not to be everywhere in the world; rather, we need to determine the minimum number of countries and cities in which we must operate in order to exercise maximum power to persuade corporations to adopt a new social compact. This means organizing janitors, security, hotel, airport, and other service workers in some of the 40 or so global cities that are central to the operations of these corporations. Such organization must take place not only in individual work sites, but across cities, corporate groups, and industry sectors to improve immediate conditions and to build a union that organizes not only where workers labor but also in their neighborhoods and communities.

4. A Moral and Economic Message

It is not enough to organize workers and their workplaces. The campaign needs a powerful message about the immorality of forcing workers to live in poverty amidst incredible wealth. Religious, community, and political leaders need to embrace and help lead the campaign because it highlights the moral issues of poverty, calls the corporations responsible for it to task, and offers solutions that are good for workers and the community as a whole.

There are signs that elements of this campaign are becoming politically fashionable. Public-opinion polls suggest there is significant concern about the growing inequality between rich and poor. In a national *Los Angeles Times*/Bloomberg poll in December 2006, nearly three-quarters of respondents said they considered the income gap in America to be a serious problem.

To organize successfully at the work site and in communities, immigrants and migrant workers need to be brought out of the shadows of second-class status in the countries where they work. This campaign needs to take the lead in each country, and globally, to defend the rights of immigrant and migrant workers. It must promote laws that give immigrant and migrant workers full legal rights so that they can organize, unite with native-born workers, and help lead this fight.

5. Disrupting—and Galvanizing—the Global City

It would be naive to imagine that traditional union activity, moral persuasion, and responsible investment policies are enough to change corporate behavior or the world. These are starting points—small steps that allow workers and their allies to win victories, solidify organization, and increase the capacity to challenge corporate power. As activity and tension increase, the global business elite will go back and forth between making minor concessions to placate workers and attacking them at the workplace, in the media, and in political circles. But in the end, we only get real change by executing a two-part strategy: (1) galvanizing workers, community leaders, and the public to lift up our communities and (2) creating a crisis that threatens the existing order.

This is why this moment is so exciting and ripe with opportunity. In the last century industrial workers learned that increasingly coordinated industrial action could cripple national economies, topple governments, and win more just and humane societies. This strategy worked for more than 50 years. But production has been redesigned and shifted across the globe to disperse the power of workers and their unions. The rapid convergence of global corporations and workers in key cities around the world—where corporations are concentrating, not dispersing—has created the conditions and contradictions that allow us to envision how organized service workers can capture the imagination of people in their communities who are disturbed by poverty and income inequality while simultaneously learning how to disrupt the "engine rooms" in cities across the globe and so gain the leverage needed to start to tip the balance of economic power in the world.

Global capitalism operates smoothly in these cities because business leaders from around the world can fly in and out of their airports, stay in their hotels, and travel their streets to offices, banks, finance houses, and stock exchanges. Global cities and the multinational corporations that have centered the economic life of the world in them cannot operate without the global workers, who literally feed, protect, and serve the richest and most powerful corporations and people in the world.

By learning how to disrupt these airports, offices, and hotels, service workers can exert their newly available and previously unimagined power—not for a day, but for weeks and months in an escalating campaign that demands decent wages and living conditions for workers and a stronger, more prosperous future for entire communities and cities. In using this power, they can take the lead in creating a new world where the incredible technological progress, wealth, and economic advances of the global economy lift up the poor, empower the powerless, and inspire all of us to fight for justice.

Recommended Resources

For more information on global union organizing, see http://www.union-network.org/unipropertyn.nsf. To learn about SEIU, go to www.seiu.org; and to find out more about the corporate accountability campaign on Group 4 Securicor, go to www.focusongroup4securicor.org and www.eyeonwackenhut.com.

Dan Clawson. 2003. *The Next Upsurge: Labor and the New Social Movements* (Cornell University Press). A progressive transformation, Clawson believes, will be difficult or impossible without the active involvement of the working class and its collective voice, the labor movement.

Rick Fantasia and Kim Voss. 2004. *Hard Work: Remaking the American Labor Movement* (University of California Press). Fantasia and Voss examine the decline of the American labor movement and the emergence of a new kind of "social movement unionism" that suggests the potential revival of unionism in the United States.

Stephen Lerner. 2003. "An Immodest Proposal: A New Architecture for the House of Labor." *New Labor Forum* 12(2)(Summer):7–30; and (2005) "A Winning Strategy to Do Justice." *Tikkun* (May/June):50–51. Drawing lessons from how SEIU remade itself so that workers could take on big, non-union employers, Lerner argues that the labor movement's structure, culture, and priorities stand in the way of workers' gains and the need to change.

Ruth Milkman. 2006. *L.A. Story: Immigrant Workers and the Future of the U.S. Labor Movement* (Russell Sage Foundation). Milkman explains how Los Angeles, once known as a company town hostile to labor, became a hotbed of unionism, and how immigrant service workers emerged as the unlikely leaders in the battle for workers' rights.

Ruth Milkman and Kim Voss, eds. 2004. *Rebuilding Labor: Organizing and Organizers in the New Union Movement* (Cornell University Press). Milkman and Voss bring together established researchers and a new generation of labor scholars to assess the current state of labor organizing and its relationship to union revitalization.

Saskia Sassen. 2006. *Cities in a World Economy* (Pine Forge Press). Sassen uses the term "global cities" to capture the growth of service firms under globalization and their concentration in a small number of cities, as well as discussing these firms' increasing dependence on low-paid service workers.

Part IX

Why Do Movements Decline?

Introduction

Not surprisingly, scholars have had much more to say about why social movements arise than why they decline, enter a period of "abeyance," or disappear altogether. Nonetheless, several hypotheses about movement decline have attained some notoriety. Most explanations for decline focus on the surrounding political environment, which may of course constrain as well as facilitate movements. Of course, the very success of a movement in changing laws or government policies may undermine the motivations that many people had for participating in that movement. Movement organizations may also be legally recognized by the government, leading to their "institutionalization" and declining reliance upon disruptive protest. Government concessions of this type, even if they do not redress all the grievances and concerns of movement participants, may nevertheless be sufficient to satisfy or placate many people, who will then drift away from the movement or from protest tactics. Social movements, in short, may become victims of their own success.

Movements may also decline as a result of their own internal dynamics and evolution. In her account of the decline of the women's movement in America, Barbara Epstein stresses how the movement gradually lost its radical élan and vision. This was a result in part of intense ideological conflicts among radical feminists within the movement, who had provided much of the movement's activist core and ideological inspiration. Gradually, and partly because of its own success in opening up new professional careers for women, the women's movement as a whole took on a middle-class outlook. It became more concerned with the career opportunities and material success of individual women than with the group solidarity of women or the concerns of poor and working-class women. A remarkably wide range of women's organizations have now been successfully institutionalized, Epstein points out, but they have not been able, and most have not been concerned, to bring about gender equality within the larger society.

The excerpt by Joshua Gamson emphasizes yet another way in which a movement's internal dynamics may lead to schism, if not decline. Movements typically

Movements in Abeyance Some political causes go through long periods of relative inactivity, disappearing from the public eye, before springing back to life. While in abeyance, they are kept alive by small groups or networks of people who remember previous mobilizations and remain committed to ideals that are generally out of favor among the broader public. Such "abeyance structures" also include formal organizations that continue to work for social change even when there is no evidence of a surrounding movement. For instance, the small and largely obscure National Woman's Party (NWP) led by Alice Paul agitated for the Equal Rights Amendment (ERA) during the 1940s and 1950s, until that cause was picked up again by the women's movement of the 1960s and 1970s. The persistence of such networks and organizations helps to explain why certain movements, ideas, and tactics can sometimes reappear quickly after decades of dormancy. See Taylor (1989).

require—or themselves attempt to create—clear and stable collective identities. How can we make claims and demands upon others, after all, if we do not know who "we" and "they" are? Many recent movements have been centrally concerned with establishing, recasting, and/or defending collective identities, including previously stigmatized identities. But collective identities, sociologists argue, are not "natural" or given once and for all; they are culturally constructed and continually reconstructed. Some identities, moreover, may obscure or devalue others. As a result, people have often attempted to blur, reconfigure, or deconstruct certain identities. Hence, Gamson's question: must identity movements self-destruct?

Gamson shows how the gay and lesbian movement has been shaken in recent years by "queer" theorists and activists who have challenged fixed sexual identities like "gay, "lesbian," and "straight." Queer activists have also challenged the "assimilationist" goals of mainstream (and generally older) gay and lesbian activists, some of whom object to the very use of a stigmatized label like "queer." To some extent, Gamson points out, queer activism developed out of the growing organization of bisexual and transgendered people, whose very existence challenges the notion of fixed sexual and gender identities.

In the end, then, the gay and lesbian movement and indeed all identity movements face a dilemma: to be politically effective they may feel a need to emphasize exclusive and secure collective identities, but this may paper over and effectively ignore important differences among movement participants—differences that may later erupt in a way that weakens the movement. How movements handle this dilemma in order to avoid self-destruction—how they weigh and balance competing and potentially disruptive identity claims—is an important question for future research.

Movements may also decline because the "political opportunities" that may have helped give rise to them begin to contract or disappear. Elite divisions may be resolved or (perhaps because of elite unity) elites may decide to harshly repress a movement. Both of these factors are usually invoked to explain the violent demise of the democracy movement in China in 1989. In *The War on Labor and the Left* (1991), Patricia Cayo Sexton also emphasizes repression as a key factor in the decline of the U.S. labor movement since the 1950s. More specifically, Sexton argues that union decline in America is largely explained by aggressive employer opposition to unions, which is in turn facilitated by laws and policies that favor employers over workers. One does not see the same type of employer resistance in Canada, Sexton points out, mainly because laws discourage it. As a result, unions have become stronger in Canada. American unions have also been hurt by factory closings in recent years; many businesses have transferred their operations to parts of the country (mainly the South) or other countries where unions are weak and wages relatively low. (Of course, as Stephen Lerner points out in chapter 33, multinational corporations remain vulnerable to organized labor.)

A primary reason for the existence of a legal framework in the United States which encourages business opposition to unions is the historic *political* weakness of the American labor movement. Unlike all other developed capitalist countries, the United States has never had a strong labor or leftist political party (although some scholars have suggested that the Democratic Party briefly functioned like one during the 1930s and 1940s). Scholars refer to the historical weakness of labor and socialist parties in the United States as "American exceptionalism." The precise reasons for this exceptionalism continue to be debated, with factors such as the two-party system, racial and ethnic antagonisms among workers, and the American creed of individualism receiving considerable emphasis.

Charles Brockett and Ian Roxborough remind us that repression sometimes works and sometimes fails. State violence sometimes demobilizes protestors and crushes insurgents, but it sometimes backfires, spurring more people to take to the streets or to take up arms. What explains this?

Looking at Central America during the 1970s and 1980s, Brockett notes that ruthless repression was most effective when authorities used it before movements had become strong—before a "cycle of protest" had begun. However, after such a cycle of protest was underway—when people were already active and organized—repression tended to backfire. Organized activists redoubled their efforts, went underground, and often turned to violence, joined by others seeking protection, justice, and sometimes revenge.

Roxborough suggests that U.S. counterinsurgency efforts in Iraq failed because they were based on a misunderstanding of insurgent social movements. U.S. officials assume that popular attitudes towards insurgents and the government are based on short-term cost-benefit calculations, failing to see how insurgencies are deeply rooted in intractable class, ethnic, or religious conflicts. Accordingly, attempts to win over the "hearts and minds" of the population by providing material benefits are insufficient. Insurgent movements are less interested in popularity or legitimacy per se than in monopolizing political control at the grassroots; such movements constitute an alternative government. Counterinsurgency, then, is about establishing local political control, a project that requires a great deal of time and manpower—something which outside powers may be unwilling to commit.

Discussion Questions

1. How might a social movement become a victim of its own success? Could this be said of the women's movement?
2. Why has the women's movement declined in recent years? Do you think this decline is permanent or is the movement simply in "abeyance," with the possibility of springing back to life under the right conditions?
3. How have "queer" activists challenged the gay and lesbian movement? Is this challenge simply destructive or potentially beneficial to that movement?
4. Why did government repression sometimes "work" in Central America and sometimes backfire?
5. How do insurgent or revolutionary movements differ from other movements? When are such movements most likely to succeed? When and how is counterinsurgency most likely to succeed?

34 The Decline of the Women's Movement

Barbara Epstein

From the late sixties into the eighties there was a vibrant women's movement in the United States. Culturally influential and politically powerful, on its liberal side this movement included national organizations and campaigns for reproductive rights, the Equal Rights Amendment (ERA), and other reforms. On its radical side it included women's liberation and consciousness raising groups, as well as cultural and grassroots projects. The women's movement was also made up of innumerable caucuses and organizing projects in the professions, unions, government bureaucracies, and other institutions. The movement brought about major changes in the lives of many women, and also in everyday life in the United States. It opened to women professions and blue-collar jobs that previously had been reserved for men. It transformed the portrayal of women by the media. It introduced the demand for women's equality into politics, organized religion, sports, and innumerable other arenas and institutions, and as a result the gender balance of participation and leadership began to change. By framing inequality and oppression in family and personal relations as a political question, the women's movement opened up public discussion of issues previously seen as private, and therefore beyond public scrutiny. The women's movement changed the way we talk, and the way we think. As a result, arguably most young women now believe that their options are or at least should be as open as men's.

Despite the dramatic accomplishments of the women's movement, and the acceptance of women's equality as a goal in most sectors of U.S. society, gender equality has not yet been achieved. Many more women work outside the home but most continue to be concentrated in low-paying jobs; women earn, on the average, considerably less than men; women are much more likely than men to be poor. Violence against women is still widespread. Responsibility for childcare remains largely the responsibility of women; despite the fact that most women work outside the home, nowhere is it seen as a societal rather than a familial responsibility. In the sixties and seventies feminists protested the imbalance in power between men and women in family and personal relations. But these continue to exist.

Worst of all, there is no longer a mass women's movement. There are many organizations working for women's equality in the public arena and in private institutions; these include specifically women's organizations such as the National Organization for Women, and in environmental, health care, social justice and other areas that address women's issues. But where there were once women's organizations with large participatory memberships there are now bureaucratic structures run by paid staff. Feminist theory, once provocative and freewheeling, has lost concern with the conditions of women's lives and has become pretentious and tired. This raises two questions. Why is there so little discussion of the near-disappearance of a movement that not so long ago was strong enough to bring about major changes in the social and cultural landscape? What are the causes of the movement's decline?

Why the Silence?

[...] It is my impression that the real reason for avoiding or suppressing criticisms within the movement is fear that discussing the movement's problems will hasten a process of unraveling that is already well underway. Movements are fragile; the glue that holds them together consists not only in belief in the causes that they represent, but also confidence in their own growing strength. Especially when a movement is in decline it is tempting to silence criticism and turn to whistling in the dark, in the hope that no one will notice that something has gone wrong. But problems that are not acknowledged or discussed are not likely to go away; it is more likely that they will worsen. Understanding why a movement has declined may not lead to the revival of that movement as it was in the past, but it may help in finding new directions.

Reluctance to look at the weaknesses of the current women's movement may also have to do with the fear that second wave, or contemporary, feminism could disappear, sharing the fate of first wave feminism. The first women's movement in the United States, which took place in the latter part of the nineteenth and the early twentieth century, was almost wiped from historical memory during the four-decade interlude between the two waves of feminist activism. It was the weaknesses of first wave feminism, most of which have not been shared by feminism's second wave, that made this possible. First wave feminism was largely confined to white, middle and upper middle class women. First wave feminism also moved, over the course of its history, toward a narrowness of vision that isolated it from other progressive movements. The first feminist movement in the United States originated in the abolitionist movement. In its early years feminism's alliance with the anti-slavery movement, and its association with other protest movements of the pre-Civil War decades, gave it a radical cast. But when the Civil War ended and suffrage was extended to former slaves but not to women, much of the women's movement abandoned its alliance with blacks. In the decades between the Civil War and the turn of the twentieth century, racist and anti-immigrant sentiment spread within the middle class. In the last decades of the nineteenth century and the first two decades of the twentieth the women's movement narrowed its focus to winning woman's suffrage, and leading feminists turned to racist and anti-immigrant arguments on behalf of that goal. Other currents in the women's movement, such as the women's trade union movement, avoided racism and continued to link feminism with a radical perspective. But by the late nineteenth century the mainstream woman's suffrage organizations dominated the women's movement. By the time woman's suffrage was won, first wave feminism had abandoned any broader agenda and had distanced itself from other progressive movements. Feminism was easily pushed aside by the conservative forces that became dominant in the twenties.

The impact of second wave feminism has been broader and deeper than that of the first wave. Whatever direction U.S. politics may take it is hard to imagine feminism being wiped off the slate as it was in the thirties, forties, and fifties. In the last three decades feminism has changed women's lives and thinking in ways that are not likely to be reversed. Where first wave feminism collapsed into a single-issue focus, second wave feminism has in many respects broadened. Second wave feminism had its limitations in its early years. Though participants included women of color and of working class backgrounds, their route into the movement was through the same student and professional circles through which white middle class women found feminism. The presence of women of color and working class women did not mean that feminism was being adopted within these communities. Second wave feminists, especially in the intoxicating early years of the movement, tended to believe that they could speak for all women. Such claims contained a small grain of truth, but ignored the composition of the movement, which was overwhelmingly young, white, college educated, heterosexual, and drawn from the post-Second World War middle class.

Unlike first wave feminism, the second wave broadened over time, in its composition and, in important respects, in its perspective. In the seventies and eighties, lesbian feminism emerged as a current within the movement. Women of color began to articulate their own versions of feminism, and working class women, who had not been part of the movement's early constituency of students and professionals, began to organize around demands for equal treatment at the workplace and in unions, for childcare, and for reproductive rights. Where first wave feminism pulled back, over time, from its early alliances with the black movement and other radical currents, second wave feminism increasingly allied itself with progressive movements, especially with movements of people of color and with the gay and lesbian movement. Second wave feminists also developed increasing sensitivity to racial differences, and differences of sexual orientation, within the women's movement.

From a Movement to an Idea

The heyday of the women's movement was in the late sixties and early seventies. During the eighties and nineties a feminist perspective, or identity, spread widely and a diffuse feminist consciousness is now found nearly everywhere. There are now countless activist groups and social and cultural projects whose goals and approaches are informed by feminism. There are women's organizations with diverse, grassroots constituencies focusing on issues of concern to working class women and women of color. There is the National Congress of Neighborhood Women, dealing with the problems of working class women and women of color. There are many local groups with similar concerns; an example from California is the Mothers of East Los Angeles, which has played an important role in environmental justice struggles. There is Women's Action for New Directions (previously Women's Action for Nuclear Disarmament), bringing women of color and white women together around issues of health and the environment. There are many others. Nevertheless, grassroots activism is not the dominant, or most visible, sector of the women's movement. Public perception of feminism is shaped by the staff-run organizations whose concerns are those of their upper middle class constituencies and by the publications of feminists in the academy. The mass diffusion of feminist consciousness, the bureaucratization of leading women's organizations, and the high visibility of academic feminism are all consequences of the acceptance of feminism by major sectors of society. But these changes have not necessarily been good for the movement. Feminism has simultaneously become institutionalized and marginalized. It has been rhetorically accepted, but the wind has gone out of its sails.

Feminist activism has not ceased, nor have the numbers of women engaged in feminist activity or discussion declined. Millions of U.S. women talk to each other about women's concerns, using the vocabulary of feminism. There are countless organized feminist projects, focusing on domestic violence, reproductive rights and women's health. There are international networks of women continuing efforts begun at the international meeting of women at Beijing in 1995. Young feminist writers are publishing books addressed to, or speaking for, their generation.

The proliferation of feminist activism is part of a broader pattern. The numbers of people involved in community, social justice, and progressive activism generally appear to have increased since the seventies (though there is no way of counting the numbers of people involved). Feminist activism is not an exception to this trend, especially if one includes in this category women's involvement in the environmental and public health movements, addressing women's issues among others. The fact that feminist perspectives have been adopted by movements outside the women's movement, by organizations that also include men, is itself an achievement. Women play a role in leadership of the environmental and anti-corporate movements that is at least equal to men's; feminism is understood by most of these groups to be a major element in their outlook. But these activist projects do not shape the public image of feminism. The organizations and academic networks that shape public perceptions of feminism have become distant from the constituencies that once invigorated them, and have lost focus and dynamism.

Feminism has become more an idea than a movement, and one that often lacks the visionary quality that it once had. The same could be said about progressive movements, or the left, generally: we now have a fairly large and respectable arena in which feminist and progressive ideas are taken for granted. And yet we seem to have little influence on the direction of politics in the United States as a whole, and a kind of "low-grade depression" seems to have settled over the feminist/progressive arena. This is both result and cause of the weakness of the left in recent decades, a response to the widespread acceptance of the view that there is no alternative to capitalism. The women's movement has been weakened along with other progressive movements by this loss in confidence in the possibility that collective action can bring about social change.

Why the Decline of the Women's Movement?

In the sixties and early seventies the dominant tendency in the women's movement was radical feminism. At that time the women's movement included two more or less distinct tendencies. One of these called itself Socialist Feminism (or, at times, Marxist Feminism) and understood the oppression of women as intertwined with other forms of oppression, especially race and class, and tried to develop a politics that would challenge all of these simultaneously. The other tendency called itself Radical Feminism. Large-R Radical Feminists argued that the oppression of women was primary, that all other forms of oppression flowed from gender inequality.

Feminist radicals of both stripes insisted that the inequality of the sexes in the public sphere was inseparable from that in private life; radical feminism demanded equality for women in both spheres. And despite disagreements among themselves about the relationship between the oppression of women and other forms of oppression, radical feminists agreed that equality between women and men could not exist by itself, in a society otherwise divided by inequalities of wealth and power. The goal of radical feminism was an egalitarian society, and new kinds of community, based on equality.

During the sixties and seventies the radical current within the women's movement propelled the whole movement forward, but it was the demand for women's entry into the workplace, on equal terms with men, that gained most ground. The more radical feminist demands for an egalitarian society and new kinds of community could not be won so easily. Though the liberal and radical wings of the women's movement differed in their priorities, their demands were not sharply divided. Radical feminists wanted gender equality in the workplace, and most liberal feminists wanted a more egalitarian society. Affirmative action was not only a tool of privileged women. In an article in the Spring 1999 issue of *Feminist Studies*, Nancy McLean points out that working women used this policy to struggle for equality at the workplace, both opening up traditionally male jobs for women and creating a working class component of the women's movement. As long as the women's movement was growing and was gaining influence, demands for equal access to the workplace and for broad social equality complemented one another.

But a movement's demands, once won, can have different consequences than intended. Affirmative action campaigns were on the whole more effective in the professions than elsewhere, and it was educated, overwhelmingly white, women who were poised to take advantage of these opportunities. This was in large part due to the failure of the labor movement to organize women and people of color. The class and racial tilt of affirmative action was also a result of the accelerating stratification of U.S. society in the seventies, eighties, and nineties, the growing gap between the lower and higher rungs of the economy. The gains made by working women for access to higher-paid jobs could not offset the effects of widening class divisions. From the early seventies on, the standard of living of workers generally declined. Women, who were poorer to begin with, suffered the worst consequences.

The radical feminist vision became stalled, torn apart by factionalism and by intense sectarian ideological conflicts. By the latter part of the seventies, a cultural feminism, aimed more at creating a feminist subculture than at changing social relations generally, had taken the place formerly occupied by radical feminism. Alice Echols' book *Daring to Be Bad: Radical Feminism in America 1967–1975* describes these developments accurately and empathetically. Ruth Rosen's recent survey of the women's movement, *The World Split Open: How the Modern Women's Movement Changed America*, includes a clear-eyed account of the impact of these developments on the women's movement generally. Ordinarily, such sectarianism occurs in movements that are failing, but the women's movement, at the time, was strong and growing. The problem was the very large gap between the social transformation that radical feminists wanted and the possibility of bringing it about, at least in the short run. The movement itself became the terrain for the construction of, if not a new society, at least a new woman. The degree of purity that feminists demanded of one another was bound to lead to disappointment and recriminations.

I think that radical feminism became somewhat crazed for the same reasons that much of the radical movement did during the same period. In the late sixties and early seventies many radicals not only adopted revolution as their aim but also thought that revolution was within reach in the United States. Different groups had different visions of revolution. There were feminist, black, anarchist, Marxist-Leninist, and other versions of revolutionary politics, but the belief that revolution of one sort or another was around the corner cut across these divisions. The turn toward revolution was not in itself a bad thing; it showed an understanding of the depth of the problems that the movement confronted. But the idea that revolution was within reach in the United States in these years was unrealistic. The war in Vietnam had produced a major crisis in U.S. society. Protest against the war, combined with protest against racism and sexism, led some to think that it had become possible to create a new society. In fact, the constituency for revolution, however conceived, was limited mostly to students and other young people, and this was not enough for a revolution. When the war ended the broad constituency of the protest movement evaporated, isolating its radical core. Radical feminism lasted longer than other insurgencies due to the continuing strength of the women's movement as a whole, and the ongoing receptivity of many feminists to radical ideas. But by the eighties radical feminism, at least as an activist movement with a coherent agenda, also became marginal to politics in the United States.

Affirmative action for women constituted an effort toward gender equality in the workplace, a goal not yet achieved. But the success of the women's movement in opening up the professions to women, ironically, has had the effect of narrowing the movement's perspective and goals. When it was mostly made up of young people, and infused with radical ideas, feminism was able to develop a perspective that was in many ways independent of, and critical of, the class from which most feminists were drawn. Now, although there are important new, younger feminist voices, the largest part of the organized women's movement consists of women of my generation, the generation that initiated second wave feminism. I am not suggesting that people necessarily become less radical as they get older. I think that what happens to people's politics depends as much on the times, and the political activity that they engage in, as it does on their age. In a period when radicalism has been made to seem irrelevant even for the young, it is easy for a movement whose leadership is mostly made up of middle aged, middle class professionals to drift into something like complacency.

This of course does not describe the whole women's movement. What we now have is a women's movement composed on the one hand of relatively cautious organizations such as the National Organization for Women, the National Women's Political Caucus, and others, as well as more daring but also less visible organizations concerned with specific issue grassroots organizing. What we do not have is a sector of the women's movement that does what radical feminism once did, that addresses the issue of women's subordination generally, and places it within a critique of society as a whole. Liberal feminism lost the ERA, but it did accomplish many things. Largely due to liberal feminist organizing efforts, young women and girls now have opportunities that did not exist a few decades ago, and expectations that would have seemed wildly unrealistic to earlier generations.

Radical versions of feminism still exist, but more in the academy and among intellectuals than among organizers. Some feminists have continued to work at bridging this gap, both in their intellectual work and in engagement with grassroots movements. The growing numbers of women, including feminists, in the academy, has meant that many students have been introduced to feminist and progressive ideas, and feminist and progressive writings have influenced the thinking of a wide audience. But on the whole, feminists in the academy, along with the progressive wing of academics generally, lack a clear political agenda, and have often become caught up in the logic and values of the university. In the arena of high theory, and to some extent cultural studies, both of which are closely associated with feminism, the pursuit of status, prestige, and stardom has turned feminist and progressive values on their head. Instead of the sixties' radical feminist critique of hierarchy, we have a kind of reveling in hierarchy and in the benefits that come with rising to the top of it.

Though the contemporary women's movement has avoided the racial and ethnic biases, and the single-issue focus, that plagued the early feminist movement, it resembles first-wave feminism in having gradually lost its critical distance from its own middle and upper middle class position. First wave feminism narrowed, over the course of its history, not only in relation to the issue of race but also in relation to the issues of capital and class. In the pre-Civil War years, first wave feminism was part of a loose coalition of movements within which radical ideas circulated, including critical views of industrial capitalism. In the late nineteenth century, as the structures of industrial capitalism hardened and class conflict intensified, feminists played important roles in the reform movements that championed poor and working class people, and some sections of the women's movement criticized capitalism and reached out to labor. The Women's Christian Temperance Union, for instance, criticized the exploitation of labor by capital and entertained support for "gospel socialism" as "Christianity in action." In the early years of the twentieth century the alliance between feminism and socialism continued within the Socialist Party. But after the turn of the century mainstream feminists moved away from any critique of capitalism, instead identifying women's interests and values with those of the upper middle class. By the time first wave feminism disappeared it had lost any critical perspective on capitalism or on its own class origins.

Feminism Has Absorbed the Perspective of the Middle Class

Like first wave feminism, contemporary feminism has over time tended to absorb the perspective of the middle class from which it is largely drawn. Meanwhile the perspective of that class has changed. Over the last several decades, under the impact of increasing economic insecurity and widening inequalities, the pursuit of individual advancement has become an increasingly important focus within the middle class. Community engagement has weakened for many, perhaps most, middle class people. For many people, especially professionals, work has become something of a religion; work is the only remaining source of identity that seems valid. Meanwhile the workplace has become, for many, more competitive and more stressful. This is not just a problem of the workplace, but of the culture as a whole. This country has become increasingly individualistic, cold, and selfish. And feminism has not noticeably challenged this. The feminist demand for equal workplace access was and remains important; for most women this demand has not been achieved. But the most visible sector of the women's movement appears to have substituted aspirations toward material success for the demand for social equality and community. This evolution, from the radical and transforming values of its early years, has been so gradual that it has been easy for those involved not to notice it. But it is a reflection of the shifting perspectives of women who were once part of a radical movement and now find themselves in settings governed by a different set of values.

In the seventies and eighties, many feminists thought that if only we could get more women into the universities, the universities would be transformed and would become less elitist, less competitive, more humane, and more concerned with addressing social problems. We now have a lot of women in the universities, and it is not clear that the universities have changed for the better. Indeed, in many respects the universities are worse, especially in regard to the growing pursuit of corporate funds and the resultant spread of the market ethos. But so far neither women in general nor feminists in particular have been especially prominent in challenging these trends and demanding a more humane, less competitive, or less hierarchical university. Feminist academics have not in recent years been particularly notable for their adherence to such values. There are some areas of academic feminism where there is open discussion, where people treat each other with respect, and where everyone involved is treated as an equal participant toward a common purpose. But in too much of feminist academia this is not the case. In the arena of high theory, the most prestigious sector of academic feminism, competition and the pursuit of status are all too often uppermost.

The shift in values that has taken place in the women's movement has been part of a broader trend. In a period of sharpening economic and social divisions, characterized by corporate demand for greater and greater profits and the canonizing of greed, a whole generation has been seized by the desire to rise to the top. Feminists are no exception to this. The image of the feminist as careerist is not merely a fantasy promulgated by hostile media. Put differently, feminists, at least those in academia and in the professions, have been no more overtaken by these values than other members of the middle class. But to say this is to admit that feminists have lost their grip on a vision of a better world.

[...]

35 The Dilemmas of Identity Politics

Joshua Gamson

Focused passion and vitriol erupt periodically in the letters columns of San Francisco's lesbian and gay newspapers. When the *San Francisco Bay Times* announced to "the community" that the 1993 Freedom Day Parade would be called "The Year of the Queer," missives fired for weeks. The parade was what it always is: a huge empowerment party. But the letters continue to be telling. "Queer" elicits familiar arguments: over assimilation, over generational differences, over who is considered "us" and who gets to decide.

> **New Social Movements** Since the 1960s, a cluster of social movements have swept through Europe and the United States which are not pursuing the economic or class interests of their members. Instead, they are pursuing issues such as the quality of life or democratic procedures. The antinuclear movement, ecology, the animal rights and peace movements, and the women's and student movements are examples. Many theorists argued that these movements were to "postindustrial" society what the labor movement – the quintessential "old" social movement – had been to "industrial" society: the central social conflict whose outcome would determine the direction of social change. These new movements were thought to be resisting corporate and government "technocrats" who make a range of decisions that, without being publicly debated, profoundly shape everyone's lives. Other scholars have argued that these movements are not so new, especially in the United States, which had non-class movements such as temperance or "anti-vice" in the nineteenth century. While these "post-class" movements use many of the same tactics as more traditional movements, they may also pay more attention to the manipulation of images on television and in other media.

On this level, it resembles similar arguments in ethnic communities in which "boundaries, identities, and cultures, are negotiated, defined, and produced" (Nagel 1994:152). Dig deeper into debates over queerness, however, and something more interesting and significant emerges. Queerness in its most distinctive forms shakes the ground on which gay and lesbian politics has been built, taking apart the ideas of a "sexual minority" and a "gay community," indeed of "gay" and "lesbian" and even "man" and "woman." It builds on central difficulties of identity-based organizing: the instability of identities both individual and collective, their made-up yet necessary character. It exaggerates and explodes these troubles, haphazardly attempting to build a politics from the rubble of deconstructed collective categories. This debate, and other related debates in lesbian and gay politics, is not only over the *content* of collective identity (whose definition of "gay" counts?), but over the everyday *viability* and political *usefulness* of sexual identities (is there and should there be such a thing as "gay," "lesbian," "man," "woman"?).

This paper, using internal debates from lesbian and gay politics as illustration, brings to the fore a key dilemma in contemporary identity politics and traces out its implications for social movement theory and research. As I will show in greater detail, in these sorts of debates – which crop up in other communities as well – two different political impulses, and two different forms of organizing, can be seen facing off. The logic and political utility of deconstructing collective categories vie with that of shoring them up; each logic is true, and neither is fully tenable.

On the one hand, lesbians and gay men have made themselves an effective force in this country over the past several decades largely by giving themselves what civil rights movements had: a public collective identity. Gay and lesbian social movements have built a quasiethnicity, complete with its own political and cultural institutions, festivals, neighborhoods, even its own flag. Underlying that ethnicity is typically the notion that what gays and lesbians share – the anchor of minority status and minority rights claims – is the same fixed, natural essence, a self with same-sex desires. The shared oppression, these movements have forcefully claimed, is the denial of the freedoms and opportunities to actualize this self. In this *ethnic/essentialist* politic, clear categories of collective identity are necessary for successful resistance and political gain.

Yet this impulse to build a collective identity with distinct group boundaries has been met by a directly opposing logic, often contained in queer activism (and in the newly anointed "queer theory"): to take apart the identity categories and blur group boundaries. This alternative angle, influenced by academic "constructionist" thinking, holds that sexual identities are historical and social products, not natural or intrapsychic ones. It is socially-produced binaries (gay/straight, man/woman) that are the basis of oppression; fluid, unstable experiences of self become fixed primarily in the service of social control. Disrupting those categories, refusing rather than embracing ethnic minority status, is the key to liberation. In this *deconstructionist* politic, clear collective categories are an obstacle to resistance and change.

The challenge for analysts, I argue, is not to determine which position is accurate, but to cope with the fact that both logics make sense. Queerness spotlights a dilemma shared by other identity movements (racial, ethnic, and gender movements, for example): Fixed identity categories are both the basis for oppression and the basis for political power. This raises questions for political strategizing and, more importantly for the purposes here, for social movement analysis. If identities are indeed much more unstable, fluid, and constructed than movements have tended to assume – if one takes the queer challenge seriously, that is – what happens to identity-based social movements such as gay and lesbian rights? Must sociopolitical struggles articulated through identity eventually undermine themselves?

Social movement theory, a logical place to turn for help in working through the impasse between deconstructive cultural strategies and category-supportive political strategies, is hard pressed in its current state to cope with these questions. The case of queerness, I will argue, calls for a more developed theory of collective identity formation and its relationship to both institutions and meanings, an understanding that *includes the impulse to take apart that identity from within.*

[...]

Social Movements and Collective Identity

Social movements researchers have only recently begun treating collective identity construction as an important and problematic movement activity and a significant subject of study. Before the late 1980s, when rational-actor models came under increased critical scrutiny, "not much direct thought [had] been given to the general sociological problem of what collective identity is and how it is constituted" (Schlesinger 1987: 236). As Alberto Melucci (1989:73) has argued, social movement models focusing on instrumental action tend to treat collective identity as the nonrational expressive residue of the individual, rational pursuit of political gain. And "even in more sophisticated rational actor models that postulate a *collective* actor making strategic judgments of cost and benefit about collective action," William Gamson points out, "the existence of an *established* collective identity is assumed" (1992:58, emphasis in original). Identities, in such models, are typically conceived as existing before movements, which then make them visible through organizing and deploy them politically; feminism wields, but does not create, the collective identity of "women."

Melucci and other theorists of "new social movements" argue more strongly that collective identity is not only necessary for successful collective action, but that it is often an end in itself, as the self-conscious reflexivity of many contemporary movements seems to demonstrate. Collective identity, in this model, is conceptualized as "a continual process of recomposition rather than a given," and "as a dynamic, *emergent* aspect of collective action" (Schlesinger 1987:237). Research on ethnicity has developed along similar lines, emphasizing, for example, the degree to which "people's conceptions of themselves along ethnic lines, especially their ethnic identity, [are] situational and changeable" (Nagel 1994:154). "An American Indian might be 'mixed-blood' on the reservation," as Joane Nagel describes one example, " 'Pine Ridge' when speaking to someone from another reservation, a 'Sioux' or 'Lakota' when responding to the U.S. census, and 'Native American' when interacting with non-Indians" (1994:155).

How exactly collective identities emerge and change has been the subject of a growing body of work in the study of social movements. For example, Verta Taylor and Nancy Whittier, analyzing lesbian-feminist communities, point to the creation of politicized identity communities through boundary-construction (establishing "differences between a challenging group and dominant groups"), the development of consciousness (or "interpretive frameworks") and negotiation ("symbols and everyday actions subordinate groups use to resist and restructure existing systems of domination") (1992: 100–111). Other researchers, working from the similar notion that "the location and meaning of particular ethnic boundaries are continuously negotiated, revised, and revitalized," demonstrate the ways in which collective identity is constructed not only from within, but is also shaped and limited by "political policies and institutions, immigration policies, by ethnically linked resource policies, and by political access structured along ethnic lines" (Nagel 1994:152, 157).

When we turn to the disputes over queerness, it is useful to see them in light of this recent work. We are certainly witnessing a process of boundary-construction and identity negotiation: As contests over membership and over naming, these debates are part of an ongoing project of delineating the "we" whose rights and freedoms are at stake in the movements. Yet as I track through the queer debates, I will demonstrate a movement propensity that current work on collective identity fails to take into account: the drive to blur and deconstruct group categories, and to keep them forever unstable. It is that tendency that poses a significant new push to social movement analysis.

Queer Politics and Queer Theory

Since the late 1980s, "queer" has served to mark first a loose but distinguishable set of political movements and mobilizations, and second a somewhat parallel set of academy bound intellectual endeavors (now calling itself "queer theory"). Queer politics, although given organized body in the activist group Queer Nation, operates largely through the decentralized, local, and often anti-organizational cultural activism of street postering, parodic and non-conformist self-presentation, and underground alternative magazines ("zines") (Berlant and Freeman 1993; Duggan 1992; Williams 1993); it has defined itself largely against conventional lesbian and gay politics. The emergence of queer politics, although it cannot be treated here in detail, can be traced to the early 1980s backlash against gay and lesbian movement gains, which "punctured illusions of a coming era of tolerance and sexual pluralism;" to the AIDS crisis, which "underscored the limits of a politics of minority rights and inclusion;" and to the eruption of "long-simmering internal differences" around race and sex, and criticism of political organizing as "reflecting a white, middle-class experience or standpoint" (Seidman 1994:172).

Queer theory, with roots in constructionist history and sociology, feminist theory, and post-structuralist philosophy, took shape through several late 1980s academic conferences and continues to operate primarily in elite academic institutions through highly abstract language; it has defined itself largely against conventional lesbian and gay studies (Stein and Plummer 1994). Stein and Plummer have recently delineated the major theoretical departures of queer theory: a conceptualization of sexual power as embodied "in different levels of social life, expressed discursively and enforced through boundaries and binary divides;" a problematization of sexual and gender categories, and identities in general; a rejection of civil rights strategies "in favor of a politics of carnival, transgression, and parody, which leads to deconstruction, decentering, revisionist readings, and an anti-assimilationist politics;" and a "willingness to interrogate areas which would not normally be seen as the terrain of sexuality, and conduct queer 'readings' of ostensibly heterosexual or non-sexualized texts" (1994:181–182).

[...]

My discussion of this and the two debates that follow is based on an analysis of 75 letters in the weekly *San Francisco Bay Times*, supplemented by related editorials from national lesbian and gay publications. The letters were clustered: The debates on the word "queer" ran in the *San Francisco Bay Times* from December 1992 through April 1993; the disputes over bisexuality ran from April 1991 through May 1991; clashes over transsexual inclusion ran from October 1992 through December 1992. Although anecdotal evidence suggests that these disputes are widespread, it should be noted that I use them here not to provide conclusive data, but to provide a grounded means for conceptualizing the queer challenge.

The Controversy over Queerness: Continuities with Existing Lesbian and Gay Activism

In the discussion of the "Year of the Queer" theme for the 1993 lesbian and gay pride celebration, the venom hits first. "All those dumb closeted people who don't like the Q-word," the *Bay Times* quotes Peggy Sue suggesting, "can go fuck themselves and go to somebody else's parade." A man named Patrick argues along the same lines, asserting that the men opposing the theme are "not particularly thrilled with their attraction to other men," are "cranky and upset," yet willing to benefit "from the stuff queer activists do." A few weeks later, a letter writer shoots back that "this new generation assumes we were too busy in the '70s lining up at Macy's to purchase sweaters to find time for the revolution – as if their piercings and tattoos were any cheaper." Another sarcastically asks, "How did you ever miss out on 'Faggot' or 'Cocksucker'?" On this level, the dispute reads like a sibling sandbox spat.

Although the curses fly sometimes within generations, many letter writers frame the differences as generational. The queer linguistic tactic, the attempt to defang, embrace, and resignify a stigma term, is loudly rejected by many older gay men and lesbians. "I am sure he isn't old enough to have experienced that feeling of cringing when the word 'queer' was said," says Roy of an earlier letter writer. Another writer asserts that 35 is the age that marks off those accepting the queer label from those rejecting it. Younger people, many point out, can "reclaim" the word only because they have not felt as strongly the sting, ostracism, police batons, and baseball bats that accompanied it one generation earlier. For older people, its oppressive meaning can never be lifted, can never be turned from overpowering to empowering.

Consider "old" as code for "conservative," and the dispute takes on another familiar, overlapping frame: the debate between assimilationists and separatists, with a long history in American homophile, homosexual, lesbian, and gay politics. Internal political struggle over agendas of assimilation (emphasizing sameness) and separation (emphasizing difference) has been present since the inception of these movements, as it has in other movements. The "homophile" movement of the 1950s, for example, began with a Marxist-influenced agenda of sex-class struggle, and was quickly overtaken by accommodationist tactics: gaining expert support; men demonstrating in suits, women in dresses. Queer marks a contemporary anti-assimilationist stance, in opposition to the mainstream inclusionary goals of the dominant gay rights movement.

"They want to work from within," says Peggy Sue elsewhere (Berube and Escoffier 1991), "and I just want to crash in from the outside and say, 'Hey! Hello, I'm queer. I can make out with my girlfriend. Ha ha. Live with it. Deal with it.' That kind of stuff." In a zine called *Rant & Rave*, co-editor Miss Rant argues that:

> I don't want to be gay, which means assimilationist, normal, homosexual.... I don't want my personality, behavior, beliefs, and desires to be cut up like a pie into neat little categories from which I'm not supposed to stray (1993:15).

Queer politics, as Michael Warner puts it, "opposes society itself," protesting "not just the normal behavior of the social but the *idea* of normal behavior" (1993:xxvii). It embraces the label of perversity, using it to call attention to the "norm" in "normal," be it hetero or homo.

Queer thus asserts in-your-face difference, with an edge of defiant separatism: "We're here, we're queer, get used to it," goes the chant. We are different, that is, free from convention, odd and out there and proud of it, and your response is either your problem or your wake-up call. Queer does not so much rebel against outsider status as revel in it. Queer confrontational difference, moreover, is scary, writes Alex Chee (1991), and thus politically useful:

> Now that I call myself queer, know myself as a queer, nothing will keep [queer-haters] safe. If I tell them I am queer, they give me room. Politically, I can think of little better. I do not want to be one of them. They only need to give me room.

This goes against the grain of civil rights strategists, of course, for whom at least the appearance of normality is central to gaining political "room." Rights are gained, according to this logic, by demonstrating similarity (to heterosexual people, to other minority groups) in a nonthreatening manner. "We are everywhere," goes the refrain from this camp. We are your sons and daughters and co-workers and soldiers, and once you see that lesbians and gays are just like you, you will recognize the injustices to which we are subject. "I am not queer," writes a letter writer named Tony. "I am normal, and if tomorrow I choose to run down the middle of Market Street in a big floppy hat and skirt I will still be normal." In the national gay weekly *10 Percent* – for which *Rant & Rave* can be seen as a proud evil twin – Eric Marcus (1993:14) writes that "I'd rather emphasize what I have in common with other people than focus on the differences," and "the last thing I want to do is institutionalize that difference by defining myself with a word and a political philosophy that set me outside the mainstream." The point is to be not-different, not-odd, not-scary. "We have a lot going for us," Phyllis Lyon says simply in the *Bay Times*. "Let's not blow it" – blow it, that is, by alienating each other and our straight allies with words like "queer."

Debates over assimilation are hardly new, however; but neither do they exhaust the letters column disputes. The metaphors in queerness are striking. Queer is a "psychic tattoo," says writer Alex Chee, shared by outsiders; those similarly tattooed make up the Queer Nation. "It's the land of lost boys and lost girls," says historian Gerard Koskovich (in Berube and Escoffier 1991:23), "who woke up one day and realized that not to have heterosexual privilege was in fact the highest privilege." A mark on the skin, a land, a nation: These are the metaphors of tribe and family. Queer is being used not just to connote and glorify differentness, but to revise the criteria of membership in the family, "to affirm sameness by defining a common identity on the fringes" (Berube and Escoffier 1991:12; see also Duggan 1992).

In the hands of many letter writers, in fact, queer becomes simply a shorthand for "gay, lesbian, bisexual, and transgender," much like "people of color" becomes an inclusive and difference-erasing shorthand for a long list of ethnic, national, and racial groups. And as some letter writers point out, as a quasi-national shorthand "queer" is just a slight shift in the boundaries of tribal membership with no attendant shifts in power; as some lesbian writers point out, it is as likely to become synonymous with "white gay male" (perhaps now with a nose ring and tattoos) as it is to describe a new community formation. Even in its less nationalist versions, queer can easily be difference without change, can subsume and hide the internal differences it attempts to incorporate. The queer tribe attempts to be a multicultural, multigendered, multisexual, hodge-podge of outsiders; as Steven Seidman points out, it ironically ends up

> denying differences by either submerging them in an undifferentiated oppositional mass or by blocking the development of individual and social differences through the disciplining compulsory imperative to remain undifferentiated (1993:133).

Queer as an identity category often restates tensions between sameness and difference in a different language.

Debates Over Bisexuality and Transgender: Queer Deconstructionist Politics

Despite the aura of newness, then, not much appears new in recent queerness debate; the fault lines on which they are built are old ones in lesbian and gay (and other identity-based) movements. Yet letter writers agree on one puzzling point: Right now, it matters what we are called and what we call ourselves. That a word takes so prominent a place is a clue that this is more than another in an ongoing series of tired assimilationist-liberationist debates. The controversy of queerness is not just strategic (what works), nor only a power-struggle (who gets to call the shots); it is those, but not only those. At their most basic, queer controversies are battles over identity and naming (who I am, who we are). Which words capture us and when do words fail us? Words, and the "us" they name, seem to be in critical flux.

But even identity battles are not especially new. In fact, within lesbian-feminist and gay male organizing, the meanings of "lesbian" and "gay" were contested almost as soon as they began to have political currency as quasi-ethnic statuses. Women of color and sex radicals loudly challenged lesbian feminism of the late 1970s, for example, pointing out that the "womansculture" being advocated (and actively created) was based in white, middle-class experience and promoted a bland, desexualized lesbianism. Working-class lesbians and gay men of color have consistently challenged "gay" as a term reflecting the middle-class, white homosexual men who established its usage (Stein 1992; Phelan 1993; Seidman 1993, 1994). They have challenged, that is, the definitions.

The ultimate challenge of queerness, however, is not just the questioning of the content of collective identities, but the *questioning of the unity, stability, viability, and political utility of sexual identities* – even as they are used and assumed. The radical provocation from queer politics, one which many pushing queerness seem only remotely aware of, is not to resolve that difficulty, but to exaggerate and build on it. It is an odd endeavor, much like pulling the rug out from under one's own feet, not knowing how and where one will land.

To zero in on the distinctive deconstructionist politics of queerness, turn again to the letters columns. It is no coincidence that two other major *Bay Times* letters column controversies of the early 1990s concerned bisexual and transgender people, the two groups included in the revised queer category. Indeed, in his anti-queer polemic in the magazine *10 Percent* (a title firmly ethnic/essentialist in its reference to a fixed homosexual population), it is precisely these sorts of people, along with some "queer straights," from whom Eric Marcus seeks to distinguish himself:

> Queer is not my word because it does not define who I am or represent what I believe in.... I'm a man who feels sexually attracted to people of the same gender. I don't feel attracted to both genders. I'm not a woman trapped in a man's body, nor a man trapped in a woman's body. I'm not someone who enjoys or feels compelled to dress up in clothing of the opposite gender. And I'm not a "queer straight," a heterosexual who feels confined by the conventions of straight sexual expression. ... I don't want to be grouped under the all-encompassing umbrella of queer... because we have different lives, face different challenges, and don't necessarily share the same aspirations (1993:14).

The letters columns, written usually from a different political angle (by lesbian separatists, for example), cover similar terrain. "It is not empowering to go to a Queer Nation meeting and see men and women slamming their tongues down each other's throats," says one letter arguing over bisexuals. "Men expect access to women," asserts one from the transgender debate. "Some men decide that they want access to lesbians any way they can and decide they will become lesbians."

Strikingly, nearly all the letters are written by, to, and about women – a point to which I will later return. "A woman's willingness to sleep with men allows her access to jobs, money, power, status," writes one group of women. "This access does not disappear just because a woman sleeps with women 'too'... That's not bisexuality, that's compulsory heterosexuality." You are not invited; you will leave and betray us. We are already here, other women respond, and it is you who betray us with your backstabbing and your silencing. "Why have so many bisexual women felt compelled to call themselves lesbians for so long? Do you think biphobic attitudes like yours might have something to do with it?" asks a woman named Kristen. "It is our community, too; we've worked in it, we've suffered for it, we belong in it. We will not accept the role of the poor relation." Kristen ends her letter tellingly, deploying a familiar phrase: "We're here. We're queer. Get used to it."

The letters run back and forth similarly over transgender issues, in particular over transsexual lesbians who want to participate in lesbian organizing. "'Transsexuals' don't want to just be lesbians," Bev Jo writes, triggering a massive round of letters, "but insist, with all the arrogance and presumption of power that men have, on going where they are not wanted and trying to destroy lesbian gatherings." There are surely easier ways to oppress a woman, other women shoot back, than to risk physical pain and social isolation. You are doing exactly what anti-female and anti-gay oppressors do to us, others add. "Must we all bring our birth certificates and two witnesses to women's events in the future?" asks a woman named Karen. "If you feel threatened by the mere existence of a type of person, and wish to exclude them for your comfort, you are a bigot, by every definition of the term."

These "border skirmishes" over membership conditions and group boundaries have histories preceding the letters (Stein 1992; see also Taylor and Whittier 1992), and also reflect the growing power of transgender and bisexual organizing. Although they are partly battles of position, more fundamentally the debates make concrete the anxiety queerness can provoke. They spotlight the possibility that sexual and gender identities are not the solid political ground they have been thought to be – which perhaps accounts for the particularly frantic tone of the letters.

Many arguing for exclusion write like a besieged border patrol. "Live your lives the way you want and spread your hatred of women while you're at it, if you must," writes a participant in the transgender letter spree, "but the fact is we're here, we're dykes and you're not. Deal with it." The Revolting Lesbians argue similarly in their contribution to the *Bay Times* bisexuality debate: "Bisexuals are not lesbians – they are bisexuals. Why isn't that obvious to everyone? Sleeping with women 'too' does not make you a lesbian. We must hang onto the identity and visibility we've struggled so hard to obtain." A letter from a woman named Caryatis sums up the perceived danger of queerness:

> This whole transsexual/bisexual assault on lesbian identity has only one end, to render lesbians completely invisible and obsolete. If a woman who sleeps with both females and males is a lesbian; and if a man who submits to surgical procedure to bring his body in line with his acceptance of sex role stereotypes is a lesbian; and if a straight woman whose spiritual bonds are with other females is a lesbian, then what is a female-born female who loves only other females? Soon there will be no logical answer to that question.

Exactly: In lesbian (and gay) politics, as in other identity movements, a logical answer is crucial. An inclusive queerness threatens to turn identity to nonsense, messing with the idea that identities (man, woman, gay, straight) are fixed, natural, core phenomena, and therefore solid political ground. Many arguments in the letters columns, in fact, echo the critiques of identity politics found in queer theory. "There is a growing consciousness that a person's sexual identity (and gender identity) need not be etched in stone," write Andy and Selena in the bisexuality debate, "that it can be fluid rather than static, that one has the right to PLAY with whomever one wishes to play with (as long as it is consensual), that the either/or dichotomy ('you're either gay or straight' is only one example of this) is oppressive no matter who's pushing it." Identities are fluid and changing; binary categories (man/woman, gay/straight) are distortions. "Humans are not organized by nature into distinct groups," Cris writes. "We are placed in any number of continuums. Few people are 100 percent gay or straight, or totally masculine or feminine." Differences are not distinct, categories are social and historical rather than natural phenomena, selves are ambiguous. "Perhaps it is time the lesbian community re-examined its criteria of what constitutes a woman (or man)," writes Francis. "And does it really matter?" Transsexual performer and writer Kate Bornstein, in a *Bay Times* column triggered by the letters, voices the same basic challenge. Are a woman and a man distinguished by anatomy? "I know several women in San Francisco who have penises," she says. "Many wonderful men in my life have vaginas" (1992:4). Gender chromosomes, she continues, are known to come in more than two sets ("could this mean there are more than two genders?"); testosterone and estrogen don't answer it ("you could buy your gender over the counter"); neither child-bearing nor sperm capacities nails down the difference ("does a necessary hysterectomy equal a sex change?"). Gender is socially assigned; binary categories (man/woman, gay/straight) are inaccurate and oppressive; nature provides no rock-bottom definitions. The opposite sex, Bornstein proposes, is neither.

Indeed, it is no coincidence that bisexuality, transsexualism, and gender crossing are exactly the kind of boundary-disrupting phenomena embraced by much post-structuralist sexual theory. Sandy Stone, for example, argues that "the transsexual currently occupies a position which is nowhere, which is outside the binary oppositions of gendered discourse" (1991:295). Steven Seidman suggests that bisexual critiques challenge "sexual object-choice as a master category of sexual and social identity" (1993:123).

[...]

The point, often buried in over-abstracted jargon, is well taken: The presence of visibly transgendered people, people who do not quite fit, potentially subverts the notion of two naturally fixed genders; the presence of people with ambiguous sexual desires potentially subverts the notion of naturally fixed sexual orientations. (I say "potentially" because the more common route has continued to be in the other direction: the reification of bisexuality into a third orientation, or the retention of male-female boundaries through the notion of transgendered people as "trapped in the wrong body," which is then fixed.) Genuine inclusion of transgender and bisexual people can require not simply an expansion of an identity, but a subversion of it. This is the deepest difficulty queerness raises, and the heat behind the letters: If gay (and man) and lesbian (and woman) are unstable categories, "simultaneously possible and impossible" (Fuss 1989:102), what happens to sexuality-based politics?

The question is easily answered by those securely on either side of these debates. On the one side, activists and theorists suggest that collective identities with exclusive and secure boundaries are politically effective. Even those agreeing that identities are mainly fictions may take this position, advocating what Gayatri Spivak has called an "operational essentialism" (cited in Butler 1990; see also Vance 1988). On the other side, activists and theorists suggest that identity production "is purchased at the price of hierarchy, normalization, and exclusion" and therefore advocate "the deconstruction of a hetero/homo code that structures the 'social text' of daily life" (Seidman 1993:130).

The Queer Dilemma

The problem, of course, is that both the boundary-strippers and the boundary-defenders are right. The gay and lesbian civil rights strategy, for all its gains, does little to attack the political culture that itself makes the denial of and struggle for civil rights necessary and possible. Marches on Washington, equal protection pursuits, media-image monitoring, and so on, are guided by the attempt to build and prove quasi-national and quasi-ethnic claims. By constructing gays and lesbians as a single community (united by fixed erotic fates), they simplify complex internal differences and complex sexual identities. They also avoid challenging the system of meanings that underlies the political oppression: the division of the world into man/woman and gay/straight. On the contrary, they ratify and reinforce these categories. They therefore build distorted and incomplete political challenges, neglecting the political impact of cultural meanings, and do not do justice to the subversive and liberating aspects of loosened collective boundaries.

[...]

References

Berlant, Lauren, and Elizabeth Freeman 1993 "Queer nationality." In *Fear of a Queer Planet*, ed. Michael Warner, 193–229. Minneapolis: University of Minnesota Press.

Berube, Allan, and Jeffrey Escoffier 1991 "Queer/Nation." *Out/Look* (Winter):12–23.

Bornstein, Kate 1992 "A plan for peace." *San Francisco Bay Times*, December 3:4.

Butler, Judith 1990 "Gender trouble, feminist theory, and psychoanalytic discourse." In *Feminism/Postmodernism*, ed. Linda J. Nicholson, 324–340. New York: Routledge.

Chee, Alexander 1991 "A queer nationalism." *Out/Look* (Winter):15–19.

Duggan, Lisa 1992 "Making it perfectly queer." *Socialist Review* 22:11–32.

Fuss, Diana 1989 *Essentially Speaking: Feminism, Nature, and Difference*. New York: Routledge.

Gamson, William A. 1992 "The social psychology of collective action." In *Frontiers in Social Movement Theory*, eds. Aldon Morris and Carol McClurg Mueller, 53–76. New Haven: Yale University Press.

Marcus, Eric 1993 "What's in a name." *10 Percent*:14–15.

Melucci, Alberto 1989 *Nomads of the Present: Social Movements and Individual Needs in Contemporary Society*. Philadelphia: Temple University Press.

Nagel, Joane 1994 "Constructing ethnicity: Creating and recreating ethnic identity and culture." *Social Problems* 41:152–176.

Phelan, Shane 1993 "(Be)coming out: Lesbian identity and politics." *Signs* 18:765–790.

Rant, Miss 1993 "Queer is not a substitute for gay." *Rant & Rave* 1:15.

Schlesinger, Philip 1987 "On national identity: Some conceptions and misconceptions criticized." *Social Science Information* 26:219–264.

Seidman, Steven 1993 "Identity politics in a 'postmodern' gay culture: Some historical and conceptual notes." In *Fear of a Queer Planet*, ed. Michael Warner, 105–142. Minneapolis: University of Minnesota Press.

—— 1994 "Symposium: Queer theory/sociology: A dialogue." *Sociological Theory* 12:166–177.

Stein, Arlene 1992 "Sisters and queers: The decentering of lesbian feminism." *Socialist Review* 22:33–55.

Stein, Arlene, and Ken Plummer 1994 " 'I can't even think straight': 'Queer' theory and the missing sexual revolution in sociology." *Sociological Theory* 12:178–187.

Stone, Sandy 1991 "The empire strikes back: A posttranssexual manifesto." In *Body Guards*, eds. Julia Epstein and Kristina Straub, 280–304. New York: Routledge.

Taylor, Verta, and Nancy Whittier 1992 "Collective identity in social movement communities." In *Frontiers in Social Movement Theory*, eds. Aldon Morris and Carol McClurg Mueller, 104–129. New Haven: Yale University Press.

Vance, Carole S. 1988 "Social construction theory: Problems in the history of sexuality." In *Homosexuality? Which Homosexuality?*, eds. Dennis Altman et al., 13–34. London: GMP Publishers.

Warner, Michael, ed. 1993 *Fear of a Queer Planet: Queer Politics and Social Theory.* Minneapolis: University of Minnesota Press.

Williams, Andrea 1993 "Queers in the Castro." Unpublished paper, Department of Anthropology, Yale University.

36 The Repression/Protest Paradox in Central America

Charles D. Brockett

The specific focus of this chapter is the often-noted paradox that regime violence smothers popular mobilization under some circumstances, but at other times similar (or even greater) levels of violence will provoke mass collective action rather than pacify the target population. This paradox remains even when the usual explanatory variables, such as the level of socioeconomic grievances or political regime type, are held constant.

The consequences of governmental repression for mass protest and rebellion have been the subject of much scholarly attention. Theories have been advanced for linear relationships, but in both negative and positive directions. Curvilinear relationships have also been proposed, again with the curves running in both directions. Each of these four models has found some empirical support—but also contradiction—from a variety of cross-national aggregate data studies.

[. . .]

The most significant argument of this essay is that the repression/protest relationship is mediated by its temporal location in what Sidney Tarrow has conceptualized as "the cycle of protest." I will demonstrate that the key to the resolution of the repression/protest paradox is its location within the protest cycle.

The case material for this chapter comes from Central America, especially the recent histories of El Salvador and Guatemala through the first third of the 1980s, which is when their protest cycles were brought to an end. The subject matter of this article has not been an abstract question for the people of these countries: a repressive response to popular mobilization has been probable throughout their histories. Indeed, tens of thousands of people innocent of any crime have been slain in recent years by the agents of state terrorism in both countries. This tragic story will be utilized to demonstrate that a protest-cycle model resolves the paradoxical relationship between repression and mobilization.

[. . .]

The Central American Reality

It is generally agreed that in the 1970s popular challenges to elite rule reached unparalleled levels in Central America. Tragically, this mass mobilization was matched by extraordinary levels of state terrorism. This contradiction was most intense in El Salvador and Guatemala. Both countries will be examined here (with limited comparisons to Nicaragua in the following section). [. . .]

Salvadoran society in the early 1970s was aptly characterized as a "culture of repression" by one scholar with substantial experience in the country (Huizer 1972: 52–61). The lack of popular opposition to the regime was not because of the lack of grievances nor because of support for the government. Instead, the paramount factor was the high level of coercion built into the system and the intermittent use of violence by public and private elites to maintain quiescence. This description applied to Guatemala as well. Although there are important differences in the histories of the two countries, these repressive structures had evolved in both across the centuries to ensure elite control of the land and labor necessary for the enrichment of the elite.

Socioeconomic grievances intensified during the 1960s and 1970s in both countries as the economic security of many people deteriorated, especially in rural areas. At the same time, new opportunities for acting on their discontent opened for nonelites, beginning in El Salvador in the late 1960s and then in Guatemala in the mid-1970s when a more moderate government came to power. Mass political activity was facilitated by the sustained efforts of outside "catalysts for change" (Pearce 1986: 108), such as church workers, some of whom brought a new biblical message of liberation here on earth. As the 1970s progressed, new forms of popular political activity appeared and new levels of popular opposition to the regimes were reached. Most important were the popular organizations with their large mass memberships and their use of nonviolent but confrontational actions, such as demonstrations, strikes, occupations of buildings, and land seizures. In response to this growing popular challenge, violence from the entrenched security forces escalated. [...] From a strategy of targeted and intermittent killings in the mid-1970s, by early 1980 the violence became widespread and indiscriminate in its scope.

[...]

In Guatemala, indiscriminate and widespread political violence crushed a popular mobilization involving many different interests, organizations, and strategies that drew on substantial support across many sectors of society. Some of these groups were mainly seeking progress toward political democracy and respect for civil liberties. The last fairly elected president had been the leftist Jacobo Arbenz, who was covertly overthrown by the United States in 1954. Since then, the military had tightened its control of the country, with military candidates winning the presidency in each election since 1970. Other groups stressed the need to reform Guatemala's grossly unequal socioeconomic structures and exploitative labor practices. Most significantly, for the first time there were groups representing the interests and needs of the country's Mayan population, still about one-half of the entire population and concentrated primarily in the rugged highlands of the west.

In its early stages the indiscriminate violence of the late 1970s and into the early 1980s did bolster active support for the opposition and especially the armed revolutionary movements operating among Indian communities, particularly in the isolated back reaches of the western highlands. But as the military violence intensified and continued virtually without restraint in the Mayan countryside, where even the young and the elderly were murdered in large numbers, and as it continued relentlessly month after month and year after year, the guerrillas were thrown on the defensive and then isolated. The military destroyed some 440 villages with the "scorched earth" tactics of 1980–84 and left up to one million Guatemalans displaced from their homes (Black 1985: 16). In the face of this unrelenting brutality, it became clear that the revolutionaries would not win and then that they could not protect their supporters. Exile to Mexico or the United States was often the only rational choice. The military's recourse to massive indiscriminate violence against innocent civilians not only won the war against the people but also created structures of control that penetrated the Indian highlands of western Guatemala far beyond that which had existed previously.

[...]

The military had directly ruled El Salvador since 1932. When civilian centrist forces looked like they might win in the elections of both 1972 and 1977, the military relied on fraud and intimidation to maintain its power. As the 1970s progressed, Salvadoran society became increasingly mobilized through a multitude of organizations representing peasants and workers, students and professionals. With the electoral path blocked, regime opponents turned to strikes, demonstrations, and occupations. In the face of this growing popular challenge, the Salvadoran regime increasingly turned to violence. A coup by junior military officers brought a reformist government to office in

October 1979 and the hope of a peaceful resolution to the crisis. The new government, however, was divided, was distrusted by the militant left, and most importantly, had no control over the security forces. As confrontational activities of the left (especially occupations of buildings and mass demonstrations) increased, regime violence escalated even further. Civilian deaths at the hands of the regime averaged over 300 a month for the remainder of the year, more than double the rate of the preceding period (Morales Velado et al. 1988: 190). In March 1980, following two virtually complete changes in the new government, an agrarian reform was promulgated. It is at this point that informed observers identify the beginning of the civil war (for example, Baloyra 1982: 137; Dunkerley 1982: 162). Regime violence accelerated again, with civilian deaths doubling to 584 during March and then more than doubling in May to 1424 (Morales Velado et al. 1988: 195). By the end of the year virtually all political space for nonviolent opposition to the regime had been eliminated (ibid.: 73), the key symbol being the November kidnapping and execution of six leaders of the nonviolent left. The remaining leadership then either went into exile or underground. Over 10,000 civilians were murdered by the security forces and their allied death squads in El Salvador in both 1980 and 1981, with 6000 more killed in 1982 (Brown 1985: 122).

The relationship between popular opposition and regime violence during these years in El Salvador was multifaceted. Generally, as regime violence grew through the late 1970s into 1980, collective actions against the regime increased in number, intensity, and militancy. During this period, the guerrilla forces remained relatively small and comparatively limited in their activities. Instead, the major vehicles for popular opposition were the popular organizations (which had semi-covert ties to the guerrilla movements) and their (largely) nonviolent confrontational tactics. As the regime violence became increasingly widespread in early 1980, many of the leaders and the rank and file of the popular organizations were killed, and the space for their forms of collective action disappeared. It was at this point that the guerrilla forces rapidly grew in size, popular support, and ability to oppose the regime. This growth in the size and actions of what became later in the year the Faribundo Marti National Liberation Front (FMLN), however, coincided with a *decline* in the total number of people who were actively engaged in all forms of oppositional activities. The civil war intensified until about early 1984. Although the war continued through 1991, the FMLN never was able to reachieve the level of threat to the regime that it represented at that time. Vital to the ability of the Salvadoran military to contain the threat from the FMLN, of course, was the tremendous financial support it received from the United States, which totaled $6 billion (Gugliotta and Farah 1993: 6), peaking in 1985 at $115 per resident of El Salvador (Congressional Research Service 1989: 25–27).

[...]

Did popular opposition to the regime decline because regime violence declined first? Or did regime violence eventually decline because it had successfully eliminated most overt popular opposition, with the exception of the guerrilla armies, and even with the armed opposition had stemmed the growth of its support? If the latter, then the indiscriminate violence was successful, not counterproductive, from the viewpoint of the regime, just as it was in Guatemala.

In reality, nonelites have another alternative besides supporting either the regime or the guerrillas as regime violence escalates. They can also flee: about one-quarter of the entire population of El Salvador were refugees by mid-1984. Close to 750,000 people had fled the country in the preceding five years (Brown 1985: 135). If nonelites believe that the opposition has a chance of winning, then active support might be rational in the face of indiscriminate violence that might strike them. If they find the program and/or the tactics of that opposition also objectionable, however, then exile might be the more rational alternative. Furthermore, when regime violence continues and intensifies to the point where victory by the opposition is doubtful, then exile might be the more likely response, regardless of agreement with the program of the guerrillas.

When calculating the probable consequences of a recourse to systematic state terrorism in response to escalating popular opposition, elites in El Salvador and Guatemala only needed to contemplate their own histories. Elites in El Salvador could look back to *la mantanza* of 1932, when 10,000 to 30,000 peasants were massacred, as "a model response to the threat of rebellion," as well as to the four decades of "peace" that the massacre brought (McClintock 1985a: 99–100; Anderson 1971). Guatemalan elites considering violence only needed to refer to 1966–72 when over 10,000 innocents were murdered or to the 22-year reign of terror of Manuel Estrada Cabrera early in the century. Going further back in time, elites in both countries evaluating violence as an instrument of control could recall the coercion employed in converting peasant food-crop land to elite-owned coffee land beginning in the latter third of the nineteenth century, or they could go all the way back to the massive violence of the Conquest itself and the consequent coercion utilized to maintain colonial society. The fundamental point has been aptly stated by Gurr (1986: 66): "Historical traditions of state terror ... probably encourage elites to use terror irrespective of ... structural factors." Although morally abhorrent, the historic reliance on violence by Guatemalan and Salvadoran elites has not been counterproductive to their interests. Violence-as-necessary has allowed a small group to maintain its privileged position to the severe disadvantage of the vast majority. From the viewpoint of those in charge, state terrorism has been a success.

Summarizing this section, I argue in partial agreement with Mason and Krane (1989) that in its early stages indiscriminate violence targeted against neutral nonelites can increase mass involvement in and support for oppositional collective action, including revolutionary activities. However, state terrorism when sustained has often had the opposite effect in Central America, smashing overt popular opposition to the terrorist regime. In the following section a superior model will be proposed for differentiating which effect regime violence will have, regardless of whether it be violence from an indiscriminate targeting strategy or from the two more limited strategies.

The Political Cycle Explanation

[...]

Socioeconomic grievances did escalate throughout Central America in the 1970s. Equally critical to the development of the mass movements of the decade, though, was the development of a more favorable opportunity structure. Mass mobilization was catalyzed and sustained by assistance from support groups and allies, such as religious groups, revolutionary organizers, political party activists, and international development workers. Also crucial was the opening of political space for oppositional activities in El Salvador and Guatemala, as well as in Nicaragua and Honduras. Repression lightened, lowering the risks of organization and action. With the possibilities for winning beneficial changes improving, mass organizations and oppositional activities proliferated.

Tarrow has demonstrated in a number of his works (for example, 1983) that such mass collective action sometimes occurs in the larger context of a protest cycle, a temporal location with significant implications for challengers. Protest cycles begin when the structure of political opportunity turns more favorable, encouraging groups to act on long-standing grievances and/or newly created ones. The activities of these early mobilizers then encourage other groups and movements to activate as well. As a result, conflict diffuses throughout society at higher than normal levels of frequency and intensity. This activity builds, peaks, and then declines to more normal levels (Tarrow 1983: 38–39). [...]

A challenger asserting claims on the upswing of the protest cycle generally will fare better than challengers late in the cycle or outside its duration. During the upswing of a cycle, many groups and movements will be asserting claims, placing greater pressure on the system than could any group individually. Systems and their elites, though, adapt only so far; short of revolutionary transformations, responsiveness eventually declines and repressive measures become more likely. Challenges made late in the cycle or afterward face a less favorable opportunity structure.

When the concept of the protest cycle is wedded to government violence, the essential argument is this: indiscriminate repression is likely to provoke further popular mobilization only during the ascendant phase of the protest cycle. In contrast, indiscriminate repression deters popular collective action before the initiation of a cycle, and it can (and does) bring protest cycles to an abrupt end. For example, the widespread and arbitrary murders of thousands of noncombatant peasants in Guatemala in the mid-1960s and in Nicaragua in the mid-1970s did not provoke mass mobilization among the survivors (see Brockett 1990). The revolutionary guerrilla organizations in their midst (which were the "justifications" for the campaigns of terror) were small and isolated from other political forces. Indeed, society itself was largely demobilized, as certainly the peasantry was even prior to the counterinsurgency campaigns. Under these circumstances, survivors in the targeted regions, no matter how sharp their pain nor how strong their rage, had no opportunities for collective action. The structure of political opportunity offered no hope for justice, no possibility for revenge.

Later, though, the political context changed. Political space for organizing and action opened for a variety of reasons in each country: in urban El Salvador in the late 1960s, slowly spreading to its rural areas; in Guatemala in the mid-1970s; and to a lesser extent in Nicaragua in the last third of the 1970s. Collective action was greatly assisted by the appearance of numerous support groups. In this more supportive context, intermittent regime violence provoked anger, determination, and resistance in each country. Popular organizations grew in number, in size, and in assertiveness. Vigorous protest cycles were initiated in El Salvador and Guatemala and to a lesser extent in Nicaragua.

Faced with this sustained threat from below, the regimes of each country turned to even more violence. Although this violence became increasingly widespread, brutal, and arbitrary, initially it did not deter popular mobilization but provoked even greater mass opposition. Opponents who were already active redoubled their efforts, and some turned to violence. Increasing numbers of nonelites gave their support to the growing revolutionary armies, many becoming participants themselves. Previously passive regime opponents were activated, and new opponents were created as the indiscriminate violence delegitimized regimes, on the one hand, and created incentives for opposition, such as protection, revenge, and justice, on the other.

The desires for justice and for revenge can find an outlet through collective action in this ascendant phase of the protest cycle (and violence as self-protection can appear rational) for at least two reasons. First, there is hope of winning. Despite the brutality of the regime's indiscriminate violence, the active opposition of large numbers of people and of many organizations from many different sectors of society sustains the belief that the regime will be defeated. This belief was widespread among the popular forces in Nicaragua during the insurrections of 1978–79 and, shortly thereafter, in El Salvador and Guatemala for a brief time at the peak of their popular mobilizations.

The second reason goes beyond rational calculation of the probability of victory to include both emotional response and location in the protest cycle. Assume two sets of regime opponents where the first set is already engaged in collective action against the regime but the second set is not. When indiscriminate repression is directed against the population, the people who are already mobilized are more likely to continue their opposition than the people who are unmobilized are likely to act on their rage by initiating oppositional activities. For the first set, although the indiscriminate violence increases the dangers of further collective action (and might even diminish the probability of success), the rage engendered by that violence provides additional motivation for action, perhaps more than enough to offset the increased danger. Since these opponents are already active, the momentum of that activity can carry them into clandestine and violent forms of resistance and retaliation as the regime closes nonviolent channels of protest. For the second set, however, the configuration of grievances and risks will be different. They had not been active before the violence, which now increases the dangers of opposition while further restricting the opportunities for action.

Furthermore, the active individuals are not isolated. The fact that they have already been involved in oppositional activities means that they are integrated, at least to some extent, into groups and organizations. These social networks provide the leadership and opportunities for continuing activity, as well as the solidarity bonds and obligations and the examples that encourage action.

As with individuals, we can posit two different situations concerning the social movement sector: organizations making demands on the political system are either numerous or few. The ascendant phase of the protest cycle is marked by the proliferation of organizations and their activities and by unusually large numbers of individuals involved in collective action. Under these circumstances (for example, Guatemala in the early 1980s), indiscriminate regime violence is likely to accelerate antiregime action, for the reasons identified above. However, prior to the initiation of a protest cycle (for example, Guatemala in the late 1960s) there are far fewer people in the active category and far fewer organizations to give direction to their grievances. Therefore, indiscriminate regime violence outside the protest cycle deters popular collective action.

The popular mobilizations in El Salvador and Guatemala during the 1970s and early 1980s, however, were met by ever more vicious repression, abruptly ending their protest cycles. The tens of thousands of murders in each country in the early 1980s were sufficient to destroy most popular organizations or drive them underground, to restore fear and passivity to much of the countryside, and to contain the revolutionary forces. The fact is, successful rebellions and revolutions are rare. Although indiscriminate violence might escalate regime opposition under some circumstances, there are limitations to a people's ability to withstand ferocious regime violence. The difference in the outcomes between these two countries and Nicaragua, where the popular forces succeeded in overthrowing the murderous Somoza regime in 1979, was the result of more than the fact that the opposition to Somoza was more widespread across classes. In addition, Somoza did not have nearly the same capacity for state terrorism as his neighbors, and the Guatemalan and Salvadoran regimes had the willingness to use their greater capacity to the extent necessary to ensure their survival.

Conclusion

The central issue dealt with in this chapter is the paradoxical relationship between regime violence and popular protest. In attempting to explain why sometimes regime violence deters mass oppositional activities but at other times it provokes further opposition, I claim here that the most important determinant is the temporal location in the protest cycle. The targeting strategy pursued by the regime is, of course, a critical variable. However, the evidence from

Central America indicates that during "normal conditions," that is, prior to the onset of a protest cycle, escalating repression will deter popular mobilization against the regime.

In contrast, in the ascendant phase of the protest cycle the same repression is likely to provoke increased mass oppositional activities. Nonetheless, if elites are willing and are capable of instituting widespread indiscriminate killing on a sustained basis, then they have often been successful in ending the protest cycle and terrorizing the population back into political passivity. [...]

References

Anderson, T. (1971) *Matanza: El Salvador's Communist Revolt of 1932*. Lincoln: University of Nebraska Press.

Baloyra, E. (1982) *El Salvador in Transition*. Chapel Hill: University of North Carolina Press.

Black, G. (1985) "Under the gun." *NACLA Report on the Americas* xix, 6: 10–24.

Brockett, C. (1990) *Land, Power, and Poverty: Agrarian Transformation and Political Conflict in Central America*. Rev. ed. Boston: Unwin Hyman.

Brown, C., ed. (1985) *With Friends Like These: The Americas Watch Report on Human Rights & U.S. Policy in Latin America*. New York: Pantheon.

Congressional Research Service (1989) "El Salvador, 1979–1989: A briefing book on U.S. aid and the situation in El Salvador." Library of Congress CRS Report for Congress.

Dunkerley, J. (1982) *The Long War: Dictatorship and Revolution in El Salvador*. London: Junction Books.

Gugliotta, G., and D. Farah (1993) "When the truth hurts: A U.N. report reopens old wounds over civil rights abuses in El Salvador." *Washington Post National Weekly Edition*, March 29–April 4: 6–7.

Gurr, T. (1986) "The political origins of state violence and terror: A theoretical analysis," in M. Stohl and G. Lopez (eds.) *Government Violence and Repression: An Agenda for Research*. New York: Greenwood: 45–71.

Huizer, G. (1972) *The Revolutionary Potential of Peasants in Latin America*. Lexington, MA: Lexington Books.

McClintock, M. (1985a) *The American Connection. Vol. 1, State Terror and Popular Resistance in El Salvador*. London: Zed Books.

—— (1985b) *The American Connection. Vol. 2, State Terror and Popular Resistance in Guatemala*. London: Zed Books.

Mason, T., and D. Krane (1989) "The political economy of death squads: Towards a theory of the impact of state-sanctioned terror." *International Studies Quarterly* 33: 175–98.

Morales Velado, O., et al. (1988) *La resistencia no violenta ante los regimenes salvadoreños que han utilizado el terror institucionalizado en el periodo 1972–1987*. San Salvador: Universidad Centroamericanos J.S. Cañas.

Pearce, J. (1986) *Promised Land: Peasant Rebellion in Chalatenango El Salvador*. London: Latin America Bureau.

Tarrow, S. (1983) *Struggling to Reform: Social Movements and Policy Change during Cycles of Protest*. Western Societies Paper no. 15. Ithaca, NY: Cornell University Press.

37 Counterinsurgency

Ian Roxborough

The most powerful military in the world has lost control of Iraq, unable to put an end to the violence or to sustain a democratic Iraqi government. A civil war simmers on the edge of catastrophe. Has the U.S. military learned nothing since Vietnam?

In military parlance, the task of suppressing revolution (insurgency) and civil war is called *counterinsurgency*. Looking at the nationalist and revolutionary guerrilla wars of the 20th century, military thinkers sought to develop ways to defeat insurgents. Counterinsurgency theory is a practitioner's guide to the sociology of revolution, only with the aim of defeating it. Forty years ago, during the Vietnam era, debate within the military produced a slew of books, articles, and official manuals on counterinsurgency. After the United States withdrew from Vietnam, these books gathered dust. The military vowed never again to get caught up in a messy war of counterinsurgency.

The current imbroglio in Iraq has forced the U.S. military to look again at theories of counterinsurgency. In this chapter I explain why the sociological dynamics of these conflicts baffle military thinkers and why a workable "solution" is so elusive.

The Shadow of Vietnam

When we think about counterinsurgency, we think first of Vietnam. American thinking about counterinsurgency began with the Maoist notion of "people's war"; all insurgencies and counterinsurgencies were then forced into this framework. Insurgencies were seen as the response of peasants to the dislocations produced by modernization; they were easily swayed by Communist promises of a better life, and Moscow could orchestrate these social movements in its global Cold War struggle against the United States.

This is too simple. While there are similarities between Iraq (or Afghanistan) and Vietnam, there are just as many differences. It is not useful to treat all insurgencies as fundamentally the same. Revolutionary romanticism on the left is as much a mistake as military technicism. Everyone has learned too well from Vietnam: Rural Maoist guerrilla war with foreign sanctuaries is not the only type of insurgency. We are like a doctor who believes that all patients suffer from the same disease and require the same course of treatment.

Because of the Vietnam model, old formulas are recirculated and old lessons reaffirmed. One thing the U.S. military learned in Vietnam—reinforced by its success in defeating a Marxist insurgency in El Salvador in the 1980s—was that counterinsurgency is essentially a struggle for the "hearts and minds" of the population. This implies that an army cannot use the same kind of overwhelming firepower it would in a traditional offensive. Both the population and insurgents who surrender need to be treated well.

Since conventional U.S. military forces are trained for high-intensity combat, the Vietnam formula suggests it is better to deploy small numbers of Special Forces soldiers who can use violence in a more discriminating manner. Rather than treat the insurgents as a military force to be destroyed in combat via "search-and-destroy" operations, it would be more effective to pacify a small region and then work outward, like a spreading ink-spot, to protect and control the population. Improvements in material standards of living would then win over the population and establish the legitimacy of the government.

But the foremost lesson of Vietnam was "never again." Never again would the U.S. military be drawn into what was essentially a civil war. After Vietnam, with the exception of a handful of Special Forces experts, the U.S. military as a whole lapsed into a bout of collective amnesia about counterinsurgency. When the Army and Marine Corps found themselves mired in a difficult conflict in Iraq, they had to relearn rapidly the lessons of counterinsurgency, dusting off and reprinting those 40-year-old books. The problem is, these lessons were based on false assumptions.

The World Is Complicated

The standard way of thinking about counterinsurgency employs a "triangular" model: the government and the insurgents compete with each other for the allegiance of the population. While this is superior to the military notion of dyadic conflict between two armies, the assumption of a triangular contest misapprehends the dynamics of most counterinsurgencies. For a start, the triangular model is based on a misleading notion of the causes of support for government and insurgents. Most people passively accept the government (or the insurgent counter-government) if they view its rule as permanent—as a de facto monopoly of violence. Active minorities have clear goals, and these vary from situation to situation. Also, the "population" is seldom an undifferentiated object. Different ethnic, political, or religious groups all seek their own goals. The conflict may resemble a many-sided "civil war" more than it does a triangular insurgency.

Moreover, both the government and the insurgents are almost always divided into hard-liners and those willing to consider accommodation with the adversary. This generates a series of dilemmas for each actor, as each seeks the most effective way to pursue its goals, while often being undercut by some of its own supporters who adopt different tactics.

No conflict can be reduced to a single, simple model. In Afghanistan, the Karzai government faces the classic problem of attempting to impose central power over regional warlords. This is the context for military operations aimed at Taliban and al-Qaeda forces. The insurgents, moreover, have a sanctuary in Pakistan, where the terrain is forbidding, the local peoples are sympathetic to the guerrillas, and the military government worries about offending a massive Islamist population.

Iraq, on the other hand, is not—at least not yet—run by warlords. Nor, despite much wild talk, do the insurgents benefit from a nearby sanctuary. There, the American invasion produced an instant failed government. The lines of political contention are largely ethnic and religious. Kurds, Sunnis, and Shia struggle to define the post-Saddam polity and maximize their position within it. Neither Iraq nor Afghanistan resembles Vietnam, where there was a largely agrarian struggle between absentee landlords and the government on the one hand and the peasantry on the other.

Political scientist Stephen Biddle argues that U.S. policymakers have made a category mistake in Iraq. The conflict in that country is not an ideological, class-based, people's war (as in Vietnam), but a sectarian communal conflict, more akin to the wars in Rwanda and the former Yugoslavia. The dynamics of the conflicts differ and require different policies.

The problem is deeper still. While a distinction between two types of conflict (Maoist peoples' war versus communal conflict) is better than the notion that all insurgencies are basically the same, it does not go far enough. In some ways it simply reproduces the central lesson drawn from Vietnam and El Salvador: "We don't do civil wars." Sociologists and practitioners who think about counterinsurgency are prisoners of their concepts. We assume too easily that insurgency–counterinsurgency is one thing, "civil war" another.

In fact, the borderlines between insurgency, terrorism, civil war, ethnic cleansing, and other forms of conflict are fuzzy. Social scientists and policymakers are apt to believe that these terms denote clear and distinct phenomena. Reality is different. Many internal wars, and certainly those in which the United States is likely to be involved, are complex, shifting, hybrid affairs that mix elements of insurgency, civil war, and regular warfare in ways that are often difficult to untangle. This makes the design of appropriate policies incredibly difficult: Counterinsurgency is a difficult business requiring a deep sociological understanding of the dynamics of conflict.

Because the Army had forgotten what little it knew of counterinsurgency except the injunction not to get embroiled in another country's internal war, the conflict in Iraq came as a rude shock. American soldiers and marines were intellectually unprepared for the challenges they faced.

Soldiers are trained to fight other soldiers; they are uncomfortable with "politics." They treat an insurgency as a purely military affair: a simple matter of killing or capturing insurgents more quickly than they can be replaced. They try to bring the insurgents to battle and/or to disrupt their organization. Early U.S. Army efforts in both Vietnam and Iraq involved large "sweep and cordon" or "area assault" operations designed to bring "the enemy" to battle and destroy him. Only later did American military thinkers scramble to relearn the techniques of fighting insurgents. They turned initially to the writings of military officers, especially the French, with experience of counterinsurgency in the 1950s and 1960s.

Once a military organization convinces itself—or is convinced by others—that standard military practice is inappropriate, the way is open to a coherent counterinsurgency strategy. But by then it is often too late to stop the fighting quickly; a long—and possibly unwinnable—war is usually necessary.

Legitimacy and Consent

In many ways, an insurgency is like other social movements. Insurgents must articulate grievances, mobilize resources, and develop a strategy. They must struggle with competitors (those willing to work peacefully within the political system) to establish authoritative claims to speak on behalf of their constituency.

But there is an important difference between insurgencies and the kinds of social movements sociologists usually study. Insurgent organizations, like governments, typically seek to monopolize the representation of their social base. Indeed, they claim to constitute an alternative government. They may therefore manage to displace their competitors not through competition but more directly by assassinating their leaders and terrorizing and coercing their supporters. Other revolutionary and reformist organizations usually contest these efforts, and the struggles within the ranks of the antigovernment forces can be intense and bloody. As a would-be government, an insurgency seeks a monopoly of political control.

Political control is not the same thing as legitimacy. When insurgents and counterinsurgents are seen as involved in a struggle for the "hearts and minds" of the population, it is not always clear what this entails and whether it is necessary. Whose hearts and minds are to be won over, how do you win them, and why will this stop the insurgency? Wars are not elections or popularity polls; individual preferences are less important than behavior. Whether individuals support the government (or the insurgents) willingly or grudgingly, because of intimidation, or because they see no realistic alternative, matters little compared to the fact of their acceptance and acquiescence in government control. Governments do not need the active support of the entire population, or even a majority; acquiescence will suffice. Although the phrase "hearts and minds" implies active support for the government, a sort of positive legitimacy, this may not always be necessary.

American counterinsurgency thinking not only stresses the importance of legitimacy; it believes that this will come about through the provision of material goods and services. American policy in Iraq (as in Vietnam) has been to restore local services, get the economy moving, and improve living conditions. Such material improvements will win hearts and minds, and legitimacy will follow. This misdiagnoses the microdynamics of internal war.

In a study of the province of Long An in Vietnam, Jeffrey Race contrasts the kinds of rewards offered to the peasantry by the government and by the insurgents. Government forces provided wells, roads, and other kinds of improvements for the peasants. But these benefits would accrue to the peasants no matter which side won the war. On the other hand, the benefits brought by the insurgents—driving out the landlords and reducing rents—would cease if government forces won the war. This was one of several practical reasons for peasants to support the insurgents. The government—until it belatedly got into the business of land reform—could not compete.

American counterinsurgency continues to operate on the incorrect assumption that improvements in material conditions are the key to winning hearts and minds and thereby gaining the legitimacy needed for victory. Throughout the conflict in Iraq, American policymakers have worried about the delivery of services to the Iraqi population: electricity, security, jobs, construction, and so on. The catastrophic failure to deliver the goods in Iraq is often seen as a major factor behind the continuing unrest. This notion that grievances can be ameliorated by improving government services or by increasing the standard of living of the population derives from a commonsense (and very Western) notion of the origins of grievances. Antigovernment behavior is seen as a response to poverty rather than to inequality and injustice. U.S. counterinsurgency thinking refuses to confront the hard reality of intractable, zero-sum conflict between classes, sects, or ethnic groups.

Competition in Coercion

Some military strategists criticize this "amelioration program" in two ways. First, they argue that security, rather than other public services such as schools, clean water, electricity, and so forth, is the most important thing a government can offer. Until the personal safety of the population is assured, no other inducements will be effective. The proponents of this approach retain the notion of winning hearts and minds by providing government services; they simply prioritize the delivery of these services, with law and order at the top of the list.

Second, they argue that the problem is not about buying the support of the population, but about winning a competition in coercion between government and insurgents. In this view, the population is asked only to comply with, not believe in, its government. What matters is a calculation on the part of the population that the government will prevail. Combining both arguments, the French counterinsurgency thinker David Galula wrote, back in 1964, "The population's attitude ... is dictated not so much by the relative popularity and merits of the opponents as by the more primitive concern for safety. Which side gives the best protection, which one threatens the most, which one is likely to win, these are the criteria governing the population's stand."

An extension of this school of thought sees massive violence as highly effective. Authoritarian regimes and their armies often decide that their best strategy is extreme violence to defeat the insurgency. This seems to have worked in El Salvador in the 1930s and perhaps also in Guatemala in the 1980s. Peasants may have been sympathetic to the insurgents, but when the army unleashed a wave of terror against whole communities suspected of favoring the insurgents, peasants turned against the insurgents, whom they saw as responsible for bringing this violence down on their heads.

Which of these schools of thought is right? Current social-science thinking suggests that neither "hearts and minds" nor "competition in coercion" accurately captures the dynamics of contention for power. What matters is control: persistent and predictable political control at the local level. Violence is necessary, and targeted, discriminate violence is more effective than indiscriminate violence. Local political control requires a massive commitment of manpower. It requires detailed local knowledge of the local population. This is something that police do well and military organizations do badly.

Counterinsurgency as Reform

The reality that material improvements will not by themselves end an insurgency has an obvious corollary. Counterinsurgents can take the wind out of insurgents' sails by reforming the government and its army, as well as by attending to the legitimate grievances of the people, usually through land reform, to address the "root causes" of the insurgency. The official 1990 Army manual on low-intensity conflict states that

> mobilization grows out of intense popular dissatisfaction with existing political and social conditions.... Insurgency arises when the government is unable or unwilling to redress the demands of important social groups.... The government must recognize conditions that contribute to insurgency and take preventive measures. Correcting conditions that make a society vulnerable is the long-term solution to the problem of insurgency.

In this view, all problems can be solved. There are no intractable, zero-sum social conflicts. The keys are the willingness and ability of the government to implement the needed reforms. Depending on the nature of the grievances, free elections, land reform, or ethnic partition will solve the problem. Many insurgent supporters can then be coopted and incorporated. As for the guerrillas themselves, a policy of restraint and correct treatment will lead all but a few hard-liners to give up. Military measures are secondary. Effective local policing and intelligence, rather than big military sweeps, are the keys to success.

In El Salvador, the insurgency ended only when the army began to reduce its abuses, and the government held elections and implemented a very modest land reform. Even relatively minor efforts to address grievances may be sufficient to undercut an insurgency. The Huk rebellion in the Philippines ended when Ramon Magsaysay promised to reduce abuses by the army, to hold meaningful elections, and to introduce agrarian reform. The amount of land actually redistributed was tiny. It was the reduction in army-induced violence, an amnesty for guerrillas, and the prospect of democratic elections that took the wind out of the insurgency.

But ruling oligarchies and praetorian armies are seldom inclined toward reform, seeing it as more of a threat than a solution. Reforms often undercut the social basis of the government itself. Alternatively, some nations may be willing to undertake reforms but be too weak to implement them. The reformist version of counterinsurgency usually needs the backing of a powerful foreign government.

Nation-Building

Effective counterinsurgency is one component of a larger project of nation-building. Because American policymakers learned from the bitter experiences of the Cold War that "nation-building" is a dauntingly complex task, they generally shrink from detailed contemplation of its intricacies. Yet, if regime change does not go smoothly, or if there is a decision to intervene in a failed nation, U.S. policymakers must engage in a task whose complexities they only dimly grasp.

As sociologists have argued, nation-building is a long-term project that takes generations, if not centuries. It entails contention. Success is far from certain. Local power holders need to be subordinated to the central government. At the same time, the organizational grip of the central government on the society must be extended. All sorts of local-level representations of the government must be created and sustained.

Moreover, policymakers need to control their nominal subordinates to ensure that their policies are actually executed. Military forces in an insurgency or civil war are seldom accountable to or under the effective control of the political leadership. They act with considerable impunity, and lower-level leadership effectively operates without restraint. It is common to talk about a "national" army, but in practice the armed forces of an embattled Third World country are neither unified nor accountable to political leaders.

It is tricky to build an army and police force composed of distinct ethnic or sectarian groups. In insurgencies and civil wars, our "normal" assumptions about military forces no longer apply. Armed force is fragmented and uncertain. It has been decentralized or dispersed in some manner so that the "state" no longer has a monopoly. This occurs in two ways: by the development of a range of militias and armed forces not under government control (and often in opposition to it); and by the fragmentation of the "national" army. The social composition of the national army is a key issue. Simply labeling it as a national army does not make it so. Counterinsurgency doctrine tiptoes around this sensitive issue.

A central part of nation-building is to establish a monopoly on organized violence. Power at a local level is often in the hands of warlords who control their own armies. There may be local "self-defense" militias and paramilitaries with variable relations to the official government forces. Bringing all these forces under the control of the central government is a delicate and risky business, full of conflict and the potential for failure.

The central government may not control enough economic resources to suppress local power centers. Where local strong men control easily tradable resources—minerals and drugs, for example—they may be able to operate independently. Where this happens, guerrilla forces often settle into permanent opposition. Their ideological aspirations become subordinated to the mechanics of daily existence and economic parasitism. They may devolve into banditry and racketeering. Even if the guerrillas lose interest in overthrowing the government, they still pose a serious problem.

Since counterinsurgency is part of nation-building, it must create the micro-foundations of political order. Counterinsurgents often do this unintentionally following a purely military logic. Various population control measures recommended by counterinsurgency thinkers—relocating people, issuing identity cards, controlling travel, and so on—together with the organization of self-defense forces build the local foundations of the government.

Counterinsurgencies often generate a variety of "self-defense" militias and "warlord" armies. Such forces are formed by local groups that oppose the insurgents. They may wish to protect themselves and their property, to wreak vengeance on the insurgents, to dispossess them, or to establish the political domination of their class, ethnic group, or religious sect. Self-defense militias provide the government with a vast pool of manpower that it can use to free up regular forces. Familiar with local conditions, militias are often effective in identifying and suppressing the insurgents.

The risk is that the conflict increasingly takes on the features of a "civil war" between armed bands of the population. Both the brutal treatment of the population that this entails and the difficulty of asserting political control over such militias pose serious problems for the government as it eventually seeks a peace agreement. Achieving peace often means controlling or disbanding pro-government militias in order to reintegrate the insurgents into the political process.

The role of self-defense organizations in defeating insurgency has often been understood in narrowly military terms. Counterinsurgents have come to appreciate that organizing the rural population to defend itself is very efficient. Local self-defense forces (together with some population reconcentration) enable villages to stave off insurgent attacks. But the political aspects of local self-defense organizations are just as important.

In places where self-defense forces are closely linked to the defense of fortified villages and where they are under the control of government agencies (often the military), a form of near-totalitarian political control over the adult male population is achieved. This may not always be intended, but it works to crowd out any space for independent organization among the villagers, subjecting them all to surveillance by the military. The local self-defense forces organized during the long war in Guatemala, along with those organized in Peru to defend against Sendero Luminoso, the Vietnamese Regional Forces and Popular Forces, and the Kikuyu Home Guard during the Mau-Mau insurgency in Kenya in the 1950s all seem to have monopolized political activity and suppressed dissent.

Population control serves several purposes. Standard military doctrine emphasizes the goal of separating the insurgents from the people. If the insurgents are like fish that swim in the sea of the people, then the sea can be drained or dykes built to keep the population away from the insurgents. Of course, this tactic presumes that insurgents are, in a physical sense, "outside" the communities under government control. If this is not the case, then population control measures are unlikely to work.

Civilians may be relocated into protected hamlets or even refugee camps. They may be required to carry identification papers. Travel may be restricted. There will be roadblocks and neighborhood searches. Food may be tightly controlled to prevent it from being passed to the insurgents. From the point of view of micro-politics, population control serves the same purpose as establishing a local self-defense militia. It imposes a totalitarian control system over the population. This is most effective when there is a dominant political party tightly linked, possibly through a militia, with the armed forces.

French counterinsurgency thinker Roger Trinquier argued in 1961 that "control of the masses through a tight organization ... is the master weapon of modern warfare." To counter the organization of the insurgent, Trinquier advocated organizing the entire population into a structured organization under government control. "We may always assure ourselves of their loyalty by placing them within an organization it will be difficult to leave." The strategy was not an amorphous appeal to hearts and minds, but totalitarian control of the population.

Despite frequent citations of Galula and Trinquier, modern American counterinsurgent thinkers seem unable to grasp the implications of their insistence on political control at the micro level. Winning a counterinsurgency means building the government at the grassroots, from the bottom up. It means creating organizational means for the political control of the population. Military strategists think of this as "politics": something to be done by someone else. Creating the micro-foundations of the government is, in fact, the key task of counterinsurgency.

At the macro level of nation-building, an effective, stable government is the goal of American counterinsurgent operations. Often, they will also at least pay lip-service to creating democracy. Social scientists disagree about the role of elections in promoting stability and reducing an insurgency. Some argue that elections reduce insurgencies by offering an alternative to antigovernment violence. Others believe that, at least in the short run, new democracies may be politically destabilizing and prone to exacerbate, rather than reduce, conflict. Where conflict is likely to be organized along ethnic or sectarian lines, holding early elections may bring communal extremists to power. But postponing elections also has grave risks, delaying the institutionalization of political conflict. Since democracy has many advantages in the long run, one of the inescapable difficulties in nation-building is to get over "the hump" of early, unstable democracy.

A Final Dilemma

Counterinsurgency involves two ticking clocks, two different sets of priorities and constraints. One is the time frame for military and police operations in the insurgent country or region. The general assumption is that counterinsurgency is a slow process that may take a decade or more. The processes of nation-building, development, and reform, possibly including democratization, do not happen overnight. The other is the political time frame in the country sending troops to the fight. Here publics are often impatient and want their troops home quickly. Democracies are also constrained by a public unwilling to tolerate atrocity and widespread killing. These distinct time frames pose a dilemma for policymakers, forming the Achilles' heel of a counterinsurgency.

Political leaders need to end the insurgency quickly, while their military commanders tell them that it will be a lengthy process. This dilemma has a tendency to produce wishful thinking on the part of policymakers; it is not surprising that they are frequently disappointed. The United States can resolve the dilemma if it commits only a handful of troops to the counterinsurgency and if they do not suffer appreciable casualties. El Salvador and Colombia are the models in this regard. The Vietnamization of the war in Southeast Asia (namely, training Vietnamese troops to do the fighting so the Americans could withdraw) was intended to produce this effect. And now Iraqification is intended to do something similar.

Iraqification, like Vietnamization before it, will not in itself defeat the insurgency. It will merely transfer the task from American to Iraqi shoulders. If and when the U.S. military leaves, the Iraqi army must still design a strategy to suppress the fighting. This will not be easy. It will require political accommodation between the rival ethnic and sectarian groups at the highest level. So long as official military thinking about counterinsurgency fails to grasp these central issues and the underlying dynamics of popular mobilization and nation-building, it will be doomed to recycle the dubious "lessons" of Vietnam.

The U.S. Army prides itself on being a "learning organization." It claims that it has, after an initial period of muddling through, learned anew the fundamentals of counterinsurgency. This may be so, but it is not the point. The central sociological assumptions upon which U.S. counterinsurgency policy is built—the notion of a struggle for "hearts and minds"; the denial of intractable class, sectarian, or ethnic conflict; the idea that nation-building is about government "legitimacy," and so on—are deeply flawed. There is something about the ideological mind-set of policymakers and the authors of military doctrine that prevents them from seeing the real dynamics of conflict.

The failure in Iraq, as in Vietnam, stems in part from the intellectual poverty of official American thinking about counterinsurgency and nation-building. In 2006 the Army and Marine Corps wrote new counterinsurgency doctrine. However, it showed little sign of breaking through the conceptual impasse. It simply refurbished the lessons of the most recent positive case, El Salvador, for a conflict involving large numbers of American troops.

There are advances in thinking, to be sure. American soldiers and marines are enjoined to do a careful analysis of the society and culture, and to treat the locals with great cultural sensitivity. There is a whole section of the new manual that reads like a sociology textbook—a rather good one, at that. But admonitions to study the local society and to behave with cultural sensitivity will not work if the fundamental sociological assumptions underlying counterinsurgency doctrine are flawed. The misguided notion that providing material benefits will increase government legitimacy and thereby erode support for the insurgency remains at the heart of current thinking.

Counterinsurgency continues to be seen as a popularity contest rather than as a competition for control between two (or more) forces that claim to be the effective government. The inherent complexity of armed conflict is reduced to a simple dichotomy of "insurgency" versus "civil war." The notion of deeply rooted group antagonisms remains a taboo area. The micro-foundations of nation-building are poorly understood. The upshot of this accumulation of conceptual errors and blind spots is that the contemporary American military is like a blind boxer, swinging wildly, hoping to land a lucky punch. Counterinsurgency is hard; it is made still harder by the inability of the military to transcend an analysis that is as mistaken now as when it was first written 40 years ago. Dusting off old books is not the same as learning.

Recommended Resources

David Galula. 1964. *Counterinsurgency Warfare: Theory and Practice* (Praeger). Written by a French officer with considerable experience in combating insurgency, this book has been widely read by American military officers in recent years.

Jeff Goodwin. 2001. *No Other Way Out: States and Revolutionary Movements, 1945–1991* (Cambridge University Press). The best sociological survey of modern insurgencies.

Stathis Kalyvas. 2006. *The Logic of Violence in Civil War* (Cambridge University Press). Exhaustive survey of violence and political control in civil wars and insurgencies, with a tightly argued theory and a case study of Greece.

Jeffrey Race. 1972. *War Comes to Long An: Revolutionary Conflict in a Vietnamese Village* (University of California Press). A detailed study of insurgency and counterinsurgency in a Vietnamese province near Saigon.

D. Michael Shafer. 1988. *Deadly Paradigms: The Failure of U.S. Counterinsurgency Policy* (Princeton University Press). A clear exposition of American military thinking about counterinsurgency, focusing on Greece, the Philippines, and Vietnam.

Roger Trinquier. 1964. *Modern Warfare: A French View of Counterinsurgency* (Pall Mall Press). Another French book newly popular with U.S. military officers.

Part X

What Changes Do Movements Bring About?

Introduction

Social movements have a number of effects on their societies, some of them intended and others quite unintended. A few movements attain many or all of their goals, others at least manage to gain recognition or longevity in the form of protest organizations, and many if not most are suppressed or ignored. But whereas scholars used to talk about the success or failure of movements, today they are more likely to talk about movement "outcomes," in recognition of the unintended consequences. Some movements affect the broader culture and public attitudes, perhaps paving the way for future efforts. Others leave behind social networks, tactical innovations, and organizational forms that other movements can use. At the extreme, some movements may simply arouse such a backlash against them that they lose ground. (The far-right mobilization against the U.S. government which led to the Oklahoma City bombing probably inspired closer surveillance and repression of their groups than had previously existed.)

Even if we concentrate on movement goals and success for a moment, we see that most movements have a range of large and small goals. They may try at the same time to change corporate or state policy, transform public attitudes and sensibilities, and bring about personal transformations in protestors themselves. What is more, within a given movement different participants may have different goals, or at least a different ranking of priorities. And these goals may shift during the course of a conflict. Goals may expand in response to initial successes, or contract in the face of failures. When a movement faces severe repression, mere survival (of the group or the literal survival of members) may begin to take precedence over other goals. We have seen that movements have different audiences for their words and actions, and we can now add that they have different goals they hope to accomplish with each of these different audiences. A group may launch a campaign designed to prove its effectiveness to its financial backers, its disruptive

Radical Flank Effects Most social movements consist of diverse organizations and networks that disagree on strategy and ideology. Often, a more radical wing emerges that is more likely to use disruptive or illegal tactics and which develops a more pure (and less compromising) distillation of the movement's guiding ideas. The existence of a "radical flank"—more threatening to authorities—can have diverse effects on a movement. In some cases, it undermines public tolerance for the movement as a whole, making it easier for its enemies to portray it as undesirable. Authorities may decide to repress the entire movement, not just its radical wing. In other cases, the radical flank is threatening enough that the forces of order take the movement more seriously, often making concessions. The moderate flank can present itself as a reasonable compromise partner, so that authorities give it power in order to undercut the radicals (although the moderates must distance themselves from the radicals to garner these benefits). If nothing else, radical flanks, by creating a perception of crisis, often focus public attention on a new set of issues and a new movement. In many cases, radical flanks have a combination of negative and positive effects on the broader movement. See Haines (1988).

capacity to state officials, and its willingness to compromise to members of the general public. It may not be possible to succeed on all these fronts at once; there may be tradeoffs among goals.

Even a movement's goals with regard to the state and its many agencies can conflict with one another. Burstein, Einwohner, and Hollander (1995) contrast six types or stages of policy effects alone: access to legislators and policymakers, agenda-setting for legislators, official policies, implementation and enforcement of those policies, achievement of the policies' intended impact, and finally deeper structural changes to the political system. And this does not even include effects on repression—in other words, a movement's relationship with the police or armed forces.

Success in the short and the long term may not coincide. In some cases, these even conflict with each other, as when a movement's initial successes inspire strong countermobilization on the part of those under attack. This happened to both the antinuclear and the animal-protection movements (Jasper and Poulsen 1993). Efforts that are quite unsuccessful in the short run may have big effects in the long, as in the case of martyrs who inspire outrage and additional mobilization.

Overall, researchers have managed to demonstrate relatively few effects of social movements on their societies. In part this is due to their concentration on direct policy effects or benefits for constituencies. A large number of movements have met with considerable repression. Others have attained some acceptance for their own organizations without obtaining tangible benefits for those they represent. Still others have found government ready to establish a new agency or regulator in response to their demands, only to conclude later that this agency was ineffectual or unduly influenced by the movement's opponents. Scholars of social movements would like to believe that the mobilizations they study affect the course of history, but usually they have had to assert this without much good evidence.

A brief excerpt from William Gamson's classic, *The Strategy of Social Protest*, is an important statement of the meaning of success, reflecting a combination of mobilization and process perspectives. The stability and institutionalization of the protest group is as important as the benefits it achieves for its constituency. The assumption behind this approach seems to be that there is a pre-defined group ready to benefit, a group whose spokespersons have been excluded in some way from full participation in politics. In a later part of the same chapter, not included here, Gamson lists consultation, negotiation, formal recognition, and inclusion as signs of the protest group's acceptance. In the 53 groups he studied, 20 received a full response and 22 collapsed, while only 5 were subject to co-optation and only 6 pre-emption (Gamson 1990:37).

The piece by David S. Meyer reviews how movements have mattered for public policy, political institutions, and activists themselves. The personal consequences of activism are further explored in the chapter by Darren E. Sherkat and T. Jean Blocker. The activist identity is itself an important effect of social movements, just one of many cultural effects of movements. These cultural effects are perhaps the hardest movement impacts to study, yet they may be some of the most profound and longest-lasting outcomes. Many movements help articulate new ways of thinking and feeling about the world. Thus animal protectionists developed widespread sympathy for nonhuman species into an explicit ideology of outrage. Other movements raise issues for public debate, forcing informed citizens to think about a topic and decide how they feel about it. A majority may reject the movement's perspective, but it can still cause them to think more deeply about their own values and attitudes. Even those who disagree with anti-abortionists have still had to decide *why* they disagreed. Still other social movements inspire scientific research or technological change, as the environmental movement has.

Ron Eyerman and Andrew Jamison have addressed some of these cultural effects in their book, *Music and Social Movements* (1998). They generally view culture as the arts. Art affects a society's collective memory and traditions, its "common sense" of how the world works. Culture is thus a bearer of truth, as they put it. They are keen to insist on the independent effects of culture in political life, on how our beliefs about the world affect our sense of what is possible and desirable.

One of the effects that Eyerman and Jamison mention is that movements create the raw materials for future movements. In their case, these are songs that movements may share with one another; the civil rights movement for instance generated a number of songs now associated generally with protest. Movements also create new tactics and other political know-how that future protestors can use. They also leave behind social ties that can be used to ignite new efforts in the future. The women's movement of the early twentieth century, for example, left a legacy of personal networks and organizations (as well as values and ideas) that the new women's movement of the 1960s could draw upon (Rupp and Taylor 1987; Taylor 1989).

There may be even broader cultural effects of social movements. On the one hand, they give people moral voice, helping them to articulate values and intuitions that they do not have time to think about in their daily lives (Jasper 1997). This is extremely satisfying for most participants. On the other hand, social movements can also generate extremely technical, scientific, and practical knowledge. They engage people in politics in an exciting way—rare enough in modern society. Unfortunately, some movements may go too far, when instead of trying to be artists they try to be engineers, telling others what is good for them rather than trying to persuade them.

The final excerpt by David Naguib Pellow and Robert J. Brulle discusses the achievements of the movement for environmental justice (EJ). They end by expressing their hope and concern for the future. The EJ movement has had many successes, but current and future challenges seems more daunting than ever. This is perhaps an appropriate note on which to end this volume. The world we live in is undoubtedly a better place thanks to past social movements (although some have certainly made us worse off). Yet current and emergent social problems—many associated with "globalization"—suggest that we need movements more than ever. Clearly, social movements will not soon disappear. We hope this volume has provided the reader with some ideas to understand them better.

Discussion Questions

1. What kinds of effects do social movements have on their societies?
2. What are the main institutional arenas in which protestors hope to have an impact?
3. Under what circumstances, or in what kind of movements, should we consider it a form of success for movement organizations to gain recognition, simply to survive?
4. How can movements contribute to a society's culture or knowledge, including its self-knowledge?
5. What kinds of unintended effects can a movement have?
6. What seem to be the main personal consequences of political protest?
7. What have been the main successes and failures of the environmental justice movement? What challenges will this movement face in the years ahead?

38 Defining Movement "Success"

William A. Gamson

Success is an elusive idea. What of the group whose leaders are honored or rewarded while their supposed beneficiaries linger in the same cheerless state as before? Is such a group more or less successful than another challenger whose leaders are vilified and imprisoned even as their program is eagerly implemented by their oppressor? Is a group a failure if it collapses with no legacy save inspiration to a generation that will soon take up the same cause with more tangible results? And what do we conclude about a group that accomplishes exactly what it set out to achieve and then finds its victory empty of real meaning for its presumed beneficiaries? Finally, we must add to these questions the further complications of groups with multiple antagonists and multiple areas of concern. They may achieve some results with some targets and little or nothing with others.

It is useful to think of success as a set of outcomes, recognizing that a given challenging group may receive different scores on equally valid, different measures of outcome. These outcomes fall into two basic clusters: one concerned with the fate of the challenging group as an organization and one with the distribution of new advantages to the group's beneficiary. The central issue in the first cluster focuses on the *acceptance* of a challenging group by its antagonists as a valid spokesman for a legitimate set of interests. The central issue in the second cluster focuses on whether the group's beneficiary gains *new advantages* during the challenge and its aftermath.

Both of these outcome clusters require elaboration, but, for the moment, consider each as if it were a single, dichotomous variable. Assume a group that has a single antagonist and a single act which they wish this antagonist to perform – for example, a reform group which desires a particular piece of national legislation. We ask of such a group, did its antagonist accept it as a valid spokesman for the constituency that it was attempting to mobilize or did it deny such acceptance? Secondly, did the group gain the advantages it sought – for example, the passage of the legislation that it desired?

By combining these two questions, as in figure 38.1, we acquire four possible outcomes: full response, co-optation, preemption, and collapse. The full response and collapse categories are relatively unambiguous successes and failures – in the one case the achievement of both acceptance and new advantages, in the other, the achievement of neither. The remainder are mixed categories: co-optation is the term used for acceptance without new advantages and preemption for new advantages without acceptance.

		Acceptance Full	None
New advantages	Many	Full response	Preemption
	None	Co-optation	Collapse

Figure 38.1 Outcome of resolved challenges

Figure 38.1 is the paradigm for handling outcomes of challenging groups, but it requires additional complexity before it can be used to handle as diverse a set of groups as the 53 represented here. Acceptance must be given a special meaning for revolutionary groups, for example, which seek not a nod of recognition from an antagonist but its destruction and replacement. Similarly, new "advantages" are not always easy to define. We must deal with cases in which a group seeks, for example, relatively intangible value changes, shifts in the scope of authority, or a change in procedures as well as the simpler case of material benefits for a well-defined group.

The Endpoint of a Challenge

The outcome measures used refer to "ultimate" outcome, to the state of the group at the end of its challenge. A given group might achieve significant new advantages at one point without receiving acceptance, but we would not consider that preemption had occurred as long as it continued to press an active challenge. Only when it eventually collapsed or ceased activity would we classify its outcome as preemption. Or, if it eventually won acceptance, its outcome would be full response instead. Similarly, the new advantages might be withdrawn and the group brutally crushed, making "collapse" the appropriate outcome. Thus, during its period of challenge, a group might appear to be in one or another cell of figure 38.1 at different times, but the outcome measures only consider its location at the end.

A challenge period is considered over when one of the following occurs:

1. *The challenging group ceases to exist as a formal entity.* It may officially dissolve, declaring itself no longer in existence. Or, it may merge with another group, ceasing to maintain a separate identity. Note, however, that a group does not cease to exist by merely changing its name to refurbish its public image. Operationally, we consider that two names represent the same challenging group if and only if:
    a. The major goals, purposes, and functions of the two groups are the same.
    b. The constituency remains the same.
    c. The average challenging group member and potential member would agree that the new-name group is essentially the old group relabeled.

2. *The challenging group, while not formally dissolving, ceases mobilization and influence activity.* A five-year period of inactivity is considered sufficient to specify the end of the challenge. If, after such a dormant period, the group becomes active again, it is considered a new challenging group in spite of its organizational continuity with the old challenger. This occurred, in fact, with two of the 53 challengers in the sample. In each case the period of dormancy was quite a bit longer than the required five years, and, in one case, the geographical location of activity was different as well.

Marking the end of a challenge is more difficult with groups that continue to exist and be active. The line between being a challenging group and an established interest group is not always sharp. The essential difference lies in how institutionalized a conflict relationship exists between the group and its antagonists. When this conflict becomes regulated and waged under some standard operating procedures, the challenge period is over. Operationally, this can be dated from the point at which the group is accepted. Hence, for continuing groups, the challenge period is over when:

3. *The challenging group's major antagonists accept the group as a valid spokesman for its constituency and deal with it as such.* In the case of unions, this is indicated by formal recognition of the union as a bargaining agent for the employees. In other cases, the act of acceptance is less clear, and, even in the case of unions, different companies extend recognition at different times.

With continuing groups, then, there is some inevitable arbitrariness in dating the end of a challenge. The compiler was instructed to err, in ambiguous cases, on the side of a later date. Thus, where acute conflict continues to exist between the group and important antagonists, the challenge is not considered over even when some other antagonists may have begun to deal with the challenger in a routinized way. Furthermore, by extending the challenge period, we include new benefits that might be excluded by using a premature termination date.

39 How Social Movements Matter

David S. Meyer

In January 2003, tens if not hundreds of thousands of people assembled in Washington, D.C. to try to stop the impending invasion of Iraq. It did not look good for the demonstrators. Months earlier, Congress authorized President Bush to use force to disarm Iraq, and Bush repeatedly said that he would not let the lack of international support influence his decision about when—or whether—to use military force. Opposition to military action grew in the intervening months; the Washington demonstration coincided with sister events in San Francisco, Portland, Tampa, Tokyo, Paris, Cairo, and Moscow. Protests, albeit smaller and less frequent, continued after the war began. Did any of them change anything? Could they have? How? And how would we know if they did?

Such questions are not specific to this latest peace mobilization, but are endemic to protest movements more generally. Social movements are organized challenges to authorities that use a broad range of tactics, both inside and outside of conventional politics, in an effort to promote social and political change. Opponents of the Iraq war wrote letters to elected officials and editors of newspapers, called talk radio shows, and contributed money to antiwar groups. Many also invited arrest by civil disobedience; some protesters, for example, blocked entrances to government offices and military bases. A group of 50 "Unreasonable Women of West Marin" lay naked on a northern California beach, spelling out "Peace" with their bodies for a photographer flying overhead. Besides using diverse methods of protest, opponents of the war also held diverse political views. Some opposed all war, some opposed all U.S. military intervention, while others were skeptical only about this particular military intervention. This is a familiar social movement story: broad coalitions stage social movements, and differences within a movement coalition are often nearly as broad as those between the movement and the authorities it challenges.

Political activists and their targets act as if social movements matter, and sociologists have been trying, for the better part of at least four decades, to figure out why, when, and how. It is too easy—and not very helpful—to paint activists as heroes or, alternatively, as cranks. It is similarly too easy to credit them for social change or, alternatively, to dismiss their efforts by saying that changes, such as advances in civil rights or environmental protections, would have happened anyway. What we have learned is that social movements are less a departure from conventional institutional politics than an extension of them—a "politics by other means." In the end, we find that movements crest and wane, often failing to attain their immediate goals, but they can lastingly change political debates, governmental institutions, and the wider culture.

It is often difficult to tell whether activism makes a difference because the forces that propel people to mobilize are often the same forces responsible for social change. For example, it is difficult to decide whether the feminist movement opened new opportunities to women or whether economic changes fostered both the jobs and feminism. Also, authorities challenged by movements deny that activism influenced their decisions. What politicians want to admit that their judgments can be affected by "mobs"? Why risk encouraging protesters in the future? Finally, movements virtually never achieve all that their partisans demand, and so activists are quick to question their own influence. As a result, proving that movements influence politics and policy involves difficult detective work.

But research shows that social movements can affect government policy, as well as how it is made. And movement influence extends further. Activism often profoundly changes the activists, and through them, the organizations in which they participate, as well as the broader culture. The ways that movements make a difference are complex, veiled, and take far longer to manifest themselves than the news cycle that covers a single demonstration, or even a whole protest campaign.

When Movements Emerge

Activists protest when they think it might help them achieve their goals—goals they might not accomplish otherwise. Organizers successfully mobilize movements when they convince people that the issue at hand is urgent, that positive outcomes are possible and that their efforts could make a difference. In the case of the war on Iraq, for example, President Bush set the agenda for a broad range of activists by explicitly committing the country to military intervention. More-conventional politics—elections, campaign contributions, and letter-writing—had already played out and it became clear that none of these activities were sufficient, in and of themselves, to stop the war. In addition, the President's failure to build broad international or domestic support led activists to believe that direct pressure might prevent war. The rapid worldwide growth of the movement itself encouraged activism, assuring participants that they were part of something larger than themselves, something that might matter. In effect, President Bush's actions encouraged antiwar activism to spread beyond a small group of perpetual peace activists to a broader public.

With peace movements, it is clear that threat of war helps organizers mobilize people. Threats generally help political opposition grow beyond conventional politics. Movements against nuclear armaments, for example, emerge strongly when governments announce they are building more weapons. Similarly, environmental movements expand when government policies toward forests, pesticides, or toxic wastes become visibly negligent. In the case of abortion politics, each side has kept the other mobilized for more than 30 years by periodically threatening to take control of the issue. In each of these cases, those who lose in traditional political contests such as elections or lobbying campaigns often take to the streets.

Other sorts of movements grow when the promise of success arises. American civil rights activists, for example, were able to mobilize most broadly when they saw signals that substantial change was possible. Rosa Parks knew about Jackie Robinson and *Brown v. Board of Education*—as well as Gandhian civil disobedience—before deciding not to move to the back of the bus in Montgomery, Alabama. Government responsiveness to earlier activism—such as President Truman's desegregation of the armed forces and calling for an anti-lynching law—though limited, fitful, and often strategic, for a time encouraged others in their efforts. And the success of African-American activists encouraged other ethnic groups, as well as women, to pursue social change through movement politics.

As social movements grow, they incorporate more groups with a broader range of goals and more diverse tactics. Absent a focus like an imminent war, activists inside and political figures outside compete with one another to define movement goals and objectives. Political authorities often respond with policy concessions designed to diminish the breadth and depth of a movement. While such tactics can divide a movement, they are also one way of measuring a movement's success.

How Movements Matter: Public Policy

By uniting, however loosely, a broad range of groups and individuals, and taking action, social movements can influence public policy, at least by bringing attention to their issues. Newspaper stories about a demonstration pique political, journalistic, and public interest in the demonstrators' concerns. By bringing scrutiny to a contested policy, activists can promote alternative thinking. By displaying a large and engaged constituency, social movements provide political support for leaders sympathetic to their concerns. Large demonstrations show that there are passionate citizens who might also donate money, work in campaigns, and vote for candidates who will speak for them. Citizen mobilization against abortion, taxes, and immigration, for example, has encouraged ambitious politicians to cater to those constituencies. In these ways, social movement activism spurs and supports more conventional political action.

Activism outside of government can also strengthen advocates of minority positions within government. Social movements—just like presidential administrations and Congressional majorities—are coalitions. Antiwar activists in the streets may have strengthened the bargaining position of the more internationalist factions in the Bush administration, most notably Colin Powell, and led, at least temporarily, to diplomatic action in the United Nations. Mobilized opposition also, for a time, seemed to embolden Congressional critics, and encouraged lesser-known candidates for the Democratic presidential nomination to vocally oppose the war.

Social movements, by the popularity of their arguments, or more frequently, the strength of their support, can convince authorities to re-examine and possibly change their policy preferences. Movements can demand a litmus test for their support. Thus, George H. W. Bush, seeking the Republican nomination for president in 1980, revised his prior support for abortion rights. A few years later, Jesse Jackson likewise reconsidered his opposition to abortion. Movements raised the profile of the issue, forcing politicians not only to address their concerns, but to accede to their demands.

Although movement activists promote specific policies—a nuclear freeze, an equal rights amendment, an end to legal abortion, or, more recently, a cap on malpractice awards—their demands are usually so absolute that they do not translate well into policy. (Placards and bumper stickers offer little space for nuanced debate.) Indeed, the clearest message that activists can generally send is absolute rejection: no to nuclear weapons, abortion, pesticides, or taxes. These admonitions rarely become policy, but by promoting their programs in stark moral terms, activists place the onus on others to offer alternative policies that are, depending on one's perspective, more moderate or complex. At the same time, politicians often use such alternatives to capture, or at least defuse, social movements. The anti-nuclear weapons movement of the late 1950s and early 1960s did not end the arms race or all nuclear testing. It did, however, lead to the Limited Test Ban Treaty, which ended atmospheric testing. First Eisenhower, then Kennedy, offered arms control proposals and talks with the Soviet Union, at least in part as a response to the movement. This peace movement established the framework for arms control in superpower relations, which subsequently spread to the entire international community.

In these ways, activists shape events—even if they do not necessarily get credit for their efforts or achieve everything they want. The movement against the Vietnam War, for instance, generated a great deal of attention which, in turn, changed the conduct of that war and much else in domestic politics. President Johnson chose bombing targets with attention to minimizing political opposition; President Nixon, elected at least partly as a result of the backlash against the antiwar movement, nonetheless tailored his military strategy to respond to some of its concerns. In later years, he suggested that the antiwar movement made it unthinkable for him to threaten nuclear escalation in Vietnam—even as a bluff. In addition, the movement helped end the draft, institutionalizing all-volunteer armed forces. And, according to Colin Powell, the Vietnam dissenters provoked a new military approach for the United States, one that emphasized the use of overwhelming force to minimize American casualties. Thus, the military execution of the 1991 Persian Gulf war was influenced by an antiwar movement that peaked more than three decades earlier. This is significant, if not the effect most antiwar activists envisioned.

Political Institutions

Social movements can alter not only the substance of policy, but also how policy is made. It is not uncommon for governments to create new institutions, such as departments and agencies, in response to activists' demands. For example, President Kennedy responded to the nuclear freeze movement by establishing the Arms Control and Disarmament Agency, which became a permanent voice and venue in the federal bureaucracy for arms control. A glance at any organizational chart of federal offices turns up numerous departments, boards, and commissions that trace their origins to popular mobilization. These include the Department of Labor, the Department of Housing and Urban Development, the National Labor Relations Board, the Environment Protection Agency, the National Council on Disability, the Consumer Product Safety Commission, and the Equal Employment Opportunity Commission. Although these offices do not always support activist goals, their very existence represents a permanent institutional concern and a venue for making demands. If, as environmentalists argue, the current Environmental Protection Agency is often more interested in facilitating exploitation of the environment than in preventing it, this does not negate the fact that the environmental movement established a set of procedures through which environmental concerns can be addressed.

Government responses to movement demands also include ensuring that diverse voices are heard in decisionmaking. In local zoning decisions, for example, environmental impact statements are a now a routine part of getting a permit for construction. Congress passed legislation establishing this requirement in 1970 in response to the growing environmental movement. Indeed, movement groups, including Greenpeace and the Sierra Club, negotiated directly with congressional sponsors. Similarly, juries and judges now routinely hear victim impact statements before pronouncing sentences in criminal cases, the product of the victims' rights movement. Both public and private organizations have created new departments to manage and, perhaps more importantly, document personnel practices, such as hiring and firing, to avoid being sued for discrimination on the basis of gender, ethnicity, or disability. Workshops on diversity, tolerance, and sexual harassment are commonplace in American universities and corporations, a change over just two decades that would have been impossible to imagine without the activism of the 1960s and 1970s. In such now well-established bureaucratic routines, we can see how social movements change practices, and through them, beliefs.

Social movements also spawn dedicated organizations that generally survive long after a movement's moment has passed. The environmental movement, for example, firmly established a "big ten" group of national organizations, such as the Wildlife Defense Fund, which survives primarily by raising money from self-defined environmentalists. It cultivates donors by monitoring and publicizing government actions and environmental conditions, lobbying elected officials and administrators, and occasionally mobilizing supporters to do something more than mail in their annual membership renewals. Here, too, the seemingly permanent establishment of "movement organizations" in Washington, D.C. and in state capitals across the United States has—even if these groups often lose—fundamentally changed policymaking. Salaried officers of the organizations routinely screen high-level appointees to the judiciary and government bureaucracy and testify before legislatures. Mindful of this process, policymakers seek to preempt their arguments by modifying policy—or at least their rhetoric.

Political Activists

Social movements also change the people who participate in them, educating as well as mobilizing activists, and thereby promoting ongoing awareness and action that extends beyond the boundaries of one movement or campaign. Those who turn out at antiwar demonstrations today have often cut their activist teeth mobilizing against globalization, on behalf of labor, for animal rights or against welfare reform. By politicizing communities, connecting people, and promoting personal loyalties, social movements build the infrastructure not only of subsequent movements but of a democratic society more generally.

Importantly, these consequences are often indirect and difficult to document. When hundreds of thousands of activists march to the Supreme Court to demonstrate their support for legal abortion, their efforts might persuade a justice. More likely, the march signals commitment and passion to other activists and inspires participants to return home and advocate for abortion rights in their communities across the country, thereby affecting the shape of politics and culture more broadly.

The 2003 anti-Iraq War movement mobilized faster, with better organizational ties in the United States and transnationally than, for example, the movement against the 1991 Persian Gulf War. But how are we to assess its influence? Many activists no doubt see their efforts as having been wasted, or at least as unsuccessful. Moreover, supporters of the war point to the rapid seizure of Baghdad and ouster of Saddam Hussein's regime as evidence of the peace movement's naïveté. But a movement's legacy extends through a range of outcomes beyond a government's decision of the moment. It includes consequences for process, institutional practices, organizations, and individuals. This antiwar movement changed the rhetoric and international politics of the United States' preparation for war, leading to a detour through the United Nations that delayed the start of war. The activists who marched in Washington, San Francisco, and Los Angeles may retreat for a while, but they are likely to be engaged in politics more intensively in the future. This may not be much consolation to people who marched to stop a war, but it is true. To paraphrase a famous scholar: activists make history, but they do not make it just as they please. In fighting one political battle, they shape the conditions of the next one.

Recommended Resources

Arkin, William M. 2003. "The Dividends of Delay." *Los Angeles Times*, February 23. Arkin details the influence of the peace movement on U.S. military strategy in the Iraq war.

Giugni, Marco, Doug McAdam, and Charles Tilly. 1990. *How Social Movements Matter* (Minneapolis: University of Minnesota Press). This collection employs diverse approaches in examining the outcomes of social movements across a range of cases.

Klatch, Rebecca. 1999. *A Generation Divided: The New Left, The New Right, and the 1960s* (Berkeley: University of California Press). Klatch traces individual life stories of activists on both ends of the political spectrum during a turbulent period and beyond.

Meyer, David S. 1993. "Protest Cycles and Political Process: American Peace Movements in the Nuclear Age." *Political Research Quarterly* 46: 451–79. This article details how government responses to peace movements affect policy and subsequent political mobilization.

Meyer, David S., Nancy Whittier, and Belinda Robnett, eds. 2002. *Social Movements: Identity, Culture, and the State* (New York: Oxford University Press). A collection that addresses the link between protesters and context across different settings and times.

McAdam, Doug, and Yang Su. 2002. "The War at Home: Antiwar Protests and Congressional Voting, 1965 to 1973." *American Sociological Review* 67: 696–721. Antiwar protests set an agenda for Congress, forcing resolutions about the war, but could not influence the outcomes of those votes.

Rochon, Thomas. 1998. *Culture Moves: Ideas, Activism, and Changing Values* (Princeton, NJ: Princeton University Press). Rochon looks at social movements as a primary way to promote new ideas and alter culture.

Tarrow, Sidney. [1994] 1998. *Power in Movement* (New York: Cambridge University Press). A broad and comprehensive review of scholarship on movements, synthesized in a useful framework.

40 The Personal Consequences of Protest

Darren E. Sherkat and T. Jean Blocker

Social movement organizations recruit adherents who are, to some degree, ideologically aligned with the goals of the movement. However, the relationship between constituents' orientations and movement participation is not unidirectional—social movements mold participants' beliefs, direct behaviors, and channel commitments. Indeed, many sociological studies of recruitment and mobilization downplay the role of ideas and beliefs, noting that organizations generate demand for their services, and that members often only grudgingly accept movements' ideologies (McCarthy and Zald 1977; Stark and Bainbridge 1980). Social movements attempt to attract like-minded individuals, while trying to change the preferences of adherents and bystanders to more closely conform with those of the organization. With such processes occurring in the dynamics of recruitment and retention, and given the temporality of most social movements (particularly in terms of mass mobilization), it is important to learn: (1) whether movement participation leaves an indelible mark on activists; and (2) how activism influences participants. The significance of these issues is underscored by theory and research suggesting that prior mobilization efforts provide consequential tactical, cultural, and tangible resources for later movements (Rupp and Taylor 1987; Taylor 1989).

A considerable body of literature has developed around the consequences of participation in social movements. Early studies on 1960s activists hypothesized that maturation and adult integration would lead to moderation (Eisenstadt 1956; Lipset and Ladd 1971, 1972; Parsons 1963), or that the defeat of the movement would drive disillusioned activists back into the middle-class mainstream from which they came (Foss and Larkin 1976, 1982; Mauss 1971). In contrast, overwhelming sociological evidence demonstrates that activists maintained liberal ideals, continued to participate in liberal social movements, and pursued lifestyles in concert with their beliefs (e.g. Fendrich 1993; McAdam 1989; Whalen and Flacks 1989). Yet, most studies of the long-term consequences of movement participation have focused on high-risk activists, and the majority target the civil rights struggles of the early 1960s (e.g., Fendrich 1993; McAdam 1989; Marwell, Aiken, and Demerath 1987). While such investigations are extremely important for identifying how participation might affect future orientations and commitments, the distinctiveness of high-commitment civil rights and antiwar activists may not generalize to the majority of activists who were involved in antiwar and student demonstrations (Sherkat and Blocker 1994). If the less-committed majority of activists—who constituted more than ten percent of the cohorts reaching adulthood in the late 1960s—maintained their ideological orientations or altered their lifestyles this would certainly magnify the impact of these movements on American society.

We explore the biographical consequences of run-of-the-mill activism—the type of protest that was characteristic of the late 1960s and early 1970s. After proposing a framework for explaining the consequences of activism, we focus on four areas of social life that might be influenced by protest participation: (1) politics, (2) status attainment, (3) religion, and (4) family. Using data from the Youth-Parent Socialization Panel Study (Jennings 1987; Jennings and Niemi 1981), we compare protesters and others in 1973 and 1982. Unlike prior studies (e.g., Jennings 1987; McAdam 1989; Marwell, Aiken, and Demerath 1987), we examine differences between activists and nonactivists controlling for class and socialization factors that predict protest participation—and which might have generated distinctive orientations and choices even in the absence of protest participation.

Explaining the Consequences of Activism

Researchers charting the continuity of liberalism among former 1960s activists have often appealed to generational unit theories. Drawing on Mannheim ([1928] 1972), scholars have argued that the unique historical experiences of protesters provided a clear break from both their parents and peers who did not have such exposure (Braungart and Braungart 1990; Demartini 1983; Fendrich 1977, 1993; Fendrich and Lovoy 1988; Fendrich and Tarleau 1973; Fendrich and Turner 1989; Jennings 1987; Marwell, Aiken, and Demerath 1987; Whalen and Flacks 1989). However, generational unit theories fail to supply a mechanism through which participation might influence individuals' orientations or actions. To this end, McAdam (1989) contends that movement participation and sustained interactions between activists lead to conversion-like experiences captured by the concept of alternation (Travisano 1970). However, the concept of alternation is problematic. Alternation implies a state of acceptance of movement principles or alternative values, but there is no way to discern when an individual has become "alternated." Further, there is no systematic explanation for why alternation generated by participation in political movements might influence other arenas of life—such as religiosity, family ties, or occupational choice. Using Sewell's (1992) reformulation of Giddens's (1984) structuration theory, we provide a perspective for explaining the influence of movement participation.

Structure and Social Movements

Participation in social movements inevitably forges opinions, orients activities, and affects the lifestyles of participants. The interactive processes occurring between individuals in social movements help transform and reenforce ideological orientations (Rochford 1985; Snow et al. 1986). Sewell's (1992) theory of structure as comprised of both schemata and resources provides an appealing framework for explaining the consequences of social movement participation. First, when individuals participate in social movements these interactions may alter informal rules or procedures applied in social settings—the schemata that constitute preferences, assumptions, and conventions that inform future decisions (Sewell 1992). Second, participation in social movements constitutes a link to a variety of resources. Resources available in social movement organizations include: tangible resources (such as networks of people, offices, events); positions within the organization (cadre worker, transitory activist, patron); and codified statements of movement goals (such as pamphlets, books, and speeches). These resources will help sustain distinctive schemata, and will be sustained by the schematic orientations that constitute the social structure of social movements. Third, individuals' commitments to particular schemata may become codified, providing cognitive resources for other decisions and understandings—thereby generating cognitive structures (Sherkat and Ellison 1997). For example, participants in the protests may come to identify with liberalism so strongly that they use it as a cognitive resource to explain novel situations, searching for a position consistent with liberal precommitments.

If social movement participation is an interactive process between organizational resources and individuals' schematic understandings, these resource interactions could motivate shifts in schemata. Further, resource interactions fostered by protest participation could result in the cognitive codification of schematic understandings supported by a social movement, thus producing a cognitive structure that will serve to inform other schemata and resource interactions. Theories of the dual nature of social structures focus on the processual dynamics that make social structures both constraining and enabling (Giddens 1984; Sewell 1992; Stryker 1994). However, asymmetries of influence often exist, typically making resources dominant in social structures. Our focus on the influence of social movements specifies a particular asymmetry—that protest resources generate identifiable effects on future schemata and resource interactions.

Importantly, schemata are transposable across diverse realms of social life (Sewell 1992). For example, orienting frameworks guiding political choices will spill over into religious choices, and vice versa. Such transposability gives a theoretical justification for examining the effects of political experiences on a variety of social realms, such as occupation, religion, and family. Further, resources may take on multiple meanings in different social contexts (Sewell 1992). Since choices made across social fields can have different interpretations, they may also serve to sustain diverse schemata. For example, the resource of holding a particular occupation could be interpreted as integration into the political-economic system ("selling out"), or it could be seen as a means to change the system by performing in a manner consistent with antisystemic schemata or cognitive resources ("acting locally"). This framework for analyzing how social movement participation could influence a variety of social fields meshes well with contemporary discussions of "new social movements," which imply that diverse interpretations of resources and generalizable schemata serve to politicize personal issues (Melucci 1980, 1985; Offe 1985). Further, this perspective allows us to probe how political structures might intersect with and influence other structural arenas such as religion, occupation, and family.

Domains of Protest Influence

Social movement participation may foster changes in orienting schemas and resource interpretations in a number of realms. The transposability of schematic orientations across structural domains implies that shifting preferences will lead to different choices among diverse resource options—such as choice of job, political affiliations, religious ties, and family structure. These shifts in schematic orientations and their concomitant influences on life choices may vary in intensity or duration across different areas of social life. By examining how activists differ from nonactivists while controlling for the factors that predicted taking part in the protests, we will be able to speculate how protest participation influences these four social realms.

Politics

The movements of the 1960s can be expected to have recruited among individuals with liberal political orientations and to have solidified and radicalized liberal beliefs and identifications. If movement participants changed their schematic orientations and resource interactions as a result of activism, they should differ substantially from nonactivists on a variety of political issues even when considering political socialization factors. We expect to find differences in both political schemata—indicated by what people believe about politics—as well as interactions with political resources—indicated by political affiliation and participation. Previous studies of activists over the life course have found that 1960s-era protesters remained more liberal in political orientations, and were more likely to be affiliated with and active in liberal organizations and parties (Fendrich 1977, 1993; Fendrich and Lovoy 1988; Fendrich and Tarleau 1973; Fendrich and Turner 1989; Jennings 1987; McAdam 1989; Marwell, Aiken, and Demerath 1987; Whalen and Flacks 1989).

Status Attainment

Anti-establishment schematic orientations fostered by protest movements of the 1960s may have influenced activists' educational pursuits and occupational trajectories. High-commitment activists from the early 1960s were more likely to drop out of college or to pursue degrees in less financially rewarding areas such as the arts, humanities, and social sciences (Braungart and Braungart 1990; Fendrich 1974, 1977). Studies have also shown that civil rights movement participation had a substantial impact on career trajectories, with movement activists entering the workforce later and changing jobs more frequently (McAdam 1989). Activists have been found to be averse to jobs in the capitalist economy, preferring instead positions in new class, knowledge, or helping occupations outside of the private sector (Fendrich 1974, 1977; Fendrich and Krauss 1978; Fendrich and Tarleau 1973; McAdam 1989; Wagner 1990; Whalen and Flacks 1989). Importantly, career choice provides a resource setting that re-enforces schematic orientations by furnishing a community of like-minded coworkers. Hence, activists' schemas not only will drive their educational and occupational choices, but these choices will help former activists maintain their distinctive views. Further, certain occupations also provide an arena in which the values promoted by protest movements can be put into practice—especially in occupations such as social work, education, public health, politics, and law (Braungart and Braungart 1990; Wagner 1990).

Religion

Religious commentators commonly refer to the 1960s as a "consciousness reformation" during which countercultural values replaced traditional religious expressions (e.g. Bellah 1976; Roof 1993; Wuthnow 1976). Protest participants should be most likely to have adopted an opposition to traditional religious orientations, and to avoid religious affiliation and participation. The association of religious institutions with conservatism (rightly or wrongly) was a common theme among activists (Flacks 1990). Conservative Protestant orientations and affiliations have been shown to foster support for obedience to authority and to hinder participation in protests (Ellison and Sherkat 1993; Sherkat and Blocker 1994). Participation in the demonstrations should influence religious beliefs, affiliation, and participation across religious "periods" and stages of the life course (Stolzenberg et al. 1995). Political activism should weaken both religious schematic orientations—such as beliefs about the Bible and support for prayer in school—as well as connections to religious resources through affiliation and participation. Movement-inspired shifts in religious affiliation and participation will also help activists maintain their radicalism. By withdrawing from traditional religious communities, former activists can embed themselves in networks supportive of nontraditional beliefs and lifestyles (Sherkat 1996).

Family

The movements of the 1960s were generally supportive of equal rights for women, showed concern for population control, and emphasized nontraditional values. Because of this, protest activists may have been more likely to delay marriage, forgo having children, or curtail their fertility. The personal had become politicized, and participation in these political movements should have an impact on the personal life choices of participants. This meshes well with the theory of schematic transposability, as well as new social movements theories (e.g. Melucci 1985, 1980; Offe 1985). Additionally, resource commitments to social movements may create conflicting claims with family relations. Parents, spouses, or even children may be seen as "part of the problem" which the social movements of the time sought to solve. We expect that activists will have higher rates of divorce than nonactivists, both because of potential conflicts generated by activism, as well as nontraditional values that will reduce the stigma of marital dissolution (McAdam 1989). Further, if activism widens the gulf between parents' and children's values, this could disrupt intergenerational affective solidarity (Dunham and Bengtson 1992; Roberts and Bengtson 1990).

Data, Measures, and Methods

Data

We analyze data from the Youth–Parent Socialization Panel Study (YPSPS), collected by the Survey Research Center at the University of Michigan (Jennings and Niemi 1981). The first wave of the study was completed in spring of 1965 and yielded interviews with 1,669 high school seniors, 99 percent of those targeted by the study. A randomly selected parent of each child was also interviewed, resulting in 1,562 interviews with parents (93 percent of those contacted). The second wave of the study was completed in 1973, and retained 1,348 (80.8 percent) of the students from the original panel. The current study will not use data from the parents in the later waves. The third panel of the study was collected in 1982, when the students were about 34 years old, and 1,135 interviews were completed. This represents a 68 percent retention rate over the 17 years of the study; adjusting for known deaths the retention rate is 70 percent (Jennings and Markus 1984). Combined with the extraordinarily high response rate of the initial study, the YPSPS yields 17 years of data that are more complete than many cross-sectional surveys which suffer from low response rates.

Since students were high school seniors in 1965, they would have been college seniors in 1969 if they followed the traditional student pattern. The YPSPS is ideal because it taps beliefs, behaviors, and background prior to the period of heavy mobilization by the antiwar and student movements of the late 1960s. This allows us to control for factors that would initially distinguish activists from nonactivists. The second panel followed up respondents shortly after the collapse of the majority of the social protests of this period. The third wave was collected nine years later when respondents were relatively settled in adult roles at the beginning of a long conservative political period.

The Activists

We distinguish respondents who participated in the antiwar, women's rights, civil rights, and student movements from respondents who were not active. We exclude respondents who participated in "problem solving" environmental activism, including movements concerning land protection, zoning, pollution problems, or general environmental issues (Sherkat and Blocker 1993). The YPSPS does not allow us to distinguish high-risk or high-involvement activists from "token" participants. These levels of involvement of protest activists will range between high-risk and relatively low-risk activism. These "average activists" should better represent the range of protest activity that took place in this period. In 1973, we compare 181 protesters with 1,111 nonactivists. In 1982, 148 of these protesters remain in the study and are compared to 935 nonactivists.

Politics

We first examine the effects of movement participation on political orientations and participation. A number of diverse measures of political orientations are available in the YPSPS. Respondents rated themselves on a scale from (1) extremely liberal to (7) extremely conservative. In 1973 an item tapping beliefs in the need for a radical change in our political system is employed, which runs from (1) "change in our whole form of government is needed," to (7) "no change is necessary." Endorsement of the welfare state is measured in both 1973 and 1982 by placement on a scale from (1) "government should guarantee a job and a good standard of living," to (7) "government should let each person get ahead on his own." Feelings of closeness to big business are measured with a 100-degree feeling thermometer. We examine political trust with a scale that measures whether or not the respondent thought that the government "wastes money," "is run by dishonest people," "can be trusted to do what is right," is "run by a few big interests looking out for themselves," or "is run by people who don't know what they are doing." Each item runs from (0) for the least trustworthy response to (2) for most trusting response. Civic tolerance is measured by agreement that communists should be allowed to hold office if elected, and that speeches against religion should be allowed. Beliefs in the rights of the accused are examined on a scale from (1) "protect the rights of the accused" to (7) "stop crime regardless of the rights of the accused."

Beliefs about government support for the economic position of blacks and other minorities is measured from (1) "government should help minorities" to (7) "minority groups should help themselves." Support for busing to achieve integration runs from (1) "busing should be used to achieve integration" to (7) "keep children in neighborhood schools," and this measure is only available in 1973. Backing school integration is measured by a dummy variable in both 1973 and 1982. Opposition to foreign involvement is tapped with a dummy indicator in both 1973 and 1982. In 1973, opposition to Vietnam is measured by a dichotomous indicator representing the belief that the U.S. should have stayed out of Vietnam. Support for abortion on demand is tapped with a dummy variable; however, it is only available in 1982.

Political party identification runs from (1) strong Democrat to (7) strong Republican. Respondents were asked if they voted in presidential elections, and for whom they voted (or would have voted for if they did not vote). Dummy variables indicate support for Richard Nixon in the 1973 study, and for Jimmy Carter and Ronald Reagan in the 1982 study. In 1982, a scale of overall political activity tallies nine activities: working to influence people on political issues; voting; working for a candidate; wearing buttons or placing bumper stickers; contributing money; writing letters or talking to officials; writing to a newspaper; participating in a demonstration; or working with others to solve community problems. Finally, we examine whether or not respondents participated in a demonstration between 1973 and 1982, focusing only on "liberal" movements (a small number of anti-abortion demonstrators are coded 0 for the dummy indicator).

Status Attainment

Educational attainment in 1973 and 1982 is measured from (1) high school, (2) some college, (3) college graduate, (4) graduate degree. We also employ a dummy indicator for higher educational pursuits between 1973 and 1982. The measure of individual income in 1973 runs from (1) none to (18) $35,000 and over. In 1982, income is measured from (0) none to (22) $80,000 and over. We examine the number of jobs a respondent had between 1965 and 1973 and between 1973 and 1982. We assess whether or not respondents were employed in a new class occupation, classifed following Macy (1988) as lawyer, artist, performing artist, social worker, teacher, social scientist, journalist, academic, writer, clergy, or librarian. We identify housewives in 1982. Because the male respondents were eligible for the draft, and nearly 400 served in the military between 1965 and 1973, we explore differences in military service between protesters and nonprotesters with a dummy indicator.

Religion

We have two indicators of religious orientations, beliefs in the Bible, and support for prayer in schools. Respondents were asked which was closest to their own view: (4) "The Bible is God's word and all it says is true"; (3) "The Bible was written by men inspired by God, but it contains some human error"; (2) "The Bible is a good book because it was written by wise men, but God had nothing to do with it"; and (1) "The Bible was written by men who lived so long ago that it is worth very little today." An indicator of support for prayer in schools is used in both 1973 and 1982. We identify respondents who had no religious affiliation in 1973 and in 1982. A two-item additive scale taps religious participation, including church attendance and participation in religious organizations. Church attendance in 1965–82 is measured from (4) almost every week, to (1) never. Participation in religious organizations is also gauged ranging from (1) no participation to (4) very active. The items are highly correlated in every panel of the study and form a reliable scale for religious participation (Sherkat 1991).

Family

We not only assessed whether or not respondents were married, divorced, or had children between 1965 and 1982. We also asked respondents to rate themselves on a scale from (1) "women and men should have an equal role" to (7) "women's place is in the home." We examine frequency of contact with parents or guardians in both 1973 and 1982 from (1) never to (7) every day. Feelings of closeness to parent(s) or guardian(s) are examined in both 1973 and 1982, from (3) very close to (1) not close at all. The measure is an average of closeness to the mother and father. If the respondent had one parent or guardian the existing score is used.

[...]

Results

Short-Term Consequences, 1973 YPSPS

Looking first at political orientations, protesters rate themselves significantly more liberal than nonactivists. Indeed, in 1973 protesters were significantly more liberal than nonactivists on every political orientation item, and they remain so when controls for socialization and education are introduced. [...] Controlling for socialization and education, protesters are significantly more aligned with the Democratic party than nonprotesters. Protesters are also significantly more likely to have voted in the 1972 presidential election, but the significance of this difference is explained by socialization factors. Both adjusted proportions and logistic regression results show that activists were significantly less likely than nonprotesters to support Nixon.

Protesters were significantly more educated than nonactivists, even controlling for parents' education, high school grades, and college tracking. Despite protesters' educational advantages, activists had significantly lower incomes. In the unadjusted proportions, twice as many activists as nonactivists were employed in new-class occupations in 1973. However, the significance of this difference is accounted for by protesters' higher educational attainment. Protesters also changed employment more often than nonprotesters, but this is explained by background factors. Interestingly, there were no differences between protesters and nonprotesters on whether or not they served in the military.

[...] Controlling for other factors—including beliefs and affiliation in high school—protesters were significantly less orthodox in their views of the Bible. Activists were significantly more opposed to prayer in public schools compared to nonprotesters. Even after controls for socialization and education, protesters were significantly less likely than nonprotesters to have a religious affiliation, evidencing their withdrawal from traditional religious resources. Demonstrators also had significantly lower levels of religious participation than nonactivists, and these differences hold up after controls for socialization factors in both the adjusted means and regression results.

Turning to family choices, we find that protesters were significantly less likely to be married than were nonactivists, even when controlling for socialization and education. Activists were also less likely to have had children, but this difference becomes insignificant when controls for education are introduced in the adjusted proportions and logistic regressions. Protesters had significantly more egalitarian views of gender roles in 1973 even after controlling for background factors and education. Activists had less frequent contact with their parents, though this dissimilarity is explained by the control variables, and protesters did not feel less close to their parents than nonprotesters.

Long-Term Consequences, 1982 YPSPS

While both protesters and nonactivists became somewhat more conservative in their political orientations between 1973 and 1982, former protesters remained significantly more liberal than nonactivists on everything except political trust and feelings toward big business. Declining political trust among the nonprotesters eliminated the difference between nonactivists and protesters. And nonactivists' and protesters' beliefs about foreign involvement switched directions. While protesters were significantly more opposed to foreign involvement in 1973, nonprotesters were more isolationist in 1982 (though controls for background factors eliminate the significance of this difference). Clearly, the nature and meaning of foreign involvement changed radically after withdrawal from Vietnam. Protesters were significantly more likely than nonprotesters to support abortion rights (an item not available in 1973).

Turning to political affiliations and participation, protesters remained significantly more aligned with the Democratic Party than the nonactivists. Logistic regression estimates and adjusted proportions show that demonstrators were significantly more likely to vote for Jimmy Carter, especially in his bid against Ronald Reagan in 1980. Indeed, only 24 percent of former protesters voted for Ronald Reagan. Further, former protesters were more active in politics, and were significantly more likely to have participated in a demonstration between 1973 and 1982, controlling for other factors.

Protesters widened the already significant educational gap with nonactivists. Controlling for other factors, protesters were more likely to receive additional education between 1973 and 1982. Despite their advantages in education, activists were not highly compensated for their efforts — though in contrast to 1973, activists did not earn significantly less than nonprotesters in 1982. Demonstrators were significantly more likely to choose jobs in the "new class," even when education and other factors are held constant. In the unadjusted results, activists are nearly five times more likely than nonactivists to be employed in new class occupations in 1982. Protesters were significantly less likely to be housewives, and this difference remains significant when socialization and education are taken into account. Finally, former activists changed jobs significantly more often than their counterparts.

In 1982 protesters remained significantly less conservative in their interpretations of the Bible compared to nonactivists, even when controls for socialization and education were added. Similarly, activists were less supportive of school prayer, even after adjustments for socialization and education. Many protesters reestablished a religious identification between 1973 and 1982, but protesters were more likely to remain unaffiliated (even when socialization and education are held constant) and were also significantly less active in religious groups compared to nonactivists.

Finally, looking at family factors, we find that protesters are less likely to be married in 1982, though this difference loses significance when controls for socialization and education are added. Demonstrators were significantly more prone to have married in the later period, and this difference holds up to multivariate scrutiny. Contrary to McAdam's (1989) findings, we do not find significant differences in the percentage of protesters who were divorced. While more activists experienced divorce between 1973 and 1982, the difference is insignificant. Protesters were significantly less likely to have children than nonactivists, and this difference remains when controls for socialization and educational attainment are added. Among those who had children, the two groups did not differ significantly in the number of children, though activists did tend to have fewer children. Nonprotesters became much more liberal in their attitudes toward women's roles, and controls for education eliminate the significance of differences from protesters (who maintained their liberal views on women's roles). Looking at family solidarity, we found no differences between activists and nonprotesters in closeness to parents. However, demonstrators had less contact with their parents, though the difference becomes insignificant when controls are introduced.

Discussion

Previous studies have shown that high-risk civil rights activists and high-commitment student protesters followed particular political and lifestyle trajectories (e.g. Fendrich 1993; McAdam 1989; Marwell, Aiken, and Demerath 1987, Whalen and Flacks 1989). Our study adds to this body of literature by showing that the activists who participated primarily in the antiwar and student movements of the late 1960s and early 1970s also remained distinctive in their politics, status attainment, religious commitments, and family choices. Our results show that participation in the protests of the late 1960s influenced each of these arenas, and that the effects of movement participation were long-lived. We explain the influence of social movement participation using a theory of structure—identifying how intersections between political structures and other social structures constitute the consequences of social movements.

The theory of structure we employ implies that political activism can be situated in a political structure by demonstrating how actors' schematic orientations direct interactions with protest resources and how those resources help reproduce or alter individuals' political schemata. We demonstrate that the protest movements of this period had an impact on political orientations throughout the early life course. Further, these invigorated political orientations led activists to interact with political resources in a distinctive way—continuing liberal affiliations and activism. Thus, even though the antiwar and student movements died out in the early 1970s, the political structures that gave rise to those movements are sustained in the schematic orientations of former participants, and through protesters' interactions with political resources currently available.

Theorists of "new social movements" have argued that one characteristic of contemporary social movements is that they are no longer confined to or emanate from the particular political questions they address (e.g. Melucci 1980, 1985; Offe 1985). As Melucci (1980:218) puts it, "The personal and social identity of individuals is increasingly perceived as a product of social action, and therefore as that which is at stake in a conflict between the exigencies of various agencies of social manipulation and the desire of individuals to reappropriate society's resources." Whether or not there is a trend or anything "new" about the relationship between personal identities and political movements, it seems clear that participation in the protests had consequences far beyond the political realm. Using Sewell's (1992) theoretical framework, the interweaving of political and personal concerns evidences the intersection of social structures through the transposition of political schemata into other realms of social life, and the reinterpretation of resources from disparate realms through the lens of politicized schemata.

First, former protesters made distinctive educational and career choices. While protesters attained significantly more education than nonprotesters, they did not convert these educational resources into income advantages. Former protesters were also disproportionately represented in the "new class" of professional and information intellectuals. Sewell's (1992) conception of polysemic resources—allowing resources to take on a variety of meanings—helps explain activists' divergent educational and occupational trajectories. It is likely that protesters and nonprotesters interpreted educational and occupational resources differently, and consequently used these resources in different ways. Nonactivists probably viewed educational and occupational resources primarily as a means to attain income. In contrast, protesters may have seen educational and occupational resources as a way to sustain political orientations, promote interactions with networks of likeminded or receptive individuals, and obtain political power and influence. It seems plausible that the desire to secure new class employment helped drive activists' educational pursuits. Demonstrators' organizational and friendship ties in and around institutions of higher education probably helped support their educational attainment, and their educational resources allowed them to obtain jobs that influenced public policy and future generations by working in largely public-sector professional and teaching fields. However, one occupational choice proscribed by the personalized politics of 1960s protest movements was becoming a housewife, and we find very few former activists in this occupation.

Second, former protesters maintained less orthodox religious orientations and were more likely to sever ties with religious organizations. Religious orientations influenced and were influenced by participation in the movements of the 1960s. Youths with fundamentalist orientations shunned participation in the demonstrations (Sherkat and Blocker 1994). Thus, religious schemata and resources helped direct who would join in the protests. After involvement in the protests, activists gravitated towards irreligion, rejected traditional religious schemata, and avoided participation in organized religion even if they did not renounce affiliation.

Finally, activists married later and were less likely to have children. Personal choices about family and gender roles were informed by schemata transposed from political structures, perhaps especially for female activists. In general, activists may have seen traditional family relations and childrearing orientations as supportive of the patriarchal culture they were fighting against. Given the political continuities evident across generations, lower rates of fertility among 1960s-era activists could have profound and long-lasting negative consequences for liberal political movements in the U.S.

Participation in the social movements of the 1960s had far reaching and multifaceted repercussions. Even the typical activists we studied were appreciably changed by participation in the movements that characterized the 1960s. Future research should explore the extent to which commitment is mediated by adult socialization and social networks. One promising avenue for future studies is the relationship between occupational choice and the maintenance of alternative values and lifestyles. Occupations and organizations (such as political institutions, religious groups, and social movements) can sustain activist networks, movement goals, and radical identities, and may serve as abeyance structures for unmobilized or undermobilized social movements during periods of limited opportunity (Taylor 1989; Whittier 1995). Subsequent studies should examine the mobilization potential these abeyance organizations provide. Further, pockets of radical resistance may foster particular organizational cultures, and radicalized professionals may have access to resources that may help activists accomplish some of the movements' goals. The presence of a significant number of former activists in certain types of professions—particularly, social work, law, public health, and education—has very likely changed these professions and the policies they influence.

References

Bellah, Robert. 1976. "New Religious Consciousness and the Crisis of Modernity." In *The New Religious Consciousness*, edited by Charles Glock and Robert Wuthnow. Berkeley: University of California Press.

Braungart, Margaret M., and Richard G. Braungart. 1990. "The Life-Course Development of Left- and Right-Wing Youth Activist Leaders from the 1960s." *Political Psychology* 11:243–82.

Demartini, Joseph R. 1983. "Social Movement Participation, Political Socialization, Generational Consciousness, and Lasting Effects." *Youth and Society* 15:195–223.

Dunham, Charlotte Chorn, and Vern L. Bengtson. 1992. "The Long-Term Effects of Political Activism on Intergenerational Relations." *Youth and Society* 24:31–51.

Eisenstadt, S.N. 1956. *From Generation to Generation*. New York: Free Press.

Ellison, Christopher G., and Darren E. Sherkat. 1993. "Obedience and Autonomy: Religion and Parental Values Reconsidered." *Journal for the Scientific Study of Religion* 32:313–29.

Fendrich, James Max. 1974. "Activists Ten Years Later: A Test of Generational Unit Continuity." *Journal of Social Issues* 30:95–118.

Fendrich, James Max. 1977. "Keeping the Faith or Pursuing the Good Life: A Study of the Consequences of Participation in the Civil Rights Movement." *American Sociological Review* 42:144–57.

Fendrich, James Max. 1993. *Ideal Citizens: The Legacy of the Civil Rights Movement*. New York: SUNY Press.

Fendrich, James Max, and Elis Krauss. 1978. "Student Activism and Adult Left-Wing Politics: A Causal Model of Political Socialization for Black, White and Japanese Students of the 1960s Generation." 231–55 in *Research in Social Movements, Conflict and Change*, edited by Louis Kriesberg. Vol. 1. Greenwich, CT: JAI Press.

Fendrich, James Max, and Kenneth L. Lovoy. 1988. "Back to the Future: Adult Political Behavior of Former Student Activists." *American Sociological Review* 53:780–84.

Fendrich, James Max, and Alison T. Tarleau. 1973. "Marching to a Different Drummer: The Occupational and Political Orientations of Former Student Activists." *Social Forces* 52:245–53.

Fendrich, James Max, and Robert W. Turner. 1989. "The Transition from Student to Adult Politics." *Social Forces* 67:1049–57.

Flacks, Richard. 1990. "Social Bases of Activist Identity: Comment on Braungart Article." *Political Psychology* 11:283–92.

Foss, Daniel A., and Ralph W. Larkin. 1976. "From 'The Gates of Eden' to 'Day of the Locust': An Analysis of the Dissident Youth Movement of the 1960s and its Heirs of the Early 1970s." *Theory and Society* 3:45–64.

Foss, Daniel A., and Ralph W. Larkin. 1982. "Seven Ways of Selling Out: Post-Movement Phenomena in Social and Historical Perspective." *Psychology and Social Theory* 3:3–12.

Giddens, Anthony. 1984. *The Constitution of Society: Outline of the Theory of Structuration*. Berkeley: University of California Press.

Jennings, M. Kent. 1987. "Residues of a Movement: The Aging of the American Protest Generation." *American Political Science Review* 81:367–82.

Jennings, M. Kent, and Gregory Markus. 1984. "Partisan Orientations over the Long Haul: Results from the Three-Wave Political Socialization Study." *American Political Science Review* 78:1000–18.

Jennings, M. Kent, and Richard Niemi. 1981. *Generations and Politics*. Princeton, NJ: Princeton University Press.

Lipset, Seymour Martin, and Everett Carl Ladd Jr. 1971. "College Generation—From the 1930's to the 1960's." *Public Interest* 25:99–113.

Lipset, Seymour Martin, and Everett Carl Ladd Jr. 1972. "The Political Future of Activist Generations." In *The New Pilgrims: Youth Protest in Transition*, edited by Philip G. Altbach and Robert S. Laufer. New York: David McKay.

McAdam, Doug. 1986. "Recruitment to High-Risk Activism: The Case of Freedom Summer." *American Journal of Sociology* 92:64–90.

McAdam, Doug. 1989. "The Biographical Consequences of Activism." *American Sociological Review* 54:744–60.

McCarthy, John D., and Mayer, N. Zald. 1977. "Resource Mobilization and Social Movements. A Partial Theory." *Amercian Journal of Sociology* 82: 1212–41.

Macy, Michael. 1988. "New Class Dissent among Social-Cultural Specialists." *Sociological Forum* 3:325–56.

Mannheim, Karl. 1928/1972. "The Problem of Generations." In *The New Pilgrims: Youth Protest in Transition*, edited by Philip G. Altbach and Robert S. Laufer. New York: David McKay.

Marwell, Gerald, Michael T. Aiken, and N.J. Demerath. 1987. "The Persistence of Political Attitudes among 1960s Civil Rights Activists." *Public Opinion Quarterly* 51:359–75.

Mauss, Armand. 1971. "On Being Strangled by the Stars and Stripes." *Journal of Social Issues* 27:183–202.

Melucci, Alberto. 1980. "The New Social Movements: A Theoretical Approach." *Social Science Information* 19:199–226.

Melucci, Alberto. 1985. "The Symbolic Challenge of Contemporary Movements." *Social Research* 52:789–816.

Offe, Claus. 1985. "New Social Movements: Challenging the Boundaries of Institutional Politics." *Social Research* 52:817–68.

Parsons, Talcott. 1963. "Youth in the Context of American Society." In *Youth, Change and Challenge*, edited by E.H. Erickson. New York: Basic Books.

Roberts, Robert E., and Vern L. Bengtson. 1990. "Is Intergenerational Solidarity a Unidimensional Construct? A Second Test of a Formal Model." *Journal of Gerontology* 45:1:s12–s20.

Rochford, E. Burke. 1985. *Hare Krishna in America*. New Brunswick, NJ: Rutgers University Press.

Roof, Wade Clark. 1993. *A Generation of Seekers: The Spiritual Journeys of the Baby Boom Generation*. New York: Harper.

Rupp, Leila, and Verta Taylor. 1987. *Survival in the Doldrums: The American Women's Rights Movement, 1945 to the 1960s*. Oxford: Oxford University Press.

Sewell, William H. Jr. 1992. "A Theory of Structure: Duality, Agency, and Transformation." *American Journal of Sociology* 98:1–29.

Sherkat, Darren E. 1991. "Religious Socialization and the Family: An Examination of Religious Influence in the Family over the Life Course." Ph.D. diss. Duke University. Durham, NC.

Sherkat, Darren E. 1996. "Counterculture or Continuity? Examining Competing Influences on Baby Boomers' Religious Orientations and Participation." Paper presented at the 1996 annual meeting of the American Sociological Association.

Sherkat, Darren E., and T. Jean Blocker. 1993. "Environmental Activism in the Protest Generation: Differentiating Sixties Activists." *Youth and Society* 25:140–61.

Sherkat, Darren E., and T. Jean Blocker. 1994. "The Political Development of Sixties Activists: Identifying the Impact of Class, Gender, and Socialization on Protest Participation." *Social Forces* 72:821–42.

Sherkat, Darren E., and Christopher G. Ellison. 1997. "The Cognitive Structure of a Moral Crusade: Conservative Protestantism and Opposition to Pornography." *Social Forces* 75:957–80.

Sherkat, Darren E., and John Wilson. 1995. "Preferences, Constraints, and Choices in Religious Markets: An Examination of Religious Switching and Apostasy." *Social Forces* 73:993–1026.

Snow, David A., E. Burke Rochford, Steven K. Worden, and Robert D. Benford. 1986. "Frame Alignment Processes, Micromobilization, and Movement Participation." *American Sociological Review* 51:464–81.

Stark, Rodney, and William Sims Bainbridge. 1980. "Networks of Faith: Interpersonal Bonds and Recruitment to Cults and Sects." *American Journal of Sociology* 85:1376–95.

Stolzenberg, Ross M., Mary Blair-Loy, and Linda J. Waite. 1995. "Religious Participation in Early Adulthood: Age and Family Life Cycle Effects on Church Membership." *American Sociological Review* 60:84–103.

Stryker, Robin. 1994. "Rules, Resources, and Legitimacy Processes: Some Implications for Social Conflict, Order, and Change." *American Journal of Sociology* 99:847–910.

Taylor, Verta. 1989. "Social Movement Continuity: The Women's Movement in Abeyance." *American Sociological Review* 54:761–75.

Travisano, Richard V. 1970. "Alternation and Conversion as Qualitatively Different Transformations." In *Social Psychology through Symbolic Interaction*, edited by Gregory Stone and Harvey Farberman. Waltham, MA: Ginn-Blaisdell.

Wagner, David. 1990. *The Quest for a Radical Profession: Social Service Careers and Political Ideology*. Lanham, MD: University Press of America.

Whalen, John James, and Richard Flacks. 1989. *Beyond the Barricades*. Philadelphia, PA: Temple University Press.

Whittier, Nancy. 1995. *Feminist Generations: The Persistence of the Radical Women's Movement*. Philadelphia, PA: Temple University Press.

Wuthnow, Robert. 1976. *The Consciousness Reformation*. Berkeley: University of California Press.

41 Environmental Justice

David Naguib Pellow and Robert J. Brulle

One morning in 1987 several African-American activists on Chicago's southeast side gathered to oppose a waste incinerator in their community and, in just a few hours, stopped 57 trucks from entering the area. Eventually arrested, they made a public statement about the problem of pollution in poor communities of color in the United States—a problem known as environmental racism. Hazel Johnson, executive director of the environmental justice group People for Community Recovery (PCR), told this story on several occasions, proud that she and her organization had led the demonstration. Indeed, this was a remarkable mobilization and an impressive act of resistance from a small, economically depressed, and chemically inundated community. This community of 10,000 people, mostly African-American, is surrounded by more than 50 polluting facilities, including landfills, oil refineries, waste lagoons, a sewage treatment plant, cement plants, steel mills, and waste incinerators. Hazel's daughter, Cheryl, who has worked with the organization since its founding, often says, "We call this area the 'Toxic Doughnut' because everywhere you look, 360 degrees around us, we're completely surrounded by toxics on all sides."

The Environmental Justice Movement

People for Community Recovery was at the vanguard of a number of local citizens' groups that formed the movement for environmental justice (EJ). This movement, rooted in community-based politics, has emerged as a significant player at the local, state, national, and, increasingly, global levels. The movement's origins lie in local activism during the late 1970s and early 1980s aimed at combating environmental racism and environmental inequality—the unequal distribution of pollution across the social landscape that unfairly burdens poor neighborhoods and communities of color.

The original aim of the EJ movement was to challenge the disproportionate location of toxic facilities (such as landfills, incinerators, polluting factories, and mines) in or near the borders of economically or politically marginalized communities. Groups like PCR have expanded the movement and, in the process, extended its goals beyond removing existing hazards to include preventing new environmental risks and promoting safe, sustainable, and equitable forms of development. In most cases, these groups contest governmental or industrial practices that threaten human health. The EJ movement has developed a vision for social change centered around the following points:

- All people have the right to protection from environmental harm.
- Environmental threats should be eliminated before there are adverse human health consequences.
- The burden of proof should be shifted from communities, which now need to prove adverse impacts, to corporations, which should prove that a given industrial procedure is safe to humans and the environment.
- Grassroots organizations should challenge environmental inequality through political action.

The movement, which now includes African-American, European-American, Latino,

Asian-American/Pacific-Islander, and Native-American communities, is more culturally diverse than both the civil rights and the traditional environmental movements, and combines insights from both causes.

Researchers have documented environmental inequalities in the United States since the 1970s, originally emphasizing the connection between income and air pollution. Research in the 1980s extended these early findings, revealing that communities of color were especially likely to be near hazardous waste sites. In 1987, the United Church of Christ Commission on Racial Justice released a groundbreaking national study entitled *Toxic Waste and Race in the United States*, which revealed the intensely unequal distribution of toxic waste sites across the United States. The study boldly concluded that race was the strongest predictor of where such sites were found.

In 1990, sociologist Robert Bullard published *Dumping in Dixie*, the first major study of environmental racism that linked the siting of hazardous facilities to the decades-old practices of spatial segregation in the South. Bullard found that African-American communities were being deliberately selected as sites for the disposal of municipal and hazardous chemical wastes. This was also one of the first studies to examine the social and psychological impacts of environmental pollution in a community of color. For example, across five communities in Alabama, Louisiana, Texas, and West Virginia, Bullard found that the majority of people felt that their community had been singled out for the location of a toxic facility (55 percent); experienced anger at hosting this facility in their community (74 percent); and yet accepted the idea that the facility would remain in the community (77 percent).

Since 1990, social scientists have documented that exposure to environmental risks is strongly associated with race and socioeconomic status. Like Bullard's *Dumping in Dixie*, many studies have concluded that the link between polluting facilities and communities of color results from the deliberate placement of such facilities in these communities rather than from population-migration patterns. Such communities are systematically targeted for the location of polluting industries and other locally unwanted land uses (LULUs), but residents are fighting back to secure a safe, healthy, and sustainable quality of life. What have they accomplished?

Local Struggles

The EJ movement began in 1982, when hundreds of activists and residents came together to oppose the expansion of a chemical landfill in Warren County, North Carolina. Even though that action failed, it spawned a movement that effectively mobilized people in neighborhoods and small towns facing other LULUs. The EJ movement has had its most profound impact at the local level. Its successes include shutting down large waste incinerators and landfills in Los Angeles and Chicago; preventing polluting operations from being built or expanded, like the chemical plant proposed by the Shintech Corporation near a poor African-American community in Louisiana; securing relocations and home buyouts for residents in polluted communities like Love Canal, New York; Times Beach, Missouri; and Norco, Louisiana; and successfully demanding environmental cleanups of LULUs such as the North River Sewage Treatment plant in Harlem.

The EJ movement helped stop plans to construct more than 300 garbage incinerators in the United States between 1985 and 1998. The steady expansion of municipal waste incinerators was abruptly reversed after 1990. While the cost of building and maintaining incinerators was certainly on the rise, the political price of incineration was the main factor that reversed this tide. The decline of medical-waste incinerators is even more dramatic (Tables 41.1 and 41.2).

Sociologist Andrew Szasz has documented the influence of the EJ movement in several

Table 41.1 Municipal waste incinerators in the United States

Year	*Number of incinerators*
1965	18
1970	25
1975	45
1980	77
1985	119
1990	186
1995	142
2000	116
2002	112

Source: Tangri 2003

Table 41.2 Medical waste incinerators in the United States

Year	*Number of incinerators*
1988	6,200
1994	5,000
1997	2,373
2003	115

Source: Tangri 2003

hundred communities throughout the United States, showing that organizations such as Hazel Johnson's People for Community Recovery were instrumental in highlighting the dangers associated with chemical waste incinerators in their neighborhoods. EJ organizations, working in local coalitions, have had a number of successes, including shutting down an incinerator that was once the largest municipal waste burner in the western hemisphere. The movement has made it extremely difficult for firms to locate incinerators, landfills, and related LULUs anywhere in the nation, and almost any effort to expand existing polluting facilities now faces controversy.

Building Institutions

The EJ movement has built up local organizations and regional networks and forged partnerships with existing institutions such as churches, schools, and neighborhood groups. Given the close association between many EJ activists and environmental sociologists, it is not surprising that the movement has notably influenced the university. Research and training centers run by sociologists at several universities and colleges focus on EJ studies, and numerous institutions of higher education offer EJ courses. Bunyan Bryant and Elaine Hockman, searching the World Wide Web in 2002, got 281,000 hits for the phrase "environmental justice course," and they found such courses at more than 60 of the nation's colleges and universities.

EJ activists have built lasting partnerships with university scholars, especially sociologists. For example, Hazel Johnson's organization has worked with scholars at Northwestern University, the University of Wisconsin, and Clark Atlanta University to conduct health surveys of local residents, study local environmental conditions, serve on policy task forces, and testify at public hearings. Working with activists has provided valuable experience and training to future social and physical scientists.

The EJ movement's greatest challenge is to balance its expertise at mobilizing to oppose hazardous technologies and unsustainable development with a coherent vision and policy program that will move communities toward sustainability and better health. Several EJ groups have taken steps in this direction. Some now own and manage housing units, agricultural firms, job-training facilities, farmers' markets, urban gardens, and restaurants. On Chicago's southeast side, PCR partnered with a local university to win a federal grant, with which they taught lead-abatement techniques to community residents who then found employment in environmental industries. These successes should be acknowledged and praised, although they are limited in their socio-ecological impacts and longevity. Even so, EJ activists, scholars, and practitioners would do well to document these projects' trajectories and seek to replicate and adapt their best practices in other locales.

Legal Gains and Losses

The movement has a mixed record in litigation. Early on, EJ activists and attorneys decided to apply civil rights law (Title VI of the 1964 Civil Rights Act) to the environmental arena. Title VI prohibits all government and industry programs and activities that receive federal funds from discriminating against persons based on race, color, or national origin. Unfortunately, the courts have uniformly refused to prohibit government actions on the basis of Title VI without direct evidence of discriminatory intent. The Environmental Protection Agency (EPA) has been of little assistance. Since 1994, when the EPA began accepting Title VI claims, more than 135 have been filed, but none has been formally resolved. Only one federal agency has cited environmental justice concerns to protect a community in a significant legal case: In May 2001, the Nuclear Regulatory Commission denied a permit for a uranium enrichment plant in Louisiana because environmental justice concerns had not been taken into account.

With regard to legal strategies, EJ activist Hazel Johnson learned early on that, while she could trust committed EJ attorneys like Keith Harley of the Chicago Legal Clinic, the courts were often hostile and unforgiving places to make the case for environmental justice. Like other EJ activists disappointed by the legal system, Johnson and PCR have diversified their tactics. For example, they worked with a coalition of activists, scholars, and scientists to present evidence of toxicity in their community to elected officials and policymakers, while also engaging in disruptive protest that targeted government agencies and corporations.

National Environmental Policy

The EJ movement has been more successful at lobbying high-level elected officials. Most prominently, in February 1994, President Clinton signed Executive Order 12898 requiring all federal agencies to ensure environmental justice in their practices. Appropriately, Hazel Johnson was at Clinton's side as he signed the order. And the Congressional Black Caucus, among its other accomplishments, has maintained one of the strongest environmental voting records of any group in the U.S. Congress.

But under President Bush, the EPA and the White House have not demonstrated a commitment to environmental justice. Even Clinton's much-vaunted Executive Order on Environmental Justice has had a limited effect. In March 2004 and September 2006, the inspector general of the EPA concluded that the agency was not doing an effective job of enforcing environmental justice policy. Specifically, he noted that the agency had no plans, benchmarks, or instruments to evaluate progress toward achieving the goals of Clinton's Order. While President Clinton deserves some of the blame for this, it should be no surprise that things have not improved under the Bush administration. In response, many activists, including those at PCR, have shifted their focus from the national level back to the neighborhood, where their work has a more tangible influence and where polluters are more easily monitored. But in an era of increasing economic and political globalization, this strategy may be limited.

Globalization

As economic globalization—defined as the reduction of economic borders to allow the free passage of goods and money anywhere in the world—proceeds largely unchecked by governments, as the United States and other industrialized nations produce larger volumes of hazardous waste, and as the degree of global social inequality also rises, the frequency and intensity of EJ conflicts can only increase. Nations of the global north continue to export toxic waste to both domestic and global "pollution havens" where the price of doing business is much lower, where environmental laws are comparatively lax, and where citizens hold little formal political power.

Movement leaders are well aware of the effects of economic globalization and the international movement of pollution and wastes along the path of least resistance (namely, southward). Collaboration, resource exchange, networking, and joint action have already emerged between EJ groups in the global north and south. In the last decade EJ activists and delegates have traveled to meet and build alliances with colleagues in places like Beijing, Budapest, Cairo, Durban, The Hague, Istanbul, Johannesburg, Mumbai, and Rio de Janeiro. Activist colleagues outside the United States are often doing battle with the same transnational corporations that U.S. activists may be fighting at home. However, it is unclear if these efforts are well financed or if they are leading to enduring action programs across borders. What is certain is that if the EJ movement fails inside the United States, it is likely to fail against transnational firms on foreign territory in the global south (see chapter 33).

Although EJ movements exist in other nations, the U.S. movement has been slow to link up with them. If the U.S. EJ movement is to survive, it must go global. The origins and drivers of environmental inequality are global in their reach and effects. Residents and activists in the global north feel a moral obligation to the nations and peoples of the south, as consumers, firms, state agencies, and military actions within northern nations produce social and ecological havoc in Latin America, the Caribbean, Africa, Central and Eastern Europe, and Asia. Going global does not necessarily require activists to leave the United States and travel abroad, because many of the major sources of global economic decision-making power are located in the north (corporate headquarters, the International Monetary Fund, the World Bank, and the White House). The movement must focus on these critical (and nearby) institutions. And while the movement has much more to do in order to build coalitions across various social and geographic boundaries, there are tactics, strategies, and campaigns that have succeeded in doing just that for many years. From transnational activist campaigns to solidarity networks and letter-writing, the profile of environmental justice is becoming more global each year.

After Hazel Johnson's visit to the Earth Summit in Rio de Janeiro in 1992, PCR became part of a global network of activists and scholars researching and combating environmental inequality in North America, South America, Africa, Europe, and Asia. Today, PCR confronts a daunting task. The area of Chicago in which the organization works still suffers from the highest density of landfills per square mile of any place in the nation, and from the industrial chemicals believed to be partly responsible for the elevated rates of asthma and other respiratory ailments in the surrounding neighborhoods. PCR has managed to train local residents in lead-abatement techniques; it has begun negotiations with one of the Big Three auto makers to make its nearby manufacturing plant more ecologically sustainable and amenable to hiring locals, and it is setting up an environmental science laboratory and education facility in the community through a partnership with a major research university.

What can we conclude about the state of the movement for environmental justice? Our diagnosis gives us both hope and concern. While the movement has accomplished a great deal, the political and social realities facing activists (and all of us, for that matter) are brutal. Industrial production of hazardous wastes continues to increase exponentially; the rate of cancers, reproductive illnesses, and respiratory disorders is increasing in communities of color and poor communities; environmental inequalities in urban and rural areas in the United States have remained steady or increased during the 1990s and 2000s; the income gap between the upper classes and the working classes is greater than it has been in decades; the traditional, middle-class, and mainly white environmental movement has grown weaker; and the union-led labor movement is embroiled in internecine battles as it loses membership and influence over politics, making it likely that ordinary citizens will be more concerned about declining wages than environmental protection. How well EJ leaders analyze and respond to these adverse trends will determine the future health of this movement. Indeed, as denizens of this fragile planet, we all need to be concerned with how the EJ movement fares against the institutions that routinely poison the earth and its people.

Recommended Resources

Robert Bullard. 2000. *Dumping in Dixie: Race, Class, and Environmental Quality* (Westview Press). The foundation of environmental justice studies, this book is a landmark work by the leading scholar in the field who is also the movement's most prominent advocate.

David Naguib Pellow and Robert J. Brulle, eds. 2005. *Power, Justice, and the Environment: A Critical Appraisal of the Environmental Justice Movement* (MIT Press). A hopeful but hard-hitting analysis of how far this young social movement has come and where it might be headed.

Andrew Szasz. 1994. *Ecopopulism: Toxic Waste and the Movement for Environmental Justice* (University of Minnesota Press). A groundbreaking study of the contemporary origins of environmental inequality in the United States and the story of how ordinary activists spearheaded a grassroots revolution to challenge this epidemic.

Neil Tangri. 2003. *Waste Incineration: A Dying Technology* (GAIA). A study commissioned by the Global Alliance for Incinerator Alternatives provides critical details concerning the rise and fall of the global waste-incineration industry.

United Church of Christ. 1987. *Toxic Wastes and Race in the United States* (UCC). The first national study to uncover the relationship between a community's racial composition and the location of waste sites.

References from Part Introductions/ Key Concepts

Adorno, Theodor W. et al. 1950. *The Authoritarian Personality.* New York: Harper.

Bob, Clifford. 2005. *The Marketing of Rebellion: Insurgents, Media, and International Activism.* Cambridge: Cambridge University Press.

Breines, Wini. 1982. *Community and Organization in the New Left, 1962–1968: The Great Refusal.* South Hadley, MA: J. F. Bergin.

Burstein, Paul, Rachel L. Einwohner, and Jocelyn A. Hollander. 1995. "The Success of Social Movements." In J. Craig Jenkins and Bert Klandermans, eds., *The Politics of Social Protest.* Minneapolis: University of Minnesota Press.

Davies, James C. 1962. "Toward a Theory of Revolution." *American Sociological Review* 27:5–19.

Evans, Sara M., and Harry C. Boyte. 1986. *Free Spaces: The Sources of Democratic Change in America.* New York: Harper and Row.

Eyerman, Ron and Andrew Jamison. 1998. *Music and Social Movements: Mobilizing Traditions in the Twentieth Century.* Cambridge: Cambridge University Press.

Gamson, William A. 1990. *The Strategy of Social Protest*, 2nd edn. Homewood, IL: Dorsey.

Gans, Herbert J. 1979. *Deciding What's News.* New York: Random House.

Gerlach, Luther P., and Virginia H. Hine. 1970. *People, Power, and Change: Movements of Social Transformation.* Indianapolis: Bobbs-Merrill.

Goode, Erich, and Nachman Ben-Yehuda. 1994. *Moral Panics: The Social Construction of Deviance.* Oxford: Blackwell.

Goodwin, Jeff. 1997. "The Libidinal Constitution of a High-Risk Social Movement: Affectual Ties and Solidarity in the Huk Rebellion, 1946 to 1954." *American Sociological Review* 62:53–69.

Goodwin, Jeff, and James M. Jasper, eds. 2003. *Rethinking Social Movements: Structure, Meaning, and Emotion.* Lanham, MD: Rowman and Littlefield.

Goodwin, Jeff, James M. Jasper, and Francesca Polletta, eds. 2001. *Passionate Politics: Emotions and Social Movements.* Chicago: University of Chicago Press.

Gurney, Joan M. and Kathleen J. Tierney. 1982. "Relative Deprivation and Social Movements: A Critical Look at Twenty Years of Theory and Research." *Sociological Quarterly* 23:33–47.

Gurr, Ted. 1970. *Why Men Rebel.* Princeton, NJ: Princeton University Press.

Haines, Herbert H. 1988. *Black Radicals and the Civil Rights Mainstream, 1954–1970.* Knoxville: University of Tennessee Press.

Hall, John R. 1988. "Social Organization and Pathways to Commitment: Types of Communal Groups, Rational Choice Theory, and the Kanter Thesis." *American Sociological Review* 53:679–92.

Hoffer, Eric. 1951. *The True Believer.* New York: Harper and Row.

Inglehart, Ronald. 1977. *The Silent Revolution: Changing Values and Political Styles among Western Publics.* Princeton, NJ: Princeton University Press.

Isaacs, Harold R. 1963. *The New World of Negro Americans.* London: Phoenix House.

Jasper, James M. 1990. *Nuclear Politics: Energy and the State in the United States, Sweden, and France.* Princeton, NJ: Princeton University Press.

Jasper, James M. 1997. *The Art of Moral Protest: Culture, Biography, and Creativity in Social Movements.* Chicago: University of Chicago Press.

Jasper, James M., and Dorothy Nelkin. 1992. *The Animal Rights Crusade: The Growth of a Moral Protest.* New York: Free Press.

Jasper, James, and Jane Poulsen. 1993. "Fighting Back: Vulnerabilities, Blunders, and

Countermobilization by the Targets in Three Animal Rights Campaigns." *Sociological Forum* 8:639–57.

Jasper, James M., and Jane Poulsen. 1995. "Recruiting Strangers and Friends: Moral Shocks and Social Networks in Animal Rights and Animal Protest." *Social Problems* 42:493–512.

Jenkins, J. Craig, and Charles Perrow. 1977. "Insurgency of the Powerless: Farm Worker Movements (1946–1972)." *American Sociological Review* 42:249–68.

Kanter, Rosabeth Moss. 1972. *Commitment and Community: Communes and Utopias in Sociological Perspective*. Cambridge, MA: Harvard University Press.

Katzenstein, Mary Fainsod. 1998. *Faithful and Fearless: Moving Feminist Protest inside the Church and Military*. Princeton, NJ: Princeton University Press.

Keck, Margaret E., and Kathryn Sikkink. 1998. *Activists Beyond Borders: Advocacy Networks in International Politics*. Ithaca, NY: Cornell University Press.

Kitschelt, Herbert. 1986. "Political Opportunity Structures and Political Protest: Anti-Nuclear Movements in Four Democracies." *British Journal of Political Science* 16:57–85.

Klandermans, Bert. 1983. "Locus of Control and Socio-political Action-taking: The Balance of Twenty Years of Research." *European Journal of Social Psychology* 13:399–415.

Klandermans, Bert. 1989. "Grievance Interpretation and Success Expectations: The Social Construction of Protest." *Social Behaviour* 4:113–25.

Klandermans, Bert, and Dirk Oegema. 1987. "Potentials, Networks, Motivations and Barriers: Steps toward Participation in Social Movements." *American Sociological Review* 52:519–31.

Kornhauser, William. 1959. *The Politics of Mass Society*. Glencoe, IL: The Free Press.

LeBon, Gustave. 1960 [1895]. *The Crowd: A Study of the Popular Mind*. New York: Viking.

Mansbridge, Jane J. 1986. *Why We Lost the ERA*. Chicago: University of Chicago Press. Excerpted in this volume.

McAdam, Doug. 1982. *Political Process and the Development of Black Insurgency, 1930–1970*. Chicago: University of Chicago Press.

McAdam, Doug. 1986. "Recruitment to High-Risk Activism: The Case of Freedom Summer." *American Journal of Sociology* 92:64–90.

McAdam, Doug. 1988. *Freedom Summer*. New York: Oxford University Press.

McAdam, Doug, John D. McCarthy, and Mayer N. Zald. 1988. "Social Movements." In Neil J. Smelser, ed., *Handbook of Sociology*. Beverly Hills, CA: Sage.

McCarthy, John D., and Mayer N. Zald. 1973. *The Trend of Social Movements in America: Professionalization and Resource Mobilization*. Morristown, NJ: General Learning Press.

McCarthy, John D., and Mayer N. Zald. 1977. "Resource Mobilization and Social Movements: A Partial Theory." *American Journal of Sociology* 82:1212–41.

Melucci, Alberto. 1996. *Challenging Codes*. Cambridge: Cambridge University Press.

Morris, Aldon D. 1984. *The Origins of the Civil Rights Movement: Black Communities Organizing for Change*. New York: Free Press.

Oberschall, Anthony. 1973. *Social Conflict and Social Movements*. Englewood Cliffs, NJ: Prentice-Hall.

Olson, Mancur. 1965. *The Logic of Collective Action: Public Goods and the Theory of Groups*. Cambridge, MA: Harvard University Press.

Piven, Frances Fox, and Richard A. Cloward. 1979. *Poor People's Movements: Why They Succeed, How They Fail*. New York: Vintage.

Polletta, Francesca. 2002. *Freedom Is an Endless Meeting: Democracy in American Social Movements*. Chicago: University of Chicago Press.

Robnett, Belinda. 1997. *How Long? How Long? African-American Women in the Struggle for Civil Rights*. New York: Oxford University Press.

Rothschild, Joyce, and J. Allen Whitt. 1986. *The Cooperative Workplace: Potentials and Dilemmas of Organizational Democracy and Participation*. Cambridge: Cambridge University Press.

Rupp, Leila J., and Verta Taylor. 1987. *Survival in the Doldrums*. New York: Oxford University Press.

Scott, James C. 1985. *Weapons of the Weak: Everyday Forms of Peasant Resistance*. New Haven: Yale University Press.

Scott, James C. 1990. *Domination and the Arts of Resistance*. New Haven: Yale University Press.

Sexton, Patricia Cayo. 1991. *The War on Labor and the Left: Understanding America's Unique Conservatism*. Boulder, CO: Westview Press.

Skocpol, Theda. 1979. *States and Social Revolutions: A Comparative Analysis of France, Russia, and China*. Cambridge: Cambridge University Press.

Smelser, Neil J. 1968. "Social and Psychological Dimensions of Collective Behavior." In Smelser, *Essays in Sociological Explanation*. Englewood Cliffs, NJ: Prentice-Hall.

Snow, David A., and Robert D. Benford. 1988. "Ideology, Frame Resonance, and Participant Mobilization." *International Social Movement Research* 1:197–217.

Snow, David A., and Susan Marshall. 1984. "Cultural Imperialism, Social Movements, and the Islamic Revival." In *Social Movements, Conflicts, and Change*, Vol. 7, edited by Louis Kriesberg. Greenwich, CT: JAI Press.

Snow, David A., Louis A. Zurcher, and Sheldon Ekland-Olson. 1980. "Social Networks and Social Movements: A Microstructural Approach to Differential Recruitment." *American Sociological Review* 45:787–801.

Snow, David A., E. Burke Rochford, Jr., Steven K. Worden, and Robert D. Benford. 1986. "Frame Alignment Processes, Micromobilization, and Movement Participation." *American Sociological Review* 51:464–81.

Tarrow, Sidney. 1998. *Power in Movement*, 2nd edn. Cambridge: Cambridge University Press.

Taylor, Verta. 1989. "Social Movement Continuity: The Women's Movement in Abeyance." *American Sociological Review* 54:761–75.

Tilly, Charles. 1978. *From Mobilization to Revolution*. Reading, MA: Addison-Wesley.

Touraine, Alain. 1977. *The Self-Production of Society*. Chicago: University of Chicago Press.

Useem, Bert. 1980. "Solidarity Model, Breakdown Model, and the Boston Anti-Busing Movement." *American Sociological Review* 45:357–69.

Walsh, Edward J. 1981. "Resource Mobilization and Citizen Protest in Communities around Three Mile Island." *Social Problems* 29:1–21.

Woodward, C. Vann. 1974. *The Strange Career of Jim Crow*, 3rd edn. New York: Oxford University Press.

Index

Note: Arabic names with the prefix "al-" have been filed under the letter immediately following the hyphen. Page numbers in *italic* indicate figures and tables.